AF889351

Recommended by **Teachers**
Trusted by **Toppers**

All in One

LEGAL STUDIES
Class 12

EVERYTHING YOU NEED TO SCORE

- Simplified Theory
- CBSE Textbook & other Imp. Ques.
- CBQs; MCQs, A-R, Case Based
- Board Questions Upto 2025
- Sample Question Papers

CBSE Exams 2026

Author
Manik Chaubey

arihant
SUCCESS AND NOTHING LESS

arihant
SUCCESS AND NOTHING LESS

ARIHANT PRAKASHAN
(School Division Series)

卐 *ADMINISTRATIVE & PRODUCTION OFFICES*

Regd. Office
'Ramchhaya' 4577/15, Agarwal Road, Darya Ganj, New Delhi -110002
Tele: 011- 47630600, 43518550; Fax: 011- 23280316

卐 *Head Office*
Kalindi, TP Nagar, Meerut (UP) - 250002, Tel: 0121-7156203, 7156204

卐 *SALES & SUPPORT OFFICES*
Agra, Ahmedabad, Bengaluru, Bareilly, Chennai, Delhi, Guwahati, Hyderabad, Jaipur, Jhansi, Kolkata, Lucknow, Nagpur & Pune.

PO No : TXT-XX-XXXXXXX-X-XX

Published By Arihant Publications (India) Ltd.

For further information about the books published by Arihant, log on to www.arihantbooks.com or e-mail at info@arihantbooks.com

Follow us on

卐 *PRICE* ₹400.00

PRODUCTION TEAM

Publishing Managers	*Cover Designer*	*Inner Designer*
Mahendra Singh Rawat & Keshav Mohan	Salman Shaikh	Ankit Tyagi
Project Head	*Page Layouting*	*Proof Reader*
Monika Bhasin	Chintoo Kumar	Anurag Vashist, Pravesh Bhagrwal

Index *cum* Study Planner

One Book- Endless Features

to Help you Succeed

01

CHAPTER

The framework of the Indian judicial system is laid down in the Indian Constitution. The Supreme Court located in New Delhi is the Apex Court of India. The High Courts at the state level follows next which function for one or more number of states.

YOUR STUDY GOALS

1.1 Structure and Hierarchy of Courts in India
1.2 Features of Indian Judiciary
1.3 Legal Officers in India
1.4 Constitution, Roles and Impartiality
1.5 Role of Indian Judiciary
1.6 Public Interest Litigation (PIL)
1.7 Tribunals

YOUR PRACTICE GOAL

- Objective Type Questions (19 Qs ; MCQs, A-R, Statements, Matching)
- Subjective Questions (14 VSAs, 6 SAs, 3 LAs)

Judiciary in India

1.1 Structure and Hierarchy of Courts in India

- The Constitution creates a single integrated system of justice that includes courts to administer both central and states laws.
- The Supreme Court is the Apex Court of India. It is followed by High Courts at state levels.
- The High Courts are followed by **District** and **Subordinate** Courts popularly known as the **lower courts** in India.
- To make justice more accessible and efficient, specialised tribunals have been established to handle specific areas of law.
- These dedicated courts addresses disputes related to employment, consumer rights and service matters, taking some of the burden away from the traditional court system.

In this Chapter

A quick information about the coverage of the chapter to explain students about what they are going to study.

1.1 Structure and Hierarchy of Courts in India

- The Constitution creates a single integrated system of justice that includes courts to administer both central and states laws.
- The Supreme Court is the Apex Court of India. It is followed by High Courts at state levels.
- The High Courts are followed by **District** and **Subordinate** Courts popularly known as the **lower courts** in India.
- To make justice more accessible and efficient, specialised tribunals have been established to handle specific areas of law.
- These dedicated courts addresses disputes related to employment, consumer rights and service matters, taking some of the burden away from the traditional court system.

Complete Theory in Each Chapter

Each chapter has Complete, Easy to Understand and Simplified theory covering latest syllabus and CBSE Textbook. Theory is developed in such a way that it perfectly rectifies the complexity of CBSE Text making it suitable for all types of learners.

Quick Test 1

1. What were the first four High Courts in India?
2. Mention any one power of the Attorney General.
3. Mention any one function of the Advocate General of State.

Quick Test

A set of 3-5 Questions given in between the text, helps students to remain connected with the text while studying. They can instantly assess themselves for their understanding.

CBSE Textbook

Complete explanations of all the questions of CBSE Textbook Exercises.

CBSE TEXTBOOK FOLDER

1. List any two Constitutional offices endowed with the function to advise and represent the government on legal matters.

Ans. The two Constitutional offices endowed with the function to advise and represent the government on legal matters are

(i) **Attorney General of India** The Government of India needs the Attorney General's advice on any legal issues that are brought to them. Additionally, they carry out additional legal obligations that the President has given them. The Attorney General is entitled to appear before all Indian courts and to take part in Parliamentary sessions, but not to vote. The Attorney General represents the Indian government in all Supreme Court actions (including lawsuits, appeals and other hearings) involving the Indian Government. Additionally, they represent the Indian Government when the President approaches the Supreme Court under Article 143 of the Constitution.

The Attorney General is assisted by a Solicitor General and Additional Solicitor Generals. The Attorney General is to be consulted only in legal matters of real importance and only after the Ministry of Law has been consulted. All references to the Attorney General are made by the Law Ministry.

as Presidential Reference and is recognised as the advisory jurisdiction of the court. Supreme Court also has other functions or jurisdication.

- **Original Jurisdiction** Original jurisdiction is given to the Supreme Court under Article 131 of the Constitution. The Supreme Court shall have original jurisdiction in any dispute between the Government of India and one or more states.
  - Between the Government of India and any state or states on one side and one or more other states on the other side.
  - Between two or more states, only if the dispute concerns any question (whether of law or fact) on which the existence or scope of a legal right is dependent. However, the jurisdiction shall not extend to any dispute arising out of any treaty, agreement, covenant, engagements or other similar instruments which have been entered into or executed before the commencement of the constitution or continues to exist after such commencement.
  - States that the jurisdiction does not apply to such a dispute.
- **Writ Jurisdiction** Article 32 of the Constitution further gives extensive original jurisdiction to the Supreme Court for the enforcement of the Fundamental Rights of the citizens, through issuing directions, orders and writs.

One Book- Endless Features

to Help you Succeed

Exam Pattern Question

Exam Pattern Question have all types of questions; such as Objective Type Questions, SA & LA Type Questions.

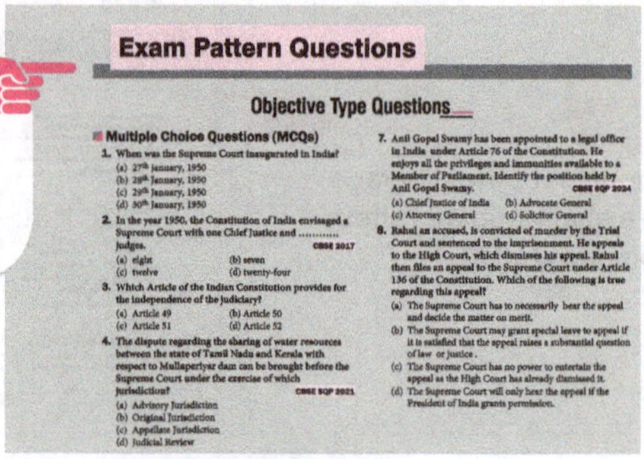

Exam Pattern Questions

Objective Type Questions

Multiple Choice Questions (MCQs)

1. When was the Supreme Court inaugurated in India?
   (a) 27th January, 1950
   (b) 28th January, 1950
   (c) 29th January, 1950
   (d) 30th January, 1950
2. In the year 1950, the Constitution of India envisaged a Supreme Court with one Chief Justice and .... judges. CBSE 2017
   (a) eight (b) seven
   (c) twelve (d) twenty-four
3. Which Article of the Indian Constitution provides for the independence of the judiciary?
   (a) Article 49 (b) Article 50
   (c) Article 51 (d) Article 52
4. The dispute regarding the sharing of water resources between the state of Tamil Nadu and Kerala with respect to Mullaperiyar dam can be brought before the Supreme Court under the exercise of which jurisdiction? CBSE SQP 2021
   (a) Advisory Jurisdictinn
   (b) Original Jurisdiction
   (c) Appellate Jurisdiction
   (d) Judicial Review
7. Anil Gopal Swamy has been appointed to a legal office in India under Article 76 of the Constitution. He enjoys all the privileges and immunities available to a Member of Parliament. Identify the position held by Anil Gopal Swamy. CBSE SQP 2024
   (a) Chief Justice of India (b) Advocate General
   (c) Attorney General (d) Solicitor General
8. Rahul an accused, is convicted of murder by the Trial Court and sentenced to the imprisonment. He appeals to the High Court, which dismisses his appeal. Rahul then files an appeal to the Supreme Court under Article 136 of the Constitution. Which of the following is true regarding this appeal?
   (a) The Supreme Court has to necessarily hear the appeal and decide the matter on merit.
   (b) The Supreme Court may grant special leave to appeal if it is satisfied that the appeal raises a substantial question of law or justice.
   (c) The Supreme Court has no power to entertain the appeal as the High Court has already dismissed it.
   (d) The Supreme Court will only hear the appeal if the President of India grants permission.

Chapter Assessment

Complete Test of chapter in Exam format.

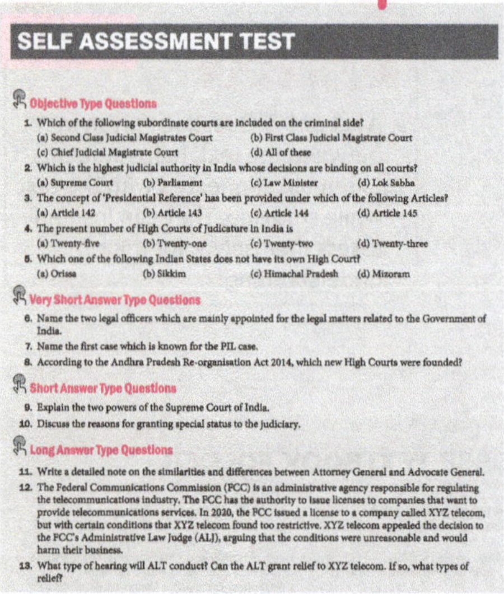

SELF ASSESSMENT TEST

Objective Type Questions

1. Which of the following subordinate courts are included on the criminal side?
   (a) Second Class Judicial Magistrates Court (b) First Class Judicial Magistrate Court
   (c) Chief Judicial Magistrate Court (d) All of these
2. Which is the highest judicial authority in India whose decisions are binding on all courts?
   (a) Supreme Court (b) Parliament (c) Law Minister (d) Lok Sabha
3. The concept of 'Presidential Reference' has been provided under which of the following Articles?
   (a) Article 142 (b) Article 143 (c) Article 144 (d) Article 145
4. The present number of High Courts of Judicature in India is
   (a) Twenty-five (b) Twenty-one (c) Twenty-two (d) Twenty-three
5. Which one of the following Indian States does not have its own High Court?
   (a) Orissa (b) Sikkim (c) Himachal Pradesh (d) Mizoram

Very Short Answer Type Questions

6. Name the two legal officers which are mainly appointed for the legal matters related to the Government of India.
7. Name the first case which is known for the PIL case.
8. According to the Andhra Pradesh Re-organisation Act 2014, which new High Courts were founded?

Short Answer Type Questions

9. Explain the two powers of the Supreme Court of India.
10. Discuss the reasons for granting special status to the judiciary.

Long Answer Type Questions

11. Write a detailed note on the similarities and differences between Attorney General and Advocate General.
12. The Federal Communications Commission (FCC) is an administrative agency responsible for regulating the telecommunications industry. The FCC has the authority to issue licenses to companies that want to provide telecommunications services. In 2020, the FCC issued a license to a company called XYZ telecom, but with certain conditions that XYZ telecom found too restrictive. XYZ telecom appealed the decision to the FCC's Administrative Law Judge (ALJ), arguing that the conditions were unreasonable and would harm their business.
13. What type of hearing will ALT conduct? Can the ALT grant relief to XYZ telecom. If so, what types of relief?

Sample Question Papers

To make students practice of examination in real sense, there are 3 Sample Question Papers at the end. All these Sample Questions Papers are exactly prepared on the latest syllabus & pattern of examination.

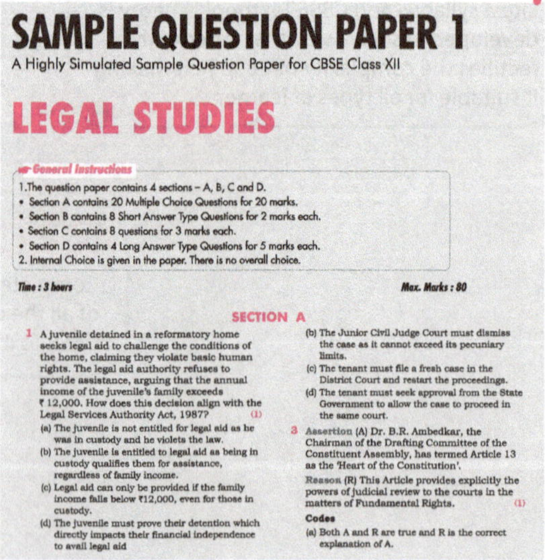

SAMPLE QUESTION PAPER 1

A Highly Simulated Sample Question Paper for CBSE Class XII

LEGAL STUDIES

General Instructions

1.The question paper contains 4 sections – A, B, C and D.
- Section A contains 20 Multiple Choice Questions for 20 marks.
- Section B contains 8 Short Answer Type Questions for 2 marks each.
- Section C contains 8 questions for 3 marks each.
- Section D contains 4 Long Answer Type Questions for 5 marks each.

2. Internal Choice is given in the paper. There is no overall choice.

Time : 3 hours *Max. Marks : 80*

SECTION A

1 A juvenile detained in a reformatory home seeks legal aid to challenge the conditions of the home, claiming they violate basic human rights. The legal aid authority refuses to provide assistance, arguing that the annual income of the juvenile's family exceeds ₹ 12,000. How does this decision align with the Legal Services Authority Act, 1987? (1)
(a) The juvenile is not entitled for legal aid as he was in custody and he violets the law.
(b) The juvenile is entitled to legal aid as being in custody qualifies them for assistance, regardless of family income.
(c) Legal aid can only be provided if the family income falls below ₹12,000, even for those in custody.
(d) The juvenile must prove their detention which directly impacts their financial independence to avail legal aid

(b) The Junior Civil Judge Court must dismiss the case as it cannot exceed its pecuniary limits.
(c) The tenant must file a fresh case in the District Court and restart the proceedings.
(d) The tenant must seek approval from the State Government to allow the case to proceed in the same court.

3 Assertion (A) Dr. B.R. Ambedkar, the Chairman of the Drafting Committee of the Constituent Assembly, has termed Article 13 as the 'Heart of the Constitution'.
Reason (R) This Article provides explicitly the powers of judicial review to the courts in the matters of Fundamental Rights. (1)
Codes
(a) Both A and R are true and R is the correct explanation of A.

Latest Course *Structure*

(BASED ON REVISED BOOK WITH NEW CHAPTERS)
(Testbook Revised in the Academic Year 2023-24)

S.No.	Units	Marks
Unit 1	Judiciary	08
Unit 2	Alternative Dispute Resolution in India (ADR)	08
Unit 3	Topics in Law - I (Business Laws)	20
	Chapter 3 (A) - Law of Contract	
	Chapter 3 (B) - Law of Torts	
	Chapter 3 (C) - Law of Property	
	Chapter 3 (D) - Intellectual Property Law	
Unit 4	Topics in Law - II (General Laws)	10
	Chapter 4 (A) -Law and Sustainable Development	
	Chapter 4 (B) - Forms of Legal Entities	
	Chapter 4 (C) - Criminal Laws in India	
Unit 5	Concept of Human Rights	10
	Chapter 5 (A) - Human Rights in India	
	Chapter 5 (B) - Human Rights Violations-Complaint Mechanism (Quasi-Judicial Bodies)	
Unit 6	International Law	08
Unit 7	Legal Profession in India	08
Unit 8	Legal Services	08
	Project	20
	Total	**100**

Theory- 80 marks (One Paper)

Internal Assessment- Project Based Assessment- 20 marks

S.No.	Unit	Topics
Unit 1	Judiciary	a) Structure, Hierarchy of Courts and Legal Officers in India b) Constitution, Roles and Impartiality c) Appointments, Retirement and Removal of Judges d) Tribunals e) Courts and Judicial Review
Unit 2	Alternative Dispute Resolution in India (ADR)	a) Adversarial and Inquisitorial Systems b) Meaning and Scope of ADR c) Arbitration d) Mediation e) Conciliation f) Lok Adalat g) Ombudsman h) Lokpal and Lokayukta
Unit 3	Topics in Law-I (Business Laws)	
Chapter 3A	Law of Contract	a) Introduction to Contract b) Formation of Contract c) Intention to Contract d) Consideration of Contract e) Capacity to Contract f) Consent g) Types of Contracts h) Discharge of Contract i) Remedies in Case of Breach
Chapter 3B	Law of Torts	a) Concept of Law of Torts b) Sources of Law of Torts c) Intentional Tort d) Defamation e) Negligence f) Strict Liability g) Absolute Liability
Chapter 3C	Law of Property	a) Types of Property b) Who can transfer property c) Essential of a valid transfer d) Types of Transfer- Sale, Lease, Exchange, Gift

Chapter 3D	Intellectual Property Law	a) Meaning of Intellectual Property b) International Obligations that have Shaped Indian IPR c) WIPO d) Copyright e) Patent f) Trademark g) Geographical Indication h) Design
Unit 4	Topics in Law-II (General Laws)	
Chapter 4A	Law and Sustainable Development	a) Introduction b) Initiatives under International Scenario c) Provisions under Indian Constitution d) Environment Protection Act, 1986 e) Pollution Control Boards
Chapter 4B	Forms of Legal Entities	Types of Legal Entities in India a) Sole Proprietorship b) Partnership c) Limited Liability Partnership d) Private Limited Company e) Public Limited Company f) One Person Company
Chapter 4C	Criminal Laws in India	a) Objectives of Criminal Law b) Legislations for Criminal Laws in India c) Distinction between Intention and Motive d) Stages of Crime e) The Indian Evidence Act, 1872 f) Admission and Confession
Unit 5	Concept of Human Rights	
Chapter 5A	Human Rights in India	a) Introduction 1. Historical Context b) Indian Constitutional Framework on Human Rights and Related Laws in India 1. The Preamble 2. Fundamental Rights-Part III of the Constitution 3. Directive Principles-Part IV- Articles 36-51 4. Fundamental Duties-Part IV(A)- Article 51 A

Chapter 5B	Human Rights Violations Complaint Mechanism (Quasi-Judicial Bodies)	a) What are Quasi-Judicial Bodies? b) Various Human Rights Commission 1. National Human Rights Commission (NHRC) 2. National Commission for Minorities 3. National Commission for Women (NCW) 4. National Commission for Scheduled Castes and Scheduled Tribes 5. National Commission for Protection of Child Rights (NCPCR)
Unit 6	International Law	a) Introduction b) Historical Evolution of International Law c) What is International Law? d) Sources of International Law e) International Human Rights f) International Law and Municipal Law g) International Law and India h) Dispute Resolution
Unit 7	Legal Profession in India	a) The Advocates Act, 1961 b) Lawyers and Professional Ethics c) Advertising by Lawyers in India d) Liberalisation and Globalisation of Legal Profession e) Women and Legal Profession f) Legal Education in India, USA and UK g) Opportunities for Law Graduates
Unit 8	Legal Services	a) Brief History of Legal Services b) Free Legal Aid under Criminal Law c) Legal Aid by the State d) Legal Aid under the Indian Constitution e) National Legal Services Authority (NALSA) f) Legal Services Authority Act, 1987 g) Legal Aid in Context of Social Justice and Human Rights

01

CHAPTER

The framework of the Indian judicial system is laid down in the Indian Constitution. The Supreme Court located in New Delhi is the Apex Court of India. The High Courts at the state level follows next which function for one or more number of states.

▼ **YOUR STUDY GOALS**

1.1 Structure and Hierarchy of Courts in India
1.2 Features of Indian Judiciary
1.3 Legal Officers in India
1.4 Constitution, Roles and Impartiality
1.5 Role of Indian Judiciary
1.6 Public Interest Litigation (PIL)
1.7 Tribunals

▼ **YOUR PRACTICE GOAL**

- Objective Type Questions (19 Qs ; MCQs, A-R, Statements, Matching)
- Subjective Questions (14 VSAs, 8 SAs, 3 LAs)

Judiciary in India

1.1 Structure and Hierarchy of Courts in India

- The Constitution creates a single integrated system of justice that includes courts to administer both central and states laws.
- The Supreme Court is the Apex Court of India. It is followed by High Courts at state levels.
- The High Courts are followed by **District** and **Subordinate** Courts popularly known as the **lower courts** in India.
- To make justice more accessible and efficient, specialised tribunals have been established to handle specific areas of law.
- These dedicated courts addresses disputes related to employment, consumer rights and service matters, taking some of the burden away from the traditional court system.

Supreme Court of India

- The Constitution of India intially in 1950, provided the Supreme Court with a Chief Justice and 7 judges.
- The Supreme Court of India was established on **28th January, 1950.**

- It replaced the **Federal Court** of India and the Judicial Committee of the **Privy Council**, which were at the top of the colonial Indian judicial system.
- The Parliament is granted with power to increase the number of judges.
- The Parliament has increased the number of judges in Supreme Court. There are **now 34 judges** in the Supreme Court, including the Chief Justice of India.

The Supreme Court (Number of Judges) Amendment Bill, 2019

- The Supreme Court (Number of Judges) Amendment Bill, 2019 was introduced in **Lok Sabha on 5th August, 2019.**
- The Bill amends the Supreme Court (Number of Judges) Act, 1956.
- The act fixes the maximum number of judges in the Supreme Court at 30 judges (excluding the Chief Justice of India). The Bill increases this number from 30 to 33.

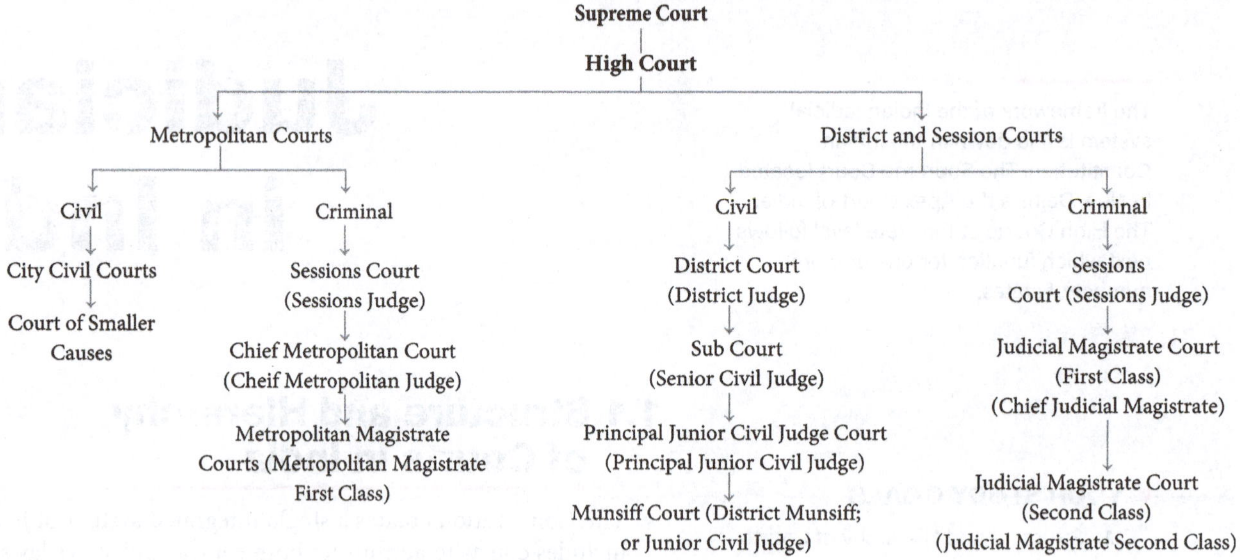

▲ *Hierarchy of Courts in India*

High Courts

- India has **25 High Courts** at the state and union territory level. Each High Court has **jurisdiction**[1] over a state, a union territory or a group of states and union territories.
- The subordinate courts that serve as **civil courts, criminal courts** and **specialised tribunals** exist below the High Courts.
- The **first four** High Courts in India are the **Madras High Court** in Chennai, the **Bombay High Court** in Mumbai, the **Calcutta High Court** in Kolkata and the **Allahabad High Court** in Allahabad.
- According to the **Andhra Pradesh Re-organisation Act, 2014**, the two new High Courts were founded on 1st January, 2019. They are the Andhra High Court and Telangana High Court.

District and Subordinate Courts

- Subordinate judiciary refers to the courts that work below the High Courts. They include district and subordinate courts.
- A **District** and **Sessions** Judge presides over the judicial districts that are established within each state.

1 **Jurisdiction** It means having a legal right over something.

- When a judge presides over a **civil matter,** he is referred to as a **District Judge** and when he preside over a **criminal case,** he is referred to as a **Sessions Judge**.
- When a judge presides over a district court in a city that has recognised as a metropolitan region by State Government, then he is also referred to as a **Metropolitan Sessions Judge**.
- District Judges may work with **Additional District Judges**, depending upon the judicial workload.
- The district judge is the highest level of judicial power below a High Court judge. All courts below the District Court are subject to its appellate authority and supervision.
- Junior Civil Judge Court, Principal Junior Civil Judge Court and Senior Civil Judge Courts are the subordinate courts on the civil side below the District Court (in descending order).
- The Second Class Judicial Magistrates Court, First Class Judicial Magistrate Court and Chief Judicial Magistrate Court are the subordinate courts on the criminal side (in descending order).

Discrict Munsiff Courts

These courts are part of subordinate courts hierarchy. These are lowest in order of hierarchy. These are lowest in order of handling matters of civil nature and function below the subordinate courts. These are controlled by district courts of respective districts.

1.2 Features of Indian Judiciary

The important features of Indian Judiciary are discussed below

India as a Common Law Jurisdiction

- India has adopted the model of common law, as similar to the British tradition.
- The **decisions**, **decrees** and **judgements** made by Indian judges under this common law system help in the creation of laws and legal principles. These principles serve as precedents that must be followed by all subordinate courts in the hierarchy.
- Courts are essential in the creation of laws, particularly when there are legal gaps and the legislative or executive branch has failed to enact laws. In addition to administering civil and criminal justice, courts and judges play a crucial role in the federal structure of the nation.
- The civil law system, which is used in nations like **Germany**, **Russia** and **Continental Europe**, is opposed to this approach. The source of law is the main basis for distinction between common law and civil law. The civil law only allows the legislature or government to enact laws and regulations. The common law allows the judiciary to do so through the judicial judgements of courts.

Adversarial Model of Dispute Resolution

- Courts in India follow adversarial form of adjudication rather than the inquisitorial approach. Under an adversarial arrangement, the role of lawyer representing the party becomes crucial.
- Lawyers of the opposing parties present their cases before an impartial judge and the judge provides a decision based on the merits of the case as given by the lawyers.
- On the other hand, judges are more proactive in making decisions under the **inquisitorial system of law.** They have the right to enquire and look into the problem, much like the police, as compared to the functioning of impartial judges.

1.3 Legal Officers in India

The executive branch of the government is advised by specific legal offices at the union and state levels. These law officers derive their authority from the Constitution or other laws and regulations.
The main legal officers in India are

Attorney General of India

▲ *M.C. Setalvad first Attorney General*

The Attorney General is **first legal officer of the country**. According to **Article 76** of the Indian Constitution, the **President of India appoints the Attorney General** of India, who **holds office during the pleasure of the President.** The Constitution stipulates that the Attorney General must be a person qualified to be appointed as a Supreme Court judge. He/she should have sufficient legal experience or have held judicial office for the required amount of time. **M.C. Setalvad** was **India's first Attorney General.**

The duties and powers of the Attorney General are

- Attorney General **gives advice to the Government of India** upon such legal matters, which are referred or assigned to him by the President.
- He also performs other duties of a legal character that are referred or assigned to him by the President or conferred on him by or under the Constitution or any other law.
- He has the right of hearing in all courts in the territory of India.
- He has the right to speak or to take part in the proceedings of both the Houses of Parliament and their joint sittings but without a right to vote.
- He has the right to speak or to take part in the meeting of any committee of the Parliament of which he is named as a member but without a right to vote.
- He enjoys all the privileges and immunities that are available to a member of Parliament.

A Solicitor General[2] and four Additional Solicitors General support the Attorney General. The Constitution does not recognise the position of the Solicitor General or Additional Solicitors General. However, they are regulated by laws passed by the Parliament.

Advocate General of State

- The position of Advocate General exists at the state level. An Advocate General is a **senior law officer** who acts as a legal advisor to the State Government. According to **Article 165** of the Constitution, Advocate General is appointed by the Governor of the respective state.
- The Advocate General is the **chief legal advisor of the state** and performs duties of a legal character. This include representing the state before the courts either through himself/herself or through the law officers or pleaders appointed by the state.
- The qualification required for appointment as an Advocate General is similar to that of a judge of a High Court.
- The office of an Advocate General is held during the pleasure of the Governor, who also determines the nature of remunerations for the Advocate General. Additional Advocate Generals are also appointed to assist the office of the Advocate General.

Quick Test 1

1. What were the first four High Courts in India?
2. Mention any one power of the Attorney General.
3. Mention any one function of the Advocate General of State.

2 Solicitor General A legal officer who is the chief representative of regional or national government in courtroom proceedings.

1.4 Constitution, Roles and Impartiality

The judiciary in India derives its powers and functions from the Constitution, which is the fundamental legal text for the functioning of Indian democracy.

Independence of Judiciary as a Constitutional Safeguard

The rule of the judiciary's independence is laid down in **Article 50** of the Indian Constitution. It provides for the independence of judiciary from the executive and legislative branches of the government. The independence of judiciary is important due to the following reasons

- The independence of **judiciary helps** in the maintenance of the rule of law, good governance and the creation of a just and free society.
- It monitors and maintains the system of **checks and balances** over the other branches of the government. Thus, the judiciary acts as a **mediator** when any organ of a government exercises excess power which tends to violate the interests of the larger society or individual.

  For example, the Indian police have extensive powers for crime detection and gathering evidence for prosecution of criminals. It is common for the police to interrogate suspect criminals in order to gather the best evidence of the crime. However, such powers should not impinge upon the rights of the accused or the **suspected criminal.**

  An accused cannot be coerced into giving statement pointing to his/her guilt. This right has been constitutionally guaranteed to the accused under **Article 20(3)** of the Constitution.
- The judiciary has been protected from **external pressures** in order to ensure that Constitutionally guaranteed freedom, such as the freedom to speak in public or to peacefully gather, are interpreted as the true Constitutional philosophy. This is especially helpful when the judge is interpreting a dispute between, the government (the political party in power) and certain civil society protesters who have peacefully expressed their ideas on social concerns like a crime against women.
- The judiciary protects the Fundamental Rights that are guaranteed to every Indian person under the country's Constitution. Independence of judiciary was created during the formation of Indian Constitution, as India was transitioning from a **feudal system**[3] to a democratic order. The constitution grants unique rights to the Indian citizens such as
  - **Civil and political rights,** e.g. the right to life, right to freedom of discrimination based on religion, race, caste, sex or place of birth.
  - **Economic, social and cultural rights**, e.g. freedom to practice any religion, protection of interests of minorities.

    An independent and impartial judiciary has empowered Indian citizens. **Article 21** of the Indian Constitution provide a general right to life and personal liberty.

    For example, within this freedom, the Supreme Court has held that a street vendor has a right to operate on streets, as selling products on street is linked to his livelihood and daily living which is protected under **Article 21.**

    Similarly, the Supreme Court has also stated that those who are aged, disabled and destitute in India, including men and women, have a right to food, which is most essential for their survival. State has a corresponding duty to provide them with food.
- Independence of judiciary is important for the respect of **due process of law**[4]. In the field of criminal law, independence of judiciary is linked to the granting of a fair trial to the accused. This becomes extremely important even when the accused are foreign nationals or persons who have committed crimes against the state, e.g. terrorists.

---

3 **Feudal system** It means the dominant social system in medieval Europe, in which the mobility held lands from the Gown in exchange for military service.

4 **Due process of law** Mean that the state must respect all the legal right that are owed to a person and confirm to the norms of fairness, liberty, Fundamental Rights, etc. Only an independent judiciary can make this concept operational.

Provisions Relating to the Judges

Independence of judges is crucial to ensuring independence of judiciary. The following legal provisions mandate judge's independence and impartiality

- Once appointed, judges are provided with a security of tenure till they reach a retirement age. This age remains **62 for the High Court judges and 65 for the Supreme Court judges.**
- Judges are not allowed to practice as advocates in the same or equivalent courts, post their retirement. For example, a retired High Court judge can practice in the Supreme Court, but is prevented from practicing in the same or other High Courts. This ensures that ex-judges practicing at the bar do not influence the decision of the bench, with whom they may have assumed familiarity.
- Judges cannot be easily removed from their office, except for proven **misbehaviour** and **incapacity**. The legal process is kept strict to ensure security of tenure of the judges.
- The **salaries** and **allowances of judges are fixed** and not subject to vote of the legislature. Judges derive their salaries from the consolidated fund of India (for the Supreme Court) and consolidated fund of state (in case of High Courts). Their emoluments cannot be changed during financial emergency.
- The conduct of judges of both the **Supreme Court and High Courts** cannot be discussed in Parliament or state legislature, except when a motion for removal of a judge is being presented to the President.
- Supreme Court of India has been authorised to have its own establishment and to have complete control over it. It is further authorised to make appointments of officers and staff of the court and determine their service conditions.

1.5 Role of Indian Judiciary

Indian judiciary comprises of the Supreme Court, High Court, Subordinate Courts and other tribunals. The composition and role of these courts are discussed below

Role of the Supreme Court of India

The Supreme Court of India primarily exercises the role of an adjudicator[5] and **interpreter.** It has the following jurisdictions

Original Jurisdiction

Original Jurisdiction is given to the Supreme Court under **Article 131** of the Constitution. The Supreme Court shall have original jurisdiction in any dispute.

- Between the Government of India and one or more states.
- Between the Government of India and any state or states on one side and one or more other states on the other side.
- Between two or more states, only if the dispute concerns any question (whether of law or fact) on which the existence or scope of a legal right is dependent.

  However, the jurisdiction shall not extend to any dispute arising out of any treaty, agreement, covenant, engagements or other similar instruments which have been entered into or executed before the commencement of the Constitution or continues to exist after such commencement.

Writ Jurisdiction

Article 32 of the Constitution further gives extensive original jurisdiction to the Supreme Court for the enforcement of the Fundamental Rights of the citizens, through issuing directions, orders and writs. This is popularly known as the **Writ Jurisdiction of the Court.**

According to **Article 32** of the Constitution, the Supreme Court is empowered to issue following writs

- **Habeas corpus** i.e. to order the release of person is unlawfully detained.
- **Mandamus** i.e. to order to a public authority to do its duty.

5 **Adjudicator** It is someone who hear formal disputes and make legally binding dicisions.

- **Prohibition** i.e. to prevent a subordinate court from continuing on a case.
- **Quo-warranto** i.e. to issue directive to a person to vacate an office wrongfully occupied. It literally means 'by what authority'.
- **Certiorari** i.e. to remove a case from a subordinate court and get the proceedings before it.

Appellate Jurisdiction

The appellate jurisdiction of the Supreme Court can be invoked by a certificate granted by the High Court. Appeal to the Supreme Court may be made against any **judgement, decree or final order** of a High Court, in both civil and criminal cases. However, these cases must involve a substantial question of law related to the interpretation of the Constitution as per the following

- **An Appeal in Constitutional Matters** According to **Article 132 (1)** of the Constitution of India, an appeal from any judgement, decree or final order of a High Court, whether in civil, criminal or other proceedings, shall be admissible to the Supreme Court, if the High Court confirms under **Article 134-A** that the case involves significant issue of law regarding the interpretation of the Constitution.
- **An Appeal in Civil Cases** According to **Article 133**, a judgement, decree or final order in a civil proceeding of a High Court may be appealed to the Supreme Court, only if the High Court certifies under **Article 134-A** that the case involves a material legal issue of public concern and that, in the High Court's view, the issue need to be decided by the Supreme Court.
- **An Appeal in Criminal Cases** According to **Article 134**, any judgement, final decision or sentence in a criminal process issued by a High Court may be appealed to the Supreme Court. There are two methods to file this appeal, i.e. without a High Court certificate and with a High Court certificate.

  An appeal without a certificate lies if the High Court
  - has reversed an order of acquittal of an accused person on appeal and sentenced him to death.
  - has withdrawn any case from any sub-ordinate court for trial before it and has convicted the accused person and sentenced him to death in such trial.
- **Special Leave to Appeal** According to **Article 136** of the Constitution, an appeal may be made directly from any court in India to the Supreme Court in certain exceptional circumstances. This is special leave petition or special leave to appeal.

  Any order, decision, decree, judgement etc. issued by any court or body in India may be appealed directly to the Supreme Court under **Article 136**. The Supreme Court has discretion over this matter and it may or may not grant someone special permission to appeal.

Advisory Jurisdiction

The President may seek advisory jurisdiction of the Supreme Court under **Article 143** of the Constitution. This method is known as **Presidential Reference** and is recognised as the advisory jurisdiction of the court. According to **Article 143** the President may refer any question for the advisory of the Supreme Court, if it appears to him/her that at any time that

- a question of law or fact has arisen or is likely to arise.
- the question is of such a nature and of such public importance that it is convenient to obtain the opinion of the Supreme Court on it. The **Supreme Court** may report to the President its opinion thereon, after such hearing as it thinks fit.

In the **Kerala Education Bill case** (1958), the Supreme Court laid down the following principles

- The Supreme Court has the freedom to refuse to express any opinion on the question submitted to it.
- The President decides what question should be referred to the court.
- The advisory opinion of the Supreme Court is not binding on courts.

In **Re-special Court Bill (1979)**, the Supreme Court ruled that its advisory authority is obligatory on all courts in India's territory. It also concluded that under **Article 143**, the Supreme Court is required to give an **advisory** opinion if the questions presented to it are neither uncertain nor of a political nature.

Supreme Court as an Activist

The Supreme Court of India is considered the **sentinel qui vie**[6] and protects the Fundamental and Constitutional Rights of the people. There have been numerous instances where Higher Court have stepped in on their own to address issues of social, political and economical importance. Sometimes these courts take action on their own to initiative, recognising the significance of a matter that demands their attention. In other cases, they many act based on a letter, a news reportor even a simple submission brought before them.

Role of High Courts and Lower Courts

The High Courts of India have several roles, including

- The High Courts function as organs of judicial administration at the state level.
- The High Courts have the power to issue within directions, orders or writs including **habeas corpus, mandamus, prohibition, quo-warranto and certiorari,** for enforcement of Fundamental Rights and any other purposes. This writ jurisdiction is similar to the Supreme Court of India.
- The role of the High Court also becomes similar to the Supreme Court in the exercise of Public Interest Litigation. Each High Court has powers of superintendence over all courts within its jurisdiction.
- High Court can also determine the manner and form in which book entries and accounts shall be kept.

The Lower Court of India has many roles, including

- The Lower Courts function as centers of civil and criminal justice at the district level.
- Lower Courts are usually courts of first instance, where litigants proceed with their disputes. These courts have set territorial and **pecuniary limits**[7] when accepting cases of civil nature.
- A similar hierarchy exists in the criminal courts at the subordinate level. Once matters are adjudicated by these courts, they proceed to the High Courts on appeal.

Court of Record

- It is a court whose judgements and proceedings are kept on **permanent record** and that has the power to **impose penalties** for contempt. The Supreme Court and High Courts are called a Court of Record. The Supreme Court and High Courts have two powers as a Court of Record.
- The judgements, proceedings and acts of the Supreme Court and High Courts are **recorded for permanent memory and witness.** These records are accepted to have evidence value and cannot be challenged. They are accepted as legal precedents and references.
- The Supreme Court and High Courts have the **power to punish contempt**[8] **of court**, either with simple imprisonment for a term of up to six months or with a fine, or with both.

1.6 Public Interest Litigation (PIL)

- Public Interest Litigation or **Janhit Yachika** is a legal action that can be filed in a court to protect the public interest. The **first ever PIL** is listed as **Hussainara Khatoon Vs. State of Bihar** and dates back to **1979**. A public interest activist lawyer filed this case on behalf of thousands of prisoners of the Bihar jail against the inhuman conditions of the prison.
- A Supreme Court bench headed by **Justice P.N. Bhagwati** declared the right for free legal aid and expeditious trial of these prisoners, which ultimately led to their release. Since then, PILs have encompassed several issues including
  - socio-economic rights (freedom from bonded labour).
  - legal entitlements (right to food, right to work).
  - environment issues (clean air and water).
  - political reforms (disclosure of assets by members of the executive, disbursement of natural resources done by the government).

---

6 **Sentinel qui vie** It means watchful guardian.
7 **Pecuniary limits** Relating to or consisting of money.
8 **Contempt** It is a legal offense that occurs when someone disobeys or shows disrespect towards a court of law or its officers.

Characteristics of PIL

The characteristics of PIL include

- PILs can be termed as **non-adversarial litigation** that sets the interest of one party over the other. PILs are recognised as **tools for social change** rather than focusing on traditional litigation of adversary[9] character.
- PILs expands the **rights of third parties** to approach the court.
- PIL from its inception is modelled on **remedial nature** which aims at creating a dynamic, welfare oriented model of judiciary. Thus, PIL incorporates the **Directive Principles** whose claims cannot be brought directly to the courts, into the domain of **Fundamental Rights** under Part III of the Constitution, which can be invoked before the courts as a matter of rights by the citizens of India.
- PIL strengthens the role of the judiciary as a monitor and watchdog agency.

Cases Related to PIL

Some of the instances where the PIL, admitted by the Supreme Court, has added a new dimension to the Indian judicial system are as follows

Ganges Pollution Case

The judgements in this case against polluting industries in the Ganga basin resulted in

- In this case, apart from industries, more than 250 towns and cities have been ordered to put sewage treatment plants.
- Six hundred tanneries operating in highly congested residential area of **Kolkata** have been shifted out of the city and relocated in a planned **Leather Complex** in the state of West Bengal.
- A large number of industries were closed down by the court and were allowed to reopen only after these industries set up effluent treatment plants and controlled pollution.

Vehicular Pollution Case

The judgements in this case in 1992 against vehicular pollution in India resulted in

- Orders for providing lead-free petrol in the country and for the use of natural gas and other mode of fuels for use in the vehicles in India have been passed and carried out.
- **Lead-free** petrol had been introduced in the **four metropolitan cities** from April 1995. All new cars registered from April 1995 onwards have been fitted with catalytic convertors.
- **COG** outlets have been set up to provide **CNG** as a clean fuel in Delhi and other cities in India, apart from Euro 2 norms.

As a result of this case, **Delhi has become the first city in the world to have complete public transportation running on CNG.**

Oleum Gas Leak Case

The judgement in this case resulted in

- The **fertiliser plant** was situated very close to human habitation and the court held that the carrying on of a hazardous industry in such proximity to population could not be permitted and the factory was relocated.
- The **Public Liability Insurance Act** was passed and the policy for the abatement of **Pollution Control** was established. The **Environment Protection Act** was passed.

Supreme Court's Guidelines for Public Interest Litigation

Letter petitions under the following categories **will be entertained** as Public Interest Litigation

- Bonded Labour matters
- Neglected children
- Non-payment of minimum wages to workers and exploitation of casual workers and complaints of violation of labour laws (except in individual cases).

9 **Adversary** It means one opponent in a contest, conflict or dispute.

- Petitions from jails complaining of harassment, for pre-mature release and seeking release after having completed 14 years in jail, death in jail, transfer, release on personal bond, speedy trial as a Fundamental Right.
- Petitions against police for refusing to register a case, harassment by police and death in police custody.
- Petitions against atrocities on women, harassment of bride, bride burning, rape, murder, kidnapping, etc.
- Petitions complaining of harassment or torture of villagers by co-villagers or by police, from persons belonging to Scheduled Caste and Scheduled Tribes and economically backward classes.
- Petitions concerning environmental pollution, disturbance of ecological balance, drugs, food adulteration, maintenance of heritage and culture, antiques, forest and wild-life and other matters of public importance.
- Petitions from riot-victims.
- Family pension.

Cases under the following categories **will not be entertained** as Public Interest Litigation and these may be returned to the petitioners or filed in the PIL cell

- Landlord-tenant matters.
- Service matter and those concerning pension and gratuity.
- Complaints against Central/ State Government Departments and local bodies, except those given above.
- Admission to medical and other educational institution.
- Petitions for early hearing of cases pending in High Courts and Sub-ordinate Courts.

In regard to the petitions concerning maintenance of wife, children and parents, the petitioners may be asked to file a petition under **Section 125 of CrPC.**

Suo Moto Action

'Suo Moto' is a Latin term that means **'on its own motion'**. The 'Suo Moto' power empowers the court to take **legal action** based on their cognisance (knowledge) of a topic without the need for a petition or an interest to be placed before them.

Courts have taken Suo Moto notice of the situation after receiving media reports, telegrams and petitions from affected parties. One of the most visible manifestations of India's Suo Moto jurisdiction is the ability to penalise for contempt of court under **Article 129** of the Indian Constitution and the **Contempt of Courts Act 1971.**

An example of Suo Moto Action was when a newspaper report on pollution in the Yamuna prompted the court to take up the case on its own in 1994. During the Covid Pandemic, a three-judge bench of the Supreme Court took Suo Moto cognisance of the non-availability of **mid-day meals** for children due to school closures caused by the coronavirus outbreak and issued notifications to all State Governments and union territories.

Provision of Legal Aid

- A person is **entitled to free legal aid** from the Supreme Court Legal Aid Committee if
  - a person belongs to the **poor section of society,** with an annual income of less than ₹ 18,000.
  - a person belong to a **Scheduled Caste or Scheduled Tribe.**
  - a person is a **victim of natural calamity.**
  - a person is a **woman or a child.**
  - a person is **mentally ill or otherwise disabled** or is an industrial worker.

- The committee's assistance includes the expense of preparing the issue and any related applications, as well as providing an advocate to prepare and argue the case. Anyone wishing to use the committee's **legal services must apply** to the secretary and provide the committee with all relevant papers. After determining the person's eligibility, the committee provides him or her with the **appropriate legal help**.
- Persons in the medium income group, with income above ₹ 18,000/- but less than ₹ 1,20,000/- per year, are entitled to legal help from the Supreme Court Middle Income Group Society on minimal payments.

Amicus Curiae

Amicus Curiae means **friend of the court**. If a petition is received from a jail or if the accused is un unrepresented in any other criminal activity, the court appoints an Advocate as Amicus Curiae to defend and argue the case of the accused.

In **civil disputes**, the court may appoint an Advocate as Amicus Curiae if it thinks, it is essential in case situation of an unrepresented party. The court may also appoint Amicus Curiae in any subject of wide public concern or in which the public at large is involved.

Quick Test 2

1. What do you mean by independence of the judiciary?
2. Identify the writs that the Supreme Court are empowered to issue.
3. Mention the advisory functions of the Supreme Court.
4. State any one functions of the High Court Judge.

1.7 Tribunals

Tribunals are **semi-judicial** bodies involved in dispute resolution. They were not part of the original Constitution, it was incorporated in the **Indian Constitution by 42nd Amendment Act, 1976.** Thus, the 42nd Amendment Act marked the era of **'tribunalisation of Indian judiciary'.**

Article 323-A deals with Administrative Tribunals and **Article 323-B** deals with tribunals for other matters. The tribunals exercise jurisdiction of service matters of employees covered by it. The appeals against the orders of the administrative tribunals lie before the division bench of the concerned High Court.

Some of the tribunals include

- **Central Administrative Tribunal** (CAT) for resolving the grievances and disputes of Central Government employees.
- **State Administrative Tribunals (SAT)** for State Government employees.
- **Telecom Dispute Settlement Appellate Tribunal (TDSAT)** for resolving disputes in the telecom sector in India.
- **National Green Tribunal** (NGT) for disputes involving environmental issues.

Central Administrative Tribunal (CAT)

The CAT was set up under the **Administrative Tribunals Act, 1985** in the year **1985**. There are **19 Benches** and **19 Circuit Benches** in the Central Administrative Tribunal all over India. The Government of India has notified organisations including Ministries and Departments of Central Government, under **Section 14** (2) of the Administrative Tribunals Act, 1985, to bring them within the jurisdiction of the Central Administrative Tribunal, from time to time.

In addition, the Central Administrative Tribunal, Principal Bench is dealing with the matters of Government of National Capital Territory of Delhi. The tribunal consists of a **Chairman, Vice Chairman** and **members.** The members of the tribunal include persons from judicial as well as administrative streams, so as to give the benefit of expertise to the tribunal in both legal and administrative spheres.

Matters over which Tribunal have Jurisdiction

Under **Article 323-B**, the Parliament and the state legislatures are authorised to provide for the establishment of tribunals for the adjudication of disputes relating to the following matters

- Taxation
- Foreign exchange and export
- Industrial and labour disputes
- Land reforms laws
- Ceiling on urban property
- Elections disputes of members of Parliament and state legislatures
- Production, procurement, supply and distribution of food stuffs and essential goods
- Rent and tenancy issues

Difference between Article 323-A and 323-B

Articles 323-A and **323-B** differ in the following two aspects

- Article 323-A is related to the establishment of tribunals for public service matters only, while Article 323-B is related to the establishment of tribunals for certain other matters.
- Tribunals under Article 323-A can be established only by Parliament, while tribunals under Article 323-B can be established both by Parliament and state legislatures with respect to matters falling within their legislative competence.

Role of Tribunals

- The tribunals are procedurally flexible and this flexibility increases their efficiency. For example, the Administrative Tribunals Act, 1985 allows the aggrieved persons to appear directly before the tribunals.
- The overall objectives of the tribunals are to **provide speedy and inexpensive justice** to the litigants. Since government is a major litigant in the courts and government related litigation has increased in the delay and pendency of litigation, such tribunals have significantly contributed in supplementing the role of the courts in adjudication of service disputes.
- The tribunals are not meant to replace the courts. In the case of **L. Chandra Kumar (1997)**, the Supreme Court decided that **tribunals would not take away the exclusive jurisdiction of the courts** and their decisions could be scrutinised[10] by the division bench of the High Courts.
- Tribunals have been constituted under specific Constitutional mandate enshrined in the Constitution of India or through legal enactments, e.g. a law passed by the legislature. Their creation **aims at increasing efficiency in resolving disputes and reducing the burden on courts.**
- Some of the tribunals function with regulators[11].

For example, one of the tribunals TDSAT (Telecom Dispute Settlement Appellate Tribunals) functions alongside the regulator, TRAI (Telecom Regulatory Authority of India) in formulating laws and policy for resolving telecom disputes in India.

Quick Test 3

1. What are the two sub-branches of Tribunals?
2. Which article is related to the establishment of tribunals for certain matters?
3. What do you mean by the regulators?
4. Under which act, the Central Administrative Tribunal was set up?

10 **Scrutinised** It means to inspect and examine closely and thoroughly.
11 **Regulators** Regulators are specialised government agencies that oversee the law and order compliance in the relevant government sectors.

Mind Map

JUDICIARY IN INDIA

1 Structure and Hierarchy of Courts in India

- It includes courts to administer both central and states laws.
- High Courts are followed by District and Subordinate Courts popularly known as the lower courts in India.
- Disputes related to employment, consumer rights and service matters, taking some of the burden away from the traditional court system.

Supreme Court
- **Establishment** January 28, 1950; replaced Federal Court of India.
- **Composition** Chief Justice + 33 judges (as per 2019 amendment).
- **Jurisdiction**
  - **Original Jurisdiction** Disputes between states or the union and states.
  - **Appellate Jurisdiction** Appeals against High Court decisions in civil, criminal and Constitutional cases.
  - **Advisory Jurisdiction** Presidential reference under Article 143.
  - **Writ Jurisdiction** Enforcement of Fundamental Rights via writs (e.g., habeas corpus, mandamus).

High Courts
- **Number** 25 High Courts.
- **Jurisdiction** State/Union Territory-specific or groups of states.
- **Functions**
  - Supervisory role over subordinate courts.
  - Power to issue writs like the Supreme Court.

District and Subordinate Courts
- **District Courts**
  - Civil cases presided over by District Judges.
  - Criminal cases presided over by Sessions Judges.
- **Subordinate Courts**
  - Civil Junior Civil Judge, Principal Junior Civil Judge, Senior Civil Judge.
  - Criminal Magistrates (First and Second Class), Chief Judicial Magistrates.

2 Features of Indian Judiciary

Independence
- Constitutional safeguards (**Article 50** Separation of judiciary from the executive).
- Judges' security of tenure and fixed salaries.
- Strict removal process.

Common Law System
- Based on precedents; judicial decisions create laws.
- Differs from civil law systems, which rely solely on legislative enactments.

Adversarial Model
- Lawyers represent parties before an impartial judge.
- Contrast with inquisitorial systems where judges investigate.

3 Legal Officers

- Attorney General is first legal officer of the country.
- M.C. Setalvad was India's first Attorney General.
- The President of India appoints the Attorney General of India according to Article 76.

Attorney General of India
- **Role** Legal advisor to the Central Government, appointed under Article 76.
- **Powers** Can participate in Parliamentary proceedings without voting rights.

Advocate General
- **Role** Legal advisor to State Governments, appointed under Article 165.
- **Powers** Represents the state in High Courts and the Supreme Court.

4 Tribunals

Overview
- Established under Articles 323-A (Administrative Tribunals) and 323-B (other matters).
- Provide specialised and speedy justice in areas like taxation, labour and environment.

For examples
- Central Administrative Tribunal (CAT)
- State Administrative Tribunals (SAT)
- National Green Tribunal (NGT)
- Telecom Disputes Settlement Appellate Tribunal (TDSAT)

5 Judiciary and Fundamental Rights

Enforcement of Fundamental Rights
- Article 32 empowers the Supreme Court to issue writs for rights enforcement.
- High Courts have similar powers under Article 226.

Other Roles of Judiciary
- **Guardian of Democracy**
  - Maintains checks and balances over legislative and executive powers.
  - Ensures fair trial and upholds the rule of law.
- **Protection of Constitutional Philosophy**
  - Resolves conflicts between civil liberties and state powers.
  - Ensures government accountability.
- **Court of Record**
  - Supreme Court and High Courts' decisions are permanent records, binding on lower court.

6 Key Concepts and Provisions

Judicial Review
- Power to determine the Constitutionality of laws and executive actions.

Independence Vs. Impartiality
- Independence ensures freedom from external pressures.
- Impartiality ensures fair and unbiased judgements.

Judges' Tenure
- High Court judges retire at 62; Supreme Court judges at 65.
- Post-retirement restrictions on practicing law in similar courts.

7 Public Interest Litigation (PIL)

- Allows third parties to approach the courts for public welfare.
- **For examples** Ganges Pollution Case, Vehicular Pollution Case, Oleum Gas Leak Case.

CBSE TEXTBOOK FOLDER

1. List any two Constitutional offices endowed with the function to advise and represent the government on legal matters.

Ans. The two Constitutional offices endowed with the function to advise and represent the government on legal matters are

(i) **Attorney General of India** The Government of India needs the Attorney General's advice on any legal issues that are brought to them. Additionally, they carry out additional legal obligations that the President has given them. The Attorney General is entitled to appear before all Indian courts and to take part in Parliamentary sessions, but not to vote. The Attorney General represents the Indian government in all Supreme Court actions (including lawsuits, appeals and other hearings) involving the Indian Government. Additionally, they represent the Indian Government when the President approaches the Supreme Court under Article 143 of the Constitution.

The Attorney General is assisted by a Solicitor General and Additional Solicitor Generals. The Attorney General is to be consulted only in legal matters of real importance and only after the Ministry of Law has been consulted. All references to the Attorney General are made by the Law Ministry.

(ii) **Advocate General** The Advocate General is the highest law officer in the state. He is responsible to assist the State Government in all its legal matters. The Advocate General defends and protects the interest of the State Government. The Advocate General can defend the State Government in front of the High Court and Supreme Court. He advises the government of the state upon such legal matters, which are referred to or assigned to him by the Governor.

2. Besides being an adjudicator and an interpreter, the Supreme Court performs another function under Article 143 of the Indian Constitution. Identify and explain the function of the Supreme Court of India.

Ans. The Supreme Court of India primarily exercises the role of an adjudicator and interpreter.

- **Advisory Jurisdiction** The President may seek advisory jurisdiction of the Supreme Court under Article 143 of the Constitution. This method is known as Presidential Reference and is recognised as the advisory jurisdiction of the court. Supreme Court also has other functions or jurisdication.
- **Original Jurisdiction** Original jurisdiction is given to the Supreme Court under Article 131 of the Constitution. The Supreme Court shall have original jurisdiction in any dispute between the Government of India and one or more states.
  - Between the Government of India and any state or states on one side and one or more other states on the other side.
  - Between two or more states, only if the dispute concerns any question (whether of law or fact) on which the existence or scope of a legal right is dependent. However, the jurisdiction shall not extend to any dispute arising out of any treaty, agreement, covenant, engagements or other similar instruments which have been entered into or executed before the commencement of the constitution or continues to exist after such commencement.
  - States that the jurisdiction does not apply to such a dispute.
- **Writ Jurisdiction** Article 32 of the Constitution further gives extensive original jurisdiction to the Supreme Court for the enforcement of the Fundamental Rights of the citizens, through issuing directions, orders and writs.
- **Supreme Court as an Activist** The Supreme Court of India is considered as the guardian of the fundamental and Constitutional Rights of the people.

3. What are tribunals? How do they play an instrumental role in rendering more effective dispute resolution mechanism?

Ans. Tribunals are semi-judicial bodies involved in dispute resolution. They were not part of the original Constitution, it was in-corporated in the Indian Constitution by 42nd Amendment Act, 1976. The tribunals are procedurally flexible and this flexibility increases their efficiency. The overall objectives of the tribunals are to provide speedy and inexpensive justice to the litigants.

Since government is a major litigant in the courts and government related litigation has increased in the delay and pendency of litigation, such tribunals have significantly contributed in supplementing the role of the courts in adjudication of service disputes.

Exam Pattern Questions

Objective Type Questions

Multiple Choice Questions (MCQs)

1. When was the Supreme Court inaugurated in India?

(a) 27th January, 1950
(b) 28th January, 1950
(c) 29th January, 1950
(d) 30th January, 1950

2. In the year 1950, the Constitution of India envisaged a Supreme Court with one Chief Justice and .... judges. CBSE 2017

(a) eight (b) seven
(c) twelve (d) twenty-four

3. Which Article of the Indian Constitution provides for the independence of the judiciary?

(a) Article 49 (b) Article 50
(c) Article 51 (d) Article 52

4. The dispute regarding the sharing of water resources between the state of Tamil Nadu and Kerala with respect to Mullaperiyar dam can be brought before the Supreme Court under the exercise of which jurisdiction? CBSE SQP 2021

(a) Advisory Jurisdiction
(b) Original Jurisdiction
(c) Appellate Jurisdiction
(d) Judicial Review

5. In 1979, a Supreme Court bench headed by Justice P.N. Bhagwati declared the right to free legal aid and expeditious trial for the prisoners who were stuck in a Bihar jail, which ultimately led to their release. This became a landmark case as it established the role of being an activist for the Supreme Court, in the form of CBSE SQP 2021

(a) Appellate Jurisdiction
(b) Advisory Jurisdiction
(c) Public Interest Litigation
(d) Original Jurisdiction

6. Indian police have extensive powers for crime detection and investigation. But such powers should not impinge upon the rights of the accused. This right has been guaranteed under .... CBSE SQP 2021

(a) Article 20(3)
(b) Article 21
(c) Article 22
(d) Article 20(4)

7. Anil Gopal Swamy has been appointed to a legal office in India under Article 76 of the Constitution. He enjoys all the privileges and immunities available to a Member of Parliament. Identify the position held by Anil Gopal Swamy. CBSE SQP 2024

(a) Chief Justice of India (b) Advocate General
(c) Attorney General (d) Solicitor General

8. Rahul an accused, is convicted of murder by the Trial Court and sentenced to the imprisonment. He appeals to the High Court, which dismisses his appeal. Rahul then files an appeal to the Supreme Court under Article 136 of the Constitution. Which of the following is true regarding this appeal?

(a) The Supreme Court has to necessarily hear the appeal and decide the matter on merit.
(b) The Supreme Court may grant special leave to appeal if it is satisfied that the appeal raises a substantial question of law or justice .
(c) The Supreme Court has no power to entertain the appeal as the High Court has already dismissed it.
(d) The Supreme Court will only hear the appeal if the President of India grants permission.

9. Which of the following statement correctly describe the power of the Supreme Court.

I. It is empowered to issue directions, orders or writs.
II. The Supreme Court also has a very wide appellate jurisdiction over all court.
III. Article 143 of the Indian Constitution empowers Supreme Court with advisory jurisdiction.
IV. The Supreme Court is a Court of Record.
V. Article 139 of the Indian Constitution gives ancillary powers to the Supreme Court.

Codes

(a) I, II, III, V (b) I, II, III, IV
(c) I, II, IV, V (d) All of these

10. Identify the correct sequence of the Indian Judiciary as per the hierarchy.

I. Munsiff Court **II. District Court**
III. Principal Junior Civil Judge Court
IV. High Court

Codes

(a) II, III, I, IV (b) IV, I, II, III
(c) IV, II, III, I (d) IV, II, I, III

11. In a landmark case, the Supreme Court was handling a highly technical environmental dispute involving multiple stakeholders and scientific complexities. Given the intricate details of environmental policies and scientific evidence, the court appointed an amicus curiae, an expert in environmental law and science, to assist by providing impartial information and insights on the matter. The amicus curiae made recommendations based on international standards, which helped the court in reaching its final decision.

Based on the concept of amicus curiae, which of the following statements is correct? **CBSE 2025**

(a) The amicus curiae advocates for the interests of the public and acts as a representative for the government.
(b) The amicus curiae serves as the legal advisor to the party that requests their assistance in the case.
(c) The amicus curiae assists the court by providing impartial expertise on complex issues, without representing any party in the case.
(d) The amicus curiae is only allowed to assist in cases related to Constitutional matters.

12. A High Court in India issues a verdict in a complex property dispute, which left one party dissatisfied with the decision. The aggrieved party now seeks to approach the Supreme Court for special leave to appeal. Under Article 136, the Supreme Court can grant special leave to appeal against any judgement, decree or order in any matter passed by .... **CBSE 2025**

(a) any court or tribunal in India
(b) only High Court
(c) only subordinate court
(d) only tribunals

13. Match the following. **CBSE 2024 C**

	Column I		Column II
A.	Article 50	1.	Appointment of Advocate General
B.	Article 131	2.	Original Jurisdiction of the Supreme Court
C.	Article 165	3.	Appointment of the Attorney General
D.	Article 76	4.	Independence of Judiciary

Codes

	A	B	C	D		A	B	C	D
(a)	4	3	2	1	(b)	2	4	1	3
(c)	4	1	2	3	(d)	4	2	1	3

14. Out of the following two statements, which is the correct one.

Statement I Judiciary's independence is linked to its role as the watchdog in a democracy.

Statement II An independent and impartial judiciary has empowered Indian citizens and performed the role of guardian of Fundamental Rights.

Codes

(a) Only Statement I is correct.
(b) Only Statement II is correct.
(c) Both the Statements are correct.
(d) Both the Statements are incorrect.

Assertion-Reason Questions

Directions (Q.Nos. 15-19) In the questions given below, there are two statements. Read the statements and choose the correct option.

Codes

(a) Both A and R are true and R is the correct explanation of A.
(b) Both A and R are true, but R is not the correct explanation of A.
(c) A is true, but R is false.
(d) A is false, but R is true.

15. Assertion (A) A retired High Court judge can practice in the Supreme Court, but is prevented from practicing in the same or other High Courts.

Reason (R) This ensures that ex-judges practicing at the bar do not influence the decision of the bench, with whom they may have presumed familiarity.

16. Assertion (A) PILs can be termed as adversarial litigation that pits the interest of one party over the other.

Reason (R) Rather than focusing on traditional litigation of adversary character, PILs are recognised as tools for social change.

17. Assertion (A) Public Interest Litigations (PILs) are based on the tenets of citizen standing and representative standing. **CBSE 2024 C**

Reason (R) PILs have strengthened the role of judiciary as a monitor.

18. Assertion (A) The salaries and allowances of judges are fixed and not subject to vote of the legislature. **CBSE SQP 2022**

Reason (R) Independence of judges is crucial to ensure independence of judiciary.

19. Assertion (A) PILs are based on the tenets of citizen standing and representative standing.

Reason (R) PILs have strengthened the role of judiciary as a monitor and watchdog agency. **CBSE 2024**

Answers

1. (b) 28th January, 1950
2. (b) seven
3. (b) Article 50
4. (b) Original jurisdiction
5. (c) Public Interest Litigation
6. (a) Article 20(3)
7. (c) Attorney General
8. (b) The Supreme Court may grant special leave to appeal if it is satisfied that the appeal raises a substantial question of law or justice.
9. (b) I, II, III, IV
10. (c) IV, II, III, I
11. (c) The amicus curiae assists the court by providing impartial expertise on complex issues, without representing any party in the case.
12. (a) any court or tribunal in India
13. (d) 4 2 1 3
14. (c) Both the statements are correct
15. (a) Both A and R are true and R is the correct explanation of A.
16. (d) A is false, but R is true.
17. (c) A is true, but R is false.
18. (d) A is false, but R is true.
19. (d) A is false, but R is true.

Subjective Questions

Very Short Answer Type Questions

1. Why is the Supreme Court called the Court of Record? Give reasons.

Ans. The Supreme Court is called a Court of Record because the judgements, proceedings and acts of the Supreme Court are recorded for permanent memory and witness. These records are accepted to have evidence value and cannot be challenged. They are accepted as legal precedents and references.

2. Covid Pandemic has brought a paradigm shift in the way people perceived information technology. Schools and colleges all adopted online mode. This gave rise to instances of cyber crimes. Cyber bullying, body shaming, hacking, stalking became very common. The cases of suicide in teenagers increased. The concern was raised in the Parliament as well. The President of India also sought the advice of the Supreme Court on the issue.

(i) Under which jurisdiction can the President seek the opinion of the Supreme Court?

(ii) On what grounds can the Supreme Court refuse to provide its opinion? **CBSE SQP 2022**

Ans. (i) Article 143 of the Indian Constitution empowered the Supreme Court with advisory jurisdiction. This procedure is termed as 'Presidential Reference' and is recognised as the 'Advisory jurisdiction' of the court.

(ii) Supreme Court can refuse to provide its opinion if it is satisfied that the questions are either socio-economic or political in nature.

3. Explain the role of High Courts in the Indian Judicial system. **CBSE 2024**

Ans. The High Courts function as organs of judicial administration at the state level. The role of the High Court becomes similar to the Supreme Court in the exercise of PIL, furthermore, each High Courts has powers of superintendence over all courts within jurisdiction.

4. Analyse the role of 'regulators' in aiding the tribunals. Substance the answer with help of an example. **CBSE SQP 2024**

Ans. Regulators play a crucial role in aiding tribunals by providing expert insights and enforcing compliance. For example, the Securities and Exchange Commission (SEC) assists securities tribunals by investigating and prosecuting cases, ensuring fair market practices.

5. What is meant by the term 'Due process of law'? How is the independence of judiciary related to due process of law? **CBSE 2023**

Ans. Due process of law is a legal principle that ensures the government follows fair procedures before taking action that could affect a person's life, liberty or property. Independence of judiciary is linked to the granting of a fair trial to the accused, as independence of judiciary is important for the respect of due process of law.

6. In the Landmark case of Marbury V.S. Madison (1803), the Supreme Court ruled that a provision of the Judiciary Act of 1789 was unconstitutional. The court held that the provision violated the principle of separation of powers and encroached on the executive branch's authority. What is the significance of this decision in establishing the principle that Supreme Court judgements are binding on all courts?

Ans. Marbury V.S. Madison decision established the power of judicial review, which holds that the Supreme Court has the final say on the Constitutionality of laws and government actions.

This decision set a precedent that all lower courts must follow the Supreme Court's interpretations of the Constitution and federal laws.

This means that Supreme Court judgements are binding on all courts, ensuring consistency and uniformity in the application of law across the country.

7. Which were the first four High Courts of India?

Ans The Madras High Court in Chennai, Bombay High Court in Mumbai, Calcutta High Court in Kolkata and the Allahabad High Court in Allahabad were the first four High Courts of India.

8. List the Subordinate Courts below the District Court on the civil as well as criminal side.

Ans. On the civil side, the Subordinate Courts below the District Court include (in ascending order)

- Junior Civil Judge Court
- Principal Junior Civil Judge Court
- Senior Civil Judge Courts (also called sub-courts) Subordinate Courts on the criminal side (in ascending order) include
- Second Class Judicial Magistrates Court
- First Class Judicial Magistrate Court
- Chief Judicial Magistrate Court

9. Analyse the relation between 'due process of law' and 'independence of judiciary.' **CBSE 2020**

Ans. Independence of the judiciary is vital for the respect of due process of law. Due process of law means that the state must respect all the legal rights that are owed to a person and confirm to the norms of fairness, liberty, Fundamental Rights, etc. Only an independent judiciary can make this concept operational.

10. Why is an independent judiciary considered to be a watchdog of democracy?

Or **Explain the role of judiciary as the watchdog in Indian democracy.** **CBSE 2023**

Ans. Independent judiciary is considered to be a watchdog of democracy as it monitors and maintains the checks and balances over the other arms of the government. Thus, the judiciary emerges as a mediator when any organ of the government exercises 'excess power' which tends to violate the larger societal or individual interest.

11. How does the judiciary act as the guardian of Fundamental Rights of citizens?

Ans. The judiciary acts as the guardian of Fundamental Rights which are Constitutionally granted to every citizen in India. Independence of the judiciary was carved out during the formation of the Indian Constitution as India was transitioning from a feudal to a democratic order. It was done to fully translate the well-knit provisions of extensive rights guaranteed under the Constitution into the lives of average citizens.

12. What are the primary objectives which an independent judiciary seeks to achieve?

Ans. Independence of judiciary helps in

- the maintenance of rule of law.
- ensuring good governance.
- creating a free and fair society.

13. What do you understand by 'Presidential Reference'? Is it binding in nature?

Ans. Under Presidential Reference, the President may refer any question of law or fact of public importance. However, it is not binding on the Supreme Court to answer questions raised in the reference.

14. Who is an 'Amicus curiae' ? Why is he/she appointed? **CBSE 2024 C**

Ans. An 'Amicus curiae' (Latin for "friend of the court") is a neutral, impartial expert appointed by the court to provide information, insight, or expertise on a specific issue or case. They assist the court in reaching a just decision, often in complex or sensitive cases.

Short Answer Type Questions

1. Rajesh, a resident of Mumbai, files a case against his employer, XYZ corporation, for unfair labour practices. The case is initially heard by the Subordinate Court (labour judge). The labour judge rules in favour of Rajesh, but XYZ corporation appeal the decision, which court will hear the appeal? Write a short note on District and Subordinate Courts.

Ans. The appeal will be heard by District court. The courts that function below the High Courts are popularly known as the Lower Courts. They consist of District and Subordinate Courts. Each state is divided into judicial districts presided over by a 'District and Sessions Judge'. The judge is known as a 'District Judge' when he presides over a civil case and a 'Sessions Judge' when he presides over a criminal case. The District Judge is also called a 'Metropolitan Sessions Judge' when he is presiding over a District Court in a city which is designated as a metropolitan area by the State Government. District judges may be working with additional district judges, depending upon the judicial workload.

The District Judge is the highest judicial authority below a High Court judge. The District Court also holds appellate jurisdiction and supervision over all Subordinate Courts below it.

2. Differentiate between Attorney General and Advocate General. **CBSE SQP 2020**

Ans. Differences between Attorney General and Advocate General are as follows

Attorney General	Advocate General
The Attorney General is first legal officer of the country.	An Advocate General is a senior law officer who acts as a legal adviser to the State Government.
According to Article 76 of the Indian Constitution, the President of India appoints the Attorney General of India, who holds office during the pleasure of the President.	According to Article 165 of the Constitution, Advocate General is appointed by the Governor of the respective state.
The constitution stipulates that the Attorney General must be a person qualified to be appointed as a Supreme Court judge. He/She should have sufficient legal experience or have held judicial office for the required amount of time.	The qualification required for appointment as an Advocate General is similar to that of a High Court.

3. "The concept of independence and impartiality of Indian Judiciary must be studied in conjunction as they aim at achieving the same goal of maintaining judicial integrity in the democratic process of the country. Comment." **CBSE SQP 2022**

Or **"Independence of judiciary and impartiality of judges exist as two distinct concepts, yet these concepts must be studied in conjunction as they aim at achieving the same goal."**

Justify stating the Constitutional provisions safeguarding both.

Ans. Independence of judges is crucial to ensuring independence of judiciary.

The following legal provisions mandate judge's independence and impartiality

- Once appointed, judges are provided with a security of tenure till they reach a retirement age. This age remains 62 for the High Court judges and 65 for the Supreme Court judges.
- Judges are not allowed to practice as advocates in the same or equivalent courts, post their retirement. For example, a retired High Court judge can practice in the Supreme Court, but is prevented from practicing in the same or other High Courts.
- This ensures that ex-judges practicing at the bar do not influence the decision of the bench, with whom they may have assumed familiarity.
- Judges cannot be easily removed from their office, except for proven misbehaviour and incapacity. The legal process is kept strict to ensure security of tenure of the judges.

4. Identify and explain which type of jurisdiction will be applied by the Supreme Court of India under the following given situations **CBSE 2016**

(i) A dispute arose between two states in India regarding the sharing of rivers.

(ii) The President of India refers a matter of public importance to the Supreme Court of India.

(iii) A civil appeal was filed by Mr. Rajan in the Supreme Court of India for which the certificate of appeal not granted by High Court.

Ans. (i) Original jurisdiction will be applied by the Supreme Court in this situation. Original jurisdiction is given to the Supreme Court under Article 131 of the Constitution.

The Supreme Court shall have original jurisdiction in any dispute

- between the Government of India and one or more states.
- between the Government of India and any state, or states on one side and one or more other states on the other side.
- between two or more states.
- states that the jurisdiction does not apply to such a dispute.

(ii) Advisory jurisdiction/role will be applied by the Supreme Court in this situation. The President may seek advisory jurisdiction of the Supreme Court under Article 143 of the Constitution.

This method is known as **Presidential Reference** and is recognised as the advisory jurisdiction of the court.

(iii) Appellate jurisdiction will be applied by the Supreme Court in this situation. The appellate jurisdiction of the Supreme Court can be invoked only by a certificate granted by the High Court.

5. "Independence of judiciary is vital for the respect of due process of law". Elaborate. **CBSE 2025**

Ans. The independence of the judiciary is essential for upholding the due process of law, ensuring that the state respects legal rights, fairness, liberty and Fundamental Rights. Only an independent judiciary can operationalise this concept.

In criminal law, it guarantees a fair trial, even for foreign nationals and individuals accused of crimes against the state, such as terrorists. Thus, judicial independence remains a vital principle in modern democracy.

6. Rohit has a Saving Bank Account with Zono Bank. Being an employee of TTS Co. Ltd, his salary and other allowances were being directly credited to his account with the bank. He alleged that the bank had issued a cheque book without his knowledge to someone else and had passed cheques which were not drawn by him. The total amount so fraudulently withdrawn from his account amounted to ₹1,00,000.

(i) Identify the agency he can approach for the redressal of his grievance.

(ii) State its functions.

Ans. (i) The agency Rohit can approach for the redressal of his grievance is Banking Ombudsman, who is a senior official appointed by the Reserve Bank of India to redress customer complaints against deficiency in certain banking services.

(ii) The function of Banking Ombudsman are as follows

- A Banking Ombudsman is responsible for matters relating to non-payment or delay in collection of cheques, bills, drafts, etc.
- Failure to issue or delay in issues of banker's cheques, failing to honour guarantee or letter of credit commitments all fall under the ambit of the responsibilities of a Banking Ombudsman.
- A Banking Ombudsman receives complaints regarding non-adherence to any of the banking guidelines laid down by the RBI.

7. "Article 50 of the Constitution of India directe the state to take stepe to separate the judiciary from the executive". In light of Article 50, discuss the importance of the separation of two powers between the judiciary and the executive. State any provisions enumerated in Article 50 that contribute to the independence of the judiciary in India. **CBSE 2025**

Ans. Article 50 of the Indian Constitution mandates the separation of the judiciary from the executive to ensure an independent judicial system. This separation helps maintain the rule of law, prevents misuse of power, and upholds citizens' rights. Two key provisions contributing to judicial independence include

(i) Judges are provided with security of tenure, ensuring they remain free from external influence.

(ii) Judges cannot be easily removed except for proven misbehaviour or incapacity, safeguarding their impartiality.

8. Harmeet, a 35-year-old lawyer who has been practicing law for 10 years. She has a strong background in criminal law and has tried numerous cases in state and federal courts. Harmeet is a member of the State Bar Association and has completed additional training in judicial ethics and procedures. Does Harmeet meet the qualifications to be appointed as a District Judge?

Ans. In India, the qualifications for a District Judge are specified in Constitution of Indian and the Judges (Inquiry) Act, 1968.

The criteria needed to qualify for a district judge are

(i) She should be 35 years old.

(ii) She should have been a practicing advocate or a pleader for at least 7 years.

Additionally the selection process include a written examination as well as viva-voce.

Long Answer Type Questions

1. The two broad models of the legal system differ in their techniques of adjudication and justice delivery mechanism. Elaborate. **CBSE 2020**

Ans. The two broad models of the legal system are inquisitorial and adversarial model.

Courts in India follow adversarial form of adjudication rather than the inquisitorial approach. Under an adversarial arrangement, the role of lawyer representing the party becomes crucial.

Lawyers of the opposing parties present their cases before an impartial judge and the judge provides a decision based on the merits of the case as given by the lawyers.

On the other hand, judges are more proactive in making decisions under the inquisitorial system of law. They have the right to enquire and look into the problem, much like the police, as compared to the functioning of impartial judges.

2. Justice Kumar, a High Court Judge is hearing a sensitive case involving a powerful politician Mr. Singh. As Justice Kumar delivers a verdict against Mr. Singh, he receives a phone call from the politician's, aide threatening to 'consequences' if he doesn't change his decision. Justice Kumar refuses to bow down and upholds his original verdict.

Discuss the legal provisions which help in maintaining a judge's independence and impartiality.

Ans. For answer, refer to text under the heading Constitution, Roles and Impartiality on page no 5.

3. Examine the role of the Supreme Court as an adjudicator and interpreter. **CBSE 2020**

Ans. For answer, refer to text under the heading Role of the Supreme Court of India on page no. 6 and 7.

SELF ASSESSMENT TEST

Objective Type Questions

1. Which of the following subordinate courts are included on the criminal side?
   (a) Second Class Judicial Magistrates Court
   (b) First Class Judicial Magistrate Court
   (c) Chief Judicial Magistrate Court
   (d) All of these
2. Which is the highest judicial authority in India whose decisions are binding on all courts?
   (a) Supreme Court (b) Parliament (c) Law Minister (d) Lok Sabha
3. The concept of 'Presidential Reference' has been provided under which of the following Articles?
   (a) Article 142 (b) Article 143 (c) Article 144 (d) Article 145
4. The present number of High Courts of Judicature in India is
   (a) Twenty-five (b) Twenty-one (c) Twenty-two (d) Twenty-three
5. Which one of the following Indian States does not have its own High Court?
   (a) Orissa (b) Sikkim (c) Himachal Pradesh (d) Mizoram

Very Short Answer Type Questions

6. Name the two legal officers which are mainly appointed for the legal matters related to the Government of India.
7. Name the first case which is known for the PIL case.
8. According to the Andhra Pradesh Re-organisation Act 2014, which new High Courts were founded?

Short Answer Type Questions

9. Explain the two powers of the Supreme Court of India.
10. Discuss the reasons for granting special status to the judiciary.

Long Answer Type Questions

11. Write a detailed note on the similarities and differences between Attorney General and Advocate General.
12. The Federal Communications Commission (FCC) is an administrative agency responsible for regulating the telecommunications industry. The FCC has the authority to issue licenses to companies that want to provide telecommunications services. In 2020, the FCC issued a license to a company called XYZ telecom, but with certain conditions that XYZ telecom found too restrictive. XYZ telecom appealed the decision to the FCC's Administrative Law Judge (ALJ), arguing that the conditions were unreasonable and would harm their business.
13. What type of hearing will ALT conduct? Can the ALT grant relief to XYZ telecom. If so, what types of relief?

02

CHAPTER

Appointments, Retirement and Removal of Judges

The appointment of judges in practice remains a complex process despite a clear Constitutional mandate. The appointment at the Supreme Court and the High Court follows a collegium model, which is a judicial creation through case-laws. It is not Constitutionally mandated.

YOUR STUDY GOALS

YOUR PRACTICE GOAL

- Objective Type Questions (21 Qs ; MCQs, Matching) Statements, A-R)
- Subjective Questions (9 VSAs, 4 SAs, 3 LAs)

2.1 Appointment of Judges

The method of appointment of judges at the Supreme Court, High Courts and District Courts has been enshrined in the Constitution of India.

Procedure for Appointing Supreme Court Judges

- According to **Article 124** of the Constitution, every judge of the Supreme Court shall be appointed by the President after consultation with such judges of the Supreme Court and of the High Courts in the states, as the President may deem necessary.
- The article also provides that in case of appointment of a judge other than the Chief Justice of India, the Chief Justice must be consulted. The article further provides for the qualifications required to become a judge at the Supreme Court.

These qualifications include

- He/She should be a **citizen of India**.
- He/She has been a **judge of a High Court** or of two or more High Courts in succession, **for atleast five years.**
- He/She has been an **advocate of a High Court** or of two or more such courts in succession, for atleast ten years.
- He/She should be a **distinguished** jurist[1] in the opinion of the President.

1 **Jurist** It is a person who is an expert in details of the legal system.

Procedure for Appointing High Court Judges

- The procedure for appointment of judges at the High Court has been enshrined in **Article 217** of the Constitution.
- Every judge of the High Court shall be appointed by the President after consultation with the Chief Justice of India, the Governor of the state and in the case of appointment of a judge other than the Chief Justice, the Chief Justice of the High Court concerned must be consulted.

  The qualifications of a High Court judge includes
  - He/She should be a **citizen of India.**
  - He/She has **held a judicial office** in India, **for atleast ten years.**
  - He/She has been an **advocate in a High Court** or of two or more such courts in succession, **for atleast ten years.**

Procedures for Appointing District and Subordinate Court Judges

- The procedure for appointment of judges for the district and subordinate courts or the lower judiciary is mentioned in Article 233 of the Constitution.
- Appointment of district judges in any state shall be made by the Governor of the state in consultation with the **concerned High Court in such state.**

  The qualifications for appointment as District Judge includes
  - He/She should be a member of judicial service of the state.
  - He/She should be a person who has had a minimum of seven years of practice as a lawyer at the bar.

2.2 Current Practice in the Appointment of Judges

- The issue of appointment has often been linked to the independence of judiciary. There has been a constant struggle between executive and judiciary over the **appointment** of judges.
- The **14th Law Commission Report** under the chairmanship of M.C. Setalvad (India's first attorney general in 1958) highlighted that several appointments were being made on political, regional, communal or other grounds, due to which the appropriate were never appointed. Thus, the commission suggested on strengthening the process of consultation between the executive and the judiciary.

  Later, a series of three judicial decisions popularly known as the **Three Judges Cases** helped in the development of the modern collegium system in the following ways

  (i) **The first judges case** (1981) gave primacy to the executive and stated that the CJI's recommendation to the President can be refused for cogent[2] reasons. It gave vast powers to the executive for the next 12 years, in making judicial appointments.

  (ii) **In the second judges case** (1993), the decision in the first case was modified. It decided that the Chief Justice of India has primacy in the matter of appointments to the Supreme Court and the High Courts. It also decided that an appointment has to be made according to the final opinion of the Chief Justice of India, while emphasising the desirability of consultation of the Chief Justice with other Judges. This decision was rendered by a **nine-judge bench** but it was only supported by **five judges** on the bench.

  (iii) In 1998, the Supreme Court in a **Presidential reference (1998 advisory decision)** emphasised upon the role of 'consultation' and held that the process of appointment of judges to the Supreme Court and the High Courts is an integrated participatory consultative process. The Chief Justice of India give his opinion after consultation with a plurality of judges. His opinion is formed by a body of senior judges.

---

2 Cogent It means something which clear, logical and convincing.

Appointment of Supreme Court Judges under the Collegium System

Under the collegium model for appointment of judges of the Supreme Court,

- The Chief Justice of India consults with **four** senior most judges of the Supreme Court.
- The Chief Justice of India sends his recommendations to the Union Minister of Law and Justice.
- Who then puts up the same to the Prime Minister.
- The Prime Minister will then advise the President.

Appointment of the Chief Justice of India

The Chief Justice of India is the senior most judge of the Supreme Court. Seniority is determined on the basis of the **date of their appointment** the Supreme Court and if **two** judges are appointed to the court on the same day, the judge **who takes the oath first** is the senior judge.

Seniority Principle in Appointment of CJI

- According to this principle, the senior most judge of the Supreme Court is appointed as the Chief Justice of India.
- The principle is an unwritten convention called the 'seniority principle' in legal, academic and judicial language.
- It aims to safeguard the judiciary's independence from any sort of political interference.
- The Constitution of India under **Article 124 (2),** grants power to the President of India to appoint the next Chief Justice in consultation with the outgoing Chief Justice.
- As per convention[3] the name suggested by the incumbent[4] Chief Justice is almost always the next senior most judge in the Supreme Court.
- The suggestion is forwarded by the Union Law Minister to the Prime Minister, who then advises the President.

Appointment of High Court Judges under the Collegium System

- For High Courts, the collegium comprises the **Chief Justice of the High Court and two senior most judges of the High Court.** The Chief Justice conveys his recommendations to the Chief Minister of the state and the Governor of the state, who in turn send their views directly to the Union Minister of Law and Justice.
- The complete material is then forwarded to the Chief Justice of India, who in consultation with a collegium of two judges of the Supreme Court, would send his recommendations to the Union Minister of Law and Justice.
- The Union Minister of Law and Justice then puts up the same to the Prime Minister who will advise the President in the matter of appointment.

Appointment of Chief Justice of High Courts

The Chief Justice of the High Court is appointed as per the policy of having Chief Justices from outside the respective states.

- High Court judges are recommended by a collegium comprising the CJI and two senior most judges in the appointment.
- The proposal is initiated by the outgoing Chief Justice of the High Court concerned, in consultation with two senior-most colleagues.
- The recommendation is sent to the Chief Minister, who advises the Governor to send the proposal to the Union Law Minister.

---

3 Convention It is a way in which something is usually done.
4 Incumbent It means an official or regime currently holding office.

Quick Test 1

1 Which article is related to the appointment of judges of the Supreme Court?
2 What does Article 233 of the Constitution provides?
3 Who appoints District Judge in any state?
4 What do you mean by collegium system?

2.3 Retirement of Judges

- The retirement age for a Supreme Court judge is **65 years.** Similarly, a High Court judge continues in his office, till the retirement age which is **62 years.** The age of retirement of District Court judges is determined by their respective State Government under special service rules.
- In 2002, the **Venkatachaliah Report** recommended that the retirement age of the judges of the High Court should be increased to 65 years and that of the judges of the Supreme Court should be increased to 68 years.
- In 2010, the **Constitution (114th Amendment) Bill** was introduced to increase the retirement age of High Court judges to 65, however, it was not taken up for consideration in Parliament and turned down with the dissolution of the 15th Lok Sabha.

Argument for Increasing the Retirement Age of Judges in India

- The **judge-population ratio** in India is among the lowest in the world. It is necessary to increase the number of judges **to enable** the Judiciary to deal with the huge pendency of cases.
- Legislations provide for retired High Court and Supreme Court judges **work at tribunals till the age of 70 as chairman and 65 as members.** Thus, there is no reason why these judges should be retired immediately.
- As the Indian **economy grows,** the ratio of **litigation to population will grow.** Advanced economies such as Australia, Canada, France, the US, the UK and Japan have much higher litigation-to-population ratios.
- Several senior lawyers with required expertise and experience decline to accept judgeship due to the lower retirement age of 62, especially in the High Courts. By an enhanced age, this problem could be rectified as advocates would have greater incentive to forgo their individual legal practice and function in the role of judges.
- The early retirement age in India is often linked to the declining quality of judicial service and the inability of a judge to properly produce the stipulated judicial work-load.

Positive Consequences of Increasing the Retirement Age of Judges

- Senior serving judges will bring with them years of experience.
- It will ensure the continued presence of a strong talented group of experienced judges.
- New judges can be appointed without displacing existing judges.
- It will address the problem of mounting arrears[5].
- It will be a safeguard against upcoming large number of litigations.
- It will strengthen the rule of law and the independence of the judiciary, both of which are crucial to sustain democracy.
- India faces the issue of backlog of cases. Increasing the age of judges will certainly help in addressing this issue.

5 Arrears It means state of being behind or late, especially in the fulfillment of a duty, promise or the obligation.

The Case in Western Democracies

A retirement age of around **70** for judges is common place in most Western liberal democracies. Some of them even opt for tenures for life. For example,

- In the Supreme Court of the United States and in Constitutional Courts in Austria and Greece, judges are appointed for life.
- In Belgium, Denmark, Ireland, the Netherlands, Norway and Australia, the retirement age for judges is 70 years.
- The practice of quitting before reaching the age of superannuation (retirement benefit) is prevailing in Zimbabwe, where a top court judge is appointed to retire at 65 years but he can opt to continue till 70 years.

2.4 Removal of Judges

- Judges of the Supreme Court and the High Courts can be removed through a process called **impeachment.** The process for removal of the judges is exactly the **same for both the Supreme Court and the High Courts.**
- The procedure for removal of the Supreme Court judge is guided by **Article 124(4)** of the Constitution of India and the Judges (Inquiry) Act, 1968. **Article 218** of the Constitution of India provides for the impeachment of High Court judges.

  The judges can be removed on two grounds as follows

  (i) Incapacity (ii) Proven misbehaviour

Procedure for Removal of Judges

The procedure for the removal of judges is explained below

Step 1 Notice of Motion for Removal of a Judge Removal proceedings against a Supreme Court or a High Court judge can be initiated in any of the Houses of Parliament.

For this

- A minimum of **100 members of Lok Sabha** may give a signed notice to the Speaker or
- A minimum of **50 members of Rajya Sabha** may give a signed notice to the Chairman.

The Speaker or Chairman may consult individuals and examine relevant content related to notice. According to this, he/she may decide to either admit or refuse to admit it.

Step 2 Constitution of an Inquiry Committee After the motion is admitted, the Speaker of the Lok Sabha or Chairman of the Rajya Sabha will form an Inquiry Committee as per **Article 3(2)** of the Judges (Inquiry) Act, 1968 to start investigating the complaint.

It will consist of the following members

- A Supreme Court judge
- A High Court Chief Justice
- A distinguished jurist as per the opinion of the Speaker/Chairman.
- If such notices have been admitted in both the Houses of Parliament, the Inquiry Committee will be formed together by the Speaker and the Chairman of the respective houses.

  In this scenario, the notice that has been on a later date will stand rejected. If such notices have been passed by both the Houses of Parliament on the same day, the Inquiry Committee will not be formed.

Step 3 Submission of the Inquiry Report After concluding its investigation, the Inquiry Committee will record its findings in a formal report and submit it to the **Speaker or Chairman.**

If the report finds misbehaviour or incapacity which makes the judge guilty, the motion for removal has to be put to vote in both the Lok Sabha and Rajya Sabha.

As per **Article 124(4)** of the Constitution, the motion is required to be adopted in each house by

- a **majority** of the total membership of the house and
- a majority of **not less than two-thirds of members present and voting.**

If the motion is adopted by this majority in one house, the motion will be sent to the other house.

Step 4 **Order by the President** As per **Article 124(4),** after the motion is adopted in both the houses by the required majority, it is placed before the President of India, who will issue an order for the removal of the judge.

Removal of Judges at District Level

At the district level, a District Judge or an Additional District Judge can be removed from his office by the State Government in consultation with the High Court.

Impeachment Proceedings Initiated against a Supreme Court or High Court Judge in India

Impeachment proceedings against Supreme Court or High Court judges was initiated a total of **five times** in Indian history as follows

- **V. Ramaswami** (Judge) was the **first judge against whom impeachment proceedings were initiated.** In 1993, the motion was brought up in Lok Sabha but **failed** to secure the required two-thirds majority.
- **Soumitra Sen** judge of the Calcutta High Court resigned in 2011 after the Rajya Sabha passed an impeachment motion against him. He was the **first judge to have been impeached by the Upper House for misconduct.**
- **P.D. Dinakaran** was the Chief Justice of the Sikkim High Court, against whom the Rajya Sabha Chairman had set up a judicial panel to look into allegations of corruption. However, he resigned in July 2011, before impeachment proceedings could be initiated against him.
- In 2015, an impeachment notice was moved by the members of Rajya Sabha against **J.B. Pardiwala** judge of the Gujarat High Court, for his objectionable remarks on the issue of reservation.
- In 2017, Rajya Sabha MPs moved a motion to initiate impeachment proceedings against **C.V. Nagarjuna Reddy** judge of the High Court for Andhra Pradesh and Telangana.
- In March 2018, opposition parties signed a draft proposal for moving an impeachment motion against **Dipak Misra** (CJI).

Quick Test 2

1. What is the retirement age for judges of Supreme Court and High Courts?
2. Mention any one consequence of increasing the retirement age of judges.
3. Which article is related to the removal of Supreme Court judge?
4. Name the first judge against whom impeachment proceedings were initiated.

Mind Map

APPOINTMENTS, RETIREMENT, AND REMOVAL OF JUDGES

1 Appointment of Judges

Supreme Court
- Governed by **Article 124**
- Appointment of judge other than the Chief Justice of India

Qualifications
- Citizen of India.
- Judge of a High Court for at least 5 years or an advocate for at least 10 years.
- Distinguished jurist in the opinion of the President.

Procedure
- Appointment by the President after consultation with the Chief Justice of India (CJI) and other judges.
- **Collegium system** CJI consults with four senior-most judges.
- **Recommendations flow** CJI → Union Law Minister → Prime Minister → President.

Chief Justice of India (CJI)
- Selected based on the seniority principle.
- President appoints based on CJI's recommendation.
- Seniority is determined by the date of appointment to the SC.

High Court
- Governed by **Article 217**

Qualifications
- Citizen of India.
- Held a judicial office for 10 years or been an advocate in one or more High Courts for 10 years.

Procedure
- President appoints after consulting the CJI, Governor, and Chief Justice of the respective High Court.
- **Collegium model** Chief Justice of the High Court consults with two senior-most judges.

District and Subordinate Courts
- Governed by **Article 233**

Qualifications
- Member of the judicial service of the state.
- Minimum of 7 years of practice as a lawyer.

Procedure
- Appointed by the Governor in consultation with the High Court.

2 Retirement of Judges

Retirement Ages
- **Supreme Court** 65 years.
- **High Court** 62 years.
- **District Courts** Determined by state service rules.

Recommendations for Change
- **Venkatachaliah Report (2002)** Increase SC judges' retirement age to 68 and HC judges' age to 65.

Arguments for Increasing Retirement Age
- Addresses backlog of cases.
- Retains experienced judges.
- Aligns with global practices (e.g., US and European democracies with higher ages or lifetime tenure).

3 Removal of Judges

- Article 218 of the Constitution of India provides for the impeachment of High Court judges.

Grounds for Removal
- Incapacity
- Proven misbehaviour

Procedure
- Article 124(4) and Judges Inquiry Act, 1968

Notice of Motion
- Initiated in House of Parliament.
- Requires support of 100 Lok Sabha members or 50 Rajya Sabha members.

Inquiry Committee Formation
- Composed of a Supreme Court judge, a High Court Chief Justice, and a distinguished jurist.
- Submits a report to the Speaker or Chairman.

Voting in Parliament
- Motion must pass in both houses with
  - Majority of total membership.
  - Two-thirds of members present voting.

President's Order
- If approved, the President issues the order for removal.

Historical Cases
- V. Ramaswami, Soumitra Sen, P.D. Dinakaran, J.B. Pardiwala, and Dipak Misra (attempted).

4 Collegium System

- Judicial creation through case laws (not explicitly mentioned in the Constitution).
- Evolved through the **Three Judges Cases.**
  - **First Case (1981)** Gave primacy to the executive.
  - **Second Case (1993)** Established CJI's primacy in appointments.
  - **Third Case (1998)** Emphasised a consultative process with senior judges.

Criticisms
- Lack of transparency and accountability.
- Political and communal considerations in appointments.

5 Challenges in the Judicial System

Appointment Issues
- Independence Vs. executive influence.
- Political, regional and communal biases.

Retirement Age Debate
- Balancing experience retention with the need for fresh perspectives.
- Comparisons with international practices.

Backlog of Cases
- India has one of the lowest judge-to-population ratios.
- Increasing retirement age may help reduce pendency.

CBSE TEXTBOOK FOLDER

1. Can 'Impeachment' proceedings be initiated against the sitting judge? If yes, Explain the grounds and procedure for 'Impeachment'. How many times has this process been successful in the history of Indian Judiciary?

Ans. Yes, impeachment proceedings can be initiated against sitting judge. The grounds for the impeachment are misbehaviour or incapacity.

The procedure for the removal of judges is explained below

- **Notice of motion for Removal of a Judge** Removal proceedings against a Supreme Court or a High Court judge can be initiated in any of the Houses of Parliament.

  For this
  - A minimum of 100 members of Lok Sabha may give a signed notice to the Speaker or
  - A minimum of 50 members of Rajya Sabha may give a signed notice to the Chairman.

  The Speaker or Chairman may consult individuals and examine relevant content related to notice. According to this, he or she may decide to either admit or refuse to admit it.
- **Constitution of an Inquiry Committee** After the motion is admitted, the Speaker of the Lok Sabha or Chairman of the Rajya Sabha will form an Inquiry Committee as per Article 3(2) of the Judges (Inquiry) Act, 1968 to start investigating the complaint.
- **Submission of the Inquiry Report** After concluding its investigation, the Inquiry Committee will record its findings in a formal report and submit it to the Speaker or Chairman.

  If the report finds misbehaviour or incapacity which makes the judge guilty, the motion for removal has to be put to vote in both the Lok Sabha and Rajya Sabha.
- **Order by the President** As per Article 124(4), after the motion is adopted in both the houses by the required majority, it is placed before the President of India, who will issue an order for the removal of the judge.

Impeachment proceedings were initiated against a Supreme Court or High Court judge 5 times in the history of the Supreme Court of India.

2. Elucidate on the current practice for the appointment of members of Higher Judiciary in India.

Ans. The appointment of Judges in practice remains a complex process despite a clear Constitutional mandate. The appointment at the Supreme Court and the High Court follows a **collegium model**, which is a judicial creation through case-laws. It is not Constitutionally mandated.

The issue of appointment has often been linked to the independence of judiciary. There has been a constant struggle between executive and judiciary over the appointment of judges.

The **14th Law Commission Report** under the Chairmanship of **M.C. Setalvad** (India's first Attorney General in 1958) highlighted that several appointments were being made on political, regional, communal or other grounds, due to which the appropriate were never appointed. Thus, the commission suggested on strengthening the process of consultation between the executive and the judiciary.

Exam Pattern Questions

Objective Type Questions

Multiple Choice Questions (MCQs)

1. The Indian Constitution outlines a clear process for appointing judges to the Supreme Court, High Courts and District Courts. As per Article 124, Supreme Court judges are appointed by the President in consultation with judges of the Supreme Court and High Courts. Article 217 provides for High Court judge appointments, requiring consultation with the Chief Justice of India, the state Governor and the concerned Chief Justice. Qualifications for judges include Indian citizenship, years of legal experience or recognition as a distinguished jurist.

Who is responsible for appointing Supreme Court judges?

(a) Prime Minister (b) Chief Justice of India
(c) President (d) Governor

2. The Chief Justice of a High Court recommends a candidate for appointment as a High Court Judge. The State Governor and Chief Minister do not provide their opinions for a prolonged period. How should the process proceed, keeping in mind judicial independence and procedural guidelines?

(a) The Chief Justice can proceed without state inputs.
(b) The collegium must suspend recommendations.
(c) The Chief Justice of India can still consider the recommendation.
(d) The Law Minister will terminate the proposal.

3. A recommendation made by a High Court Collegium reaches the Chief Justice of India. However, one member of the Supreme Court Collegium raises concerns about the candidate's impartiality. What should happen next, considering procedural norms?

(a) The Chief Justice of India overrides the concerns and forwards the recommendation.
(b) The recommendation is sent back for review to the High Court Collegium.
(c) The candidate is automatically rejected.
(d) A detailed inquiry into the candidate's background is conducted.

4. Which article of the Constitution provides for the appointment of High Court judges?

(a) Article 216
(b) Article 217
(c) Article 218
(d) Article 219

5. Dinkar wants to be appointed as a District Judge in the state of Delhi. Under Article 233, the Governor decides on the appointment in consultation with the High Court. The minimum qualification required is .... **CBSE SQP 2021**

(a) eminent jurist
(b) member of judicial service of state
(c) minimum 10 years experience at bar
(d) minimum 5 years as Advocate of High Court

6. Mr. Satish Kumar was a Supreme Court judge. It was discovered that he was embroiled in the misappropriation of funds.
An inquiry under the Judges Inquiry Act was done by a committee of three members, out of which **CBSE SQP 2021**

(a) Two were judges- one from Supreme Court and one Chief Justice of High Court.
(b) Three were judges- two judges from Supreme Court and one from High Court.
(c) Two were judges- one Chief Justice of India and one Chief Justice of the High Court.
(d) Three were judges- one judge of the Supreme Court and two judges from the High Court.

7. The declining quality of judicial service and inability of judges to properly effectuate the stipulated judicial workload has been attributed to .... **CBSE SQP 2021**

(a) relatively lower salary
(b) relatively early retirement age
(c) enhanced retirement age
(d) collegium model

8. The sitting Chief Justice of India, Justice 'A', is retiring in two months. Justice B, who is currently the senior-most judge of the Supreme Court, is widely regarded as the next probable Chief Justice. However, a controversy arises regarding Justice B's integrity, leading to significant public and media debate. The President of India, as per Constitutional provisions, is scheduled to appoint the next Chief Justice in consultation with Justice 'A', the outgoing Chief Justice.

In light of the situation, which of the following statements regarding the appointment of the next Chief Justice is most accurate?

(a) The President is bound by the recommendation of Justice 'A', and cannot disregard it, even if there is a public controversy surrounding Justice 'B'.
(b) The President can independently appoint a new Chief Justice without consulting the outgoing Chief Justice if the controversy is deemed significant.
(c) The President can only appoint Justice 'B' as the next Chief Justice, as they are the senior-most judge, irrespective of any public controversies.
(d) The President has the discretion to consult with other senior judges of the Supreme Court apart from Justice 'A', in the event of a public controversy, but must ultimately base the decision on the recommendation of the outgoing Chief Justice.

9. Nilanjan, is a citizen of India and a qualified advocate. In the year 2000, he was appointed as a Judicial Magistrate in Uttar Pradesh. But in 2006, he resigned from the post of Judicial Magistrate. He started practicing as an advocate in Delhi High Court, in the year 2006. In 2016, Nilanjan is eligible to be appointed as .... **CBSE 2016**

(a) High Court judge only
(b) Both Supreme Court and High Court judge
(c) District Judge only
(d) Supreme Court judge only

10. Additional District Judge Mr. Gupta, is accused of corruption and misconduct. An inquiry is conducted by the High Court, which finds him guilty of the charges. The High Court recommends his removal to the ....

(a) Governor of the state
(b) Chief Justice of India
(c) President of India
(d) Legislative Assembly of the state

11. **The Supreme Court of India needs to appoint new High Court judge. The Chief Justice of India, Justice Sharma, consults with a term of senior judges, including justicis Kumar, Singh and Gupta to select a candidate. They consider factors like merit, seminority and diversity. Once they reach a consensus, they recommend the name to the ....**

(a) President of India (b) Prime Minister of India
(c) Law Minister of India (d) Governor of the state

12. **Match the following.**

Column I	Column II
A. Judge of Supreme Court	1. 1981
B. Judge of High Court	2. He/She has been for atleast five years as a judge of a High Court
C. First Judges Case	3. 65 years
D. Supreme Court judge retirement	4. He/She has been held a judicial office in India for atleast two year

Codes

	A	B	C	D		A	B	C	D
(a)	2	4	1	3	(b)	3	4	1	2
(c)	2	3	4	1	(d)	4	2	1	3

13. **For the process of removal of judges in India. Identify the correct sequence in ascending order.**

I. Constitution of an inquiry committee.
II. Order by the President.
III. Notice for motion for removal of a judge.
IV. Submission of the inquiry report. **CBSE 2024**

Codes

(a) III, IV, I, II (b) III, I, IV, II
(c) IV, III, I, II (d) III, II, I, IV

14. **Arrange the following steps in the correct order for the appointment of Supreme Court judges under the collegium system.**

I. President of India notifies the vacancy.
II. Collegium recommends a name to the President.
III. CJI convenes a collegium meeting.
IV. Collegium deliberates and selects a candidate.
V. President appoints the recommended candidate as a Supreme Court judge.

Codes

(a) I, III, IV, II, V (b) II, I, IV, III, V
(c) IV, III, I, II, V (d) II, III, I, IV, V

15. **Which of the following statements is/are correct regarding the removal of judges in India?**

Statements I The President can remove a Supreme Court judge on the recommendation of the Parliament.

Statements II A Supreme Court judge can be removed by an impeachment motion passed by a two-third majority in both the Lok Sabha and the Rajya Sabha.

Codes

(a) Only Statement I is correct.
(b) Only Statement II is correct.
(c) Both the Statements are correct.
(d) Both the Statements are incorrect.

Assertion-Reason Questions

Directions (Q. Nos. 16-21) In the questions given below, there are two statements. Read the statements and choose the correct option.

Codes

(a) Both A and R are true and R is the correct explanation of A.
(b) Both A and R are true, but R is not the correct explanation of A.
(c) A is true, but R is false.
(d) A is false, but R is true.

16. **Assertion** (A) The impeachment process in the Parliament is governed under Article 124(4) of the Constitution.

Reason (R) Under this scheme, the motion of impeachment has to be passed by the two-third majority members present and voting must be done separately in each House of the Parliament.

17. **Assertion** (A) The retirement age for a Supreme Court judge is 62 years.

Reason (R) The National Judicial Education Strategy (NJES) was established in 2006 to provide Judicial Education to High Court judges, District Judiciary and State Judicial Academies.

18. **Assertion** (A) The Supreme Court and High Court judges cannot be easily removed from their office except for proven misbehaviour and insolvency.

Reasoning (R) The legal process for removing Supreme Court and High Court judges is kept stringent to ensure security of tenure of the judges.

19. **Assertion** (A) A Supreme Court judge is appointed by the President.

Reasoning (R) There should be minimum interference of the executive body.

20. **Assertion** (A) The District Judge is the highest judicial authority in the district.

Reasoning (R) The District Judge has both judicial and administrative powers. He has also supervisory powers over all the subordinate courts in the district.

21. **Assertion** (A) There is an urgent need to increase the retirement age of judges in India. **CBSE 2024 C**

Reason (R) It will be a buffer against impending litigation explosion.

Answers

1. (c) President
2. (c) The Chief Justice of India can still consider the recommendation.
3. (b) The recommendation is sent back for review to the High Court Collegium.
4. (b) Article 217
5. (b) member of judicial service of state.
6. (a) two were judges-one from Supreme Court and one Chief Justice of High Court.
7. (b) relatively early retirement age
8. (d) The President has the discretion to consult with other senior judges of the Supreme Court apart from Justice A, in the event of a public controversy, but must ultimately base the decision on the recommendation of the outgoing Chief Justice.
9. (b) Both Supreme Court and High Court judge.
10. (c) President of India
11. (a) President of India
12. (a) 2 4 1 3
13. (b) III, I, IV, II
14. (a) I, III, IV, II, V
15. (b) Only statement II is correct.
16. (a) Both A and R are true and R is the correct explanation of A.
17. (d) A is false, but R is true.
18. (d) A is false, but R is true.
19. (a) Both A and R are true and R is the correct explanation of A.
20. (a) Both A and R are true and R is the correct explanation of A.
21. (a) Both A and R are true and R is the correct explanation of A.

Subjective Questions

Very Short Answer Type Questions

1. Write down any two qualifications required to become a Supreme Court judge in India.

Ans. Qualification required to become a Supreme Court Judge in India are

- He/She should be a citizen of India.
- He/She has been a judge of a High Court or of two or more High Courts in succession or, for atleast five years.

2. Which article of the Constitution provides for the appointment of High Court judges?

Ans. The procedure for appointment of judges at the High Court has been enshrined in Article 217 of the Constitution.

3. Rahul and Ramesh are both lawyers woh have been practicing law for several years. Rahul has been a district judge for 5 years and has a reputation for his impartiality and legal expertise. Ramesh, on the other hand has been a successful lawyer with 10 years of experience but have never been a judge before. What are the two qualifications required to be a High court judge in India?

Ans. The two qualifications of High Court judge in India are

- He/She should be an Indian citizen.
- He/She should be served as a judge for atleast 10 years in any Indian court.

4. Explain the seniority principle in the appointment of CJI. How is the seniority determined? **CBSE SQP 2024**

Ans. According to the seniority principle, the senior-most judge of the Supreme Court is appointed as the Chief Justice of India. The seniority is determined by the length of service as a High Court judge and subsequently as a Supreme Court judge. If two judges are appointed to the court on the same day, the judge who takes the both first is the senior judge.

5. The constant tussle between the executive and judiciary over the appointment of judges led to the development of a new system for appointment of judges.

(i) Identify the system **CBSE SQP 2022**

(ii) Why does this system invoke scepticism?

Ans. (i) The constant tussle between the executive and judiciary over the appointment of judges led to the development of a new system for appointment of judges known as collegium model.

(ii) As per the 14th Law Commission Report under the chairmanship of M.C. Setalvad, the appointment or rejection of appointment of judges by the executive, in contrary to what the judiciary suggested, creating rather awkward situations. The report highlighted that several appointments were being made on political, regional, communal or other grounds as a result of which the fittest of the lot were never appointed. Thus, this system invoked scepticism.

6. How does the collegium model of appointment of judges work?

Or **How are judges of the Supreme Court of India appointed under the collegium model for judicial appointment?** **CBSE 2024**

Ans. Under the collegium model for appointment of judges of the Supreme Court, the Chief Justice of India consults with four senior most judges of the Supreme Court. The Chief Justice of India sends his recommendations to the Union Minister of Law and Justice, who then puts up the same to the Prime Minister. The Prime Minister will then advise the President.

7. How can a judge from the lower judiciary be removed from his office? **CBSE 2020**

Ans. Judge from the lower judiciary can be removed by the Central Government in consultation with the High Court.

8. Describe the procedure of impeachment as given in Article 124(4) of the Indian Constitution. **CBSE 2020**

Ans. The impeachment process in the Parliament is governed under Article 124(4) of the Constitution. Under this scheme, the motion of impeachment has to be passed by the two-third majority members present and voting must be done separately in each House of the Parliament. If the motion is passed, then the formal announcement is done by the President of India. Therefore, the overall process of impeachment is lengthy and complex.

9. Ashok aspires for an appointment as a District Judge. State the qualification for the said post in India. **CBSE 2023**

Ans. To be appointed as a District Judge, Ashok has to be

(i) a member of judicial service of the state or

(ii) any person who has had a minimum of seven years of practice as a lawyer at bar.

Additionally the procedure for appointment has been mentioned under Article 233 of Constituion. A district judge in any state shall be made by the governor of the state in consultation with the High Court exercising jurisdiction in relation to such state.

Short Answer Type Questions

1. State the rationale behind increasing the retirement age of judges in India. **CBSE SQP 2024**

Ans. Rationale behind increasing the retirement age of judges in India are

(i) It is necessary to increase the number of judges in the pool to enable the judiciary to deal with enormous pendency of cases.

(ii) Legislations provide for retired High Court and Supreme Court judges to work for tribunals till the age of 70 as chairman and 65 as members. There is no reason why these judges should be retired so early.

(iii) As the Indian economy grows, the ratio of litigation to population will increase exponentially.

(iv) The relatively early retirement age in India is often linked to declining quality of judicial service and the inability of a judge to properly effectuate the stipulated judicial work-load.

2. Briefly discuss the procedure of appointing a High Court judge.

Ans. The procedure for appointment of Judges at the High Court has been enshrined in Article 217 of the Constitution. This Article prescribes that every judge of the High Court shall be appointed by the President after consultation with the Chief Justice of India, the Governor of the state, and in the case of appointment of a judge other than the Chief Justice, the Chief Justice of the High Court concerned.

The qualifications of a High Court judge includes

(i) He/She should be a citizen of India.

(ii) He/She has held a judicial office in India for atleast ten years.

(iii) He/She has been an advocate in a High Court or of two or more such courts in succession for atleast ten years.

3. How has the series of three judicial decisions, popularly known as the Three Judges Case, helped in the development of the modern collegium system? **CBSE 2017**

Ans. A series of three judicial decisions popularly known as the Three Judges Cases helped in the development of the modern collegium system in the following ways

(i) The first judges case (1981) gave primacy to the executive and stated that the CJI's recommendation to the President can be refused for cogent reasons. It gave vast powers to the executive for the next 12 years, in making judicial appointments.

(ii) In the second judges case (1993), the decision in the first case was modified. It decided that the Chief Justice of India has primacy in the matter of appointments to the Supreme Court and the High Courts.

(iii) In 1998, the Supreme Court in a Presidential reference (1998 advisory decision) emphasised upon the role of 'consultation' and held that the process of appointment of judges to the Supreme Court and the High Courts is an integrated participatory consultative process.

4. How is the Chief Justice of India appointed? Explain the 'seniority principle' applied in the appointment of the Chief Justice of India. **CBSE 2024 C**

Ans. The Chief Justice of India (CJI) is appointed by the President of India, in consultation with the outgoing CJI and other senior judges.

The 'seniority principle' is traditionally followed, where the most senior judge of the Supreme Court is appointed as the CJI. This principle ensures a smooth transition and respects the hierarchy within the judiciary. However, the President has the discretion to deviate from this principle in exceptional circumstances.

5. Justice Kumar a Supreme Court judge who has been serving for 15 years. He was appointed as a High Court judge at the age of 40 and elevated to the Supreme Court at 55. For how long Justice Kumar will serve in the Supreme Court.

Ans. Since Justice Kumar is currently 55 years old and the retirement age of a Supreme Court judge is 65 years, he will serve for another 10 years . In India Supreme Court judges retire at the age of 65 while the high Court judges retire at 62. This ensures that experienced judges continue to serve and contribute to the judiciary for a significant period by getting along with tribunals as well.

Long Answer Type Questions

1. Priyansh, an advocate practicing in the Calcutta High Court, aspires to become the Chief Justice of the High Court some day. Identify the specific steps in the elevation to the said post in the collegium model. **CBSE 2018**

Ans. Under the collegium model for appointment of judges of the Supreme Court, the Chief Justice of India consults with four senior most judges of the Supreme Court. The Chief Justice of India sends his recommendations to the Union Minister of Law and Justice, who then puts up the same to the Prime Minister. The Prime Minister will then advise the President.

For High Courts, the collegium comprises the Chief Justice of the High Court and two senior most judges of the High Court. The Chief Justice conveys his recommendations to the Chief Minister of the state and the Governor of the state, who in turn send their views directly to the Union Minister of Law and Justice.

The complete material is then forwarded to the Chief Justice of India, who in consultation with a collegium of two judges of the Supreme Court, would send his recommendations to the Union Minister of Law and Justice. The Union Minister of Law and Justice then puts up the same to the Prime Minister who will advise the President in the matter of appointment.

The seniority of a judge plays a vital role in his/her elevation or appointment as Chief Justice. For initial appointment as a judge in a High Court for those from the lower judiciary inter-se (among themselves), seniority does matter; and for elevation of advocates from the bar, relative merit matters. The collegium model considers the relative merits of those judges/advocates in the zone of consideration for elevation with reference to their judgements and cases.

2. Trace the historical debate on the issue of the evolution of judges.

Ans. The issue of appointment has often been linked to the independence of judiciary. There has been a constant struggle between executive and judiciary over the appointment of judges.

The 14th Law Commission Report under the chairmanship of M.C. Setalvad (India's first Attorney General in 1958) highlighted that several appointments were being made on political, regional, communal or other grounds, due to which the appropriate were never appointed. Thus, the commission suggested on strengthening the process of consultation between the executive and the judiciary.

Current practice in the appointment of judges

For answer, refer to Q. No. 3 of Short Answer Type Questions.

3. Imagine a scenario where serious allegations of misconduct are raised against a sitting Supreme Court judge. A group of Parliamentarians presents a notice for judges, removal.
Following this, an inquiry committee is set-up and the committee find the judge guilty of the alleged misconduct. What steps must be followed in Parliament for the removal of the judge?
Can the judge be removed immediately based on the inquiry committee's finding or is there a further process to follow under the Constitution of India?

Ans. For answer, refer to text under the heading Removal of Judges on page no. 26 and 27.

SELF ASSESSMENT TEST

Objective Type Questions

1. Which committee was formed to review the working of the Constitution (2000) and suggested to increase the retirement age of Supreme Court judges from 65 to 68 ?
   (a) Venkatachaliah Committee
   (b) Mandal Commission
   (c) R.C. Krishna Committee
   (d) None of these
2. A High Court judge continues in his office, till the retirement age which is
   (a) 62 years
   (b) 60 years
   (c) 65 years
   (d) 70 years
3. Provisions with respect to tribunals were added by which Amendment Act?
   (a) 44th (b) 24th (c) 42nd (d) 25th
4. The age of retirement of a High Court Judge in India is
   (a) 65 (b) 60 (c) 62 (d) 58
5. Which of the following is not the essential qualification for appointment as a judge of the Supreme Court of India?
   (a) He/She should be a citizen of India.
   (b) He/She should have practiced for atleast 10 years as an advocate in one or more High Court.
   (c) He/She should be an eminent jurist.
   (d) He/She should be at least 35 years of age.

Very Short Answer Type Questions

6. What is the collegium system for the Supreme Court judges?
7. In which article procedure for appointment of district judge is given under Constitution?

Short Answer Type Questions

8. What are the two grounds where judges can be removed easily? Discuss them.
9. Discuss the Constitutional provisions regarding the impeachment of judges.
10. Justice Patel, a Supreme Court judge is accused of misconduct and misuse of office . The motion for impeachment is moved in the Lok Sabha with 150 MPs supporting it. The speaker of the Lok Sabha constitutes a 3 member committee to investigate the charges. After investigation the committee finds that Justice Patel is guilty of misconduct. What is next step in the impeachment process?

Long Answer Type Question

11. A public debate arises about increasing the retirement age of Supreme Court judges in India from 65 to 70 years. Proponents argue that extending the retirement age would retain experienced judges for longer and address the backlog of cases. However, opponents claim it may hinder fresh perspectives in the judiciary and block opportunities for younger legal minds. Analyse both arguments and suggest whether increasing the retirement age would be beneficial for the judicial system in India. Should the focus be on increasing efficiency or retaining experience?
12. Explain the current practice of appointment of judges using the collegium model.

03

CHAPTER

Judicial review is a principle or a legal doctrine or a practice whereby a **court can examine or review** an executive or a legislative act, such as law or some other governmental or administrative decision and determine if the act is inconsistent with the Constitution.

▼ **YOUR STUDY GOALS**

3.1 Meaning of Judicial Review
3.2 Doctrine of Basic Structure

▼ **YOUR PRACTICE GOAL**

- Objective Type Questions (19 Qs ; MCQs, A-R, Statements, Matching)
- Subjective Questions (10 VSAs, 5 SAs, 3 LAs)

Court and Judicial Review

3.1 Meaning of Judicial Review

- In certain countries, such as the United States, France and Canada, judicial review enables the court to annual or nullify legislation or an executive act if it violates the Constitution.
- In the United Kingdom, judicial review powers are restricted. The courts do not have the jurisdiction to overturn or invalidate Parliamentary legislation.
- India, which has a parliamentary system of government, follows the Indian Constitution's requirements for the separation of powers among the three branches Executive; Legislative and Judiciary of the government. These are
  - **Executive Branch** The President, the Prime Minister and the bureaucracy make up the **executive branch.**
  - **Legislative Branch** The both chambers of Parliament, Lok Sabha and Rajya Sabha are part of the **legislative branch**.
  - **Judiciary** The Supreme Court is the final authority for interpreting the Constitution in the judiciary, which is completely independent of the other two branches.
- Constitution provides checks and balances[1] to ensure that no branch misuse the authority granted to it or asserts its dominance over the others.

1 Checks and Balances It is a system that prevents any one part of organisation from becoming too powerful.

- In this way, each branch puts a check on the other whenever there is an encroachment[2] or conflict of powers among them and thus preventing any concentration[3] of powers in one branch.

Scope of Judicial Review in India

- **Article 13** of the Indian Constitution describes judicial review.
- It has helped in maintaining the ideals and principles of the Constitution as well as its supremacy.
- In cases involving **legislative and administrative activities,** the Supreme Court and the High Courts in several states have the authority of judicial review.
- Courts have used doctrines including proportionality, legitimate expectation, reasonableness and the principles of natural justice with respect to judicial review on matters of executive or administrative actions.

The scope of judicial review in courts in India has developed with respect to **three** issues

(i) Protection of **Fundamental Rights** as guaranteed in the Constitution.

(ii) Matters concerning the **legislative** competence between the centre and states.

(iii) Fairness in **executive** acts.

Individual and Group Rights

- According to **Article 13(2)** of the Indian Constitution, the state shall not make any law which takes away the rights conferred by this Part III (Fundamental Rights).
- This clause has been referred to as the **heart of the Constitution** by B.R. Ambedkar, the Chairman of the Drafting Committee of the Constituent Assembly.
- In the matters of Fundamental Rights, this Article expressly grants the authority to the courts to conduct judicial reviews.
- Additionally, Article 32 grants the authority to the Supreme Court to enforce Fundamental Rights and grants right to the individuals to petition the Supreme Court for the enforcement of such rights.
- The Supreme Court derives authority from this article to issue directives or orders or writs like
  - **Habeas corpus** i.e. to order the release of a person who is unlawfully detained.
  - **Mandamus** i.e. to order a public authority to do its duty.
  - **Prohibition** i.e. to prevent a subordinate court from continuing on a case.
  - **Quo-warranto** i.e. to direct a person to leave an unlawfully held office.
  - **Certiorari** i.e. to take a matter from a lower court and bring the proceedings before it.
- **Article 226** is a similar provision for High Courts in states, like **Article 32.** It allows a person to initiate similar writs in the High Courts for the enforcement of Fundamental Rights.
- High Court's power to issue writs is wider or extensive than the Supreme Court. Because the Supreme Court can issue writs only for the enforcement of Fundamental Rights, the High Courts can issue writs for the enforcement of Fundamental Rights as well as any ordinary legal right.
- Courts have liberalised the doctrine of locus standi[4] for the enforcement of Fundamental Rights of those who lack access to courts due to poverty or social and economic limitations.
- This strategy resulted in the establishment of Public or Social Action Litigation (PIL or SAL), in which any person can petition or submit letters to courts on behalf of victims or aggrieved parties whose human rights are violated.

---

2 Encroachment It means intrusion on someone's rights, territory etc.

3 Concentration It means the action or power is concentrated in a single center.

4 Locus Standi It means the right to appear before or petition the court.

Centre-State Relations

- Judicial review has also been employed in cases involving legislative competence in the context of Centre-State relations. **Article 246** outlines the division of legislative authority between the Parliament and State Legislature.
- Constitution states that the Parliament has exclusive legislative authority over items listed in the **union list** (List 1 of the Seventh Schedule of the Constitution).
- It further states that both the Parliament and the legislature of any state have the authority to pass legislation on the subjects included in the **concurrent list** (List III of the Seventh Schedule of the Constitution).
- The Legislature of any **state has the authority** to make laws over the items listed in the **state list** (List II of the Seventh Schedule of the Constitution).
- Judicial review ensures that centre does not exert its supremacy over the state matters and similarly, states do not interfere in the matters within the scope of the centre.

Fairness in Executive Actions

- **Audi alteram partem** is a Latin phrase which means to **listen to the other side**. This phrase is a principle in Indian legal practice and it has been used by the Supreme Court in various cases, especially in the case of **Maneka Gandhi Vs. Union of India**.
- Using its judicial review powers in administrative matters, the Supreme Court held that in the matter of **confiscation**[5] of passport a hearing should have been given to the petitioner in the interest of the principles of natural justice.
- Consequently the court applied the idea of a post-decision hearing in cases of urgency where a previous hearing is not possible and accepted that a chance of hearing cannot be fully removed.

Quick Test 1

1. In which country, judicial review powers are restricted?
2. Name the case in which the principle of judicial review was applied for the first time.
3. Which writ is related to the power of court to order a public authority to do its duty?
4. In which case the principle of audi alteram partem was used?

3.2 Doctrine of Basic Structure

- The doctrine of basic structure is an evolution of the judiciary and has been regarded an important component of judicial review.
- The doctrine of basic structure declares any Constitutional change as unlawful if it destroys or harms a fundamental or important aspect of the Constitution, such as secularism, democracy or federalism.
- The Supreme Court has also declared judicial review to be a fundamental structure or element of the Constitution.
- As a result, any constitutional change that abolishes or ignores judicial review in matters involving the Fundamental Rights of citizens, can be invalidated.
- This doctrine is used when it is believed that the administration and legislature have crossed the boundary specified by the Constitution underlying the spirit of separation of powers.

5 **Confiscation** It means the action of taking or seizing someone's property with authority.

Evolution of Basic Structure Concept

The landmark judgements that have helped in the evolution of the concept of the basic structure are as follows

Shankari Prasad Case (1951)

In this case, the Supreme Court decided that the Parliament's power to amend the Constitution under **Article 368** also included the power to amend the Fundamental Rights provided in Part III.

Golaknath Case (1967)

- In this case, the court changed its previous decision that Fundamental Rights can be amended. It claimed that **Fundamental Rights are not subject to the Parliamentary restrictions** established in **Article 13** and a new Constituent Assembly would be required to amend the Fundamental Rights.
- **Article 368** also specifies the method for amending the Constitution but does not provide Parliament the authority to do so. Fundamental Rights now have a **transcendental standing**[6] as a result of this case.
- The people had reserved these Fundamental Rights for themselves. As the Constitution gives a place of permanence to the fundamental freedoms of the citizens. The Preamble recites that "hereby adopt, enact and give to ourselves this Constitution."

Kesavananda Bharati Case (1973)

- In this case, concept of the basic structure doctrine was defined.
- The Supreme Court decided that no part of the Constitution, including Fundamental Rights was beyond the Parliament's amending power, however, the basic structure of the Constitution could not be repealed even by a Constitutional Amendment.
- The decision meant that **Parliament could only change the Constitution, not rewrite it.**
- In Indian law, the judiciary can strike down any amendment passed by Parliament that conflicts with the basic structure of the Constitution. This case was heard by the largest Constitutional bench in the history of judiciary, by 13 judges of the Supreme Court.

Indira Nehru Gandhi Vs. Raj Narain Case (1975)

- In this case, the Supreme Court used a theory of basic structure to struck down **Clause(4) of Article 329-A.** It was adopted by the 39th Amendment in 1975 because it exceeded Parliament's amending power as it destroyed the Constitution's basic features.
- During the emergency period, Parliament passed the 39th Amendment Act.
- This act **exempted**[7] the election of the President, Vice President, Prime Minister and Speaker of the Lok Sabha from judicial scrutiny. The 39th Amendment Act was held valid by the Supreme Court, four out of five judges on the bench upheld its validity.

Minerva Mills Case (1980)

- In this case, the **doctrine of basic structure was strengthened.** The judgement **repealed two changes** made to the Constitution by the 42nd Amendment Act of 1976 declaring them to be violative of the basic structure. The judgement makes it clear that the **Constitution, and not the Parliament, is superior.**
- The Court **added two features** to the list of basic structure features. They were judicial review, and the balance between Fundamental Rights and the DPSP. The judges determined that a **limited amending power** is a basic feature of the Constitution.

---

6 **Transcendental Standing** It means something which is beyond ordinary and everyday experience.

7 **Exempted** It means free or released from some liability or requirement.

Indra Sawhney and Union of India Case (1992)

- In this case, the Supreme Court examined the scope and extent of Article 16(4). It provides job reservation in favour of backward classes. It provides for **27% reservation** for OBCs with certain conditions (such as creamy layer exclusion, no reservation in promotion and total reserved quota should not exceed 50%).
- **Rule of Law** was added to the list of fundamental Constitutional elements in this case.

S.R. Bommai Case (1994)

- In this case, the Supreme Court attempted to stop the misuse of **Article 356** (concerning the imposition of the President's Rule on states).
- It was not an issue of a Constitutional Amendment, but the concept of the basic doctrine was applied. The Supreme Court ruled that a State Government's policies against a basic structure of the Constitution would be a valid **ground** for the exercise of central power under Article 356.

Conclusion about Judgements of Supreme Court

- The judgements of Supreme Court frequently mention the sovereign, democratic and secular nature of the rule of law, the independence of the judiciary, the Fundamental Rights of individuals, etc., as essential elements of the Constitution.
- All laws and Constitutional changes are now subject to judicial review and measures that breach the fundamental framework are likely to be overturned by the Supreme Court.
- In essence, **Parliament has limited authority to modify the Constitution,** and the Supreme Court ultimately decides, reviews and interprets all the Constitutional Amendments. It can be concluded from the Supreme Court's judgements in the Kesavananda Bharati, Indira Gandhi Election and Minerva Mills cases that the **Parliament's ability to amend the Constitution** is limited and the **Parliament cannot violate the basic structure of the Constitution,** in the exercise of its constituent power.

Madison Vs. Marbury

In the weeks before Thomas Jefferson's inauguration as President in March 1801, the Federalist Congress created 16 new circuit judgeships and an unspecified number of new judgeships, which Adams proceeded to fill with federalists in an effort to preserve his party's control of the judiciary. William Marbury, a federalist party leader from Maryland, **did not receive his commission** before Jefferson became President. Once in office, Jefferson directed his secretary of state, James Madison to **withhold the commission,** and Marbury petitioned the Supreme Court to issue writ of Mandamus to compel Madison to act.

Decision

The court held that, "Having this legal title to the office, Marbury has a consequent right to the commission, a refusal to deliver which is a plain violation of that right, for which laws of the country afford him a remedy." The provision of Judiciary Act of 1789 was itself unconstitutional.

Conclusion

Marshall's masterful verdict has been widely hailed. Surrendering the power derived from the 1789 statute, Marshall gained for the court a far-more-significant power, that of judicial review. So, the concept of judicial review dates back to 1800.

Quick Test 2

1. When did the Shankari Prasad case take place?
2. What does Article 368 of Indian Constitution discusses?
3. In which case, the Supreme Court used a theory of basic structure to struck down clause (4) of Article 329-A?
4. How much percentage of reservations to OBCs was provided through Indra Sawhney case?

Mind Map

COURT AND JUDICIAL REVIEW

1 Judicial Review

- Legal principle allowing courts to examine and nullify executive or legislative acts violating the Constitution.
- **Varies globally** expansive in the US, limited in the UK.
- Ensures checks and balances among the executive, legislative and judiciary.

Scope in India

- Governed by **Article 13**.
- **Extends to**
  - Protection of Fundamental Rights.
  - Legislative competence between the centre and states.
  - Fairness in executive actions.
- **Judicial Doctrines Used** Proportionality, legitimate expectation, reasonableness and natural justice.

Powers of Judicial Review

- **Supreme Court Article 32** for enforcing Fundamental Rights (writs: Habeas Corpus, Mandamus, Prohibition, Quo -Warranto, Certiorari).
- **High Courts Article 226** for enforcing fundamental and legal rights.

Key Cases

- **Maneka Gandhi Vs. Union of India** Applied "audi alteram partem" (right to be heard) for natural justice.

2 Doctrine of Basic Structure

- **Judicially Evolved Doctrine** protects essential features of the Constitution from amendments that would destroy its core.
- Key elements include secularism, democracy, federalism and judicial review.

Evolution Through Cases

- **Shankari Prasad Case (1951)** Allowed Parliament to amend fundamental rights.
- **Golaknath Case (1967)** Declared Fundamental Rights unamendable without a Constituent Assembly.
- **Kesavananda Bharati Case (1973)** Established the basic structure doctrine.
- **Indira Nehru Gandhi Vs. Raj Narain Case (1975)** Struck down laws exempting elections from judicial review.
- **Minerva Mills Case (1980)** Reinforced balance between Fundamental Rights and directive principles.
- **Indra Sawhney Case (1992)** Added "Rule of Law" to the basic structure.

3 Separation of Powers

Three Branches

- **Executive** President, Prime Minister, bureaucracy.
- **Legislative** Lok Sabha, Rajya Sabha.
- **Judiciary** Supreme Court, High Courts, subordinate courts.
- Ensures no branch encroaches on another's powers.

4 Centre-State Relations

Governed by Article 246

- **Union List (List I)** Exclusive Parliament jurisdiction.
- **State List (List II)** State legislatures' jurisdiction.
- **Concurrent List (List III)** Shared legislative authority.
- Judicial review resolves disputes over legislative competence.

5 Key Constitutional Articles

- **Article 13** Prohibits laws infringing on Fundamental Rights.
- **Article 32** Supreme Court's writ jurisdiction.
- **Article 226** High Court's writ jurisdiction.
- **Article 368** Parliament's amendment powers (limited by basic structure doctrine).

6 Fairness in Executive Actions

- **Principle** "Audi alteram partem" (listen to the other side).
- Courts ensure executive actions follow natural justice.
- **For example** Maneka Gandhi Case fairness in administrative decisions.

7 Global Perspective

- Originated in Marbury Vs. Madison (1803), USA.
- Widely recognised in democratic countries but varies in scope.

Judicial Review

Supreme Court

CBSE TEXTBOOK FOLDER

1. The power of judicial review is available to the Supreme Court and High Courts of states in the matters of both administrative and legislative actions. How far has the judicial review principle been successful in ensuring the fairness in executive actions? Discuss by referring to a decided case law.

Ans. The power of judicial review is available to the Supreme Court and the High Courts in different states in the matters of both legislative and administrative actions. With respect to judicial review on matters of executive or administrative actions, courts have employed doctrines such as proportionality legitimate expectation, reasonableness and the principles of natural justice.

In the executive actions, the principle of audi alteram partem, which literally means 'listen to the other side', was applied by the Supreme Court in several cases including the landmark decision of **Maneka Gandhi Vs. Union of India.**

In this case, passport of Maneka was confiscated by the governmental authorities without giving her any chance of prior hearing. Invoking its judicial review powers in administrative matters, the Supreme Court held that in the matter of confiscation of passport a hearing should have been given to the petitioner in the interest of the principles of natural justice. Consequently, a hearing was given and the passport was returned to her.

Concluding remark

In the life of the citizens of a state, judiciary is a source of confidence and fearlessness. The common man depends upon judiciary for getting justice. Without a security of rights and freedom guaranteed by the judiciary, they cannot really hope to carry out their jobs and enjoy their living. They are more dependent upon judiciary than the legislature and the executive. Without judicial protection, their lives can become miserable. From citizens point of view, judiciary is the most important organ of the government.

With the power of judicial review, the courts act as a custodian of the Fundamental Rights, Thus, the power of judicial review is recognised as the part of the basic structure of the Constitution of India. The activist role of the judiciary is implicit in the said power.

Exam Pattern Questions

Objective Type Questions

Multiple Choice Questions (MCQs)

1. Which is a principle or a legal doctrine or a practice whereby a court can examine or review an executive or a legislative act?

(a) Judicial review
(b) Executive review
(c) Delegated legislation
(d) None of the above

2. Which of the following is/are included in the scope of judicial review in courts in India?

(a) Protection of Fundamental Rights as guaranteed in the Constitution.
(b) Matters concerning the legislative competence between the centre and states.
(c) Fairness in executive acts.
(d) All of the above

3. A Constitutional Amendment was passed by the Indian Parliament which abridged rights conferred in Part III of the Indian Constitution. The Supreme Court of India invalidated the said amendment by using the power of .... **CBSE 2016**

(a) Locus Standi (b) Judicial review
(c) Public Interest Litigation (d) Writs

4. Which type of writ is issued to order the release of a person who is unlawfully detained?

(a) Mandamus (b) Certiorari
(c) Habeas corpus (d) Quo warranto

5. Which Article of the Constitution provide for judicial review?

(a) Article 32 (b) Article 246
(c) Article 13 (d) Article 368

6. The Central Government legislates on a matter listed under the state list given in the Seventh Schedule of the Indian Constitution. The Supreme Court determines that such an action is incompatible with the Constitution and is .... **CBSE SQP 2021**

(a) valid (b) invalid
(c) voidable (d) justiciable

7. Concurrent List has been given under which of the following?

(a) List-I (b) List-II
(c) List-III (d) None of these

8. Article 368 of the Constitution confers power to the Parliament to amend the Constitution. Article 13 (2) states that the state shall not make any law which takes away the Fundamental Rights. To overcome this restriction, the Parliament adopted the 24th amendment to the Constitution which altered Articles 13 and 368 in such a way that allowed itself with unlimited powers of amendment, including the authority to amend Fundamental Rights.

Identify the case which restricted this power in 1973 by establishing the doctrine of basic structure.

(a) Maneka Gandhi Vs. Union of India **CBSE SQP 2021**
(b) Three Judges Case
(c) Kesavananda Bharati Vs. State of Kerala
(d) Hussainara Khatoon Vs. State of Bihar

9. In which of the following case, the Supreme Court applied the theory of basic structure and struck down Clause (4) of Article 329 A?

(a) Kesavananda Bharati Case
(b) Indira Nehru Gandhi Vs. Raj Narain Case.
(c) Indra Sawhney Case
(d) Shankari Prasad Case

10. Article 329 A of Indian Constitution was inserted by which Amendment?

(a) 24th Amendment Act (b) 39th Amendment Act
(c) 42nd Amendment Act (d) 44th Amendment Act

11 Which statement best reflects scope of judicial review in India?

(a) The scope of judicial review in India has developed with protection of Fundamental Rights as guaranteed in the Constitution, centre-state relations, fairness in executive actions.
(b) The scope of judicial review in India has developed with protection of legal and statutory rights, fairness in judicial actions.
(c) The scope of judicial review in India has developed through the case laws only.
(d) The scope of judicial review in India has developed with protection of Constitutional rights and fair judicial diecisions.

12. The Minister of Education has passed an order cancelling the recognition of a private school, citing non-compliance with certain regulations. The school's management challenges the order in court, arguing that minister had no authority to pass such an order and that it violates their Fundamental Rights. What type of judicial review is the court likely to conduct in this case?

(a) Substantive (b) Procedural
(c) Judicial activism (d) legislative

13. Match the following.

Column I		Column II
A. Habeas corpus	1.	To prevent a Subordinate Court from continuing on a case.
B. Mandamus	2.	To order the release of person is unlawfully detained.
C. Prohibition	3.	To issue directive to a person to vacate an office wrongfully occupied.
D. Quo-warranto	4.	Order to a public authority to do its duty.

Codes

	A	B	C	D		A	B	C	D
(a)	1	2	3	4	(b)	2	4	1	3
(c)	2	1	4	3	(d)	1	3	4	2

14. Match the following Case Laws with its year.

Column I		Column II	
A.	Golaknath Case	1.	1992
B.	Shankari Prasad Case	2.	1994
C.	Indra Sawhney Case	3.	1980
D.	S.R. Bommai Case	4.	1951
E.	Minerva Mills Case	5.	1967

Codes

	A	B	C	D	E		A	B	C	D	E
(a)	2	1	5	4	3	(b)	5	4	1	2	3
(c)	4	1	5	3	2	(d)	1	5	2	4	3

15. Analyse the two statements given below and select the correct option.

Statement I Judicial review has been used in matters concerning the legislative competence with regards to the centre-state relations.

Statement II Article 264 of the Constitution delivers clear division of law-making powers (division of powers) as well as room for intersection between the centre and the state.

Choose the correct statement.

(a) Only Statement I is correct.
(b) Only Statement II is correct.
(c) Both the Statements are correct.
(d) Both the Statements are incorrect.

Assertion-Reason Questions

Directions (Q. Nos. 16-19) In the questions given below, there are two statements. Read the statements and choose the correct option.

Codes

(a) Both A and R are true and R is the correct explanation of A.

(b) Both A and R are true, but R is not the correct explanation of A.

(c) A is true, but R is false.

(d) A is false, but R is true.

16. **Assertion** (A) Dr. B.R. Ambedkar, the Chairman of the Drafting Committee of the Constituent Assembly, has termed Article 13 as the 'Heart of the Constitution'.

Reason (R) This article provides explicitly the powers of judicial review to the courts in the matters of Fundamental Rights.

17. **Assertion** (A) Fundamental Rights are enforceable by any court.

Reason (R) The Supreme Court has the authority to issue directions, orders or writs for the enforcement of any Fundamental Right.

18. **Assertion** (A) The scope of judicial review is limited in India.

Reasoning (R) Indian Constitution is 'a bag of borrowing'.

19. **Assertion** (A) High Courts are in better position to protect rights of Indian Citizens than the Supreme Court.

Reasoning (R) Supreme Court can issue writs only for the protection of Fundamental Rights and legal rights.

Answers

1. (a) Judicial review
2. (d) All of the above
3. (b) Judical review
4. (c) Habeas corpus
5. (c) Article 13
6. (b) invalid
7. (c) List-III
8. (c) Kesavananda Bharati Vs. State of Kerala
9. (b) Indira Nehru Gandhi Vs. Raj Narain Case
10. (b) 39th Amendment Act
11. (a) The scope of judicial review in India has developed with protection of Fundamental Rights as guaranteed in the Constitution, centre-state relations, fairness in executive actions.
12. (b) Procedural
13. (b) 2 4 1 3
14. (b) 5 4 1 2 3
15. (a) Only Statement I is correct.
16. (b) Both A and R are true, but R is not the correct explanation of A.
17. (a) Both A and R are true and R is the correct explanation of A.
18. (a) Both A and R are true and R is the correct explanation of A.
19. (c) A is true, but R is false.

Subjective Questions

Very Short Answer Type Questions

1. A government order bans a political party's rally, citing public safety concerns. The party claims, the order violates their Fundamental Right to freedom of assembly. What legal remedy can the political party seek to challenge the government's order?

Ans. The political party can seek judicial review, where a court examines the government's order for legality, reasonableness and Constitutionality and strikes it down if found violative of Fundamental Rights.

2. How has the Supreme Court diluted the provision of 'locus standi'?

Ans. The Supreme Courts has diluted the doctrine of locus standi (right to appear before or petition the court) through its judicial review practice, for the enforcement of Fundamental Rights of those who lack access to courts due to poverty or social and economic disabilities.

3. How does Article 13(2) of the Constitution safeguard the Fundamental Rights?

Ans. Article 13(2) of the Constitution of India provides that the state shall not make any law which takes away or abridges the rights conferred by this Part (Part III - Fundamental Rights) and any law made in contravention of this clause shall, to the extent of the contravention, be void. In this way, it safeguards the Fundamental Rights.

4. Differentiate between Article 32 and Article 226 in one point only.

Ans.

Article 32	Article 226
Article 32 provides a person to initiate writs (Habeas corpus, Mandamus, Prohibition, Quo-warranto and Certiorari) in the Supreme Court for the enforcement of Fundamental Rights.	Article 226 provides a person to initiate similar writs in the High Courts for the enforcement of Fundamental Rights.

5. Explain the principle of judicial review. **CBSE 2025**

Ans. The principle of judicial review means that courts can check if a law or government action follows the Constitution. If a law goes against the Constitution, courts can cancel it. This helps protect people's rights and ensures fairness in government decisions.

6. Which are the five types of writs used as remedies for Fundamental Rights?

Ans. The writs used as remedies for Fundamental Rights are
(i) Habeas corpus i.e. to order the release of a person who is unlawfully detained.
(ii) Mandamus i.e. to order a public authority to do its duty.
(iii) Prohibition i.e. to prevent a subordinate court from continuing on a case.
(iv) Quo-warranto i.e. to direct a person to leave an unlawfully held office.
(v) Certiorari i.e. to take a matter from a lower court and bring the proceedings before it.

7. Which Constitution article gives the concept of center-state relations?

Ans. Article 246 gives the concept of centre-state relations.

8. Maneka Gandhi Vs. Union of India provided clarity on what procedure established by law meant under Article 21 of the Indian Constitution. Explain the observation of the court in context with adversarial system of justice dispensation in India. **CBSE SQP 2022**

Ans. In this case, the Supreme Court significantly expanded the scope and interpretation of Article 21 of the Indian Constitution and thereby received the name 'watchdog of democracy'. In an adversarial system, the parties in a legal proceeding develop their own theory of the case and gather evidence to support their claims.

9. Mr. 'X', an employee, was terminated from his job without being given a chance to explain his side of the story. The management had made a decision based on a complaint from a colleague. Has the principle of Audi Alteram Partem been violated in this scenario?

Ans. Yes, the principle of Audi Alteram Partem has been violated as Mr. 'X' was not given an opportunity to be heard and present his side of the story.

10. The doctrine of basic structure has evolved with the time kindly name the main cases and its year as they were decided.

Ans. The doctrine of basic structure has evolved with time and there are some landmark judgements which have helped the doctrine grow with the time. The judgements are as follows
(i) Shankari prasad case (1951)
(ii) Golaknath case (1967)
(iii) Kesavananda Bharati case (1973)
(iv) Indira Nehru Gandhi Vs. Raj Narain case (1975)
(v) Minerva Mills case (1992)
(vi) Indra Sawhney case (1992)
(vii) S.R. Bommai case (1994)

Short Answer Type Questions

1. Judicial review has helped to preserve the Constitutional principles and values in India.
In the given context answer the following questions.
(a) To whom is the power of judicial review available in India?
(b) Examine the scope of judicial review in the matters concerning the legislative competence between the centre and states.
(c) Can practice of judicial review extend to Article 368 of the Constitution of India? If yes, how? **CBSE 2023**

Ans. Judicial review has helped to preserve the Constitutional principles and values in India.
(a) The power of judicial review in India is vested in both the Supreme Court and the High Courts.
(b) Article 246 provides for the legislative competence between centre and states, it clarifies the scope of Judicial review as it derives clear division of law making powers as well as room for intersection between the centre and the state.
Judicial review helps demarcate the legislative competencies and ensures that centre does not exert its supremacy over the state matters and like wise states do not enroach upon matters within the ambit of the centre.
(c) Yes, the practice of judicial review extend to Article 368 of the Constitution of India. As, it is said that Fundamental Rights are not amenable to the Parliamentary restriction as stated in Article 13 and that to amend the Fundamental Rights a new Constituent Assembly would be required. Article 368 gives the procedure to amend the Constitution but does not confer on Parliament the power to amend the Constitution.

2. What is the general procedure for the division of powers between centre and states?

Ans The general procedure for the division of powers between centre and states are as follows

- Article 246 of the Constitution states that the Parliament has exclusive legislative authority over items listed in the 'Union List' (List 1 of the Seventh Schedule of the Constitution).
- It further states that both the Parliament and the legislature of any state have the authority to pass legislation on the subjects included in the 'Concurrent List' (List III of the Seventh Schedule of the Constitution).
- With respect to states, the legislature of any state has the authority to make laws over the items in the 'State List' (List II of the Seventh Schedule of the Constitution).

Article 246 provides for a clear separation of law-making authorities (division of powers) as well as opportunities for convergence between the centre and the state.

3. "The decision in the landmark 1973 Supreme Court Case of Kesavananda Bharati Vs. the State of Kerala was an answer to the 24th Amendment Act to the Constitution affecting Article 13 and Article 368." Explain. **CBSE 2017**

Ans The landmark 1973 Supreme Court Case of Kesavananda Bharati Vs. State of Kerala discussed the question about the unlimited Constitutional Amendment powers of the Parliament (24th Amendment Act) and established the doctrine of the basic structure or feature of the Constitution. This doctrine invalidates any Constitutional amendments that destroys or harms a basic or essential feature of the Constitution, like secularism, democracy and federalism.

The Supreme Court has also decided judicial review to be the basic structure or feature of the Constitution, as a result, it can nullify any Constitutional Amendment that abolished or disregards judicial review in issues concerning Fundamental Rights of citizens.

4. Discuss the landmark judgement of the OBC reservation case.

Ans. For answer refer to text under the heading Indra Sawhney and Union of India Case (1992) on page no. 40.

5. A group of farmers challenge a government notification acquiring their land for an industrial project. They argue that the notification violates their Fundamental Rights to equality livelihood and environmental protection. Which Article of Indian Constitution would the farmers likely invoke for protection of their group rights?

Ans. The farmers would likely invoke Article 21, which guarantees the right to life and personal liberty including the right to livelihood and environmental protection. This article has been interpreted by the Indian judiciary to include the right to protection of livelihood and environment protection making it a crucial provision for group rights and can come under ambit of judicial review.

Long Answer Type Questions

1. What do you understand by judicial review? What are the features of judicial review?

Ans. Judicial review refers to the power of the judiciary to interpret the Constitution and to declare any such law or order of the legislature and executive void if it finds them in conflict with the Constitution of India.

The features of judicial review are

- Judicial review can be conducted in respect of all Central and State laws, the orders and ordinances of the executives and Constitutional Amendments.
- Judicial review cannot be conducted in respect of the laws incorporated in the 9th Schedule of the Constitution.
- Both the Supreme Court and High Courts exercise the power of judicial review. But the final power to determine the Constitutional validity of any law is in the hands of the Supreme Court of India.
- Judicial review applies only to the questions of law. It cannot be exercised in respect of political issues.
- The Supreme Court does not use the power of judicial review of its own. It can use only when any law or rule is specifically challenged before it or when during the hearing of a case the validity of any law is challenged before it.

2. Discuss the role of center-state relations in judicial review.

Ans. For answer refer to text under the heading Centre-State Relations on page no. 38.

3. A High Court quashes a state government's decision to grant a mining lease to a private company, citing environmental concerns. What is the legal basis for the High Court's intervention?

Ans. The High Court exercised its judicial review power through a writ of mandamus which commands a public authority to perform its legal duty and act in accordance with the law, in this case, protecting the environment.

The High Courts intervention was based on the principle of judicial review, which allows courts to review administrative decisions to ensure they are

(i) Made in accordance with the law.

(ii) Reasonable and not arbitrary.

(iii) Not violating the individual or group rights.

SELF ASSESSMENT TEST

Objective Type Questions

1. To deal with the questions of secrecy and related inefficiency and corruption in the administration, courts have adopted the judicial method of

(a) disclosure (b) reasonableness (c) proportionality (d) None of these

2. In which of the following cases was it held that in the matter of confiscation of passports, a hearing should have been given to the petitioner in the interest of the principles of natural justice. Consequently, a hearing was given and the passport was returned to her?

(a) Maneka Gandhi Vs. Union of India (b) Kharak Singh Case

(c) Three judges Cases (d) Kesavananda Bharati Case

3. The doctrine of judicial review originated from which country?

(a) UK (b) France (c) USA (d) Russia

4. The Supreme Court of India enunciated the doctrine of 'Basic Structure of the Constitution in

(a) the Golaknath Case in 1967 (b) the Sajjan Singh Case in 1965

(c) the Shankari Prasad Case in 1951 (d) the Kesavananda Bharati Case in 1973

5. Which of the following writs can be used against a person believed to be holding a public office to which he is not entitled?

(a) Habeas Corpus (b) Mandamus (c) Prohibition (d) Quo warranto

Very Short Answer Type Questions

6. In a federal setup, agriculture is a subject listed under the State list in the Indian Constitution. However, the Central Government passes a law regulating the sale and marketing of agricultural products, which some states infringes infuingeson their jurisdiction. The states challenge the law, claiming it violates the principles of federalism by encroaching on a subject reserved for them. Can the Central government legislate on a matter in the state list under certain circumstances? Explain, how the balance is made in such situations between centre and state? **Competency Based Que**

7. Which Article deals with the state in the Constitution of India?

8. State the meaning of the Doctrine of Locus Standi and why is it important?

Short Answer Type Questions

9. State some examples wherein the court has adopted judicial review to ensure fairness in executive actions.

Long Answer Type Questions

10. What do you understand about basic structure doctrine? Trace the evolution of this doctrine in the Indian context.

11. William Marbury sues James Madison for refusing to deliver his commission as a justice of the peace. The Supreme Court rules that the law giving the Supreme Court the power to issue writs of Mandamus is unconstitutional. What is the significance of this ruling? **Competency Based Que**

04 CHAPTER

Alternative Dispute Resolution and Administrative Tribunal

Every legal system in this world can be broadly classified into two models i.e. Adversarial and Inquisitorial. Both the systems aim at delivering justice, but they differ in their techniques of adjudication and justice delivery mechanisms. Therefore, this classification becomes important.

YOUR STUDY GOALS

4.1 Adversarial System
4.2 Inquisitorial System
4.3 Alternative Dispute Resolution (ADR)
4.4 Types of ADR

YOUR PRACTICE GOAL

- Objective Type Questions (32 Qs ; MCQs, A-R, Statements, Matching)
- Subjective Questions (10 VSAs, 10 SAs, 7 LAs)

4.1 Adversarial System

- In an adversarial system, the parties in a legal proceeding develop their own theory of the case and gather evidence to support their claims.
- Parties are assisted by their lawyers who take a proactive role in **delivering** justice to the litigants.
- The **lawyers** gather evidence and even participate in cross-examination and scrutiny of evidence, presented by the other disputing party.
- The **role of the judge/decision maker is passive** as the judge decides the claims only on the basis of the evidence and arguments presented by the parties and their lawyers.
- The adversarial system is generally adopted in **common law countries.** Common law jurisdictions include the UK, U.S., Australia and India.

Advantages of Adversarial System

The main advantages of an adversarial system are

- The use of **cross-examination**[1] can be an effective way to test the credibility (genuineness) of witnesses presented.

1 **Cross-examination** It means the examination of a witness who has already testified in orders to check or discredit the witness's testimony, knowledge or credibility.

- The parties may be more willing to accept the results when they are given effective control over the process.
- The adversarial system protects individual rights by ensuring that defendants have a strong advocate and by placing the burden of proof on the prosecution.
- This system upholds the principle that the accused is presumed innocent until proven guilty, placing the burden of proof on the prosecution.
- Both the sides have the opportunity to challenge evidence and arguments presented, helping to prevent wrongful convictions.

Disadvantages of Adversarial System

The disadvantages of an adversarial system are

- The cost of the justice system falls upon the parties. This creates an in-built discrimination amongst the litigants. Parties with better resources are able to access justice by hiring competent lawyers
- The role of lawyers and the procedural formalities, e.g. cross-examination may extend the trial and lead to delays in several matters.
- Judges play a less active role. A judge is not duty bound to ascertain the truth, but only to evaluate the matter on the basis of evidence presented before him/her.
- The focus on outplaying the opposition may lead to a lack of focus on finding the truth and achieving justice.
- Requires each side to contest each other, possibly leading to questionable tactics.

4.2 Inquisitorial System

- In an inquisitorial system, the judge/decision maker has the central role in delivering justice.
- The **role of the judge/decision maker is active** as he/she determines the facts and issues in dispute.
- The judge/decision maker also decides the manner in which the evidence must be presented before the court. For example, the judge may decide for presentation of a specific form of evidence i.e., oral (witness statement) or documentary (correspondence between the parties through letters/e-mails) or a combination of both.
- In this system, less reliance is placed on cross-examination, and other techniques are often used by lawyers to evaluate evidence of their opposing counsel.
- Continental Europe which follows the **civil law system** (i.e. those deriving from Roman law or the Napoleonic Code) has adopted the inquisitorial system.

Advantages of Inquisitorial System

The advantages of an inquisitorial system are

- This system offers procedural efficiency as the active role of judges prevents delays and prolonged trials.
- This system preserves equality between the parties as even the stronger party with more resources and expert lawyers may not be able to influence the judges.
- Minor errors in procedure are ignored if the purpose of justice is served.
- The defense and the judge have access to all evidence collected by the government. This helps to prevent a defendant from being convicted without enough evidence.

Disadvantages of Inquisitorial System

The disadvantages of inquisitorial system are

- In this system, since the judge act like an investigator, he/she can no longer remain neutral to evaluate the case with an open mind.
- In this system, there may be a lack of an incentive structure for judges to involve themselves in proper fact finding.
- Inquisitorial investigations often occur behind closed doors, making it difficult for the public to scrutnise the process.
- In an inquisitorial investigation, there is no party advocating for the accused, which can lead to questioning of evidence.

4.3 Alternative Dispute Resolution (ADR)

- Alternative Dispute Resolution (ADR) system refers to the use of non-adversarial techniques of adjudication of legal disputes.
- ADR is an attempt to devise a machinery which should be capable of providing an alternative to the conventional methods of resolving disputes in the court system.
- The history of ADR in India pre-dates the modern adversarial model of Indian judiciary.
- The modern Indian judiciary was introduced with the advent of the British colonial era, as the English courts and the English legal system influenced the practice of Indian courts, advocates and judges.
- Courts in India were established to have a uniform legal system on the basis of the English courts.
- Even before the advent of such formalistic models of courts and judiciary, the Indian legal system was characterised by several native ADR techniques.

The Vedic age in India, witnessed the flourishing of specialised tribunals such as

- **Kula** For disputes of family, community, tribe, castes, races.
- **Shreni** For internal disputes in business, corporation of artisans.
- **Puga** For association of traders/commerce branches.

In these institutions, interest based negotiations dominated with a neutral third party which seeks to identify the underlying needs and concerns of the parties in dispute. Similarly, **People's Courts** or **Panchayats** continued to be responsible for dispute resolution in villages.

ADR Outside India

In ancient times, **ADR outside India** often involved referring disputes to private individuals for resolution.

Under Roman law, this was known as compromysm (compromise). Arbitration, as a way to settle conflict, was highly regarded across the civil law systems of Europe. For the Greeks, arbitration was particularly important and widely respected as a method for resolving disputes outside of formal court settings.

However, in England the attitude towards arbitration was more complex. The common law courts were often protective of their authority and were wary of any agreements that by passed the judicial system, leading to a fluctuating stance - ranging from strong opposition to a more open, yet cautions, acceptance of arbitration.

Source Russel on Arbitration, 22nd Edn, 2003

Needs of ADR

ADR is needed due to the following problems confronted by the law courts

- The lack of number of courts and judges which creates an inadequacy within the justice delivery system.
- The increasing litigation in India due to increasing population, complexity of laws and obsolete continuation of some pre-existing legal statutes.
- The increasing cost of litigation in prosecuting or defending a case, increasing court fees, lawyer's fees and incidental expenses.
- Delay in disposal of cases resulting in huge pendency in all the courts.
- Access to justice is a challenge for marginalised groups.

Benefits of ADR

The ADR techniques are **speedier, informal and cheaper** mode of delivering justice, as compared to the conventional judicial procedure. Following are the benefits of ADR

- It is less time consuming as people resolve their disputes expeditiously[2] in a short period as compared to courts.
- It is **less costly** than litigation.
- It is **free from technicalities** of courts as informal ways are applied in resolving disputes.
- It can be **used at any time,** even when a case is pending before a court of law.
- It provides a **more convenient** forum[3] to the parties who can choose the time, place and procedure for conducting the preferred dispute redressal process.
- If the dispute is technical in nature, parties have an **opportunity to select the expert** who possesses the relevant legal and technical expertise.
- ADR provides the **flexibility** to even refer disputes to non-lawyers. For example, several disputes of technical character i.e. disputes pertaining to the regulation of the construction industry are usually referred to engineers rather than lawyers.
- ADR is based on more **direct participation** by the disputants rather than being run by lawyers and judges.

Statutory Recognition of ADR

- Alternative Dispute Resolution obtained statutory[4] recognition with the enactment of **Arbitration and Conciliation Act, 1996 and the Legal Services Authority Act, 1987.**
- The ADR mechanisms were incorporated under **Section 89 of Code of Civil Procedure Code, 1908.** The purpose of this section is to enable the courts to legally refer the matters of ADR, to resolve the cases quickly and to reduce the pendency of cases.
- Section 89 is a provision inserted by the **2002 Amendment** of the Civil Procedure Code, 1908. The code is the primary legislation governing the method, procedure and legal practice of civil disputes.
- Section 89 of the code only deals with court referred mediation.
  According to **Section 89** in cases where the elements of a settlement exist which may be acceptable to the parties, the court shall formulate the terms of settlement and give them to the parties for their observation. After receiving the observations of the parties, the court may reformulate the terms of a possible settlement and refer the same for

- Arbitration
- Mediation
- Conciliation
- Judicial settlement including settlement through Lok Adalat

---

2 **Expeditiously** It means with speed and efficiency.
3 **Forum** It means a court or tribunal.
4 **Statutory** It means required, permitted or enacted by statute.

Quick Test 1

1 In which legal system the role of judges/decision makers is passive?
2 Which type of legal system is based on the interventionist/investigative model?
3 Which country's legal system influenced the practice of Indian courts?
4 Name the acts through which ADR obtained statutory recognition.

4.4 Types of ADR

Arbitration

Arbitration is a term derived from the nomenclature of Roman law. Arbitration is a private arrangement of taking disputes to a less adversarial, less formal and more flexible forum and abiding by judgement of a selected person, **instead of carrying** it to the established courts of justice.

- The law relating to arbitration is contained in the Arbitration and Conciliation Act, 1996.
- **It came into force on the 25th day of January, 1996.** It provides for domestic arbitration, international commercial arbitration and also enforcement of foreign arbitral awards.
- The Arbitration and Conciliation Amendment Act, 2015 has come into force to meet the requirements of alternative resolutions.
- The Arbitration and Conciliation Act of 1996 provides for an elaborative codified recognition of the concept of arbitration, which has largely been influenced by significant movements of judicial reforms and conflict management across the world.
- The international convention entitled, United Nations Commission on International Trade Law (UNCITRAL) model law on International Commercial Arbitration, 1985. After this, the United Nations General Assembly recommended that all countries must duly consider it, in order to bring uniformity in the law and practice of international arbitration.

Process of Arbitration

- The process of dispute resolution through arbitration is confidential, unlike the court proceedings which are open to the public. This feature of arbitration makes it popular especially for commercial disputes where business secrets revealed during the process of dispute resolution are protected and preserved.
- The companies also can maintain their commercial reputation by preventing the general public and their customers from discovering the details of their on-going legal disputes.

The stepwise process of arbitration is discussed below

Step 1 **Notice** Aggrieved party send a notice to the defaulting party initiating arbitration.

Step 2 **Choose an Arbitrator** The parties in an arbitration have the freedom to select a qualified expert as an arbitrator.

- **Arbitration Agreement** An agreement where parties mutually decide to resolve any current or future disputes through arbitration, instead of going to court. This agreement can be made in writing or through other forms of communication, reflecting the intention of both parties to settle their differences in a more efficient, private and flexible manner.
- **Court Referral to Arbitration** If one party takes the dispute to court, despite having an arbitration agreement in place, the other party can inform the court about the existing agreement. In such cases the court is required to refer the dispute back to arbitration, as originally agreed upon by both the parties. This process, where the court directs the matter to arbitration, is known as court referral to arbitration. It ensures that the agreed - upon method of resolving disputes is respected.

Step 3 **Statement of Claim** The initial documents are filled by claimants enlisting the issues raised to be resolved in an arbitration.

Step 4 **Statement of Counter Claim** Respondent's reply to the claim presented by the claimant.

Step 5 **Proceeding Start** Decide the place and time to meet.

Step 6 **Award** The decision rendered by an arbitrator is known as an **arbitral award.**

Arbitral Award

- An arbitral award is **similar to a judgement given by a judge.** It is binding on the disputing parties.
- Once an arbitral award is rendered, it is recognised and enforced (given effect to), like a judgement or order of the court.
- In addition to an arbitral award, the arbitrator also holds power and authority to grant interim[5] **measures,** like a judge in the court.
- These interim measures are temporary relief and may be granted while the legal proceedings are on-going, in order to preserve and protect certain rights of the parties, till the final award is rendered.
- However, unlike a judgement rendered by a judge in the court, the award **does not hold** precedential[6] **value** for future arbitrations. It does not act as the doctrine of stare decisis which means 'stand by the decision'.
- Arbitrators are free to base their decisions on their own conception of what is fair and just.
- Thus, unlike judges, they are not strictly required to follow the law or the reasoning of earlier case decisions.
- An arbitral award rendered in an arbitration may be struck down or invalidated by the courts. The grounds of such invalidation are limited to
  - incapacity of a party to enter into arbitration agreement in the first place.
  - improper appointment of arbitrator.
  - dispute falling outside the terms of the arbitration agreement.
  - bias on the part of arbitrator, award violating public policy at large.

Types of Arbitration

The types of arbitration are discussed below

- **Domestic Arbitration** It is an arbitration with Indian parties, where the **place of arbitration is in India** and laws applicable are Indian.
- **Foreign Arbitration** It is an arbitration where proceedings are conducted in a **place outside India** and the award is required to be enforced in India.
- **Ad-hoc Arbitration** It is an arbitration which is governed by parties themselves, without recourse to a formal arbitral institution. It may be domestic or international in character. Ad-hoc arbitration means that the arbitration should not be conducted according to the rules of an arbitral institution.
- **Institutional Arbitration** It is an arbitration where **parties select a particular institution,** which in turn takes the arbitration forward by selecting an arbitrator and laying out the rules applicable within an arbitration, e.g., mode of obtaining evidence, etc.
  There are several institutions to govern arbitration. Examples of prominent institutions of arbitration include the **London Chamber of International Arbitration** (LCIA) which has its offices across the world, including New Delhi, India, etc.
- **Statutory Arbitration** It is an arbitration which is mandatorily imposed on the parties by the operation of a particular law or statute, applicable to them. For example, the **Defence of India Act, 1971** is one such legislation that mandates a recourse to arbitration in case of any dispute arising within the act.
- **International Commercial Arbitration** According to **Section 2(1)(f)** of the Arbitration and Conciliation, 1996, international commercial arbitration is an arbitration in which **atleast one of the disputing parties is a resident/body corporate of a country other than India.** Arbitration with the government of a foreign country is also considered to be an international commercial arbitration.

5 Interim It means something which is temporary.

6 Precedential It means having the character of, or constituting precedent.

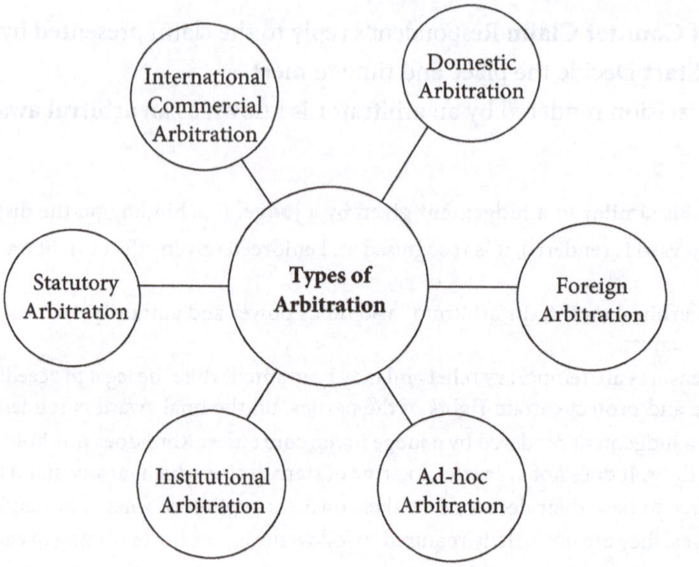

▲ *Types of Arbitration*

Quick Test 2

1. What does an arbitration which is governed by the parties themselves called?
2. What is the decision rendered by an arbitrator known as?
3. In which arbitration, the parties select a particular institution?
4. In which year, the Arbitration and Conciliation Act was passed?

Mediation

- Mediation is a method of ADR in which parties **appoint a neutral third party** who facilitates the mediation process in order to assist the parties in achieving an acceptable, voluntary agreement.
- Mediation is based on the voluntary will of the parties and is a flexible and informal technique of dispute resolution. The features of mediation are
  - Mediation is **more formal** than negotiation, but **less formal** than arbitration or litigation.
  - Mediation is relatively **inexpensive, fast and confidential** unlike litigation and similar to arbitration.
  - Mediation and arbitration differ on the grounds of the nature of an award rendered.
  - The outcome of mediation **does not have similar binding like an arbitral award.**
  - Mediation gives the participants an opportunity to raise and discuss any issues they might wish to settle.
  - Mediation can handle any number of outstanding issues. It offers a way to discuss (and solve) the problems underlying a dispute and **create a truly lasting peace.**

Process of Mediation

- Mediator is the neutral third party facilitating the process of mediation.
- Mediation does not follow a uniform set of rules, though **mediators typically explain the rules** that the mediation will observe at the beginning of the process.
- Successful mediation often reflects not only the parties' willingness to participate, but also the mediator's skill.
- There is no uniform set of rules for mediators to become licensed and rules vary by state regarding requirements for mediator certification.

Mediation may be existed in three ways

- Parties may agree to resolve their claims through a **pre-agreed mediation agreement** without initiating formal judicial proceedings (pre-litigation mediation).
- Parties may agree to mediate, at the beginning of formal court proceedings, popularly known as **court referrals.**
- Mediation may be taken **after formal court proceedings** have started, or **even post trial** i.e. at the appellate stage.

Scope of Mediation

Under the Indian law, following have been held to be most suited for mediation

- Contractual dispute (including money claims)
- Disputes arising from strained relationships (from matrimonial to partnership)
- Disputes which need a continuity of relationship (neighbour's easement rights)
- Consumer disputes
- For example, A suburban home owner might find that the formal legal system offers no realistic way to deal with his neighbour's overly bright driveway lights that shine in his bedroom window. Such disputes however can be mediated. Mediation gives the participants an opportunity to raise and discuss any issue they might wish to settle.
- In the case of **Afcons Infrastructure Ltd. Vs. Cherian Varkey Construction Co. (P) Ltd., (2010),** the Supreme Court clarified that representative suits, election disputes, criminal offenses, cases against specific classes of persons (minors, mentally challenged) have been excluded from the scope of mediation.

Types of Mediation

Mediation can be classified into the following categories

- **Evaluative Mediation** It focused on providing the parties with an **evaluation of their case** and directing them towards settlement. During an evaluative mediation process, the mediator will express a viev on what might be a fair or resonable settlement. The evaluative mediator has an advisory role that he /she evaluates the strengths and weaknesses of each side's arguments and makes some predictions about what would happen if they go to court.
- **Facilitative Mediation** Facilitative mediators typically **do not evaluate a case** or direct the parties to a particular settlement. Instead, they **facilitates the conversation.** These mediators act as guardians of the process, not the content or the outcome.
  During a facilitative mediation session, the parties in dispute control both what will be discussed and how their issues will be resolved.
  The facilitative mediator is focused on helping the parties to find a resolution to their dispute. The facilitative mediator further provides a structure and agenda for the discussion.
- **Transformative Mediation** It focused on **supporting empowerment and recognition shifts,** by allowing and encouraging deliberation, decision-making and perspective-taking.

  A competent transformative mediator practices with a main focus on communication, identifying opportunities for empowerment and recognition as those opportunities appear in the parties, own conversations and responding in ways that provide an opening for parties to choose what, to do with them.
- Mediation with arbitration mediation has sometimes good effect when coupled with arbitration, particularly binding arbitration, in a process called **'mediation/arbitration'.** The process **begins as a standard mediation,** but if mediation fails, the mediator becomes an arbitrator.

This process is more appropriate in civil matters where rules of evidence or jurisdiction are not in dispute. In some respects, it resembles, the criminal plea bargaining and confucian judicial procedure, wherein the judge also plays the role of prosecutor.

- **Online Mediation** It employs online technology to provide disputants access to mediators and each other despite geographic distance, disability or other barriers to direct meeting.

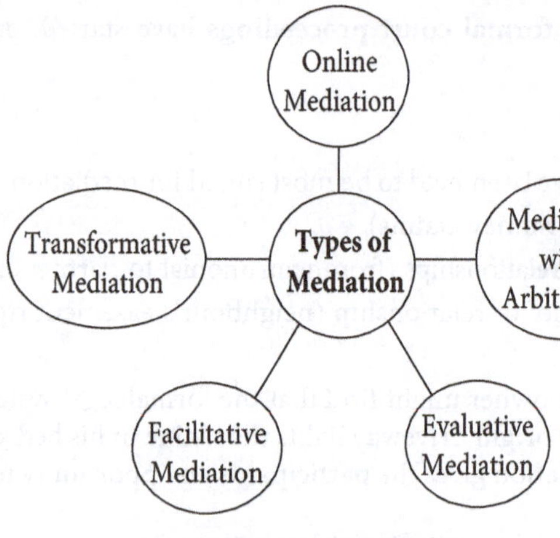

▲ *Types of Mediation*

Conciliation

- Conciliation means **settling of disputes without litigation.**
- Conciliation is a process by which discussion between parties is kept going through the participation of a conciliator.
- Conciliation process is similar to mediation as parties appoint a **neutral third party** out of their own will, to resolve their disputes.
- The key difference between mediation and conciliation lies in the role of the neutral third party.
- A mediator only performs a facilitative role and provides a platform for the parties to reach a mutually agreeable solution.
- However, the role of a conciliator goes beyond that of a mediator. A conciliator may be **interventionist** in the sense that he/she may suggest potential solutions to the parties, in order to resolve their claims and disputes.
- Conciliation is also governed by **Section 89,** Civil Procedure Code, 1908. The process and methods within conciliation have been described in the Arbitration and **Conciliation Act,** 1996.
- Further, the Industrial Disputes Act, 1947 also provides for conciliation as a **viable means** of resolving disputes in the labour sector.

Settlement Agreement

If the parties reach agreement on the settlement of a dispute, a written settlement agreement will be drawn up and signed by the parties. According to **Section 73(2)** of the Arbitration and Conciliation Act, 1996, if the parties request, the conciliator may draw up or assist the parties in drawing up the settlement agreement. According to **Section 73(3)** of the Act, when the parties have signed the settlement agreement, it becomes final and binding on the parties and persons claiming under them respectively.

In the case of **Haresh Dayaram Thakur Vs. State of Maharashtra** (2000), it was ruled that the settlement agreement shall have the same status and effect as an arbitral award. This means it shall be treated as a decree of the court and shall be enforceable.

Cases about Arbitration and Conciliation Act, 1996

Bharat Aluminium Co. Ltd. (BALCO) Vs. Kaiser Aluminium Technical Service, Inc. (Kaiser) (2012 SC), the Supreme Court dealt with some significant issues

- It was observed that object of Section 2 (7) of the act is to distinguish the 'domestic award' from the 'foreign award'.
- It was held that there is a clear distinction between part I (domestic award) and part II (foreign award) as being applicable in completely different field and on overlapping provisions.
- The court has also drawn a distinction between a 'seat' and 'venue'.
- The court dissented with the observations made in Bhatia International case and further observed on a logical construction of the act' that the Indian courts do not have the power to grant interim measures when the seat of arbitration is outside India.
- The court further held that in foreign related international commercial arbitration no application for interim relief will be maintainable in India, either by arbitration or by filing a suit.

In the case of **Konkan Railways Corp. Ltd. Vs. M/s Mehul Construction Co.** (2000), the Supreme Court emphasised that the increasing growth of global trade and the delay in disposal of cases in courts made it **imperative**[7] to have the perception of an alternative dispute resolution system.

The act provides for domestic as well as international commercial arbitration. It aim to resolve dispute as quickly as possible with minimum interference of a court of law.

The Supreme Court affirmed that the Arbitration and Conciliation Act, 1996 was introduced in order to attract the 'international mercantile community'.

In the case of **Fuerst Day Lawson Ltd. Vs. Jindal Exports Ltd.** 2001, the Supreme Court observed that the object of the Arbitration and Conciliation Act of 1996 is to provide speedy and alternative solution to the dispute and avoid extension of litigation.

Quick Test 3

1. In which method of ADR parties appoint a neutral third party?
2. The scope of mediation is expressly clarified by Supreme Court in which case law?
3. What is the key difference between mediation and conciliation?

7 **Imperative** It means something which is of vital importance; crucial.

Mind Map

ALTERNATIVE DISPUTE RESOLUTION AND ADMINISTRATIVE TRIBUNAL

1 Adversarial and Inquisitorial Systems

Adversarial System
- Parties develop their own case theories and gather evidence.
- Lawyers play a key role; judges are passive decision-makers.
- Common in the UK, US, Australia and India.

Advantages of Adversarial System
- Effective use of cross-examination ensures evidence reliability.
- Defendants have strong advocates; burden of proof on prosecution.

Disadvantages of Adversarial System
- Costly and resource-dependent, leading to discrimination.
- Focus on winning may overshadow truth-seeking.
- Role of lawyers and the procedural formalities

Inquisitorial System
- Judges actively investigate and decide how evidence is presented.
- Common in civil law countries like those in Continental Europe.

Advantages of Inquisitorial System
- Procedurally efficient, prevents delays.
- Promotes equality, minimising resource based disparities.

Disadvantages of Inquisitorial System
- Judges may lose neutrality due to active involvement.
- lack of an incentive structure for judges to involve themselves in proper fact finding.
- Limited public scrutiny; behind-closed-doors investigations.

2 Alternative Dispute Resolution (ADR)

- Non-adversarial methods to resolve disputes outside courts.
- Historically significant in India and globally (e.g., Panchayats, Roman Law).
- Vedic age in India, witnessed the flourishing of specialised tribunals such as.
- **Kula** For disputes of family, community.
- **Shreni** For internal disputes in business.
- **Puga** For association of traders.

Problems Addressed by ADR
- Overburdened judiciary, limited judges.
- Rising litigation cost and delays.
- Ensures justice for marginalised groups.

3 Types of ADR

Arbitration
- Private dispute resolution by an agreed arbitrator.
- Governed by Arbitration and Conciliation Act, 1996.

Types
- Domestic Arbitration
- International Commercial Arbitration
- Foreign Arbitration
- Ad-hoc Arbitration
- Institutional Arbitration
- Statutory Arbitration Imposed on the parties by the operation of a particular law or statute
- **Arbitral Award** Binding decision; not precedent-based.
- **Grounds for Invalidation** Bias, jurisdiction issues, public policy violation.

Mediation
- Neutral third-party facilitates voluntary agreement.

Types
- Evaluative Mediation
- Facilitative Mediation
- Trans formative Mediation
- Online Mediation
- Best for contractual, consumer, or relationship disputes.

Conciliation
- Similar to mediation but allows the conciliator to suggest solutions.
- Recognised under the Arbitration and Conciliation Act, 1996.
- Provides for conciliation as a viable means of resolving disputes in the Labour Sector Act, 1947.

Judicial Settlement
- Includes Lok Adalats.
- Courts may refer cases under Section 89 of the CPC.

4 Administrative Tribunals

- Established for specialised and speedy justice in administrative matters.
- Operate under Articles 323-A and 323-B of the Constitution.

5 Benefits of ADR

- Faster, cost-effective, and informal dispute resolution.
- Preserves relationships through mutual agreements.
- Parties can select experts for technical disputes.
- Flexible process; accommodates non-lawyers for technical cases.

6 Case Studies and Precedents

Konkan Railways Vs. Mehul Construction Co.
- Importance of arbitration for international commercial disputes.

Afcons Infrastructure Vs. Cherian Varkey Construction
- Clarified mediation scope; excluded cases like election disputes and offenses.

7 Comparative Analysis

Arbitration Vs. Mediation
- **Arbitration** Binding decision by arbitrator.
- **Mediation** Non-binding; parties control outcomes.

Mediation Vs. Conciliation
- **Mediation** Facilitative role.
- **Conciliation** Suggestive, interventionist role.

CBSE TEXTBOOK FOLDER

1. Ram and Sikander agreed in writing to resolve the disputes arising out of their contract by way of arbitration. A dispute arose between Ram and Sikander. Ram filed a case in the court. Will the court stay the legal proceedings filed by Ram? Discuss.

Ans. The court will not stay the legal proceedings filed by Ram because if a party to the dispute approches the court despite the presence of an arbitration agreement, the other party raise a claim before the court. The court then must refer the dispute back to arbitration, if it has been previously agreed by the party.

2. Mr. Hari and his friend, Mr. Suresh entered into a partnership deed to carry on the business of creative designing. After a year of starting a successful partnership firm, creative differences arose between Mr. Hari and Mr. Suresh, which created a rift between them.

To help resolve the dispute, Mr. Sharma, the secretary of a reputed firm, is facilitating them to help them achieve an acceptable agreement. Which dispute resolution method is Mr. Sharma resorting to? Explain.

Ans. The dispute resolution method Mr. Sharma is resorting to is known as mediation. It is a method of ADR in which parties appoint a neutral third party who facilitates the mediation process in order to assist the parties in achieving an acceptable, voluntary agreement.

3. Sita and Reena are business partners. After sometime a dispute arose between them. Both of them agreed to submit the dispute between them to Mr. Bajaj, a senior member of a law firm. Sita subsequently came to know that Reena and Mr. Bajaj are related to each other. Can Sita challenge the authority of Mr. Bajaj as an arbitrator? Discuss.

Ans. Yes, Sita can challenge the authority of Mr. Bajaj as an arbitrator because the Arbitration and Conciliation Act says that an arbitral award rendered in an arbitration may be struck down or invlidated on the ground of

- incapacity of a party to enter into arbitration agreement in the first place.
- improper appointment of arbitrator.
- dispute falling outside the terms of arbitration agreement.
- bias on the part of arbitrator.
- award violating public policy at large.

4. A dispute arose between Rakesh and his employer regarding some incident of injustice to Rakesh by some senior members of the management during the course of his employment. They appointed Mr. Kumar to resolve the dispute. Mr. Kumar not only facilitated the conversation but also suggested potential solutions. Identify and explain the role played by Mr. Kumar.

Ans. The role played by Mr. Kumar is of conciliator. Conciliation is a process by which discussion between parties is kept going through the participation of a conciliator. A conciliator may be interventionist in the sense that he/she may suggest potential solutions to the parties, in-order to resolve their claims and disputes.

Exam Pattern Questions

Objective Type Questions

Multiple Choice Questions (MCQs)

1. In a criminal trial in a country in continental Europe, the judge, Judge Helena plays an active role in investigating the case. She questions the witnesses, evaluates the evidences presented by the parties and orders additional forensic test. The defense lawyer, Mr. Jameson, expresses concern that the judge's active involvement in the investigation may undermine the fairness of the trial.

In the given content, identify the probable disadvantage of the justice dispensation system that is concerning for the defense lawyer. **CBSE 2025**

(a) The active role of judge would prevent delays and prolonged trials.
(b) Stronger party in the case, with more resources and expert lawyers may not be able to influence the judges.
(c) The judge can no longer remain neutral to evaluate the case with an open mind.
(d) Less reliance is placed on cross examination and other techniques used by lawyers.

2. Omega Builders and Delta Constructions have a dispute over project delays. The court suggest mediation, but Omega Builders is unsure if their case qualifies. According to the Afcons Infrastructure Ltd. Vs. Cherian Varley Construction Co. ruling, which disputes are generally excluded from mediation? **CBSE 2025**

(a) Commercial contracts
(b) Matrimonial and Custody issues
(c) Criminal offenses
(d) Consumer disputes

3. Sandeep and Sarika were involved in a business transaction where a dispute arose and the same was referred to arbitration. The award given by the arbitrator was in the form of a wager. Identify the ground on which the award can be set aside. **CBSE SQP 2021**

(a) Bias of arbitrator
(b) Dispute outside the scope of arbitration agreement
(c) Award violates public policy
(d) Improper appointment of arbitrator

4. An arbitration which is governed by parties themselves, without recourse to a formal arbitral institution are called

(a) institutional arbitration
(b) ad-hoc arbitration
(c) international arbitration
(d) domestic arbitration

5. Which form of arbitration has been specifically defined under Section 2(1)(f) of the Arbitration and Conciliation Act, 1996? **CBSE SQP 2021**

(a) Domestic arbitration
(b) Institutional arbitration
(c) International commercial arbitration
(d) Foreign arbitration

6. The Arbitration and Conciliation Laws in India have been largely influenced by significant movements of judicial reforms and conflict management across the world. The Indian Arbitration and Conciliation Act, 1996 is modelled on which law? **CBSE SQP 2021**

(a) Universal Declaration of Human Rights
(b) United Nations Commission on International Trade Law Model Law on International Commercial Arbitration
(c) United Nations Commission on International Trade Law Model Law on Arbitration
(d) Vienna Convention

7. Two companies ABC and XYZ have a contractual dispute regarding non-payment of services rendered. Instead of going to court, they decide to pursue ad-hoc arbitration to resolve their dispute. Which of the following is a key feature of ad-hoc arbitration? **CBSE 2024**

(a) The process is conducted by an arbitral institution.
(b) The process follows a pre-determined set of rules established by a recognised arbitration
(c) The parties have the flexibility to tailor the arbitration process to their specific needs and preferences.
(d) The process is conducted by a sole arbitrator appointed under the statutory provisions.

8. An informal dispute resolution method where the two parties discuss the issues before a neutral third party who will assist the parties to reach an agreement. **CBSE SQP 2021**

(a) Mediation (b) Arbitration
(c) Conciliation (d) Judicial determination

9. Mohan purchases a mixer-grinder from M/s Makil and Bros. The grinder malfunctions within the warranty period. Both the manufacturer and the seller fail to rectify the problem and a dispute ensues. The dispute may best be resolved through ....

(a) mediation (b) conciliation
(c) arbitration (d) negotiation

10. Mr. Lal and his friend, Mr. Kumar entered into a partnership to carry on the business of creating digital products like print-on-demand posters, greeting cards, T-shirts, etc and online courses. After a year of launching a successful partnership firm, creative differences and other issues arose between Mr. Lal and Mr. Kumar that created a rift between them. To help resolve their dispute, Mr. Borwanker, the Secretary of a Law firm, is facilitating Mr. Lal and Mr. Kumar to exchange ideas and to give possible alternative solutions.

Mr. Borwanker is resorting to which dispute resolution method? **CBSE SQP 2021**

(a) Arbitration (b) Negotiation
(c) Mediation (d) Conciliation

11. Nita Industries Ltd. went through an arbitration process with Mira Ltd. to resolve a dispute over the supply of raw materials. The arbitrator was the former CEO of Mira Ltd. Nita Industries was not satisfied with the arbitral award. What remedy is available to Nita Industries Ltd.? **CBSE SQP 2024**

(a) No remedy as an arbitral award is binding.
(b) Nita Industries Ltd. can file an appeal before the SCI.
(c) Nita Industries Ltd. can ask for setting aside the arbitral award.
(d) Nita Industries Ltd. has no reason to doubt the arbitrator, so it will have to accept the award.

12. Identify the form of arbitration that has been defined specifically under Section 2 (1)(f) of the Arbitration and Conciliation Act, 1996. **CBSE 2023**

(a) Institutional arbitration
(b) Statutory arbitration
(c) International commercial arbitration
(d) Ad-hoc arbitration.

13. Saba and Hamid are an estranged couple seeking mediatory help to resolve their disputes. Being in different countries, however, is proving to be a major hurdle. Identify which of the following is a suitable recourse. **CBSE 2023**

(a) Facilitative mediation (b) Arbitration
(c) Online mediation (d) Mediation with arbitration

14. Mr. Akash stood as an independent candidate in the State Assembly elections. On losing, he raised an objection to the counting of the votes and thus an election dispute arose. He brought the dispute before a mediator, Mr. Verma, but Mr. Verma expressed his incapacity to mediate the matter. For the given situation, choose the correct statement. **CBSE SQP 2021**

(a) Election disputes are expressly excluded from the scope of mediation.
(b) Mr. Verma should mediate the matter as it is the best suited alternative dispute resolution mechanism.
(c) Mr. Verma should not mediate the matter as the outcome of mediation is not binding.
(d) Mr. Verma should mediate the matter only when it is Court referred.

15. Rohit, aged 13 years and Kartik, aged 20 years entered into a sale agreement wherein Rohit agreed to sell his farmhouse to Kartik for ₹ 5,00,000. After execution of the sale agreement, Rohit avoided the agreement of sale stating that the farmhouse is involved in a litigation pending before the Hon'ble Delhi High Court and he cannot transfer the farmhouse. Aggrieved by this, Rohit and Kartik agreed to appoint a mediator to resolve their dispute.

Given the dispute, which of the following statement is correct?

(a) The dispute can be referred to arbitration as contractual disputes are best suited for arbitration.
(b) The dispute cannot be referred to mediation as claims against minors are excluded from the scope of mediation.
(c) The dispute can be referred to mediation as property disputes are best suited for mediation.
(d) The dispute cannot be referred to mediation as the property is lis pendens.

16. This type of mediation is focused on providing the parties with an evaluation of their case and directing them towards settlement.

(a) Evaluative mediation
(b) Facilitative mediation
(c) Transformative mediation
(d) None of the above

17. In which of the following situations do parties out of their own free will, appoint a neutral third party to resolve their disputes? **CBSE 2018**

(a) Lok Adalat
(b) Family Court
(c) Conciliation
(d) Arbitration

18. Section 89 of the Civil Procedure Code only deals with .... **CBSE SQP 2021**

(a) mediation with arbitration
(b) pre-litigation mediation
(c) appellate mediation
(d) court referred mediation

19. There was a dispute between Ms. Shreya and Ms. Piyabli regarding the title and possession of a plot of land. The parties to the dispute appointed a neutral third party. Ms. Liam who suggested potential solutions. Identify the role of Ms. Liam in this situation. **CBSE 2020**

(a) Arbitrator (b) Negotiator
(c) Mediator (d) Conciliator

20. **The SCI in its judicial decision in Afcons Infrastructure Ltd. Vs. Cherian Varkey Construction Co. (P) Ltd. has expressly clarified the ambit of mediation.**
Who among the following falls within the preview of mediation? **CBSE SQP 2024**
(a) Representative suits
(b) Election disputes
(c) Criminal offenses
(d) Cases involving International mercantile community

21. **Jagdish and Susheela, neighbours in the same residential complex, are experiencing a disagreement regarding the boundary wall between their houses. They would like to resolve this dispute through a method that encourages open communication and mutual agreement.**
Which of the following options is best suited to their situation? **CBSE 2024**
(a) Litigation (b) Negotiation
(c) Lok Adalat (d) Mediation

22. Green Tech Inc. and Eco Power Corp., two competing companies in the renewable energy sector are embroiled in a complex commercial dispute over alleged patent infringement. Green Tech claims that Eco Power has unlawfully used their patented technology in their new product. Eco Power vehemently denies the allegation asserting that their technology is original and not infringing. They wish to resolve their dispute through an ADR method that combines mediation and arbitration.
Which of the following options is best suitable for their situation? **CBSE 2024 C**
(a) Filing a lawsuit
(b) Negotiating a settlement agreement
(c) Mediation-arbitration hybrid
(d) Conciliation

23. **Shreya and Sandhya are involved in a heated dispute over the ownership of a valuable piece of artwork. They have decided to engage in evaluative mediation to resolve their conflict. What is the primary role of the mediator in this situation?** **CBSE 2024 C**
(a) Facilitate open communication and encourage parties to reach a mutually agreeable solution.
(b) Provide an objective evaluation of the parties' position and potential outcomes to assist them in reaching a settlement.
(c) Focus on understanding the underlying interests and needs of the parties to facilitate a creative solution
(d) Act as neutral facilitator and guide the parties through a structured process of negotiation and problem-solving.

24. **Match the following.**

Column I	Column II
A. An arbitration with Indian parties, where the place of arbitration is in India.	1. Ad-hoc Arbitration
B. An arbitration which is governed by parties themselves, without recourse to a formal arbitral institution.	2. Domestic Arbitration
C. An arbitration where proceedings are conducted in a place outside India and the award is required to be enforced in India.	3. Institutional Arbitration
D. An arbitration where parties select a particular institution, which in turn takes the arbitration forward by selecting an arbitrator and laying out the rules applicable within an arbitration.	4. Foreign Arbitration

Codes

	A	B	C	D		A	B	C	D
(a)	2	1	4	3	(b)	1	2	3	4
(c)	3	1	2	4	(d)	4	2	3	1

25. **Match the following.**

Column I	Column II
A. Use of non-adversarial techniques of adjudication of legal disputes.	1. Evaluative Mediation
B. Mediation focused on providing the parties with an evaluation of their case and directing them towards settlement.	2. Arbitration Agreement
C. An agreement whereby parties agree to submit their present or future disputes/ differences to arbitration.	3. ADR
D. Process similar to mediation.	4. Conciliation

Codes

	A	B	C	D		A	B	C	D
(a)	3	1	4	2	(b)	1	2	3	4
(c)	3	1	2	4	(d)	4	2	3	1

26. **Which of the following statements best describes the adversarial system in law?**
Statement I The adversarial system relies on an impartial judge or jury to decide the outcome of a case.
Statement II The adversarial system requires the prosecution and defense to present their cases and evidence in a collaborative effort to reach a verdict.

Codes
(a) Statement I best describes the adversarial system in law.
(b) Statement II best describes the adversarial system in law.
(c) Both the Statements are correct and best describes the adversarial system in law.
(d) Both the Statements are incorrect and neither of the two best describes the adversarial system in law.

27. Which of the following statements best describes the benefits of ADR?

Statement I ADR methods, such as mediation and arbitration are often less expensive than traditional litigation.

Statement II ADR methods, such as mediation and arbitration, can lead to more formal and rigid outcomes than traditional litigation.

Codes
(a) Only Statement I is correct.
(b) Only Statement II is correct.
(c) Both Statements are correct.
(d) Both Statements are incorrect.

Assertion-Reason Questions

Directions (Q. Nos. 28-32) In the questions given below, there are two statements. Read the statements and choose the correct option.

Codes
(a) Both A and R are true and R is the correct explanation of A.
(b) Both A and R are true, but R is not the correct explanation of A.
(c) A is true, but R is false.
(d) A is false, but R is true.

28. Assertion (A) In an adversarial system, the parties in a legal proceeding develop their own theory of the case and gather evidence to support their claims.

Reason (R) In an adversarial system, cross examination is an effective way to test the credibility of the witnesses presented. **CBSE SQP 2021**

29. Assertion (A) In an adversarial system, the cost of justice is borne by the parties to the dispute.

Reason (R) Accessibility and affordability to justice are important challenges for the adversarial system of dispute resolution.

30. Assertion (A) Arbitration is a private arrangement of taking disputes to a less adversarial, less formal and more flexible forum and abiding by judgement of a selected person, instead of carrying it to the established courts of justice.

Reason (R) The primary objective of arbitration is to reduce the burden on courts and promote more flexibility in its operations.

31. Assertion (A) International Commercial Arbitration has been defined specifically under Section 2(1)(f) of the Arbitration and Conciliation Act, 1996.

Reason (R) The decision rendered by a mediator is known as an award.

32. Assertion (A) Conciliation is a process similar to mediation as parties out of their own free will appoint a neutral third party to resolve their disputes.

Reason (R) A mediator merely performs a facilitative role and provides a platform for the parties to reach a mutually agreeable solution but the role of a conciliator goes beyond the mediator.

Answers

1. (c) The judge can no longer remain neutral to evaluate the case with an open mind.
2. (c) Criminal offenses
3. (c) Award violates public policy
4. (b) ad-hoc arbitration
5. (c) International commercial arbitration
6. (b) United Nations Commission on International Trade Law Model Law on International Commercial Arbitration
7. (c) The parties have the flexibility to tailor the arbitration process to their specific needs and preferences.
8. (a) Mediation
9. (a) mediation
10. (c) Mediation
11. (c) Nita Industries Ltd. can ask for setting aside the arbitral award.
12. (c) International commercial arbitration
13. (c) Online mediation
14. (a) Election disputes are expressly excluded from the scope of mediation.
15. (b) The dispute cannot be referred to mediation as claims against minors are excluded from the scope of mediation.
16. (a) Evaluative mediation
17. (c) Conciliation
18. (d) court referred mediation

19. (d) Conciliator
20. (d) Cases involving International mercantile community
21. (d) Mediation
22. (c) Mediation-arbitration hybrid
23. (b) Provide an objective evaluation of the parties' position and potential outcomes to assist them in reaching a settlement.
24. (a) 2 1 4 3
25. (a) 3 1 4 2
26. (a) Statement I best describes the adversarial system in law.
27. (a) Only Statement I is correct.
28. (a) Both A and R are true and R is the correct explanation of A.
29. (b) Both A and R are true, but R is not the correct explanation of A.
30. (a) Both A and R are true and R is the correct explanation of A.
31. (c) A is true, but R is false.
32. (a) Both A and R are true and R is the correct explanation of A.

Subjective Questions

Very Short Answer Type Questions

1. Jonathan Leeman and Jared Wilson are co-owners of a restaurant. The former files a case against the latter for fraudulent transactions. In the legal system of their country, the judge determines the facts and issues in dispute.

Identify the legal system of this country and state one of its disadvantages. CBSE 2019

Ans. The system followed here is an inquisitorial system. The disadvantage of this model is that in an inquisitorial system, since the judge acts like an investigator, he/she can no longer remain neutral to evaluate the case with an open mind.

2. There is a dispute between an M/S Rohtash Bros., an Indian Body Corporate and M/S Garry and Fern Bros. a Canadian Body Corporate, regarding breach of contractual terms. Both companies appointed an institution for initiating the process required for settlement of their dispute. Arbitration proceedings were conducted in Canada and the award was enforced in India.

Identify and explain any two types of arbitration mentioned in the above situation. CBSE 2016

Ans. The two kinds of arbitration mentioned in the above situation area.

(i) **Foreign Arbitration** It is an arbitration where proceedings are conducted in a place outside India and the award is required to be enforced in India.

(ii) **International Commercial Arbitration** It is an arbitration in which atleast one of the disputing parties is a resident/body corporate of a country other than India. Arbitration with the government of a foreign country is also considered to be an international commercial arbitration.

3. Anand, a student of international commercial law is reviving a case involving a construction dispute between a contractor and sub-contractor. The contract between the parties includes an arbitration clause stating that any disputes arising from the contract shall be resolved through arbitration. However, the contract does not specify any particular arbitral institution/set of rules to govern the process.

Identify the type of arbitration opted for in this instance. How is arbitration a better mode for dispute resolution in commercial disputes ? CBSE 2024 C

Ans. The type of arbitration opted for in this instance is ad hoc arbitration, where the parties have agreed to arbitrate their disputes without specifying a particular arbitral institution or set of rules. Arbitration is a better mode for dispute resolution in commercial disputes because it offers flexibility, confidentiality, and expertise, allowing for faster and more cost-effective resolution of complex commercial disputes.

4. A utility company digs up a section of the lawns of Mr. Sanjeev Kumar to repair the telephone lines. Soon, his neighbour, Mr. Walia, starts to grow tomatoes in the dug-up patch. Mr. Sanjeev requested Mr. Walia shifted the plants to his kitchen garden, but he refused to do so.

Identify and explain the alternative dispute resolution technique that is best for resolution of the dispute that ensues. CBSE 2019

Ans. The method followed here is mediation.

Mediation is a method of ADR in which parties appoint a neutral third party. This neutral third party facilitates the mediation process in-order to assist the parties in achieving an acceptable, voluntary agreement. Mediation is based on the voluntary will of the parties and is a flexible and informal technique of dispute resolution.

5. Why is mediation a better method of resolution of disputes arising from strained resolutions? **CBSE 2020**

Ans. Mediation gives the participants an opportunity to raise and discuss any issues they might wish to settle. Mediation can handle any number of outstanding gripes or issues. It offers a way to discuss (and solve) the problems underlying a dispute and create a truly lasting peace.

6. There was a dispute between Ms. Udita and Mr. Bhavesh regarding title and possession of an immovable property. The parties to the dispute, out of their own free will appointed Mr. Mohan, a neutral third party to resolve their dispute. Mr. Mohan acted not only as an interventionist, but also suggested potential solutions to the parties, in order to resolve their claims and disputes. State the role of Mr. Mohan as an Alternative Dispute Resolution (ADR) in the above situation. **CBSE 2016**

Ans. Mr. Mohan played the role of a mediator. Mr. Mohan will facilitate the mediation process in-order to assist the partics in achicving an acceptable, voluntary agreement.

7. Write down any two ways in which mediation can be triggered.

Ans. Mediation may be triggered in the following ways

(i) Parties may agree to resolve their claims through a pre-agreed mediation agreement without initiating formal judicial proceedings (pre-litigation mediation).

(ii) Parties may agree to mediate, at the beginning of formal court proceedings (popularly known as court referrals).

8. What are the matters best suited for mediation in the Indian context?

Ans. Under the Indian law, the following are the matters best suited for mediation in the Indian context

(i) Contractual dispute (including money claims)

(ii) Disputes arising from strained relationships (from matrimonial to partnership).

(iii) Disputes which need a continuity of relationship (neighborur's easement rights).

(iv) Consumer disputes

9. A dispute arose between Mr. Shalu Kapahi, MD of a glass factory and its workers' union. The disputing parties appointed Mr. Manoj George (a retired High Court judge) as a neutral third party to intervene and resolve the matter. Mr. George suggested potential solutions to the parties.
Identify and explain which ADR is followed in the given situation. **CBSE 2019**

Ans. The ADR method followed in this case is conciliation.

Conciliation is a process similar to mediation as parties out of their own free will appoint a neutral third party to resolve their disputes.

10. Sunil and Asha are co-founders of a tech-startup. Recently they had a contractual disagreement with their software vendor regarding the delivery timeline of a critical project. Sunil insisted on filing a lawsuit whereas Asha suggested resolution by appointing a neutral third party who could facilitate the parties in achieving an acceptable, voluntary agreement. Sunil agreed and their matter was resolved within two weeks. **CBSE 2025**

(i) Identify the method of dispute resolution adopted by Sunil and Asha.

(ii) Give any two advantages of adopting alternate disputes resolution mechanism by the parties.

Ans. (i) The method of dispute resolution adopted by Sunil and Asha is Mediation. In this process, a neutral third party helps both sides communicate and reach a mutually acceptable solution without going to court.

(ii) Two advantages of Alternate Dispute Resolution (ADR) are

(a) **Saves Time** It is less time consuming as people resolve their disputes expeditiously in a short period as compared to courts.

(b) **Cost-Effective** It is less costly than litigation.

Short Answer Type Questions

1. Explain how the adversarial system in India made access to justice difficult? **CBSE 2019**

Ans. The disadvantages of an adversarial system that made access to justice difficult are

- The cost of the justice system falls upon the parties. This creates an in-built discrimination amongst the litigants. Parties with better resources are able to access justice by hiring competent lawyers and presenting sophisticated evidence which may not be immediately available for parties that lack these resources.
- Accessibility and affordability to justice are important challenges for the adversarial system of dispute resolution.
- The role of lawyers and the procedural formalities, e.g. cross examination may prolong the trial and lead to delays in several matters.
- Judges play a less active role, a judge is not duty bound to ascertain the truth, but only to evaluate the matter based on the evidence presented before him/her.

2. In a criminal trial the judge takes an active role in investigating the case, gathering evidence and questioning witnesses, while the accused has a limited say in the proceedings. Identify the system and state the main advantages of this system. **CBSE 2024**

Ans. The judge/decision maker if takes an active rols in investigating, gathering evidence, etc. such a system is inquistiorial system.

The main advantages of this system include

(i) The system offers procedural efficiency as the active role of judges prevents delays and prolonged trials.

(ii) The system preserves equality between the parties as even the stronger party with more resources and expert lawyers may not be able to influence the judges.

3. A commercial dispute has arisen between two companies over a breach of contract. They have to pursue arbitration as a means of resolving the conflict. Outline the process of arbitration. **CBSE 2019**

Ans. The process of arbitration includes the following steps

Step 1 The party aggrieved will send a notice to the defaulting party initiating arbitration.

Step 2 The parties in an arbitration have a freedom to select a qualified expert known as arbitrator, either through arbitration agreement or through court referral.

Step 3 This intial documents filed by the claimant enlisting issues raised to be resolved in an arbitration. (statement of claim)

Step 4 Respondent will reply to the claim presented by the claimant. (statement of counter-claim)

Step 5 Proceedings start (decide the place and time to meet)

Step 6 The decision rendered by an arbitrator is known as arbitral award which given at the end, similar to judgment.

4. How is an arbitral award both similar and different from a court pronounced judgment or order? **CBSE 2025**

Ans. An arbitral award is similar to a court judgment as it is binding on the parties and can be enforced like a court order. Arbitrators also have the authority to grant interim relief, similar to judges.

However, an arbitral award lacks precedential value, meaning future arbitrations are not bound by previous awards, unlike judicial rulings that follow the doctrine of stare decisis. redressal process.

5. Analyse the reasons that paved the way for Alternate Dispute Resolution techniques in the Indian judicial system. **CBSE 2020**

Or **Discuss the main problems confronting law courts that have resulted in the rise of Alternate Dispute Resolution (ADR) mechanisms.** **CBSE 2018**

Or **What are the problems confronted by the law courts in India? How can ADR help in resolving these problems?** **CBSE SQP 2024**

Ans. The reasons that paved the ways for the rise of ADR mechanisms or techniques are

- The lack of number of courts and judges which creates an inadequacy within the justice delivery system.
- The increasing litigation in India due to increasing population, complexity of laws and obsolete continuation of some pre-existing legal statutes.
- The increasing cost of litigation in prosecuting or defending a case, increasing court fees, lawyer's fees and incidental expenses.
- Delay in disposal of cases resulting in huge pendency in all the courts.
- The ADR can help as the ADR techniques are a speedier, informal and cheaper mode of dispensing justice when compared to conventional judicial procedure.

6. Differentiate between arbitration and mediation process. State any two values communicated by these two forms of ADR. **CBSE 2017**

Or **Give any three difference between arbitrations and mediation as Alternative Dispute Resoluti** **CBSE SQP 2024**

Ans. Three difference between arbitration and mediations are as follows

Basis	Arbitration	Mediation
Meaning	Arbitration is a private arrangement of taking disputes to a lets adversarial, less formal and more flexible forum and abiding the judgment of a selected person.	Mediation is a method of ADR in which parties appoint a neutral third party who facilitates the mediation process in order to assist the parties in achieving an acceptable voluntary agreement.
Role	Role of an arbitrator is that of an adjudicator	Role of a mediator is that of a facilitator.
Nature of Proceeding	Arbitration proceeding end with binding award by the arbitrator.	Mediation proceedings are successful when the disputing parties mutually arrive at a decision mediator does not suggest any solution to the parties.

The two values communicated by the two forms of ADR are
(i) The ADR methods are speedier, informal and cheaper modes of dispensing justice when compared to the conventional judicial procedure.
(ii) ADR provides a more convenient forum to the parties who can choose the time, place and procedure for conducting the preferred dispute

7. What is conciliation? In what ways does the role of a conciliator go beyond that of a mediator? **CBSE 2018**

Ans Conciliation is a process similar to mediation as parties out of their own free will appoint a neutral third party to resolve their disputes. The key difference between mediation and conciliation lies in the role of the neutral third party.

A mediator only performs a facilitative role and provides a platform for the parties to reach a mutually agreeable solution. The role of a conciliator goes beyond that of a mediator. A conciliator may be interventionist in the sense that he/she may suggest potential solutions to the parties, in-order to resolve their claims and disputes.

8. In a workplace conflict scenario, two employees are engaged in a heated dispute over a misunderstanding that has escalated between them. The management decides to implement transformative mediation to address the issues and restore a positive work environment. Identify the key features of transformative mediation that will be employed in the conflict resolution process **CBSE 2024 C**

Ans. In transformative mediation, the key features employed in the conflict resolution process are

- **Empowerment** Encouraging employees to take responsibility for resolving their conflict.
- **Recognition** Helping employees understand and acknowledge each other's perspectives, needs and emotions.
- **Non-judgmental facilitation** The mediator facilitates a neutral and supportive conversation, without imposing a decision or solution.
- **Focus on interaction and communication** The mediation process emphasises improving communication and interaction between the employees.
- **Goal of transforming the relationship** The ultimate aim is to transform the relationship between the employees, promoting a positive and productive work environment.

9. In a family dispute, two siblings have a prolonged argument over the division of their late parents' assets. The situation has become emotionally charged and they struggle to settle the matter. Explain how conciliation and mediation may be applied to this situation. Discuss the distinct roles of the neutral third party facilitators in both processes. **CBSE 2024 C**

Ans. In the family dispute, conciliation and mediation can be applied to resolve the issue

- **Conciliation** A conciliator facilitates a settlement by proposing terms of agreement. They play an evaluative role, making recommendations to help the siblings reach a mutually acceptable agreement.
- **Mediation** A mediator facilitates a discussion, helping the siblings to identify common goals and find their own solution. The mediator plays a facilitative role, guiding the conversation without making recommendations or imposing a decision.

In both processes, the neutral third-party facilitator helps the siblings communicate effectively, manage their emotions, and work towards a mutually beneficial agreement.

10. State the features of ad-hoc arbitration. **CBSE 2025**

Ans. Ad-hoc arbitration is governed by the parties themselves without involving a formal arbitral institution. It can be domestic or international. The parties are not bound by institutional rules and have the freedom to set their own arbitration procedures. This type of arbitration is cost-effective and provides flexibility in choosing arbitrators, timelines, and procedures. However, it may face delays due to the absence of a structured framework and administrative support.

Long Answer Type Questions

1. The two broad models of legal systems differ in their techniques of adjudication and justice delivery mechanism. Elaborate. **CBSE 2020**

Ans The two broad models of legal systems are adversarial system and inquisitorial system

In an adversarial system, the parties in a legal proceeding develop their own theory of the case and gather evidence to support their claims. The parties are assisted by their lawyers who take a proactive role in delivering justice to the litigants.

The lawyers gather evidence and even participate in cross-examination and scrutiny of evidence presented by the other disputing party. The role of the judge/decision-maker is rather passive as the judge decides the claims solely based on the evidence and arguments presented by the parties and their lawyers.

In an inquisitorial system, the judge/decision- maker takes a centre-stage in dispensing justice. The role of the judge/decision-maker is active as he/she determines the facts and issues in dispute. The judge/decision-maker also decides the manner in which the evidence must be presented before the court.

2. Evaluate the adversarial system of justice dispensation. **CBSE 2023**

Ans. In an adversarial system, the parties in a legal proceeding develop their own theory of the case and gather evidence to support their claims. They are assisted by their lawyers who take a proactive role in delivering justice to the litigants. The lawyers gather evidence and even participate in cross-examination and scrutiny of evidence, presented by the other disputing party.

The role of the judge is passive here, as the judge decides the claims only on the basis of the evidence and arguments presented by the parties and their lawyers. This system is adopted in common law countries like the UK, US and India.

There are some advantages of this system as well as disadvantages too.

Advantages are as follow

(i) The parties may be more willing to accept the results when they are given effective control over the process.

(ii) The use of cross-examination can be an effective way to test the credibility (genuineness) of witness presented.

Disadvantages are as follows

(i) The cost of justice system falls upon the parties. This creates an in-built discrimination between the parties. Better resources and money may get competent lawyers and access to justice will be easier.

(ii) The role of lawyers and procedural formalities, e.g. cross-examination may extend the trial and lead to delays in several matters.

3. What is arbitration? Describe its types.

Ans Arbitration is a private arrangement of taking disputes to a less adversarial, less formal and more flexible forum and abiding by judgement of a selected person, instead of carrying it to the established courts of justice.

For answer refer to text under the heading Types of Arbitration on page no. 53.

4. Deep Mohanty and Raghav Nair are neighbours in an apartment complex. Large flowering pots kept on the balcony of Deep's flat have caused seepage and weakened the ceiling above Raghav's balcony. The latter demands that Deep remove the plants and a dispute ensues.

Identify and explain the alternative dispute resolution mechanism that is best suited in the given situation. Also explain its process. **CBSE 2018**

Ans. The method best suited in this situation is mediation.

Mediation is a method of ADR in which parties appoint a neutral third party.

This neutral third party facilitates the mediation process in-order to assist the parties in achieving an acceptable, voluntary agreement.

Mediation is premised (based) on the voluntary will of the parties and is a flexible and informal technique of dispute resolution.

Process of Mediation

Mediator is the neutral third party facilitating the process of mediation. Mediation does not follow a uniform set of rules, though mediators typically explain the rules that the mediation will observe at the beginning of the process.

Successful mediation often reflects not only the parties' willingness to participate, but also the mediator's skill. There is no uniform set of rules for mediators to become licensed and rules vary by state regarding requirements for mediator certification.

Mediation may be triggered in three ways

(i) Parties may agree to resolve their claims through a pre-agreed mediation agreement without initiating formal judicial proceedings (pre-litigation mediation).

(ii) Parties may agree to mediate, at the beginning of formal court proceedings (popularly known as court referrals).

(iii) Mediation may be taken recourse of, after formal court proceedings have started or even post trial i.e. at the appellate stage.

5. Ramesh and Suresh are business partners who have a dispute over the management of their company. They approach a neutral third party, Mr. Kumar to resolve their dispute. Mr. Kumar facilitates a discussion between Ramesh and Suresh, helping them to identify common goals and interests. He then proposes a solution that is acceptable to both the parties. Is Mr. Kumar acting as a mediator or a conciliator?

What are the key differences between mediation and conciliation?

Ans. Mr. Kumar is acting as a mediator because he facilitated the discussion but the parties remain in control of the decision-making process.

The following are the key differences between mediation and conciliation

Basis	Mediation	Conciliation
Definiton	The process of dispute resolution in which a third party intervenes in an attempt to resolve it, by enabling communication between parties is called mediation.	Conciliation implies a process of settling the dispute between the parties, in which a neutral third party provides potential solutions to the parties so as to resolve the issue.
Regulates	Mediation is governed by code of Civil Procedure Act, 1908.	The Arbitration and Conciliation Act, 1996 regulates conciliation.
Role of Third Neutral Party	In mediation, the role of the third party is a facilitator, who facilitates interaction between the parties.	In conciliation, the role played by the third party is beyond facilitator, who not only facilitate communication but also provide solutions to their problem as an expert.
Nature of Procedure	Mediation process completes with an agreement between the parties concerned.	Conciliation ends with a settlement agreement between the parties.
Agreement	The contract of agreement between the parties under mediation is enforceable by law.	The settlement agreement between the parties is binding upon parties like an arbitral award.

6. Discuss any four kinds of mediation.

Ans. Mediation can be classified into the following categories

- **Evaluative Mediation** It focused on providing the parties with an evaluation of their case and directing them towards settlement. During an evaluative mediation process, the mediator will express a viev on what might be a fair or resonable settlement. The evaluative mediator has an advisory role that he /she evaluates the strengths and weaknesses of each side's arguments and makes some predictions about what would happen if they go to court.
- **Facilitative Mediation** Facilitative mediators typically do not evaluate a case or direct the parties to a particular settlement. Instead, they facilitates the conversation. These mediators act as guardians of the process, not the content or the outcome.
  During a facilitative mediation session, the parties in dispute control both what will be discussed and how their issues will be resolved.
  The facilitative mediator is focused on helping the parties to find a resolution to their dispute. The facilitative mediator further provides a structure and agenda for the discussion.
- **Transformative Mediation** It focused on supporting empowerment and recognition shifts, by allowing and encouraging deliberation, decision-making and perspective-taking.
  A competent transformative mediator practices with a main focus on communication, identifying opportunities for empowerment and recognition as those opportunities appear in the parties, own conversations and responding in ways that provide an opening for parties to choose what, to do with them.
- Mediation with Arbitration Mediation has sometimes good effect when coupled with arbitration, particularly binding arbitration, in a process called 'mediation/arbitration'. The process begins as a standard mediation, but if mediation fails, the mediator becomes an arbitrator.
  This process is more appropriate in civil matters where rules of evidence or jurisdiction are not in dispute. In some respects, it resembles, the criminal plea bargaining and confucian judicial procedure, wherein the judge also plays the role of prosecutor.

7. In Konkan Railways Corp. Ltd. Vs. Mehul Construction Co., the Hon'ble Supreme Court affirmed that the Arbitration and Conciliation Act, 1996 was introduced in order to attract the 'international mercantile community'. Analyse the affirmation of the court.

CBSE SQP 2022

Ans. The Indian Arbitration and Conciliation Act of 1996 provides for an elaborate codified recognition of the concept of arbitration. In the Konkan Railways Corp. Ltd. Vs. Mehul Construction Co. the Supreme Court of India has affirmed that the Arbitration and Conciliation Act, 1996 was introduced in order to attract the 'international mercantile community' because of

- minimisation of supervisory role of courts.
- providing speedy disposal of the disputes.
- amicable, swift and cost-efficient settlement of disputes.
- resolving the dispute by a formal award. Ensuring that arbitration proceedings are just, fair and effective.
- comprehensively cover international commercial arbitration and conciliation as also domestic arbitration and conciliation.
- permit an arbitrator to use mediation, conciliation or other procedure during the arbitral proceedings to encourage settlement of disputes.

SELF ASSESSMENT TEST

Objective Type Questions

1. Which of the following countries has a common law jurisdiction?
   (a) U.S. (b) UK (c) Australia (d) All of these
2. In an adversarial system, the cost is borne by
   (a) the parties themselves (b) the judge
   (c) the political system (d) All of these
3. Which of the following is the most formal process?
   (a) Litigation (b) Mediation (c) Conciliation (d) Arbitration
4. This system gives the participants an opportunity to raise and discuss any issues they might wish to settle.
   (a) Mediation (b) Litigation (c) Conciliation (d) None of these
5. Which Constitutional Amendment added Articles 323-A and 323-B to the Constitution of India?
   (a) 41st Constitutional Amendment (b) 42nd Constitutional Amendment
   (c) 13th Constitutional Amendment (d) None of these

Very Short Answer Type Questions

6. Mention the differences between adversarial and inquisitorial system.
7. What were the specialised tribunals during the Vedic age in India.
8. Asha and Raj, business partners, have disagreement over the interpretation of their contract. Their agreement contains a clause stating : "Any dispute arising out of the contract shall be resolved through arbitration in accordance" with the rules of the Indian Arbitration Association". What is the significance of this clause in the event of a dispute between Asha and Raj?

Short Answer Type Questions

9. Discuss the process of arbitration. Why is it beneficial in solving commercial disputes?
10. What do you understand by conciliation? State the laws on conciliation.
11. Rohan and Siya, neighbours have dispute over a boundary wall. They agree to conciliate the matter, where a neutral third party facilitates a settlement. The conciliator helps them reach a mutually acceptable agreement. In India, which law governs the conciliation process and settlement agreement reached by Rohan and Siya?

Long Answer Type Questions

12. Elaborate the two kinds of judicial system and state three advantages and disadvantages.
13. What are the benefits of mediation? State three different types of mediation.
14. Emma and Ryan, business partners, have a dispute over the direction of their company. They opt for mediation, where a neutral mediator helps them communicate and find a mutually beneficial solution. After several sessions, they reach a settlement avoiding a costly lawsuit. What benefit of mediation is exemplified in Emma and Ryan's situation?

05

CHAPTER

Lok Adalats, Ombudsman & Lokpal and Lokayukta

'Lok' stands for people and the term 'Adalat' means court as the very name suggests, means people's court. The concept of Lok Adalat is an innovative Indian contribution to the global legal jurisprudence.

YOUR STUDY GOALS

5.1 Lok Adalat
5.2 Ombudsman
5.3 Lokpal and Lokayukta

YOUR PRACTICE GOAL

- Objective Type Questions (20 Qs ; MCQs, A-R, Statements, Matching)
- Subjective Questions (8 VSAs, 6 SAs, 6 LAs)

5.1 Lok Adalat

- In ancient times, the disputes were referred to **panchayats** which were established at village level. Panchayats used to resolve the dispute through arbitration.
- This concept of settlement of dispute through mediation, negotiation or through the arbitral process known as decision of **Nyaya Panchayat,** is conceptualised and institutionalised in the philosophy of Lok Adalat.
- Lok Adalat involves people who are directly or indirectly affected by dispute resolution.
- The evolution of Lok Adalat was a part of the strategy to relieve heavy burden on the courts with pending cases and to **give relief to the litigants** who were in a queue to get justice.
- The modern institution of Lok Adalat is presided over by a sitting or retired judicial officer such as the **Chairman**, with usually two other members i.e. a **lawyer** and a **social worker**.
- A Lok Adalat has jurisdiction to settle any matter pending before any court, as well as matters at pre-litigative stage[1], i.e., disputes which have not yet been formally instituted in any Court of Law. Such matters may be in the nature of **civil** or **non-compoundable criminal disputes.**

1 **Pre-litigative Stage** It means disputes which have not yet been formally instituted in any court of law.

- Participation, accommodation, fairness, voluntariness, neighbourliness, transparency, efficiency and lack of animosity are the salient features of Lok Adalat.

The first Lok Adalat was held on 14th March, 1982 at Junagarh in Gujarat. Lok Adalats have been very successful in settlement of claims including motor accident claims, matrimonial/family disputes, labour disputes, disputes relating to public service, such as telephone, electricity, bank recovery cases, etc.

Benefits of Lok Adalat

The benefits of Lok Adalat are

- There is **no court fee** and even if the case is already filed in the regular court, the fee paid will be refunded if the dispute is settled at the Lok Adalat.
- There is **no strict application of the procedural laws** and the disputing parties can directly interact with the judges.
- The decision of Lok Adalat is **binding on the parties** and its order is capable of execution through legal process.

5.2 Ombudsman

- Ombudsman is an indigenous Swedish, Danish and Norwegian term, which is derived from the word 'umboosranor' meaning **'representative'**.
- Ombudsman can be appointed by a legislature, the executive or an organisation. The typical duties of an ombudsman are
  - **Investigate the complaints** and attempt to resolve them, usually through recommendations (binding or not) or mediation.
  - To **identify systemic issues** leading to poor service or breaches of people's rights.
  - Most ombudsman have a wide mandate at the national level, to **deal with the entire public sector,** and sometimes also elements of the private sector, for example, contracted service providers.
  - The Government of India has designated several ombudsmen (sometimes called Chief Vigilance Officer, CVO) for the redress of grievances and **complaints from individuals** in the banking, insurance and other sectors, being serviced by both private and public bodies and corporations.
  - The **Central** Vigilance[2] **Commission** (CVC) was set up on the recommendation of the Santhanam Committee (1962-64). It is has been conceived to be the apex vigilance institution.
- The major advantage of an ombudsman is that he/she **examines complaints from outside the offending state institution,** thus avoiding the conflicts of interest existing in self-policing.

Banking and Insurance Ombudsman

- The **Banking Ombudsman** is a senior official **appointed by the Reserve Bank of India** to redress customer complaints against deficiency in certain banking services.
- The **Banking Ombudsman Scheme** is an **expeditious and inexpensive forum** for bank customers for resolution of complaints relating to certain services rendered by banks. Presently, the **Banking Ombudsman Scheme, 2006 (as amended up to 1st July, 2017)** is in operation.
- The **Insurance Ombudsmen** are appointed by the **Council for Insurance Ombudsman** according to Insurance Ombudsman Rules, 2017. They are empowered to receive and consider complaints claiming deficiency in performance required of an insurer (including its agents and intermediaries) or an insurance broker.

2 **Vigilance** It means the action or state of keeping careful watch for possible danger of difficulties.

Quick Test 1

1 How many members are there in the institution of Lok Adalat?
2 The first Lok Adalat was held on 14th March, 1982 in which state?
3 Which committee was responsible for the set-up of CVC?
4 Which officer is responsible for redressing grievances and complaints from individual in banking, insurance sectors?

5.3 Lokpal and Lokayukta

- A **Lokpal** (caretaker of people) is an ombudsman in India. **The Lokayukta** (appointed by the people) is also a similar anti-corruption ombudsman organisation in the Indian states.
- The institutions of Lokpal and Lokayukta were given formal recognition by passing of the **Lokpal and Lokayukta Act, 2013.**
- This legislation aims to reduce or resoule acts of bribery and corruption of public servants. The act **applies to the public servants in and outside India.**
- The act includes the **current and ex-Prime Ministers of India** under it, except in matters international relations, external and internal security, public order, atomic energy and space.
- Besides the Prime Minister, it also includes any person who is or has been a Minister of the Union and any person who is or has been a member of either House of Parliament.

Lokpal

A Lokpal is an anti-corruption authority who represents the public interest in the Republic of India.

- According to the Lokpal and Lokayukta Act, **atleast two-thirds** of the members of Lokpal must give approval to an inquiry about a public servant.
- It further provides that any such inquiry shall be held **in camera**[3] in private and if the Lokpal comes to the conclusion that the complaint deserves to be dismissed, the records of the inquiry shall not be published or made available to anyone.
- As provided under the provisions contained in **clause (2) of Article 105** of the Constitution, the Lokpal shall not inquire against the statement or vote given by any member of either House of Parliament, in matter involving or arising from, or connected with any allegation of corruption.
- In relation to bureaucracy, it includes any Group 'A', 'B', 'C' or 'D' official or equivalent public servants, defined in the Prevention of Corruption Act, 1988 who has served in connection with the affairs of the union.
- The Lokpal and Lokayukta Act also provides for the **manner in which the public-servants must declare their assets.**

Composition of Lokpal

According to the Lokpal and Lokayukta Act, the Lokpal shall consist of a **Chairperson** who has been either of the following

- Chief Justice of India
- A Judge of the Supreme Court

3 **In Camera** It is a latin term that means 'in private' or 'in chambers'.

- An eminent[4] judicial member of who has special knowledge and expertise of not **less than 25 years** in matters relating to anti-corruption policy, public administration, vigilance or finance.
- Further, the total members of Lokpal shall not exceed 8, out of whom 50 per cent shall be judicial members.

Powers of Lokpal

The powers of Lokpal are as follows

- The powers of the Lokpal are extensive and equivalent to the superintendence, inquiry and investigative powers of the police and the Central Vigilance Commission.
- The Lokpal shall consist of an inquiry and prosecution wing to take necessary steps in **prosecution of public servants,** in relation to offences committed under the Prevention of Corruption Act, 1988.
- Lokpal can even **recommend** the government **to create Special Courts** to decide cases arising from the Prevention of Corruption Act, 1988.

Lokayukta

- The Lokpal and Lokayuktas Act, 2013 provides for the establishment of **Lokayukta in every state** in order to deal with complaints of corruption against public functionaries.
- The act provides that all states must institute Lokayuktas **within one year** from the date of the commencement of the Lokpal and Lokayuktas Act, 2013.
- Even before the enactment of this act, some states in India, for example, Delhi, Karnataka, Kerala, etc. had the institutions of Lokayukta.

> Only 19 Indian states have Lokayukta. **Maharashtra** was the first state to introduce the institution of Lokayukta in 1971.

Quick Test 2

1. In which year the Lokpal and Lokayukta Act was passed?
2. How many member should be there in Lokpal?
3. Which states have Lokayuktas even before the enactment of the act?
4. Which state was the first state of India to introduce Lokayukta in 1971?

---

4 **Eminent** It means a person famous or respected in a particular sphere.

Mind Map

1 Lok Adalats

- **Meaning** "Lok" = People, "Adalat" = Court. A people's court offering alternative dispute resolution.

Historical Background
- Originates from ancient Nyaya Panchayats resolving disputes through arbitration.
- Modern Lok Adalats institutionalised to reduce court burdens.

Key Features
- Flexible procedures; no strict application of procedural laws.
- No court fees; refund of previously paid fees if resolved.
- Decisions are binding and executable legally.

Composition
- Chaired by a sitting/retired judicial officer.
- Two additional members - a lawyer and a social worker.

Jurisdiction
- Civil disputes and non-compoundable criminal cases.
- Includes pre-litigative and pending cases.

Benefits
- Speedy resolutions.
- Encourages compromise, maintaining cordial relationships.
- Cost-effective with no animosity.

Notable Fact
- First Lok Adalat held on 14th March 1982, Junagarh, Gujarat.

2 Ombudsman

- **Meaning** Derived from Swedish "umboosrnaor" meaning "representative."

Role
- Investigates complaints against public/private entities.
- Resolves issues through mediation or recommendations.
- Identifies systemic issues and breaches of rights.

Types in India
- **Banking Ombudsman** Appointed by RBI, handles banking service complaints.
- **Insurance Ombudsman** Appointed under Insurance Ombudsman Rules, 2017.

Central Vigilance Commission (CVC)
- Established on Santhanam Committee's recommendation.
- Monitors vigilance activities, free from executive control.

Advantages
- Independent investigations prevent conflicts of interest.
- Ensures accountability and transparency.

LOK ADALATS, OMBUDSMAN, & LOKPAL AND LOKAYUKTA

3 Lokpal and Lokayukta

- **Lokpal** Central anti-corruption authority.
- **Lokayukta** State-level anti-corruption authority.

Formalisation
- Lokpal and Lokayukta Act, 2013.

Scope
- Covers public servants, including current and ex-Prime Ministers (with specific exceptions).
- Applies to Union Ministers, MP, and Group A-D public servants.

Composition

Lokpal
- **Chairperson** Chief Justice of India, Supreme Court Judge, or an expert with 25+ years of experience.
- Up to 8 members, 50% must be judicial members.

Lokayukta
- Established in states like Maharashtra, Karnataka, Kerala.
- Maharashtra was the first state (1971).

Powers
- Inquiry and prosecution powers similar to the police and CVC.
- Can recommend special courts for corruption cases.
- Requires two-thirds approval for inquiries, conducted privately.

Objectives
- Combat corruption and bribery.
- Foster accountability in public administration.

4 Comparison of Lok Adalat, Ombudsman, and Lokpal or Lokayukta

Aspect	Jurisdiction	Authority	Purpose
Lok Adalat	Civil and non-compoundable criminal cases.	Judicial officer + lawyer + social worker.	Speedy and cost-effective dispute resolution.
Ombudsman	Public or private grievances	Appointed by government or organisations	Accountability and service improvement
Lokpal or Lokayukta	Corruption cases	Central or state authorities	Anti-corruption

CBSE TEXTBOOK FOLDER

1. The concept of Lok Adalat is an innovative Indian contribution to the global legal jurisprudence. Analyse the features of Lok Adalat that make it a suitable forum for alternative dispute resolution. CBSE SQP 2022

Ans. The concept of Lok Adalat is an innovative Indian contribution to the global legal jurisprudence in the following ways

- **Procedural Flexibility** There exist considerable procedural flexibility as major procedural laws such as the Code of Civil Procedure, 1908 or the Indian Evidence Act, 1882 are not strictly enforced. The parties can interact directly through their counsels which is not possible in a regular court of law. This dynamic nature of Lok Adalat allows them to conciliate both party interests and pass awards which are acceptable to both parties.
- **No Court Fees** There is no court fee payable when a matter is filed in a Lok Adalat. If a matter pending in the court of law is referred to the Lok Adalat and is settled subsequently, the court fee originally paid in the court on the complaints/petition is also refunded back to the parties.
- **Final and Binding Award** Under Section 21 of the Act, the award passed by the Lok Adalat stand final and binding. As no appeal lies to this conclusive determination, the cases are put to rest on first instance.
- **Maintenance of Cordial Relationships** The main thrust of Lok Adalat is on compromise between parties. Its role is to persuade the parties to reach a solution and help in reconciling their contesting differences. This encourages consensual arrangements. Therefore, disputes are not only settled but also the cordial relations between parties can be retained. Hence, it is a very healthy way of dispute resolution.

2. What is the meaning of Ombudsman? Identify equivalent institutions within India. Discuss their roles and limitations.

Ans. An ombudsman is an official, usually appointed by the government, who investigates complaints (usually lodged by private citizens) against businesses, financial institutions, universities, government departments or other public entities and attempts to resolve the conflicts or concerns raised, either by mediation or by making recommendations.

The Government of India has designated several ombudsmen (sometimes called Chief Vigilance Officer, CVO) for the redress of grievances and complaints from individuals in the banking, insurance and other sectors being serviced by both private and public bodies and corporations.

For example, the Central Vigilance Commission was set up on the recommendation of the Santhanam Committee (1962-64). CVC has been conceived to be the apex vigilance institution, free of control from any executive authority, monitoring all vigilance activity under the Central Government and advising various authorities in Central Government organisations in planning, executing, reviewing and reforming their vigilance work.

3. A Lokpal is an ombudsman in India while a Lokayukta is a similar anti-corruption ombudsman organisation in the Indian states.

(i) Elaborate on the scope of the Lokpal and Lokayukta Act, 2013.

(ii) Explain the composition of Lokpal under the Act.

Ans. (i) The Lokpal and Lokayukta Act, 2013. This legislation aims to combat acts of bribery and corruption of public servants. The act applies to the public servants in and outside India.

The act includes the current and ex-Prime Ministers of India under it, except in matters international relations, external and internal security, public order, atomic energy and space.

Besides the Prime Minister, it also includes any person who is or has been a Minister of the Union and any person who is or has been a member of either House of Parliament.

(ii) According to the Lokpal and Lokayukta Act, the Lokpal shall consist of a Chairperson who has been a either of the following

- Chief Justice of India or
- A Judge of the Supreme Court or
- An eminent judicial member of who has special knowledge and expertise of not less than 25 years in matters relating to anti-corruption policy, public administration, vigilance or finance.
- Further, the total members of Lokpal shall not exceed 8, out of whom 50 per cent shall be judicial members.

Exam Pattern Questions

Objective Type Questions

Multiple Choice Questions (MCQs)

1. Which of the following is an innovative Indian contribution to global jurisprudence?

(a) Ombudsman (b) Lok Adalat
(c) Arbitration (d) Mediation

2. Disputes in Lok Adalat are resolved by **CBSE SQP 2021**

(a) Mediation only
(b) Negotiation only
(c) Arbitral process
(d) Mediation, negotiation or through arbitral process

3. Who among the following is the Chairman of the Lok Adalat? **CBSE SQP 2021**

(a) Sitting/Retired Judge (b) Lawyer
(c) Activist (d) Retired Judge only

4. The Lokpal and Lokayukta Act, 2013 aims to combat acts of bribery and corruption of public servants- a term that has been given a fairly wide interpretation in the act. As per the legislation, an enquiry of corruption can be initiated against which of the following persons? **CBSE SQP 2021**

(a) Against the ex-Prime Minister of India accused of corruption in matters pertaining to international relations.
(b) Against the ex-Prime Minister of India accused of corruption in matters relating to internal security.
(c) Against any person who has been a member of either House of the Parliament.
(d) Against any member of the Parliament against whom allegation of corruption is raised for anything said or a vote given by him in the Parliament.

5. An advantage of .... is that there is no strict application of the procedural laws and the disputing parties can directly interact with the judges. **CBSE 2025**

(a) Mediation (b) Lok Adalat
(c) Conciliation (d) Tribunal

6. Kishore was contacted by a customer representative of a digital wallet company, MTM.
The representative informed Kishore that his KYC is due and to complete the KYC, Kishore is required to download an application and submit the form with his card details. Kishore downloaded the application and submitted the form with his card details.
Immediately after submitting the form, Kishore's card was charged for ₹ 5 lacs.
Kishore immediately called the helpline number of MTM and informed them about the charge on his card. However, MTM's representative said that he cannot help Kishore in this regard.
What remedy does Kishore have?

(a) File a criminal case against MTM
(b) File a complaint with Ombudsman
(c) File a complaint with Lokpal
(d) There is no remedy

7. Allegations of bribery and corruption were made against the ex-Prime Minister of India in matters pertaining to international relations under Lokpal and Lokayukta Act, 2005. The Lokpal **CBSE 2016**

(a) can conduct inquiry against ex-Prime Minister as even ex-Prime Minister is within the purview of Lokpal and Lokayukta Act, 2005.
(b) cannot conduct inquiry against ex-Prime Minister as only the conduct of acting Prime Minister is within the purview of Lokpal and Lokayukta Act, 2005.
(c) can conduct inquiry as provisions of Article 105 of Indian Constitution will be applicable which will bring the conduct of ex-Prime Minister within the purview of Lokpal and Lokayukta Act, 2005.
(d) cannot conduct inquiry as the alleged conduct of ex-Prime Minister is related to international relations which is outside the purview of Lokpal and Lokayukta Act, 2005.

8. Aadarsh, a young and dedicated Police Officer known for his competence and integrity, was assigned to a district plagued by a low literacy ratio and controlled by an education mafia involved in extorting money from students for facilitating cheating in exams.
He initiated stringent measures against them and conducted raids to dismantle the illegal operations. In one of the raids, he caught the examination incharge of the school leaking the exam paper for money. He was arrested. Aadarsh also arrested a Head Constable for taking bribes to allow the students to cheat in the examination. Unaccustomed to such resistance, the mafia became alarmed, with some office employees tipping them off about Aadarsh's determination to eradicate birbery and cheating in the district.

Against whom can an action be taken under the Lokpal and Lokayukta Act 2013 ? **CBSE SQP 2024**

(a) Examination incharge of the school
(b) Mafia
(c) Head Constable
(d) Employees of his office

9. **The aim of the Lokpal and Lokayukta Act, 2013 is ....** **CBSE 2024**

(a) to prevent instances of corruption through stringent measures.
(b) to eradicate corruption for betterment of society.
(c) to foster a culture of accountability within the public sector.
(d) to combat acts of bribery and corruption of public servants.

10. **A citizen files a complaint against a Union Minister for allegedly accepting a bribe. The complaint is investigated and found to have merit. Under the Lokpal and Lokayukta Act, 2013, what is the next step in the process?**

(a) The case is directly sent to a special court for trial.
(b) The Lokpal recommends the case to the Prime Minister for action.
(c) The Lokpal conducts a preliminary inquiry and may initiate prosecution.
(d) The case is closed due to insufficient evidence.

11. Ayan in an online transaction did a purchase of ₹ 500. Within an hour of the transaction, he received a message of a transaction of rupees one lakh done on his card. Ayan realised that someone has fraudulently used his card for online shopping. He immediately reported the matter to the bank manager. The manager expressed his inability to resolve the matter due to lockdown leading to poor service.

Identify the best remedy available to Ayan

(a) File a civil case
(b) File a complaint with Ombudsman
(c) File a complaint with Lokpal
(d) There is no remedy

12. **Under the Lokpal and Lokayukta Act, 2013 the powers of the Lokpal can be related to which of the following personnel?**

(a) Lokpal has inquiry and investigative powers of Central Vigilance Commission.
(b) Lokpal has powers equivalent to that of the President of India.
(c) Lokpal is not a strong institution and has no powers.
(d) Lokpal can only recommend to the Government of India to initiate enquiry like a civil body.

13. The word 'Lokpal' was first used by a Member of Parliament, Laxmi Mall Singhvi in 1963 during a debate on grievance redressal mechanisms. The Lokpal Bill was first introduced in the Lok Sabha in 1968. The version enacted in 2013 was from a draft prepared in 2010.

Which of the following is Not a salient feature of Lokpal and Lokayukta Act 2013?

(a) The Lokpal consists of a Chairperson with a maximum of 8 members of which 50% shall be judicial members.
(b) The Prime Minister has been brought under the purview of the lokpal .
(c) The selection of the Chairperson and the members of Lokpal shall be through a selection committee.
(d) Lokpal's jurisdiction will cover all categories of public servants including group 'A', group 'B' and group 'C' excluding group 'D'.

14. Ashok, a government official, is accused of taking a bribe from a contractor to award a contract. The contractor who was asked to pay the bribe, files a complaint with the Central Vigilance Commission (CVC). The CVC initiates an inquiry and finds prima facie evidence of misconduct against Ashok.

Which of the following statement is Not correct about the Central Vigilance Commissioner of India?

(a) The Central Vigilance Commissioner is to be appointed by the President of India.
(b) Tenure of Central Vigilance Commissioner is 5 years.
(c) Central Vigilance Commissioner can be removed or suspended from the office by the President on the ground of misbehaviour but only after the Supreme Court has held an inquiry into his case and recommended action against him.
(d) The Central Vigilance Commission is mainly an advisory body and has no adjudicatory functions.

15. **Match the following.**

Column A	Column B
A. Ombudsman	1. Ombudsman in India
B. Lokpal	2. People's Court
C. Lokayukta	3. Ombudsman in Indian States
D. The Lok Adalat	4. Chief Vigilance Officer in the banking sector

Codes

	A	B	C	D		A	B	C	D
(a)	1	2	3	4	(b)	4	1	3	2
(c)	2	4	3	1	(d)	1	3	4	2

16. Which of the following statements best describes the role of a banking ombudsman?

Statement I A banking ombudsman is an independent authority that investigates and resolves disputes between banks and their customers.

Statement II A banking ombudsman is an official appointed by the bank to represent the bank's interests in legal proceedings.

Codes
(a) Only Statement I is correct.
(b) Only Statement II is correct.
(c) Both Statements are correct.
(d) Both Statements are incorrect.

17. Which of the following statements describes the composition of Lokpal in India?

Statement I Lokpal consists of a Chairperson and upto 8 members, with 50% of them being judicial members.

Statement II Lokpal consists of a Chairperson and upto 4 members, with all members being bureaucrats.

Codes
(a) Only Statement I is correct.
(b) Only Statement II is correct.
(c) Both Statement are correct.
(d) Both Statements are incorrect.

Assertion-Reason Questions

Directions (Q.Nos. 18-20) In the questions given below, there are two statements. Read the statements and choose the correct option.

Codes
(a) Both A and R are true and R is the correct explanation of A.
(b) Both A and R are true, but R is not the correct explanation of A.
(c) A is true, but R is false.
(d) A is false, but R is true.

18. **Assertion** (A) Panchayats used to resolve the dispute through arbitration.

Reason (R) It has proved to be a very effective alternative to litigation.

19. **Assertion** (A) The major advantage of an ombudsman is that he/she avoids the conflicts of interest inherent in self-policing.

Reason (R) Duties of an ombudsman are to investigate complaints and attempt to resolve them, usually through recommendations (binding or not) or mediation.

CBSE SQP 2021

20. **Assertion** (A) The Government of India has designated several ombudsmen, sometimes called Chief Vigilance Officer (CVO)).

Reason (R) The CVC (Central Vigilance Commission) was set up on the recommendation of the Santhanam Committee (1962-64).

Answers

1. (b) Lok Adalat
2. (d) Mediation, negotiation or through arbitral process
3. (a) Sitting/Retired Judge
4. (c) Against any person who has been a member of either House of the Parliament.
5. (b) Lok Adalat
6. (b) File a complaint with Ombudsman.
7. (d) cannot conduct inquiry as the alleged conduct of ex-Prime Minister is related to International relations which is outside the purview of Lokpal and Lokayukta Act, 2005.
8. (c) Head Constable
9. (d) to combat acts of bribery and corruption of public servants.
10. (c) The Lokpal conducts a preliminary inquiry and may initiate prosecution.
11. (b) File a complaint with Ombudsman
12. (c) Lokpal is not a strong institution and has no powers.
13. (d) Lokpal's jurisdiction will cover all categories of public servants including group 'A', group 'B' and group 'C' excluding group 'D'.
14. (b) Tenure of Central Vigilance Commissioner is 5 years.
15. (b) 4 1 3 2
16. (a) Only Statement I is correct.
17. (a) Only Statement I is correct.
18. (a) Both A and R are true and R is the correct explanation of A.
19. (b) Both A and R are true, but R is not the correct explanation of A.
20. (b) Both A and R are true, but R is not the correct explanation of A.

Subjective Questions

Very Short Answer Type Questions

1. Name an innovative Indian contribution to global legal jurisprudence.

Ans. The concept of Lok Adalat (People's Court) is an innovative Indian contribution to the global legal jurisprudence.

2. What does the term 'Lok Adalat' stand for?

Ans. 'Lok' stands for 'people' and the term 'Adalat' means court. The institution of Lok Adalat in India, means People's Court.

3. Who presides over the modern institutions of Lok Adalat? State its composition as well.

Ans. The modern institution of Lok Adalat is presided over by a sitting or retired judicial officer such as the chairman, with usually two other members i.e. a lawyer and a social worker.

4. Rohan, a consumer purchased a defective electronic product from a company. He filed a complaint in a Consumer Court, which is still pending. Can Rohan's dispute be resolved through Lok Adalat?

Ans. Yes, Rohan's dispute can be resolved through Lok Adalat. Since the complaint is pending in a Consumer Court, which is a Civil Court, Lok Adalat has the jurisdiction to settle the matter. Lok Adalat can consider civil cases pending in any court, including Consumer Courts and provide a speedy and conciliatory resolution.

5. Rahul and Ramesh are involved in a civil dispute concerning a property. They decide to approach a Lok Adalat for resolution. What benefits will they likely experience by choosing this alternative dispute resolution mechanism?

Ans. By choosing Lok Adalat, Rahul and Ramesh can expect the following benefits

(i) Speedy resolution of their dispute, as Lok Adalats are known for their expeditious disposal of cases.

(ii) They won't have to pay any court fees, and if they had already paid fees in a regular court, they will get a refund.

(iii) The procedure will also be flexible, with no strict application of procedural laws and the Evidence Act.

6. Who is a Lokpal? Give the name of its similar organisation in States.

Ans. A Lokpal (caretaker of people) is an ombudsman in India. The Lokayukta (appointed by the people) is a similar anti- corruption ombudsman organisation in the Indian states.

7. The government of India wants to establish an anti-corruption body to investigate complaints against public servants. The established the institutions of Lokpal and Lokuyukta, how are these institutions formally recognised?

Ans. The institutions of Lokpal and Lokayukta were given formal recognition, by passing of the Lokpal and Lokayukta Act, 2013.

8. What is the primary objective of the Lokpal and Lokayukta Act?

Ans. The primary objective of the Lokpal and Lokayukta Act is the legislation aims to combat acts of bribery and corruption of public servants a term that has been given a fairly wide interpretation in the act. The act applies to the public servants in and outside India.

Short Answer Type Questions

1. In 1982, a legal aid movement in India led to the establishment of an ADR mechanism called Lok Adalat. How does the concept of Lok Adalat came into being, briefly describe?

Ans. In ancient times, the disputes were referred to 'panchayats' which were established at village level. Panchayats used to resolve the dispute through arbitration. It has proved to be a very effective alternative to litigation.

This concept of settlement of dispute through mediation, negotiation or through the arbitral process known as decision of 'Nyaya Panchayat', is conceptualised and institutionalised in the philosophy of Lok Adalat.

It involves people who are directly or indirectly affected by dispute resolution. The evolution of the movement called Lok Adalat was a part of the strategy to relieve heavy burden on the courts with pending cases and to give relief to the litigants who were in a queue to get justice.

2. Raju, Manoj and Anil are brothers who are joint owners of a plot of land. In course of time, there was a tussle over the ownership and partition of the said plot. They decide to take the matter to the Lok Adalat for expeditious resolution.

Identify three benefits of a Lok Adalat in the given situation. CBSE 2023

Ans. The matter has been taken to the Lok Adalat for expeditious resolution, there are several other benefits of Lok Adalat, three of them are given below.

(i) There is no court fee and even if the case is already filed in the regular court, the fee paid will be refunded if the dispute is settled at the Lok Adalat.

(ii) There is no strict application of the procedural laws and the disputing parties can directly interact with the judges.

(iii) The decision of Lok Adalat is binding on the parties and its order is capable of execution through legal process.

3. When can a case be refered to Lok Adalat? State the powers of Lok Adalats while trying a suit. CBSE 2022

Ans. Lok Adalat takes up cases which are civil in nature (including marriage and family disputes) and compoundable criminal cases. It accepts cases pending in regular court under their jurisdiction.

The Lok Adalat shall have the same powers as are vested in a Civil Court under the Code of Civil Procedure (1908). Further, a Lok Adalat shall have the requisite powers to specify its own procedure for the determination of any dispute coming before it.

4. What do you understand by the concept of Ombudsman? What are its primary duties?

Ans Ombudsman is an indigenous Swedish, Danish and Norwegian term, which is derived from the word 'umboosranor' meaning 'representative'.

Ombudsman can be appointed by a legislature, the executive or an organisation. The typical duties of an ombudsman are

- Investigate complaints and attempt to resolve them, usually through recommendations (binding or not) or mediation.
- To identify systemic issues leading to poor service or breaches of people's rights.
- At the national level, most ombudsman have a wide mandate to deal with the entire public sector, and sometimes also elements of the private sector (for example, contracted service providers).

5. The Indian Government has established several ombudsmen to address citizen grievances. The Lokpal and Lokayukta Act, 2013 provides for the establishment of Lokpal at the Central level and Lokayukta at the State level. The Central Vigilance Commission (CVC) oversees vigilance administration. The Central Information Commission (CIC) implements the Right to Information Act, 2005. The National Human Rights Commission (NHRC) protects human rights. The Central Government sanctions the working of these ombudsmen.

How do these ombudsmen contribute to the Indian Government's accountability and transparency?

Ans. These ombudsmen play a crucial role in ensuring government accountability and transparency. Lokpal and Lokayukta address corruption cases, CVC tackles corruption in government departments, CIC ensures access to information and NHRC protects human rights.

The Central Government's sanctioning of these ombudsmen demonstrates its commitment to transparency and accountability, enabling citizens to seek redressal and promoting good governance. By establishing and empowering these institutions, the government ensures that citizens grievances are heard and addressed, fostering trust and accountability in the democratic system.

6. Nupur maintained an account with Bena Bank. She withdrew an account of ₹ 5,000 from the ATM of Kotak Bank on 28th July, 2015. The cash dispensed by the machine was only ₹ 4,000. However, her account was debited by ₹ 5,000. She immediately lodged the complaint with her bank officials but ₹ 1,000 was not credited back to her account even after repeated complaints. CBSE 2016

(i) Identify the ombudsman within India to investigate and resolve complaints related to the banking sector.

(ii) Can Nupur approach this ombudsman identified in part (i) above? Give reasons for your answer.

(iii) If the functioning of the entire banking sector is to be put under a vigil to avoid any issue of poor service, which institution has the authority to do so? State the area activities to be performed by it.

(iv) State one advantage of the ombudsman in the dispute resolution mechanism.

Ans. (i) Chief Vigilance Officer is the right officer to investigate and resolve complaints related to the banking sector.

(ii) Yes, complaints can also be lodged by addressing the letter/e-mail directly to the Central Vigilance Commission (CVC) by giving specific facts of the matter relating to corruption.

(iii) CVC has been conceived to be the apex vigilance institution, free of control from any executive authority, monitoring all vigilance activity under the Central Government and advising various authorities in Central Government organisations in planning, executing, reviewing and reforming their vigilance work.

(iv) The major advantage of an ombudsman is that he/she examines complaints from outside the offending state institution, thus avoiding the conflicts of interest inherent in self-policing.

Long Answer Type Questions

1. **(i) When can a case be referred to Lok Adalat?**
(ii) State the powers of a Lok Adalat. **CBSE 2019**

Ans (i) The following cases can be referred to Lok Adalat
- When any case pending before any court.
- When any dispute which has not been brought before any court and is likely to be filed before the court.

(ii) The Lok Adalat are similar powers of a Civil Court. It includes the following
- It has the power to summon and enforce the attendance of a witness.
- It has the power to receive evidence regarding a particular case.
- The Lok Adalat has the power to follow its own procedure for determining any dispute.
- The proceedings of a Lok Adalat are considered to be judicial proceedings.

2. **Examine the role of permanent Lok Adalats in providing speedy and cost-effective resolution of disputes in India.** **CBSE 2024 C**

Ans. Permanent Lok Adalats (PLAs) play a significant role in providing speedy and cost-effective resolution of disputes in India

The following key features are
- **Free of cost** No court fees or litigation expenses.
- **Speedy resolution** Disputes resolved within a few months.
- **Conciliatory approach** Emphasis on settlement through mutual agreement.

The benefits of Lok Adalat are
- **Reduced litigation** Decreases burden on courts and promotes alternative dispute resolution.
- **Increased access to justice** Provides affordable and accessible justice to marginalised communities.
- **Improved efficiency** Encourages parties to settle disputes amicably, reducing the need for lengthy court proceedings.

Overall, PLAs offer an efficient and cost-effective mechanism for resolving disputes, aligning with the Indian Government's goal of promoting accessible and affordable justice.

3. **Literal meaning of ombudsman is 'representative'. With respect to India, answer the following questions.** **CBSE 2017**

(i) Identify the anti-corruption ombudsman in the Indian states and in India.
(ii) State the composition of anti-corruption ombudsman in India.
(iii) Identify the banking and insurance ombudsman in India and state its role.

Ans. (i) A Lokpal is an anti-corruption authority or body of ombudsman who represents the public interest in the Republic of India.

The Lokpal has jurisdiction over the Central Government to inquire into allegations of corruption against its public functionaries and for matters connected to corruption.

Likewise, the Lokpal and Lokayuktas Act, 2013 provides for the establishment of Lokayukta in every state in order to deal with complaints of corruption against public functionaries.

(ii) According to the Lokpal and Lokayukta Act, the Lokpal shall consist of

(a) a chairperson who has been a either of the following
- Chief Justice of India or
- A Judge of the Supreme Court or
- An eminent judicial member of who has special knowledge and expertise of not less than 25 years in matters relating to anti-corruption policy, public administration, vigilance or finance.

(b) Further, the total members of Lokpal shall not exceed 8, out of whom 50 per cent shall be judicial members.

(iii) The banking ombudsman is a senior official appointed by the Reserve Bank of India to redress customer complaints against deficiency in certain banking services.

The Banking Ombudsman Scheme is an expeditious and inexpensive forum for bank customers for resolution of complaints relating to certain services rendered by banks. Presently, the Banking Ombudsman Scheme, 2006 (as amended up to 1st July, 2017) is in operation.

4. **A citizen files a complaint with the Lokpal against a Union Minister for allegedly accepting a bribe, can the Lokpal investigate and take action against the minister? If yes, what powers does the Lokpal have?**

Ans. Yes, the Lokpal has the power to investigate and take action against the minister. The Lokpal and Lokayukta Act, 2013 empowers the Lokpal to
- receive complaints of corruption against public servants, including the Prime Minister, Ministers and MPs.
- conduct preliminary inquiry and investigations
- summon and examine witnesses.
- order searches and seizures.

- impose penalties, including fines and imprisonment.
- recommend disciplinary action, including dismissal or removal from office.

The Lokpal's powers extend to all public servants including those in the highest echelons of power, ensuring accountability and transparency in governance. The Lokpal's investigation and actions are independent of government's influence, ensuring fair and impartial process.

5. 'The legislation aims to combat the acts of bribery and corruption of public servants'. A term that has been given a fairly wide interpretation in the act. **CBSE 2019**

(i) Identify this legislation.

(ii) State the categories of public servants included within the purview of this legislation and the exceptions therein.

(iii) Examine the conduct of inquiry under this legislation.

Or **Examine the purpose and scope of the Lokpal and Lokayukta Act, 2013.** **CBSE 2023**

Ans. (i) The Lokpal and Lokayukta Act, 2013.

(ii) The act includes the following categories of public servants within its purview

- Group 'A', Group 'B', Group 'C' or Group 'D' official equivalent public servants defined in the Prevention of Corruption Act, 1988 who has served in connection with the affairs of the union.
- any person who is or has been a Minister of the Union and any person who is/has been a member of either House of Parliament.
- The act also includes the current and ex-Prime Ministers of India, except in matters pertaining to international relations, external and internal security, public order, atomic energy and space.

(iii) Inquiry shall be held in camera (must be recorded) by atleast two-thirds of the members of Lokpal, and if the Lokpal comes to the conclusion that the complaint deserves to be dismissed, the records of the inquiry shall not be published or made available to anyone.

6. Mr. Kumar, a citizen, files a complaint with the ombudsman against a government department alleging delay in processing his pension papers, audeness by a government official and corruption in granting licenses.

Describe the role of an ombudsman in investigating complaints against government departments, including the types of issues they can investigate and the powers they have to redress grievances.

Ans. An ombudsman is an independent and impartial institution that investigates complaints against government departments, agencies and public officials. Their role includes

(i) Investigating complaints related to mala administration, misconduct, corruption, neglect, injustice and dis-crimination.

(ii) Examining decision, actions and policies of government department.

(iii) Identifying systematic issues and recommending reforms.

(iv) Providing recommendations to government departments for redressal of grievances.

(v) Ensuring accountability and transparency in government.

The ombudsman has the power to

(i) Subpoena documents and witnesses.

(ii) Conduct hearings and interviews.

(iii) Access government records and files.

(iv) Make binding recommendations to government departments.

(v) Report findings and recommendations to the government and legislature.

SELF ASSESSMENT TEST

Objective Type Questions

1. Which act also provides for the manner in which the public-servants must declare their assets?

(a) Lokpal and Lokayukta Act (b) NALSA

(c) Both (a) and (b) (d) None of these

2. With respect to bureaucracy, the Lokayukta Act includes any Group 'A', 'B', 'C' or 'D' official or equivalent from amongst the public servants defined in the ....

(a) Prevention of Corruption Act, 1988 (b) Lokpal Act itself

(c) Civil Rights Act (d) NALSA

3. When did the first Lok Adalat held?

(a) 1984 (b) 1982 (c) 1970 (d) 1994

4. Which of the following was the first state to introduce the institution of Lokayukta?

(a) Gujarat (b) Maharashtra (c) Bihar (d) Andhra Pradesh

Very Short Answer Type Questions

5. Under which rules, the Insurance Ombudsman are appointed by the Council for Insurance Ombudsman?

6. A citizen files a complaint with the Lokpal against a Cabinet Minister for allegedly misusing their position to gain undue benefits? The minister is accused of allocating government contracts to their relative's companies. What power does the Lokpal have in this situation?

Short Answer Type Questions

7. State the benefits of Lok Adalat.

8. What are the major advantages of an ombudsman?

Long Answer Type Questions

9. A citizen complaints to the Lokayukta about a State Government official who demanded a bribe to approve a building plan. The official is a member of the State's Revenue Department. What action can the Lokayukta take against the official?

10. How does the ombudsman function? What is its major advantage?

06 CHAPTER

Law of Contract

Contracts are an important part of commercial law because all commercial law transactions usually begin with an agreement or a contract.

YOUR STUDY GOALS

YOUR PRACTICE GOAL

- Objective Type Questions (28 Qs ; MCQs, A-R, Statements, Matching)
- Subjective Questions (14 VSAs, 10 SAs, 3 LAs)

6.1 Introduction to Contracts

- It has been a common practice to exchange things of utility in the ancient times. However, with the arrival of money as a common medium of exchange that is fair and uniformly valued at a given place, it has become easy to enter into transactions. In the modern times, these definite transactions are known as **contract**.
- Business transactions involving sale-purchase or exchange of services have become an integral part in day-to-day activities. for example buying groceries, booking a cab, eating at a restaurant, paying for internet, purchasing clothes, etc.
- In such instances, an agreement or a contract is necessary for determining the rights, obligations and liabilities of parties when they enter into any business transaction. The Indian Contract Act, 1872 is the law governing contracts in India.
- The agreements that create a **legal obligation** are only contracts, but the agreements that do not seek to create a legal relationship are not contracts. All contracts are agreements, but all agreements are not contracts.

Formation of Contract

- The Indian Contract Act, 1872 (referred to as the ICA) defines a contract as a legally enforceable agreement [**Section 2(h)**].
- An agreement is the result of a **proposal** or an offer by one party and its **acceptance** by the other.

- Agreements must meet certain criteria to become a contrat, which are as follows
  - **Competent Parties** The parties to the agreement must be legally capable of entering into a contract.
  - **Lawful Consideration and Lawful Object** The agreement must have a legitimate object and a lawful consideration.
  - **Free consent** The parties' assent must be free of coercion, undue influence, fraud, misrepresentation and mistakes.
  - **Not Expressly Declared Void by the Law** The agreement must not have been declared void by the law in force, at the time of the entering into the agreement.
- **By Virtue of Provisions of Section 10 of ICA** It is true that all contracts are enforceable agreements while the vice-versa may not be true when an agreement is not enforceable by law for want of lawful consideration or lawful object.

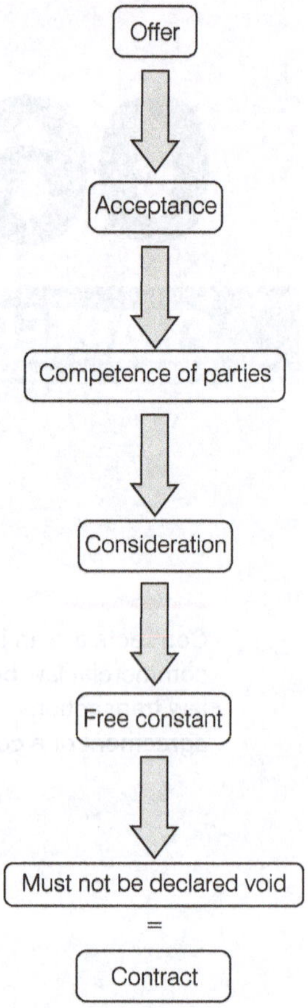

Offer and Acceptance of Contract

- The offer or proposal is the **first step** in the formation of a contract. According to **Section 2(a)** of Indian Contract Act, when one person signifies to another his willingness to do or not to do certain things, it is called an **offer.**
- The person making the proposal or offer is called the **offeror** and the person to whom the offer is made is called the **offeree.**
- The offer given must be with an **intention to create a legal relationship.**
- According to **Section 2(b)** of the Indian Contract Act, an assent or consent (consent means to agree) given to an offer by the offeree is known as **acceptance**. Saying 'yes', 'ok' or clicking on 'I agree' on an offer on a website also amounts to acceptance.
- An offer when accepted becomes an agreement. An agreement is also called a **promise.**

offer + acceptance = agreement

For example, 'A' expresses his willingness to sell his cottage to 'B' for `5 lakhs. Here, A's willingness to sell his cottage to 'B' is called an offer. 'A' is the offeror and 'B' is the offeree. 'B' accepts the offer to purchase the cottage. This is called acceptance. A's offer, when accepted by 'B', becomes an agreement.

- Both **offer and acceptance must be definite and certain.** If the offer or acceptance is not clear enough to conclude a contract, it is considered **invalid.**
- An offer and acceptance must be **communicated** to the other person in order to be valid.
- An offer expires by revocation or withdrawal.

Intention to Contract

In contract law, intention to contract means that both the parties to an agreement must intend to create a legally binding contract. If this intention is not present, the contract is not binding and can not be enforced.

General Offer

In the general offer, there is no need for communicating acceptance to the offeror. Only fulfilling the conditions of the offer itself is treated as acceptance to create a contract.

Consideration of Contract

Consideration is an important element in a contract.

- Consideration means **'something in return'** quid pro quo for an offer.
- Consideration can be in the nature of an act or forbearance[1].
- An **agreement without consideration is void** and not enforceable by law. This is because in such cases, one party is getting something from the other without giving anything to the other.
- There should always be mutual consideration.

  For example, 'A' offers to sell his car for ₹ 50,000 to 'B', 'B' accepts the offer. In this case, the consideration of 'A' is his car and the consideration of 'B' is ₹ 50,000.
- However, in certain situations such as a written and registered agreement **out of natural love** is not void, even if it is without consideration.
- Consideration is not required to be adequate, but should be real.
- Consideration may be **past, present or future** and should not be illegal, immoral or opposed to public policy.

  For example, 'A', for natural love and affection, promises to give his son, 'B', ₹ 1,000. 'A' puts his promise to 'B' in writing and registers it. This is a contract and the absence of consideration does not make it void.

Capacity to Contract

According to **Section 10 of ICA,** one of the essentials of a valid contract is that the parties must be **competent to contract.** Following are not competent to a contract

- **Minor** i.e. persons who are less than 18 years of age
- Persons with **unsound** mind
- Persons **disqualified by law**

Minor Under Indian Law

- It was the Indian Majority Act that laid down the age of majority as 18 years except in cases where guardian has been appointed by the court, it was 21 years. An amendment to the said act has amended the majority age to 18 years for all cases.

  For e.g 'A' (major) offers to sell his coat for ₹ 3000/- to 'B' (minor). 'B' accepts the offer and pays ₹ 3000/-. 'A' states that the contract is entered into with a minor and hence void. In this case, even if the contract is entered into with a minor, it is enforceable because it is beneficial to the minor and the minor has performed his part of the obligation in the contract.

Indian Contract Act does not answer whether an agreement by a minor is void or voidable? Nature of minor's agreement has been analysed by the courts from time to time based on the facts and circumstances of the case in light of general principles of equity and natural justice .

Consent to Contract

- Consent is an important criterion while entering into a contract.
- According to **Section 13,** when two persons agree on the same thing in the same sense (consensus ad idem), it is termed as **consent.**
- Consent should be free and not caused by coercion, undue influence, misrepresentation, fraud or mistake.

1 Forbearance It means not doing an act.

- If consent is obtained by the influence of any one of the above said factors, the consent so obtained is **not free**. It becomes voidable for the person whose consent is not free.
- It means that the person whose consent was not freely given has the option to **rescind**[2] the contract. For example, 'A' threatened to kill 'B' if he does not sell his house to 'A'. 'B', out of fear, signs the contract for selling his house to 'A'. Here, the consent of 'B' is not free. 'B' can later avoid the sale on the ground that he was compelled to agree to the sale and the consent given was not free consent.

Quick Test 1

1. What are the three basics of a contract?
2. Who are not competent to enter into a contract?
3. When does a minor attain the age of majority?
4. In which section of the Indian Contract Act, 1872, consent is defined?

6.2 Types of Contracts/Agreements

As discussed previously, all agreements may not be contracts and vice versa. There are situations when agreements turn into contracts at the start, but at a later stage due to change in any of the essential conditions of a contract, a contract ceases to be enforeable under the law and thus becomes void at the option of any of the parties to the contract.

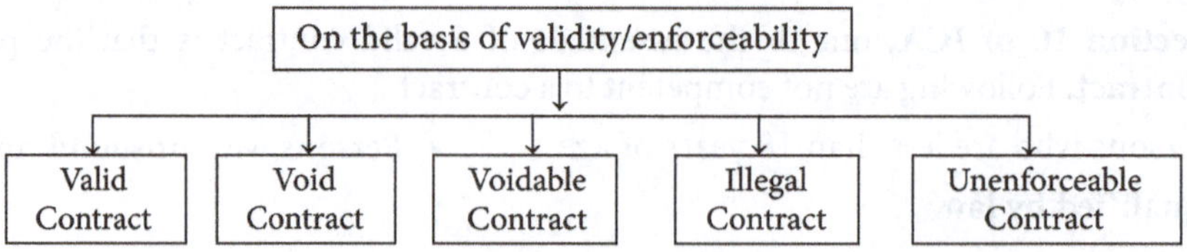

▲ *Types of Contracts*

Some important valid and enforceable contracts are discussed below

Void Contracts

- According to **Section 2(j)** of ICA, a contract becomes void when it **ceases to be enforceable** by law.
- A void contract is allowed only to the extent to restore any benefit received by the party, on the grounds of equity.
- If any contract becomes void, it cannot become valid thereafter.

Voidable Contracts

- According to **Section 2(i)** of ICA, voidable contract is a contract which may **either be affirmed or rejected** by one of the parties to the contract, on ground of coercion, undue influence, fraud or mis-representation.
- It remains enforceable till the time it is not **declared void by a competent court**.
- Under this contract, the injured has the right to initiate action for damages.
- A voidable contract may become valid upon lapse of time, affirmation, **ratification**[3], waiver of right and acceptance of the party whose consent was not free.

---

2 **Rescind** It means to revoke, cancel or repeal.
3 **Ratification** It means the action of signing or giving formal consent to a treaty.

Contingent Contracts

- According to **Section 31** of ICA, a **contingent**[4] contract is a contract **to do or not to do something** depending upon the happening or non-happening of a **future uncertain event**. However, the uncertain future event does not determine the outcome of the contract. It is only **collateral to the contract**.
- A contingent contract is enforceable under the law. There may or may not be reciprocal promise in a contingent contract.
- For example, 'A' promises to buy 'B' the Indian cricket team's jersey, if they win the match today. Now, this is a contingency as there's no guarantee whether India will win the match.
- In the same example, 'A' promises to buy 'B' the jersey if he pays him the money, then this will be a promissory condition that depends on the performance of a duty.

Wagering Contracts

- **Section 30** of ICA declares **wagering**[5] agreements to be void but **does not** define wagering agreements.
- Under this agreement, the parties have opposite views regarding an uncertain event and equal chances of gain or loss.
- The uncertain future event decides who wins the wager.
- There is no other interest of the parties in the agreement, except for winning or loosing it.
- It is **simply a bet** and thus is based on reciprocal promise.
- A wagering agreement is not enforceable under the law.

  For example, 'X' enters into a wager with 'Y'. If X's food tech start-up gains at least 50,000 customers in 6 months, then 'Y' shall pay 'X' a certain monetary sum, and if it doesn't hit the target, then 'X' shall pay 'Y' the same amount.

Illegal/Unlawful Agreements

- According to **Section 10** of ICA, a contract must be made for a lawful consideration and lawful object. If the consideration or the object is an action or omission prohibited by law, it results into an illegal contract.
- According to **Section 24** of ICA, the agreements that are entered into for any unlawful or illegal object or consideration cannot be enforced under the law and are thus void.
- However, there is a possibility that the object or the consideration with which the contract was formed initially, later turns unlawful or illegal. In this case, it becomes void.

  For example, 'A' enters into an agreement with 'B' to share the profits by giving false assurance to the public to get them a job in Singapore. The agreement involves cheating which is a fraudulent act. The agreement is unlawful and hence it is void.

6.3 Discharge of Contract

Discharge means termination of the contractual relations of the parties to the contract. In a contract, mutual obligations of parties are created. When the mutual obligations of the parties are fulfilled, the contract comes to an end. When the **contract is ended, it is said to be discharged.** Discharge of a contract may be done by the following ways

- **Discharge by Performance** When parties to a contract perform their obligations and **fulfill their promises,** the contract gets discharged by performance.

  For example, 'A' offer to sell his dining set to 'B' for ₹10,000. 'B' pays ₹ 10,000 to 'A' and 'A' delivers his dining set to 'B'. Here, the contract gets discharged by performance as both the parties fulfilled their promises.

4 **Contingent** It means occurring on if (certain circumstances) are the case.
5 **Wagering** It means risk against someone else's on the basis of the outcome of an unpredictable event.

- **Discharge by Agreement or Consent** There are several ways in which a contract can be discharged by an agreement or consent. These are
  - **Novation** A new contract is substituted for an old contract.
    For example, 'A' is indebted to 'B' and 'B' to 'C'. By mutual agreement B's debt to 'C' and A's debt to 'B' is cancelled and 'C' accepts 'A' as his debtor. This is new contract substituting the old one and hence, novation.
  - **Rescission** The **cancellation** of some or all of the conditions of a contract. For example, 'A' enters into an agreement with 'B' for buying certain machine parts for their project. Before the agreement ends, 'A' and 'B' change certain terms of the agreement.
  - **Remission Acceptance** of an agreement but not on the full conditions.
    For example, 'A' owes 'B' ₹ 5000/-. 'A' pays to 'B' and 'B' accepts ₹ 2,000/- in full satisfaction to the whole debt. The old debt is discharge but to a lesser fulfillment of the promise.
  - **Merger** With an approval of the parties, certain provisions of a contract or all terms of a contract are **merged into another contract.**
    For example, 'A' enters into a contract with 'B' for the supply of 50 bags of wheat on a specified date. Later it was realised by 'A' that he needs 10 bags of mixed pulses also at the same time. 'A' and 'B' merge the two contracts to supply 50 bags of wheat and 10 bags of mixed pulses on the same date and at the same place.
- **Discharge by Impossibility of Performance** Performance of a contract can become impossible **with or without the knowledge of the parties to the contract.** It can also become impossible subsequently after the parties have entered into a contract. This is known as supervening impossibility **(as per Section 56).** Supervening[6] impossibility takes place by any of the following
  - Destruction of the subject matter
  - Death or incapacity
  - Non-existence of state of things having an effect directly or indirectly on the contract
  - Outbreak of war
  - Change or amendments in law

  For example, 'X' agreed to sell his car to 'Y' for ₹ 1 lakh and deliver it after two months. After a week, 'X' met with an accident and the car got completely destroyed. The contract gets discharged by impossibility of performance as the car was completely destroyed.
- **Discharge by Lapse of Time** Time is very significant while entering into a contract. If the contract is not performed within the specified time and the other party does not resort[7] to any action within the limitation period, he is **deprived** of his remedy and the contract gets discharged by lapse of time.
- **Discharge by Operation of Law** The following are instances where a contract gets discharged by operation of law
  - Death of either of the parties
  - Insolvency
  - Merger
  - Unauthorised (not agreed to by the other party) alteration of the terms of the agreement
- **Discharge by Breach of Contract** Breach[8] means failure to perform the obligation by a party. According to **Section 73** of the Contract Act, when a party to a contract does not perform his part of the obligation due to which the contract becomes broken, then the person who suffers because of the breach is entitled to receive compensation or damages from the party who has breached the contract.

6 Supervening It means occurring as an interruption or change to an existing situation.
7 Resort It means turn to and adopt (a course of action, especially an extreme or undesirable one) so as to resolve a difficult situation.
8 Breach It means an act of breaking or failing to observe an agreement, contract.

For example, 'A' agrees to supply 20 litres of oil to 'B' on 1st June, 2014. On 1st June, 2014, 'A' does not supply the oil. Then 'A' has breached the contract. Suppose 'A' has supplied the oil, but 'B' does not accept the oil, then 'B' has breached the contract.

In the first instance, 'B' is entitled to receive compensation from 'A'. In the latter instance, 'A' is entitled to receive compensation from 'B'.

6.4 Remedies in Case of Breach

- A remedy implies a **relief** given by law to ensure the enforcement of contractual rights or to provide sufficient compensation for the non-performance. In the matters of breach of contract, the remedies available are **damages** and **specific performance**.
- Damages are the most common remedy available to the injured party. It entitles them to recover the money compensation for the losses suffered due to the breach. It is covered in **Section 73** of ICA in India.
- The purpose of a contract is to enforce the rights of the parties, in event of breach the promisee can request the performance of specific obligations.

For example, 'A' agrees to deliver 40 bags of rice to 'B' for ₹

Quick Test 2

1. When did the voidable contract become void?
2. Under which section of Indian Contract Act, 1872 is contingent contract defined?
3. What is discharge of contract by performance?
4. In which section of Indian Contract Act, remedies in case of breach is covered?

REFERENCE CASES

Intention to Contract

In a leading case **Balfour Vs. Balfour** (1919, 5KB 571), the validity of an agreement entered between a husband and wife was in question.

The husband and wife went on leave to England and the wife fell ill in England. The doctors who treated the wife advised her to take full bed rest and remain in England in order to continue the treatment.

The wife stayed in England. When the leave was over, the husband went to Ceylon where he was employed and promised to send a sum of £ 30 to the wife every month for her stay in England. He sent amount for sometime and later on due to differences and mis-understanding between them, the husband stopped sending the amount.

The wife initiated action to recover, the arrears due to her. The court dismissed it on the ground that the agreement entered into between the husband and wife was not a contract. The arrangement between the husband and wife was only a moral obligation and the parties never intended to create any legal relationships.

The decision clearly shows that agreements that create a **legal obligation** are only contracts and those agreements that do not intend to create legal relationship are not contracts.

General Offer

In a leading English case **Carlill Vs. Carbolic Smoke Ball Co.** (1893, 1 QB 256), facts the company was the manufacturer of a medicine called Smoke Ball which was used for the treatment of influensa.

The company believed that the medicine completely cured influensa. An advertisement was put up offering a reward of £ 100 to anyone who got influensa again after using the Smoke Ball medicine continuously for fifteen days.

In the advertisement, it was also stated that £ 1000 was deposited in a bank, namely. Alliance Bank for paying the reward if such situation arose. Seeing the advertisement, Mrs. Carlill bought the Smoke Ball medicine and used it as per the directions, provided. Mrs. Carlill got a fresh episode of influensa. Mrs. Carlill sued the company for the reward of £ 100.

The manufacturing company stated that (i) there was no intention to enter into a legal relationship with anyone through the advertisement and the advertisement was put up only to boost the marketing of the Smoke Ball medicine; (ii) the advertisement was not an offer as it was not made to any particular person and an offer cannot be made to the public at large or to the whole world; (iii) acceptance by the offeree had not been communicated, and so there was no binding contract.

The court rejected these contentions of the company and allowed Mrs. Carlill's claim for £ 100. The court also stated that the deposit of £ 1000 in the Alliance Bank by the Smoke Ball Company was evidence that the company had real intention to enter into a legal relationship with anyone who accepted the offer. An offer can also be made to the world at large. It is called a general offer and it is valid.

Consideration of Contract

In leading Indian case **Durga Prasad Vs. Baldeo (1880, 3A 11221)**, the Plaintiff constructed some shops at the request of the district collector in a town. The constructed shops where given on rent for doing business to the defendant, the shopkeeper.

The defendant apart from the rent, promised to give 5% commission to the Plaintiff on all articles sold through the shop in consideration of the huge amount spent by the Plaintiff in the construction of the building. The defendant failed to pay the commission and the Plaintiff initiated action to recover the commission. The court rejected the action of the Plaintiff on the ground that the construction of the shop was done at the desire of the District Collector and hence there was no consideration to give commission. Accordingly, there is no valid contract to pay commission to the Plaintiff.

Capacity of Contract

The controversy initially, was set at rest by the decision of privy council in **Mohori Bibee Vs. Dharmodas Ghose.** The minor Plaintiff mortgaged his property in favour of the defendant who was a money lender, to secure his loan. The money lender had knowledge about the minority of the Plaintiff. The court held against the contentions of the defendant that no estoppel could apply against the Plaintiff as both the parties were aware of the minor's minority. Also, the defendant asked for the refund of loan taken under the provisions of ICA if mortgage is cancelled. Court held that an agreement by a minor is void ab initio

In anothe case, **Kalus Mittelbachert Vs. East India Hotels Ltd.,** there was a contract between Lufthansa, a German airline and hotel Oberoi, New Delhi that crew of the airline will stay in Latter's hotel. The Plaintiff, a co-pilot of the airline stayed in the hotel and sustained serious head injuries on diving in the swimming pool of the hotel. This resulted in paralysis and after a battle of 13 years with his health conditions, he died. Though he head no direct contract with hotel but he succeeded as a beneficiary and was awarded compensation for the damage caused. Being a 5-star hotel extra care and caution was expected out of the hotel and thus exemplary damages of 50 lac were awarded.

Mind Map

LAW OF CONTRACT

1 Introduction

- **Definition** Contract = Agreement enforceable by law (Section 2(h) of the Indian Contract Act, 1872).

Key Points

- Based on agreements, rights, obligations and liabilities.
- **Legal Vs. Social/Moral Agreements** Only legal agreements are contracts.
- All contracts are agreements, but not all agreements are contracts.

2 Formation of Contracts

Steps

- **Offer and Acceptance** Proposal by one party and its acceptance by another.
- **Competent Parties** Legally capable parties to enter a contract.
- **Lawful Consideration** Must have value but not necessarily adequate.
- **Free Consent** Without coercion, fraud, undue influence, or misrepresentation.
- **Not Declared Void** Agreement must comply with the law.

3 Types of Contracts

Based on Validity

- **Valid Contract** Legally enforceable.
- **Void Contract** Not enforceable (e.g., unlawful objects).
- **Voidable Contract** Enforceable at one party's discretion (due to coercion, fraud, etc.).
- **Illegal Contract** Prohibited by law; void.
- **Unenforceable Contract** Cannot be enforced due to technical defects.

Special Contracts

- **Contingent Contracts** Based on uncertain future events.
- **Wagering Agreements** Betting on uncertain outcomes; void.
- **Quasi-Contracts** No agreement but obligations imposed by law.

4 Essential Elements of a Valid Contract

Offer and Acceptance

- Offer = Willingness to do/refrain from doing something.
- Acceptance = Consent to the offer.
- **For example** Clicking "I agree" on a website.

Consideration
Something of value exchanged (money, goods, promises). May be past, present, or future.

Capacity to Contract
Minors, persons of unsound mind, or disqualified persons cannot contract.

Free Consent
Agreement on the same thing in the same sense (Consensus ad idem).

5 Discharge of Contracts

By Performance Fulfillment of contractual obligations.

By Agreement

- **Novation** Substitution of a new contract.
- **Rescission** Cancelling the contract.
- **Remission** Acceptance of less fulfillment.

By Impossibility of Performance

- Destruction, incapacity, legal amendments, war.

By Lapse of Time Failure to act within the limitation period.

By Breach

- Party fails to perform; the aggrieved can seek damages.

6 Remedies for Breach of Contract

Damages

- Compensation for losses.
- **Types** Ordinary, exemplary and special damages.

Specific Performance

- Court order to perform the contract.

Injunction

- Preventive relief to stop a party from doing something.

7 Key Legal Doctrines

- **Consensus Ad Idem** Meeting of minds; essential for consent.
- **Doctrine of Frustration** Contract becomes impossible due to unforeseen events.

General Vs. Specific Offers

- **General** Made to the public at large (e.g., advertisements).
- **Specific** Directed to a particular person.

8 Landmark Cases

Balfour Vs. Balfour

- No legal obligation in domestic agreements.

Carlill Vs. Carbolic Smoke Ball Co.

- General offers are binding if conditions are met.

Mohori Bibee Vs. Dharmodas Ghose

- Agreement with a minor is void.

CBSE TEXTBOOK FOLDER

1. Ramesh sells his bike to his friend Suresh for a consideration of ₹ 50,000/-, whereas the market price of the said bike is ₹ 65,000/-. Examine if the agreement is enforceable under Law of Contract.

Ans. This agreement is enforceable under the Law of Contract as according to Section 25(1), when an agreement is made on account of natural love and affection between the parties standing in near relation to each other, the agreement is enforceable, even though, the consideration is absent.

2. 'D', a minor borrowed a sum of money from 'M' by executing a mortgage of his property in favour of 'M'. Subsequently, 'D' sued for cancellation of mortgage. Is the contract of mortgage valid? Can 'M' recover the sum advanced to 'D' ?

Ans. In the given case, 'D' is a **minor** who borrowed a sum from 'M' by mortgaging his property. But as per the provisions, 'D' is not competent to contract and any contract entered will be void and hence, the mortgage here is not valid. Also, due to the void contract 'M' will not succeed in recovering the amount from 'M'.

3. Apexx Chemicals entered into an agreement with Moonled Pharma Ltd. to supply them with 16 units calcium and 8 units of magnesium powder for its medicine unit. By the time Apexx Chemicals supplied 12 units of calcium and 4 units of magnesium, the government restricted free sale of chemicals for life saving drugs. Every dealer was supposed to get his supply sanctioned from the government to a maximum of 10 units of each chemical. Apexx Chemicals found it difficult to complete the order of Moonled Pharma Ltd., brings a suit for breach of contract against Adarsh Chemicals. Will it succeed? Analyse by referring to relevant provisions.

Ans. In this situation, Moonled Pharma Ltd. can easily bring a suit for breach of contract because Apexx Chemicals failed to perform the obligation of agreement and that situation become a breach of contract.

Section 73 of the Indian Contract Act deals with the damages for the breach of contract. If the court analyses this situation in favour of Moonled Pharma Ltd., then, they will succeed in this case.

4. 'X' enters into a contract with 'Y' to pay him ₹ 10,000 if the books are delivered to him by friday. This is an example of contingent contract. Explain why.

Ans. This is an example of contingent contract as it is a contract to do or not to do something depending upon the happening or non-happening of a future uncertain event. A contingent contract is enforceable under the law. There may or may not be reciprocal promise in a contingent contract.

Exam Pattern Questions

Objective Type Questions

Multiple Choice Questions (MCQs)

1. Which of the following statements is true for 'Considaration' as an important element in contract? **CBSE 2024**

(a) A contract without consideration is voidable.
(b) Consideration must be adequate and real.
(c) Consideration can be in the nature of an act or forbearance.
(d) Consensus ad idem is the pre-requisite for consideration

2. In which of the following cases, was the validity of an agreement entered between a husband and wife was in question?

(a) Balfour Vs. Balfour (b) Carlill Vs. Carbolic Smoke Co.
(c) Durga Prasad Vs. Baldeo (d) All of these

3. Which of the following definitions is the right definition of contract as per Section 2(h) of Contract Act?

(a) Agreement enforceable by law
(b) Agreement enforceable by morality
(c) Agreement enforceable by social relations
(d) All of the above

4. **Raj signs a contract to perform at a music festival. A few days before the festival, Raj develops a severe illness and doctors advise him complete rest. He misses the performance. Organisers of the event had to cut a sorry figure as Raj's performance was the highlight of the music festival.**

Which of the given statements best describes Raj's inability to perform at the festival? **CBSE 2025**

(a) It is breach of contract as Raj failed to fulfill his obligation.
(b) It is discharge due to impossibility of performance because the illness makes performance impossible.
(c) It is discharge by performance as Raj was willing to perform if he hadn't been ill.
(d) It is breach of contract as a health issue does not discharge a contract.

5. **Raj signs a contract with Suman, agreeing to sell his laptop for ₹ 30,000. Suman is 17 years old. They both agree on the terms, and Suman promises to pay the amount in two weeks. However, before the payment is made, Suman decides to cancel the deal.**

Which of the following is most accurate regarding the validity of the contract? **CBSE SQP 2024**

(a) The contract is valid because both the parties agreed to the terms.
(b) The contract is void because Suman is a minor.
(c) The contract is valid because it involves the sale of goods.
(d) The contract is invalid because the payment was not made in advance.

6. **An insane man, who is delirious from fever or who is so drunk that he cannot understand the terms of a contract, or form a rational judgement as to its effect on his interests. Can he be said to be competent to contract in such a state of delirium or drunkenness?**

(a) Yes, if he is able to understand the terms of contract.
(b) No
(c) Yes, as he was voluntarily drunk.
(d) No, as he cannot be said to understand the terms of contract whilst such delirium or drunkenness lasts.

7. **In the English Case of ...., the court held that an offer can also be made to the world at large. It is called a general offer and it is valid.**

(a) Balfour Vs. Balfour
(b) Carlill Vs. Carbolic Smoke Ball Co.
(c) R. V. Wheeler
(d) None of the above

8. **'A' makes an offer to 'B' to buy his car for ₹ 10 lakhs, 'A' has the option of revoking or cancelling his offer ....**

(a) after 'B' receives it.
(b) after 'A' has put it in course of transmission.
(c) before 'B' accepts it.
(d) Either (b) or (c)

9. **Ravi is a sculptor and makes idols of all popular deities. Naresh places an order for an idol be delivered in time for an auspicious gathering. Ravi is able to deliver the idol a week later than agreed. Naresh was unable to conduct Pooja on the appointed date and sues Ravi for damages.** **CBSE 2023**

(a) Discharge by performance.
(b) Discharge by breach of contract.
(c) Discharge by lapse of time.
(d) Discharge by impossibility of performance.

10. **When certain terms or all terms of a contract are cancelled it is known as ....**

(a) novation (b) rescission
(c) waiver (d) merger

11. **Bhoora, a poor farmer, forced by hunger and destitution, loans ₹ 10,000 from Ajay provided Bhoora undertakes to work for him without pay for all his life. After a year of hard labour, Bhoora stops working for Ajay.**

Which of the following will apply in this instance? **CBSE 2023**

(a) Ajay can move the court as Bhoora has breached the contract.
(b) Ajay cannot enforce contract as Bhoora's consent was not free.
(c) Ajay cannot enforce contract because agreement was without consideration.
(d) Ajay can sue Bhoora as he hasn't done enough work, since the agreement was for life.

12. **Ashwin agreed to supply 20 litres of oil to Bholu on 1st June, 2014. On 1st June, 2014, Ashwin did not supply the oil.**

Which of the following is correct?

(a) Bholu cannot recover compensation from Ashwin.
(b) Bholu can recover compensation from Ashwin for 10 litres of oil.
(c) Bholu cannot recover compensation as the suit is barred by limitation.
(d) Bholu is entitled to receive compensation as there is a breach of contract.

13. **Anuj owes Rajiv ₹, 000. Anuj pays ₹, 00 to Rajiv in full settlement of the whole debt. This contract is discharged by ....** **CBSE 2024 C**

(a) rescission (b) remission (c) remittance (d) Novation

14. **Adheer is indebted to Bhanu and Bhanu is indebted to Chitranjan. By mutual agreement among the three, Bhanu is absolved of the liability to pay Chitranjan and Chitranjan accepts Adheer as his debtor. This understanding is converted into a contract.**

Which of the following options correctly describes the effect of this new arrangement on the already existing contract between the parties? **CBSE 2024 C**

(a) The existing contract is discharged by rescission as all terms of the contract are cancelled.
(b) The existing contract is discharged by novation as the new contract will substitute the old one.
(c) The existing contract is automatically discharged by performance.
(d) The existing contract is discharged by operation of law as the parties have merged terms of contract.

15. Aadwik sells his bike for a consideration of ₹ 50,000 to his friend Sandeep, whereas the market price of the said bike is ₹ 75,000.

The above agreement is ....
(a) not enforceable as Aadwik can not sell his bike below the market price.
(b) enforceable as the consideration need not be adequate, but should be real.
(c) not enforceable as it is an unlawful consideration.
(d) enforceable as the consideration is adequate and reasonable as the bike is not brand new.

16. Herbicure Limited, a paint manufacturing company advertised their soil proof paint, Mericuren and claimed that the coating of this paint would prevent termite attack for a minimum period of 2 years after applying the paint. The company also claimed that it would give a reward of ₹ 10,000 to anyone who purchased the paint and followed the instructions for the application of the paint and still got a termite attack. The company deposited an amount of ₹ 10 lakhs in State Bank of India towards the reward. Ms. Shruti, upon seeing the advertisement, purchased the paint and applied it as per the instructions. Within a year of applying the paint, she saw a termite attack on her walls.

What established the fact that the company had any real intention to enter into a legal relationship with anyone who accepted the offer?
(a) The offer of a reward of ₹ 10,000
(b) Putting up of the advertisement
(c) Deposit of ₹ 10 lakhs in the bank
(d) Instructions given in the advertisement

17. Section 4 of the Indian Contract Act states that the communication of a proposal is complete when it comes to the knowledge of the person to whom it is made. In Lalman's case, the defendant's nephew absconded from home. The Plaintiff who was defendant issued handbills announcing a reward of ₹ 501 to anyone who might find out the boy. The Plaintiff who was unaware of this reward, was successful in searching the boy. When he came to know of the reward, which had been announced in his absence, he brought an action against the defendant to claim this reward. It was held that since the Plaintiff was ignorant of the offer of reward, his act of bringing the lost boy did not amount to the acceptance of the offer and therefore he was not entitled to claim the reward.

How is this judgement contradictory to the Carlill Vs. Carbolic Smokeball Company Case?
(a) No intention to enter into legal relationship.
(b) The need for acceptance of the offer was emphasised.
(c) Knowledge of the offer is important.
(d) There was intention to enter into legal relationship.

18. Sheena was a builder. She constructed a shopping complex at the request of the District Collector on government land and gave shops on lease to earn revenue. Ajit took a shop on rent and promised to pay 5% commission above the rent. However, later-on he refused to pay the commission. Sheena sued Ajit for breach of contract.

Choose the best option.
(a) Ajit is liable to pay as it was a valid contract.
(b) Ajit is not liable to pay as consideration was missing in this particular promise.
(c) Ajit is not liable to pay as this was not a valid offer.
(d) Ajit is liable to pay as Sheena is related to the District Collector.

19. Rupa and Ravi entered into a contract for the sale of illegal substances. Both were fully aware of the illegality of the contract at the time of its formation. Which of the following options correctly describes the status of the contract? **CBSE 2024 C**
(a) The contract is legally enforceable despite the illegality of the subject.
(b) The contract is voidable at the discretion of either party due to its unlawful nature.
(c) The contract is void and cannot be enforced by either party due to its unlawful nature.
(d) The contract is valid, but both parties may face criminal charges for engaging in an illegal transaction.

20. Match the following.

Column I	Column II
A. New contract substituted for old contract	1. Remission
B. Acceptance is made to a promise but not on the complete terms of the promise but to a lesser fulfillment of the promise.	2. Waiver
C. Parties abandon their mutual rights	3. Alteration
D. Certain terms of a contract are altered or modified with the mutual consent of the parties.	4. Novation

Codes

	A	B	C	D		A	B	C	D
(a)	1	2	3	4	(b)	3	2	1	4
(c)	2	1	4	3	(d)	4	1	2	3

21. **Analyse the two statement given below and select the consent option.**

Statement I A wagering agreement is a type of contract where two parties bet on the outcome of an uncertain event.

Statement II Wagering agreements are legally enforceable in India.

Which of the following is true?

(a) Both the Statements are true.
(b) Only Statement I is false.
(c) Only Statement II is false.
(d) Both the Statements are false.

22. **Analyse the two statement given below and select the consent option.**

Statement I An agreement that is opposed to public policy is considered an illegal agreement.

Statement II All illegal agreements are void and un-enforceable.

Which of the following is true?

(a) Both the Statements are true.
(b) Only Statement I is true.
(c) Only Statement II is true.
(d) Both the Statements are false.

23. **Analyse the two statement given below and select the consent option.**

Statement I Damages are a legal remedy available to the injured party in case of a breach of contract.

Statement II Specific performance is a remedy that can be granted by the court to compel the breaching party to perform their obligations.

Keeping in mind the above statements, mark the correct option.

(a) Both the Statements are false.
(b) Only Statement I is true.
(c) Only Statement II is true.
(d) Both the Statements are true.

Assertion-Reason Questions

Directions (Q. Nos. 24-28) In the questions given below, there are two statements marked as Assertion (A) and Reason (R). Read the statements and choose the correct option.

Codes

(a) Both A and R are true and R is the correct explanation of A.
(b) Both A and R are true, but R is not the correct explanation of A.
(c) A is true, but R is false.
(d) A is false, but R is true.

24. **Assertion** (A) All contracts are agreements but all agreements, are not contracts.

Reason (R) An agreement must be enforceable by law in order to be a contract.

25. **Assertion** (A) When parties to a contract perform their obligations and fulfill their promises, the contract gets discharged by performance.

Reason (R) Discharge by performance can take place through novation.

26. **Assertion** (A) Wager is an invalid contract.

Reason (R) Contingent contracts are valid.

27. **Assertion** (A) A void agreement is not necessarily illegal.

Reason (R) Every illegal contract is void.

28. **Assertion** (A) The effect of frustrating event is to discharge the contract immediately after the event.

Reason (R) A frustrating event is one which renders the performance of the contract impossible by no fault of either party.

Answers

1. (c) Consideration can be in the nature of an act or forbearance.
2. (a) Balfour Vs. Balfour
3. (a) Agreement enforceable by law
4. (b) It is discharge due to impossibility of performance because the illness makes performance impossible.
5. (b) The contract is void because Suman is a minor.
6. (d) No, as he cannot be said to understand the terms of contract whilst such delirium or drunkenness lasts.
7. (b) Carlill Vs. Carbolic Smoke Ball Co.
8. (c) before 'B' accepts it.
9. (c) Discharge by lapse of time.
10. (b) rescission
11. (b) Ajay cannot enforce contract as Bhoora's consent was not free.
12. (d) Bholu is entitled to receive compensation as there is a breach of contract.
13. (b) remission
14. (b) The existing contract is discharged by novation as the new contract will substitute the old one.
15. (d) enforceable as the consideration is adequate and reasonable as the bike is not brand new.
16. (c) Deposit of the ₹ 10 lakhs in the bank

17. (c) Knowledge of the offer is important.
18. (b) Ajit is not liable to pay as consideration was missing in this particular promise.
19. (c) The contract is void and cannot be enforced by either party due to its unlawful nature.
20. (d) 4 1 2 3
21. (c) Only Statement II is false.
22. (a) Both the Statements are true.
23. (d) Both the Statements are true.
24. (a) Both A and R are true and R is the correct explanation of A.
25. (c) A is true, but R is false.
26. (b) Both A and R are true, but R is not the correct explanation of A.
27. (b) Both A and R are true, but R is not the correct explanation of A.
28. (b) Both A and R are true, but R is not the correct explanation of A.

Subjective Questions

Very Short Answer Type Questions

1. What is the meaning of a contract under the Indian Contract Act?

Ans. A contract is an agreement made with the free consent of parties with the capacity to contract, for a lawful consideration and with a lawful object, to be legally bound.

2. State the meaning of acceptance under the Indian Contract Act.

Ans. According to Section 2(b) of the Indian Contract Act, 1872, an assent or consent given to an offer by the offeree is known as acceptance.

3. Arjun threatened to kill Bhim if he does not sell his house worth ₹ 1 crore to Arjun for ₹ 50 lakhs. Bhim, out of fear, signs the contract for selling his house to Arjun.
(i) Identify the essential of valid contract missing in the above situation.
(ii) What remedy, if any, is available to Bhim in the given case? **CBSE 2024**

Ans. (i) There are five essentials of a valid contract, one essential which is missing in the above situation is the **consent** freely given by the parties. If consent is influenced by coercion, fraud, undue influence and mis-representation, then the consent is said to be not given freely.

(ii) Bhim in such a case go to the court and get the contract declared as void because such contracts are voidable.

4. What is the general rule regarding an agreement without consideration?

Ans. The general rule is that an agreement without consideration is void and not enforceable by law.

5. 'A', for natural love and affection, promises to give his son, 'B', ₹ 1,000. 'A' puts his promise to 'B' in writing and registers it. Is this a valid contract?

Ans. This is a valid contract and the absence of consideration does not make it void as an agreement out of natural love and affection, even if it is without consideration.

6. 'A' agrees to give ₹ 1,000 to 'B' as penalty, if the minor daughter is not given to 'A' in marriage. Is the agreement valid?

Ans. This agreement is opposed to public policy and not enforceable.

7. 'A' enters into an agreement with 'B' to share the profits by giving false assurance to the public to get them a job in Singapore.

Ans. The agreement involves cheating which is a fraudulent act. Thus, the agreement is unlawful and void.

8. Arjun offers to sell his bicycle to Bhavana for ₹ 3000, Bhavana agrees to buy the bicycle at the said price and promises to pay the amount the following week. They decide to write down their agreement on a piece of paper, which both sign.
Identify the four essentials of a valid contract in the situation given above. **CBSE SQP 2024**

Ans. The four essentials of a valid contract are
(i) An agreement is the result of a proposal or an offer by one party and acceptance by the other.
(ii) The parties to the agreement must be competent to enter into a contract.
(iii) There must be lawful object and lawful consideration in respect of the agreement.
(iv) There must be free consent of the parties that is free from coercion, undue influence, fraud, mis-representation and mistake, when they enter into agreement.

9. Pramod paid ₹ 10 lakh to Alex as bribe to secure a seat for his son in the government dental college. Alex is eventually unable to secure the seat and Pramod sues him to recover the amount. Assess whether Pramod has a valid basis to recover the amount from Alex. **CBSE 2023**

Ans. Pramod has paid 10 lakh rupees to Alex as bribe and bribe is not a lawful consideration. Also, an object of the contract is not lawful. Since the consideration and object of the contract is not lawful, the agreement will be void and therefore Pramod will not be able to recover the amount from Alex, as there was no contract at all.

10. Raman and Mohit entered into a contract where Raman promises to supply 20 bags of sugar to Mohit, a sweet shop proprietor, on 5th September, 2021. The sugar was to be supplied by 15th September, 2021. The mode of transport available to their places is roadways only. A landslide happened on 7th September, 2021 and the connecting road was completely damaged and could not be repaired within 15 days. Raman offered to supply the sugar by 25th September, 2021. Mohit refused to accept the sugar. Raman filed a claim for ₹ 10,000 on Mohit for refusal of the order. **CBSE SQP 2022**

(i) Identify the mode of discharge of this contract?

(ii) What remedy is available to Raman?

Ans. (i) The mode of discharge of this contract is by impossibility of performance. Performance of a contract can become impossible with or without the knowledge of the parties to the contract. It can also become impossible subsequently after the parties have entered into a contract.

(ii) The objective of awarding damages by the court is to put the injured party in the same position as he would have been if the contract had not been breached.

This is called the 'doctrine of restitution'. the basis of this doctrine is awarding damages for the pecuniary loss incurred by the party to the contract.

11. What are the various ways for discharge of a contract?

Ans. A contract can be discharged in any of the following ways

- Discharge by performance
- Discharge by agreement or consent
- Discharge by impossibility of performance
- Discharge by lapse of time
- Discharge by operation of law
- Discharge by breach of contract

12. State the ways in which supervening impossibility can take place.

Ans. Supervening impossibility takes place by any of the following

- Destruction of the subject matter
- Death or incapacity
- Non-existence of state of things having an effect directly or indirectly on the contract
- Outbreak of war
- Change or amendments in law

13. Rahul agrees to sell his laptop to Rohan on April 15*th* but fails to deliver it on that date. Rohan sends a notice to Rahul on April 20*th*, stating that he will not accept the laptop if it's not delivered within 7 days. Rahul delivers laptop on April 25*th*. Is the contract discharged by breach? Why or why not?

Ans. Yes, the contract is discharged by breach. Rahul failed to perform his obligation within the stipulated time (April 15th) and Rohan gave a notice for extending the time limit, which Rahul still failed to meet. Time was the of essence in this contract.

14. Jai, a business owner, enters into an agreement with Sana, a government official. Jai promises to pay Sana ₹ 10 lakhs in exchange for her influence in securing a lucrative government contract for his company. Both parties sign the agreement and begin to execute it. Identify the nature of this agreement and discuss the legal consequences for both parties involved. **CBSE 2025**

Ans. The agreement between Jai and Sana is illegal and void under the Indian Contract Act, as it involves unlawful consideration and object, i.e., bribery. Such contracts cannot be enforced by law. Both parties may face legal consequences under the Prevention of Corruption Act, 1988, which penalises bribery and corruption involving public servants.

Short Answer Type Questions

1. What is the objective behind the enactment of the Indian Contract Act, 1872?

Ans. The objective behind the enactment of the Indian Contract Act, 1872 is that a contract is necessary for determining the rights, obligations and liabilities of parties when they enter into any business transactions involving sale-purchase or exchange of services.

The Indian Contract Act, 1872 is the law governing contracts in India. It defines a contract as a legally enforceable agreement [Section 2(h)]. Contracts are an important part of commercial law because all commercial law transactions usually begin with an agreement or a contracts.

The agreements that create a legal obligation are only contracts, but the agreements that do not seek to create a legal relationship are not contracts. All contracts are agreements, but all agreements are not contracts.

2. Susheela is a minor who looks older than her age. Subroto is a major who enters into a contract with Susheela thinking that she is a major too. Later, Subroto found that Susheela is a minor.

(i) Is the contract valid ? Give reasons.

(ii) State the exception to the rule regarding capacity to contract by a minor as stated in the Indian Contract Act, 1872. **CBSE 2020**

Ans. (i) As per the Indian Contract Act, 1872, a contract entered into with a minor is void. In the given situation, the contract is void as Susheela is a minor. The fact that she looked older cannot validate the contract.

(ii) As per the Indian Contract Act, 1872, a contract entered into with a minor is void in all cases except where the contract has been entered into for the benefit of the minor. For example, a contract to provide essential supplies to the minor till he attains the age of 18.

3. Briefly discuss the case of Durga Prasad Vs. Baldeo on consideration.

Ans. In Durga Prasad Vs. Baldeo (1880), the plaintiff constructed some shops at the request of the District Collector in a town. The constructed shops were given for rent for doing business to the defendant. The defendant, apart from the rent, promised to give 5% commission to the plaintiff on all articles sold through the shop in consideration of the huge amount spent by the plaintiff in the construction of the building.

The defendant failed to pay the commission and the plaintiff initiated action to recover the commission. The court rejected the action of the plaintiff on the ground that the construction of the shop was done at the desire of the District Collector and not on the desire of the defendant and hence, there was no consideration to give commission. Accordingly, there is no valid contract to pay commission to the plaintiff.

4. Ramesh agrees to give ₹ 5000 to his friend, Suresh, as a gift. However, Suresh insists that Ramesh should give the money as a loan, promising to repay ₹ 6000 in a year. Ramesh agrees and hands over the ₹ 5000. Can Suresh demand repayment of ₹ 6000 from Ramesh?

Ans. No, Suresh cannot demand repayment. Initially the agreement was a gift, which is a gratuitous transaction without consideration.

Later, Suresh proposed a loan with a promise to repay, but Ramesh's consent was already given for the gift. There is no valid consideration to support the loan agreement. Suresh cannot enforce the promise to repay.

5. Gagan enters into a contract with Nikhil to murder his wife, Preity for a sum of ₹ 5 lakhs. Gagan agrees to pay the amount to Nikhil in return for the murder. Any contract made for an unlawful consideration is void in law.

(i) Is it a valid contract?

(ii) What is the consideration in the contract act?

Ans. (i) In the present case, the contract is void as the consideration of the same i.e. murdering of Preity is unlawful. No obligations arise out of a void contract. Section 24 of the Indian Contract Act, 1872 states that a contract whose object or consideration is unlawful is void.

(ii) Anything of value promised by one party to the other when making a contract can be treated as 'consideration'.

6. Briefly discuss consent as an important element of a contract.

Ans. Consent is an important criterion while entering into a contract. According to Section 13, when two persons agree on the same thing in the same sense (consensus ad idem), it is termed as consent.

Consent should be free and not caused by coercion, undue influence, misrepresentation, fraud or mistake. If consent is obtained by the influence of any one of the above-mentioned factors, the consent so obtained is not free. It becomes voidable (the enforcement of the contract can be avoided) for the person whose consent is not free. It means that the person whose consent was not freely given has the option to repudiate/cancel the contract.

7. Saurabh took a comprehensive fire insurance for protecting his shop and godown against fire. AIG Insurance Company insured his shop and godown. The term of insurance stated that the claim amount will be paid only when the insured properties are destroyed by fire within the period of insurance cover. Identify the type of contract entered between Saurabh and AIG Insurance Company. State any two characteristics of this type of contract.

Ans. Fire insurance is a type of contingent contract entered between Saurabh and AIG Insurance Company. A contingent contract is an agreement between two or more parties to do or not to do something if a collateral event happens or doesn't happen.

The two characteristics of a contingent contract are

(i) It can only be enforced after a future event occurs.

(ii) The contract is depend upon an uncertain event, and the action required is based on the occurrence of that event. The event must be unpredictable and not in the control of any party.

8. Vidya Bharti Appliances Ltd. was a manufacturer of laptops. It claimed to have developed a laptop which did not need to be charged for 7 days, if it was charged overnight as per directions. It put up an advertisement offering a reward of ₹ 10,000 to anyone who had a contrary experience after charging the laptop in the prescribed manner.

Mr. Ramakant bought the said laptop, and charged it as per directions, but the battery did not last for even 2 days. He claimed the reward offered by Vidya Bharti Appliances Ltd., but the company refused to pay the amount, saying that no offer was made to Mr. Ramakant. Mr. Ramakant sued the company for the amount.

Giving valid reasons if Mr. Ramakant is entitled to compensation.

Ans. Mr. Ramakant will not be entitled to compensation as the offer was a buff.

There was no intention of the manufacturer to enter into a legal relationship with anyone through the advertisement, and the advertisement was put up only to boost the marketing of the laptop. The advertisement was not an offer as it was not made to any particular person and an offer cannot be made to the public at large or to the whole world. The acceptance by the offeree had not been communicated, and so there was no binding contract.

9. A contract can be discharged by many ways, how can a contract be discharged by impossibility of performance, briefly explain with the relevant provision .

Ans. Performance of a contract can become impossible with or without the knowledge of the parties to the contract. A contract may later become unenforceable under the law due to impossibility of performance.

It can became impossible to perform the contract subsequently after the parties have entered into the contract, that is known as supervening impossibility [Section 56 ICA].

It can take place by the following ways

(i) Destruction of the subject matter

(ii) Death or incapacity

(iii) Nin-existence of state of things having an effect directly or indirectly on the contract

(iv) Outbreak of war

(v) Change or amendments in law.

10. Rahul and Ravi, college students and friends, start a music club together. Ravi promises to pay Rahul 20 per cent of the club's profits for his guitar skills. The club becomes successful, but Ravi stops paying Rahul. Rahul sues Ravi, calming a valid contract based on Durga Prasad. vs. Baldeo. Analyse if there is a valid consideration and its significance on forming a legally enforceable contract. CBSE 2024 C

Ans. In this scenario, there is a valid consideration. Ravi's promise to pay Rahul 20 per cent of the club's profits provides something of value in exchange for Rahul's guitar skills.

This consideration is significant in forming a legally enforceable contract. As per the Indian Contract Act, 1872, consideration is one of the essential elements of a valid contract. Rahul can sue Ravi for breach of contract, and the court may order Ravi to pay the promised share of profits.

Long Answer Type Questions

1. All agreements per se are not contracts. They must meet certain criteria to qualify as such. Elaborate. CBSE 2025

Ans. According to the Indian Contract Act, 1872, an agreement becomes a contract only when it meets certain legal criteria. An agreement is formed when one party makes an offer and another accepts it. However, for an agreement to be legally enforceable as a contract, it must fulfill the following essential conditions

(i) **Competent Parties** Both parties must be legally capable of entering into a contract.

(ii) **Lawful Consideration and Object** The agreement must involve a valid exchange that is not illegal.

(iii) **Free Consent** Both parties must agree without coercion, fraud, or misrepresentation.

(iv) **Not Expressly Declared Void** Certain agreements, like those against public policy, are unenforceable.

2. (a) What is the contract?

(b) Explain the four types of contracts based on the validity of contracts. CBSE SQP 2024

Ans. (a) As per section 2(h) of the Indian Contract Act, 1872 an agreement enforceable by law is a contract.

(b) The four types of contract based on the validity and enforceability of contracts are

(i) **Valid Contract** According to the Indian Contract Act 1872, an agreement that is enforceable by law is a contract [Section 2(h)]. A valid contract is a legally binding agreement between two or more parties that is enforceable by law. This implies, all agreements per se are not contracts.

(ii) **Void Contract** A contract which ceases to be enforceable by law becomes void.

(iii) **Voidable Contract** It is a contract that may either be affirmed or rejected at the option of one of the parties to the contract on grounds of coercion, undue influence, fraud or misrepresentation.

(iv) **Illegal Contract** According to section 10 of ICA, Contract must be made for a lawful consideration and lawful object. If either the consideration or the object is an action or omission prohibited by law, it results in an illegal contract.

3. Ramesh contracts with Sunil to supply 1000 kg of wheat on Ist May. Due to unforseen circumstances, Ramesh is unable to supply the wheat. Sunil agrees to accept 800 kg of wheat on 10th May as a full and final settlement. Ramesh supplies the 800 kg of wheat. Is the contract discharged?

Ans. Yes, the cotnract is discharged by mutual agreement (novation). Initially, Ramesh was unable to perform his obligation, which would have led to a breach of contract. However, Sunil agreed to accept a reduced quantity of wheat as a full and final settlement, which discharged the original contract. By accepting the reduced quantity, Sunil waived his rights to claim the original quantity or damages. The contract is not discharged and Ramesh is no longer liable for the original obligation.

SELF ASSESSMENT TEST

Objective Types Questions

1. Anand enters into a contract with Raman to supply 5 bags of cement for ₹2000. He delivers 5 bags of cement on the decided date and receives ₹ 2000 from Raman as consideration, leading to discharge of the contract. What was the mode of discharge of contract in the above situation?
   (a) Discharge by Breach of Contract (b) Discharge by Performance
   (c) Discharge by Operation of Law (d) Discharge by Lapse of Time.
2. This form of discharge of contract takes place when one of the parties fails or refuses to perform their part of the promise. In this event, the party that suffers due to the other party's non performance of promise becomes entitled to monetary compensation. What is the name given to the monetary compensation for the loss suffered by the injured party in this form of discharge?
   (a) Remuneration (b) Damages (c) Discharges (d) Consideration
3. As per the Indian Contract Act, it is a contract where one person promises to pay money to other person on the happening of an uncertain future event and the other person promises to pay on the non-happening of the event.
   (a) Conditional Contract (b) Contingent Contract (c) Wagering Agreement (d) All of these
4. A contract can become impossible to perform .... entering into a contract.
   (a) before (b) after (c) Either (a) or (b) (d) None of these

Very Short Answer Type Questions

5. What are general and specific offers under Indian Contract Act?
6. Ramesh contracts with Sunil to sell his motorcycle for ₹ 15,000. The contract specifies that the payment will be made in two installments, ₹ 7000 on 1st September and ₹ 8000 on 20th September. On September 1st, Ramesh hands over the motorcycle to Sunil and receives ₹ 7000. On 20th September, Sunil pays Ramesh ₹ 8000. Has the contract discharged by performance? Why or why not?

Short Answer Type Questions

7. Rohan agrees to sell his old guitar to his friend, Aryan, for ₹ 5000. They shake hands on it, but Rohan says, "Just between friends, no legal fuss, okay?" Aryan pays Rohan ₹ 5000 but later Rohan refuses to hand over the guitar, saying it was just a friendly promise. Is there an intention to create a legal relation in this contract? Would Aryan have a valid claim against Rohan?
8. Explain any two methods by which a contract can be discharged.
9. Offer and acceptance, backed by legal enforcement result in a contract. Discuss.

Long Answer Type Question

10. What do you understand by 'Damages'? Discuss the objective of grating damages.
11. Rahul contracts with Kumar to supply 1000 kg of mangoes on May 1st. However, due to a sudden nationwide ban on mango exports, Rahul is unable to supply the mangoes. Kumar sues Rahul for breach of contract. Can Rahul claim impossibility of performance due to the change in circumstances? Would Kumar's claim for damages succeed? Consider the situation and decide.

07

CHAPTER

In law, tort is defined as a civil wrong or a wrongful act done to a person, either intentionally or accidentallly, that results in injury or harm to him. In turn, the person has option to civil remedies for damages or a court order or injunction.

▼ **YOUR STUDY GOALS**

7.1 Meaning of Tort
7.2 Kinds of Wrongful Acts
7.3 Fault-based and No-fault Liability
7.4 Kinds of Harms

▼ **YOUR PRACTICE GOAL**

- Objective Type Questions (30 Qs ; MCQs, A-R, Matching, Statements)
- Subjective Questions (11 VSAs, 9 SAs, 5 LAs)

Law of Torts

7.1 Meaning of Tort

- Tort is derived from the Latin word **tortum**, which means **twisted** or **crooked.** There are three fundamental elements of a tort
  - wrongful act
  - damage
  - remedy
- The remedy for tort is often in the nature of **unliquidated damages** and the purpose of damages under law of torts are act essentially compensatory and seek to place the defendent in the position that he would have been had the wrongful act not been performed.
- Unliquidated damages can be defined as the **sum of money that cannot be foreseen** or assessed by a fixed or predecided formula. Damages may be categorised as unliquidated when the amount of damages is unidentifiable or subject to an unforeseen event due to which the amount could not be calculated.

Definition of Tort

- According to **Sir John Salmond,** an English legal scholar, "Tort is a civil wrong for which the remedy is a common law action for unliquidated damages, and which is not exclusively a breach of contract, a breach of trust or other merely equitable obligation".
- According to **M.C. Setalvad**, the first Attorney General of India, "Law of torts is an instrument for making people adhere to standards of reasonable behaviour and respect the rights and interests of one another".
- It should be clearly specified that tort is a civil wrong as distinguished from criminal wrong.

- In a criminal case, the state initiates legal proceedings in a criminal court on behalf of the victim and is punished if found guilty by the court.
- A civil case like tort is imitated in a civil court where the person aggrieved or his representatives or survivors prosecute the wrong-doer usually for compensation in the form of monetary damages and also at times for other relief or **injunction**[1]
- Tort cases aim at compensating the victim while criminal lawsuits often result in punishments, for example, prison sentences.

Difference between Tort and Breach of Contract

Tort	Breach of Contract
A tort is a civil wrong in which the remedy is **action for damages**.	Breach of contract is a breach of a promise in which the primary remedy is **performance of the contract**.
Damages are always **unliquidated** in a tort.	In breach of contract, the damages are **liquidated**[2].
In tort, motive may be **taken into consideration.**	In breach of contract, the motive is **irrelevant.**
In tort, **duty** is bound **towards** the **persons generally.**	In breach of contract, the duty is bound towards a **specific person or persons.**
In tort, the damages may be **compensatory** or even **exemplary damages** may also be awarded.	In breach of contract, nature of damages is **compensatory.**

Sources of Law of Torts

- Law of tort seeks to provide **restorative justice**[3] as it does not aim to punish the wrongdoer, rather it aims to help the aggrieved person to reach to the position at which he/she was, before the cause of action arose.
- The law of torts did not develop from a statute or an act passed by the Parliament. It is the result of **past judicial decisions** which are based on case decisions in English courts as well as in courts of other countries that follows the **common law system**, such as India, Canada, Australia or the United States of America.
- In India as well as in other jurisdictions both criminal law and contract law are based on **statutes**[4]. For example, the Indian Penal Code (Bhartiya Nayaya Sanhita) and the Indian Contract Act respectively. However, there is **no single statute or a group of statutes that comprehensively deal with tort law** as a separate area of law.
- However, in many jurisdictions, including in India, there is a move to enact statutes concerning tortious wrongs which were earlier governed only by case laws.

  For example, in India, **automobile accidents** as well as harm caused to **consumers of goods and services** are covered by the **Motor Vehicle Act of 1988** (as amended) and the **Consumer Protection Act of 1986** (as amended), respectively.

7.2 Kinds of Wrongful Acts

In tort cases, the victim or the plaintiff (complainant) claims that the defendant or the wrong-doer has conducted a wrongful act or is liable for injury incurred by the plaintiff.

Generally, there are three kinds of wrongs in tort law. The wrongful act can occur

- either intentionally,
- negligently on part of the wrong-doer or
- the defendant is strictly liable for the wrongful act.

1 **Injunctions** are court orders that, for example, may prohibit the wrong-doer from harming the victim or prevent the former from trespassing the latter's property.

2 **Liquidated** are those damages which are predecided by the parties doing agreement.

3 **Restorative Justice** It is a kind of justice provided to the aggrieved person to restore his/her original position before the wrong happened.

4 **Statutes** It means a written law passed by a legislative body.

A tort can be intentional or accidental. It includes wrongful acts such as

- battery and assault (physical or mental injury to the claimant)
- nuisance (an act which is harmful or offensive to the public or an individual)
- defamation (where claimant's reputation is injured)
- property damage
- trespass (to claimant's land or property)
- negligence (careless behaviour) and others.

Intentional Tort

- An intentional tort requires the claimant to show that the defendant caused the **injury on purpose.**
- The claimant must also show that he or she suffered a particular consequence or injury, and the defendant's actions caused that consequence or injury.
- Different intentional torts deal in different consequences and intents. On the basis of the contexts and situations, there are various kinds of intentional torts. These include assault, battery, false imprisonment, unlawful harassment, invasion of privacy and so on.

The kinds of intentional torts are discussed below

Battery and Assault

- The tort of **battery** occurs when the defendant shows an intentional and direct application of **physical force** of the claimant with the intent to cause harm or offense.
- For the occurrence of tort of battery, both **intent** and **causation** are required.
- It is not necessary that the act of touching have to be done always with the defendant's hands, it could be anything touching the plaintiff such as throwing hot water at someone.
- The tort of **assault** occurs when the defendant intends to **cause reasonable apprehension** (feeling of anxiety or fear) in the mind of a claimant about harmful or offensive touching; and when this causes the claimant to suffer a reasonable apprehension of a harm.

  For example, if the defendant throws an iron ball at the claimant and misses his head as the claimant moves his head away from the direction of the iron ball, this will be regarded as assault.

  For example, if the defendant points an unloaded gun at the claimant who does not know that it is unloaded and he thinks he is about to get shot, this will be regarded as assault, which can take place without battery.

False Imprisonment

- The intentional tort of false imprisonment is satisfied whenever there is an **intent to confine or restrain** the claimant unlawfully in a bounded area, and when the claimant come to know about this confinement in a bounded area unlawfully.
- This leads to the total restraint on liberty of a person. For example, the defendant intentionally locks the claimant in the classroom **without having the legal authority** to do so, and the claimant knows he is trapped.
- Sometimes courts allow the actual harm to replace the awareness of the claimant about the imprisonment. This means that even if the claimant is unaware that he is trapped but suffers injury, the tort of false imprisonment is satisfied. However, the **claimant should not be trapped willingly.**

Trespass to Land

- The tort of **trespass to land** occurs when the defendant has the intent to interfere with the possession of land belonging to the claimant.
- This is done when the defendant physically invade the property of the claimant without the approval or consent of the claimant.
- The invasion can happen with objects or by people. It includes invasion of some area of air above the land and some area below the land. For example, if the defendant litter the claimant's land or create a drainage outlet below the land of the claimant, then it will be regarded as trespass to land.

Trespass to Chattels

- The tort of trespass to chattels[5] occur when the defendant has the intent to and interfere with the lawful possession of goods belonging to the claimant.
- This is done when the defendant uses or interfere with a chattel (moveable personal property), which was possessed by the claimant and **causes significant dispossession,** deprivation of use, or damage to condition, quality, or value of the chattel, or some other harm to claimant's legally secured interest.

  For example, if the defendant paints the car of claimant that was parked on the side of the street, without the consent of the claimant while the claimant was away, this will be regarded as trespass to chattels.

Conversion

- The tort of **conversion** is somewhat related with the tort of trespass to chattels.
- Conversion is defined as an **act of willful interference** with any chattel, **without lawful justification,** through which the other is deprived of the use and possession of it.
- It occurs when the defendant intentionally uses or interferes with the chattel of the claimant in such a serious way that it becomes fair to ask for compensation or money payment for the total original value of the chattel.
- In other words, the defendant is forced to buy the chattel for a purchase price based on the original value.
- The remedy in conversion is forced sale. Conversion is applicable in many situations including where the chattel is **taken, transferred to someone else, changed, misused or damaged.**

Unlawful Harassment and Intentional Infliction of Emotional Distress

- The defendant may be liable for any act of **intentional physical harm** done to the victim even when **no battery or assault is involved.** For example, if the defendant lies to the claimant that his son met with a road accident, which causes nervous shock to the claimant resulting in illness, then it will be regarded as tort of unlawful harassment.
- **Sexual harassment may also be regarded as tort of unlawful harassment.** For example, if one follows another person, sends unwanted messages or phone calls; although there is no violence or threat of violence involved, then this act will be regarded as a tort of harassment.

Defamation

- Defamation can be defined as any intentional false communication, either written or spoken, that harms a person's reputation and decreases the respect, regard or confidence of that person in the view of society.
- **Defamation can be both a tort as well as a crime**
  - **Criminal Defamation** is an act of defaming a person by **committing a crime or offence.** For criminal defamation, the liable person can be prosecuted. It is studied in IPC (BNS) as a criminal act.
  - **Civil Defamation** It involves no criminal offence, but the **claimant can sue the wrongdoer for compensation.** It is studied under law of torts as a civil wrong.

---

5 **Chattels** It means an item of property other than freehold land, including tangible goods.

- According to English law, actions for defamation are divided into **libel** and **slander**.
  - **Libel** refers to causing defamation in a **permanent form**, i.e. writing or pictures. It is recognised as an offence under the English Criminal Law.
  - **Slander** refers to causing defamation in a transient form such as **spoken words or gestures.** Slander is actionable under law of torts in the English law.

Negligence

- Negligence is defined as the **breach (violation) of the duty to take care,** which results in damages. It means the wrong-doer or the defendant has been **careless** in a way that harms the interest of the victim or the claimant.

  For example, when the defendant carries out an act of constructing something on her premises, she owes a duty of care towards the claimant (and **anyone in proximity**).
- The standard of duty of care depends on whether the claimant was on the site or in the neighbourhood, as well as whether the claimant was a lawful visitor or a trespasser.
- Generally, the victim or the claimant must establish **three elements** against the defendant in a tort of negligence case. These are
  (i) The **defendant owes a duty of care** to the victim.
  (ii) There has been a **breach of duty of care** on part of the defendant.
  (iii) The **breach of the duty** to care **resulted** in the **harm suffered** by the claimant.

Element of Negligence

These elements are discussed below

Duty of Care

The duty of care is owed to those whom one can foresee reasonably as being potentially harmed.

For example, a landlord owes a duty of care with reasonable foresight to his tenants and should ensure that no hazardous substance like petrol is stored by him in the basement of the apartment where tenants stay.

Breach of Duty of Care

Once the **duty of care is proven** the claimant then must prove that the **duty of care was broken**, i.e. the defendant was unsuccessful in fulfilling the duty of care in accordance with the standard of reasonableness (reasonable conduct or reasonable foresight).

Harm to the Claimant

In the case of **Donoghue Vs. Stevenson**, the negligence on part of the manufacturer of the soft drink resulted in the illness or injury to the claimant.

Quick Test 1

1 What are the three fundamental elements of a tort?
2 In case of tort, what is the nature of damages?
3 When does the tort of trespass to land occur?
4 What are the three elements of negligence?

7.3 Fault-based and No-fault Liability

- In **fault-based liability,** the legal right of the claimant is violated due to a **mistake of the defendant,** and the defendant is liable to pay compensation.
- In **no-fault liability**, the defendant is liable to pay compensation even if the violation of the claimant's right is **not done by the defendant, but there is a violation of the claimant's right.** In other words, liability arising without any fault is a no-fault liability. It covers two kinds of liability that are **strict liability** and **absolute liability**.

Strict Liability

- It is a standard of liability under which a **person is legally responsible** for the consequences of an activity, even in the **absence of fault or criminal intent** from the defendant.
- Under the strict liability law, if the defendant possesses anything that is dangerous, as specified under the **ultra-hazardous activity**, then the defendant is **strictly liable** for any damages caused by such possession.
- The claimant does not have to establish any sort or level of blame to the defendant on the basis of intention or the degree of carelessness.
- The rule of strict liability evolved in the year 1868, in the case of **Rylands Vs. Fletcher** which took place in England.

Ultra-hazardous Activity

The general rule with respect to ultra-hazardous activity is that when the defendant carries out a hazardous activity on his/her building or involves in an activity that offers a danger of injury to the claimant or his/her property, the defendant could be responsible for the damage caused even if the defendant has exercised reasonable care to prevent the harm.

Exceptions to Strict Liability

- **Plaintiff's Own Fault** When the cause of the damage is an act or fault of the claimant himself, no remedy would be available to the plaintiff in that case.
- **Act of God** When the escape is caused directly by natural causes without any human intervention, then the defendant can use 'Act of God' as a defence.
- **Mutual Benefit** When the plaintiff expresses or gives consent to the presence of the source of damage or danger, and there is no negligence on the part of the defendant, then the defendant will not be held liable.
- **Act of Stranger** When the cause of harm is the act of a stranger or third party, then no remedy would be available to plaintiff. Here, it should be noted that the third party is neither the servant of the defendant, nor he is having any control over that person.
- **Statutory Act** When it is an act of the government or corporation, then no remedy would be available to plaintiff.

Absolute Liability

- In India, principle of Absolute Liability was introduced by the Supreme Court after the two instances of gas leaks from factories.
- The industry cannot plead that all safety measures were taken care of by them and that there was no negligence on their part. **They will not be allowed any exceptions neither can they take up any defence like that of 'Act of God' or 'Act of Stranger'.**
- The basic principles of absolute liability that emerged from the above cases are
  - Enterprise (commercial objective)
  - Hazardous or inherently dangerous activity
  - Escape is not necessary

Differences between Strict Liability and Absolute Liability

Basis For Comparison	Strict Liability	Absolute Liability
Meaning	Strict liability implies the legal responsibility of a person for compensating the injured or aggrieved[6], even when he or she was not at fault or negligent.	Absolute liability arises from inherently hazardous activities like keeping dangerous animals or using explosives.
Talks about	It is applicable to persons.	It is applicable to enterprises, i.e., commercial undertakings.
Escape	In strict liability, the escape of hazardous or dangerous components from the premises of the owner is necessary.	Escape is not necessary in absolute liability.
Exceptions	In the case of strict liability, the defendant has got certain exceptions that he/she can use to prevent himself from the liability.	No exceptions are provided in the case of absolute liability to the defendant. This means that, if any person faces damages due to the hazardous element, then the defendant would be absolutely liable for the same.
Payment of compensation	The compensation is as per the nature and quantum[7] of damages incurred in case of strict liability.	In absolute liability, the quantum of damages relies on the magnitude and financial capability of the organisation.

7.4 Kinds of Harms

Some examples of the ways in which the claimant may suffer injuries are

- **Property Interests in Land** The claimant may also suffer harm by the damage caused due to carelessness or negligence of the defendant. When the defendant interferes with the claimant's right to enjoy his/her land, the defendant commits the tort of nuisance.

  The law of tort protects the claimant's interests in his/her landed property by preventing intentional intrusions or trespass of the property by the defendant or the wrong-doer.

  Other Types of Property The damage to the property may occur due to carelessness or negligence. Law of tort prohibits taking away of tangible property deliberately, which amounts to the tort of 'conversion'.
- **Bodily Injury** Harm may be caused by negligence as well as any breach of statutory duty like, traffic laws, health laws and so on. Mental distress is an element in bodily injury which raises any compensation to the victim.

  Law of tort protects the claimant against any harm to his/her interests of bodily integrity. Tort of battery and assault applies to any intentional harm caused to the body.
- **Economic Interests** Injury caused by both **intentional act as well as negligence** can cause economic harm to the claimant. The economic interests are also protected by the law of tort to a lesser extent.

Quick Test 2

1. What is fault-based liability?
2. What are the three basic principles regarding strict liability?
3. Which case led to the introduction of principle of absolute liability?
4. When was the defendant use Act of God as a defence?

6 **Aggrieved** It means feeling resentment at having been unfairly treated.
7 **Quantum** It means an amount of money legally payable in damages.

REFERENCE CASES

Duty of Care

The duty of care principle can be explained by citing landmark case. In **Donoghue Vs. Stevenson,** a case decided in England, the plaintiff. Donoghue drank a soft drink (ginger beer) manufactured by the defendant Stevenson. The **drink had a decomposed snail** in the bottle that made the claimant ill. The court held that the **manufacturer owed duty of care** to those who are reasonably foreseeable to be affected by the product.

"In a case like the present, where the goods of the defenders are widely distributed throughout Scotland, it would seem little short of outrageous to make them responsible to members of the public for the condition of the contents of every bottle which issues from their works. It is obvious that, if such responsibility attached to the defenders, they might be called on to meet claims of damages which they could not possibly investigate or answer."

Harm to the Claimant

In **MacPherson Vs. Buick Motor Co** (1914) a famous American case, the Plaintiff bought a car from a retail dealer, and was injured when a **defective wheel** collapsed. The plaintiff sued the defendant, Buick Motor Co., the original manufacturer of the car, for negligence. The **wheel was not made by the defendant**; it was bought from another manufacturer. The defendant, however, failed to inspect the wheel.

It was **observed by the court that the defendant was responsible** for the finished product. It was not at liberty to put the finished product on the market without subjecting the components to tests. In order to establish duty of care in relation to ultimate purchasers, it must be proved that

- nature of the product must be such that it is **likely to place life and limb in danger if negligently made**. This knowledge of danger must be probable, not merely possible.
- there must be knowledge that **in the usual courses of events, the danger will be shared by people other than the buyer**. This may be inferred from the nature of the transaction and the proximity or remoteness of the relation.

Strict Liability

The rule of strict liability evolved in the year 1868, in the case of **Rylands Vs. Fletcher** which tool place in England. Rylands and Fletcher were neighbours. Rylands owned a mill for whose energy requirement he **constructed a water reservoir on his land**. The work of construction was done by an independent contractor who was negligent in his work. Due to this negligence, the water escaped and leaked into Fletcher's mines, causing **heavy losses** to him. Fletcher sued Rylands for the damage caused.

Rylands took the defence that the construction work was carried out by an agency and was inspected by an engineer. It was contended that Rylands was not a part of the work and was also not informed about the security regarding the construction. The **court held** that it does not matter what care the appellant took but he was **responsible** for the damage as he **brought such an article to his premises which could be dangerous if it escapes**. Rylands was thus held liable for the loss incurred by Fletcher and had to pay compensation.

In the above case, three basic principles regarding strict liability were established.

- **Dangerous Thing** non-natural use of the land
- **Escape** the escape of water from Rylands land
- **Liability** as the thing escaped, it caused damage

If someone brings on his land something that is dangerous and **it escapes and because of this escape damage is caused**, the person is strictly liable.

Absolute Liability

The first case was the infamous **Bhopal gas leak disaster of 1984** where a factory of the Union Carbide Corporation located in Bhopal had a major leakage of the gas **methyl isocyanate** that killed 2260 and injured around 6,00,000 people.

- In the second incident of 1985 in Delhi, a factory of the Shri Ram Foods and Fertiliser Industries leaked oleum gas that killed one person that had few other hospitalised and created huge panic among the residents.
- The then Chief Justice of India P.N. Bhagwati, in the famous 1987 case of M.C. Mehta Vs. Shri Ram Foods and Fertiliser Industries, held:
- "We are of the view that an enterprise, which is engaged in a hazardous or inherently dangerous industry, which poses a potential threat to the health and safety of the persons working in the factory and residing in the surrounding areas owes an absolute and non-delegable duty to the community to ensure that no harm results to any one on account of hazardous or inherently dangerous activity in which it is engaged must be conducted with the highest standards of safety and if any harm is done on account of such activity, the enterprise must be absolutely liable to compensate for such harm and it should be no answer to the enterprise to say that it had taken all reasonable care and that the harm occurred without any negligence on its part".
- It an industry/enterprise is engaged in some inherently dangerous activity from which it is deriving commercial gain and that activity is capable of causing catastrophic damage then the industry officials are absolutely liable to pay compensation to the aggrieved parties.

Mind Map

LAW OF TORTS

1 Meaning of Tort

- **Derived from** Latin word "Tortum" = Twisted or Crooked.

Definition

- A civil wrong, not a criminal offense.
- Involves a breach of duty resulting in harm or injury.

Elements

- Wrongful act.
- Damage (harm caused).
- Remedy (compensation in unliquidated damages).

2 Types of Wrongful Acts

Intentional Acts

- **For examples** Assault, battery, defamation, trespass.

Negligent Acts

- Failure to act responsibly, resulting in harm.

Strict Liability Acts

- Liability without proving intent or negligence.

3 Remedies in Tort

Damages

- Unliquidated and compensatory.
- Exemplary in some cases.

Injunctions

- Court orders to prevent or stop wrongful acts.

4 Sources of Tort Law

Common Law

- Originated in judicial decisions from courts.

Statutory Laws

- **For examples** Motor Vehicles Act, Consumer Protection Act.

5 Objectives of Tort Law

Compensation

- Restore the victim's position.

Deterrence

- Prevent future wrongful acts.

Safeguarding Interests

- Protect rights like property, bodily safety, etc.

6 Landmark Cases

Donoghue Vs. Stevenson (1932)

- Established duty of care.

Rylands Vs. Fletcher (1868)

- Developed strict liability principles.

M.C. Mehta Vs. Union of India (1987)

- Introduced absolute liability in India.

7 Differences

Tort Vs. Breach of Contract

- **Tort** Duty to society; unliquidated damages.
- **Contract** Duty to specific person; liquidated damages.

Strict Liability Vs. Absolute Liability

- **Strict** Some exceptions allowed.
- **Absolute** No exceptions; complete liability.

8 Summary of the Kinds of Harm

- **Property Interest in Land** Tort law protects the tangible property.
- **Bodily Injury** Tort law protects against any harm.

M.C. Setalvad

Sir John Salmond

CBSE TEXTBOOK FOLDER

1. Define what is the law of tort. What is the difference between tort law and criminal law?

Ans. The word 'tort' has been derived from the Latin word, 'tortum' which means 'twisted or crooked'. It essentially means a 'wrong'.

In law, tort is defined as a civil wrong or a wrongful act, of one, either intentional or accidental, that results in injury or harm to another, who in turn has recourse to civil remedies for damages or a court order or injunction.

The differences between tort law and criminal law are

Tort Law	Criminal law
It is a wrong against a private person (civil wrong).	It is a wrong against the society at large.
The suit is brought by the party whose interests were affected.	Proceedings are initiated by the state.
Compensation is generally awarded to the party whose interest was affected.	Focus is more on punishing the offender to prevent other people in the society from committing a crime.

2. What are the sources of tort law?

Ans. The law of torts did not develop from a statute or an act passed by the Parliament. It is the result of past judicial decisions which are based on case decisions in English courts as well as in courts of other countries that follows the common law system, such as India, Canada, Australia or the United States of America.

The law of torts includes both statutes and case laws and cannot be traced to a single source. However, in many jurisdictions, including in India, there is a move to enact statutes concerning tortious wrongs which were earlier governed only by case laws. For example, in India, automobile accidents as well as harm caused to consumers of goods and services are covered by the Motor Vehicle Act of 1988 (as amended) and the Consumer Protection Act of 1986 (as amended), respectively.

3. What is intentional tort? Explain atleast three different kinds of intentional tort.

Ans. An intentional tort requires the claimant to show that the defendant caused the injury on purpose.

Furthermore, the claimant must show that he/she suffered a particular consequence or injury and that the defendant's actions caused the consequence or injury.

Different intentional torts deal in different consequences and intents.

Three different kinds of intentional torts are

(i) **False Imprisonment** The intentional tort of false imprisonment is satisfied whenever there is an intent to unlawfully confine or restrain the claimant in a bounded area, and when this actually causes the claimant to be knowingly confined or restrained in a bounded area unlawfully. For example, the defendant intentionally locks the claimant in the classroom without having the legal authority to do so and the claimant knows he is trapped.

(ii) **Tort of Trespass to Land** The tort of trespass to land occurs when the defendant has the intent to physically attack real property of the claimant and does invade physically without the claimant's approval or consent. The invasion can happen with objects or by people and includes invasion of some area of air above the land and some area below the land. For example, the defendant may create a drainage outlet below the land of the claimant.

(iii) **Conversion** The tort of conversion is somewhat related with the tort of trespass to chattels. Conversion occurs when the defendant intentionally uses or intermeddles with the chattel of the claimant in such a serious way that it becomes fair to ask for compensation or money payment for the total prior value of the chattel.

In other words, the defendant is forced to buy the chattel for the claimant based on its original value. So, the remedy in conversion is forced sale. Conversion is applicable in many situations including where the chattel is wrongfully taken, transferred to someone else, changed, misused or damaged.

4. What is tort of negligence and how does duty of care relate with negligence?

Or **What constitutes tort of negligence?** **CBSE 2016**

Ans. The basic understanding of negligence is that the wrong-doer or the defendant has been careless in a way that harms the interest of the victim or the claimant. For example, when the defendant carries out an act of constructing something on her premises, she owes a duty of care towards the claimant. The standard of duty of care depends on whether the claimant was on the site or in the neighbourhood, as well as whether the claimant was a lawful visitor or a trespasser.

Generally, the victim or the claimant must establish three elements against the defendant in a tort of negligence case

- The defendant owes a duty of care to the victim.
- There has been a breach of duty of care on part of the defendant.
- The breach of the duty to care resulted in the harm suffered by the claimant.

In a 1932 English case of Donoghue Vs. Stevenson, the claimant Donoghue drank a soft drink manufactured by the defendant Stevenson. The drink had a decomposed snail in the bottle that made the claimant ill. The court held that the manufacturer owed duty of care to those who are 'reasonably foreseeable' to be affected by the product. So, the duty of care is owed to those whom one can reasonably foresee as being potentially harmed.

5. What is the strict liability principle? Give one example.

Ans. Strict liability torts do not care about the intention or carelessness of the defendant when the defendant caused the injury. The claimant does not have to establish any sort of or level of blame attributable to the defendant based on the intention or the degree of carelessness.

Strict liability is available in a very limited context. For example, where the defendant's animals may cause an injury to the claimant or where the defendant is involved in an unusually hazardous activity like blasting dynamite.

Thus, in the first case, if the defendant possesses an animal with a known and unusual dangerous tendency, say a dog that bites, the defendant is strictly liable for the harm resulting from the dangerous tendency of the dog.

However, in the case of the defendant possessing a bull that harms, the claimant is not strictly liable as the act of the bull is not considered to be unusual, rather a normal dangerous tendency.

6. Some basic principles regarding strict liability were established in Ryland Vs. Fletcher. Discuss these principles.

Ans. Three basic principles regarding strict liability that were established in Ryland Vs. Fletcher were

(i) **Dangerous Thing** Non-natural use of the land.

(ii) **Escape** The escape of water from Rylands land.

(iii) **Liability** As the thing escaped, it caused damage.

It means if someone bring a dangerous thing on his land, and it escapes, and because of this escape damage is caused, then the person is strictly liable.

7. There are certain exceptions to strict liability which are not available in a case of absolute liability. List these exceptions.

Ans. Exceptions to strict liability which are not available in a case of absolute liability are

(i) **Plaintiff's Own Fault** When the cause of the damage is an act or fault of the claimant himself, no remedy would be available to the plaintiff in that case.

(ii) **Act of God** When the escape is caused directly by natural causes without any human intervention, then the defendant can use 'Act of God' as a defence.

(iii) **Mutual Benefit** When the plaintiff expresses or gives consent to the presence of the source of damage or danger, and there is no negligence on the part of the defendant, then the defendant will not be held liable.

(iv) **Act of Stranger** When the cause of harm is the act of a stranger or third party, then no remedy would be available to plaintiff. Here, it should be noted that the third party is neither the servant of the defendant, nor he is having any control over that person.

(v) **Statutory Act** When it is an act of the government or corporation, then no remedy would be available to plaintiff.

8. What are the objectives behind having tort law?

Ans. The objectives behind having tort law are

(i) **Compensation** Compensation is one of the most fundamental ideas behind tort law. The whole law of torts focuses on compensating the victim or the grieved party through various available remedies.

(ii) **Safeguarding Interests** Another primary objective that the law of torts serves is safeguarding or protecting an individual's interest in his integrity or his property.

(iii) **Deterrence** Deterrence theory about law says that the threat or the fear imposed by law will demotivate and discourage people from committing certain acts which are tagged as unlawful. This eventually prevents the further commission of unlawful acts. Although the law of torts doesn't penalise the guilty, the unliquidated nature of the damages or the compensation which she/he might have to pay acts as a deterrence.

9. Discuss the main differences between strict liability and absolute liability, with the help of relevant case law.

Ans. The main differences between strict liability and absolute liability are as follows

Meaning	Strict liability implies the legal responsibility of a person for compensating the injured or aggrieved, even when he or she was not at fault or negligent.	Absolute liability arises from inherently hazardous activities like keeping dangerous animals or using explosives.
Talks about	It is applicable to persons.	It is applicable to enterprises, i.e., commercial undertakings.
Escape	In strict liability, the escape of hazardous or dangerous components from the premises of the owner is necessary.	Escape is not necessary in absolute liability.
Exceptions	In the case of strict liability, the defendant has got certain exceptions that he/she can use to prevent himself from the liability.	No exceptions are provided in the case of absolute liability to the defendant. This means that, if any person faces damages due to the hazardous element, then the defendant would be absolutely liable for the same.
Payment of Compensation	The compensation is as per the nature and quantum of damages incurred in case of strict liability.	In absolute liability, the quantum of damages relies on the magnitude and financial capability of the organisation.
Case law	The rule of strict liability evolved in the year 1868, in the case of Rylands Vs. Fletcher which took place in England. In this case, three basic principles regarding strict liability were established which are dangerous thing, escape and liability.	It was introduced after two instances. First was the case of infamous Bhopal gas leak disaster of 1984. Second was the incident gas leakage in 1985 from a factory of the Shri Ram Foods and Fertiliser Industries in Delhi.

10. Explain the meaning of the following terms.

(i) Unliquidated damages **(ii) Defamation**

(iii) Conversion

Ans. (i) Unliquidated damages are awarded by the courts or arbitral tribunals after assessing the loss or injury caused to the party suffering from such breach of contract.

(ii) Defamation is a legal term that refers to any statement or communication that harms the reputation of a person, business, or organisation. It is a common type of tort law that protects individuals from false or harmful statements that can cause them to suffer economic or reputational damages.

(iii) Conversion is defined as an act of willful interference with any chattel, without lawful justification, through which the other is deprived of the use and possession of it.

Exam Pattern Questions

Objective Type Questions

Multiple Choice Questions (MCQs)

1. The word 'tort' has been derived from ....
   (a) Greek word 'torte' (b) Latin word 'tortum'
   (c) Greek word 'torque' (d) Spanish word 'torto'

2. **Mohan lends his rare antique vase to his friend Sumit for a week. Instead of returning it, Sumit accidentally drops and shatters the vase while showing it to another friend. When Mohan asks for his vase to be returned, Sumit apologises but says there is nothing he can do now that the vase is destroyed. Mohan decides to take legal action. Identify the legal claim he should pursue?** CBSE 2025
   (a) He should file a claim for trespass to chattels because Sumit damaged the vase while it was in his possession.
   (b) He should file a claim for trespass to chattels because Sumit used the vase without permission.
   (c) He should file a claim for conversion because Sumit destroyed the vase, depriving him of its use permanently.
   (d) He should file a claim for conversion because Sumit delayed returning the vase.

3. **Ajay was facing Chitra and Binny's back was towards Chitra, who was aiming a gun towards Binny. Ajay informed Binny of the same and even though Chitra did not fire a shot, Binny sues Chitra for tort of assault. Choose the best option.**
   (a) Chitra is not liable for assault as Binny had her back towards Chitra and she could not perceive the threat.
   (b) Chitra is not liable for assault as there was no imminent threat.
   (c) Chitra is liable as through Ajay an imminent threat was created in the mind of Binny.
   (d) Chitra is liable for battery.

4. **What do you understand by trespass to chattel?** CBSE SQP 2021
   (a) Damage to a person's personal movable property.
   (b) Damage to a person's personal immovable property.
   (c) Transfer of movable property to another person.
   (d) Physically invading another person's property.

5. **Ravi, at a local market, was involved in an argument with Mohan over a disputed transaction. In the heat of the argument, Ravi suddenly pushed Mohan forcefully, causing Mohan to stumble backward and fall. Mohan suffered a minor injury to his back as a result of the fall. Mohan believes that Ravi's action was an intentional physical contact that resulted in harm, and he is considering suing Ravi for the tort of battery. Which of the following statements is correct regarding the tort of battery in this case?** CBSE 2025
   (a) Ravi's action of pushing Mohan constitutes battery, as it was an intentional and direct application of physical force.
   (b) Ravi is not liable for battery because the physical contact was not severe enough to cause significant injury.
   (c) The tort of battery requires that the defendant's action must cause permanent injury, which is not the case here.
   (d) Ravi is not liable for battery because his action was a part of self-defense act, even if there was no immediate threat to his safety.

6. **The concept that an enterprise must be absolutely liable to compensate for the harm and there should be no answer that the enterprise had taken all reasonable care and that harm occurred without any negligence on its part, was developed in which of the following cases?**
   (a) M.C. Mehta Vs. Shri Ram Foods and Fertiliser Industries
   (b) Kartar Singh Vs. State of Punjab
   (c) Shanta Bai Vs. State of Bombay
   (d) Hussainara Khatoon Vs. Union of India

7. **Which among the following is not an outcome of the Oleum gas leak case?** CBSE SQP 2024
   (a) Deep pocket principle
   (b) Principle of absolute liability in tort
   (c) Policy for the abatement of pollution control.
   (d) Introduction of lead-full petrol in the country.

8. **A company, XYZ Corp. operates a large dam to generate electricity. Due to an unforeseen design flaw the dam suddenly bursts, causing massive flooding in a nearby town. The company had taken all standard safety measures and had no knowledge of the design flaw. The affected residents sue the company for damages, Which of the following is applicable in this instance ?** CBSE 2025
   (a) The company is not liable because the flaw was unforeseen.
   (b) The company is absolutely liable because the operation of the dam is inherently dangerous and the damages occurred regardless of the fault.
   (c) The company is liable only if it is proven that they ignored warning signs of the flaw.
   (d) The company is not liable because it followed all safety protocols.

9. Mr. Gupta owns an apartment building where several families reside as tenants. He decides to store a large quantity of petrol in the basement of the building for his personal use , for fueling his collection of vintage cars. A month later, a minor leakage from the petrol containers led to a fire outbreak in the basement. Although, the fire is quickly controlled and no one is hurt, the incident causes significant panic and stress among the residents. Is Mr. Gupta liable for causing harm to the tenants? CBSE SQP 2024

(a) Mr. Gupta is not liable since he did not intend to cause harm to his tenants.
(b) Mr. Gupta cannot be held liable because the fire did not result in any physical injuries.
(c) Mr. Gupta is liable for negligence as he breached his duty to care by storing a hazardous substance in the basement.
(d) Mr. Gupta is only liable if the tenants had previously warned him about the risk of fire.

10. Sheela bought a packet of potato chips from the brand Crispy. While eating the chips, she noticed a dead cockroach in the packet. Consequently, she fell sick and sued the company, Crispy, for compensation. Which of the following elements needs to be established by Sheela to win the claim against the company? CBSE SQP 2021

(a) Duty of care (b) Non-natural use of land
(c) Inherently dangerous activity (d) Intention

11. Yash owns a large farmland in the village where he decides to construct a reservoir to supply water for irrigation purposes. The construction work was done by an independent contractor who was negligent in his work. Due to this negligence, the water escaped and flooded Manya's neighbouring house and crops, this resulted in heavy losses to her. Under what legal principle is Yash liable for causing damage to Manya's property? CBSE SQP 2024

(a) Negligence (b) Strict liability
(c) Trespass to land (d) Nuisance

12. During a neighbourhood dispute, Kabir verbally threatens Veer with immediate physical harm while holding a hockey stick in a threatening manner. Kabir is within striking distance of Veer, causing Veer to fear for his safety. There is no physical contact between them during this incident.

In the above scenario, Kabir is guilty of committing which Tort? CBSE SQP 2024

(a) Tort of Battery (b) Invasion of Privacy
(c) Tort of Assault (d) Unlawful Harassment

13. Which of the following principles was developed by the Supreme Court after the Bhopal Gas Tragedy case?

(a) Strict Liability (b) Absolute Liability
(c) Both (a) and (b) (d) None of these

14. In automobile insurance, all drivers are required to pay insurance premiums, which are then used by insurance companies to compensate victims. In the above case, which object or purpose of tort law is being achieved?

(a) Deterrence so that the victims can be compensated for a wrongful act.
(b) Fair and Just response to compensate the victims and to satisfy the end of justice.
(c) Loss-spreading to a wider community to compensate the victims.
(d) There is no object or purpose of tort law that is being achieved.

15. Which of the following statements correctly describe features of Tort law?
I. Tort is a civil law subject.
II. Damages under tort law are always unliquidated.
III. Tort is an instrument for making people adhere to standards of reasonable behaviour.
IV. Tort is an intentional criminal activity.
V. Tort is a civil wrong. CBSE SQP 2024

Codes
(a) I, III, IV (b) II, III, V (c) II, IV, V (d) I, III, V

16. A few week after a surgery, Lata complained of excruciating pain in her abdomen. A scan revealed that a piece of gause had been left inside and had led to a severe infection. Which of the following is applicable in this instance? CBSE SQP 2023

(a) The surgeon is liable for unlawful harassment, this cannot be mistake.
(b) The surgeon is liable for negligence.
(c) The surgeon is not liable since nothing major has happened.
(d) The surgeon is liable for tort of assault.

17. 'X' painted the car of 'Y' that was parked on the side of the street, without the consent of 'Y' while he was away. What does the act of 'X' amounts to?

(a) Trespass to lant (b) Trespass to chattels
(c) Nuisance (d) Conversion

18. Raj was in his car when he was approached by a police officer who told him to move the vehicle. Raj did so, reversed his car and rolled it on the foot of the police officer. The officer forcefully told him to move the car off his foot at which point Raj swore at him and refused to move his vehicle and turned the engine off. Raj was convicted for assaulting a police officer in the execution of his duty.

Is he liable for battery or assault?

(a) He is not liable because there cannot be an assault in omitting to act and that driving on the foot of the officer was accidental, meaning that he had no interntion to cause that harm.
(b) He is not liable as the act neither amounted to an attempt nor a threat to commit battery which amounts to an actionable tort of assault.

(c) Raj's crime was not the refusal to move the car but that of having driven on the foot of the officer and decided not to cease the act, so he had committed the continual act of battery.
(d) He is neither liable for assault nor battery as he accidentally drove his car on the police officer's foot.

19. 'A', an industrialist, stored 1,000 litres of liquid ammonia in a tank in his premises for industrial use. There was a leakage from a tank due to which there was ammonia vapour in the surroundings. Many workers in other industries as well as his own industry and some members from the public suffered serious health hazards. Examine A's liability.

(a) 'A' may be liable for the injury sustained by his workers only and not others.
(b) 'A' is liable as he is responsible for the injury caused by the leakage of ammonia from his premises.
(c) 'A' is not liable because there was no fault on his part for the escape of the dangerous substance.
(d) 'A' is not liable because he did not expect a leakage from the tank.

20. Battery refers to the .... use of force against another without any lawful justification.

(a) intentional (b) unintentional
(c) mental (d) physical

21. In the case of ...., the negligence on part of the manufacturer of the soft drink resulted in the illness or injury to the claimant.

(a) Rylands Vs. Fletcher
(b) M.C. Mehta Vs. Union of India
(c) Donghua Vs. Stevenson
(d) MacPherson Vs. Buick Motor Co.

22. The tort of .... occurs when the defendant intentionally uses or intermeddles with the chattel of the claimant in such a serious way that it becomes fair to ask for compensation or money payment for the total prior value of the chattel.

(a) nuisance (b) conversion
(c) negligence (d) trespass

23. Match the following

Column I	Column II
A. Tort law ensures that the defendant compensates the victim for the wrongful act.	1. Sexual harassment
B. A form of unlawful harassment.	2. Trespass to land
C. Intent to physical invade the claimant's physical property.	3. Conversion
D. Defendant intentionally interferes with the chattel of the claimant.	4. Deterrence

Codes

	A	B	C	D		A	B	C	D
(a)	1	3	2	4	(b)	4	3	2	1
(c)	4	1	3	2	(d)	4	1	2	3

24. Match the following

Column I	Column II
A. False imprisonment	1. Donoghue vs. Stevenson
B. Absolute Liability	2. Intentional Tort
C. Harm to the claimant	3. Evolved in India
D. Remedy in conversion	4. Forced Sale

Codes

	A	B	C	D		A	B	C	D
(a)	2	3	1	4	(b)	2	1	3	4
(c)	1	3	4	2	(d)	4	3	1	2

25. Statement I The intentional tort of battery occurs when the defendant causes the touching of the claimant with the intent to cause harm or offense.

Statement II The act of touching doesn't necessarily have to be done with defendant's hands always. **CBSE SQP 2022**

Choose the correct option.

(a) Both Statement I and Statement II are correct.
(b) Both Statement I and Statement II are incorrect.
(c) Statement I is correct, but Statement II is incorrect.
(d) Statement I is incorrect, but Statement II is correct.

26. Which of the following statement is true regarding sexual harassment under tort law?

Statement I Sexual harassment is considered a form of battery under tort law.

Statement II Sexual harassment is only considered a form of intentional infliction on emotional distress under tort law.

Choose the correct option.

(a) Both Statement I and Statement II are correct.
(b) Both Statement I and Statement II are incorrect.
(c) Statement I is correct, but Statement II is incorrect.
(d) Statement I is incorrect, but Statement II is correct.

27. Which of the following statements is true regarding strict liability?

Statement I Strict liability applies to cases where the defendant has acted with negligence or intent.

Statement II Strict liability applies to cases where the defendant is responsible for harm caused, regardless of fault or intent.

Choose the correct option.

(a) Only Statement I is true.
(b) Only Statement II is true.
(c) Both Statement I and Statement II are true.
(d) Neither Statement I nor Statement II is true.

Assertion-Reason Questions

Directions (Q. Nos. 28-30) In the questions given below, there are two statements. Read the statements and choose the correct option.

Codes

(a) Both A and R are true and R is the correct explanation of A.
(b) Both A and R are true, but R is not the correct explanation of A.
(c) A is true, but R is false.
(d) A is false, but R is true.

28. Assertion (A) A contract lawyer would look up the Contract Act to look for rules to be applicable in a given fact situation. A tort lawyer would look for rules as developed by courts in similar cases.
Reason (R) Torts are mostly a common law subject.

29. Assertion (A) The basic understanding of negligence is that the wrongdoer or the defendant has been careless in a way that harms the interest of the victim or the claimant.
Reason (R) When the defendant carries out an act of constructing something on her premises, she owes a duty of care towards the claimant and that the standard of duty of care depends on whether the claimant was on the site or in the neighbourhood as well as whether the claimant was a lawful visitor or a trespasser.

30. Assertion (A) When the defendant carries out or keeps an unusually hazardous situation or activity on his/her building premises or involves in an activity that offers an inevitable danger of injury to the claimant or his/her property, the defendant could be responsible for the damage caused.
Reason (R) The liability arises due to the violation of the principle established under Donoghue Vs. Stevenson.
CBSE SQP 2022

Answers

1. (b) Latin word 'tortum'
2. (c) He should file a claim for conversion because Sumit destroyed the vase, depriving him of its use permanently.
3. (a) Chitra is not liable for assault as Binny had her back towards Chitra and she could not perceive the threat.
4. (a) Damage to a person's personal movable property.
5. (a) Ravi's action of pushing Mohan constitutes battery, as it was an intentional and direct application of physical force.
6. (a) M.C. Mehta Vs. Shri Ram Foods and Fertiliser Industries
7. (d) Introduction of lead-free petrol in the country.
8. (b) The company is absolutely liable because the operation of the dam is inherently dangerous and the damages occurred regardless of the fault.
9. (c) Mr. Gupta is liable for negligence as he breached his duty to care by storing a hazardous substance in the basement.
10. (a) Duty of care
11. (b) Strict liability
12. (c) Tort of assault
13. (b) Absolute Liability
14. (c) Loss-spreading to a wider community to compensate the victims.
15. (b) II, III, V
16. (b) The surgeon is liable for negligence.
17. (b) Trespass to chattels
18. (c) Raj's crime was not the refusal to move the car but that of having driven on the foot of the officer and decided not to cease the act, so he had committed the continual act of battery.
19. (b) 'A' is liable as he is responsible for the injury caused by the leakage of ammonia from his premises.
20. (a) intentional
21. (c) Donoghue Vs. Stevenson
22. (b) conversion
23. (d) 4 1 2 3
24. (d) 4 3 1 2
25. (a) Both Statement I and Statement II are correct.
26. (d) Statement I is incorrect, but Statement II is correct.
27. (b) Only Statement II is true.
28. (a) Both A and R are true and R is the correct explanation of A.
29. (a) Both A and R are true and R is the correct explanation of A.
30. (a) Both A and R are true and R is the correct explanation of A.

Subjective Questions

Very Short Answer Type Questions

1. List down any two essential features of tort.

Ans. The essential features of tort include the following

(i) Tort is a civil wrong wherein the legal right of a person is violated. Thus, there is a breach of duty towards him.

(ii) It is different from a breach of contract or a breach of trust.

2. How common law is a source of tort law?

Ans. Torts are mostly a common law subject in the sense that tort law or the rules of tort law developed not from a statute or an act passed by the Parliament, but from centuries of judicial decisions of countries following common law systems like UK, India and the US.

3. What do you understand by 'intentional tort'?

Ans. An intentional tort requires the claimant to show that the defendant caused the injury on purpose. Furthermore, the claimant must show that he/she suffered a particular consequence or injury and that the defendant's actions caused the consequence or injury.

4. Ram a store owner, falsely accuses Shyam, a customer, of shoplifting and detains him against his will. Shyam is embarrassed and suffers emotional distress. Which intentional tort has Ram committed, please explain.

Ans. Ram's actions constitute the intentional tort of false imprisonment, as he detained Shyam against his will without reasonable cause. This intentional tort violates Shyam's right to freedom and causes emotional distress.

5. What do you understand by 'assault'?

Ans. Assault refers to any intentional act which causes another person to be fearful of immediate harm. In other words, it should cause the plaintiff to fear that the plaintiff is about to be physically attacked and can make him the victim of the assault.

6. Rahul, a neighbour, enters Priya's property without permission to retrieve his stray football. Priya objects, but Rahul claims he had no other option. Is Rahul liable for trespass to land? Since he had intention only to retrieve his football.

Ans. Rahul's unauthorised entry onto Priya's property constitutes trespass to land, despite his intention to retrieve his football. Consent was not obtained and Priya's objection establishes a violation of her exclusive possession rights.

7. 'X' litters the property of 'Y'. What can he be liable for?

Ans. 'X', by littering the property of 'Y', causes an unlawful interference with Y's land. Thus, he can be held liable for trespass to land.

8. Ramesh, a pawnbroker, refuses to return a laptop to its rightful owner, Suresh, despite repeated demands Ramesh claims the laptop was pledged as security for a loan that remains unpaid. Which tort has Ramesh committed? Explain.

Ans. Ramesh's refusal to return the laptop constitutes conversion, as he has exercised unauthorised control over Suresh's property, depriving him of its use and possession. This is a tortious act, even if Ramesh claims a rightful lien or security interest.

9. Write a short note on negligence.

Ans. The term 'negligence' denotes carelessness. The basic understanding of negligence is that the wrongdoer or the defendant has been careless in a way that harms the interest of the victim or the claimant.

10. Mention the three elements required to prove to constitute a tort of negligence.

Ans. The three elements required to constitute a tort of negligence are

(i) The defendant owes a duty of care to the victim.

(ii) There has been a breach of duty of care on part of the defendant.

(iii) The breach of the duty to care resulted in the harm suffered by the claimant.

11. How does a tort protect a claimant's interest in property?

Ans. The law of tort protects the claimant's interests in her landed property by preventing intentional intrusions or trespass of the property by the defendant or the wrongdoer. The claimant may also suffer harm by the damage caused due to carelessness or negligence of the defendant.

Short Answer Type Questions

1. What are the differences between tort and breach of contract?

Ans. For answer refer to text under the heading Difference between Tort and Breach of Contract on page no. 104.

2. Pramod, an advocate in the Patna High Court specialises in commercial transactions. He is very hardworking and can go to any extent to bring justice to his clients. **CBSE 2022**

In one case, he is defending Mr. Raghav for breach of contract. Mr. Raghav offers him a contingency fee as an incentive to win. He also urges Pramod to meet the judge in person for managing a favourable decision. Pramod refuses to carry on with the case. Mr. Raghav moves a complaint against Pramod.

(i) **Is Pramod justified in refusing to carry on as a defense lawyer for Mr. Raghav? If yes why, if no why not?**

(ii) **Who has the authority to take an action against Pramod?**

(iii) **State the consequences faced by an advocate for breach of professional duties.**

Ans. (i) Yes, Pramod is justified in refusing to carry on as a defense lawyer for Mr. Raghav because the Bar Council of India rules encompass professional standards for lawyers. An advocate has a duty to act in a dignified manner, to respect the court, not to communicate with a judge in private and impair impartiality.

(ii) Bar Council of India has the authority to take an action against Pramod. It performs the regulatory function by prescribing standards of professional conduct and etiquette and by exercising disciplinary jurisdiction over the bar.

(iii) The consequences faced by an advocate for breach of professional duties are

- Reprimand the advocate.
- Suspend the advocate from practice for such period as it deems fit.
- Remove the name of an advocate from the state roll of advocates.

3. Suresh is an employee of a private firm and nurses a grudge against his colleague Atul. One morning at work, Suresh pulls back Atul's chair just as he is about to sit down causing Atul to be seriously injured. Identify the tort in this instance and explain its main features. **CBSE 2023**

Ans. Suresh's feeling of grudge against Atul with the intent to cause harm or offence is an example of tort of battery as both 'intent' and 'causation' are required and they are fulfilled here, Atul got seriously injured.

Tort of battery can take place without assault that means without causing reasonable apprehension to the claimant, there can be intent fulfilled and that intent is to cause harm or offense. In the given question there was an intent as well as, it was to cause harm (Atul got seriously injured). Hence, it is a tort of battery.

There are few main features of tort of battery

(i) intentional and direct application of physical force.

(ii) intent to cause harm or offense.

(iii) the act of touching doesn't necessarily have to be done with the defendant's hands always.

4. Discuss the tort relating to trespass to chattels.

Ans. The tort of trespass to chattel occurs when the defendant has the intent to and interfere with the lawful possession of goods belonging to the claimant. This is done when the defendant uses or interfere with a chattel (moveable personal property), which was possessed by the claimant, and causes significant dispossession, deprivation of use, or damage to condition, quality, or value of the chattel, or some other harm to claimant's legally secured interest.

For example, if the defendant paints the car of claimant that was parked on the side of the street, without the consent of the claimant while the claimant was away, this will be regarded as trespass to chattels.

5. What is 'defamation'? Distinguish between the two forms of defamation under Indian law. **CBSE 2024 C**

Ans. Defamation is the act of making false and damaging statements about someone, harming their reputation.

Under Indian law, there are two forms of defamation

(i) **Libel** Written or published defamation, such as articles, social media posts or books.

(ii) **Slander** Spoken defamation, such as verbal accusations or insults.

Both forms of defamation are punishable under the Indian Penal Code (IPC), with libel being considered more serious.

6. Explain with reasons whether the following act constitutes 'negligence'.
The employees of Care Cell Telecom opened a manhole in the street and in the evening left that manhole open. They covered it with canvas shelter, but left it unattended. Prince, 8 years an old boy, who was playing there, stumbled over it and fell into the manhole and sustained injuries. **CBSE 2016**

Ans. To constitute the tort of negligence, three important essentials are

(i) The defendant owes a duty of care to the victim,

(ii) There has been a breach of duty of care on part of the defendant, and

(iii) The breach of the duty to care resulted in the harm suffered by the claimant.

Since the Care Cell Telecom did owe a duty of care to Prince and there was a breach of that duty which caused harm to him, they will be held liable for the tort of negligence.

7. A company operates a nuclear power plant in a residential area. Despite safety measures, a radioactive leak occurs, causing harm to nearby residents.
Which rule will apply?

Ans. The rule of strict liability will apply, as the company is strictly liable for the harm caused by the radioactive leak, as operating a nuclear power plant is an ultra-hazardous activity. This means that the company is responsible for the damage, regardless of fault or intent. The general rule is that a person who engages in an ultra-hazardous activity is strictly liable for any harm resulting from it, even if they have taken all reasonable care to prevent it. This is because such activities pose an inherent risk of harm to others and the operator must bear the responsibility for any resulting damage.

8. In the famous 1987 case of M.C. Mehta Vs. Shri Ram Food and Fertiliser industries, Justice P.N. Bhagwati, developed a new principle evolving from the concept of strict liability. **SQP 2022**

(i) Identify the new principle.

(ii) Against whom is the principle applicable?

(iii) Under what conditions can this principle be applied?

Ans. (i) The new principle evolved from the strict liability is absolute liability in the aftermath of the two instances of gas leaks from factories.

(ii) The famous 1987 case of M.C. Mehta vs. Shri Ram Foods and Fertiliser Industries, held that the principle of absolute liability is applicable to those who engaged in a hazardous or inherently dangerous industry, which poses a potential threat to the health and safety of the persons working in the factory and residing in the surrounding.

(iii) Under the conditions of hazardous or inherently dangerous activity in which there is lack of highest standards of safety and if any harm is done on account of such activity, the enterprise must be absolutely liable to compensate for such harm and it should be no answer to the enterprise to say that it had taken all reasonable care and that the harm occurred without any negligence on its part.

9. Briefly discuss the English case of Donoghue Vs. Stevenson.

Ans. In a 1932, English case of Donoghue Vs. Stevenson, the claimant Donoghue drank a soft drink manufactured by the defendant Stevenson. The drink had a decomposed snail in the bottle that made the claimant ill. The court held that the manufacturer owed duty of care to those who are 'reasonably foreseeable' to be affected by the product. So, the duty of care is owed to those whom one can reasonably foresee as being potentially harmed.

Long Answer Type Questions

1. What is 'tort'? Explain four main characteristics features of tort law. **CBSE 2023**

Ans. 'Tort' essentially means a 'wrong'. It is derived from the Latin word 'tortum' which means 'twisted' or 'crooked'. Tort is defined as a civil wrong or a wrongful act, of one, either intentional or accidental, that results in injury or harm to another who in turn has recourse to civil remedies for damages or a court order or injunction.

A civil action, like the tort suit, is pursued in a civil court where the person aggrieved or his representatives or survivors prosecute the wrong doer usually for compensation in the form of monetary damages and also at times for other relief or injunction.

Damages under law of torts are essentially compensatory and seek to place the defendant in the position that he would have been had the wrongful act not been performed. The remedy is often in the nature of unliquidated damages, which can be defined as the sum of money that cannot be foreseen or assessed by a fixed or predecided formula.

The four main characteristic features of tort law are

(i) **Civil Wrong** A tort is a civil wrong, not a criminal offence.

(ii) **Fault-based Liability** In most of the tort cases, liability is based on fault.

(iii) **Harm or Injury** Torts can result in physical, emotional or financial harm.

(iv) **Causation** A tort required a casual link between the wrongful act or omission and the harm suffered.

2. Heena, a hair dresser treated Selena's hair with hair colour and as a result Selena contracted dermatitis. The manufacturers of the hair colour Beauty Blossom Company had delivered the product to Heena in properly labelled bottles together with a small brochure of instructions. Both the label and the brochure contained a warning that the hair colour might be reactive on certain skin types and a patch test on skin was recommended before it was used. Selena sues the manufacturer Beauty Blossom Company for negligence. **Would the manufacturers of the hair colour be held liable to Selena? Discuss with the help of decided case. Also discuss the liability of Heena towards Selena.** **CBSE 2024**

Ans. To analyse the liability of negligence, we will look at the legal principles related to duty of care, breach of duty and causation. For Selena to succeed in a claim against Beauty Blossom Company, the following elements need to be satisfied.

- **Duty of Care** Under the law, a manufacturer has a duty of care towards the consumer. This principle was established in the landmark case of **Donoghue Vs. Stevenson** (1932). Which set the precedent that manufacturers owe a duty of care to the ultimate consumer.
- **Breach of Duty** The manufacturers must have breached its duty of care. In this case, manufacturer has done its duty by labelling on the product as well as recommending to conduct a patch test before using the product.

- **Causation** Selena's dermatitis was caused by using her colour but it will be considered to be a contributory negligence on her part as she did not get the patch test done. Hence, Beauty Blossom Company is unlikely to be held liable for negligence because they provided sufficient warnings and safety instructions fulfilling their duty of care. As a professional providing services, Heena owes a **duty of care** to Selena to perform her services with reasonable skill and care. Since, Heena failed to perform a patch test, despite the manufacturer's instructions recommending it. She has **breached her duty of care.** If it is proved that Selena suffered dermatitis as a result of Heena's breach of duty of care, then the causation of harm or injury is proved. Therefore, Heena is likely to be held liable for negligence, as she failed to carry out the necessary patch test, which directly caused Selena's injury.

3. A fertiliser plant, owned by XYZ Ltd., is located in a densely populated area. On a windy day, the plant's negligence causes a massive ammonia gas leak affecting several nearby villages. Many people are hospitalised and crops are damaged. The company claims they took all necessary safety measures, but the incident was an Act of God.

Which Indian principle will the court apply, briefly discuss about it?

Ans. In India, principle of absolute liability was introduced by the Supreme Court in the aftermath of the two instances of gas leaks from factories injuring many.

The first case was about the infamous Bhopal gas leak disaster of 1984 where a factory of the Union Carbide Corporation located in Bhopal had a major leakage of the gas methyl isocyanate that killed and injured many people.

In the second incident of 1985 in Delhi, a factory of the Shri Ram Foods and Fertiliser Industries leaked oleum (acid) gas that killed one person that had few others hospitalised and created huge panic among the residents.

In the second case, the court decided that if an industry/enterprise is engaged in some inherently dangerous activity for commercial gain and that activity is capable of causing unfortunate damage, then the industry officials are absolutely liable to pay compensation to the aggrieved parties.

The industry cannot plead that all safety measures were taken care of by them and that there was no negligence on their part. They will not be allowed any exceptions neither can they take up any defence like that of 'Act of God' or 'Act of Stranger'.

4. (i) What is 'no fault liability' in tort law? **CBSE 2024 C**

(ii) Mr. Sarkar is an Ayurvedic medical practitioner who spends most of his time in research and experimentation on different herbs and spices. His mission is to develop new and effective medicines in Ayurveda. In his latest project, Mr. Sarkar was working to find a cure for cancer. After extensive study, he got some wild plants from the nearby forest area to test its viability. On lab testing, he found that the extract from the herbs was highly poisonous and could cause serious impact on the nervous system of the person if contacted without adequate precautions. Mr. Sarkar was very cautious and took utmost care to keep the extract safe and out of reach of his students. One day, when he was busy with his experiments, three of his students accidentally came into contact with the herb and two suffered from brain stroke and one got facial palsy. The family of the three students sued Mr. Sarkar for damages.

Citing the decided case law, decide if Mr. Sarkar is liable for the condition of the three students and the damage caused.

Ans. (i) In tort law, 'no fault liability' refers to a situation where a person is held liable for damages or injuries caused to another, regardless of whether they were at fault or not. This principle shifts the focus from fault to strict liability, ensuring compensation for victims.

(ii) Mr. Sarkar is liable for the damage caused to the three students. The principle of 'strict liability' applies, as established in the case of Rylands Vs. Fletcher (1868). Mr. Sarkar had a duty to ensure the safety of his students and take adequate precautions to prevent harm. His failure to do so, despite taking some precautions, renders him liable for the damages.

5. Discuss how tort law protects us against the different kinds of harms.

Ans. Tort law protects us against the different kinds of harms in the following ways

- **Property Interests in Land** The law of tort protects the claimant's interests in her landed property by preventing intentional intrusions or trespass of the property by the defendant or the wrong-doer.
- **Other Types of Property** Law of tort prohibits taking away of tangible property deliberately, which amounts to the tort of 'conversion'.
- **Bodily Injury** Law of tort protects the claimant against any harm to his/her interests of bodily integrity. Tort of battery and assault applies to any intentional harm caused to the body.
- **Economic Interests** Injury caused by both intentional act as well as negligence can cause economic harm to the claimant. The economic interests are also protected by the law of tort to a lesser extent.

SELF ASSESSMENT TEST

Objective Type Questions

1. A very old clock tower situated right in the middle of a crowded area of Chandni Chowk suddenly collapsed thereby causing the death of many people. The clock tower was 80 years old although the normal lifespan of the clock tower should have been 40-45 years. The clock tower was under the control of the municipal corporation of Delhi and they had a duty of care towards the citizens. By ignoring to repair the clock tower, they had breached their duty of care toward the public and were thereby liable

(a) trespass (b) strict liability (c) negligence (d) nuisance

2. 'A' abuses 'B' while he was sitting in a moving train, by aggressively shaking his fists when 'B' was standing on the railway platform at a distance.

(a) 'A' has caused fear of assault in the mind of 'B'. (b) 'A' has committed assault against 'B'.
(c) 'A' has not committed assault against 'B'. (d) 'A' has caused apprehension of assault in the mind of 'B'.

3. 'A' part of a public road had been closed for spectators of a boat race. 'P' wanted to enter but he was prevented by 'D' and other policemen because he had not paid the admission fee. 'P' was able to enter the enclosure by other means but he was unable to go where he wanted to go. The policemen refused access to where he wanted to go but allowed him to remain where he was or to go back. 'P' remained within the enclosure and refused to leave. Subsequently, 'P' sued 'D' for false imprisonment.

(a) It was a case of false imprisonment, but 'D' could not be made liable for it.
(b) 'D' could not be held liable for false imprisonment as he did not completely restrict P's movement.
(c) 'D' could be made liable as he did restrict P's movements.
(d) 'D' could not be made liable for false imprisonment as he did not touch 'P'.

Very Short Answer Type Questions

4. What is the rule of strict and absolute liability?

5. A newspaper publishes an article accusing Dr. Smith, a local physician, of being 'negligent and in competent' in his medical practice. The article is based on an anonymous source and has not been verified. Dr. Smith denies the allegations and claims the article has damaged his reputation and caused him financial loss. Is the newspaper liable for defamation? What are the kinds of defamation?

Short Answer Type Questions

6. Raj, a store security guard, suspects Sameer, a customer of shoplifting. Without sufficient evidence, Raj detains Sameer in a store room for two hours, preventing him from leaving. During this time, Raj calls the police, who arrive and search Sameer's belongings. However, no stolen items are found and Sameer is released without charges. Has Raj committed the tort of false imprisonment? Explain, considering the elements of false imprisonment and any possible defences Raj might raise.

7. Discuss the essentials and the sources of the law of torts.

Long Answer Type Question

8. What is the principle of absolute liability? What did Justice P.N. Bhagwati hold in the famous 1987 case of M.C. Mehta Vs. Shri Ram Foods and Fertilisers Industries regarding this principle?

08

CHAPTER

Law of Property

The Transfer of Property Act came into force in 1882 and provided the basic principles for transfer of both movable and immovable properties.

▼ **YOUR STUDY GOALS**

8.1 Meaning of Property
8.2 Types of Property
8.3 Transfer of Property
8.4 Principles Related to Transfer of Property
8.5 Modes of Transfer of a Property

▼ **YOUR PRACTICE GOAL**

- Objective Type Questions (26 Qs ; MCQs, A-R, Statements, Matching)
- Subjective Questions (11 VSAs, 8 SAs, 4 LAs)

Before the arrival of the British kingdom, each community in India was governed by its respective customary law in matters relating to transfer of property.

The English judges applied the common law of England and the rules of equity, justice and good conscience with respect to disputes relating to transfer of property. However, these provisions were unsuitable to the Indian conditions. Therefore, it became necessary to enact a legislation.

A separate enactment titled the Sale of Goods Act, 1930, was passed to deal with transfer of movable property by sale.

8.1 Meaning of Property

- According to **Section 2** (c) of the **Benami Transactions (Prohibition) Act, 1988,** property means property of any kind, whether movable or immovable, tangible or intangible, and includes any right or interest in such property.
- According to **Section 2 (11)** of the **Sale of Good Act, 1930,** property means the general property in goods, and not merely a special property.

8.2 Types of Property

- The word property has not been defined in the act, but it has a very wide meaning and includes properties of all descriptions.
- It includes movable properties such as cases, books, etc. and immovable properties such as lands or houses. It also includes intangible properties such as ownership, tenancy, copyrights, etc.

Movable Property

- Transfer of movable property is regulated by **Sales of Goods Act, 1932.** The movable property can easily be transported from one place to another, without changing its shape, capacity, quantity or quality.
- **Registration of movable property is optional** under the Registration Act, 1908.

Transfer of Property Act, 1882

- Matters relating to the property are governed by the Transfer of Property Act, 1882 in India.
- The object of the Transfer of Property Act is to **regulate the transfer of property between living persons.**
- The Transfer of Property Act, 1882 contains the general principles of transfer of property and detailed rules with respect to specific transfer of immovable property by sale, exchange, mortgage, lease and gift.

Immovable Property

- Transfer of immovable property is regulated by Transfer of Property Act, 1882.
- The immovable property cannot be transported easily from one place to another.
- **Registration** of immovable property is compulsory/ mandatory under the Registration Act, 1908, if its value **exceeds ₹100.** It must be registered in the name of the transferee.
- As per **Section 3,** the immovable property **does not** include standing timber, growing crop and grass. Standing timbers are trees fit for use for building or repairing houses.
- The **fruit-bearing trees are not standing timber,** and they are immovable properties. (Fatima bibi Vs. Arrfana Begum AIR 1980).
- Growing crop includes all vegetable growths which have no existence apart from their produce such as pan leave, sugarcane, etc. Grass is a movable property, but if it is right to cut grass it would be an interest in land and hence forms immovolde property.
- As per Section 3(25), General Clauses Act, 1897, immovable property shall include land, benefits to arise out of land and things attached to the earth or permanently fastened to anything attached to the Earth.

Difference between Movable and Immovable Property

Basis	Movable Property	Immovable Property
Movement of property	The movable property can easily be transported from one place to another, without changing its shape, capacity, quantity or quality.	The immovable property cannot easily be transported from one place to another.
Transfer	Mere delivery with intention to transfer the movable property completes the transter.	Mere delivery is not suffcient for a valid transfer. The property must be registered in the name of the transferee.
Registration	Registration of movable property is optional under the Registration Act 1908.	Registration of immovable property is compulsory/mandatory under the Registration Act 1908, subject to the condition that its value exceeds ₹ 100.
Lagal provision	Transfer of movable property is regulated by Sales of Goods Act 1932.	Transfer of immovable property is regulated by Transfer of Property Act, 1882

8.3 Transfer of Property

It is an act of conveying property from one person to another, in the present or future.

- Any person who is **competent to contract** and **authorised to dispose of property** i.e. owner of the property or any person authorised to sell the property, can make a transfer.
- The person who transfers the property is called the **transferor** and the person to whom the transfer is made is called the **transferee.**
- According to **Section 8** of the Transfer of Property Act, 1882, by transferring property, the transferor transfers all rights in a property.
- The transfer of property may also take place by inheritance and succession. The laws relating to such transfer are governed by the respective religious laws or practices, as the case may be.

Essentials of a Valid Transfer

A transfer is the process of conveying the rights and liabilities with respect to a property by one person to another. The transfer of property takes place with the formation of an agreement culminating into a contract.

The following are the essentials for a valid transfer of property

- The transfer should be between **two or more living persons.**
- The property that is going to be transferred should be **free from hindrances** and of a **transferable nature**.
- The transfer should not be for an **unlawful object** or an **unlawful consideration**.
- It should not involve a **person legally disqualified** to be a transferor or transferee.
- The transferor who transfers the property must be competent to make the transfer entitled to the transferable property, authorised to dispose off the property if the property is not his own property.
- The transfer should be made according to the **appropriate mode of transfer** with necessary formalities like registration, attestation, etc.
- In the case of a **conditional transfer**, where an interest is created on the fulfillment of a condition, the **condition should not be illegal, immoral, impossible or opposed to public policy.**

Procedure for Transferring a Property

- **Mode of Transfer** The mode of transfer of property varies according to the value of the property. If the value of the property is **more than ₹ 100,** then transfer has to be made **only by a registered instrument**.

  If the property is **tangible** where the value of the property is **less than ₹ 100,** then transfer has to be made **only by delivery,** whereas for **intangible** property, transfer has to be made only by **registered instrument.** A registered instrument contains the records of the owner of the property, for example shares, bonds, etc.
- **Attestation** According to **Section 3** of the Transfer of Property Act, 1882, attestation means **affixing the signature to the instrument** for the transfer of property. A registered instrument must be attested at least by **two witnesses** to the transfer.

  The witnesses should also mark their signature on the instrument with the intention to attest. The **intention** behind including this provision was **to ensure that transfer was done with the free will** of the executant.

- **Registration** Registration means recording of the contents of the document. Registration of the instrument is an essential legal formality. During registration, the parties to the transfer must be present to affix[1] their signatures to the document and complete the transaction with regard to immovable property. The rights, obligations and liabilities of the parties to the transfer must be clearly mentioned in the document, for the transfer.

  Registration shall take place by finally **affixing a seal of the Registrar's office** which shall be subsequently included in the official records.

  Indian Registration Act, 1908 is an act to consolidate the enactments relating to the registration of documents. **Section 17** of this act deals with the documents that are compulsory to be registered.
- **Mutation** Once a property has been transferred by way of relinquishment[2], sale, or gift deed in the 'name' of the recipient, **it is important to have the transfer recorded in the municipal records** by way of mutation.
- **Payment of Fee** A **stamp duty** on transfer is **to be paid** as per applicable state laws.

8.4 Principles Related to Transfer of Property

Doctrine of Election

- Doctrine of election is mentioned in **Section 35** of the TPA.
- According to this principle, if a person to the transfer gets two selections (a benefit and a burden), then he has to **accept both the benefit and the burden**. He cannot accept the benefit and reject the burden in a single transaction.
- In other words, while accepting the advantage of an instrument, the burden of the instrument should also be accepted.

  For example, 'A' sells his garden as well as his house through one instrument to 'B'. However, 'B' wants to retain only the house and wants to cancel the transfer regarding the garden. According to the Doctrine of Election, 'B' has to retain the garden if he wants to retain the house, or cancel the whole transaction. 'B'cannot retain the house and cancel the transfer regarding the garden.
- The doctrine of election is based on the principle of equity that one cannot take what is beneficial to him and disapprove what is against him, under the same instrument.
- **The Latin phrase 'quod approbo non reprobo'** is one of the underlying principles of doctrine of election. It means that no one can approbate (to approve) and reprobate (to disapprove). 'That which I approv, I cannot disapprove'. The principle of the doctrine of election was explained by the House of Lords in the case of **Cooper Vs. Cooper.**

Doctrine of Lis Pendens

- Doctrine of lis pendens is mentioned in **Section 52** of the Transfer of Property Act, 1882. Lis pendens literally means a **pending suit**.
- According to this doctrine, a property should not be transferred to a third-party during a pending suit in such a way that it affects the rights of any party concerned with the property.
- In other words, **no new interest should be created** by way of transfer of a property during the pendency of a suit relating to it.
- The doctrine of Lis Pendens emerged from the Latin phrase 'ut lite pendent nihil innoveteur' which means 'nothing new should be introduced in a pending litigation'.
- The objective of this doctrine is to suppress all parties to a pending litigation of a property.

1 Affix It means to attach physically.

2 Relinquishment It means the act of giving up something, such as responsibility claim or prossession.

To constitute Lis Pendens, the following conditions should be satisfied

- A suit or proceeding involving the immovable property should be pending.
- The right to the immovable property must be in question in the suit or proceeding and the property is involved in litigation.

  For example, 'A' has litigation in determining the title of the property with 'X'. During the period of litigation, 'A' initiates a sales of the property in favour of 'B'. According to the Doctrine of Lis Pendens, the property cannot be sold because the property is involved in litigation.

  The Supreme Court (SC) in the case of **Dev Raj Dogra and others Vs. Gyan Chand Jain and others, interpreted the meaning of the Section 52** of the TPA and laid down the pre-conditions as follows
  - A suit or a proceeding in which any right to immovable property must be directly and specifically in question, must be pending.
  - The suit or the proceeding shall not be a collusive (un-disclosed) one.
  - Any transfer of property or any dealing with such property during the pendency of the suit is prohibited except under the authority of court, if such transfer or dealing affects the right of any other party to the suit.

Quick Test 1

1 Which act is related to property?
2 How many types of property are there in law?
3 Who are transferor and transferee?
4 Which act is related to consolidate the enactments relating to the registration of documents?

8.5 Modes of Transfer of a Property

Sale

- According to **Section 54 of TPA**, sale means a transfer of ownership (right to possess something) of the property in exchange for a price (money).
- **Seller** is the person who **transfers the property** and **buyer** is the person to whom **the property is transferred.** The consideration in a sale is usually money.

  For example, 'A' sells his house for ₹ 2 lakhs to 'B'. This is called sale. Here, 'A' is the seller and 'B' is the buyer and ₹ 2 lakhs is the consideration which is money.

  The essentials for a sale to become valid are
  - There should be **two different parties** - the seller and the buyer.
  - Both the parties should be **competent** to transfer.
  - The property to be transferred should be in **existence**.
  - Consideration for the transfer should be **money**.
  - The contract should be in **accordance with law**.

Lease

- According to **Section 105 of TPA,** a lease is a contract by which one party transfer the right to enjoy the land, property, services, etc to another party for a specified time, usually in return for a periodic payment.
- A lease can be done only of immovable property. The **lessor** is the person who lets out the property for lease or transferor, and the **lessee**
- **The lessee can also sub-let the lease and the relation between the lessee and the sub-lessee will be that of the lessor and lessee.**

- A sub-lease is the renting of property by a tenant to a third party for a portion of the tenant's existing lease contract.
- In other words, when a tenant whose name is on the lease rents a room, a portion of the property, or all of the property to another, it is referred to as **sub-leasing** (or sub-letting).
- If a tenant sub-leases a property, the original tenant is still liable for the obligations stated in the lease agreement, such as the payment of rent each month.
- **In India, subleasing with the consent of the landlord is legal.** If the agreement allows the tenant to sub-lease it, the tenant can sub-lease a portion of the property to a third party.

  For example, 'A' for a period of 3 years lets out his property for use to 'B' for a sum of ₹ 50,000. This is called a lease. 'A' is the lessor and 'B' is the lessee. If 'B' sub-lets the property to 'C', then 'B' will be the lessee and 'C' will be the sub-lessee. The relation between 'B' and 'C' will be similar to that of the relationship between 'A'and 'B'.

Exchange

- According to **Section 118 of TPA,** when two persons transfer ownership of one thing for the ownership of another, it is called exchange.
- **Transfer of property by exchange can be made only by way of sale.**
- The rights and liabilities of the parties to exchange shall be that of the rights and liabilities of the buyer to the extent of receiving, and the seller to the extent of giving.

  For example, 'A' offers to sell his cottage to 'B'. 'B' in consideration of the cottage sells his farm to 'A'. Instead of getting money for his cottage, 'A' has received a farm from 'B'. This is an example for exchange.

Gift

According to **Section 122 of TPA,** a transfer of ownership of property that is **made voluntarily** and **without consideration** is called gift.

The person making the transfer is called the **donor** and the person to whom it is made is called the **donee.** If the donee expires before accepting the gift, it becomes void.

For example, 'A' gives his car to 'B'. 'B' accepts the car but 'B' does not pay anything in return for the car. This is known as Gift. In this case, 'A' is the donor and 'B' is the donee.

Sale, Lease, Exchange and Gift

Basis	Sale	Lease	Exchange	Gift
Transfer	Transfer of ownership for price	Transfer of limited ownership for rent	Transfer of ownership for some other property	Transfer of ownership without consideration
Consideration	Price	Rent	Another property	No consideration
Mode	Sale deed should be registered	Lease deed should be registered	Sale deed should be registered	Gift of immovable property should be registered
Parties	Buyer and Seller	Lessor and Lessee	Party to an exchange	Donor and Donee

Quick Test 2

1 Name the modes of transfer of property.
2 Under which section of Transfer of Property Act, exchange is covered?
3 Give an example of exchange.
4 Who is called as the donor?

REFERENCE CASES

Immovable Property

Whether trees can be regarded as movable or immovable depends upon the circumstances of the case. If the intention is that trees should continue to have the benefit of further sustenance or nutriment by the soil (land) e.g enjoining their fruits, then such tree is immovable property. But if the intention is to cut them down sooner or later for the purpose utilising the wood for building or other industrial proposes, they would be timber and accordingly be regarded as movable property. **(Shanta Bai Vs. State of Bombay AIR 1958 SC 532).**

In the case of **Sukry Kurdepa Vs. Goondakull (1872)** court has explained that movability may be defined to be a capacity in—a thing of suffering alteration. On the other hand, if a thing cannot change its place without injury to the quality it is immovable.

In **Marshall Vs. Green (33 LT 404)**, there was a sale of trees where they were Cut and taken away. The court held that the sale was not that of immovable property.

Procedure for Transfering of a property

In **Madam Pillai Vs. Badar Kali (45 Mad 612 (FB),** the plaintiff being the first wife made a claim for maintenance to her husband. The husband orally transferred his lands of the value of ₹ 100/- to the plaintiff. Later, he executed an instrument of sale in favour of the defendant for the same property. The plaintiff initiated a suit stating that the transfer was initially made in her favour and the subsequent sale to the defendant was not valid. The defendant stated that the transfer in favour of the plaintiff failed for a want of a registered, instrument.

The court held that the plaintiff acquired a title by way of oral transfer and she is entitled to the property though the instrument of sale was not registered.

Doctrine of Election

In this case Lord Heather explained the principle underlying the doctrine of election in the following words, "There is an obligation on him who takes a benefit under a will or other instrument to give full effect to that instrument under which he takes a benefit and if it be found that instrument purports to deal with something which is beyond the power of the donor or settler to dispose of, but to which effect can be given by the concurrence of him who receives a benefit under the same instrument, the law will impose on him who takes the benefit of the obligation of carrying the instrument into full and complete force and effect."

Doctrine of Lis Pendens

In **Hardev Singh Vs. Gurmail Singh,** the Supreme Court observed that **Section 52** of an act does not declare a pendents lite transfer by a party to the suit as void or illegal, but only makes the pendents like purchaser bound by the decision of the pending litigation.

Thus, if during the pendency of any suit in a court of competent jurisdiction, in which any right of an immovable property is in question, such immovable property cannot be transferred by any party to the suit so as to affect the rights of any other party to the suit under any decree that may be made in such a suit.

Mind Map

LAW OF PROPERTY

1 Introduction

Historical Background
- Communities governed by customary law pre-British rule.
- English law applied common law and equity, often unsuitable for Indian conditions.
- Enactments like the Transfer of Property Act, 1882, and Sale of Goods Act, 1930, introduced.

2 Meaning of Property

Definition
- **Section 2(C) Benami Transactions Act** Defines property as movable/immovable, tangible/intangible.
- **Section 2(11) Sale of Goods Act** Defines property as general property in goods.

Types

Movable Property
- Governed by the Sale of Goods Act, 1930.
- Transfer via delivery; registration optional.

Immovable Property
- Governed by the Transfer of Property Act, 1882.
- Compulsory registration for properties valued above ₹100.

3 Essentials of Valid Property Transfer

Key Requirements
- Competent transferor and transferee.
- Lawful object and transferable property.
- Proper mode of transfer (e.g., registration, attestation).

4 Principles in Property Law

Doctrine of Election
- Accept benefits and burdens or none from the same transaction.
- It is based on the principle of equity.
- **Latin Maxim** "quod approbo non reprobo".

Doctrine of Lis Pendens
- Prohibits property transfer during litigation.
- Ensures litigation integrity (Latin Maxim: "utlitependente nihil innoveteur").

5 Modes of Property Transfer

Sale (Section 54)
- Transfer of ownership for money.

Lease (Section 105)
- Temporary transfer for rent.

Exchange (Section 118)
- Reciprocal property transfer.

Gift (Section 122)
- Voluntary transfer without consideration.

6 Landmark Cases

Shanta Bai Vs. State of Bombay (1958)
- Differentiated movable/immovable property.

Marshall Vs. Green
- Sale of cut trees as movable property.

Madam Pillai Vs. Badar Kali
- Validity of oral transfer upheld.

7 Procedures for Transfer

Registration
- Required for immovable properties exceeding ₹100.

Attestation
- Signature by at least two witnesses.

Mutation
- Records transfer in municipal documents.

8 Distinctions in Property Law

Movable Vs. Immovable
- Movable property can easily be transported from one place to another.
- Immovable property cannot easily be transported from one place to another.

Sale Vs. Lease
- **Sale** Transfer of ownership for price.
- **Lease** Transfer of limited ownership for rent.

Transfer of Property

9 Legal Objectives

- Ensure clarity in ownership.
- Prevent endless litigation.
- Uphold justice and public interest.

Movable and Immovable Property

CBSE TEXTBOOK FOLDER

1. 'X' is an owner of mango groves where exceptional quality of mangoes are produced by hybrid mode. He is one of the largest exporters of mangoes. Till the year 2020, he has been into exporting mangoes. Due to setback to his business because of covid, from 2021 he shifted to selling mango wood in local markets.

Identify if there is any difference in the type of property he has been dealing with in the year 2020 and in 2021 respectively.

Ans. Yes, there is a difference in the type of property he has been dealing in the year 2020 and 2021, as in 2020 it was immovable property as he was exporting mangoes and now since he was into selling mango wood in local markets, it is considered as standing timber and it will be movable property.

2. 'A' has a matter pertaining to the title of immovable property situated at Bangalore with 'B'. The matter is subjudice in the court of Civil Judge at Bangalore. During the period of pendency of suit, A's mother was to be operated for open heart surgery and to accommodate the financial need, he sold this property situated at Bangalore to 'C'.

Decide the validity of the transfer made by 'A' to 'C'. Explain the requisites of principle of law involved.

Ans. In this situation, doctrine of Lis Pendens is used because of the principle of law. When a suit or litigation is pending on an immovable property, then that immovable property cannot be transferred. To constitute Lis Pendens, the following conditions should be satisfied

- A suit or proceeding involving the immovable property should be pending.
- The right to the immovable property must be in question in the suit or proceeding.
- The property in litigation should be transferred.
- The transferred property should affect the rights of the other person to the transfer.

3. Manan and Ketan enter into an agreement of lease of property for a tenure of 24 months at a consideration of ₹ 9000/- per month. Ketan is expected to return the property at the expiry of this term in the condition in which he received it. Ketan was transferred to another city but for a short span. He sub-lets the property to Manoj for a sum of ₹ 10,000/-. Manoj carries such alterations as would depreciate the property.

Decide if Ketan is authorised to make such transfer by sub-lease. Also highlight the remedy available to Manan.

Ans. No, Ketan is not authorised to make such a transfer by sublease. The lease agreement between Manan and Ketan is a contract between two parties, and Ketan does not have the right to transfer that contract to a third party without Manan's consent.

If Ketan has sublet the property to Manoj, then Manan has a number of remedies available to him. He can

- Demand that Ketan terminate the sublease and return the property to him.
- Sue Ketan for damages for breach of contract.
- Sue Manoj for damages for interference with his contractual rights.

4. Elucidate on the importance of attestation as an important step preceding registration.

Ans. The importance of attestation is to ensure that transfer was done with the free will of the executant.

According to Section 3 of the Transfer of Property Act, 1882, attestation means affixing the signature to the instrument for the transfer of property. A registered instrument must be attested at least by two witnesses to the transfer. The witnesses should also mark their signature on the instrument with the intention to attest.

Exam Pattern Questions

Objective Type Questions

Multiple Choice Questions (MCQs)

1. The Transfer of Property Act was enacted in ....

(a) 1880 (b) 1881 (c) 1882 (d) 1883

2. Which of the following describes the objective of the Transfer of Property Act?

(a) Regulate the transfer of property between all persons.
(b) Regulate the transfer of property between living persons.
(c) Regulate the transfer of property through a will
(d) None of the above

3. As per Section 3 of the Transfer of Property Act, 1882, immovable property include ....

(a) standing timber (b) grass
(c) land (d) growing crops

4. The concept of 'sale' has been embodied in which of the following sections of the Transfer of Property Act?

(a) Section 52 (b) Section 53
(c) Section 54 (d) Section 55

5. .... refers to the transfer of ownership of one thing for the ownership of another.

(a) Lease (b) Sale
(c) Gift (d) Exchange

6. Transfer of property by exchange can happen only by way of ....

(a) sale (b) lease (c) gift (d) will

7. From the options given below, which statement accurately describes the process of property registration in India? **CBSE 2025**

(a) The buyer and seller exchange property documents without involving any government authority.
(b) The property is officially transferred from the seller to the buyer through a government-authorised deed, affixed by a seal of the Registrar's office.
(c) The buyer must pay property taxes before the sale is completed without the need for any legal documentation.
(d) The property ownership is verified by a local official but no formal record is kept.

8. Arjun, at the request of the local community leader, builds a playground for the children in his neighborhood, spending a considerable amount of his own money. Later, Ravi, a local snack vendor, sets up a stall near the playground to sell snacks to children and promises to give Arjun 10% of his profits from all sales as a token of appreciation for building the playground. However, Ravi fails to pay Arjun the promised percentage, and Arjun decides to take legal action to recover it. Based on contract law principles, which of the following is correct? **CBSE 2025**

(a) Arjun is entitled to the percentage of profits as Ravi benefited from his efforts in building the playground.
(b) Arjun cannot claim the percentage of profits, as the playground was built at the request of the community leader and not Ravi.
(c) Ravi must pay Arjun the promised percentage since he made a verbal commitment to do so.
(d) Ravi has to pay Arjun only if Arjun can prove the playground was built specifically for his benefit.

9. The sale of trees wherein the trees were cut and taken away and the Court held that the sale was not that of immovable property was in the case of ....

(a) Marshall Vs. Green
(b) Shanta Bai Vs. State of Bombay
(c) Cooper Vs. Cooper
(d) None of the above

10. The distinction between movable and immovable property was made in the case of ....

(a) Marshall Vs. Green
(b) Shanta Bai Vs. State of Bombay
(c) Cooper Vs. Cooper
(d) None of the above

11. Saba inherited a valuable painting from her late grandmother. She decided to sell the painting to her friend Lata, who is an art collector. They both agreed on a price and Saba handed over the painting to Lata. However, a dispute arose, when another individual Mahesh claimed that he is the rightful owner of the painting.
Which of the following conditions must be satisfied for the transfer of property to Lata to be considered valid? **CBSE 2024 C**

(a) Saba must have legal ownership and the capacity to transfer the painting and the transfer must be done with the intention to transfer ownership to Lata.
(b) Lata must have the financial means to purchase the painting and both parties must sign a written agreement stating the transfer of ownership.

(c) Saba must notify Mahesh about the intended sale of the painting and obtain his consent before transferring the property to Lata.
(d) Lata must pay the full purchase price upfront and Saba must provide a certificate of authenticity for the painting to validate the transfer of ownership.

12. Saloni inherits a property under a will that also imposes certain obligations on her regarding maintaining another property. She decides to accept the inheritance but refuses to fulfill the maintenance obligations.
Identify the lagal principle that would apply to the given situation. **CBSE SQP 2024**
(a) 'Ut lite pendent nihil innovateur'
(b) 'Quod approbo non reprobo'
(c) Stare decisis
(d) Audi alteram partem

13. Kindly arrange the following modes of transfer of property as per their provisions.
I. Lease II. Gift III. Sale IV. Exchange
Codes
(a) II, III, I, IV (b) III, I, II, IV
(c) III, I, IV, II (d) II, I, III, IV

14. 'A' sells his garden as well his house through one instrument to 'B'. Whereas, 'B' wants to retain only the house and wants to cancel the fransfer regarding the garden. According to the Doctrine of Election which of the following is correct option?
Codes
(a) 'B' has to retain the garden if he wants to retain the house.
(b) 'B' can avoid to retain the garden if he want although he can reain the house.
(c) 'B' cannot retain house and can retain garden.
(d) None of the above

15. Monika wanted to gift her farm house in Chandigarh to her sister Somita. She offered the gift to Somita, but before it could be acepted by her, unfortunately, Somita passed away. The gift is ....
(a) valid (b) void (c) illegal (d) unlawful

16. Match the following.

	Column I		Column II
A.	Transfer of ownership of one thing for ownership of another	1.	Intellectual Property
B.	Doctrine of Lis Pendens	2.	Sale of Goods Act
C.	Property which does not involve movable or immovable property	3.	Exchange
D.	Movable Property	4.	Section 52

Codes

	A	B	C	D		A	B	C	D
(a)	3	4	1	2	(b)	2	1	3	4
(c)	3	2	4	1	(d)	1	2	3	4

17. Match the following and choose the correct option **CBSE 2024 C**

	Column I		Column II
A.	Lis Pendens	1.	General principle of transfer of property
B.	Transfer of Property Act, 1882	2.	Transfer of movable property
C.	Doctrine of Election	3.	Subjugate parties to a pending litigation of a property to court's decision
D.	Sale of Goods Act, 1930	4.	No one can approbate and reprobate

Codes

	A	B	C	D		A	B	C	D
(a)	4	2	1	3	(b)	2	1	3	4
(c)	3	4	1	2	(d)	3	1	4	2

18. What is included in immovable property?
Statement I Immovable property includes land, buildings and rights over land.
Statement II Immovable property also encompasses any permanent structures attached to the land or building.
Codes
(a) Only Statement I is correct.
(b) Only Statement II is correct.
(c) Both Statement are correct.
(d) Both Statement are incorrect.

19. What characterizes a gift in terms of transfer of ownership?
Statement I A gift involves the voluntary transfer of ownership of movable or immovable property.
Statement II No consideration or compensation is expected or given in return for a gift.
Choose the correct option.
(a) Involuntary transfer of ownership with consideration.
(b) Voluntary transfer of ownership without consideration.
(c) Transfer of ownership with expectation of inheritance.
(d) Conditional transfer of ownership with future obligations.

20. What constitutes an exchange under the transfer of Property Act?
Statement I Exchange involves reciprocal transfer of ownership of one property for another.
Statement II Exchange requires mutual consideration, where each party transfer ownership and receives ownership in return.
Codes
(a) Only Statement I is correct.
(b) Only Statement II is correct.
(c) Both the Statements are correct.
(d) Both the Statements are incorrect.

Assertion-Reason Questions

Directions (Q. Nos. 21-25) In the questions given below, there are two statements. Read the statements and choose the correct option.

Codes

(a) Both A and R are true and R is the correct explanation of A.
(b) Both A and R are true, but R is not the correct explanation of A.
(c) A is true, but R is false.
(d) A is false, but R is true.

21. **Assertion** (A) The doctrine of Lis Pendens emerged from the Latin Maxim, 'ut lite pendent nihil innovetelur'

Reason (R) Its objective is to avoid endless litigation.

22. **Assertion** (A) Madam Pillai Vs. Badar Kali was a case law that determined the validity of oral transfer.

Reason (R) The court held that the plaintiff acquired a title by way of oral transfer and she is entitled to the property though the instrument of sale was not registered.

23. **Assertion** (A) Property is a comprehensive term and includes copyright.

Reason (R) Transfer of property include all kinds of properties including patents.

24. **Assertion** (A) Transfer of Property Act, 1882, it also, serve as the code of contract law governing immovable property.

Reason (R) The term 'Property' or 'transfer of property' are not defined in the Transfer of Property Act, 1882.

25. **Assertion** (A) The most important power of an owner is the right to exclude others.

Reason (R) The owner may grant to another many of his rights and get remain an owner.

26. **Read the viven excerpt and answer the questions that follow**

Rohit and Roma have filed for divorce and the distribution of their real estate is yet to be settled. A flat that is jointly owned by them is demanded by Rohit. Before the matter is resolved in court, Rohit sells off the flat.

In this context answer the following questions CBSE 2023

(i) The sale of the flat by Rohit is ....

(a) valid
(b) invalid
(c) contingent
(d) legal

(ii) The legal principle applicable here is ....

(a) doctrine of election
(b) doctrine of severability
(c) doctrine of Lis Pendens
(d) doctrine of restitution

(iii) Which of the essentials of a valid transfer are affected in the given case? CBSE 2023

I. Transfer should be between two or more living persons.
II. Property transferred should be free encumbrances.
III. Transferor must be authourised to transfer the property.
IV. Transfer should not be for an unlawful object.

(a) I and IV
(b) II and III
(c) I and III
(d) II and IV

(iv) The mode of transfer of property varies according to ....

(a) value of property
(b) net worth of transferor
(c) net worth of transferee
(d) preference of the parties

(v) Which of the following is an immovable property ?

(a) Timber
(b) Standing crops
(c) Grass
(d) Benefits arising out of land

Answers

1. (c) 1882
2. (b) Regulate the transfer of property between living persons.
3. (c) land
4. (c) Section 54
5. (d) Exchange
6. (a) sale
7. (b) The property is officially transferred from the seller to the buyer through a government-authorised deed, affixed by a seal of the Registrar's office.
8. (b) Arjun cannot claim the percentage of profits, as the playground was built at the request of the community leader and not Ravi.
9. (a) Marshall Vs. Green
10. (b) Shanta Bai Vs. State of Bombay
11. (a) Saba must have legal ownership and the capacity to transfer the painting and the transfer must be done with the intention to transfer ownership to Lata.
12. (b) 'Quod approbo non reprobo'
13. (c) III, I, IV, II
14. (a) 'B' has to retain the garden if he wants to retain the house.
15. (b) void
16. (a) 3 4 1 2
17. (c) 3 4 1 2
18. (c) Both Statements are correct.

19. (b) Voluntary transfer of ownership without consideration.
20. (c) Both the Statements are correct.
21. (a) Both A and R are true and R is the correct explanation of A.
22. (a) Both A and R are true and R is the correct explanation of A.
23. (c) A is true, but R is false.
24. (b) Both A and R are true, but R is not the correct explanation of A.
25. (b) Both A and R are true, but R is not the correct explanation of A.
26. (i) (b) invalid (ii) (c) doctrine of Lis Pendens
(iii) (b) II and III (iv) (a) value of property
(v) (d) Benefits arising out of land

Subjective Questions

Very Short Answer Type Questions

1. What is the major objective of the Transfer of Property Act?

Ans. The major objective behind the enactment of Transfer of Property Act is to regulate the transfer of property between living persons.

2. Who can transfer the property under the Transfer of Property Act?

Ans. Every person, who is competent to contract and competent to transfer property, which can be transferred in whole or in part.

3. How can an immovable property of a value more than ₹ 100 be transferred?

Ans. An immovable property whose value is more than ₹ 100 can only be transferred by a registered instrument.

4. Give any two differences between a movable property and an immovable property. CBSE 2024 C

Ans. Here are two differences between movable and immovable property

(i) **Transferability** Movable property can be easily transferred from one place to another, whereas immovable property is fixed to a specific location and cannot be moved.

(ii) **Registration** Movable property does not require registration, whereas immovable property requires registration with the relevant authorities to establish ownership and transfer rights.

5. Ramesh inherits a property from his father, who had gifted it to Ramesh's brother, Rohan, with a condition that if Ramesh accepts the gift, Rohan will forfeit his right to inherit 50 per cent of their father's estate. Ramesh wants to inherit the 50 per cent share but also keep the gifted property.

Can Ramesh accept the gift and still inherit the 50 per cent shares?

Ans. No, Ramesh must choose between the gift and inheritance. The doctrine of election requires Ramesh to choose between accepting the gift and inheriting 50 per cent share. Since the gift and inheritance are mutually exclusive. Ramesh cannot have both. He must elect whether to take the gift or inherit the 50 per cent share, thereby forfeiting the other. This doctrine prevents a person from taking advantage of conflicting benefits.

6. Rahul files a suit against his uncle, Ravi, claiming ownership of a disputed property. During the pendency of the suit, Ravi sells the property to Rohan. Rahul's suit is eventually successful, and the court declares him the rightful owner. Can Rohan claim ownership of the property?

Ans. No, Rohan cannot claim ownership of the property, as the doctrine of Lis Pendens apply. This doctrine prohibits transfer of property during pending litigation. Since Rahul's suits was pending, Ravi's sale to Rohan is void.

Rohan cannot claim ownership as he was aware of the pending suit. The doctrine protects parties' interests during litigation.

7. What is the major difference between a sale and an exchange?

Ans. The major difference between a sale and exchange is in the form of consideration. In a sale, the consideration is money while in exchange, the consideration is ownership of another property.

8. What happens to the validity of a gift if the donee dies before accepting the gift?

Ans. If the donee dies before accepting the gift, the gift becomes void.

9. Which legislation regulates the sale of movable property?

Ans. The sale of movable property is regulated by the Sale of Goods Act, 1930.

10. Can a lessee sub-lease the lease property?

Ans. The lessee can sub-lease the lease property with the consent of the lessor.

11. Mr. P.L. wants to start a business to export bananas in the cities. But, he is confused about the registration process and he doesn't know about the laws as well. How will he start his business? In this situation, some question is raised in his hand. If you are his lawyer how will you help him?

(i) What kind of property is used in this business?

(ii) Which act is used in this situation?

Ans. (i) Movable property

(ii) Registration Act

Short Answer Type Questions

1. Write a short note on the doctrine of Lis Pendens.

Ans. The doctrine of Lis Pendens emerged from the Latin maxim 'ut lite pendent nihil innoveteur' which means that 'nothing new should be introduced in a pending litigation'. When a suit or litigation is pending on an immovable property, that immovable property cannot be transferred.

The main objectives of doctrine of Lis Pendens are

- To avoid endless litigation.
- To protect one of the parties to the litigation against the order of the court.
- To avoid the abuse of any legal process.

Further, to constitute Lis Pendens, the following conditions should be satisfied

- There must be a suit or proceeding involving the immovable property.
- Such a suit or proceeding must be pending before the court that is competent to try it.
- The right to the immovable property must be in question in the suit or proceeding.
- The property in litigation should be transferred.
- The transferred property should affect the rights of the other person to the transfer.

2. Briefly explain the concept of lease. Can sub-lessee can sue the original lessor for damages for violation of quiet enjoyment of the property. Explain with a case study.

Ans. Lease is a transfer of right to enjoy a property for a specific period of time in consideration for a price. The lessee can also sub-let the lease and the relation between the lessee and the sub-lessee will be that of lessor and lessee.

In Gajadhar Vs. Rombhaee (1938), a theatre was sub-leased and the sub-lessee was prevented from using the theatre by the original lessor on the ground that a notice was served on the lessee for determining the lease. The sub-lessee had to pay an additional amount to the proprietor (the original lessor) and then take the lease. It was held that there is violation on the part of the original lessor and the sub-lessee can sue the original lessor for damages for violation of quiet enjoyment of the property.

3. Identify and explain the type of transfer that is being done in each of the following cases

(i) Mr. Singh owns a piece of land and decides to sell it to Mrs. Jolly. They both agree on a price, and the transaction is completed with a signed contract.

(ii) Uday has a beach house and Lalita has a small lodge in the mountains, Uday's dream is to own that lodge and Lalita wants to own the beach house. They both agree that the properties have similar values and want to fulfill their dreams.

(iii) Priyanka has a valuable collection of antique jewellery that she inherited from her grandmother. She decides to give a portion of this collection to her daughter, Malti, as a token to their bond and shared memories with their grandmother with no monetary exchange involved. **CBSE SQP 2024**

Ans. (i) Mr. Singh has transferred his piece of land to Mrs. Jolly by sale. Sale means transfer of ownership of the property in exchange for a price. [Section 54 of the TPA]

(ii) Uday and Lalita have transferred their respective properties to each other by exchange.

When 2 persons transfer ownership of one thing for the ownership of another, it is called exchange. [Section 118 of the TPA]. Transfer of property by exchange can only be made by way of sale. The rights and liabilities of the parties to exchange shall be that of the rights and liabilities of buyer to the extent of receiving and that of the seller to the extent of giving.

(iii) Priyanka has given inherited jewellery as a gift to her daughter, Malti.

A transfer of ownership of property that is made voluntarily and without consideration is called gift. [Section 122 of the TPA]

4. Mrs. Kapoor, an elderly landowner, verbally expressed her wish to transfer her agricultural land worth ₹ 20 Lakhs to her son Raj without any legal documentation.

Her other son Aman, who has been managing the land wants it to be transferred in his name as had been incharge of the land. Additionally, a neighbour, Mr. Sharma, offers Aman money to buy the land directly.

In the given situations, who has the right to transfer the property under the provisions of Transfer of Property Act (TPA) 1882? State any two essentials for a valid transfer based on the scenario given above. **CBSE 2025**

Ans. Under the Transfer of Property Act, 1882, only a competent owner or an authorised individual can transfer property. Mrs. Kapoor's verbal expression lacks legal validity as a transfer must be formalised through proper documentation. Aman cannot claim ownership merely by managing the land. A sale to Mr. Sharma would require valid ownership proof and a registered deed.

Two essentials of a valid transfer include

(i) The transfer must be between two or more living persons.

(ii) It must comply with necessary formalities like registration .

5. Mr. Kumar will give his flat to his son, Rohan, on condition that Rohan pays ₹ 10 lakhs to his daughter, Rhea. Rohan accepts the flat but refuses to pay ₹ 10 lakhs to Rhea. Later, Rohan claims that the condition is invalid. Can Rohan retain the flat without paying ₹ 10 lakhs? What do you mean by doctrine of election?

Ans. No, Rohan cannot retain the flat without paying ₹ 10 lakhs to Reha. Doctrine of election is mentioned in Section 35 of the TPA. According to this principle, if a person to the transfer gets two selections (a benefit and a burden), then he has to accept both the benefit and the burden. He cannot accept the benefit and reject the burden in a single transaction. In other words, while accepting the advantage of an instrument, the burden of the instrument should also be accepted.

For example, 'A' sells his garden as well as his house through one instrument to 'B'. However, 'B' wants to retain only the house and wants to cancel the transfer regarding the garden. According to the Doctrine of Election, 'B' has to retain the garden if he wants to retain the house, or cancel the whole transaction. B'cannot retain the house and cancel the transfer regarding the garden.

The doctrine of election is based on the principle of equity that one cannot take what is beneficial to him and disapprove what is against him, under the same instrument.

6. Jyoti is selling her residential property to Jagat. Describe in brief, the process of how the ownership of the property will be transferred. CBSE 2024

Ans. There are few steps involved in transferring the ownership of the property.

(i) If the value of the property is more than ₹ 100. then transfer has to be made only by a registered instrument. A registered instrument contains the records of the owner of the property.

(ii) A registered instrument must be attested at least by two witnesses to the transfer. Attestation means affixing the signature to the instrument for the transfer of property. The witnesses should mark their signature too on the instrument with the intention to attest. The intention behind including this step was to ensure that transfer was done with the free will of the executant.

(iii) Registration of an instrument is an essential legal formality. While registration, the parties to the transfer must be present to affix their signatures. Registration shall take place by finally affixing a seal of the registrar's Office which shall be subsequently included in the official records.

(iv) Once property has been transferred by way of relinquishment, sale in the name of the recipient. It is also important to have the transfer recorded in the municipal records by way of mutation.

(v) The stamp duty is to be paid as per applicable state laws, on the transfer of property.

7. Briefly discuss the two cases on movable and immovable property.

Ans. A movable property is a property that can be moved from one place to another. It is governed by the Sale of Goods Act. Immovable Property refers to a property that cannot be moved from one place to another. It is governed by the Transfer of Property Act.

Two cases on movable and immovable property are

- In Shanta Bai Vs. State of Bombay (1958), the distinction between movable and immovable property was observed. If the intention is to reap fruits from the trees, it will be regarded as an immovable property. But if the intention is to cut down the tree and use it as timber, it would be regarded as movable property.
- In Marshall Vs. Green, there was sale of trees wherein the trees were cut and taken away. The court held that the sale was not that of immovable property.

8. Rahul, a major transfers his property of ₹ 1 lakh to his friend, Rohan, due to affection. However the transfer deed is not registered, and Rahul did not receive any consideration. Later Rahul claims that the transfer is void. Is Rahul's claim valid? What are the essentials of a valid transfer?

Ans Yes the claim of Rahul is valid as registration and consideration are essential for a valid transfer.

The following are the essentials for a valid transfer of property

- The transfer should be between two or more living persons.
- The property that is going to be transferred should be free from hindrances and of a transferable nature.
- The transfer should not be for an unlawful object or an unlawful consideration.
- It should not involve a person legally disqualified to be a transferor or transferee.

- The transferor who transfers the property must be competent to make the transfer entitled to the transferable property, authorised to dispose off the property if the property is not his own property.

Long Answer Type Questions

1. Who can transfer property? Explain the ways in which an immovable property can be transferred? CBSE SQP 2022

Ans. Any person who is competent to contract (person above 18 years of age, having sound mind and not disqualified by any law in force) and authorised to dispose off property viz. owner of the property or any person authorised to sell the property, can make a transfer. The person who transfers the property is called the Transferor and the person to whom the transfer is made is called the Transferee.

An immovable property can be transferred permanently through various modes.

- Relinquishment
- Sale
- Gift
- Mortgage
- Lease
- Leave and license agreement

2. Rahul is the sole owner of his flat in Mumbai, he wants to transfer it to Rohan through sale. Outline the procedure and steps Rahul should follow.

Ans The procedure for transferring a property is

- **Mode of Transfer** The mode of transfer of property varies according to the value of the property. If the value of the property is more than ₹ 100/-, then the transfer has to be made only by a registered instrument. If the property is tangible and the value of the property is less than ₹ 100/-, then the transfer has to be made only by delivery, whereas for intangible property, the transfer has to be made only by a registered instrument.
- **Attestation** Attestation means affixing the signature to the instrument for the transfer of property. A registered instrument must be attested at least by two witnesses to the transfer. The witnesses should mark their signature too on the instrument to attest. The intention behind including this provision was to ensure that the transfer was done with the free will of the executant.
- **Registration** Registration of the instrument is an essential legal formality. During registration, the parties to the transfer must be present to affix their signatures to the document and complete the transaction about the immovable property. While doing so, the document for transfer must mention the rights, obligations, and liabilities of the parties to the transfer. Registration shall take place by finally affixing a seal of the Registrar's office which shall be subsequently included in the official records.
- **Mutation** Once a property has been transferred by way of relinquishment (giving possession), sale, or gift deed in the 'name' of the recipient, it is important to have the transfer recorded in the municipal records by way of mutation.
- **Payment of Fee** A stamp duty on transfer is to be paid as per applicable state laws.

3 Briefly discuss the difference between sale and lease in points.

Ans The differences between sale and lease are

- A sale is a transfer of ownership of a property or item from the seller to the buyer in exchange for payment. At the same time, a lease is an agreement in which the lessee pays the lessor for the right to use a property or item for a specified period.
- In a sale, the buyer becomes the property owner, while the lessor retains ownership of the property in a lease.
- Sales are typically permanent, while leases are temporary and may be renewable.
- Selling is shifting the ownership to the purchaser. On the other hand, leasing holds the owner the same. The purchaser gets a lease from the owner briefly.
- In selling, expenses are high in rates on the other hand, in lease expenses are fewer and not much high in rate.
- Selling is permanent and cannot be turned back.On the other hand, leasing is for a temporary period. The possession of the property is not given up.

4. 'A' proper could not be transferred 'a' to third-party during a pending suit in such a way that it affects the right of any party concerned.

Identify this doctrine and explain it.

Ans. The given doctrine is the doctrine of Lis Pendens.

Doctrine of Lis Pendens is mentioned in Section 52 of the Transfer of Property Act, 1882. Lis Pendens literally means a pending suit. According to this doctrine, a property should not be transferred to a third-party during a pending suit in such a way that it affects the rights of any party concerned with the property. In other words, no new interest should be created by way of transfer of a property during the pendency of a suit relating to it. The doctrine of Lis Pendens emerged from the Latin phrase 'ut lite pendent nihil innoveteur' which means 'nothing new should be introduced in a pending litigation'. The objective of this doctrine is to suppress all parties to a pending litigation of a property.

The doctrine reflects the control that a court acquires over the property involved in a pending suit, until its final judgment. When a suit or litigation is pending on an immovable property, then that immovable property cannot be transferred.

SELF ASSESSMENT TEST

Objective Types Questions

1. Who among the following has the right to receive rent?
   (a) Lessee (b) Lessor
   (c) Seller (d) Both (b) and (c)
2. If the property is given voluntarily, it is called ...., while if it is given for a price, it is called ....
   (a) gift, sale (b) sale, gift
   (c) exchange, lease (d) gift, exchange
3. Which of the following can be considered to be the objective(s) of the doctrine of Lis Pendens?
   (a) To avoid endless litigation.
   (b) To protect one of the parties to the litigation against the order of the court.
   (c) To avoid the abuse of any legal process
   (d) All of the above
4. Temporary transfer of property for a price is called ....
   (a) exchange (b) gift
   (c) sale (d) lease
5. Kavita gave possession of her farm house to Rajeev for some period of time for money. What type of relationship exists between Kavita and Rajeev?
   (a) Donor and Donee (b) Seller and Buyer
   (c) Lessor and Lessee (d) Lessor and Sub-lessee

Very Short Answer Type Questions

6. State the meaning of immovable property under Transfer of Property Act, 1882.
7. What do you mean by movable property?
8. Aman sells his ancestral property to Neeraj. Aman's name is removed from the revenue records, and Neeraj's name is added. What is this process called, briefly explain.

Short Answer Type Questions

9. Discuss the procedure for registration of a property of the value above ₹ 100.
10. Explain sale and lease by distinguishing between them.

Long Answer Type Question

11. Discuss the concept of gift and exchange.
12. 'A' sells his garden as well as his house through one instrument to 'B'. However, 'B' wants to retain only the house and wants to cancel the transfer regarding the garden. Which doctrine will come into picture here, please explain its provision and principles related to it with one landmark case law.

09

CHAPTER

Intellectual Property Law

The term 'Intellectual Property Rights' (IPR) refers to the rights conferred by law on a creator/owner of intellectual property.

▼ **YOUR STUDY GOALS**

9.1 Meaning of Intellectual Property
9.2 Historical Perspective of Intellectual Property Law
9.3 Copyright
9.4 Patent
9.5 Trademark
9.6 Geographical Indication
9.7 Designs

▼ **YOUR PRACTICE GOAL**

- Objective Type Questions (27 Qs ; MCQs, A-R, Statements, Matching)
- Subjective Questions (9 VSAs, 10 SAs, 6 LAs)

9.1 Meaning of Intellectual Property

- Intellectual property refers to the creation of the mind or products of **human intellect** such as inventions, designs, artistic work, names, symbols, images etc.
- It is an intangible or untouchable property that comes into existence through huma intellect.

Intellectual Property Rights

These rights are the rights given to persons over the creations of their minds. The importance of these rights are

- They usually give the creator an **exclusive right** over the use of his/her creation for a certain period of time.
- They seek to protect the interests of the creators by rewarding their mental labour and allowing them to retain property rights over their creations.
- That by granting these rights, it is to encourage inventions and creations that promote social, economic, scientific and cultural development of society.

Intellectual property is divided into **two** categories

- **Industrial Property** This includes inventions (patents), trademarks, industrial designs and geographic indications of source.
- **Copyright** This includes literary and artistic works such as novels, poems and plays, films, musical works, artistic works such as drawings, paintings, photographs and sculptures and architectural designs.
- The management of **Intellectual Property** (IP) and **Intellectual Property Rights** (IPR) is a complex task that requires a combination of functions and strategies, aligned with both national laws and international agreements.
- Forms of IPR can vary and require varying approaches, including specialised knowledge in areas such as science, engineering, medicine, law, finance, marketing and economics.
- The handling and management of these forms of IPR involve different strategies and require consideration of their social, economic, technical and political impacts.

International Obligations that have Shaped Indian IPR

The Paris Convention for the Protection of Industrial Properties

- The Paris Convention was **adopted** on **20th March, 1883 in Paris** and was enforced on **7th July, 1884.** It follows the principles of national treatment and framework of priority.
- In the context of legal protection for industrial property, the principle of **national treatment** requires each member country of the Paris Convention to provide equal legal protection for the inventions of nationals from other member countries, as it would provide for its own nationals.
- The principle of **priority framework** allows an inventor to protect their invention simultaneously in various countries.

The Berne Convention for the Protection of Literary and Artistic Works

- The Berne Convention was adopted on **9th September, 1886** and came into force on **4th December, 1887**. The Berne Convention was **originally signed in 1886** at **Berne** in Switzerland. It follows principles of national treatment, automatic protection and independence of protection.
- According to principle of **national treatment** under this convention, any work originating in a contracting state, including works of authors who are nationals of that state or works first published in that state, should receive the same legal protection in every other contracting state as the latter state grants to its own nationals.
- The principle of **automatic protection** under this convention mandated that legal protection should not be subject to compliance with any formalities.
- The principle of **independence of protection** under this convention decreed that legal protection should be independent of the existence of protection in the country of origin of the work.

The Universal Copyright Convention (UCC)

- It was **established** in the year **1952**. It follows the principles of national treatment, the term of the work and minimum rights.
- The UCC adheres to the principle of **national treatment** rather than automatic protection, which implies that contracting countries are not obligated to provide foreign works with automatic protection if the national requirements are not met.
- As per the UCC's provisions, the contracting countries must provide a specific set of **minimum rights** to the lawful owner of the work, provided that they do not create any conflict with the 'spirit' of the convention.

World Intellectual Property Organisation (WIPO)

The WIPO Convention was **signed** on **14th July, 1967**, in **Stockholm**. It is the primary instrument of the World Intellectual Property Organisation. It came into **effect** in **1970** and was subsequently **amended in 1979**. In 1974, the WIPO became one of the specialised agencies of the United Nations (UN) system.

The WIPO had **two** primary objectives, which were

(i) To promote the legal protection of intellectual property worldwide.

(ii) To facilitate administrative cooperation between the intellectual property unions created by treaties administered by the WIPO.

9.2 Historical Perspective of Intellectual Property Law

The importance and role of intellectual property protection got clear with the establishment of the World Trade Organisation (WTO) in the **Trade-Related Intellectual Property Systems (TRIPS) Agreement.** It was negotiated at the end of the **Uruguay Round** of the General Agreement on Tariffs and Trade (GATT) treaty in **1994**.

- The **TRIPS Agreement** came into **effect** on **1st January, 1995** and is the most comprehensive[1] multilateral agreement on intellectual property.
- It encompasses[2] all forms of intellectual property and **aims at harmonising and strengthening standards of protection,** and providing effective enforcement of intellectual property rights at both national and international levels.
- India being signatory to the TRIPS Agreement has passed several legislations for the protection of intellectual property rights to meet the international obligations.
- Some of these legislations are listed below
  - Trade Mark Act, 1999
  - Designs Act, 2000
  - Copyright Act, 1957 (as amended)
  - Patents Act, 1970 (as amended)
  - Geographical Indications of Goods (Registration and Protection) Act, 1999
  - Protection of Plant Varieties and Farmers' Rights Act, 2001
- The history of patent law dates back to **1911**. The Indian Patents and Designs Act, **1911** was enacted around this time.
- The Patents Act, 1970 in India came into **force** in **1972**. It amended and consolidated the existing law relating to patents in India.
- The act went through an **amendment** in **2005** and is now known as the Patents (Amendment) Act, 2005.
- Through this amendment, product payment was extended to all fields of technology including food, drugs, chemicals and micro-organisms.

Quick Test 1

1. What are the two categories of intellectual property?
2. When did the Paris Convention for the protection of industrial properties adopt?
3. Where was the World Intellectual Property Organisation signed on 14th July, 1967?
4. When did the Patents Act came into force in India?

---

1 Comprehensive means including or dealing with all or nearly all elements or aspects of something.

2 Encompass means surround and have or hold within.

9.3 Copyright

- Copyright is a right given by the law to creators of literary, dramatic, musical and artistic works and producers of cinematograph films and sound recordings.
- It is a bundle of rights including, rights of reproduction, communication to the public, adaptation and translation of the work.
- This protection is automatic (upon creation of the work) and does not depend on registration.

Scope of Protection in the Copyright Act, 1957

- In India, the law relating to copyright is governed by the **Copyright Act, 1957**. A work must be **original** to get the protection of copyright.
- Only ideas, knowledge or concepts are not copyrightable. It protects the original expression of information and ideas.
- Copyright can be claimed either by the **creator** or the **person** who has **inherited the rights of ownership** from the original creator or an **agent** who is allowed to act on behalf of the creator.
- All subject matters protected by copyright are called **protected works. Section 2(y)** of the act defines 'work'. It includes work such as literary, dramatic, musical, artistic, cinematographic and sound recording works.
- A work is protected by copyright when
    - it falls within the category of 'work' under the act.
    - the work must be recorded/fixed in material form (tangible form).
    - the work must be original.

Registration of Copyright

- Acquisition[3] **of copyright is automatic and it does not require any formality.** However, certificate of registration of copyright and the entries made therein serve as clear evidence in a court of law with reference to dispute relating to ownership of copyright.
- Copyright comes into existence as soon as a work is created and **no formality is required** to be completed for acquiring copyright.

Term of Copyright

- Copyright is protected for a limited period of time.
- The general rule is that **copyright lasts for 60 years.**
- In the case of original literary, dramatic, musical and artistic works, **the 60 years period is counted from the year following the death of the author.**
- In the case of cinematograph films, sound recordings, photographs, **posthumous**[4] publications, anonymous and pseudonymous publications, works of government and works of international organisations, the **60 years period is counted from the date of publication.**

3 Acquisition means something which is bought or detained.
4 Posthumous It means occurring, awarded or appearing after the death of the originator.

Rights of the Owner of a Copyright

Rights of the owner of a copyright can be categorised into **two** groups, **economic rights** and **moral rights**. Economic rights allow owner to derive financial reward from the use of their works by others.

Economic Rights

This allows the rights' owner to derive financial reward from the use of their works by others.

It includes the following rights.

- **Right to Reproduce the Work** Reproduction is an act of copying from the previously finished works or giving it a differential form by adding, editing or modifying the same. Such right shall **exclusively be exercised by the owner** of the work and shall not be violated by any other person, since the act of reproduction of the work may economically make benefits to its owner.
- **Right to Distribute in Market** The owner of the copyrighted work also has a right to distribute in the market and make money out of it. The act of distribution may be in the form of sale, lending for free or for a consideration, rental or free distribution by the way of gift.
- **Right to Communication to the Public** It means letting or making the product/work **available to the public** by way of broadcasting, **simulcasting**[5] or webcasting.
- **Right of Adaptation** It includes conversion, alteration, **transcription**[6] or rearranging a copyrighted work.
- **Right to Translate** The owner of the copyrighted work has a right to translate his work to any other languages.

Moral Rights

Moral rights are personal ties between an author and their work. They afford control over the creation and protect against modification or alteration, preserving the work's integrity. This right would stand a step ahead of an economic right.

It includes the following

- **Right of Paternity** It means the right of an owner of copyright to claim and **prevent others to claim the ownership** of his copyrighted work.
- **Right of Integrity** It means the right of the owner of the copyright to protect the **reputation** of his own work from exploitation.
- **Right to Retraction** Retraction is an act of **taking back** the previous assertion made.

Importance of Copyright in Modern Society

Copyright is **required** in modern society **to provide legal protection** for creators of original works, such as literature, music, software and art. The importance of copyright is as follows

- Copyright helps to ensure that creators are **fairly compensated** for their work and that their work is not used or copied without permission.
- Copyright also **promotes creativity and innovation** by giving creators the exclusive right to control to use and distribute their works.
- Copyright plays a role in **stopping plagiarism** by providing legal protection for original works and giving the creators exclusive rights to control the use and distribution of their work.
- When someone is found to have plagiarised, they can be held liable for copyright violation, which can result in legal action, fines and other consequences.
- However, it is important to note that all instances of **plagiarism are not necessarily copyright violation,** as copyright law only applies to original works that are fixed in a tangible form.

---

5 **Simulcasting** means to broadcast simultaneously.

6 **Transcription** means a written or printed version of something.

9.4 Patent

- The patent grants an inventor absolute and exclusive ownership right over the invention, the freedom to use and sell the invention for a stipulated time period.
- A patent is a **legal document** which is issued by the government to the inventor. It is a **statutory right granted for an invention by the government** to the patentee for a limited period of time.
- It is given in exchange of full disclosure of his invention for excluding others, from making, using, selling, importing the patented product or process for producing that product for those purposes without his consent.
- **The term of every patent granted in India is 20 years from the date of filing of application.**
- The patent system in India is governed by the **Patents Act, 1970** as amended by the Patents (Amendment) Act, 2005 and the Patents Rules, 2003.
- The **purpose** of patent law is to **encourage scientific research, new technology and industrial progress.**
- There are **three** requirements which are required to be fulfilled for an idea to qualify as a patentable matter
  (i) **Novelty** The invention must contain one or more unique and new elements.
  (ii) **Non-obviousness** Simple or obvious changes to an existing invention cannot be called an invention. The invention must be a **notable**[7] change in the field. The particular feature must add to existing technical knowledge, in terms of uniqueness and commercial viability.
  (iii) **Industrial Application** The invention must have some utility. The invention is patentable if it is capable of commercialisation.

Examples of Patents Granted in India

Some interesting patents granted in India are

- **Memory Cells, Semiconductor Devices and Methods of Fabrication Gurtej Sandhu** has expertise and creativity in the field of inventing semiconductor devices and fabrication methods. He has filed over 1170 patent applications and is known as the **Indian who owns the highest number of patents.** His recognition as one of the most prolific inventors in the world is a **testament**[8] to his contributions to the field of semiconductor technology and his impact on the industry.
- **Susant's Breathing Sensor Apparatus** The Breathing Sensor Apparatus is a **unique** solution that allows people with disabilities to perform tasks independently, using only their breath. The collaboration between **Susant Pattnaik and the National Innovation Foundation** is also noteworthy, as it highlights the importance of partnerships between inventors and organisations in bringing innovative ideas to market.

  These patents showcase India's innovation and creativity in a variety of fields and demonstrate the importance of intellectual property protection in promoting and rewarding innovation.

7 **Notable** means worthy of attention or notice; remarkable.
8 **Testament** means something that serves as a sign or evidence of a specified fact, event or quality.

9.5 Trademark

- A 'mark' is a **distinguishing symbol** which any person can use to exert public attention or to create some kind of impression in the minds of the people.
- Trademark is a brand entity which has a capability to distinguish one's goods and services from another person's goods and services.
- Trademark includes **word, design, logo, shape of goods, their packaging and combination of colours.**
- Trademark rights in India are statutorily protected by the **Trademark Act, 1999.** The functions of a trademark are
  - It identifies the goods or services and its origin.
  - It guarantees its unchanged quality.
  - It advertises the goods or services.
  - It creates an image for the goods or services.
- The Registered Proprietor of a trademark can **create, establish and protect the goodwill of his products or services.** He can stop other traders from unlawfully using his trademark, sue for damages and secure destruction of infringing goods and or labels.

Difference between Trade Name and Trademark

- Both trade names and trademarks are important elements of a company's brand and play a crucial role in building and protecting the company's reputation and identity.
- **In many cases, a company's trade name becomes its trademark,** such as the example of Google. Registering a trademark offers additional protection and helps to secure the brand's identity.

Trade Name	Trademark
A trade name is the official name under which a company operates and is also known as a **doing business** as name or **assumed** name.	A trademark is the name, symbol, logo, slogan or sound that a business uses to market its products and services. It is a unique identifier that helps consumers to differentiate the products and services of one company from those of another.
A trade name does not provide brand name protection on its own, but registering it is an important step in protecting the name.	A trademark provides protection for a brand name and helps to distinguish a company's products and services from those of others.

Trade Secret

- Trade secrets can include a **wide range of confidential** information that is important for the success and survival of a business.
- This information can be in the form of strategies, designs, client databases, formulas, programmes or any other confidential information.
- This information must be kept secret to maintain the competitive advantage of the business.
- According to a landmark decision by the Delhi High Court in the case of **Burlington Home Shopping Pvt. Vs. Rajnish Chibber** (1995), a trade secret is defined as any information with commercial value, which is not available in the public domain and the disclosure of which would cause significant harm to the owner.
- According to the Trade Related Aspects of Intellectual Property Rights (TRIPs) Agreement, trade secret is defined as **information which is kept secret, has a commercial value and the owner of the information takes reasonable steps to keep it secret.**
- There is no specific legislation that provides protection for trade secrets, but they can be protected under various provisions of different statutes, such as Section 27 of the Contract Act, 1872. Indian courts have also recognised trade secret protection based on equity principles and common law remedies for breach of confidence and breach of contract.

9.6 Geographical Indication

- A Geographical Indication (GI) is a **legal designation** that identifies a product as originating **from a specific region or geographical location** and having certain qualities, characteristics or reputation that are unique to that place.
- GI protects the product's authenticity and quality, and helps consumers to identify the product's origin and reputation.
- It is a name or sign used on certain products which corresponds to a geographic origin of the product.
- The **Geographical Indications of Goods (Registration and Protection) Act, 1999** provides for registration and better protection of geographical indications relating to goods in India. Some examples of product with GI tag are Phulkari Handicraft of Punjab, Haryana and Rajasthan, Warli Painting of Maharashtra, Gujarat and Daman & Diu, Malabar Robusta Coffee of Kerala and Karnataka, Darjeeling Tea of West Bengal, Pochampally Ikkat of Telangana, etc.

Geographical Origin

- Geographical origin refers to the specific place or region where a product or item originates from.
- This can include the location where raw materials are sourced, where production takes place, or where a particular process or technique is used to create the product.
- Geographical origin can have a significant impact on the quality, reputation and cultural identity of a product. It is often used as a way of distinguishing and promoting products with unique characteristics and qualities. In some cases, geographical origin is also protected by intellectual property laws, such as geographical indications.

9.7 Designs

- Design intellectual property refers to **original and unique creations of the mind** that can be used commercially. The **Designs Act, 2000** is the law relating to the **protection of designs in India.**
- The law helps creators to earn recognition and financial benefits for their products. It also helps to prevent others from using their creations without permission.
- A design right protects the original and aesthetically unique appearance of a manufactured item, as long as it is new and not obvious. This type of protection only covers the ornamental aspects and does not extend to the functional or structural elements.
- Any design invented by a person shall be protected by designs.
- Shape, colour, line, pattern, etc are covered under designs.
- A design may not be eligible for registration if it lacks individual character, or if its appearance is solely dictated by its function.
- These criteria are used to assess the registrability of a design and ensure that it meets the necessary standards for protection under intellectual property law.
- Some examples of design intellectual property are design of the wrapper of a biscuit or chocolate, design of a car, design of the shape of a cold drink bottle, etc.

Quick Test 2

1. Under which section of the Copyright Act, the term work is defined?
2. What is the time period for every patent granted in India?
3. What is trademark?
4. Which act is provided for registration and better protection of geographical indications relating to goods in India?

REFERENCE CASES

Right to Retraction

Amarnath Sehgal Vs. Union of India 117 (2005) DLT 717

The plaintiff Amarnath Sehgal is a renowned artist and sculptor, who created a mural in the lobby of Vigyan Bhawan, Delhi on the direction of appropriate authority.

In 1979, the mural was pulled down and consigned to the store room of the union without notice or permission or authorisation of Amarnath. He filed a petition U/S 57 of the Copyright Act, 1957 in the DHC.

The court termed the moral rights as the soul of the author's work. "The author has a right to preserve, protect and nurture his creations through his moral rights. A creative individual is uniquely invested with the power and mystique of original genius, creating a privileged relationship between a creative author and his work".

Moral rights which define the essence of an author's work, cannot be taken away from the author, even if the work is sold.

Copy Right in Modern Society

Eastern Book Company and Others Vs. D.B. Modak Another, AIR 2008 SC 809

The extent of originality necessary to obtain copyright protection was the subject of inquiry. The plaintiff a renowned publisher, alleged that the defendants had infringed its work, a publication of SC orders and judgements, known as SCC, in a substantial manner. The defendants, in turn argued that there is a minimal level of creativity involved in such work, thus it is not eligible for copyright protection. The Supreme Court held that "The inputs put in the original text by the appellants in

- segragating the existing paragraphs in the original texts by breaking them into separate paragraphs,
- adding internal paragraph numbering within a judgement after providing uniform paragraph numbering to the multiple judgements and
- indicating in the judgement the judges who have dissented or concurred by introducing the phrases like concurring, 'party concurring', 'party dissenting', 'dissenting', 'supplementing', majority expressing no opinion, etc. have to be viewed in different light. The task of paragraph numbering and internal referencing requires skill and judgement in great measure. The editor who inserts para numbering must know how legal argumentation and legal disclosure is conducted and how a judgement of a court of law must read... In these inputs put in by the appellants in the judgements reported in SCC, the appellants have a copyright and nobody is permitted to utilise the same".

Mind Map

INTELLECTUAL PROPERTY LAW

1 Meaning of Intellectual Property

Definition
- Intellectual Property (IP) refers to creations of the human mind such as inventions, literary and artistic works, designs, symbols, names, and images used in commerce.

Key Characteristics
- Intangible in nature.
- Exists through human intellect and creativity.

Purpose of IP
- Encourage innovation by protecting the creator's rights.
- Promote economic, social and cultural development.

2 Forms of Intellectual Property Rights (IPR)

Copyright
- **Protects** Original works of authorship (literary, dramatic, musical, and artistic works, films and sound recordings).
- **Key Rights**
  - Reproduction of the work.
  - Communication to the public.
  - Adaptation and translation.
- **Duration**
  - Lifetime of the author + 60 years for literary, dramatic and artistic works.
  - 60 years from publication for sound recordings, films and government works.
- **Importance** Promotes creativity and prevents unauthorised copying.

Patent
- **Protects** Novel inventions with industrial utility.
- **Criteria for Grant**
  - **Novelty** Unique and new idea.
  - **Non-obviousness** Inventive step beyond prior art.
  - **Industrial Application** Practical utility or commercial viability.
- **Duration** 20 years from the filing date.
- **For example** Susant Pattnaik's breathing sensor apparatus.

Trademark
- **Governed by** Trademark Act, 1999.
- **Protects** Distinctive names, symbols, logos, designs and even sounds.
- **Functions**
  - Differentiates products and services in the market.
  - Ensures brand recognition and consumer trust.
- **For examples** Nike's shoes logo, Google's name.

Geographical Indications (GI)
- **Governed by** Geographical Indications of Goods (Registration and Protection) Act, 1999.
- **Protects** Products tied to a specific geographical region known for unique qualities.
- **For examples**
  - Darjeeling Tea (West Bengal)
  - Pochampally Ikkat (Telangana)

Designs
- **Governed by** Designs Act, 2000.
- **Protects** Ornamental or aesthetic aspects of an article.
- **For examples**
  - Unique packaging designs for products.
  - Shape of Coca-Cola bottles.

3 International Conventions

Paris Convention (1883)
- **Principles**
  - **National Treatment** Equal rights for foreign and domestic creators.
  - **Priority Framework** Simultaneous protection across member countries.

Berne Convention (1886)
- **Principles**
  - **Automatic Protection** Legal protection without formalities.
  - **Independence of Protection** Rights are not tied to the country of origin's laws.

Universal Copyright Convention (1952)
- **Principles**
  - **National Treatment** If the national requirements are not met then the contracting countries are not obligated to provide foreign works an automatic protection.
  - **Minimum Rights** Ensures uniform protection.

WIPO (1967)
- **Objectives**
  - Promote legal protection.
  - Facilitate administrative co-operation.

TRIPS Agreement (1995)
- **Aim** Harmonise global IP standards.
- **Scope** Covers all forms of IP.
- **Key Contribution** Strengthened enforcement measures globally.

4 Specific Acts in India

Copyright Act, 1957
- Protects original literary, artistic and musical works.

Patents Act, 1970 (Amended in 2005)
- Covers product and process patents.

Trademark Act, 1999
- Provides for registration and protection of trademarks.

Geographical Indications of Goods (Registration and Protection) Act, 1999
- Ensures legal protection for GI-tagged products.

Designs Act, 2000
- Protects the unique aesthetic design of products.

5 Key Case Studies

Amarnath Sehgal Vs. Union of India (2005)
- **Issue** Moral rights violation of a sculptor.
- **Ruling** Highlighted the importance of preserving the artist's integrity and creation.

Eastern Book Company Vs. D.B. Modak (2008)
- **Issue** Originality in copyright protection for legal commentaries.
- **Ruling** Recognised the skill and effort required in editing and organising content.

Burlington Home Shopping Vs. Rajnish Chibber (1995)
- **Issue** Misuse of trade secrets.
- **Ruling** Upheld the importance of confidentiality in business practices.

6 Importance of Intellectual Property

For Creators
- Provides exclusive rights and monetary rewards.
- Prevents unauthorised use and infringement.

For Society
- Encourages innovation and creativity.
- Enhances economic and cultural development.

CBSE TEXTBOOK FOLDER

1. What is meant by Intellectual Property? Why does intellectual property need to be promoted and protected?

Ans. Intellectual Property (IP) refers to creations of the mind, such as inventions literary and artistic works, designs, symbols, names and images used in commerce.

According to specific circumstances, you can use patents, trademarks or copyrights, all of which cover different areas of intellectual property, to protect any unique products or services that you own.

If you are a small business, it's important to protect any unique products or services that you own as competitors can use your success to take away market share, result in a loss of revenue and cause other problems.

Protecting your intellectual property may first appear tough or time-consuming, but it is worth the effort and isn't as challenging as you may believe. While you cannot protect an idea itself, you can protect the methods you use to carry out the idea, and this is what Intellectual Property (IP) is used to protect.

2. Discuss the concept of National Treatment and its evolution through the various international conventions on Intellectual Property Rights.

Ans. An international legal principle known as 'national treatment' states that if a state gives certain rights and benefits to its residents, it also provides the same rights and privileges to foreigners who are already residing in the country. Giving strangers the same treatment as one's nationals is known as the 'national treatment' principle.

One of the key principles of the international treaties protecting intellectual property is national treatment. It is outlined in the most significant conventions, including TRIPS, the Paris Convention, the Berne Convention, the Rome Convention and the Universal Copyright Convention.

Paris Convention Through Articles 2 and 3, the convention assures national treatment. According to the convention, national treatment provides each member state to provide qualified foreigners with the same level of protection for the intellectual property listed in the convention as it provides for its citizens.

Berne Convention Nationals of the Berne Union, people who have their habitual residence in one of these nations, individuals who are not nationals of these countries and people whose works were first published in one of these countries (or at the same time in a country outside the union and a country of the union), are all eligible for national treatment.

3. Describe copyright and the works protected under Copyright Act.

Ans. The term copyright is a combination of the terms 'copy' and 'right'. To be more specific, copyright refers to the 'right to copy', which indicates that only the creator or his approved person has the right to duplicate work.

The different types of works protected by copyright are as follows

- **Literary Works** The term 'literary works' refers to any original or distinctive work of literature, including fiction, technical publications or papers, biographies, plays, theses, scripts, research projects, compilations, tables and computer programmes, including databases.
- **Dramatic Work** Another category of literary work is dramatic work. Any arrangement of acting in a play, a role for recitation, choreography, dumb show entertainment, a beautiful structure or acting work based on a fixed writing work is included in the category of dramatic works. However, there are no cinematograph films included in the dramatic works.
- **Musical Work** A musical work is a unique creation that is protected by copyright. There are no sounds or lyrics in the musical works they are a requirement for the creation of works linked to sound recordings. Each musical work must be registered with the copyright office separately to be protected.
- **Artistic Work** Under Section 2 of the Copyright Act, 1957, an original artistic work that includes castings for sculptures, paintings, cartoons, graphics, lithographs, etchings, plans, photographs, diagrams, models of buildings, charts, buildings and maps, are protected by copyright.

4. You are an author who has written a novel in Hindi. The novel has become immensely popular and now podcasters, serial producers and youtubers are trying to adapt the story to be telecast on various forms of media. There are some authors who also want to translate your novel into English.

Discuss how you will negotiate in this situation given that you have certain economic rights as a copyright owner.

Ans. As the copyright owner, only I can economically gain from my creation. So if someone wants to make a serial from the novel, they have to take my permission and give me monetary compensation for using my creations.

In detail I will only give a certain right to a certain individual. If I have permitted you to make a television serial on it then you can only make a serial and all other rights will be with me and if you want to again make a movie on the novel, you will have to again take my permission and again give me monetary compensation for using my copyright work.

I will also be eligible to take royalty from the profits earned from the adaptation of my novel. If there is a sequel to be made of my work, again my prior approval and separate contract will be entered into for that purpose.

There will be a fixed time limit for making the serial or youtube video and if the time is expired then again the right will be with me to give to some other individual to adapt my novel.

For the people who want to translate it will also have to give me monetary compensation and royalty in the book translated in a particular language and if you want to translate it in any other language again, similar process will be followed.

Proper credit must be given to me for writing the novel in every serial, youtube video and book translated from my novel. Only particular rights will be awarded to one person and all the other rights will vest in me.

No changes will be made to the story, its characters, its names and its storyline without my prior written permission in any of the serial, youtube videos and book translated from my novel.

5. There was a recent tiff between the states of Odisha and West Bengal over the origin of the ever-popular sweet dish 'Rasgulla'. Both states argued that the 'Rasgulla' had been invented in their respective states. However, the registrar of the Chennai GI office gave the GI tag to the Banglar Rasogolla of West Bengal. This caused a rift between the states as both were competing to get the GI tag for Rasgolla for their respective states. In light of the above case discuss

(i) **What rights does a geographical indication provide? How would Orissa be adversely affected by the order of the Chennai GI office?**

(ii) **For which types of products can GI tags be used?**

Ans. (i) The GI provides the following

- A exclusive right to access or use GI's products which are registered geographical indications.
- Authorised user has the right to sue for infringement.
- Legal protection is available to geographical signs in India.
- There can be no unauthorised use of registered geographical indications by others.
- The economic prosperity of the area in which the registered product is produced increases.

Orissa cannot claim that the registered product originated there and it can not market that product in the domestic and international markets exclusively. Bengal now has the right to exclusively enjoy the GI tag and it has the legal claim on the origin of Banglar Rasogolla.

(ii) Geographical indications are typically used for agricultural products, foodstuffs, wine and spirit drinks, handicrafts and industrial products.

6. Valganciclovir hydrochloride is a medicine that is stable when stored as a solid-state under normal conditions. The applicant tried to make a liquid form of the medicine, but it was unstable for the required shelf life. Therefore, they focused on a powder form that could be mixed with water to make a liquid form. The powder form was very similar to the solid form and their patent claim was rejected.

Discuss why the patent claim was rejected in view of the essential ingredients of a successful patent claim.

Ans. If the essential part of patent claims is not found properly, then, patent claims can become unsuccessful easily. The three essential patent claims parts are

- **Preamble** It is the first component of a patent claim and specifies the type of invention, such as an apparatus, item, substance method or procedure.
- **Transitional Phrases** It refer to the phrases that connect the preamble of a claim to the components mentioned in the claim (which explains the functioning of an invention).
- **The Body** It provides a detailed description of the claims. It attempts to interlink and describe the relationship between the components of the invention.

Exam Pattern Questions

Objective Type Questions

Multiple Choice Questions (MCQs)

1. Rajiv is an artist who has created a unique logo for his small business. Without his permission, another company begins using a similar logo for its products, causing confusion among customers. Rajiv wants to take legal action, but he did not formally register his logo under trademark law.

Under which of the following circumstances can Rajiv still claim protection for his intellectual property?

(a) Rajiv cannot claim any protection since his logo is not registered as a trademark.
(b) Rajiv can claim protection if he has evidence that his logo has acquired distinctiveness through extensive use in the market.
(c) Rajiv can only seek protection if his logo is patented as intellectual property.
(d) Rajiv can claim protection only if the company using his logo agrees to settle the dispute out of court.

2. A patent can be granted for ....

(a) process (b) product
(c) ideas (d) Both (a) and (b)

3. A photographer captures a unique image of a natural phenomenon and shares it on their personal social media account without watermarks or restrictions. An advertisement agency downloads the photograph and uses it in a commercial campaign without the photographer's consent.

Under the Copyright Act, 1957, what legal course of action does the photographer have?

(a) The photographer cannot take legal action as the photograph was shared publicly without restrictions.
(b) The photographer can claim copyright infringement as the work is automatically protected under the Copyright Act upon creation.
(c) The agency can argue fair use since the photograph was already shared publicly on social media.
(d) The agency must only credit the photographer to avoid liability for copyright infringement.

4. Rohit is a filmmaker who creates a documentary and grants exclusive streaming rights to Platform 'A'. Another platform, Platform 'B', broadcasts the documentary without obtaining permission from either Rohit or Platform 'A'. Rohit files a complaint claiming his economic rights have been violated.

Which specific right has been infringed upon in this case?

(a) Right of adaptation
(b) Right to communication to the public
(c) Right to distribute in the market
(d) Right of paternity

5. Which of the following is not patentable?

(a) Which involves inventive steps.
(b) Product which is used for medical treatment of human beings and animals.
(c) Process of medical treatment of human beings and animals.
(d) None of the above

6. Which of the following conditions needs to be fulfilled by Sakshi's invention to be eligible for protection under intellectual property ? **CBSE 2024**

(a) Invention should fall within the category of 'work'.
(b) Invention has a special scheme of shape, colour, line, pattern, etc.
(c) Invention must be a notable change in the field and has commercial viability.
(d) Invention must be indicative of its geographic origin.

7. An author, Priya, writes a novel and allows a publisher to distribute printed copies. Without her knowledge, the publisher converts the novel into an audiobook and begins selling it. Priya claims this is a violation of her copyright.

Which specific right does this scenario address?

(a) Right of adaptation
(b) Right to distribute in the market
(c) Right of integrity
(d) Right to reproduce the work

8. The main essentials of the trademark include ....

(a) easy to pronounce (b) invented word
(c) distinctiveness (d) it should be short

9. A software developer writes an original piece of code for a program. Another developer modifies a small portion of the code and integrates it into their own commercial software, claiming that the modification makes it a new creation.

What is the likely legal outcome if the original developer files a complaint under the Copyright Act, 1957?

(a) The modified code is considered a new creation, so no infringement has occurred.
(b) The original developer can claim copyright infringement if it is proven that the new code substantially relies on the original work.

(c) The second developer is free to use the code as long as they credit the original developer.
(d) The second developer can avoid liability by demonstrating that only a minor portion of the code was copied.

10. Which of the following scenarios best demonstrates the importance of registering a trademark for a business?
(a) A local bakery wants to ensure that its unique recipe for sourdough bread is not copied by other bakeries.
(b) A software company seeks to protect the source code of its innovative application from being used by competitors.
(c) A fashion designer wishes to secure the exclusive design pattern used in their clothing line against replication.
(d) A new coffee shop aims to protect its brand name and logo from being used by others.

11. Trademark Act, came into force in ....
(a) 1957 (b) 2000 (c) 1970 (d) 1999

12. Athelix Co. has been successfully selling its unique line of sports apparel under the brand name 'Athlo Gear' for several years. The company wants to ensure that its brand is protected from unauthorised use and imitation.
Which of the following is the best option for the company to safeguard its brand name? **CBSE 2024 C**
(a) Register the brand name 'Athlo Gear' as a trademark to secure exclusive rights and prevent others from using the same or similar name in the sports apparel industry.
(b) Maintain a record of the brand name's usage and advertise campaigns to establish a common law trademark based on reputation and customer recognition.
(c) Collaborate with other sports apparel companies to refrain from using similar brand names, ensuring protection against unauthorised use and confusion in the market.
(d) Combine the brand name 'Athlo Gear' with a generic term to create a descriptive trademark, maintaining exclusivity while conveying product features.

13. Emma a talented photographer, discovers that her original photograph has been reproduced without her permission and is being sold at an art gallery. The gallery has financial loss and diminishing the value of her artistic creation.
Which of the following intellectual property right of Emma is being violated by the art gallery?
(a) Patent (b) Trademark
(c) Copyright (d) Trade Secret

14. Microhand Co. has created a new software programme that provides unique user interface and advanced features. They want to protect their software from being copied or used without their permission.
Identify the IPR type that Microhand Co. should seek to protect their software programme. **CBSE 2024 C**
(a) Trade Secret (b) Trademark
(c) Patent (d) Copyright

15. Geographical Indication (GI) tag is given as per the ......
(a) Indian Copyright Act, 1957
(b) New Design Act, 2000
(c) Patent Act, 1970
(d) Geographical Indications (Registration and Protection) Act,1999

16. Which is not a type of intellectual property?
(a) Trade secrets (b) Trademarks
(c) Home loans (d) Copyrights

17. Which of the following identifies as a trademark?
(a) Name, symbol (b) Symbol, logo
(c) Logo, name (d) Name, symbol, logo

18. After his death in 2035, how many years will his heirs enjoy copyright protection over the novel?
(a) 50 years from publication
(b) 60 years from publication
(c) 60 years from author's death
(d) 50 years from author's death

19. A tech startup, "Innovate X", develops a proprietary algorithm for predicting stock market trends. They keep the algorithm's source code confidential, limiting access to a small team of developers. They also implement strict security measures to protect the code from unauthorised access.
What type of intellectual property best protects Innovate X's algorithm?
(a) Patent (b) Trademark (c) Copyright (d) Trade Secret

20. Match the following.

Column I	Column II
A. The Paris Convention	1. 14th July 1967
B. The Berne Convention	2. 20th March 1883
C. The Universal Copyright Convention	3. 9th September 1886
D. World Intellectual Property Organisation	4. 6th September 1952

Codes

	A	B	C	D
(a)	2	3	4	1
(b)	1	3	2	4
(c)	2	1	4	3
(d)	3	2	1	4

21. Match the following.

Column I	Column II
A. Copyrights	1. Name and logo of a product
B. Patents	2. Books
C. Trademark	3. Information
D. Trade Secrets	4. Mobile phones

Codes

	A	B	C	D
(a)	4	1	2	3
(b)	2	4	3	1
(c)	2	4	1	3
(d)	3	4	1	2

22. **What is the primary purpose of Paris Convention?**

Statement I The Paris Convention provides a framework for protecting industrial property rights across member countries.

Statement II The convention establishes common rule for copyright protection.

Options

(a) Only Statement I is correct.
(b) Only Statement II is correct.
(c) Both the Statements are incorrect.
(d) Both the Statements are correct.

23. **What was the primary objective of General Agreement on Tariffs and Trade (GATT)?**

Statement I GATT sought to establish a multilateral framework for international trade, promoting co-operation and fair competition among nations.

Statement II GATT aimed to promote international trade by reducing tariffs and other trade barriers.

Codes

(a) Only Statement I is correct.
(b) Only Statement II is correct.
(c) Both the Statements are incorrect.
(d) Both the Statements are correct.

Assertion-Reason Questions

Directions (Q.Nos. 24-27) In the questions given below, there are two statements. Read the statements and choose the correct option.

Codes

(a) Both A and R are true and R is the correct explanation of A.
(b) Both A and R are true, but R is not the correct explanation of A.
(c) A is true, but R is false.
(d) A is false, but R is true.

24. **Assertion** (A) Intellectual property means ownership of ideas.

Reason (R) Patents, copyright and trademark are intellectual property rights.

25. **Assertion** (A) Trademark registration gives exclusive proprietary rights to the trademark owner.

Reason (R) A trademark is a recognisable sign, design or expression which identifies products or services of a particular source from those of others. And are used to claim exclusive proprietary rights to products or services.

26. **Assertion** (A) An American company is allowed as the company to sell a 'new' variety of Basmati rice.

Reason (R) Indian Basmati was crossed with semi dwarf varieties and claimed as a novelty.

27. **Assertion** (A) That part of brand, which can be spoken, is called a brand name.

Reason (R) That part of brand which can be recognised but which is not utterable is called trademark.

Answers

1. (b) Rajiv can claim protection if he has evidence that his logo has acquired distinctiveness through extensive use in the market.
2. (d) Both (a) and (b)
3. (b) The photographer can claim copyright infringement as the work is automatically protected under the Copyright Act upon creation.
4. (b) Right to communication to the public
5. (c) Process of medical treatment of human beings and animals.
6. (c) Invention must be a notable change in the field and has commercial viability.
7. (a) Right of adaptation
8. (c) distinctiveness
9. (b) The original developer can claim copyright infringement if it is proven that the new code substantially relies on the original work.
10. (d) A new coffee shop aims to protect its brand name and logo from being used by others.
11. (d) 1999
12. (a) Register the brand name 'Athlo Gear' as a trademark to secure exclusive rights and prevent others from using the same or similar name in the sports apparel industry.
13. (c) Copyright
14. (d) Copyright
15. (d) Geographical Indications (Registration and Protection) Act, 1999
16. (c) Home loans
17. (d) Name, symbol, logo
18. (c) 60 years from author's death
19. (d) Trade Secret
20. (a) 2 3 4 1
21. (c) 2 4 1 3
22. (a) Only Statement 1 is correct.
23. (d) Both the Statements are correct.
24. (b) Both A and R are true, but R is not the correct explanation of A.
25. (a) Both A and R are true and R is the correct explanation of A.
26. (b) Both A and R are true, but R is not the correct explanation of A.
27. (c) A is true, but R is false.

Subjective Questions

Very Short Answer Type Questions

1. Describe the meaning of intellectual property and how this property is different from other property.

Ans. Intellectual property is a type of property that incorporates intangible human intelligence creations. Patents, copyrights, trademarks and trade secrets are the most well-known categories.

This property is different from other properties because it is only used in the creation and associated with the human mind only.

2. Alisha writes a novel "The Hidden Treasure" in 2018. She publishes it in 2020. In 2022 a playwright adapts her novel into a play without her permission. Alisha had registered her novel with the copyright office in 2019. What is the legal recourse available to Alisha against the playwright?

Ans. Alisha can sue the playwright for copyright infringement, seeking damages and an injunction to stop the play's production. Her registration serves as a proof of ownership and adaptation without permission violates her exclusive rights under the Copyright Act, 1957.

3. Which type of work is covered under the Copyright Act?

Ans. Copyright Act protects the rights of authors or those who create intellectual property in the form of literary, musical, dramatic or artistic works, as well as cinematograph films and sound recordings.

4. What are the two other conventions included in the Universal Copyright Convention?

Ans. The Universal Copyright Convention (UCC), adopted in Geneva, Switzerland, in 1952, is one of the two principal international conventions protecting copyright, the other is the Berne Convention.

5. Maya, a talented writer, composes a captivating short story and publishes it on her personal blog. Later, she discovers that a well known author Ravi, has copied substantial portions of her story and published it under his name in a bestselling book. Explain the basis of legal action that Maya can take in this situation. **CBSE 2024 C**

Ans. Maya can take legal action against Ravi for copyright infringement. As the original author, Maya owns the copyright to her short story. Ravi's unauthorised copying and publication of substantial portions of her work constitute a violation of her exclusive rights under the Copyright Act.

6. Discuss different types of intellectual property rights in India and specify their names only in the answer.

Ans. There are seven different kinds of IP rights recognised in India. They are copyright, trademarks, patents, geographical indications, plant varieties, industrial designs and designs for semi-conductor integrated circuits.

7. A successful start-up, Tech Genius has developed a cutting-edge software that has gained immense popularity in the market. To protect their unique brand identity and product, they are considering whether to register a trademark or maintain it as a trade secret. Explain the fundamental difference between trademark and trade secret to Tech Genius, that would help them in decision-making. **CBSE 2024**

Ans. To protect their unique brand identity and product, they should consider to register a trademark because trademark provides protection for brand name and helps to distinguish a company's products and services from those of others. Whereas on the other hand if the company wants to maintain it as a trade secret, then the company cannot protect their brand identity whereas it can protect wide range of confidential information that must be secret to maintain competitive advantage.

8. Shagun designs a unique shape for a smartphone case in 2020. His design is titled "Curve pro" and has become popular. He files a design application in 2022 and receives registration certification in 2023. In 2024, a manufacturer produces identical cases without Shagun's permission. What is Shagun's legal recourse?

Ans. Under the Design Act, 2000. Shagun's registered design is protected for 10 years. He can sue the manufacturer for infringement, seeking damages and an injunction, as the identical reproduction violates his exclusive rights (Section 11). Registration provides prima facie evidence of ownership (Section 46).

9. Which is the first international organisation which promotes international intellectual property rights?

Ans. World Intellectual Property Organisation is the first international organisation which promotes international intellectual property rights.

Short Answer Type Questions

1. Which rights are given to the owner of the copyright under the Copyright Act, 1957?

Ans. Rights of the owner of a copyright can be categorised into two groups, economic rights and moral rights. Economic rights allow owner to derive financial reward from the use of their works by others.

Economic rights are as follows

- Right to Reproduce the Work
- Right to Distribute in Market
- Right to Communication to the Public
- Right of Adaptation
- Right to Translate

Moral rights are personal ties between an author and their work. They afford control over the creation and protect against modification or alteration, preserving the work's integrity. It includes the following

- Right of Paternity
- Right of Integrity
- Right to Retraction

2. A group of students working on a school project decide to use an image they found on the Internet to enhance their presentation. The image is a beautiful artwork they believe will enhance the visual appeal of their project. However, they are unsure about using it due to copyright concerns. Explain the moral rights of the owner of the copyright in this situation. **CBSE 2024 C**

Ans. The moral rights of the copyright owner in this situation include

- **Right of Paternity** The right to be credited as the creator of the artwork.
- **Right of Integrity** The right to protect the artwork from distortion, mutilation, or modification that could harm its reputation.

Using the artwork without permission or proper attribution would infringe on these moral rights, potentially causing harm to the creator's reputation and artistic integrity.

3. Why trademark should be necessary to be registered in this 21st century?

Ans. Trademark should be necessary to be registered due to the following

- Startups can safeguard their brand through trademarking. By registering a company name as a trademark, one makes its services and goods stand out from those of its rivals and turns it into intellectual property.
- If a company doesn't register a trademark, businesses that have the same name, sign, slogan or design as them may file legal claims against them.
- A trademark is perpetual and requires only sporadic renewal.
- Utilise a trademark in marketing campaigns to help build brand awareness and attract more customers.

4. Describe the role of the Berne Convention in the international development of intellectual property rights.

Ans. The Berne Convention was adopted on 9th September, 1886 and came into force on 4th December, 1887. It follows principles of national treatment, automatic protection and independence of protection.

According to principle of national treatment under this convention, any work originating in a contracting state, including works of authors who are nationals of that state or works first published in that state, should receive the same legal protection in every other contracting state as the latter state grants to its own nationals.

The principle of automatic protection under this convention mandated that legal protection should not be subject to compliance with any formalities.

The principle of independence of protection under this convention decreed that legal protection should be independent of the existence of protection in the country of origin of the work.

5. Suresh creates a unique smartphone case design and writes a user manual with original illustrations. He registered the design under the Design Act, 2000 and copyrighted the manual under the Copyright Act, 1957. Suresh's design and manual are reproduced without permission. What are the key differences in protection offered to Rahul?

Ans. Original literary, dramatic, musical, and creative works are protected by the automatic right known as copyright. A design right safeguards an object's or a component of an object's exterior look.

Any creative work that gives the author an exclusive right over it has a copyright, according to the Copyright Act, 1957. According to the Designs Act, 2000, a design is an applied external element that is mainly judged by the vision.

When a work takes on an actual form, it becomes protected by copyright however, a design is not protected until it is registered. Design is a legislative right, whereas copyright is an inherent right.

6. Discuss the principle followed by the Paris Convention for the protection of industrial properties.

Ans. The Paris Convention was adopted on 20th March, 1883 in Paris and was enforced on 7th July, 1884. It follows the principles of national treatment and framework of priority. In the context of legal protection for industrial property, the principle of national treatment requires each member country of the Paris Convention to provide equal legal protection for the inventions of nationals from other member countries, as it would provide for its own nationals.

The principle of priority framework allows an inventor to protect their invention simultaneously in various countries.

7. What is required to qualify as a patentable matter? Discuss.

Ans. There are three requirements which are required to be fulfilled for an idea to qualify as a patentable matter

- **Novelty** The invention must contain one or more unique and new elements.
- **Non-obviousness** Simple or obvious changes to an existing invention cannot be called an invention. The invention must be a notable change in the field. The particular feature must add to existing technical knowledge, in terms of uniqueness and commercial viability.
- **Industrial Application** The invention must have some utility. The invention is patentable if it is capable of commercialisation.

8. Mr. 'X' purchased his shoes from the Yikee company. After some days Mr. Y's showroom launched the Nikee name shoe brand. And Mr. 'X' noticed that the trademark which is used by the Nikee company arrow mark is similar to the Yikee company. after that, Mr. 'X' complained about this situation in the Yikee company. Explain in this situation what will be the Yikee company will do.

(i) What are the remedies available to the Yikee company in the infringement of a trademark?

(ii) Which type of punishment is given to the accused for such acts?

(iii) In which act is used for the case for filing in the court?

Ans. (i) The party who was damaged can file for damages because his or her business has suffered losses as a result of losing the exclusive right to use the trademark that he or she owns.

Section 29 and Section 30 of the Trade Marks Act, 1999 gives remedies for infringement of trademarks.

(ii) The punishment could be 6 months of imprisonment which could be extended to a time frame of 3 years for infringing trademark rights.

(iii) Trademark Act, 1999

9. 'A' who has written his novel. 'B' wants to take credit for this novel and copy-paste all the material which is written in the novel. He wants to publish this novel by his name. In this situation 'A' how to save his novel through this infringement issue?

(i) What are the solutions available to 'A' in this infringement issue?

(ii) Is anyone have a right to take creator material without their consent and is it illegal?

(iii) Which type of copyright work is covered under this situation? Also name other works covered under the Copyright Act, 1957.

Ans. (i) 'A' can file a case against 'B' for the copyright infringement issue.

For infringement of copyright, the criminal remedies provided under Section 63 are

- Imprisonment, not less than 6 months which may extend up to 3 years.
- A fine may not be less than ₹ 50,000 which may extend up to ₹ 2,00,000
- Search and seisure of copyrighted goods.
- Delivery of copyrighted goods to the copyrighted owner.

(ii) No, anyone cannot take any part of their work details without consent. They can become accused of the copyright issue. It is completely illegal in the eye of the law.

(iii) Literary work is covered under this situation. Some other works covered under the Copyright Act, 1957 are musical, dramatic, and artistic works and cinematograph films and sound recordings.

10. Sneha started a beauty care brand called "Glow Essence", offering organic skin care products. Within a year her brand gained popularity for its quality and natural ingredients. However, Sneha discovered that another company was selling low quality skin care products under the similar name leading to confusion among customers. This damaged her brand's reputation. **CBSE 2025**

On consulting a legal expert Sneha learned that "Glow Essence" is a trade name and not a trade mark. She initiated the registration process.

(i) Differentiate between a trade name and a trade mark .

(ii) Explain, how registration of "Glow Essence" benefit Sneha.

Ans. (i) A trade name is the official name under which a company operates, while a trademark is a distinctive mark, logo, symbol, or phrase that differentiates a company's goods or services from others. A trade name does not provide brand protection, whereas a trademark ensures legal security for brand identity.

(ii) Registering "Glow Essence" as a trademark will prevent unauthorised use by others, helping Sneha secure her brand identity and reputation. It grants her exclusive rights, allowing legal action against infringers and protecting customers from confusion.

Long Answer Type Questions

1. Describe the historical background and development of intellectual property rights.

Ans. The importance and role of intellectual property protection emerged with the establishment of the World Trade Organisation (WTO) in the **Trade-Related Intellectual Property Systems (TRIPS) Agreement.** It was negotiated at the end of the Uruguay Round of the General Agreement on Tariffs and Trade (GATT) treaty in 1994.

The TRIPS Agreement came into effect on 1st January, 1995 and is the most comprehensive multilateral agreement on intellectual property. It encompasses all forms of intellectual property and aims at harmonising and strengthening standards of protection and providing effective enforcement of intellectual property rights at both national and international levels.

India being signatory to the TRIPS Agreement has passed several legislations for the protection of intellectual property rights to meet the international obligations.

Some of these legislations are listed below

- Trade Mark Act, 1999
- Designs Act, 2000
- Copyright Act, 1957 (as amended)
- Patents Act, 1970 (as amended)
- Geographical Indications of Goods (Registration and Protection) Act, 1999
- Protection of Plant Varieties and Farmers' Rights Act, 2001

2. (i) **What is meant by intellectual property?**
(ii) **Explain the evolution of Indian IPR Laws through any three international conventions on IPR.**
CBSE SQP 2024

Ans. (i) Intellectual property is an intangible property that comes into existence through human intellect. It refers to the creation of the mind or products of human intelligence such as inventions, designs, artistic work, names, symbols, images etc.

(ii) (a) The Paris Convention for the protection of Industrial Properties

- **National Treatment** In the context of legal protection for industrial property the principle of National Treatment requires each member country of the Paris Convention to provide equal legal protection for the inventions of nationals from other member countries, as it would for its own nationals.
- **Framework of Prioity** The Paris Convention also upholds the principle of 'priority framework' allowing an inventor to protect their invention simultaneously in various countries.

(b) The Berne Convention for the protection of Literary and Artistic Works

- **National Treatment** Stipulated that any work originating in a contracting state including works of authors who are nationals of that state or works first published in that state or works first published in that state, should receive the same legal protection in every other contracting state as the latter state grants to its own nationals.
- Automatic Protection mandated that legal protection should not be subject to compliance with any formalities.
- Independence of protection decreed that legal protection should be independent of the existence of protection in the country of origin of the work.

(c) The Universal Copyright Convention (UCC)

- **National Treatment** The UCC adheres to the principle of national treatment rather than automatic protection, which implies that contracting countries are not obligated to provide foreingn works with automatic protection if the national requirements are not met.
- The term of the work under the UCC, original literary, artistic and scientific works are eligible for protection. To provide reasonable notice of UCC stipulates that protection for a work lasts for the duration of the author's lifetime and an additional 25 years following the author's death.
- **Minimum Rights** As per the UCC's provisions, the contracting countries must provide a specific set of 'minimum rights' to the lawful owner of the work, provided they do not create any conflict with the 'spirit' of the convention.

3. What is a trademark and how is it different from a trade name?

Ans. Trademark is a brand entity which has a capability to distinguish one's goods and services from another person's goods and services.

Trademark includes word, design, logo, shape of goods, their packaging and combination of colours. Trademark rights in India are statutorily protected by the Trademark Act, 1999.

Both trade names and trademarks are important elements of a company's brand and play a crucial role in building and protecting the company's reputation and identity.

A trade name is the official name under which a company operates and is also known as a **doing business as** name or **assumed** name. On the other hand, a trademark is the name, symbol, logo, slogan or sound that a business uses to market its products and services. It is a unique identifier that helps consumers to differentiate the products and services of one company from those of another.

A trade name does not provide brand name protection on its own, but registering it is an important step in protecting the name. On the other hand, a trademark provides protection for a brand name and helps to distinguish a company's products and services from those of others. In many cases, a company's trade name becomes its trademark, such as the example of Google. Registering a trademark offers additional protection and helps to secure the brand's identity.

4. Explain the concept of 'trade secrets' in intellectual property law. Discuss the legal protection provided to trade secrets under Indian law. How do these protections differ from patents and copyrights in terms of duration and scope? **CBSE 2025**

Ans. Trade secrets in intellectual property law refer to confidential business information that provides a competitive edge. This includes formulas, processes, client lists and business strategies.

In India, there is no specific legislation for trade secrets, but they are protected under contract law, equity principles and common law remedies. Section 272 of the Indian Contract Act, 1872, offers legal recourse for breach of confidentiality.

Unlike patents and copyrights, trade secrets do not have a fixed duration and remain protected as long as they remain undisclosed. Patents require public disclosure and last 20 years, while copyrights protect creative works for the author's lifetime plus 60 years .

5. Discuss patents granted in India through examples.

Ans. Some interesting patents granted in India are

- **Memory Cells, Semi-conductor Devices and Methods of Fabrication** Gurtej Sandhu has expertise and creativity in the field of inventing semi-conductor devices and fabrication methods. He has filed over 1170 patent applications and is known as the Indian who owns the highest number of patents. His recognition as one of the most prolific inventors in the world is a testament to his contributions to the field of semiconductor technology and his impact on the industry.
- **Susant's Breathing Sensor Apparatus** The Breathing Sensor Apparatus is a unique solution that allows people with disabilities to perform tasks independently, using only their breath. The collaboration between Susant Pattnaik and the National Innovation Foundation is also noteworthy, as it highlights the importance of partnerships between inventors and organisations in bringing innovative ideas to market.

These patents showcase India's innovation and creativity in a variety of fields and demonstrate the importance of intellectual property protection in promoting and rewarding innovation.

6. Which intellectual property right is used to protect original and unique creations of the mind that can be used commercially? Explain.

Ans. Design itellectual property is used to protect original and unique creations of the mind that can be used commercially.

The Designs Act, 2000 is the law relating to the protection of designs in India. The law helps creators to earn recognition and financial benefits for their products. It also helps to prevent others from using their creations without permission.

A design right protects the original and aesthetically unique appearance of a manufactured item, as long as it is new and not obvious. This type of protection only covers the ornamental aspects and does not extend to the functional or structural elements. Any design invented by a person shall be protected by designs. Shape, colour, line, pattern, etc. are covered under designs.

A design may not be eligible for registration if it lacks individual character, or if its appearance is solely dictated by its function. These criteria are used to assess the registrability of a design and ensure that it meets the necessary standards for protection under intellectual property law.

Some examples of design intellectual property are design of the wrapper of a biscuit or chocolate, design of a car, design of the shape of a cold drink bottle etc.

SELF ASSESSMENT TEST

Objective Type Questions

1. What is the main purpose of IP?
   (a) Encourage new creation (b) More marketing
   (c) More investment (d) All of these
2. 'A' who is like to do graphic designing and usually does this for paid purposes as well. One day another company employee use their design without his consent and present his idea and sell his design to their client. 'B' who is the friend of 'A', told him about this situation. Now in this situation, which type of IPR issue arose for the 'A' scenario?
   (a) Copyright (b) Trademark (c) Design (d) Patent
3. Which of the following organisations in India is involved in IPR?
   (a) The Ministry of Commerce and Industry, Ministry of Human Resource Development
   (b) Ministry of Information and Broadcasting
   (c) Federation of Indian Chambers of Commerce and Industries
   (d) All of the above
4. Which of the following can be constituents of a design under the Designs Act, 2000?
   (a) Shape or configuration (b) Composition of lines or colours
   (c) Pattern or ornament (d) All of these

Very Short Answer Type Questions

5. Are computer software, Instagram reels and online published articles copyrightable under the copyright act 1957?
6. What is a geographical indication and which statute and act is used for the issues in India?

Short Answer Type Questions

7. Do intellectual property rights work for the creators and safeguard their rights and give them some relief for their losses?
8. Ajay, an Indian author publishes his novel "The quest" in India in 2020. His novel is translated and published in country 'A', 'B' and 'C' without permission. He wants to protect his work globally. Country 'A' is signatory the Paris Convention (PC) and Universal Copyright Convention (UCC) country 'B' is signatory of (UCC) only, Country 'C' is signatory of (PC) only. Identify the international agreement's framework and objective in each country accordingly.

Long Answer Type Questions

9. Mr. Ram is a music composer and works in the XYZ company. Mr. Ravi is a new composer in the music industry and he always tries to copy Ram in the music composition. He launched one song which is composed by Ram. He took every credit for his song. When this situation arises for Ram then what should Ram will do in this situation? How should Ram safeguard his rights with the help of IPR and what penalty will impose on Ravi for this offence? State your answer with the help of a law perspective.
10. What are the economic and moral rights of the owner of a copyright?

10

CHAPTER

Law and Sustainable Development

Sustainable development is defined as economic development that meets the needs of the present without compromising the ability of the future generations to meet their own needs.

▼ **YOUR STUDY GOALS**

▼ **YOUR PRACTICE GOAL**

- Objective Type Questions (21 Qs ; MCQs, A-R, Matching, Statements)
- Subjective Questions (7 VSAs, 5 SAs, 4 LAs)

10.1 Introduction

- The **aim** of sustainable development is to achieve **long term economic growth** by lowering the impact on the environment by **reducing air, water and soil pollution,** so that a better life is ensured for the future generations.
- Some examples of sustainable practices are **harnessing**[1] solar energy to reduce pollution in the environment and planting different types of crops on the same land on a rotational basis for improving soil fertility.
- In law, sustainable development is an approach to economic planning that attempts to promote economic growth while preserving the quality of the environment for future generations.

Sustainable Development Goals (SDGs)

These are a collection of **17** interlinked goals that provide a shared programme for peace and prosperity for people and the planet, now and into the future. SDGs are also known as **Global Goals.**

In 2015, the SDG framework was **adopted** by the **United Nations** as a universal call to protect the planet, end poverty, and ensure that all people enjoy peace and prosperity by 2030.

1 **Harnessing** It means to control and make use of (natural resources) especially to produce energy.

To achieve SDGs, the creativity, knowledge, technology and financial resources from all of society are necessary. The 17 Sustainable Development Goals (SDGs) to transform our world are

- **Goal 1** No poverty
- **Goal 2** Zero hunger
- **Goal 3** Good health and wellbeing
- **Goal 4** Quality education
- **Goal 5** Gender equality
- **Goal 6** Clean water and sanitation
- **Goal 7** Affordable and clean energy
- **Goal 8** Decent work and economic growth
- **Goal 9** Industry, innovation and infrastructure
- **Goal 10** Reduced inequality
- **Goal 11** Sustainable cities and communities
- **Goal 12** Responsible consumption and production
- **Goal 13** Climate action
- **Goal 14** Life below water
- **Goal 15** Life on land
- **Goal 16** Peace and justice strong institutions
- **Goal 17** Partnerships to achieve the goal

Stockholm Declaration, 1972

- The Stockholm Convention is a global treaty that **aims to protect human health and the environment** from the effects of persistent organic pollutants[2] (POPs). It was the **first convention** to discuss environmental issues on a global scale.
- The declaration proclaims truths relating to man and the environment such as man is the creator and spoiler of his surroundings. The declaration also reiterates[3] the importance of preservation of the environment.

10.2 Initiatives under International Scenario

Rio Declaration 1992

- The United Nations Conference on Environment and Development (UNCED), also known as the **Earth Summit** was held in **Rio de Janeiro, Brazil** in 1992.
- The conference marked the 20th anniversary of the first ever International Human Environment Conference in Stockholm, Sweden, 1972.
- The conference was attended by representatives from **179 countries** to discuss the impact of human socio-economic activities on the environment.
- The objective of the Rio 'Earth Summit' was to formulate a programme for global action on environment and development issues.
- It recognised that integrating and balancing the **economic, social and environmental** concerns in meeting our needs, is vital for sustaining human life on the planet the Earth.
- This led to actions through governments from across the globe on how to ensure sustainability with development.
- The Earth Summit resulted in some major actions that were taken by countries from across the globe in the form of conventions and resolutions. Some of them were
  - Agenda 21
  - United Nations Framework Convention on Climate Change (UNFCCC)
  - Convention on Biological Diversity
  - The Declaration on the Principles of Forest Management
  - Commission on Sustainable Development

2 Pollutants It means a substance that pollutes something like air or water.

3 Reiterates It means to say something again or a number of times, typically for emphasis or clarity.

Agenda 21

- Agenda 21 focussed on new methods of education, new ways of preserving natural resources and new ways of participating in a sustainable economy.
- **The implementation of Agenda 21 was reaffirmed in the World Summit on sustainable development held in Johannesburg, in 2002.**
- Agenda 21 focuses on **community participation** as one of the major **prerequisites**[4] for sustainable development. Thus, attaining sustainability requires addressing the fundamental issues and challenges related to development at local, regional and global levels simultaneously, by all segments of society.
- Agenda 21 focuses on the key objective of sustainable development to improve human well-being and to sustain these improvements over a period of time.

Quick Test 1

1. How many goals are there in sustainable development?
2. Which convention was the first one to discuss environmental issues on a global scale?
3. What other name is given to the Earth Summit? What are its objectives?
4. What does Angenda 21 focuses on briefly explain.

10.3 Provisions under Indian Constitution

- The Constitution of India under **Article 21** enshrine the **Right to Life**. This article in its wider interpretation **include 'Right to clean environment'** as an important facet of 'life'.
- Further, **Article 38** make the state responsible for maintaining social order for ensuring a welfare state.
- This is only possible with the people living in a pollution free environment.
- According to **Article 48A, inserted by the 42nd amendment** to the Constitution of India, the state shall endeavour to **protect** and **improve** the environment and safeguard the forests and wild life of the country. It requires the state to adopt the **Protectionist Policy** as well as **Improvinistic Policy.**
- **Protectionist[5] policy imposes ban on those things which lead to environmental degradation,** e.g. ban on use of leaded petrol, ban on use of plastic bags etc.
- Improvinistic policy refers to alternatives that can be used for improvement of environment, e.g. use of CNG or low sulphur fuel, tree plantation in industrial areas, etc.
- A duty has also been imposed on all citizens to protect our environment.
- According to **Article 51A(g)** of the Indian Constitution, it shall be the duty of every citizen of India to protect and improve the natural environment including forests, lakes, rivers and wild life, and to have compassion for living creatures. The state has been directed by way of provision under Part III and Part IV to ensure the protection of environment by suitable legislations, regulations and otherwise.
- To strengthen environment protection at grass root level it further imposes fundamental duty on every citizen "To protect and improve the natural environment including forests, lakes, rivers and wild life".
- In the case of **K.M. Chinnappa Vs. Union of India,** the supreme court defined 'environmental law' as an instrument to protect and improve the environment and control or prevent any act or omission polluting or likely to pollute the environment.
- A concrete step has been taken with the enactment of Environment Protection Act, 1986 for combating modern day challenges in environment protection and improvement.

4 **Prerequisite** It means a thing that is required as a prior condition for something else to happen or exist.
5 **Protectionist** It means relating to the theory or practice of shielding a country's domestic industries from foreign competition by taxing imports.

- There are many other legislations and regulatory bodies in India.
  - Environment Protection Act, 1986
  - Air (Prevention and Control of Pollution) Act, 1981
  - National Green Tribunal Act, 2010
  - Energy Conservation Act, 2001
  - Water (Prevention and Control of Pollution) Act, 1974
  - The Noise Pollution (Regulation and Control) Rules, 2000

10.4 Environment Protection Act, 1986

- The Government of India enacted the Environment Protection Act of 1986 under **Article 253** of the Constitution, after the Bhopal gas tragedy. The purpose of the act is to implement the decisions of the United Nations Conference on the human environment, relating to the protection and improvement of the human environment.
- The act is designed to provide a framework for the Central Government to co-ordinate the activities of various central and state authorities established under previous laws, such as the Water Act and the Air Act.
- India as well, like other developing nation, is facing an alarming concern in environmental degradation due to economic activities. Control mechanisms to guard against hazardous substances, new chemicals in the environment are weak.

10.5 Pollution Control Board

The Central Pollution Control Board

- The Central Pollution Control Board is a statutory organisation under the **Ministry of Environment and Forest Protection.**
- It is constituted under the Water (Prevention and Control of Pollution) Act, 1974.
- The principal functions of the CPCB are mentioned in the Water (Prevention and Control of Pollution) Act, 1974, and the Air (Prevention and Control of Pollution) Act, 1981.
- The main functions of this board are
  - **Advise the Central Government** on any matter concerning prevention and control of water and air pollution and improvement of the quality of air.
  - **Plan and cause to be executed** a nation-wide programme for the prevention, control or abatement of water and air pollution.
  - **Co-ordinate** the activities of the state board and resolve disputes among them.
  - **Provide technical assistance and guidance** to the state boards. Carry out and sponsor investigation and research relating to problems of water and air pollution and for their prevention, control or abatement.
  - **Plan and organise training** of persons engaged in programme on the prevention, control or abatement of water and air pollution.
  - **Organise a comprehensive mass awareness programme** through mass media, on the prevention, control or abatement of water and air pollution.
  - **Collect, compile and publish technical and statistical data** relating to water and air pollution and the measures devised for their effective prevention, control or abatement.
  - **Prepare manuals, codes and guidelines** relating to treatment and disposal of sewage and trade effluents as well as for stack gas cleaning devices, stacks and ducts.
  - **Spread information** in respect of matters relating to water and air pollution and their prevention and control.

- **Lay down, modify or invalidate** the standards, in consultation with the State Governments concerned, for stream or well and lay down standards for the quality of air.
- Perform such **other functions** as may be prescribed by the Government of India.

The State Pollution Control Boards

- State Pollution Control Board is a statutory organisation established under the Water (Prevention and Control of Pollution) Act 1974.
- **It works under the supervision of the Central Pollution Control Board** to implement the environmental laws and rules within the respective state for the protection of the environment.
- It is mandatory for every business, either new or existing, to obtain necessary authorisation from the respective State Pollution Control Board in order to carry out the activities of the business in a state.
- The objectives of this board are
  - **Preservation of natural resources**
  - **Promotion of sustainable development** for economic growth of the nation along with environmental protection and social equity.
  - **Effective waste management** for the protection of the environment.
  - **Spreading Awareness** about the protection of the environment among the consumers.
  - **Encouraging the general public** for the use of environment-friendly products like paper bags, public transport, CFL, etc. to help reduce the environmental pollution.
- The primary motive of the board is to assist the entrepreneurs and industries in the fulfillment of

  The functions of the board are as follows
  - **Issue NOC** (No-Objection Certificates) from the perspective of the environmental pollution.
  - Assessment of quality ambient air.
  - Assessment of inland surface waters' quality.
  - Issuance of the consent under provisions of **Section 21** of the Air (Prevention and Control of Pollution) Act, 1981.
  - Issue of consent under provisions of **Section 25/26** of the Water (Prevention and Control of Pollution) Act, 1974.
  - **Collection and assessment of Water Cess,** under the provision of Water (Prevention and Control of Pollution) Cess Act, 1977.
  - Assessment and identification of municipal and industrial pollution sources and control.
  - Conducting mass awareness programmes.
  - Development of pollution control technologies.
  - Notification of emission and effluent standards.
  - Instituting legal action against defaulters.
  - Implementing Biomedical Waste Rules, 1998.
  - **Issuance of authorisation** under the Hazardous Waste Management Rule, 1989.
  - **Identifying the onsite crisis management** plans, isolated storage, etc. under the Manufacture, Storage and Import of Hazardous Chemicals Rules, 1989.

Quick Test 2

1. Under which Article of the Constitution, the Government of India enacted the Environment Protection Act?
2. When was Environment Protection Act enacted? What is the main purpose of this act?
3. State the main objectives of State Pollution Control Board?
4. What are the functions of Central Pollution Control Board?

Mind Map

LAW AND SUSTAINABLE DEVELOPMENT

1 Introduction

Definition
- Sustainable development aims for long-term economic growth with minimal environmental impact.

Key Goals
- Reduce air, water and soil pollution.
- Ensure better living conditions for future generations.

Examples of Practices
- Harnessing solar energy.
- Crop rotation for soil fertility.

Role in Law
- Economic growth while preserving environmental quality.

2 Sustainable Development Goals (SDGs)

- **Adoption** 2015 by the United Nations.
- **Objective** Achieve peace, prosperity, and environmental sustainability by 2030.

17 Goals Include
- No poverty, zero hunger, quality education, gender equality.
- Affordable clean energy, climate action and life on land.
- Partnerships to achieve goals etc.

3 International Initiatives

Stockholm Declaration (1972)
- First global treaty on environmental protection.
- **Focus** Human health and environmental preservation.

Rio Declaration (1992)
- UN Earth Summit in Brazil.
- Integrated economic, social, and environmental concerns.
- Resulted in conventions like
  - **Agenda 21** Community participation in sustainability.
  - **UNFCCC** Addressing climate change.
  - Convention on Biological Diversity.

Agenda 21
- Promotes education, resource preservation, and local-global actions for sustainable development.

4 Provisions in Indian Constitution

Article 21
- Right to life includes the right to a clean environment.

Article 38
- Welfare state ensuring pollution-free living conditions.

Article 48A
- State must protect and improve the environment and safeguard forests and wildlife.

Article 51A(g)
- Citizens' duty to protect and improve the natural environment.

5 Environment Protection Act, 1986

Purpose
- Enacted after the Bhopal Gas Tragedy.
- Co-ordinated framework for environmental protection.

Provisions
- Implement decisions from UN conferences.
- Prevent hazards from human activities.

6 Pollution Control Boards

Central Pollution Control Board (CPCB)
- **Functions**
  - Advise on air and water pollution control.
  - Plan nationwide pollution control programmes.
  - Co-ordinate with state boards and resolve disputes.
  - Conduct research and spread awareness.
  - Develop pollution standards and guidelines.

State Pollution Control Boards
- **Functions**
  - Issue NOCs for businesses.
  - Assess air and water quality.
  - Promote waste management and environmental-friendly practices.
  - Implement legal actions and regulations.

7 Key Case Laws

K.M. Chinnappa Vs. Union of India
- Defined environmental law as an instrument to prevent pollution.

M.C. Mehta Vs. Union of India
- Landmark case emphasising fundamental duties towards environmental protection.

8 Importance of Sustainable Development

Economic Aspect
- Balance growth with resource conservation.

Social Aspect
- Inclusivity and equity for present and future generations.

Environmental Aspect
- Focus on renewable resources and reducing ecological footprints.

CBSE TEXTBOOK FOLDER

1. What is the meaning of sustainable development? What does it aim to achieve?

Ans. According to the United Nations Conference on Environment and Development, sustainable development refers to development that sustains over a long period and meets the needs of the present generation without compromising the ability of the future generation to meet their own needs.

Aims of sustainable development are

- It aims at the potential average quality of life for both present and future generations.
- It emphasises protecting the future generation.
- It emphasises sustainable, equitable and rational use of resources to meet the needs of present and future generations.

2. When and why was the SDG framework adopted? How can these SDGs be achieved?

Ans. The Sustainable Development Goals (SDGs), also known as the Global Goals, were adopted by the United Nations in 2015 as a universal call to action to end poverty, protect the planet, and ensure that by 2030 all people enjoy peace and prosperity.

To achieve sustainable development, three key factors must be balanced i.e. economic growth, social inclusion, and environmental conservation. These factors are all interrelated, and they are all important for the well-being of individuals and civilisations.

3. Identify the SDG Goals which provide for the protection of the environment.

Ans. The SDG Goals which provide for the protection of environment are

- **Goal 6** Clean water and sanitation
- **Goal 7** Affordable and clean energy
- **Goal 9** Industry, innovation and infrastructure
- **Goal 12** Responsible consumption and production
- **Goal 13** Climate action
- **Goal 14** Life below water
- **Goal 15** Life on land

4. Describe the legal framework in India for environmental protection.

Ans. The Constitution of India under Article 21 enshrine the 'Right to Life'. This article in its wider interpretation include 'Right to clean environment' as an important facet of 'life'.

Further, Article 38 make the state responsible for maintaining social order for ensuring a welfare state. This is only possible with the people living in a pollution free environment.

According to Article 48A, inserted by the 42nd amendment to the Constitution of India, the state shall endeavour to protect and improve the environment and safeguard the forests and wild life of the country. It requires the state to adopt the **Protectionist Policy** as well as **Improvinistic Policy.**

A duty has also been imposed on all citizens to protect our environment. According to Article 51A(g) of the Indian Constitution, it shall be the duty of every citizen of India to protect and improve the natural environment including forests, lakes, rivers and wild life, and to have compassion for living creatures.

5. What are the main functions of

(i) Central Pollution Control Board

(ii) State Pollution Control Board

Ans. (i) The main functions of Central Pollution Control Board are

- Advise the Central Government on any matter concerning prevention and control of water and air pollution and improvement of the quality of air. Plan and cause to be executed a nation-wide program for the prevention, control or abatement of water and air pollution.
- Co-ordinate the activities of the state board and resolve disputes among them. Provide technical assistance and guidance to the state boards. Carry out and sponsor investigation and research relating to problems of water and air pollution, and for their prevention, control or abatement.
- Plan and organise training of persons engaged in programme on the prevention, control or abatement of water and air pollution. Organise a comprehensive mass awareness programme through mass media, on the prevention, control or abatement of water and air pollution.
- Collect, compile and publish technical and statistical data relating to water and air pollution and the measures devised for their effective prevention, control or abatement.
- Prepare manuals, codes and guidelines relating to treatment and disposal of sewage and trade effluents as well as for stack gas cleaning devices, stacks and ducts.

- Spread information in respect of matters relating to water and air pollution and their prevention and control.
- Lay down, modify or invalidate the standards, in consultation with the State Governments concerned, for stream or well and lay down standards for the quality of air.
- Perform such other functions as may be prescribed by the Government of India.

(ii) The main functions of State Pollution Control Board are
- Issue NOC (No-Objection Certificates) from the perspective of the environmental pollution.
- Assessment of quality ambient air.
- Assessment of inland surface waters' quality.
- Issuance of the consent under provisions of Section 21 of the Air (Prevention and Control of Pollution) Act, 1981.
- Issue of consent under provisions of Section 25/26 of the Water (Prevention and Control of Pollution) Act, 1974.
- Collection and assessment of water cess, under the provision of Water (Prevention and Control of Pollution) Cess Act, 1977.
- Assessment and identification of municipal and industrial pollution sources and control.
- Conducting mass awareness programmes.
- Development of pollution control technologies.
- Notification of emission and effluent standards.
- Instituting legal action against defaulters.
- Implementing Biomedical Waste Rules, 1998.
- Issuance of authorisation under the Hazardous Waste Management Rule, 1989.
- Identifying the onsite crisis management plans, isolated storage, etc. under the Manufacture, Storage and Import of Hazardous Chemicals Rules, 1989.

Exam Pattern Questions

Objective Type Questions

Multiple Choice Questions (MCQs)

1. The United Nations has established a total .... Sustainable Development Goals (SDGs).

(a) 12 (b) 4
(c) 17 (d) 20

2. Where was the first Earth Summit for the 'Convention on Biological Diversity' held?

(a) Rio de Janeiro (1992), Brazil
(b) New York (2000), USA
(c) Dehradun (1992), India
(d) Johannesburg (2022), South Africa

3. Which of the following cities is associated with the organisation of the 'Earth Summit'?

(a) Rio de Janeiro (b) Geneva
(c) Sydney (d) France

4. The concept of 'Sustainable Development' was first introduced in ....

(a) Rio Declaration
(b) Stockholm Declaration
(c) Brundtland Report
(d) None of the above

5. Which of the following acts is popularly known as umbrella legislation?

(a) The Water Prevention and Control of Pollution Act, 1974
(b) The Air Prevention and Control of Pollution Act, 1981
(c) The Factories Act, 1948
(d) The Environmental Protection Act, 1986

6. When did the Central Pollution Control Board established?

(a) 1970 (b) 1972 (c) 1974 (d) 1976

7. Which convention and resolution is not related to environmental protection?

(a) Convention on biological diversity
(b) Paris Agreement
(c) Earth Summit
(d) Stockholm Declaration

8. M.C. Mehta Vs. UoI is the landmark supreme case related to which case?

(a) Fundamental Duties
(b) Fundamental Rights
(c) Directive Principles of State Policy
(d) Environmental Protection

9. **Environment Protection Act was enacted in ………… in India.**
(a) 1983 (b) 1984 (c) 1985 (d) 1986

10. **Neha, a photographer, takes a beautiful photograph of a sunset and posts it on her personal blog. A local travel magazine uses the image without Neha's permission. The publishers credit Neha as the photographer but do not pay her or seek her consent. Neha considers taking legal action against the magazine. In this context which of the following options is correct?** CBSE 2025
(a) Neha cannot take legal action because the magazine credited her as the photographer.
(b) Neha can take legal action because her photograph is protected by copyright and the magazine used it without permission.
(c) Neha cannot take legal action because the photograph was available for the general public on her blog.
(d) Neha can only take legal action if she had registered the photograph with a copyright office.

11. **The Rio Declaration, adopted in 1992, states: "In order to achieve sustainable development, environmental protection shall constitute an integral part of the development process". Which of the following principles is embodied in the above statement from the Rio Declaration?**
(a) Polluter Pays Principle
(b) Precautionary Principle
(c) Integration of Environment and Development
(d) Intergenerational Equity

12. **A group of residents living near a polluted river sue the State Government for failing to prevent the pollution, which has caused health problems and harmed the local ecosystem. The court rules in their favour, citing the right to life and clean environment. Which Article of the Indian Constitution did the court likely rely on?**
(a) Article 21 (b) Article 32
(c) Article 48A (d) Article 51A

13. **The Central Pollution Control Board (CPCB) has categorised industries into four categories - Red, Orange, Green and White - based on their pollution potential.**

Category	Pollution Potential
Red	High
Orange	Moderate
Green	Low
White	Minimal

According to the CPCB categorisation, which category of industries requires stringent regulations and controls due to their high pollution potential?
(a) Green (b) Orange (c) Red (d) White

14. **Match the SDG Number with its corresponding Description.**

Column I (SDG Number)	Column II (SDG Description)
A. SDG 1	1. Affordable and Clean Energy
B. SDG 6	2. Climate Action
C. SDG 11	3. Sustainable Cities and Communities
D. SDG 7	4. No Poverty
E. SDG 13	5. Clean Water and Sanitation

Codes

	A	B	C	D	E
(a)	4	5	3	1	2
(b)	5	1	4	2	3
(c)	4	5	3	2	1
(d)	3	2	5	4	1

15. **Match the following.**

Column I	Column II
A. Sustainable Development Goals	1. Fundamental Rights
B. Right to clean environment	2. Clean water sanitation
C. Energy Conservation Act	3. Development in the environment
D. UNFCC	4. Environment Act

Codes

	A	B	C	D		A	B	C	D
(a)	1	2	3	4	(b)	2	1	4	3
(c)	3	4	2	1	(d)	4	3	2	1

16. **Statement I** The Sustainable Development Goals (SDGs) are a set of 17 global goals adopted by the UN in 2015 to end poverty. Protect the planet, and ensure peace and prosperity for all people.
Statement II The SDGs are scheduled to be achieved by the year 2030 and are designed to be implemented by governments, businesses and civil society organisations working together.
Which of the following options best describes the SDGs?
(a) A set of 10 global goals focused solely on economic development.
(b) A set of 17 global goal addressing social, economic and environmental challenges.
(c) A set of 5 global goals focused solely on environment protection.
(d) A set of 20 global goals addressing only social and economic challenges.

17. Statement I The Earth Summit, also known as the United Nation Conference on Environment and Development (UNCED), was held in Rio de Janeiro, Brazil in 1992.

Statement II The Earth Summit resulted in the adoption of the United Nations Framework Convention on Climate Change (UNFCCC) and the Convention on Biological Diversity (CBD) among other key international agreements.

Which of the following options best describes the significance of the Earth Summit?

(a) It led to the establishment of the United Nations Environment Programme (UNEP) and the signing of the Montreal Protocol.
(b) It resulted in the adoption of the Kyoto Protocol and the Paris Agreement.
(c) It marked a major turning point in international co-operation on environmental issues and sustainable development.
(d) It led to the creation of the WTO and the signing of the Rio Declaration.

Assertion-Reason Questions

Directions (Q. Nos. 18-21) In the questions given below, there are two statements. Read the statements and choose the correct option.

Codes

(a) Both A and R are true and R is the correct explanation of A.
(b) Both A and R are true, but R is not the correct explanation of A.
(c) A is true, but R is false.
(d) A is false, but R is true.

18. Assertion (A) Sustainable development is essential for the economic growth of the countries.

Reason (R) Sustainable development ensures that environment-friendly measures are adopted for carrying out production processes.

19. Assertion (A) Sustainable development is important for the well-being of human society.

Reason (R) Sustainable development is a kind of development that meets the needs of the present without compromising the ability of future generations to meet their own needs.

20. Assertion (A) The United Nations' Sustainable Development Goal 6 (SDG 6) focuses on providing clean water and sanitation to all.

Reason (R) This goal is crucial for reducing water-borne diseases and promoting hygiene in developing countries.

21. Assertion (A) Achieving Sustainable Development Goal 13 (SDG 13) on Climate Action requires immediate reduction of greenhouse gas emissions.

Reason (R) SDG 13 primarily focuses on promoting sustainable agriculture practices.

Answers

1. (c) 17
2. (a) Rio de Janeiro (1992), Brazil
3. (a) Rio de Janeiro
4. (c) Brundtland Report
5. (d) The Environmental Protection Act, 1986
6. (c) 1974
7. (b) Paris Agreement
8. (d) Environmental Protection
9. (d) 1986
10. (b) Neha can take legal action because her photograph is protected by copyright and the magazine used it without permission.
11. (c) Integration of Environment and Development
12. (a) Article 21
13. (c) Red
14. (a) 4 5 3 1 2
15. (b) 2 1 4 3
16. (b) A set of 17 global goal addressing social, economic and environmental challenges.
17. (c) It marked a major turning point in international co-operation on environmental issues and sustainable development.
18. (a) Both A and R are true and R is the correct explanation of A.
19. (a) Both A and R are true and R is the correct explanation of A.
20. (a) Both A and R are true and R is the correct explanation of A.
21. (c) A is true, but R is false.

Subjective Questions

Very Short Answer Type Questions

1. How sustainable development is developed in society with the help of law?

Ans. Sustainable development is an approach to economic planning that attempts to foster economic growth while preserving the quality of the environment for future generations.

2. What is the role of the Rio Earth Summit in environmental protection?

Ans. The United Nations Conference on Environment and Development (UNCED), commonly known as the 'Earth Summit', was held from 3rd June to 14th June, 1992, in Rio de Janeiro, Brazil. On the 20th anniversary of the first Human Environment Conference in Stockholm, Sweden, in 1972, this global conference brought together political leaders, diplomats, scientists, media representatives, and Non-Governmental Organisations (NGOs) from 179 countries for a massive effort to focus on the impact of human socio-economic activities on the environment.

3. A local government is developing a plan to reduce its carbon footprint and promote sustainable development. It aims to increase public transportation, promote renewable energy and reduce waste. What principle of Agenda 21 is the local government most likely to be applying?

Ans. Agenda 21 is a global plan of action for sustainable development adopted at the Earth Summit in 1992. The principle 'Think Global, Act Local' is a key concept in Agenda 21, emphasising the importance of local action to address global environmental and developmental challenges.

4. The right to a clean environment is a Fundamental Right under the Constitution. State the meaning of the term.

Ans. The right to a clean and healthy environment is also a Fundamental Right that has been incorporated under Article 21 through various judicial pronouncements. If a person infringes any other person's right to live in a clean and healthy environment he shall be liable to be punished.

5. What are the objectives of the Environment Protection Act, 1986?

Ans. The objectives of the Environment Protection Act, 1986 are

- To protect the environment from degradation and take action to improve the current condition.
- Co-ordinate the work of the agencies for the protection of the environment under existing laws.

6. Give the names of the statues which are used for environmental protection in India.

Ans. The statutes used for environmental protection in India are

- The Air Prevention and Control of Pollution, 1981
- The Water Prevention and Control of Pollution, 1974

7. Why are indicators important in sustainable development?

Ans. Indicators can provide crucial guidance for decision-making in a variety of ways. They can translate physical and social science knowledge into manageable units of information that can facilitate the decision-making process. They can help to measure and calibrate progress towards Sustainable Development Goals.

Short Answer Type Questions

1. What was the primary objective of the Stockholm Declaration 1972?

Or **State the significance of the Stockholm Declaration, 1972. Establish the relationship between Stockholm Declaration, 1972 and Earth Summit, 1992.** **CBSE 2025**

Ans. The Stockholm Convention is a global treaty that aims to protect human health and the environment from the effects of Constant Organic Pollutants (POPs). It was the first convention to discuss environmental issues on a global scale.

The declaration proclaims truths relating to man and the environment such as man is the creator and spoiler of his surroundings.

The declaration also restate the importance of preservation of the environment. The Earth Summit of 1992 in Rio de Janeiro built upon this by formulating a global action plan, Agenda 21, to promote sustainable development. The Earth Summit marked the 20th anniversary of the Stockholm Declaration and reinforced concerns in to sustainable development goals.

2. What are the significances of the United Nations Conference on Environment and Development?

Ans. The United Nations Conference on Environment and Development established the concept of 'major groups'—Business and Industry, Children and Youth, Farmers, Indigenous Peoples, Local Authorities, NGOs, the Scientific and Technological Community, Women, Workers, and Trade Unions—whose participation is required to achieve sustainable development.

The conference also acknowledged that integrating and balancing economic, social and environmental dimensions necessitated new perspectives on how we produce and consume, live and work, and make decisions.

The Earth Summit was the first United Nations Conference to openly welcome representatives from Non-governmental Organisations (NGOs), business and industry.

3. Name the statutory body that was constituted under the Water (Prevention and Control of Pollution) Act, 1974. State the two principal functions to be performed by this body. **CBSE 2025**

Ans. The statutory body constituted under the Water (Prevention and Control of Pollution) Act, 1974, is the Central Pollution Control Board (CPCB). It functions under the Ministry of Environment and Forest Protection. Two of its principal functions include

(i) Advising the Central Government on matters related to the prevention and control of water and air pollution, along with improving air quality.

(ii) Planning and executing nationwide programmes for the prevention, control, or abatement of water and air pollution .

4. What are the roles of fundamental duties in protecting and promoting environmental protection in India?

Ans. Fundamental duties are the moral responsibilities of all citizens. They are meant to instill patriotism in the public. They would also be beneficial in maintaining India's unity. These are contained in Article 51A of Part IV A of the Indian Constitution. Initially, the 42nd Amendment Act of 1976 introduced ten essential obligations to the Indian Constitution. The 86th Amendment Act adds the 11th basic obligation to the list. These basic responsibilities cannot be enforced by a court.

A court can only do this if the parliament passes legislation making it enforceable.

One of the important fundamental duties is to protect and improve the natural environment. As per Article 51A (g), every citizen of India has to protect and improve the natural environment. This includes forests, lakes, rivers, wildlife and compassion for living creatures.

5. (i) In the wake of Bhopal Gas Tragedy, which act was passed by the Government of India under Article 253 of the Constitution? State the main provisions of this act. **CBSE SQP 2024**

(ii) Name the statutory organisation established under the Water (Prevention and Control of Pollution) Act 1974 , which works under the supervision of the Central Pollution Control Board to implement the environmental laws. List the objectives and functions of this statutory organisation for the protection of the environment.

Ans. (i) In the wake of the Bhopal Tragedy , the Government of India enacted the Environment Protection Act of 1986 under Article 253 of the Constitution.

(a) The purpose of the act is to implement the decisions of the United Nations Conference on the Human Environment, relating to the protection and improvement of the human environment and the prevention of hazards of human activites for economic development to human beings, other living creatures, plants and property.

(b) The act is an 'umbrella' legislation designed to provide a framework for the Central Government to co-ordinate the activities of various central and state authorities established under previous laws, such as the Water Act and the Air Act.

(ii) The State Pollution Control Board is a statutory organisation established under the Water (Prevention and Control of Pollution) Act 1974.

Objectives

(a) Preservation of natural resources.

(b) Promotion of sustainable development for economic growth of the nation along with environmental protection and social equity.

Long Answer Type Questions

1. Discuss briefly about the provisions under Constitution of India for sustainable development became important in the context of the environment.

Ans. For answer, refer to text under the heading Provisions under Indian Constitution on page no. 164.

2. (i) Analyse the purpose of Environment Protection Act, 1986.

(ii) State three provisions of the Indian Constitution that demonstrates a commitment to sustainability and environmental stewardship.

Ans. (i) The purpose of the Environment Protection Act, 1986 is to implement the decisions of the United Nations Conference on the Human Environment, relating to the protection and improvement of the human environment and the prevention of hazards of human activities for economic development to human beings, other living creatures, plants and property. This act is an 'umbrella' legislation designed to provide a framework for the Central Government to co-ordinate the activities of various central and state authorities established under previous laws, such as the Water Act and the Air Act.

(ii) The three provisions of the Indian Constitution that demonstrates a commitment to sustainability and environmental stewardship are as follows

(a) **Article 21** Article 21 enshrine the 'Right to Life'. This article in its wider interpretation encompasses 'Right to clean environment' as an important facet of 'life'.

(b) **Article 38** This article shoulders the state with responsibility of maintaining social order for ensuring a welfare state. This is only possible with the people living in a pollution free environment.

(c) **Article 48 A** This article was inserted by the 42nd Amendment to the Constitution of India, states 'Protection and improvement of environment and safeguarding of forests and wildlife'. The state shall endeavour to protect and improve the environment and to safeguard the forests and wildlife of the country.

A duty has also been imposed on all citizens to protect our environment. Article 51A(g) provides for the same.

3. Write about the functions of the Central Pollution Control Board?

Ans. The main functions of this board are

(i) **Advise the Central Government** on any matter concerning prevention and control of water and air pollution and improvement of the quality of air.

(ii) **Plan and cause to be executed** a nation-wide programme for the prevention, control or abatement of water and air pollution.

(iii) **Coordinate** the activities of the state board and resolve disputes among them.

(iv) **Provide technical assistance and guidance** to the State Boards. Carry out and sponsor investigation and research relating to problems of water and air pollution and for their prevention, control or abatement.

(v) **Plan and organise training** of persons engaged in programme on the prevention, control or abatement of water and air pollution.

(vi) **Organise a comprehensive mass awareness programme** through mass media, on the prevention, control or abatement of water and air pollution.

(vii) **Collect, compile and publish technical and statistical data** relating to water and air pollution and the measures devised for their effective prevention, control or abatement.

(viii) **Prepare manuals, codes and guidelines** relating to treatment and disposal of sewage and trade effluents as well as for stack gas cleaning devices, stacks and ducts.

(ix) **Spread information** in respect of matters relating to water and air pollution and their prevention and control.

(x) **Lay down, modify or invalidate** the standards, in consultation with the State Governments concerned, for stream or well and lay down standards for the quality of air.

4. (i) How do the Sustainable Development Goal (SDGs) contribute to addressing global challenges and fostering a more sustainable and equitable future for both, people and the planet?

(ii) Outline the main objective and impact of the Rio Summit. **CBSE 2024 C**

Ans. (i) The Sustainable Development Goals (SDGs) contribute to addressing global challenges and fostering a sustainable and equitable future by

- **Addressing interconnected issues** 17 goals covering poverty, climate, inequality and more.
- **Promoting integrated solutions** Encouraging holistic approaches to development.
- **Fostering global cooperation** Engaging governments, businesses and civil society.
- **Ensuring no one is left behind** Prioritising vulnerable populations and promoting equality.

The SDGs provide a shared blueprint for a more sustainable, equitable, and prosperous future for all.

(ii) The Rio Summit (1992) aimed to address global environmental and development challenges. Its main objectives

- **Sustainable development** Balance economic growth, social equity and environmental protection.
- **Climate change** Address greenhouse gas emissions and mitigate climate change impacts.

Key outcomes

- **Agenda 21** A global action plan for sustainable development.
- **United Nations Framework Convention on Climate Change (UNFCCC)** A treaty to stabilise greenhouse gas concentrations.
- **Convention on Biological Diversity** A treaty to conserve biodiversity.

SELF ASSESSMENT TEST

Objective Type Questions

1. Which of the following options is not included in the sustainable development parameters?
   (a) Gender inequality and diversity
   (b) Intergenerational and intragenerational equity
   (c) Growing annually
   (d) None of these
2. What is the definition of sustainable development?
   (a) The growth that satisfies current demands without jeopardising future generations' ability to fulfill their own needs.
   (b) Conserve mineral wealth and explore alternative energy sources while decreasing pollution and environmental impact.
   (c) It is the process of creating land and building projects in such a way that they have a lower environmental effect by enabling them to produce fuel-efficient self-sufficiency patterns.
   (d) All of the above
3. Which one of the following United Nations Commissions is in charge of monitoring progress on Agenda 21 as well as the Rio Agreement on Environmental issues?
   (a) The Disarmament Commission of the United Nations
   (b) United Nations Statistical Commission
   (c) Committee on Environmental Sustainability of the United Nations
   (d) Human Rights Tribunal of the United Nations
4. Sustainable development may be divided into three categories: economic, social and environmental.
   (a) The natural environment, the economy and society
   (b) The environment, the economy and fairness
   (c) Civilisation, ecology and environment
   (d) Ecology, economy and environment

Very Short Answer Type Questions

5. Define sustainable development with the help of an example.
6. What is the objective of the United Nations Framework Convention on Climate Change, 1972?

Short Answer Type Questions

7. Discuss the need and significance of environmental education in the Indian education system.
8. What are the emerging challenges in the protection of the environment at the national and international level?

Long Answer Type Questions

9. State the inter-relationship between Fundamental Duties and Directive Principles of State Policies for the protection of the environment in India.
10. 'The right to a clean environment is a Fundamental Right'. Explain this term with relevant case laws.

11 CHAPTER

A legal entity refers to any business or organisation that has legally recognised rights and obligations, such as the obligation to file taxes.

Forms of Legal Entities

▼ **YOUR STUDY GOALS**

11.1 Legal Entity
11.2 Sole Proprietorship
11.3 Partnership
11.4 Private Limited Company
11.5 Public Limited Company
11.6 One Person Company (OPC)

▼ **YOUR PRACTICE GOAL**

- Objective Type Questions (24 Qs ; MCQs, A-R, Statements, Matching)
- Subjective Questions (11 VSAs, 4 SAs, 5 LAs)

11.1 Legal Entity

- Legal entities have the capacity to enter into agreements as either a vendor or supplier, can initiate or be a party to lawsuits in a court of law.
- Choosing the right legal structure is aligned to the goals of the entity and the local and central laws where it desires to establish its base.

Objective of Law Regulation of Legal Entities

- The **purpose of law** regulation of forms of legal entities is to provide a framework for the creation, management and dissolution of different types of organisations, such as corporations, partnerships and sole proprietorships.
- These regulations aim to protect the rights and interests of stakeholders, including shareholders, employees, customers and creditors, and to ensure the fair and transparent functioning of these entities within the legal and economic system.
- The regulations may also promote competition, prevent fraud and misconduct, and provide a clear understanding of responsibilities and liabilities.

A legal entity is a recognised party with rights and responsibilities under commercial law in India. Different types of legal entities in India are discussed in further pages.

11.2 Sole Proprietorship

- Sole proprietorship[1] refers to a form of business organisation which is owned, managed and controlled by an individual who is the recipient of all profits and bearer of all **risks.**
- The word '**sole**' implies '**only**' and 'proprietor' refers to 'owner'. Hence, a sole proprietor is the one who is the only owner of a business.
- Sole proprietorship is a popular form of business organisation and is the most suitable form for small businesses, especially in their initial years of operation.
- It is the easiest type of business to establish or take apart, due to a lack of government regulation.
- Most small businesses start as sole proprietorships and either remain small or expand and transition to a limited liability entity or corporation.
- This form of business is particularly common in areas of personalised services such as beauty parlours, hair salons and small scale activities like running a retail shop in a locality.

Salient Features of Sole Proprietorship

The salient features of a sole proprietorship are as follows

- **No Separate Entity** There is no difference in the view of the law between the owner and business in sole proprietorship.
- **Formation** No specific law and formal registration are required to form sole proprietorship. Business is owned by single person.
- **No. of Members** Minimum one and maximum one member is required in sole proprietorship.
- **Liability** There is unlimited liability in sole proprietorship. Owner is responsible for all losses, debts and liabilities.
- **Profit** If the business is successful, the owner enjoys all the profits.
- **Control and Decision-Making** The right to run the business and make all decisions lies absolutely with the sole proprietor.
- **Limited Life of the Business** As the business is owned and controlled by one person, death, insanity, imprisonment, physical/mental incapacity or bankruptcy[2] will have a direct impact on the business and lead to its closure.
- **Confidentiality** Sole decision-making authority enables the proprietor to keep all information related to business operations confidential and maintain secrecy.

Advantages and Disadvantages of Sole Proprietorship

The advantages of sole proprietorship are as follows

- Quick decision-making
- Confidentiality of information
- Owner receives all the profits
- Owner makes all decisions and is in complete control of the company
- It is the easiest and least expensive form of ownership to organise
- Its formation and closure is easy
- The business does not pay separate taxes. All income passes directly to the owner and is taxed at the owner's personal tax rate.

---

1 **Proprietorship** It means state or right of owning a business or holding property.

2 **Bankruptcy** It means the state of being not able to repay debts to creditors may seek relief from some or all of their debts.

The disadvantages of sole proprietorship are as follows

- There is unlimited liability in sole proprietorship if anything happens in the business.
- It is limited in raising funds.
- It has no separate legal status.
- It has limited funds and resources.
- The skills and managerial ability of the proprietor are limited.

11.3 Partnership

- According to the **Indian Partnership Act, 1932**, partnership is the relation between persons who have agreed to share the profit of the business carried on by all or any one of them acting for all.
- Persons who have entered into partnership with one another are individually called as **partners** and collectively called a **firm**, and the name under which their business is carried on is called the **firm-name**.
- Partnership serves to the needs of greater capital investment, varied skills and sharing of risks. A successful partnership can help a business to grow by allowing the partners to reserve their labour and resources. However, in addition to sharing profits, the partners may also assume responsibility for any losses or debts from the other partners.

Strategic Partnership

Strategic partnerships are formed when two or more businesses or individuals come together to achieve mutual goals and enhance their respective brands. By co-branding and combining resources, strategic partnerships can provide benefits such as increased brand awareness, improved brand trust, and access to new markets and customers. Some well-known examples of successful strategic partnerships include Spotify and Google, Sherwin-Williams and Pottery Barn, and McDonald's and Coca-Cola.

Salient Features of a Partnership

The salient features of a partnership are as follows

- **No Separate Entity** A partnership firm has no separate legal existence of its own i.e., the partnership firm and the partners are one and the same in the eyes of law.
- **Formation** There are two types of partnership firms, registered and unregistered. It is not compulsory to register a partnership firm. Registration is to be done through the Registrar of Firms under the Indian Partnership Act, 1932. In order to enter into partnership, a clear agreement with respect to the terms, conditions and all aspects concerning the partners is essential so that there is no misunderstanding later among the partners. This written agreement is called a **Partnership Deed.**
- **No. of Partners** There can be minimum 2 and maximum 50 partners in a partnership.
- **Liability** There is unlimited liability in partnership and partners are jointly and severally[3] liable for the liabilities of the firm.
- **Profit** Partners share profits in a mutually agreed ratio.
- **Control and Decision-Making** Partners enjoy shared responsibility amongst each other. This may sometimes raise conflicts in decision making.
- **Dissolution** Partnership firm can be dissolved by way of compulsory dissolution or by way of agreement.
- **Funds** Capital is contributed by the partners. This makes it possible to use larger amounts of funds.

3 **Severally** It means separately.

Advantages and Disadvantages of Partnership

The advantages of partnership are as follows

- It is easy to establish with the exception of developing a partnership agreement.
- It has separate legal status to give liability protection.
- Partners may have complementary skills in partnership.
- The start up cost of partnership is low.
- More capital is available for business in a partnership.

The disadvantages of partnership are as follows

- Partners are jointly and individually liable for the actions of the other partners.
- Profits must be shared with the partners.
- There will be division in decision-making.
- Business can suffer if the detailed partnership agreement is not in place.

Limited Liability Partnership

- A Limited Liability Partnership (LLP) is a type of business that combines the benefits of limited liability with the flexibility of a partnership.
- A Limited Liability Partnership (LLP) is a body corporate formed and incorporated under the **Limited Liability Partnership Act, 2008.**
- It allows members to organise their internal structure based on an agreement.
- This type of business is suitable for entrepreneurs, professionals and enterprises that provide services or engage in scientific and technical disciplines.
- It is also a good option for small enterprises and for investment by venture capital due to its flexible structure and operation.

Salient Features of a Limited Liability Partnership

The salient features of a limited liability partnership are as follows

- **Separate Entity** LLP is a separate legal entity from that of its partners. It shall have perpetual[4] succession. Any change in the partners shall not affect the existence, rights or liabilities of the LLP.
- **Formation** A written agreement known as a **limited liability partnership** agreement is entered into between the partners of the LLP or between the LLP and its partners. This agreement determines the mutual rights and obligations.
- **No. of Partners** There is no limit on the number of partners but the minimum members should be 2.
- **Liability** Liability of the partners is limited to their agreed contribution in the LLP. No partner is liable on account of the independent or unauthorised actions of other partners.
- **Capital** An LLP can be started with no minimum amount of capital contribution.
- **Less Registration Cost** The cost of registration is lesser as compared to a private limited company or public limited company.

Advantages and Disadvantages of an LLP

The advantages of an LLP are as follows

- The terms and conditions of an LLP are based on a mutually agreed LLP agreement, providing greater flexibility and ease.
- The cost of registering an LLP is lower than incorporating a public or private limited company.

4 Perpetual It means never ending or changing.

- Partners are only liable up to their agreed contribution and there is no joint liability created by the actions of another partner.
- The registration process is simpler compared to that of a company.
- Remuneration, voting rights and other aspects are clear and defined in the LLP agreement.
- The **LLP can sue and be sued** in its own name, protecting partners from being personally sued for the LLP's debts.
- There is greater flexibility for becoming a partner, leaving the LLP or transferring interest in the LLP.
- Partners are free to enter into any contract, and the LLP enjoys higher credit-worthiness compared to a partnership, although lower than a company.
- There is no mandatory requirement for auditing accounts, and the LLP can raise funds from private equity investors and financial institutions.

The disadvantages of an LLP are as follows

- Actions taken by one partner without the consent of others can bind the LLP. In some cases, partners may also be personally liable for the LLP's debts.
- The winding-up process, as mentioned in the Limited Liability Partnership (Winding Up and Dissolution) Rules, 2012, can be lengthy and costly.
- LLPs have **lower credit-worthiness** as compared to companies.
- LLPs are required to file annual statements of accounts and solvency, as well as an annual return with the Registrar of Companies, which is not a requirement for partnerships.

Quick Test 1

1. How many members are required in sole proprietorship?
2. Who is called as partner?
3. When did the partnership firm dissolve?
4. What is the nature of the liability of partners in partnership?

11.4 Private Limited Company

- Private Limited Company is a type of business entity that is owned by a small group of individuals and registered for specific business objectives.
- A Private Limited Company is a popular business structure amongst growing businesses and companies.
- A Private Limited Company is a separate legal entity registered under the **Companies Act, 2013**.
- It offers limited liability protection to shareholders and also provide flexibility in terms of ownership and management structure. Some examples of popular Private limited companies are Flipkart, Freecharge, Cafe Coffee Day, etc.

Features of Private Limited Company

The salient features of a private limited company are as follows

- **Separate Entity** A private limited company is said to be a separate legal entity. Therefore, the company can sue and can also be sued under its name.
- **Formation** The private limited company is to be registered under the Companies Act, 2013. Incorporated documents such as Memorandum of Association and Articles of Association are required.
- **No. of Members** There can be **minimum 2 and maximum 200** in a private limited company.
- **Liability** The liability of each member or shareholder is limited. The personal, individual assets of the shareholders are not at risk.

- **Capital** It must have a minimum paid-up capital of such amount which may be prescribed from time to time.
- **Borrowing Capacity** A private limited company enjoys the privileges of borrowing more funds.
- **Easy Exit** Private limited companies can be sold or transferred, either partially or in full, to another individual or entity without any disruption to the current business.
- **Perpetual Succession** The company keeps on existing in the view of law even in the case of death, insolvency, the bankruptcy of any of its members.

11.5 Public Limited Company

- As per **Section 2(71)** of the Companies Act, 2013 a public company means a company which is not a private company.
- A public limited company is recognised as a separate entity from its owners and has the ability to enter into agreements in its own name.
- It operates independently from its owners and has its own set of rules, obligations, regulations and legal rights.
- The owners run the company but have limited liability for its debts and obligations. This legal separation provides a higher level of protection to the owners and makes it easier for the company to raise capital through the sale of shares to the public.
- The owners of a public limited company are referred to as **shareholders or stakeholders,** and the ownership of the company is divided into units known as shares[5] or **equity shares.**
- These units of ownership can be held by multiple individuals or corporations which makes it easier for the company to raise capital by selling shares to the public.
- The shareholders have a right to participate in the decision-making process of the company and receive dividends from the company's profits.
- Some popular public limited companies in India are Indian Oil Corporation Ltd., Bharat Petroleum Corporation Ltd., State Bank of India, etc.
- In comparison to sole proprietorship and partnership forms of organisations, a company has larger financial resources.
- Further, capital can be attracted from public as well as through loans from banks and financial institutions.

Features of Public Limited Company

The salient features of a public limited company are as follows

- **Separate Entity** Public Limited Company is a separate legal entity registered under the Companies Act, 2013.
- **Formation** The public limited company is to be registered under the Companies Act, 2013. Incorporated documents such as Memorandum of Association and Articles of Association are required. Public limited companies could be listed in the stock market or could be unlisted.
- **No. of Members** There is no limit on the number of partners but the minimum members should be 7.
- **Limited Liability** The liability of the shareholders is limited to their stake only.

5 Shares It means units of ownership in a company.

- **Capital** A public limited company is required to have a **minimum paid-up capital** of an amount as prescribed under the act. Public Limited Company can relish an increased ability to raise capital through the stock market by issuing **debentures**[6] and **bonds**[7] from the public.
- **Perpetual Succession** The life span of the public limited company is not affected by the death of any member or shareholder.
- **Strict Regulation** A Public Limited Company is strictly regulated and is required to publish its true financial health to its shareholders.
- **Transparency** All information relating to a public limited company is available to the public including detailed financial statements and structure of the management.
- **Transferability of Shares** The shareholders are free to buy or sell/trade shares to anyone through the stock market if the company is listed, and through dealers and other platforms if the company is unlisted.

Difference between Public and Private Company

Basis	Public Company	Private Company
Members	There is no limit on the number of members but minimum members should be 7.	There can be minimum 2 and maximum 200 in a private company.
Transfer of shares	There is no restriction on transfer of shares in a public company.	There is restriction on transfer shares in a private company.
Invitation to public to subscribe to shares	A public company can invite the public to subscribe to its shares.	A private company cannot invite the public to subscribe to its securities.

11.6 One Person Company (OPC)

As per **Section 2(62)** of the Companies Act 2013, one person company means a company that has only one person as a member.

The salient features of a one person company are as follows

- **Separate Entity** The OPC receives a separate legal entity status from the member.
- **Liability** The liability of the member is limited to his/her shares, and he/she is not personally liable for the loss of the company.
- **Formation** OPC is incorporated by a single person. It is incorporated as a private company under the Companies Act, 2013.
- The director and member can be the same person.
- **No. of Members** There can be **minimum one** and **maximum one member** in an OPC.
- **Easy to Obtain Funds** Since OPC is a private company, it is easy to go for fund raising through venture capitals, angel investors, incubators etc.
- **Perpetual Succession** The OPC has the feature of perpetual succession even when there is only one member. While incorporating the OPC, the single-member needs to appoint a nominee. Upon the member's death, the nominee will run the company in the member's place.
- **No Minimum paid-up Share Capital** Companies Act, 2013 has **not prescribed** any amount as **minimum paid-up capital** for OPCs.

6 **Debentures** It means a long-term security yielding, a fixed rate of interest, issued by company.
7 **Bonds** It means an official paper given by the government or a company to show that you have lent them money.

- A sole proprietorship form of business might seem very similar to one-person companies because they both involve a single person owning the business, but actually some differences exist between them. The main difference between the two is the nature of the liabilities they carry.

Comparative Evaluation of Some Forms of Business Entities

Basis of Comparison	Sole Proprietorship	Partnership	Company
Formation	Its formation is easy and it requires minimum legal formalities.	Its formation is easy and registration is optional.	Its formation process is lengthy and expensive, and registration is compulsory.
Members	There is only one member in sole proprietorship i.e. the owner.	There can be minimum 2 and maximum 50 members.	In private company there can be minimum 2 and maximum 200 members. In a public company, there can be unlimited members but the minimum members should be 7.
Capital Contribution	Limited finance is required in a sole proprietorship.	Funds can be raised/contributed by partners in a partnership.	Large financial resources are required in a company.
Liability	There is unlimited liability in a sole proprietorship.	There is unlimited and joint liability in a partnership.	There is limited liability in a company.
Control and Management	The decision making process is quick as owner takes all decisions.	Partners take decisions and consent of all partners is needed.	There is a separation between ownership and management.
Continuity	It is unstable. The business and owner are regarded as one.	It has more status but affected by status of partners.	It is stable because of separate legal status.

Conclusion

A legal entity is an individual, group of persons or organisation that has legal rights and obligations related to agreements, contracts, payments, penalties, etc. The term legal entity refers to any organisation which is constituted as per the regulations and laws under the Government of India. There are different types of legal entities with specific privileges and responsibilities. Companies registered under the Companies Act 2013 are the most common types of legal entities in India.

Quick Test 2

1. Under which act, a Private Limited Company is registered?
2. What is the nature of the liability of the member or shareholder?
3. Who is called as shareholders or stakeholders?
4. How many members are required in case of public limited company?

Mind Map

FORMS OF LEGAL ENTITIES

1 Introduction to Legal Entities

Definition
- Legally recognised organisations or individuals with rights and responsibilities.
- **Examples** Corporations, partnerships, sole proprietorships, etc.

Objective of Regulation
- Framework for creation, management and dissolution.
- Protect stakeholders' rights (shareholders, employees, customers, creditors).
- Promote fair and transparent economic practices.

2 Types of Legal Entities

Sole Proprietorship
- Owned, managed, and controlled by one individual.

Key Features
- No separate legal entity.
- Unlimited liability.
- Confidentiality and ease of formation.

Advantages
- Quick decision-making.
- Minimal legal formalities.

Disadvantages
- Limited funds and resources.
- Liability for all business debts.

Partnership
- Governed by the Indian Partnership Act, 1932.

Key Features
- Minimum 2, maximum 50 partners.
- Joint and several liabilities.
- Partnership deed for mutual agreements.

Advantages
- Shared responsibilities and resources.
- Easier formation than corporations.

Disadvantages
- Potential conflicts in decision-making.
- Profit-sharing among partners.

Limited Liability Partnership (LLP)
- Combines limited liability and partnership flexibility.

Key Features
- Governed by LLP Act, 2008.
- Separate legal entity.
- Liability limited to contributions.

Advantages
- Flexible structure.
- No minimum capital requirement.

Disadvantages
- Requires annual filings.
- Lower credit-worthiness compared to companies.

Private Limited Company
- Registered under the Companies Act, 2013.

Key Features
- Separate legal entity.
- Minimum 2, maximum 200 members.
- Limited liability for shareholders.

Advantages
- Ease of ownership transfer.
- Higher borrowing capacity.

Disadvantages
- More regulatory requirements than LLPs.

Public Limited Company
- Defined under Section 2(71) of the Companies Act, 2013.

Key Features
- Separate legal entity with unlimited members.
- Shares traded on stock markets.

Advantages
- Access to public funding.
- Limited liability for shareholders.

Disadvantages
- Stringent regulatory requirements.
- Higher transparency obligations.

One Person Company (OPC)
- A single-member company under the Companies Act, 2013.

Key Features
- Separate legal entity.
- Limited liability for the owner.

Advantages
- Easy to obtain funding.
- Perpetual succession with nominee.

Disadvantages
- Limited scalability.
- Specific restrictions under the law.

3 Comparative Overview

Formation
- **Sole Proprietorship** Minimal formalities.
- **Partnership** Requires partnership deed.
- **LLP/Companies** Registration mandatory.

Liability
- **Sole Proprietorship/Partnership** Unlimited.
- **LLP/Companies** Limited.

Continuity
- **Sole Proprietorship** Ends with owner's incapacity.
- **LLP/Companies** Perpetual succession.

Capital Requirements
- **Sole Proprietorship/Partnership** Limited funds.
- **LLP/Companies** Flexible options.

4 Case Studies and Scenarios

- **Case 1** Weavers in a village form a public limited company for scalability and investment.
- **Case 2** Partnership disputes due to absence of a written agreement.
- **Case 3** Individual seeking to start a sole proprietorship for personalised services.

5 Legal Provisions

Key Acts
- Companies Act, 2013.
- Indian Partnership Act, 1932.
- LLP Act, 2008.

Regulatory Bodies
- Registrar of Companies.
- Ministry of Corporate Affairs.

CBSE TEXTBOOK FOLDER

1. State the differences between a private limited company and a public limited company.

Ans. The differences between a private limited and a public limited company are

Difference between Private and Public Company

Basis	Private Company	Public Company
Members	There can be minimum 2 and maximum 200 in a private company.	There is no limit on the number of members but minimum members should be 7.
Transfer of shares	There is restriction on transfer shares in a private company.	There is no restriction on transfer of shares in a public company.
Invitation to public to subscribe to shares	A private company cannot invite the public to subscribe to its securities.	A public company can invite the public to subscribe to its shares.

2. Ajay and Nilam decide to contribute ₹ 10,000 and ₹ 20,000 respectively in order to start a partnership firm selling saris. Since they are good friends they forgo registering the partnership and have only a verbal agreement to share profits and losses. In the first year itself due to Covid, the firm suffered a loss of ₹ 30,000. Now, Ajay insists that the losses should be borne in the same ratio as the initial contribution i.e. he should bear ₹ 10,000 of the loss and Nilam should bear ₹ 20,000 of loss. Whereas Nilam wants them to bear the losses equally.

In this regard, discuss the nature and essential characteristics of partnership firms, the types of partnership firms, and why it is important to have a written agreement or partnership deed between partners.

Ans. When two or more people join hands to set up an enterprise and share its gains and losses, they are said to be in a partnership.

Section 4 of the Indian Partnership Act, 1932 states partnership as the association between people who have consented to share the profits of an enterprise carried by all or any of them acting for all.

People who have entered into a partnership with one another are independently termed as 'partners' and comprehensively termed as 'firms'. The name under which the trade is carried is called the 'Name of the Firm'. A partnership enterprise has no distinct legal entity apart from the partners comprising it.

Essential characteristics of partnership are

- **Two More Persons** In a partnership, there should be at least two persons possessing a common goal.
- **Agreement** Partnership is the outcome of an accord between two or more people to regulate a business and share its gains and losses. The agreement becomes the basis of the association between the partners.
- **Sharing of Profit** Partnership is the agreement between partners to share the gains and losses of a trading concern.

There are two types of partnership which are as follows

- **Partnership at Will** A partnership by will is a partnership where there is no provision made by contract between the partners for the duration of their partnership, or the determination of their partnership.
- **Particular Partnership** A particular partnership is when a person becomes a partner with another individual in a particular business enterprise or for a particular business venture or undertaking, such as the construction of a road, laying a railway line, etc. This sort of partnership shall come to an end on the completion of the task for which it was initially formed.

It is important to have a written agreement or partnership deed between partners because it gives business partners a clear understanding of the rules and arrangements applying to their business relationship. Unless there is an agreement in place, all partners are equal and must share the business profits and cover losses, equally.

3. The people of a village in India make a special kind of silk dress. Due to social media's influence, the dress has become immensely popular in India and abroad and designers are willing to pay crores of rupees for bulk orders.

Since it is not possible for the individual weavers to handle such large orders, they sought the help of a benevolent lawyer who belonged to their village. They want to form a legal entity to enter into the supply business formally. They are also aware that if they come together, their bargaining power will increase. They are ready to contribute a fixed amount initially.

They also realise that they will require to raise capital from investors in order to fulfill their orders. A few of them have adult educated children who are ready to take up the management of the formal entity.

There are about a hundred weavers who are willing to come together to form the entity.

If you are the lawyer they have approached, suggest which will be the best form of legal entity in this case and why.

Ans. In this situation, the public company is the best form of the legal entity for them. Reasons for this are

- The business can raise additional finance through share capital.
- The shareholders have limited liability.
- There will be increased negotiation opportunities with suppliers in terms of prices because larger businesses can achieve economies of scale.
- They become part owners of the business and have a voice in how it operates.

4. Raj owns a small provisions store. He has borrowed a sum of ₹ 70,000 from a moneylender to run his business. Raj dies from Covid before returning the amount. Can the moneylender recover his money? Discuss the liabilities of a sole proprietorship firm and its advantages and disadvantages.

Ans. The moneylender can recover his money. In this situation, the deceased borrower's family or a co-applicant is the appropriate party to seek to reclaim the personal loan.

To repay the personal loan, a certain payback time is established. If the legal heirs do not repay the debt, the lender has the right to seize the borrower's actual possession, such as a property or a car, and auction it off to collect the personal loan.

Liabilities of Sole Proprietorship Firm

Sole proprietors are personally liable indefinitely. The owner and the business have no legal distinction. This implies that creditors of the company and persons with other claims against the owner can seize both the company's and the owner's assets.

Advantages of a Sole Proprietorship

- Less paperwork to get started
- Quick decision-making
- Owner receives all the profits
- Confidential of information
- Easy of formation and closure

Disadvantages of a Sole Proprietorship

- There is no liability protection
- It is harder to get financing and business credit
- Limited skills and managerial ability of the proprietor

5. A giant cola company wants to enter the Indian market. They have a huge market in foreign countries. They also want to raise more funds from the public in India. What is the best way for them to enter the markets? What legal entity should they form to be able to do business in India? Discuss the characteristics of such an entity.

Ans. The public company is the best solution for them to enter the markets and form their business in India.

The characteristics of public limited company are as follows

- **Separate Entity** Public limited company is a separate legal entity registered under the Companies Act, 2013.
- **Formation** The public limited company is to be registered under the Companies Act, 2013. Incorporated documents such as Memorandum of Association and Articles of Association are required. Public limited companies could be listed in the stock market or could be unlisted.
- **No. of Members** There is no limit on the number of partners but the minimum members should be 7.
- **Limited Liability** The liability of the shareholders is limited to their stake only.
- **Capital** A public limited company is required to have a minimum paid-up capital of an amount as prescribed under the act. Public limited company can relish an increased ability to raise capital through the stock market by issuing debentures and bonds from the public.
- **Perpetual Succession** The life span of the public limited company is not affected by the death of any member or shareholder.
- **Strict Regulation** A public limited company is strictly regulated and is required to publish its true financial health to its shareholders.
- **Transparency** All information relating to a public limited company is available to the public including detailed financial statements and structure of the management.
- **Transferability of Shares** The shareholders are free to buy or sell/trade shares to anyone through the stock market if the company is listed and through dealers and other platforms if the company is unlisted.

Exam Pattern Questions

Objective Type Questions

Multiple Choice Questions (MCQs)

1. Which of the following best describe the sole proprietorship?
(a) A business owned by different companies
(b) A business owned by a President
(c) A business owned by a company
(d) A business owned by a person

2. A person cannot incorporate more than .... OPC.
(a) three (b) four (c) two (d) one

3. Shubham runs a small bakery in his neighbourhood. He takes all the decisions related to the small business, manages the daily operations and receives all the profits. However, he is also responsible for covering any financial losses incurred.

What type of business structure does Shubham's bakery represent?
(a) Partnership (b) Corporation
(c) Sole proprietorship (d) Co-operative

4. Neha owns a beauty salon where she works independently without any partners or shareholders. Her salon has minimal government regulation and she is responsible for both profits and losses. Neha is considering expanding her salon by introducing a limited liability structure.

What is her current business structure?
(a) Sole proprietorship (b) Joint venture
(c) Private limited company (d) Limited liability partnership

5. What are the maximum limits of the members in a private company?
(a) Fifty (b) Seven (c) Twenty (d) Two hundred

6. XYZ Ltd., a public limited company, issued a notice for its Annual General Meeting (AGM) to discuss critical matters, including the appointment of new directors. However, one of its shareholders, Aprajita, claims that the notice was served only 10 days prior to the meeting instead of the statutory 21 days required.

What is the legal standing of this AGM and its resolutions?
(a) The AGM is valid, as Aprajita can waive the requirement for notice.
(b) The AGM is invalid, as the company failed to meet the statutory notice period of 21 days.
(c) The AGM is valid, but Aprajita can challenge any resolutions passed in the meeting.
(d) The validity of the AGM depends on the nature of the resolutions passed.

7. Which of the following is not a characteristic of a public company?
(a) It has a separate legal entity
(b) It has a perpetual succession
(c) It has a common seal and separate property
(d) Its shares are non-transferable

8. Flipkart, Freecharge and Cafe Coffee Day is the example of which legal entity in India?
(a) Public limited company (b) Private limited company
(c) One-person company (d) Sole proprietorship

9. Meera, a partner in a law firm, decides to leave the partnership due to personal reasons. Before her departure, Meera had taken a loan of ₹5,00,000 in the firm's name to expand operations, without notifying the other partners. Months after her departure, a creditor sues the firm to recover the loan.

Under the provisions of the Indian Partnership Act, 1932, how will the liability for the loan be handled?
(a) Meera will solely be responsible for repaying the loan since she initiated it.
(b) All partners, including Meera, will be jointly liable for the loan repayment, as it was initiated during her partnership.
(c) The partners who continued the firm will be solely liable for the loan repayment.
(d) Meera and the creditor must independently resolve the liability without involving the firm.

10. Three individuals, Ananya, Kabir and Sohail, form a partnership to run a technology consultancy firm. Ananya contributes 40 per cent of the total capital, Kabir contributes 30 per cent and Sohail contributes the remaining 30 per cent. Their partnership agreement specifies that profits and losses will be shared in the ratio of their capital contributions. During a financial year, the firm incurs a loss of ₹ 10,00,000. Later, it is discovered that Kabir had taken a high-risk decision without informing Ananya and Sohail, which led to the loss.

According to the Indian Partnership Act, 1932, who is legally liable for the loss?

(a) Kabir is solely liable for the entire loss.
(b) Kabir is liable for 50 per cent of the loss, and the remaining loss will be shared equally by Ananya and Sohail.
(c) The loss will be shared in the ratio of 40:30:30 by Ananya, Kabir and Sohail, irrespective of Kabir's actions.
(d) The firm is not liable to pay any losses caused due to individual decisions of a partner.

11. The word 'sole' refers to 'only' and 'proprietor' refers to ……
(a) partners (b) owner (c) team (d) businessman

12. Choose one reason you would use to convince a private limited company trying to expand its business to convert to a public limited company. CBSE SQP 2024
(a) It is easier for the company to raise capital through the sale of shares to the public.
(b) It becomes more well known.
(c) It gets regulated by the government.
(d) It becomes part of the Public Limited Companies Association of India.

13. Ms. XYZ, a professional consultant, wants to start a business that offers IT services, she has limited funds and wants to maintain control over the business. Which type of company structure would be most suitable for her?
(a) Sole proprietorship (b) Partnership firm
(c) One-person company (d) Private limited company

14. Rahul, a software developer, wants to start a business with his two friends. They plan to invest ₹ 5 lakhs each and have a shared management. Rahul consults a lawyer, who suggests registering the business as a private limited company. Which of the following characteristics applies to Rahul's company?
(a) Minimum 7 shareholders and no limit on maximum shareholders
(b) Minimum 2 and maximum 200 shareholders
(c) Minimum 7 shareholders and no limit on maximum shareholders
(d) Only 1 shareholder and 1 director

15. One Person Company (OPC) has the feature of perpetual succession even with one member because CBSE 2024 C
(a) It is incorporated under Companies Act, 2013.
(b) Its compliance requirements are less than a private company.
(c) It is a separate legal entity, distinct of its members.
(d) It has the provision of appointment of a nominee during in-corporation.

16. Amit, an entrepreneur, wants to raise funds from the general public for his e-commerce venture. He plans to issue shares to at least 100 investors and list the company on the stock exchange. Identify the type of company Amit should register
(a) One Person Company (OPC)
(b) Private Limited Company
(c) Public Limited Company
(d) Partnership Firm

17. Sonia, a freelance writer, wants to register her solo venture as a separate legal entity. She has limited funds and doesn't plan to raise capital from external investors. What type of company is most suitable for Sonia?
(a) Public Limited Company
(b) Private Limited Company
(c) One Person Company (OPC)
(d) Sole Proprietorship

18. Match the following.

Column I (Legal Entities)	Column II (Maximum Members)
A. Partnership	1. No limit
B. Sole Proprietor	2. 50
C. Public Company	3. 200
D. Private Company	4. 1

Codes

	A	B	C	D		A	B	C	D
(a)	1	2	3	4	(b)	2	4	1	3
(c)	3	1	2	4	(d)	4	3	2	1

19. Statement I A company is considered a legal person. Separate from its shareholders and can enter into contracts, own assets and incur liabilities in its own name.
Statement II As a legal person, a company can sue and be sued in its own name, and its shareholders have limited liability protection, meaning their personal assets are protected in case the company incurs any debts or liabilities.
Choose the correct statement
(a) Both the Statement are correct.
(b) Both the Statement are incorrect.
(c) Statement I is correct, but Statement II is not correct.
(d) Statement II is correct, but Statement I is not correct.

Assertion-Reason Questions

Directions (Q. Nos. 20-24) In the questions given below, there are two statements. Read the statements and choose the correct option.

Codes
(a) Both A and R are true and R is the correct explanation of A.
(b) Both A and R are true, but R is not the correct explanation of A.
(c) A is true, but R is false.
(d) A is false, but R is true.

20. **Assertion** (A) A one-person company always managed by one person.

Reason (R) This is a recent invention to facilitate entrepreneurs to own and manage companies alone.

21. **Assertion** (A) Limited liability partnership is different from a normal partnership.

Reason (R) It is a type of legal entity that combines the limited liability and flexibility of a partnership.

22. **Assertion** (A) Limited Liability Partnership (LLP) provides its partners with limited liability protection.

Reason (R) It allows members to organise their internal structure based on an agreement.

23. **Assertion** (A) In a partnership firm, all partners have unlimited personal liability.

Reason (R) Partnership firms are not separate legal entities from their partners.

24. **Assertion** (A) Sole proprietorship refers to a form of business organisation which is owned and controlled by one person.

Reason (R) It does not require registration.

Answers

1. (d) A business owned by a person
2. (d) one
3. (c) Sole proprietorship
4. (a) Sole proprietorship
5. (d) Two hundred
6. (b) The AGM is invalid, as the company failed to meet the statutory notice period of 21 days.
7. (d) Its shares are non-transferable
8. (b) Private limited company
9. (b) All partners, including Meera, will be jointly liable for the loan repayment, as it was initiated during her partnership.
10. (c) The loss will be shared in the ratio of 40:30:30 by Ananya, Kabir and Sohail, irrespective of Kabir's actions.
11. (b) owner
12. (a) It is easier for the company to raise capital through the sale of shares to the public.
13. (c) One-person company
14. (b) Minimum 2 and maximum 200 shareholders
15. (d) It has the provision of appointment of a nominee during incorporation.
16. (c) Public Limited Company
17. (c) One Person Company (OPC)
18. (b) 2 4 1 3
19. (a) Both Statements are correct.
20. (a) Both A and R are true and R is the correct explanation of A.
21. (a) Both A and R are true and R is the correct explanation of A.
22. (a) Both A and R are true and R is the correct explanation of A.
23. (b) Both A and R are true, but R is not the correct explanation of A.
24. (b) Both A and R are true, but R is not the correct explanation of A.

Subjective Questions

Very Short Answer Type Questions

1. State the two salient features of a limited liability partnership.

Ans. The features of limited liability partnership are

- **Separate Entity** LLP is a separate legal entity from that of its partners. It shall have perpetual succession. Any change in the partners shall not affect the existence, rights or liabilities of the LLP.
- **Formation** A written agreement known as a limited liability partnership agreement is entered into between the partners of the LLP or between the LLP and its partners. This agreement determines the mutual rights and obligations.

2. What are the laws governed for legal entities in India?

Ans. The Companies Act, 2013 is the primary legislation that governs legal entities in India.

3. Define the term of partnership under the partnership act.

Ans. According to Section 4 of the Partnership Act of 1932, a partnership is an arrangement between two or more people who have decided to split the profits and losses of a business that will be run by all of them acting collectively or by any one of them acting for all of them.

4. Two friends, Neha and Nisha, are passionate about baking and dream of starting a small bakery together. They have limited funds but plenty of enthusiasm. Considering their situation, why might they find partnership a viable option to start a bakery? CBSE 2024

Ans. Neha and Nisha would find partnership a viable option to start a bakery because, it is easy to establish, partners may have complementary skills, start up cost is low, to give liability protection partners have separate legal status.

5. "As per Section 2(71) of the Companies Act, 2013 a public company means "A company which is not a private company". Justify the given statement.

Ans. A public company, as per Section 2(71) of the Companies Act, 2013, is one that is not a private company.

This means it can sell shares to the public, has no restriction on shareholders, and must follow stricter regulations than private companies.

6. State the difference between a public company and a private company.

Ans. A private company is owned by the founders, the management or a collection of individual investors.

On the other hand, a business entity that has sold all or a portion of itself to the general public through an initial public offering is referred to as a public company.

7. What are the liabilities of one person's company and sole proprietorship?

Ans. One person company is only liable for limited liability under the OPC, as compared to unlimited liability under a sole proprietorship.

8. Mr. 'X' wants to start a new company that will offer shares to the public and list on a stock exchange. He has already convinced 3 friends to invest in the company. How many more members does Mr. 'X' need to appoint to meet the minimum requirement for forming a public company?

Ans. In India, a public company requires a minimum of 7 members to be incorporated. Mr. 'X' already has 3 friends who are willing to invest, so he needs to appoint 4 more members to meet the minimum requirement. However, since he is already one of the members, he only needs to appoint 3 more.

9. Differentiate between a sole proprietorship and one person company. Give any one reason.

Ans. One key difference between a sole proprietorship and a one person company (OPC) is

- **A Sole Proprietorship** is not a separate legal entity from its owner, meaning the owner is personally liable for all debts and liabilities.
- **A One Person Company (OPC)** is a separate legal entity under the Companies Act, 2013, providing limited liability protection to its sole member.

10. Which type of legal entity comes under the Company Act, 2013?

Ans. Private Limited Company, Public Company, Sole Proprietorship, One-Person Company, Partnership, Limited Liability Partnership (LLP) comes under Company Act, 2013.

11. Anil and Suresh want to open the mall in the XYZ area. They are good friends as well. But they are confused about the legal entity which suits them for their business. They are looking for an advocate who can advise them in this situation.

(i) What is the right legal entity good for them according to this situation?

(ii) State one key advantage of choosing a partnership.

Ans. (i) A partnership firm would be a good legal entity for Anil and Suresh. A partnership allows them to share responsibilities.

(ii) One key advantage of a partnership is easy formation—it requires fewer legal formalities, making it simpler and quicker to start the business.

Short Answer Type Questions

1. What are the role of proprietorship in society? Explain in points.

Ans. The role of sole proprietorship are

- **An Answer to the Unemployment Issue** A sole proprietorship company organisation helps to solve the problem of unemployment in society by providing many job chances to those with little or no education.
- **Offers Investment Options** Small investors with limited cash have the opportunity to use their savings in the production line through sole proprietorships.
- **Providing Items at a Discount** Sole traders typically sell products for less than the Maximum Retail Price (MRP) listed on the product packaging. This is feasible because of poor management.
- **Aids Small Farmers** The majority of the commodities offered by sole proprietors are bought from regional suppliers. The solo dealers thus gain from the tiny local producers.

2. Define partnership under the Partnership Act and also explain the salient features of partnership.

Ans. The Indian Partnership Act, 1932 governs partnership forms of business in India. Section 4 of this act defines a partnership as the relationship between partners who have agreed to share the firm's profits carried on by all or any one of them acting for all.

The salient features of partnership are

- **Agreement** When partners decide to launch a firm, they must formally agree with one another. Typically, this agreement is written per governmental act standards.

- **Number of Partners** The maximum number for a partnership firm can be 50.
- **Sharing of Profits** The profit is shared among the members according to certain percentages. If there is no provision in the agreement stating there, the revenue shall be allocated equally.

3. ABC ltd. is a company that manufactures and sells electronics. It has a large number of shareholders and its shares are listed on a stock exchange. The company has a board of directors who are elected by the shareholders. Kindly summarise the public limited company and also provide examples of public limited company.

Ans. As per Section 2(71) of the Companies Act, 2013 a public company means a company which is not a private company. A public limited company is recognised as a separate entity from its owners and has the ability to enter into agreements in its own name.

It operates independently from its owners and has its own set of rules, obligations, regulations and legal rights.

Some popular public limited companies in India are Indian Oil Corporation Ltd., Bharat Petroleum Corporation Ltd., State Bank of India, etc.

4. Mr. France wants to start his business and in-home space. But he is confused about the legal entity. In this above situation, which legal entity is good for him and write advantages of that entity also?

Ans. A sole proprietorship is a good fit for him. In this situation, it shows that he is a single owner without any partner. A sole proprietorship is a business, owned, controlled and managed by a single individual.

Advantages of the sole proprietorship are

- **Quick Decisions** A solo proprietor is solely responsible for making business decisions. As there is no need to consult multiple parties for every minor issue, the business can make decisions more quickly.
- **Confidentiality** As there is single decision-maker in the firm, a single owner can keep all business-related information to themselves. The law does not require them to make accounts of sole proprietorship public.
- **Profit-sharing** Sole proprietors own all earnings generated by business activities. They are not required to share gains with others.
- **Fulfillment** A single owner is personally accountable for both the risks and benefits of their firm, even little success can provide a higher sense of pride and pleasure than other business formats.

Long Answer Type Questions

1. State the meaning and objectives of the legal entity and objectives of legal entity.

Ans. A legal entity is the business entity or person in which the employer conducts its business or transaction. It includes a corporation, limited liability company, partnership and proprietorship. A legal entity is an organisation with a collective group of individuals working together under a common identity with some rights and obligations. They get to exercise these responsibilities under the business legal entity.

Objectives of legal entity are

- The goal of legal entity regulation is to establish a framework for the formation, operation and dissolution of various types of organisations, such as corporations, partnerships and sole proprietorships.
- Its aim is to safeguard the rights and interests of stakeholders, including owners, employees, consumers, and creditors, and to ensure the fair and transparent functioning of these entities within the legal and economic framework.
- The fundamental goal of this business is to operate under a single name and to enforce its rights during litigation or critical rulings.

2. Ravi and Deepa decide to open a Gourmet Coffee shop in Bengaluru: Ravi contributes ₹ 1,50,000 and Deepa contributes ₹ 2,50,000 to the startup capital. They do not formalise their business agreement in writing, instead rely on their strong personal trust and mutual understanding. They verbally agree to share profits and losses equally. The coffee shop thrives in the first six months, generating a substantial profit. However, disagreements soon arise: Ravi feels he should receive a larger share of the profits to compensate for his active day-to-day shop management. At the same time, Deepa argues that their initial agreement to share profits equally should stand.

In light of the above scenario, answer the following question. CBSE SQP 2024

(i) Identify the type of legal entity formed by Ravi and Deepa.

(ii) State the salient features of this type of entity.

(iii) Discuss the potential issues arising from their lack of formal written agreement under Indian Partnership Law. What could have done differently to prevent these disputes, and how should they proceed to resolve their current disagreement?

Ans. (i) Partnership firm is the legal entity formed by Ravi and Deepa.

(ii) The sailent features of this type of entity are

(a) **No Separate Entity** A partnership firm has no separate legal existence of its own i.e. the partnership firm and the partners are the same in the eyes of law.

(b) **Unlimited Liability** Partners are jointly and severally liable for the liabilities of the firm.

(c) **Profit** Partners share profits in a mutually agreed ratio.

(d) **Liability** Unlimited liability and partners are jointly and severally liable for the liabilities of the firm.

(e) **Control and Decision-Making** Partners enjoy shared responsibility amongst each other. This may sometimes raise conflicts in decision-making.

(iii) Since Ravi and Deepa did not create a formal written agreement, disputes can arise about profit sharing and responsibilities. Under Indian partnership law, verbal agreements are valid, but a written agreement helps prevent misunderstandings. To avoid such conflicts, they should have drafted a partnership deed specifying roles, profit-sharing, and dispute resolution. Now, they can resolve their disagreement through open discussion or mediation. If needed, they can legally draft a partnership agreement to clarify future terms.

3. Vikram, a skilled graphic designer, has been running his design studio as a sole proprietorship. Over time, his business has grown, and he started handling larger projects with higher risks. While he enjoys the simplicity of managing his sole proprietorship, he is worried about his personal liability if something goes wrong. On the advice of his friend, Vikram is considering converting his business into a One Person Company (OPC) to limit his liability and improve his business's credibility.
Based on the above case, compare sole proprietorship and One Person Company (OPC). Which form of business entity would be better for Vikram and why?

Ans. A sole proprietorship is a business owned and managed by a single individual. It has minimal legal formalities, no separate legal identity, and the owner has unlimited liability, meaning personal assets can be used to cover business debts. Decision-making is quick, and profits go directly to the owner. However, it has limited financial resources and lacks continuity.

On the other hand, a One Person Company (OPC), as per the Companies Act, 2013, is a private company with a single member. It has a separate legal entity, limited liability, and better access to funding. Unlike a sole proprietorship, an OPC provides perpetual succession, as a nominee takes over in case of the owner's demise.

For Vikram, shifting to an OPC would be a better option as it provides limited liability protection while allowing him to continue managing the business alone.

Since his business is growing and handling bigger projects with higher risks, an OPC will offer financial security and help build a stronger business reputation.

4. Mr. 'X' and Mr. 'Y' have good businesses. But they want to grow more in the business world. They are good in relations as well. They want to come together for business purposes. They cant choose which legal entity will help them with their business growth.
In this above situation, some questions are raised.

(i) Wich legal entity or business will help them with their growth? Explain its advantages and disadvantages.

(ii) Which set will help them understand business roles and responsibilities?

Ans. (i) Partnership will be a good option for them for their business growth because they want to grow their business together.

The advantages of partnership are

- It is easy to establish with the exception of developing a partnership agreement.
- It has separate legal status to give liability protection.
- Partners may have complementary skills in partnership.
- The start up cost of partnership is low.
- More capital is available for business in a partnership.

The disadvantages of partnership are

- Partners are jointly and individually liable for the actions of the other partners.
- Profits must be shared with the partners.
- There will be division in decision-making.
- Business can suffer if the detailed partnership agreement is not in place.

(ii) Partnership Act, 1932 is the legal act that helps them to understand the role of partners and the responsibility and duties of partners.

5. **(i) What are the main features and regulatory requirements associated with operating a Public Limited Company?**

(ii) How does a Public Limited Company differ from a Private Company? **CBSE 2024 C**

Ans. (i) For answer, refer to text under the heading 'Features of Public Limited Company' on page no. 181.

(ii) For answer, refer to text under the heading 'Difference between Public and Private Company' on page no. 182.

SELF ASSESSMENT TEST

Objective Type Questions

1. In which legal entity do partners take decisions and consent of all partners is needed?
   (a) Limited liability partnership
   (b) Sole proprietorship
   (c) Partnership
   (d) Private company
2. What is the legal remedy solution available to the businessman, company members in India?
   (a) Suit file in the court
   (b) Demand for the compensation
   (c) Mutually agreed for the settlement
   (d) All of these
3. Apple company recently opened its store in India. Identify which type of legal entity will helps them.
   (a) Private company
   (b) Public company
   (c) Sole proprietorship
   (d) Partnership
4. Which company keeps on existing in the case of death, insolvency, and bankruptcy of its members?
   (a) Partnership
   (b) Limited liability partnership
   (c) Public company
   (d) Private company
5. Ram has a grocery shop and one day some person claims that they will take his shop. Ram felt afraid because he will lose his shop because of the threatening issue. In this situation, how will Ram save his shop from the people?
   (a) He will compensate with them
   (b) Take advice from the advocate
   (c) Fight with them
   (d) He will give his shop to them

Very Short Answer Type Questions

6. In which type of legal entity formation there is no limit?
7. 'State Bank of India' is a legal entity. State the type of this legal entity.

Short Answer Type Questions

8. Write two disadvantages of limited liability partnership and partnership.
9. Which kind of legal entity can be started with no minimum amount of capital contribution? State its two advantages.

Long Answer Type Question

10. Mr. Ramu is a milk diary shop and he wants to try to open his shop in other states as well. His diary shop becomes immensely popular in just a few months.
    (i) In this situation, what he will decide for his business stability?
    (ii) Give relevant reasons for how he can solve this problem and also explain the legal entity.

12

CHAPTER

The body of laws which deals with imposing punishments on crimes is known as criminal laws.

Criminal Laws in India

▼ **YOUR STUDY GOALS**

12.1 Meaning of Crime
12.2 Criminal Laws in India
12.3 Criminal Procedure Code, 1973

▼ **YOUR PRACTICE GOAL**

- Objective Type Questions (31 Qs ; MCQs, A-R, Statements, Matching)
- Subjective Questions (13 VSAs, 5 SAs, 6 LAs)

12.1 Meaning of Crime

- The term 'crime' denotes an unlawful act and this unlawful act is punishable by a state.
- Several countries provide statuary definitions of various kinds of unlawful activities, which can be identified as crimes.
- A common principle about criminal law is that, unless an activity is prohibited by law, it does not qualify as a crime.
- Incidents of crime hurt not only the individual but also, the state. Such acts are forbidden and punishable by law.

Objectives of Criminal Law

With the change in social structure, society has witnessed various punishment theories and the radical changes that they have undergone from the traditional to the modern level and the crucial problems relating to them.

There are **five objectives** that are widely accepted for enforcement of the criminal law by punishments. These are discussed below

- **Retribution**[1] This theory basically deals with **righting of balance**. If a criminal has done a wrong towards a person or property, he needs to be given a penalty in a manner which balances out the wrong done. For example, if a person has committed murder, he can be delivered capital punishment to balance out the suffering caused to the victim and his/her family.

1 **Retribution** It Literally means punishment inflicted on someone as vengeance for a wrong or criminal act.

- **Deterrence** It serves as a major instrument in maintaining the general law and order in the society, especially from the perspective of crime. Criminal acts are penalised so as to deter[2] individuals from **repeating** it or even entering into it in the first place.
- **Incapacitation** The objective of this theory is to separate the criminals (from the rest of the society). They suffer a kind of banishment by staying in prisons for the crimes committed. In some cases, they are also subject to capital punishment.
- **Rehabilitation** It aims at transforming an offender into a valuable member of society. Its primary goal is to prevent further offense by convincing the offender that his/her conduct was wrong.
- **Restoration** It is a **victim-oriented theory** of punishment. Its aim is to restore any injury inflicted upon the victim by the offender, through state authority. For example, one who steals will be required to repay the amount improperly acquired. Restoration is commonly combined with other main goals of criminal justice and is closely related to concepts in the civil law, i.e. returning the victim to his/her original position before the injury.

Ignorantia Juris Non Excusat (Ignorance of Law is no Excuse)

It is a Latin phrase meaning ignorance of law or lack of knowledge or mistake of law about legal requirement is not an excuse and hence liability arises in such cases. If a wrongdoer says that he was ignorant of the consequences of the act done by him, he would not be excused because everybody is supposed to know the law of the land.

Quick Test 1

1. What is a common principle about criminal law?
2. Write the meaning of the words 'Ignorantia Juris Non Excusat.
3. Under which section of the Indian Penal Code, punishment for theft is defined?

12.2 Criminal Laws in India

Criminal laws in India are broadly covered by the following legislations

- Indian Penal Code, 1860 (Bhartiya Nyaya Sanhita)
- Criminal Procedure Code, 1973 (Bhartiya Nagrik Suraksha Sanhita)
- Indian Evidence Act, 1872 (Bhartiya Sakshya Adhiniyam.)

Indian Penal Code

- The Indian Penal **Code (IPC)** 1860 covers the substantial part of criminal law in India. It defines various common criminal offences. For example, it defines murder, theft, assault and a number of other offences and also stipulates appropriate punishments for each offence such as the offence of 'theft' is defined in the **Section 378** of the IPC.
- According to it, a crime of theft is committed if someone intends to take someone else's property or takes that property without the other person's consent.
- Only intending to take somebody's property without actually going ahead with the act does not amount to theft.
- The punishment for theft is defined in the **Section 379** which states a person who commits theft shall be punished with imprisonment for a term which may extend to three years or with fine, or both.

2 Deter It means to make somebody decide not to do something, especially by telling him/her that it would have bad results.

- Different crimes carry different punishments according to the severity[3] of the offence. For example, the punishment for murder is either death or life imprisonment. In this way, most of the IPC is organised i.e. first, a definition of an offence is provided, and next the punishment for that offence is stipulated.

- A Parliamentary Committee recently reviewed the Bharatiya Nyaya Sanhita (BNS) 2023 Bill, suggesting key changes to India's Criminal Justice System, including a gender-neutral law on adultery.
- The BNS Bill, introduced by the Ministry of Home Affairs, aims to replace the colonial-era IPC (Indian Penal Code). It also proposes stricter punishments for organised crime, terrorism, and mob lynching, along with reforms to speed up trials and ensure victim protection in serious offences.

Elements of Crime

There are **two** fundamental elements of a crime

(i) **Mens rea or Guilty Intention** Mens rea generally means '**ill intention**', guilty mind/intent. The constituents of mens rea are
- There must be a mind at fault/intention to constitute a crime.
- The act becomes criminal when the actor does it with a guilty mind. For any crime to exist, the physical element of crime needs to be complemented by the mental element.

- The concept of mens rea evolved in **England** during the **17th century.** During this period, the judges began to hold that, an act could not create criminal liability unless it was accompanied by a guilty state of mind. For framing a charge for an offence under the IPC, the traditional rule of existence of mens rea is to be followed. This was reiterated by the Supreme Court in **State of Maharashtra Vs. Mayer Hans George, AIR 1965 SC 722.**

(ii) **Actus reus or Illegal Act or Omission** Actus reus in common language means a guilty act. It is made up of three constituent parts, namely
- An action or a conduct
- The result of that action or conduct
- Such act/conduct being prohibited by law

- Therefore, actus reus is an act which is bad or prohibited, blameworthy or culpable. There are certain unique situations when the act in itself may appear to be a criminal act, yet it cannot be termed as actus reus. For example, An executioner's job is to hang (no actus reus). Another example, an army man kills as a part of his duty (no actus reus).
- Section 32 of the Indian Penal Code (IPC) clarifies that acts which may be considered as crime include 'illegal omissions'. But mere moral omissions of not doing something would not complete the requirement of actus reus.

  For example, a boy is drowning in the swimming pool of a resort. A man who is beside the pool does not make any attempt to save this boy. This is a moral omission of not saving someone's life. The man cannot be held criminally liable for such an omission. But in the same scenario, if there is a lifeguard on duty at this resort, and if he does not make any attempt to save the boy drowning in the pool, then he can be held criminally liable for such omission.
  - The principle of actus reus and mens rea are derived from a Latin phrase, actus non facit reum nisi mens sit rea which means that an act does not make one guilty unless the mind is also legally blameworthy.
  - To be classified as a crime, the act of doing something bad (actus reus) must be usually accompanied by the intention to do something bad (mens rea). Generally, a crime exists when both these elements are present.
  - In other words, for a physical act to be termed a crime, it must be accompanied by the necessary mental element.

3 **Severity** It means the fact or condition of being serious.

Distinction between Intention and Motive

- Intention in criminal law means something that is done wilfully and not accidentally or mistakenly. The person doing the act is well aware of the consequences or the outcomes of his action or omission. If the act which is prohibited (actus reus) is done wilfully, knowingly or with awareness of the resulting consequences then the same will cause liability in criminal law.
- On the other hand, motive is the secondary objective behind doing an act. It is the driving force behind intention or commission of an act. The criminal law does not take into account motive in affixing criminal liability.
- Thus, the criminal law does not care whether one has stolen a loaf of bread to fed a starving person or stolen medicine to save someone's life, as long as it is a prohibited act, done knowingly.

Stages of Crime

A crime has different stages, but the first two-intention and preparation are usually not punishable. This means just thinking about a crime or getting ready for it is not a crime. Legal action starts only when a person goes beyond preparation and tries to commit the act.

The stages of crime are discussed below

- **Intention** The first stage in committing a crime is to have criminal intent and this is known as mental stage. The law does not take notice of an intention. Only intention to commit an offence not followed by any act, cannot constitute an offence.
- **Preparation** The second stage refers to arranging all the essential steps to carry out the intended criminal act. Preparation is not unlawful in itself because it is difficult to prove that the essential preparations were made for the commission of the crime. However, in some exceptional circumstances, mere preparation is also punished.
- **Attempt** The third stage in the conduct of a crime is attempt, and it is punishable. The criminal liability arises only when the crime has reached the stage which is gone beyond preparation and has entered into the domain of attempt.
  Section 511 of the IPC does not define the term 'attempt', even it impose a penalty for attempting to commit an offence. An attempt is defined as a direct step towards the commission of a crime, after making necessary preparations.
- **Commission of Crime** Committing the crime is the final step in the process. If the accused succeeds in his attempt, he commits a crime and will be found guilty of it. If he fails, he will only be charged with attempting the crime.
  If the crime is complete, the offender will be tried and punished as per the specific provisions provided in the Indian Penal Code.

Conditions when Preparation is Punishable

When the offence is regarded as a serious offence, preparation to commit offences is penalised under the Indian Penal Code. Some of these offences are mentioned below

- Collecting arms, etc. with intention of waging war against the government of India (Section 122 of IPC).
- Preparing Indian coins or government stamps for counterfeiting (Sections 233 to 235, 255 and 257 of IPC).
- Possession of counterfeit coin, counterfeit government stamp or false weight or measure (Sections 242, 243, 259, 266 of IPC).
- Making preparations to commit dacoity (Section 399 of IPC).

Crimes under the Special and Local Laws

Some acts are considered to be criminal acts even when they are **not to be found in IPC.** This is because they have been identified as crimes in special and local laws. These include

- Arms Act, 1959
- Gambling Act, 1867
- Prohibition Act
- Immoral Traffic (Prevention) Act, 1956
- Registration of Foreigners Act, 1930
- Indian Passport Act, 1967
- Terrorist & Disruptive Activities Act
- Dowry Prohibition Act, 1961
- Copyright Act, 1957
- SC/ST (Prevention of Atrocities) Act,1989
- Narcotic Drugs & Psychotropic Substances Act, 1985
- Excise Act, 1944
- Explosives & Explosive substances Act, 1884 &1908
- Railways Act, 1989
- Protection of Civil Rights Act, 1955
- Essential Commodities Act, 1955
- Antiquities & Art Treasures Act, 1972
- Child Marriage Restraint Act, 1929
- Sati Prevention Act,1987
- Forest Act, 1927
- Indecent Representation of women (Prohibition) Act, 1986

Other crimes (not specified above) under special and local laws including cyber laws under Information Technology Act (IT), 2000.

12.3 Criminal Procedure Code, 1973

- The objective of the Criminal Procedure Code is to provide a mechanism for the investigation and trial of offenders.
- It lays down the rules for conduct of investigation into offences by the police, and proceedings in court against any person who has committed an offence under any criminal law, whether it is IPC or a crime classified under any other law.

Types of Offences Covered

- All such offences are covered by CrPC which are mentioned in Indian Penal Code.
- The procedure of initiating proceeding/prosecution for a criminal offence is provided in Criminal Procedure Code (CrPC).
- CrPC provides the manner and place, where investigation, inquiry and trial of an offence shall take place.
- Most of the accused persons do not lead defence evidence in India.
- One of the major reasons for this is that in India, the burden to prove the offence is on the prosecution and the degree of proof required in a criminal trial is 'proof beyond reasonable doubt'.

It is not enough for the prosecution to assert that the accused has committed the offence. The judge must be convinced beyond reasonable doubt that the accused had actually committed the offence. This was known as the golden thread principle of criminal law.

- **Reverse** onus[4] clauses shift the burden of proof from the prosecution to the defendant when the prosecution has shown certain essential facts.
- The definition of a reverse onus provision is, "One that shifts the burden of proof from the prosecution to the accused, once the prosecution establishes a fundamental truth that justifies the shift in burden".
- There are some categories of violation as well to the existence of the golden rule.

4 **Onus** It means something that is one's duty or responsibility.

- In some situations, the burden of proof is placed on the accused to present evidence supporting his innocence or to raise a reasonable doubt about his guilt.
- The accused is evidently considered guilty.
- In India, the presumption of innocence is overturned in two situations which are
  - (i) First, when a specific law explicitly reverses the burden of proof.
  - (ii) Second, when the accused files an appeal against a lower court's decision in which his assumption is guilt rather than innocent.
- Dowry death is the most popular example of a reversal onus provision in India. In dowry death cases, the accused is believed to be in a guilty mental state, in which a presumption of guilt is established rather than the ordinary presumption of innocence.

The Indian Evidence Act, 1872

- The Indian Evidence Act specifies how facts can be proved through evidence. The function of the law of evidence is to lay down rules according to which the facts of a case can be proved or disproved before a court of law.
- The Evidence Act lays down the rules of evidence for the purposes of the guidance of the courts. It plays a crucial role in the establishment of facts during the court proceedings.
- It governed the matters like what evidence can be admitted, how it can be admitted, how the burden of proof has to be discharged, etc.
- One of the main objectives of the Evidence Act is to prevent the inaccuracy in the admissibility of evidence and to introduce a more correct and uniform rule of practice.
- The main principles which form the foundation of law of evidence are
  - Evidence must be confined to the matter at hand
  - Evidence must not be admitted
  - Evidence must be given in all cases
- The act is divided into three parts

Part I It includes **Sections 5 to 55.** It deals with the relevancy of facts or what facts may or may not be proved. These are dealt with in detail of the act.

Part II It includes **Sections 56 to 100.** It deals with matters, which need not be proved under law and also how facts-in-issue or relevant facts are proved through oral and documentary evidence.

Part III It includes **Sections 101 to 167.** It deals with the manner in which and by whom must the evidence be produced. In other words, it deals with the procedure for production of evidence and the effects of evidence.

Admission and Confession

- **Sections 17 to 31** of the Evidence Act deals with admission, and **Sections 24 to 30** deals with confession.
- According to **Section 17**, an admission is a statement either oral or documentary or contained in electronic form, which suggests an inference related to any fact in issue or relevant fact.
- The term 'confession' is not defined in the Evidence Act. Justice Stephen in his **Digest of the Law of Evidence** states that, "A confession is an admission made at any time by a person charged with a crime, stating or suggesting that he committed that crime".
- Confession appears for the first time U/s 24 of the IEA. This section comes under the heading of admission, so it is clear that the confessions are merely one species of admission.

Forms of Confession

A confession may occur in many forms. Major among these are

- **Judicial Confession** When a confession is made to the court itself then it will be called judicial confession. Judicial confessions are made before a magistrate or court in the due course of legal proceedings.

  A judicial confession has been defined to mean plea of guilty on arrangement (made before a court), if made freely by a person in a fit state of mind.

- **Extra-judicial Confession** When a confession is made to anybody outside the court, it will be called extra-judicial confession. Extra-judicial confessions are made by the accused elsewhere than before a magistrate or in court. It is not necessary that the statements should have been addressed to any definite individual. It may have taken place in the form of a prayer. It may be a confession to a private person.

  An extrajudicial confession has been defined to mean a free and voluntary confession of guilt by a person in a fit state of mind, in the course of conversation with persons other than judge or magistrate. It may even consists of conversation to oneself, which may be produced in evidence if overhead by another.

  For example, a man after the commission of a crime may write a letter to his relative or friend expressing his grief over the matter. This may amount to confession.

- Extra-judicial confession can be accepted and can be the basis of a conviction only if it passes the tests of credibility as laid down in the procedural laws.

Difference between Confession and Admission

Confession	Admission
Sections 24 to 30 of Indian Evidence Act deal with confession. A confession is only a species of admission.	Sections 17 to 31 of Indian Evidence Act deal with admission. Since the provisions relating to confessions occur under the heading 'admission', it follows that the word 'admission' is more comprehensive and includes a confession also.
If a statement is made by a party charged with crime in criminal proceeding, it will be called confession.	If a statement is made by a party in civil proceeding, it will be called admission.
The expression 'confession' means a statement made by an accused admitting his guilt. Confession is a statement made by an accused person which is sought to be proved against him in criminal proceeding to establish the commission of an offence by him.	The expression 'admission' means voluntary acknowledgment of the existence or truth of a particular fact.
If the confession made is free and voluntary, then it may be accepted as conclusive proof of the matters confessed.	Admissions are not conclusive proof as to the matters admitted.
Confessions always go against the person making it.	Admissions may be used on behalf of the person making it.
Under Section 30, the confession of an accused person is relevant against all his co-accused who are being tried with him for the same offence.	In admission, statements of a co-plaintiff or those of a co-defendant are no evidence against the others.

Dying Declaration

- **Section 32** of the Indian Evidence Act deals with the admissibility of dying declaration. Dying declaration is a legal concept that refers to the statement which is made by a dying person explaining the circumstances of his death. It deals with cases in which statements of relevant fact by person who is dead or cannot be found, etc. is relevant.
- A statement made by a person about the cause or circumstances of their death is relevant in legal cases where their death is in question. It holds value as evidence, regardless of whether the person expected to die when making the statement or the type of legal case involved.
- The court must be satisfied that the deceased was in a fit state of mind while making the statement and he was making the statement without any influence. Once the Court is satisfied that the dying declaration is true and voluntary, it can be sufficient to found the conviction even without any further corroboration.
- The court laid down the following general propositions about dying declaration
  - In the case of **R. Mani Vs. State of T.N. (2006)**, the court declared that if the dying declaration is coherent, consistent and trustworthy and appears to have been made voluntarily, then conviction can be based on it even if there's no corroboration.
  - Each case must go by its own facts.
  - A dying declaration is not a weaker kind of evidence than any other piece of evidence.
- A dying declaration which has been properly recorded by a competent Magistrate, in the form of questions and answers, is reliable.

Quick Test 2

1 What is the objective of Criminal Procedure Code?
2 Which section of the Indian Evidence Act deals with the admissibility of dying declaration?
3 When does the liability in criminal law arise?
4 How many stages are there in a crime?
5 What are the two fundamental elements of crime?

REFERENCE CASES

Mens rea or Gulity Intention

State of Maharashtra Vs. Mayer Hans George, AIR 1965 SC 722

Facts of the case

Mayer Hans George, a German National and Sailor, became involved in the transport of gold from Geneva to Far East. After meeting a contact in Hamburg. George took on assignments to carry gold, wearing a specially designed jacket that could hold 34 bars of gold. He successfully completed a mission delivering gold to Tokyo before being apprehended in India. On 27th November, 1962, George arrived at Santa Cruz Airport in Bombay (now Mumbai) from Zurich, intending to travel onward to Manila. Customs officers, acting on prior intelligence, located George on the plane and questioned him about carrying gold. Initially evasive, George was searched and approximately 34 kilos of gold were found concealed in a jacket with 28 pockets, 19 of which contained gold. George denied ownership and claimed he had no interest in the gold.

Issues presented before the court Whether the respondent is guilty of bringing gold in India under Sec 8(1) and 23 (1-A) of the FERA which was published in the Gazette of India on 24th November, 1962? The state of Maharashtra contended that the act was passed keeping in mind the pirating of gold since it has become the major financial concern of the nation. Moreover, looking at the importance of the act it can be inferred that the mens rea is an irrelevant element in assuming the culpability of the offender. The strict adherence of the act refutes such assumptions and demonstrates that mens rea is not a fundamental element of the offence.

However, the respondents were of the view that mens rea is a fundamental element of any criminal offence and George was not aware of the notification published by the Reserve Bank. It was contended that a person who was not aware of the Indian Provision and has no intention to bring gold in India cannot be said to possess the intent to break the law and hence should not be prosecuted under the act.

Decision It was held in this case that, "Mens rea by necessary implication can be excluded from a statute only where it is absolutely clear that the implementation of an object of a statute would otherwise be defeated and its exclusion enables those put under strict liability by their act or omission to assist the promotion of the law".

The court said that even though mens rea is an essential requirement to commit a crime but regardless of that the statutory provision can exclude the mental element. The express words of the statute can exclude the mens rea as an essential ingredient of the crime. This may be done for various reasons, for instance, to promote public welfare and activities or to eradicate social evils. The Statute which complies strict liability helps the offender to assist the state in the enforcement of the law.

Extra Judicial Confession

Sahoo Vs. State of U.P. AIR 1996 SC 40, the accused who was charged with the murder of his daughter-in-law with whom he was always quarrelling, was seen on the day of the murder going out of the house, saying words to the effect. "I have finished her and with her the daily quarrels." The statement was held to be a confession relevant in evidence for it is not necessary for the relevancy of a confession that it should be communicated to some other person.

Dying Declaration

In **K.R. Reddy Vs. The Public Prosecutor SC 1976 AIR 1994,** The evidentiary value of dying declaration was observed as under

"The dying declaration is undoubtedly admissible Vs. 32 of JEA and not being a statement on oath so that its truth could be tested by cross-examination, the court has to apply strictest scrutiny before acting upon it". While great solemnity and sanctity is attached to the words of a dying man because a person on the verge of death is not likely to tell lies or to concoct a case so as to implicate an innocent person yet the court has to be on guard against the statement of the decreased being a result of either quoting, promoting or a product of his imagination.

Distinction between Intention and Motive

Important case laws of distinction between intention and motive In Re Sreerangayee Case (1973) 1 MLJ 231, the woman in sheer destitution and impoverishment attempted to kill herself after failing in all the ways to arrange food for her starving children, but since she knowingly did a prohibitive act of attempting suicide, she was held guilty by the court.

In Nathuni Yadav and Ors Vs. State of Bihar and another 1997 SC, the court held that "Motive for doing a criminal act is generally a difficult area of prosecution. One cannot normally see into the mind of another. Motive is the emotion which impels a man to do a particular act. Such impelling cause need not necessarily be proportionally grave to do grave crimes. Many a murder have been committed without any known or prominent motive". The motive for an offence need not be necessarily proportionately grave to commit the grave offence. Therefore, establishing a sufficient motive for committing the offence is not a prerequisite for conviction.

Mind Map

CRIMINAL LAWS IN INDIA

1 Introduction to Criminal Law

Definition
- Criminal law deals with unlawful acts punishable by the state.

Objectives
- Maintain social order.
- Protect individuals and society from harm.

Principle
- An act is not a crime unless it is prohibited by law.

2 Objectives of Criminal Law

Retribution
- Balances harm caused by punishment proportionate to the crime.
- **For example** Capital punishment for murder.

Deterrence
- Prevents crime by instilling fear of consequences.

Incapacitation
- Separates offenders from society through imprisonment.

Rehabilitation
- Reforms offenders to prevent future crimes.

Restoration
- Focuses on victim compensation and repairing harm.

3 Criminal Laws in India

Indian Penal Code (IPC), 1860
- Defines crimes such as theft, murder and assault.
- Specifies punishments for offences.

Criminal Procedure Code (CrPC), 1973
- Outlines procedures for investigation, trial and prosecution.

Indian Evidence Act, 1872
- Regulates admissibility of evidence in legal proceedings.

4 Elements of Crime

Mens Rea (Guilty Intention)
- Ill intent or guilty mind essential for a crime.
- **For example** State of Maharashtra Vs. Mayer Hans George.

Actus Reus (Guilty Act)
- A prohibited action or omission constituting a crime.
- Includes physical acts and illegal omissions.

Principle
- Actus non facitreum nisi mens sit rea (An act does not make one guilty unless there is a guilty mind).

5 Stages of Crime

Intention
- Mental decision to commit a crime (not punishable).

Preparation
- Arranging means to commit a crime (usually not punishable, except in serious cases).

Attempt
- Direct action towards committing a crime (punishable).

Commission
- Completion of the criminal act (punishable as per law).

6 Key Criminal Offences and Laws

Special and Local Laws
- Arms Act, 1959.
- NDPS Act, 1985.
- Dowry Prohibition Act, 1961.
- SC/ST Prevention of Atrocities Act, 1989.

For examples
- **Section 378** Definition of theft.
- **Section 379** Punishment for theft.

7 Evidentiary Principles

Admissions and Confessions
- Sections 17–31 of the Indian Evidence Act.
- Judicial and extrajudicial confessions.

Dying Declaration
- Section 32 of the Indian Evidence Act.
- Statement by a person explaining circumstances of imminent death.

8 Case Laws

State of Maharashtra Vs. Mayer Hans George
- Discussed relevance of mens rea in statutory offences.

Sahoo Vs. State of UP
- Relevance of extrajudicial confession.

R. Mani Vs. State of Tamil Nadu
- Importance of a trustworthy dying declaration.

9 Criminal Law and Society

Ignorantia Juris Non Excusat
- Ignorance of law is not an excuse.

Presumption of Innocence
- Accused is presumed innocent until proven guilty.

CBSE TEXTBOOK FOLDER

1. "Crime is a revolt against whole society and an attack on the civilisation of the day." Elucidate and discuss the essential elements of crime.

Ans. There are two fundamental elements of a crime

(i) **Mens rea or Guilty Intention** Mens rea generally means 'ill intention', guilty mind/ intent. The constituents of mens rea are

- There must be a mind at fault/intention to constitute a crime.
- The act becomes criminal when the actor does it with a guilty mind.

The concept of mens rea evolved in England during the 17th century. During this period, the judges began to hold that, an act could not create criminal liability unless it was accompanied by a guilty state of mind. For framing a charge for an offence under the IPC, the traditional rule of existence of mens rea is to be followed.

(ii) **Actus reus or Illegal Act or Omission** Actus reus in common language means a 'guilty act'. It is made up of three constituent parts, namely

- An action or a conduct
- The result of that action or conduct
- Such act/conduct being prohibited by law

Therefore, actus reus is an act which is bad or prohibited, blameworthy or culpable. Section 32 of the Indian Penal Code (IPC) clarifies that acts which may be considered as crime include 'illegal omissions'.

2. Explain mens rea as an element of criminal liability. Is mens rea relevant in crimes of strict liability? Discuss with the help of decided case law.

Ans. Mens rea means to have a 'guilty mind.' Mens rea or the mental element of crime is a very important part of criminal law in India as well as other countries. Most laws in India contain the element of guilty mind to make an act by a person criminally liable for punishment. Mens rea is constructed from a person's thought process, motive and intention. Motive and intention are two separate ideas.

Motive is the reason behind the act whereas intention is a person's state of mind and willingness to break the law.

A strict-liability doctrine is a rule of criminal responsibility that authorises the conviction of a morally innocent person for violation of an offense, even though the crime, by definition, requires proof of a mens rea.

An example is the rule that a person who is ignorant of, or who misunderstands the meaning of a criminal law may be punished for violating it, even if her ignorance or mistake of law was reasonable.

In JK Industries Ltd Vs. Chief Inspector of Factories and Boilers, the Supreme Court observed that the offences under the Act, (the Factory Act 1948) are not a part of general penal law but arise from the breach of a duty provided in a special beneficial social defence legislation, which creates absolute or strict liability without proof of any mens rea.

The offences are strict statutory offences for which the establishment of mens rea is not an essential ingredient. The omission or commission of the statutory breach is itself the offence. A similar type of offences based on the principle of strict liability, which means liability without fault or mens rea, exists in many statutes relating to economic crimes as well as in-laws concerning the industry, food adulteration, prevention of pollution, etc.

3. Vijay is accused of the murder of his friend, Ajay. Vijay, who was missing since the death of Ajay is alleged to have phoned the police, in a repentant mood after consuming some liquor from a hotel nearby city, confessing his crime. Prosecution wants to prove the alleged murder on the basis of this statement. Can the prosecution do so? Discuss.

Ans. Yes, the prosecution can do so as a confession obtained by intoxicating the accused is equally relevant. The law is a matter that is voluntary and not forced by anyone. It is all about the discretion of the court in this situation if the court allows it or not in the form of confession.

4. 'A', an alleged offender of rape, while in police remand felt pain in his chest. He was admitted in a hospital, where a police constable was kept on the gate to keep a watch on him. 'A', confessed his guilt before another patient 'X', who was also in the same room. The statement was overheard by police man also. Prosecution wants to make this statement of 'A' as 'confession'.

Ans. In this situation, A's confession can be considered an extra-judicial confession. It may be used as evidence in court if the law permits its admissibility and finds it valid.

5. State the correct proposition of law together with precautions that courts should take in dealing with dying declarations.

Ans. The court laid down the following general propositions about dying declaration

- In the case of R. Mani Vs. State of T.N. (2006), the court declared that if the dying declaration is coherent, consistent and trustworthy and appears to have been made voluntarily, then conviction can be based on it even if there's no confirmation.
- Each case must go by its own facts.
- A dying declaration is not a weaker kind of evidence than any other piece of evidence.
- A dying declaration which has been properly recorded by a competent magistrate, in the form of questions and answers, is reliable.

6. 'X' was convicted under Section 302 of IPC for having committed murder of his wife 'Y'. The judgement of trial court is based on the dying declarations made by 'Y' to the police officer and Metropolitan Magistrate who visited the hospital later on. Can the accused be convicted solely on the basis of the dying declaration given by 'Y'? Explain with the help of relevant case.

Ans. Yes, the accused 'X' can be convicted solely on the basis of the dying declaration given by 'Y' if it is found to be true, voluntary and reliable. The Supreme Court in K.R. Reddy Vs. The Public Prosecutor (1976) held that a dying declaration is admissible under Section 32 of the Indian Evidence Act. If the person making the statement was in a fit mental state and spoke without any influence, the court can convict the accused even without additional evidence.

In R. Mani Vs. State of T.N. (2006), the court ruled that if a dying declaration is clear and consistent, it can be the sole basis for conviction. Since 'Y' gave her statement to both a police officer and a magistrate, it holds strong evidentiary value. However, the court must ensure that 'Y' was conscious and made the statement voluntarily before relying on it for conviction.

Exam Pattern Questions

Objective Type Questions

Multiple Choice Questions (MCQs)

1. Segregating the wrongdoer from the rest of the society by giving him imprisonment serves which objective of criminal law? **CBSE SQP 2021**

(a) Retribution (b) Incapacitation
(c) Rehabilitation (d) Restoration

2. During his visit to the home of 'C', 'A' asks 'B', the son of 'C', to accompany 'A' to a forest. Neither 'A' nor 'B' inform 'C' in this regard. 'B' accompanies 'A' to the forest.

(a) 'A' has committed theft.
(b) 'A' has not committed theft.
(c) 'A' has committed theft as soon as he entered the home of 'C'.
(d) 'A' has not committed theft till 'B' did not accompany him.

3. 'A' dishonestly puts a bait for dogs in his pocket, and thus induces Z's dog to follow it.

(a) 'A' has committed theft
(b) 'A' has not committed theft
(c) Theft can not be committed on dogs
(d) None of the above

4. A security guard at a museum shoots an armed intruder who tries to breach the security barrier. Which of the following is true in this situation? **CBSE 2019**

(a) Using force to prevent a crime as part of one's duty is not a criminal act.
(b) Causing injury to an assailant in self-defence is not a crime.
(c) The injury is caused with the intent to take revenge and thus, the act is criminal.
(d) Both the elements of 'actus reus' and 'mens rea' are present so the security guard is criminally liable.

5. Bimal, in a fit of anger, killed his wife over a heated argument. In a state of drunkenness, he confessed to the crime before his own brother who is also a Magistrate. The statement made by Bimal before his brother would be regarded as **CBSE SQP 2021**

(a) Judicial confession as it is made before the Magistrate.
(b) Extra-judicial confession as it is made before his brother.
(c) The statement is not a confession as it is not made in a fit state of mind.
(d) The statement will be regarded as admission.

6. In which section the provision of dying declaration in the evidence act is given?

(a) Section 32 (b) Section 23
(c) Section 89 (d) Section 45

7. Brij was caught red-handed while travelling without a ticket in a train by the travelling ticket officer. CBSE SQP 2020

(a) Brij has to pay a fine as the TT officer is compounding the offence.
(b) Brij has to be imprisoned as this is a non-compoundable offence.
(c) Brij can't pay a fine at all, but has to be imprisoned by the officer.
(d) The travelling ticket officer can allow Brij to travel without a ticket.

8. 'A' acquires a pistol to kill his arch business rival 'B'. 'A' keeps the loaded pistol in his pocket, but does nothing to kill 'B'. CBSE SQP 2020

(a) 'A' is guilty of a criminal act as he kept the loaded gun in his pocket.
(b) 'A' is guilty of a criminal act as there he acquired a pistol.
(c) 'A' is not guilty as he has made no attempt to kill 'B'.
(d) 'A' is guilty because he had the intention to kill 'B'.

9. In which of the following cases was it held that 'Mens rea by necessary implication can be excluded from a statute only where it is absolutely clear that the implementation of the object of a statute would otherwise be defeated and its exclusion enables those put under strict liability by their act or omission to assist the promotion of the law'?

(a) State of Maharashtra Vs. M.H. George
(b) Kartar Singh Vs. State of Punjab
(c) McNaughten's case
(d) None of the above

10. What is common among UK, USA, Australia and India? CBSE 2024 C

(a) All of these countries are Civil Law jurisdiction.
(b) All of these countries follow Inquisitorial System of Justice Dispensation.
(c) All of these countries are Common Law jurisdiction.
(d) All of these countries follow the Napoleonic code.

11. Ajit is accused of stealing a motorcycle. During the investigation, he confesses his crime to a police officer while being interrogated in custody. However, later in court, he denies the confession. Which of the following is most accurate regarding the admissibility of his confession?

(a) The confession is valid because Aman admitted to the crime.
(b) The confession is inadmissible because it was made to a police officer in custody.
(c) The confession is valid only if it was made in front of a judge.
(d) The confession is inadmissible unless Aman provides supporting evidence.

12. "Most accused persons do not lead defence evidence in India."
Identify the reason for this from the options given below. CBSE 2025

(a) The burden to prove the offence beyond reasonable doubt is on the prosecution.
(b) The nudge decides the case on its merit according to the evidences presented by the defence.
(c) The assertion that the accused has committed offence is sufficient to prove the guilt by prosecution.
(d) The accused is presumed guilty at the first instance when the trial begins.

13. Sameer fires a gun at Ravi intending to kill him, but the bullet misses. Which of the following is most accurate regarding mens rea?

(a) Mens rea is absent because Ravi was not harmed.
(b) Mens rea is present because Sameer intended to kill.
(c) Mens rea is irrelevant as no crime was committed.
(d) Mens rea applies only if the act was successful.

14. In which of the following cases is 'X' guilty of attempting to commit an offence?

(a) 'X', in order to forge a document purporting to be executed by 'Y', sends his servant to buy a stamp paper in the name of 'Y'. As the servant reaches the shop, he is arrested.
(b) 'X' shoots at 'Y' whose back is towards him. 'Y' is not hurt as he is beyond the range of the gun.
(c) 'X' pours half a pint of substance from a bottle marked 'poison' into the drink of 'Y'. 'Y' is not aware of it. Later, it turns out that the bottle did not contain any poison.
(d) 'X' administers some noxious substance to Ria so that an abortion results. The woman was not pregnant.

15. Amar applied for the post of a PG teacher in a government school and submitted his application along with his degrees. He was called for the interview on 10th June, 2018.
But the school authorities on 10th May, 2018, discovered that the copy of the degrees attached with Amar's application were forged and so the application was rejected. Identify the offence committed by Amar.

(a) Amar is guilty of cheating
(b) Amar is guilty of preparation to cheat
(c) Amar is guilty of attempt to cheat
(d) Amar is not guilty of any offence as he is not called for the interview.

16. **'A', under the influence of madness, attempts to kill 'B'. 'B', to save his life, kills 'A'.**

(a) 'A' has committed the offence of attempt to murder.
(b) 'A' has committed an offence of being mad.
(c) 'B' has committed an offence.
(d) 'B' has not committed an offence.

17. **'A' jumps into a swimming pool to save 'C' from drowning. While pulling the boy from water 'A' was hit by 'C'. 'A' left the boy in the water and attacked 'C'. The boy died in the water.**

(a) 'A' has not committed the offence of killing the boy.
(b) 'A' has committed the offence of killing the boy.
(c) The boy has committed the offence of suicide.
(d) The boy has committed the offence of drowning.

18. **In the case of State Vs. Bhuvan, the accused Bhuvan was convicted under Section 302 of the IPC for the murder of his wife, Jaya. The conviction was primarily based on the dying declarations made by Jaya. A police officer recorded these declarations and were subsequently also recorded by a Metropolitan Magistrate who visited Jaya in the hospital. Can Bhuvan be convicted of murder based on Jays's dying declaration ?** **CBSE SQP 2024**

(a) Bhuvan cannot be convicted solely based on Jaya's dying declaration, as dying declarations are not admissible as an evidence under the Indian Evidence Act.
(b) Bhuvan can be convicted solely based on Jaya's dying declaration, provided the declaration is found to be true, voluntary and made in a fit state of mind.
(c) Bhuvan can only be convicted if there is corroborative evidence in addition to Jaya's dying declaration, as dying declarations alone are insufficient for conviction under Section 302 of the IPC.
(d) The conviction of Bhuvan based solely on Jaya's dying declaration is valid only if the dying declaration was made in writing and signed by Jaya.

19. **Which of the following scenarios best exemplifies the concept 'deterrence is an objective of criminal law'?** **CBSE 2024**

(a) After consuming alcohol at a party, Suresh chooses to hire a taxi and arrive home safely.
(b) Manya, a habitual shoplifter, receives a warning from a store owner to stop her from stealing again.
(c) Alex caught driving under the influence of alcohol, faces a hefty fine, license suspension and mandatory education programme.
(d) Sana refrains from cheating in an exam- being aware of the punitive consequences.

20. **Detective Jones is investigating a complex case where the victim was found dead in his apartment. During the investigation, Detective Jones uncovers a series of conflicting evidence suggesting multiple possible motives and varying levels of intent among the suspects. One such evidence is a note by the deceased that explained the circumstances of his death. Detective Jones will use this note as** **CBSE 2024 C**

(a) Admission
(b) Dying declaration
(c) Extra-judicial confession
(d) Judicial confession

21. **Match the following** **CBSE SQP 2020**

Column I	Column II
A. In Re Sreerangayee case	1. Extra judicial confession
B. State of Maharashtra Vs. Mayor Hans George	2. Mens rea must be read into a statutory penal provision unless expressly excluded.
C. Kartar Singh Vs. State of Punjab	3. Both mens rea and actus reus required for affixing criminal liability.
D. Sahoo Vs. State of UP	4. Mens rea can only be excluded if the implementation of the statute would be otherwise defeated.

Codes

	A	B	C	D
(a)	3	4	2	1
(b)	1	2	3	4
(c)	3	4	1	2
(d)	4	3	2	1

22. **Jai is accused of stealing a valuable item from a store. During the trial, the prosecution argues that he acted with a particular mental state regarding the alleged theft. Which of the following legal concepts relates to the mental state of Jai and plays a role in determining his culpability?** **CBSE 2024**

(a) Actus reus (b) Mens rea
(c) Motive (d) Ignorance of law

23. **Analyse the two statements given below and select the correct option.** **CBSE SQP 2024**

Statement I The physical element of crime needs to be complemented by the mental element.

Statement II "Mens rea by necessary implication can be excluded from a statute only where it is absolutely clear that the implementation of an object of a statute would otherwise be defeated and its exclusion enables those put under strict liability by their act or omission to assist the promotion of the law".

(a) Both Statements are correct.
(b) Both Statements are incorrect.
(c) Statement I is correct, but Statement II is not correct.
(d) Statement II is correct, but Statement I is not correct.

24. **Statement I** The retributive theory of justice focuses on punishing the offender for their wrong doing, with the goal of providing justice and closure to the victim and their family.

Statement II According to the retributive theory, the severity of the punishment should be proportionate to the severity of the crime and the offender should be held accountable for their actions.

Choose the correct statement.

(a) Both Statements are correct.
(b) Both Statements are incorrect.
(c) Statement I is correct, but Statement II is not correct.
(d) Statement II is correct, but Statement I is not correct.

25. **Situation I** A boy is sinking in the swimming pool of a resort. A man who is standing beside the pool does not make any attempt to save this boy.

Situation II A lifeguard on duty at a resort. A boy is sinking in the swimming pool of a resort. He does not make any attempt to save the boy sinking in the pool.

Which of the following statements describe both the situations? **CBSE SQP 2022**

(a) In both the situations there is actus reas though mens rea is missing.
(b) In both the situations none can be held liable for criminal omission.
(c) Situation I shows moral omission, whereas Situation II shows illegal omission.
(d) An act of not doing anything does not accrue any criminal liability as actus rea is not there.

26. **Statement I** The Evidence Law helps the judges to separate the "Wheat from the Chaff".

Statement II The function of the law of evidence is to provide a mechanism for the investigation and trial of offenders. **CBSE 2025**

Choose the correct statement.

(a) Both Statements are correct.
(b) Both Statements are incorrect.
(c) Statement I is correct, but Statement II is not correct.
(d) Statement II is correct, but Statement I is not correct.

Assertion-Reason Questions

Directions (Q. Nos. 27-31) In the questions given below, there are two statements. Read the statements and choose the correct option.

Codes

(a) Both A and R are true and R is the correct explanation of A.
(b) Both A and R are true, but R is not the correct explanation of A.
(c) A is true, but R is false.
(d) A is false, but R is true.

27. **Assertion** (A) IPC is a substantive law.

Reason (R) It defines various common criminal offences.

28. **Assertion** (A) There are some exceptions to the thumb rule of mens rea to be present for an act to be considered as crime.

Reason (R) These are generally the offences which arise due to a 'strict liability'.

29. **Assertion** (A) A person who unintentionally causes harm to another person cannot be held criminally liable.

Reason (R) The word actus can notes a 'deed' which is a physical result of human conduct.

30. **Assertion** (A) Preparation to commit a crime is not punishable unless it is accompanied by an attempt to commit the crime.

Reason (R) The stage of preparation is not considered sufficient to establish criminal liability, but it becomes relevant only when it progresses to the stage of attempt.

31. **Assertion** (A) An extra-judicial confession, if voluntarily made, is admissible as evidence even if it is retracted later.

Reason (R) The Indian Evidence Act, 1872, under Section 29, provides that a confession made by an accused person is relevant and admissible as evidence, regardless of whether it was made in court or outside of court.

Answers

1. (b) Incapacitation
2. (b) 'A' has not committed theft.
3. (a) 'A' has committed theft
4. (a) Using force to prevent a crime as part of one's duty is not a criminal act.
5. (c) The statement is not a confession as it is not made in a fit state of mind.
6. (a) Section 32
7. (a) Brij has to pay a fine as the TT officer is compounding the offence.
8. (c) 'A' is not guilty as he has made no attempt to kill 'B'.
9. (a) State of Maharashtra Vs. M.H. George
10. (c) All of these countries are Common Law jurisdiction.
11. (b) The confession is inadmissible because it was made to a police officer in custody.

12. (a) The burden to prove the offence beyond reasonable doubt is on the prosecution.
13. (b) Mens rea is present because Sameer intended to kill.
14. (b) 'X' shoots at 'Y' whose back is towards him. 'Y' is not hurt as he is beyond the range of the gun.
15. (c) Amar is guilty of attempt to cheat
16. (b) 'A' has committed an offence of being mad.
17. (a) 'A' has not committed the offence of killing the boy.
18. (b) Bhuvan can be convicted solely based on Jaya's dying declaration, provided the declaration is found to be true, voluntary and made in a fit state of mind.
19. (d) Sana refrains from cheating in an exam-being aware of the punitive consequences.
20. (b) Dying declaration
21. (a) 3 4 2 1
22. (b) Mens rea
23. (a) Both Statements are correct.
24. (a) Both Statements are correct.
25. (c) Situation I shows moral omission, whereas Situation II shows illegal omission.
26. (c) Statement I is correct, but Statement II is not correct.
27. (a) Both A and R are true and R is the correct explanation of A.
28. (a) Both A and R are true and R is the correct explanation of A.
29. (b) Both A and R are true, but R is not the correct explanation of A.
30. (a) Both A and R are true and R is the correct explanation of A.
31. (a) Both A and R are true and R is the correct explanation of A.

Subjective Questions

Very Short Answer Type Questions

1. State the meaning of the admission in the Evidence Act. **CBSE 2020**

Ans. According to Section 17, an admission is a statement either oral or documentary or contained in electronic form, which suggests an inference related to any fact in issue or relevant fact.

2. What is the meaning of crime under the criminal law in India? **CBSE SQP 2020**

Ans. Crime in Indian criminal law refer to an unlawful act punishable by the state, requiring both a guilty act (actus reus) and intent.

3. What do you understand about the concept of restoration?

Ans. Concept of restoration is a victim-oriented theory of punishment. The goal is to repair, through state authority, any injury inflicted upon the victim by the offender.

4. Has mens rea been explicitly defined in the IPC?

Ans. In India, the word mens rea, is not defined in the IPC, but its essence is reflected in almost all the provisions of the Code. For framing a charge for an offence under the IPC, the traditional rule of existence of mens rea is to be followed.

5. What is the intention under the criminal law in India? **CBSE SQP 2020**

Ans. An intention is a subjective state of mind (mens rea) that must accompany the acts of certain crimes to constitute a violation.

6. What do you understand by the maxim 'actus non facit reum nisi mens sit rea'?

Ans. Latin maxim 'actus non facit reum nisi mens sit rea' means that an act does not make one guilty unless the mind is also legally blameworthy.

7. What are the two essential elements to constitute a crime?

Ans. The two essential elements to constitute a crime are
(i) Actus reus (ii) Mens rea

8. In a hostel for school children, the canteen staff failed to properly check the ingredients of a meal. They were aware of some of the severe food allergies of some hostellers. As a result a student consumes a food item containing the allergen and suffers a severe allergic reaction. Assess whether such a scenario could be considered an 'omission' and whether it constitutes 'actus reus'. **CBSE 2024 C**

Ans. Yes, the scenario can be considered an omission, as the canteen staff failed to properly check the ingredients, despite being aware of the students' severe food allergies. This omission constitutes actus reus (guilty act), as it resulted in harm to the student. The staff's failure to act (omission) led to a breach of their duty of care, making them liable for the consequences.

9. Analyse the two situations given below and assess the criminal liability of the individuals.

(i) Ramawati in sheer destitution and impoverishment attempted to kill herself after failing in all ways to arrange for food for her starving children.

(ii) A boy is sinking in a swimming pool of a resort. A man who is besides the pool does not make any attempt to save this boy.

Would Ramawati and the man beside the swimming pool be criminally liable? **CBSE 2023**

Ans. Since Ramawati knowingly (mens rea) did a prohibitive act of killing herself (actus reus). She will be held liable. On the other hand the man beside the swimming pool will not be held liable as it was not his legal obligation to save the child, it was only his moral obligation.

10. Explain the stages involved in the commission of a crime.

Ans. The four stages involved in the commission of a crime are

(i) Intention (ii) Preparation
(iii) Attempt (iv) Commission

11. "The prosecution in a criminal trial must meet quite high standards and it is not enough for the prosecution to only assert that the accused has committed the offence". Comment with reasons. **CBSE SQP 2022**

Ans. The prosecution in a criminal trial must meet quite high standards because most of the accused persons do not lead defence evidence in India. One of the major reasons for this is that in India, the burden is cast on the prosecution to prove the offence and the degree of proof required in a criminal trial is 'Proof beyond reasonable doubt'.

12. Rohit is accused of accepting a bribe while working as a government officer. During interrogation, he confesses to the crime in front of the police. Later, in court, the prosecution presents this confession as the primary evidence against him.

(i) Identify any two errors in the prosecution's approach regarding the confession.

(ii) Explain when a confession is legally admissible in court under the Indian Evidence Act, 1872.

Ans. (i) Two errors in the prosecution's approach regarding the confession are

(a) A confession made to a police officer is not valid evidence in court (Section 25, Indian Evidence Act).

(b) A confession alone cannot be the main proof; other evidence is needed.

(ii) A confession is valid if made freely before a Magistrate or in court, without pressure or threats.

13. A man after the commission of a crime wrote a letter to his relative or friend expressing his grief over the matter. Will this amount to a confession?

Ans. Yes, this will amount to a confession and it will be known as an extra-judicial confession.

Short Answer Type Questions

1. 'Z' is going on a journey. Entrusts his plate to the possession of 'A' the keeper of a warehouse, till '7' shall return. Then 'A' carries the plate to a goldsmith and sells it.

(i) Will this act of 'A' amount to the offence of theft under Section 378 of IPC? Give reasons.

(ii) Would your answer be different if 'Z' had not entrusted the plate to 'A' and he had himself taken it out of his kitchen with a dishonest intention?

(iii) What is the punishment prescribed for theft under IPC?

Ans. (i) The act of 'A' of selling the plate entrusted to him by 'Z' will not amount to theft within the meaning of Section 378 of IPC. This is because the property was already entrusted to 'A' by 'Z' and 'A' did not move the plate out of 'Z's possession without his consent.

(ii) Yes, because in that case, all the ingredients of Section 378 would have been satisfied and 'A' would be liable for the offence of theft.

(iii) The punishment for theft is stipulated in the following Section 379 which states that a person who commits theft shall be punished with imprisonment for a term which may extend to three years, or with fine, or both.

2. Identify and explain the stage of crime in each of the following cases.

(i) Ravi plans to rob a jewellery store. He creates a detailed map of the store, gathers tools, and discusses the plan with his friend. However, he has not yet taken any action to execute the robbery.

(ii) Neha decides to poison her rival. She buys a bottle of poison and mixes it into a drink but is caught before she can serve it.

(iii) Arjun sets fire to a neighbour's car in a fit of rage. The car burns completely, causing damage to nearby property as well.

Ans. In the given cases, each situation represents a different stage of crime

(i) **Preparation Stage** Ravi is at the preparation stage because he is planning and gathering tools for the robbery. However, since he has not taken any action to commit the crime, he is not yet criminally liable unless the crime falls under exceptions like preparing for dacoity.

(ii) **Attempt Stage** Neha has crossed preparation and entered the attempt stage because she has mixed the poison, but her plan was stopped before completion. Attempting a crime is punishable even if it fails.

(iii) **Commission Stage** Arjun has completed the crime by setting the car on fire. This is the commission stage, where the crime is fully carried out, and he will be punished for arson and property damage.

3. Raghav and his two friends, Ravi and Prakash, were arrested by the police on the charges of kidnapping and abduction of a minor girl. A conversation between Raghav and his friends was overheard by a ragpicker while they were discussing the further course of action in a junkyard. The ragpicker informed the police and the three were arrested.

During investigation, Ravi told the Inspector that if taken to Kodaikanal, he would show the spot where the minor girl was kept. **CBSE 2020**

(i) **Analyse the nature of evidence presented in the given situation. Can this evidence form the basis of conviction?**

(ii) **What is the position of Ravi's statement in evidence law.**

(iii) **If the statement was made by Ravi before a Magistrate instead of the Inspector, would it have the same impact as an evidence ? Explain.**

Ans. (i) Yes, these evidence will form the basis of conviction as Ravi's statement amounts to a confession and the ragpicker's statement is oral evidence.

(ii) Ravi's statement is an extra-judicial confession as it is made to a person other than the Magistrate. Extra-judicial confession can be accepted and can be the basis of a conviction only if it passes the tests of credibility as laid down in the procedural laws (laws which establish the procedure, (e.g. CrPC).

(iii) If the statement was made by Ravi before a Magistrate instead of the Inspector, it would have amounted to a judicial confession and not an extra-judicial confession. Judicial confessions are always valid.

4. A newly wedded woman joined the new house of her husband and after sometime the accused murdered his daughter-in-law and after murdering her, he screamed 'I have finished her'. Many of his neighbours heard his statement stating "I have finished her".

(i) **Whether the statement made by the man amounts to a confession or not? Give reasons.**

(ii) **Is murder a compoundable offence? Discuss.**

Ans. (i) The self conversation made by the man shall be considered as a confession to prove his guilt and such confession should be recognised as relevant in evidence in administering justice.

(ii) Certain offences are so serious that any police officer can investigate and arrest an accused person without obtaining a warrant (legal permission to arrest) from a court, e.g. murder. These are cognisable offences (arresting without warrant). Cognisable offences are not compoundable in nature because the gravity of the offence is very serious.

5. Write a note on extra-judicial confessions.

Ans. Extra-judicial confessions are made by the accused elsewhere than before a Magistrate or in court. It is not necessary that the statements should have been addressed to any definite individual. They may have taken place in the form of a prayer.

It might may be a confession to a private person. An extra-judicial confession has been defined to mean a free and voluntary confession of guilt by a person accused of a crime in the course of conversation with persons other than the judge or Magistrate.

For example, a man after the commission of a crime may write a letter to his relative or friend expressing his grief over the matter. This may amount to confession.

Extra-judicial confession can be accepted and can be the basis of a conviction only if it passes the tests of credibility as laid down in the procedural laws.

Long Answer Type Questions

1. Explain the objectives that are widely accepted for enforcement of criminal law. **CBSE SQP 2022**

Or **Explain the objectives of criminal law in India** **CBSE 2023**

Ans. Five objectives that are widely accepted for enforcement of the criminal law are as follows

(i) **Retribution** This theory basically deals with 'righting of balance'. If a criminal has done a wrong towards a person or property he needs to be given a penalty in a manner which balances out the wrong done.

(ii) **Deterrence** Deterrence serves as a major tool in maintaining the general law and order in the society, especially from the perspective of crime. Criminal acts are penalised so as to deter individuals from repeating it or even entering into it in the first place.

(iii) **Incapacitation** The objective of this theory is to segregate the criminals from the rest of the society. For the crimes committed, they suffer a kind of banishment by staying in prisons and in some cases they are also subject to capital punishment.

(iv) **Rehabilitation** Aims at transforming an offender into a valuable member of society. Its primary goal is to prevent further offense by convincing the offender that their conduct was wrong.

(v) **Restoration** This is a victim-oriented theory of punishment. The goal is to repair, through state authority, any injury inflicted upon the victim by the offender.

2. It is a common misconception that motive and intention are the same concepts when it comes to crime. Thus, it is important to understand distinction between these two term. Explain the distinction.

Ans. For answer, refer to text under the heading 'Distinction between Intention and Motive' on page no. 197.

3. Amit and Neha are neighbours in Mumbai. One evening, while returning from work, Amit hears a loud scream from Neha's house. He rushes inside and finds an unknown man attacking Neha. In an attempt to save her, Amit picks up a heavy vase and strikes the attacker on the head, causing fatal injuries. The police arrive and arrest Amit for causing the man's death.

In light of the above scenario, answer the following questions

(i) Identify whether Amit's act constitutes a crime under Indian law.

(ii) Explain the role of mens rea and actus reus in determining criminal liability in this case.

(iii) Discuss the legal concept of self-defence in Indian criminal law. Could Amit claim self-defence as a justification for his actions? What conditions must be met for his defence to be valid?

Ans. (i) Amit's act of hitting the attacker caused death, which normally falls under the category of homicide. However, not all homicides are crimes. If Amit acted in self-defense, his action may be justified under Section 96 of the Indian Penal Code (IPC), which states that self-defense is not a crime if done to protect oneself or others from harm.

(ii) For a crime to be established, there must be a guilty act (actus reus) and a guilty mind (mens rea). Amit committed a physical act (actus reus) by striking the attacker, but he had no criminal intent (mens rea). His intention was not to kill but to protect Neha, which is an important factor in deciding criminal liability.

(iii) Under Section 100 of the IPC, a person can use force, even causing death, if they believe their life or someone else's is in danger. Amit's action was immediate and necessary to prevent harm. Since he did not use excessive force beyond what was needed, he can claim self-defense.

4. Palvinder Kaur was arrested for murder of her husband along with their family friend Arvinder Singh. Her husband was a hobbyist photographer and used to keep handy photo developing material which is quick poison. One day, her husband was ill and she brought him some medicine. The medicine was kept near the liquid developer and her husband swallowed it by mistake and died. She got afraid and with the help of Arvinder Singh, she dumped the body in the well. When she was in police custody, she told the whole story to one of the lady constables and expressed her grief over the matter. **CBSE 2016**

(i) Will the statement given by Palvinder Kaur amount to confession or admission? Give reason for your answer.

(ii) State any four differences between admission and confession.

Ans. (i) In the given situation, Palvinder Kaur's statement to the police officer will amount to an extra judicial confession as it was not made to a police officer. However, it will not be an admission since the statement admits to the commission of a crime (dumping the body by mistake).

Justice Stephen in his digest of the law of evidence states, "Confession is an admission made at any time by a person charged with a crime stating or suggesting the inference that he committed that crime."

(ii) For answer, refer to text under the heading 'Differences between Admission and Confession' on page no. 200.

5. In the context of criminal law, explain the term 'Preparation'. Under what circumstances is preparation punishable under the IPC?

Ans. Preparation is the second stage that refers to arranging of all the essential steps to carry out the intended criminal act. Preparation is not unlawful in itself since it is difficult to prove that the essential preparations were made for the commission of the crime.

However, some exceptional circumstances, mere preparation is also punished. Preparation under IPC is punishable when the offence is regarded as serious offence. A few of them are mentioned below

- Collecting arms etc., with intention of waging war against the government of India (Section 122 of IPC).
- Preparing Indian coins or government stamps for counterfeiting (Section 233 to 235, 255 and 257 of IPC).
- Possession of counterfeit coin, counterfeit government stamp or false weight or measure (Sections 242, 243, 259, 266 of IPC).
- Making preparations to commit dacoity (Section 399 of IPC).

6. What is the dying declaration and what are the elements of the dying declaration?

Ans. For answer, refer to text under the heading 'Dying Declaration' on page no. 201.

SELF ASSESSMENT TEST

Objective Type Questions

1. Arjun was caught by the police for carrying a gold bar without a valid permit at the Mumbai airport. He claimed that he was unaware of the law requiring a permit for gold imports. However, the authorities proceeded with legal action against him. What could be the probable reason for this?

(a) Arjun intended to smuggle the gold
(b) Ignorance of the law is not an excuse under Indian law
(c) Arjun did not declare the gold at customs
(d) Arjun exceeded the allowed gold limit for personal use

2. **Assertion (A)** A person cannot be held criminally liable for merely having an intention to commit a crime.

Reason (R) Under Indian law, criminal liability arises only when a person goes beyond intention and attempts or commits a prohibited act.

Codes

(a) Both A and R are true and R is the correct explanation of A.
(b) Both A and R are true but R is not the correct explanation of A.
(c) A is true, but R is false.
(d) A is false, but R is true.

3. In which section admission is defined under the Evidence Act, 1872?

(a) Section 17 (b) Section 18 (c) Section 19 (d) Section 20

4. Rohan was arrested for attempting to commit a bank robbery but failed before he could take any money. He argued that since he did not succeed, he should not be punished. Why can he still be held legally accountable?

(a) Only successful crimes are punishable.
(b) Attempt to commit a crime is also punishable under Indian law.
(c) Bank robberies are only punishable if someone is injured.
(d) He should be punished under civil law, not criminal law.

5. Relevancy of facts have been discussed under which Part of the Evidence Act?

(a) Part I (b) Part II (c) Part III (d) All of these

Very Short Answer Type Questions

6. Does an act in actus reus include omissions (not doing an act) as well?

7. What are the elements of crime under Indian Penal Code?

8. State the difference between actus rea and mens rea.

Short Answer Type Questions

9. Mr. 'X', a business man, fires an employee, Mr. 'Y', because he believes Mr. 'Y' is not performing well and is causing harm to the company. However, it is later revealed that Mr. 'X' had a personal grudge against Mr. 'Y' and had been looking for an excuse to terminate him. In this scenario what is the difference between Mr. X's intention and motive?

10. Discuss the various categories of crime.

Long Answer Type Questions

11. What types of offences are covered in Criminal Procedure Code, 1973?

12. Explain the phrase 'Actus non facit reum nisi mens sit rea'.

13

CHAPTER

Human Rights in India

A 'Right' is a moral or legal entitlement to have or do something.
The modern society recognised certain rules of respecting human dignity and their well-being have been acknowledged and established as human rights.

YOUR STUDY GOALS

YOUR PRACTICE GOAL

- Objective Type Questions (41 Qs ; MCQs, A-R, Statements, Matching)
- Subjective Questions (18 VSAs, 13 SAs, 8 LAs)

13.1 Meaning of Right

A right is a justified claim on others. In other words, rights are reasonable privileges or claims of people which are accepted by society and affirmed by statue law. Rights include **human rights** and **Fundamental Rights.**

Human Rights

- Human rights are basic rights that we have because we exist as human beings. These are not granted by any state.
- Generally, the word **'Rights'** denote that these rules are entitlements or claims of all to be recognised ones and are protected through duties and obligations. Further, the state ensures that human rights of all are guaranteed.
- Human rights are based on values that keep society fair, just and equal. They include the right to life the right to health and right to freedom from torture etc.

Origin of Human Rights

- Historically varied religious and social traditions as well as philosophical writings have recognised in different ways and with diverse perspectives the inherent rules of being humans, particularly the principles that ensure respect for human dignity. Such principles have commonly been understood as basic and unalienable.

- The origin of human rights began in the year 539 BC when troops of Cyrus the Great, conquered Babylon.
- After winning the war, Cyrus freed the slaves to return home. He also declared that all people had the right to choose their own religion.
- In the 20th century, during the Second World War, the world saw cruel acts that enraged the conscience of mankind.
- This resulted in the adoption of Universal Declaration of Human Rights (UDHR) in December 1948 by the then newly established United Nations.
- It recognised human rights to be the foundation for freedom, justice and peace.

Features of Human Rights

The features of human rights are

- Human rights belong to all human beings irrespective of their nationality, race, caste, creed, gender, etc. All individuals enjoy same human rights, without any discrimination.
- Human rights are safeguards that a human being seeks in order to live with dignity and equality. Therefore, human rights are universal and inalienable rights.
- The principle of universality of human rights means that we are all **equally entitled** to our human rights.
- Human rights are inalienable; therefore, these **should not** be taken away, except in specific situations and according to due process. For instance, the right to liberty[1] may be restricted if a person is found guilty of a crime by a court of law.
- A few examples of human rights are those basic rights that **ensure fairness, equality, freedom and respect to all people.** These rights abolish various unjust practices like exploitation, discrimination and inequality.
- Human rights include most Fundamental Rights like right to life, rights to food, education, work, health and liberty, etc.

International Human Rights

- In 1948, the United Nations General Assembly adopted the **Universal Declaration of Human Rights** (UDHR) as 'A common standard of achievement for all people and nations'.
- The Universal Declaration of Human Rights provides and defines the various kinds of human rights that are applicable to all human beings.
- These include the fundamental, civil, political, economic, social and cultural rights.

Sustainable Development Goals and Human Rights

The Sustainable Development Goals (SDGs) and human rights are interlinked. Over 90 per cent of the goals of the SDGs relate to human rights obligations.

When a state makes progress towards achieving SDGs they move forward to fulfill their human rights obligations. Few SDGs that are linked to human rights are no poverty, gender equality and zero hunger.

1 **Liberty** It means the freedom of to go anywhere we want to go and do whatever we want to do.

Fundamental Rights

- Fundamental Rights are basic rights of the citizens of a country. Fundamental Rights are enshrined in the Constitution and they are enforceable in the court of law.
- If there is any kind of violation of Fundamental Rights, one can approach the court for protection of such rights.

Features of Fundamental Rights

Some of the salient features of Fundamental Rights are

- They are enforceable by the higher courts in India.
- **Article 32** provides that the aggrieved person, whose Fundamental Rights have been violated or denied, has the right to petition the Supreme Court for the enforcement of Fundamental Rights.
- **Article 13** elevates the authority of Fundamental Rights. It ensures that the state or other competent authority does not make laws including ordinances, orders, bye laws, rules, regulations, notifications, customs or usages, that contradicts or takes away or violates breaches the Fundamental Rights.
- Fundamental Rights are mostly enforceable against the state and in some cases against private persons. An example of the rights enforceable against the state is the right to freedom of speech and expression, for the rights enforceable against private persons, is the prohibition of employment of children below the age of fourteen years in factories, mines and in places of hazardous activities.

What is a State?

Article 12 defines the term State.

Articale 12 of the Indian Constitution states that : "Definition in this part, unless the context otherwise requires, the State includes the Government and Parliament of India and the Government and the Legislature of each of the states and all local or other authorities within the territory of India or under the control of the Govemment of India".

Difference between Fundamental Rights and Human Rights

The main difference between Fundamental Rights and human rights is that the Fundamental Rights are specific to a particular country, whereas human rights have worldwide acceptance. Other differences between human rights and Fundamental Rights are

Basis For Comparison	Human Rights	Fundamental Rights
Meaning	Human Rights are the basic rights that all human beings can enjoy, regardless of their nationality, ethnicity and religion etc.	Fundamental Rights are the basic rights of citizens of a country which are stated in the Constitution and enforced by law. These may slightly vary from country to country.
Scope	It is universal.	It is country specific.

Quick Test 1

1. The origin of human rights began in which year?
2. Mention any one feature of human rights.
3. How human rights are inalienable?
4. In which year the Universal Declaration of Human Rights was adopted?
5. Mention any one feature of Fundamental Rights.

13.2 Constitutional Framework and Related Laws in India

- In India, human rights are embedded in the Constitution like in many other countries (e.g., US, South Africa, and so on), The Indian Constitutional human rights framework involves the following
  - The Preamble
  - Part III of the Constitution containing the Fundamental Rights provisions.
  - Part IV offering the Directive Principles.
  - Part IV(A) consisting of the fundamental duties.

The Preamble

- The Constitution of India begins with the Preamble affirming its aims, objectives and the guiding principles.
- The principles laid out in the Preamble are used for interpreting provisions of the Constitution that are vague and ambiguous.
- Preamble is the **basic structure** of the Constitution.
- The doctrine of 'basic structure' takes away the amendment power of the Parliament with regards to certain features of the Constitution such as democracy, rule of law, secularism, separation of powers and judicial review.

Part III : Fundamental Rights

Articles 12-35 in Part III of the Constitution contain the provisions on Fundamental Rights.

Fundamental Rights are largely civil and political rights and consist of

- Right to equality (Articles 14-18)
- Right to freedom (Articles 19-22)
- Right against exploitation (Articles 23 and 24)
- Right to freedom of religion (Articles 25-28)
- Cultural and educational rights (Articles 29-30)
- Right to constitutional remedies (Articles 32)

Definition of State

Article 12 of the Indian Constitution defines the term 'State' as including the Government of India, Parliament, State Governments, State Legislatures, and all local or other authorities within India or under its control.

For Part III of the Constitution, the 'State' includes

- The Government and Parliament of India (Union Executive and Legislature)
- The Government and Legislature of each State (State Executive and Legislature)
- All local or other authorities within India's territory
- All local and other authorities under the control of the Government of India

Right to Equality (Articles 14-18)

Article 14

- According to Article 14, the state shall not deny to any person equality before the law or the equal protection of the laws within the territory of India, on grounds of religion, race, caste, sex or place of birth.
- In other words, Article 14 provides the right to equality before law and equal protection of the law to all the persons.
- It means that law treats everyone equally without consideration of their rank or status or other backgrounds.

- The principle of equality means that one uniform law cannot be applied to all equally as some may not be similarly placed as others. So 'equality' treats equals similarly and unequals differently.

  For example, the **Prohibition of Child Marriage Act, 2006** prescribes the marriage age of girl as 18 years and that of boy as 21 years. This restricts a minor from getting married.
- However, if the marriage between two parties were to be disallowed based on the classification of religion, race, caste, sex or place of birth, it would result in discrimination and violation of the right to equality.

Article 15

- Article 15 is based on the equality principle. It prohibits state from discriminating against anyone based on grounds of religion, race, caste, sex or place of birth.
- Article 15 also, prohibits anyone and the state from using these grounds to restrict (restrain) any citizen from entering shops, public restaurants, hotels and places of public entertainment or the use of wells, tanks, bathing ghats, roads and places of public resort.

Article 16

- Article 16 is also based on the equality principle. According to this article, there shall be **equality of opportunity** for all citizens in matters relating to employment or appointment to any office under the state.
- It provides for equality of opportunity in matters of public or state employment and bars any discrimination to any citizen on grounds of religion, race, caste, sex, descent, place of birth or residence.
- However, this article allows the state to provide reservation or affirmative (positive) action programs for government jobs to backward classes like Schedule Castes and Scheduled Tribes, who have not been adequately represented in the services under the state because of historical and continued disadvantages based on caste, status and otherwise.

Article 17

- Under Article 17, untouchability is abolished and its practice in any form is forbidden. This article can be enforced against both the state as well as private individuals, and the offence is punishable in accordance with special laws like the Protection of Civil Rights Act, 1955, Scheduled Caste and Scheduled Tribe (Prevention of Atrocities) Act, 1989.
- The abolition of untouchability in Article 17 is made operationalised by these two special laws that attempt to remove any form of harassment and abuses to 'Dalits' and 'Adivasis' by the state or private individuals.

Article 18

Article 18 provides about the abolition of titles. It states that

- No title, not being a military or academic distinction, shall be conferred by the state.
- No citizen of India shall accept any title from any foreign state.
- No person who is not a citizen of India shall accept any title from any foreign state without the consent of the President, while he holds any office of profit or trust under the state.
- No person holding any office of profit or trust under the state shall accept any present, emolument or office of any kind from or under any foreign state, without the consent of the President.

Right to Freedom (Articles 19-22)

Article 19

- Article 19 prescribes and protects the following kinds of freedoms to all citizens
  - Freedom of speech and expression
  - Freedom to assemble peaceably and without arms

- Freedom to form associations or unions
- Freedom to move freely throughout the territory of India.
- Freedom to reside and settle in any part of the territory of India.
- Freedom to practice any profession, or to carry on any occupation, trade or business.

- Article 19 also provides **reasonable restrictions** on these freedoms, which means that these rights are conditional. The state can 'reasonably' limit or take away the right to 'Freedom of speech and expression' when there is a threat to either of the following
  - the sovereignty and integrity of India
  - the security of the state
  - friendly relations with foreign states
  - public order, or decency or morality
  - in relation to contempt of court
  - defamation
  - incitement (provocation to commit) to an offence

  For example, the state can prohibit someone from making inciting speeches that may provoke others to commit violence. However, at times, the Supreme Court can invalidate state's restrictions if it finds them to be unreasonable. As an instance, the state cannot put restriction as an excuse because it is unable to maintain public order.
- The various conditions under which the state can limit or take away freedoms are given in the table below

Freedoms	**Restrictions** (grounds)
Freedom of speech and expression	Sovereignty and integrity of India, or the security of the state, or friendly relations with foreign states, or public order, or decency or morality, or contempt of court, or defamation, or incitement to an offence.
Freedom to assemble peaceably and without arms	Sovereignty and integrity of India, or public order.
Freedom to form associations or unions	Sovereignty and integrity of India, or public order or morality.
Freedom to move freely throughout the territory of India Freedom to reside and settle in any part of the territory of India	Interests of the general public, or for the protection of the interests of any Scheduled Tribe.
Freedom to practice any profession, or to carry on any occupation, trade or business	Interests of the general public, or the state prescribed professional or technical qualifications, or state run trade, business, industry or service, that excludes participation of citizens or others either completely or partially.

Article 20

- Article 20 provides for safeguards to persons who are accused of having committed crimes. This article provides the human rights framework to the criminal justice system.
- The rights of persons accused of crimes are
  - Firstly, Article 20 provides that no person can be convicted for the commission or omission of an act that does not amount to an offence by any law in force at the time of such act. In other words, a person can only be punished for an act which was an offence at the time, the act was committed.

    In **2009, Section 377** was declared **invalid** and **unconstitutional** by the Delhi High Court to protect rights to privacy, non-discrimination and liberty of lesbian, gay, bisexual and transgender people. However, in 2013, the Supreme Court reversed the High Court's decision.

    The Supreme Court in 2018 reversed its 2013 judgement and declared Section 377 as unconstitutional.

    In this example, sodomy law will not apply to any consensual homosexual conduct committed in 2011, but will apply to commissions that take place post-Supreme Court judgement of 2013.

Article 20 prohibits application of laws retrospectively (dealing with events that happened before the enactment of the provision) and **prospectively** (events that happened after a provision came into force).

- Secondly, Article 20 provides that any person who is convicted of a crime should not receive a penalty greater than what is provided in the law in force at the time of the act of offence.
- Thirdly, Article 20 provides that no person shall be prosecuted and punished for the same offence more than once.
- Fourthly, Article 20 states that no person accused of any offence shall be compelled or forced to be a witness against himself. This provision safeguards the accused's right against self-incrimination (to give evidence against himself).

Article 21

- Article 21 states that no person shall be deprived of his life or personal liberty except according to procedure established by law. This article is the most fundamental and expansive.
- It covers many other rights and is applicable to both the citizens as well as non-citizens.
- The meaning of **right to life** includes
  - right to human dignity
  - right to basic requirements of life
  - right to participate in activities and expression
  - right to tradition, heritage and culture and so on.
- **Personal liberty** means various rights that provide for personal liberty of a person i.e., everyone has the right to do his or her will freely.
- The meaning of 'right to life and personal liberty' is broad and embraces many aspects including
  - Human dignity
  - Basic necessities of life
  - Engaging in activities and expression
  - Tradition, heritage and culture
  - Privacy
  - Pollution free environment
  - Livelihood
  - Against sexual harassment
  - Against solitary confinement
  - Legal aid
  - Speedy trial
  - Against delayed execution in capital punishment
  - Against custodial violence
  - Shelter, healthcare and medical provisions
  - Against bonded labour
  - Against cruel and unusual punishment

A person can be deprived of his or her 'right to life or personal liberty' only by procedure established by law. This means that any law that limits or takes away one's right to life and personal liberty must contain a procedure that is fair and reasonable and not **arbitrary**[2].

For example, the Indian Penal Code prescribes death penalty for certain crimes. This involves established procedures like

- death penalty is awarded only in 'rarest of rare' cases.
- there should not be delay in executing the prisoner waiting in death row.

Indian Penal Code also allows for appeal where the wait period is longer than **five years**.

Article 21 A

- Article 21A states that the state shall provide free and compulsory education to all children of the age of six to fourteen years in such manner as the state may, by law, determine.
- Before 2002, the Indian Constitution considered elementary education for children between the age of six to fourteen as a policy goal provision in the Directive Principles of State Policy.
- However, Directive Principles of State Policy are **not enforceable in a court of law** as they are aspirational goals to be achieved over a period of time.

2 **Arbitrary** It means based on random choice or personal whim rather than any reason or system.

- In 1992-93, the Supreme Court affirmed that depriving one from education amounts to depriving one's right to life.
- In 2002, Article 21A providing the right to elementary education was created as a Fundamental Right, by the Constitution 86th Amendment Act, 2002

The Right of Children to Free and Compulsory Education (RTE) Act, 2009

- The Right of Children to Free and Compulsory Education Act 2009, also known as the RTE Act, was enacted by the Parliament of India in 2009. It provides that every child has a Right to Free and Compulsory Education till completion of elementary education in a neighbourhood school.
- This act places a legal obligation on the state and Central Governments to implement the Fundamental Rights of a child according to the provisions of the RTE Act.
- However, implementing this right requires state's financial and budgetary expenditures of enormous amounts to meet the demand of a high illiteracy rate, which has been inadequate so far.

Article 22

Article 22 provides safeguards against arrest and detention in following ways

- No one can be detained in custody without providing grounds for arrest.
- The arrested and detained person has a right to consult and to be defended by a legal practitioner of his/her choice.
- A person who is arrested and detained in custody should be produced before the nearest magistrate within a period of twenty-four hours. The travel time is not counted towards the twenty-four hours.
- No such person can be detained in custody beyond twenty-four hours without the authority of a Magistrate.
- The above safeguards do not apply to a person from an enemy country. They also do not apply to persons arrested or detained under preventive detention laws.
- Generally, preventive detention laws allow for detaining persons on suspicion who have not been found guilty of any crime, but their release may be detrimental to society.

Difference between Arrest and Detention

- A person is arrested when she/he is charged with a crime. On the other hand, if the police have reasonable suspicion against a person that she/he may have engaged in a crime or may commit crime, they may detain that person for questioning.
- The main difference between detention and arrest is whether the accused is charged with a crime or not. When a person is detained for questioning, she/he is not charged with a crime.

Quick Test 2

1 What are the three main parts of the Indian Constitutional framework on human rights?
2 Which part of the Indian Constitution contains Fundamental Rights?
3 What does Article 12 of the Indian Constitution define?
4 Name any two Fundamental Rights guaranteed under Part III of the Constitution.
5 What is the doctrine of 'basic structure' in relation to the Indian Constitution?

Right Against Exploitation (Articles 23-24)

- **Article 23** It prohibits human trafficking, begar. Begar is a system of forced labour.
- **Article 24** It prohibits employment of children below the age of fourteen years in factories, mining and other **hazardous employment**[3].

3 **Hazardous Employment** It is a work that involves extra danger or risk. This type of work require special safety precautions or equipment to protect workers from harm.

Human Trafficking

The act + means + purpose gives the result of trafficking. Human trafficking involves the act of recruitment, transfer, transport, harbouring, receipt of persons with the means of threat, use of force, coercion, abduction, fraud deception, abuse of power of vulnerability, giving payments or benefits and with the purpose of exploitation including prostitution of others, sexual exploitation, forced labour, slavery or similar practices, removal of organs, other type of exploitation.

Right to Freedom of Religion (Articles 25-28)

Article 25

- Under Article 25, all persons have the **right to freedom of conscience** and **freedom to profess, practice** and **propagate religion**, as long as their acts do not threaten public order, morality and health.

  For example, on the issue concerning the use of loudspeakers for religious purposes, the Supreme Court has stated that no religion prescribed that prayers should be performed by disturbing the peace of others nor does it preach that they should be through voice-amplifiers or beating of drums.
- In the name of religion nobody can be permitted to add to noise pollution or violate noise pollution norms.
- Even if there is religious practice to use voice amplifiers, it should not adversely affect rights of others, including that of being not disturbed in their activities. Noise Pollution (Regulation and Control) Rules, 2000 should be followed.
- The state may regulate or restrict economic, financial, political or other secular activities that are associated with a religious practice.
- The state can also provide social welfare and reforms in Hindu, Sikh, Jain or Buddhist religious institutions.
- The state can also open their religious institutions like temples to all classes and sections of that religious society. The wearing and carrying of **kirpans** is part of the profession of the **Sikh religion** and does not threaten public order, morality or health.

Article 26

Article 26 provides the right to every religious denomination, including their sub-sections or sects, to

- establish and maintain institutions for religious and charitable purposes
- manage their own matters of religious affairs
- acquire movable (e.g., vehicles, furniture) and immovable (e.g., house, trees) property and administer such property in accordance with law.

These rights are conditional because they should not endanger public order, morality and health.

Article 27

Article 27 prohibits forcing anyone to pay any taxes on revenues which are used in payment of expenses for the promotion or maintenance of any religion or section. For example, donations in temples that are used for the upkeep of the temple cannot be taxed.

Article 28

- Article 28 prohibits religious instructions in educational institutions that are wholly maintained out of state funds.

  For example, government run schools like Sainik Schools and Kendriya Vidyalaya Schools cannot impart religious instructions to students.
- However, some educational institutions are exempted from this rule which are administered by the state but are established by endowments or trusts that require religious instruction in such educational institutions.

- Trust is a body registered under the Trust Act, 1882 (now 1961) and is run on the the basis of no profit no loss.
- Furthermore, the educational institutions recognised or aided by state cannot force any student to take part in any religious instruction or to attend any religious worship conducted in such institutions unless he/she has given consent for the same. In the case of minors, the guardians should have given consent for the same.

Wholly funded by state	Recognised by state	Aided by state	Administered by state but established under a trust
Institution whose entire expenditure is borne by the state/government.	Institutions that are recognised by the state for imparting instruction or awarding degrees under the state laws.	Institutions that are receiving aid out of the state funds.	Institutions whose day-to day administration is in the hands of government.
Government educational institutions-for instance government schools and colleges.	Without recognition the degree of such institutions shall not be recognised for the public employment.		
Religious instruction cannot be imparted in the edcational institutions that are wholly funded by state.	Cannot force students to take part in religious instruction/religious worship. In the case of minors, consent of the parent is required.	Cannot force students to take part in religious instruction/ religious worship. In the case of minors, consent of the parent is required.	Institutions that were originally established by a trust which required religious instructions to be imparted, the religious instructions may be imparted in such institution irrespective of the fact that it is administered by the state.

These provisions and others make India a secular state.

Cultural and Educational Rights (Articles 29-30)

Article 29

- According to **Article 29**, the minority sections of citizens have the right to conserve their distinct language, script or culture.
- It also prohibits educational institutions, maintained by the state or receiving aid out of state funds, from denying admissions to any citizen on grounds of religion, race, caste or language.

Article 30

- **Article 30** provides the right to all minorities, whether based on religion or language, establish to and administer educational institutions of their choice.
- It also prohibits state from discriminating educational institutions, while granting them aid, on grounds of religion or language.

Right to Constitutional Remedies (Article 32)

Article 32

- Article 32 guarantees the aggrieved ones, whose Fundamental Rights have been violated or denied, to petition directly to the Supreme Court for the enforcement of Fundamental Rights.
- Unlike cases of other matters where one has to go through remedies of lower courts, one can approach the Supreme Court directly in matters of Fundamental Rights violation.
- Article 32 allows for the practice of **Public Interest Litigation**, also known as **Social Action Litigation.** It is a process by which letters written to Supreme Court or High Courts by public-spirited persons or organisations asserting Fundamental Rights violations are converted into petitions.

- The author of the letter asserting violations of Fundamental Rights of the weaker sections of Indian society who are unable to approach the court.
- They include people in custody, victims of police violence, forced bonded labours, migrant and contracted labours, child workers, rickshaw pullers, hawkers, pensioners, pavement dwellers and slum dwellers. Courts can also act upon newspaper reports declaring Fundamental Rights violations of victims.

Article 226

Article 226 authorises High Courts to take up matters of Fundamental Rights violations directly for their enforcement.

Part IV : Directive Principles

Articles 36-51 in Part IV of the Constitution lay down the guiding principles of governance for the state called the 'Directive Principles of State Policy'.

Features of Directive Principles of State Policy

Some salient features of the directive principles are

- It is the duty of the state to apply these principles in making laws and policies on social and human development.
- These principles are largely of the nature of economic and social rights.
- The provisions of Directive Principles are not enforceable by any court of law, but they provide guidance in carrying out and drafting laws and policies regarding human and social development.
- The Supreme Court has raised the status of many provisions of directive principles to that of Fundamental Right by suggesting that they violate one's right to life (**Article 21**).
- Directive principles aim at promoting the welfare of the people. They intend to secure and protect social, economic and political justice of its citizens.
- These principles endeavour to minimise income inequalities and to eliminate inequalities based on status, facilities and opportunities amongst both individuals and groups of people.

The Directive Principles of State Policy are given below

- Right to adequate means of livelihood for both men and women.
- Equal pay for equal work for both men and women.
- Right to healthy working conditions for men, women and children.
- Protection to children against exploitation and against moral and material abandonment.
- Legal aid for securing justice for those with economic or other disabilities.
- Village panchayats vested with powers and functions as units of self-government.
- Right to work, to education and to public assistance in cases of unemployment, old age, sickness and disablement, etc.
- Provision for just and humane conditions of work and for maternity relief.
- Living wage and conditions of work to agricultural, industrial or other workers that ensures a decent standard of life and full enjoyment of leisure, and social and cultural opportunities.
- Promoting cottage industries on an individual or co-operative basis in rural areas.
- Participation of workers in management of industries.
- Uniform civil code for the citizens-one uniform law for family law matters.
- Provision for early childhood care and education to children below the age of six years.
- Promotion of educational and economic interests of Scheduled Castes, Scheduled Tribes and other weaker sections and protection from social injustice and all forms of exploitation.

- Raising level of nutrition, standard of living and improving public health and prohibition of the consumption of intoxicating drinks and drugs injurious to health.
- Organisation of agriculture and animal husbandry in a modern and scientific way, and preserving and improving the breeds, prohibiting the slaughter of cows.
- Protection and improvement of the environment and safeguarding of forests and wildlife.
- Protection of monuments and places and objects of artistic or national importance.
- Separation of judiciary from executive in the public services of the state.
- Promotion of international peace and security, maintaining just and honourable relations between nations, fostering respect for international law and treaty obligations, and encouraging settlement of international disputes by arbitration.

Part IV (A) : Fundamental Duties Article 51A

Article 51A of the Constitution prescribes fundamental duties of every citizen.

The fundamental duties are given below

- Respecting the Constitution and institutions, the National Flag and the National Anthem.
- Cherishing and following the noble ideals of the national struggle for freedom.
- Upholding and protecting the sovereignty, unity and integrity of India.
- Defending the country and rendering national service when called upon to do so.
- Promoting harmony amongst religious, linguistic and regional diversities and renouncing practices derogatory to women's dignity.
- Valuing and preserving the rich heritage and culture.
- Protecting the natural environment including forests, lakes, rivers and wildlife.
- Developing the scientific temper, humanism and the spirit of inquiry and reform.
- Safeguarding public property and abjuring violence.
- Striving for excellence and raising the nation to higher levels of endeavour and achievement.
- Providing opportunities for education to children by their parents between the age of six and fourteen years.

Quick Test 3

1. What does Article 23 of the Indian Constitution prohibit?
2. Under which article is child labour in hazardous industries prohibited?
3. Name any two forms of human trafficking.
4. What does Article 25 guarantee?
5. Under which article do religious groups have the right to manage their own affairs?

REFERENCE CASES

Directive Principle

Supreme court has raised the status of many provisions of directive principles to that of Fundamental Rights by suggesting they also violate one's right to life (Article 21)

Directive Principle	Raised to Fundamental Right as violates one's right to life (Article 21)
Elementary education for children between age six fourteen was a policy goal provision.	Right to education for children between age six and fourteen is now a Fundamental Right under Article 21A.

The Supreme Court in the case of **Mohini Jain** ruled that right to education is a Fundamental Right that flows from right to life in **Article 21** of the Constitution.

Another example is that of right to livelihood, which is a directive principle often read with right to life, as a Fundamental Right. The Supreme Court has often direction states to rehabilitate slum dwellers whenever they are evicted on grounds of encroachment.

Eviction without rehabilitation closer to their workplace amounts to violation of their right to livelihood and in turn the right to life. Livelihood can include basic shelter, food education, occupation and medical care.

The Supreme Court in **Olga Tellis and Ors. Vs. Bombay Municipal Corporation and Ors, popularly known as the 'Pavement Dwellers Case'** held that 'right to livelihood' is borne out of 'right to life', as no person can live without means of living, that is means of livelihood. It recognised right to livelihood to be part of **Article 21**.

The court also held that it is the duty of the authorities to provide slum dwellers with an alternative if their house is to be demolished.

Fundamental Duties-Part IV (A) Article 51A

Part IV (A)- **Article 51A** of the Constitution prescribes fundamental duties of every citizen. In that, certain conduct and behavior are expected of the citizens. The salient features of fundamental duties are given below

- The fundamental duties cannot be enforced in a court of law for violation of the duties and no one can be punished for violation.
- Fundamental duties contain standards to be followed by the citizens.
- They remind citizens not be behave irresponsible but help to build a free, democratic and strong society.

It may be possible that, just like some provisions of the directive principles, courts may raise the status of these duties in future.

Mind Map

HUMAN RIGHTS IN INDIA

1 Meaning of Rights

Definition
- Justified claims or reasonable privileges accepted by society and affirmed by statute law.
- Includes human rights and Fundamental Rights.

Key Features
- Rights are universal, protected by law, and essential for human dignity and equality.

2 Human Rights

Definition
- Basic rights inherent to all human beings, not granted by any state.

Origin
- Ancient traditions and philosophical writings.
- First codified in 539 BC by Cyrus the Great (e.g., freedom of religion).
- **Modern Foundation** Universal Declaration of Human Rights (UDHR), 1948.

Features
- Universal, inalienable, and equal for all.
- Includes right to life, health, and freedom from torture.

For examples
- Right to education, work and liberty.

International Framework
- UDHR provides fundamental, civil, political, economic and social rights.

3 Fundamental Rights (India)

Definition
- Basic rights enshrined in the Constitution and enforceable by law.

Features
- Enforceable by courts (Article 32 for Supreme Court, Article 226 for High Courts).
- Prohibit laws violating Fundamental Rights (Article 13).
- Some rights enforceable against individuals (e.g., child labour prohibition).

Key Articles
- **Articles 14–18** Right to Equality.
- **Articles 19–22** Right to Freedom.
- **Articles 23–24** Right against Exploitation.
- **Articles 25–28** Right to Freedom of Religion.
- **Articles 29–30** Cultural and Educational Rights.
- **Articles 32–35** Right to Constitutional Remedies.

4 Differences between Human Rights and Fundamental Rights

Scope
- **Human Rights** Universal.
- **Fundamental Rights** Country-specific.

Enforcement
- **Human Rights** Protected through international frameworks.
- **Fundamental Rights** Enshrined in a country's Constitution and enforced by its judiciary.

5 Constitutional Framework in India

Parts of Constitution
- **Preamble** Sets guiding principles of justice, liberty, equality and fraternity.
- **Part III** Fundamental Rights (Articles 12–35).
- **Part IV** Directive Principles of State Policy.
- **Part IVA** Fundamental Duties.

Directive Principles (Articles 36–51)
- Non-justiciable but promote social and economic welfare.
- Include principles like equal pay, education, health and environmental protection.

Fundamental Duties (Article 51A)
- Expectations from citizens to uphold national unity, environment and scientific temper.

6 Key Case Laws

Olga Tellis Vs. Bombay Municipal Corporation
- Recognised the right to livelihood as part of the right to life (Article 21).

Kesavananda Bharati Vs. State of Kerala
- Established the doctrine of the basic structure of the Constitution.

M.C. Mehta Cases
- Strengthened environmental laws.

7 Sustainable Development Goals (SDGs) and Human Rights

Connection
- Over 90% of SDG targets correspond to human rights obligations.

For examples
- No poverty, gender equality and zero hunger.

Implementation
- Progress on SDGs leads to fulfillment of human rights.

8 Key Provisions and Articles

Right to Equality
- **Article 14** Equality before law.
- **Article 16** Equality of opportunity in public employment.

Right to Freedom
- **Article 19** Freedom of speech, movement, profession, etc., with reasonable restrictions.
- **Article 21** Right to life and personal liberty.

Right against Exploitation
- **Article 23** Prohibition of human trafficking.
- **Article 24** Prohibition of child labour.

Right to Education
- **Article 21A** Free and compulsory education for children aged 6–14.

9 Importance of Rights

For Individuals
- Protects dignity, equality and freedom.
- Ensures justice and fair treatment.

For Society
- Promotes social harmony and development.
- Prevents exploitation and injustice.

CBSE TEXTBOOK FOLDER

1. 'Human rights and SDGs are two sides of the same coin.' Explain.

Ans. Human rights and SDGs are two sides of the same coin because over 90 per cent of the goals and targets of the SDGs correspond to human rights obligations. As member states make progress on the SDGs, they make progress on their human rights obligations.

2. Explain states' obligations to respect, protect and fulfill human rights.

Ans. According to International Human Rights Law, the obligation of states to respect means that states must refrain from interfering with or curtailing the enjoyment of human rights. The obligation to protect requires states to protect individuals and groups against human rights abuses. The obligation to fulfill means that states must take positive action to facilitate the enjoyment of basic human rights.

3. Identify any two features in the Preamble of the Indian Constitution that indicates its objective of protecting human rights.

Ans. Two features in the Preamble that indicates the Constitution's objective of protecting human rights are

(i) Securing justice-social, economic and political

(ii) Ensuring liberty of thought, expression, belief, faith and worship.

4. Describe any three salient features of Fundamental Rights in the Indian Constitution.

Ans. Some of the salient features of Fundamental Rights that are

(i) They are enforceable by the higher courts in India.

(ii) Article 32 provides the right to the aggrieved ones, whose Fundamental Rights have been violated or denied, to petition the Supreme Court for the enforcement of Fundamental Rights.

(iii) Article 13 elevates the authority of Fundamental Rights. It ensures that the state or other competent authority does not make laws including ordinances, orders, bye laws, rules, regulations, notifications, customs or usages that contradicts or takes away or breaches the Fundamental Rights.

5. What is right to equality? How is a reservation or affirmative action for government jobs to Schedule Castes and Scheduled Tribes protected by the right to equality?

Ans. The right to equality before law and equal protection of the law is defined in Article 14. It prohibits discrimination on grounds of religion, race, caste, sex or place of birth. Article 16 is also based on the equality principle of Article 14. It provides for equality of opportunity in matters of public or state employment and bars any discrimination to any citizen on grounds of religion, race, caste, sex, descent, place of birth or residence.

However, this article allows the state to provide reservation or affirmative (positive) action programmes for government jobs to backward classes like Schedule Castes and Scheduled Tribes who because of historical and continued disadvantages based on caste status and otherwise have not been adequately represented in the services under the state.

6. Why do you think it was necessary to abolish the practice of untouchability ?

Ans. It was necessary to abolish untouchability as the backward class people were not treated equally and were denied of their Fundamental Rights.

Under **Article 17** 'Untouchability' is abolished and its practice in any form is forbidden. This article can be enforced against both the state as well as private individuals. The abolition of untouchability in Article 17 is made operationalised by these two special laws that attempt to remove any form of harassment and abuses to 'Dalits' and 'Adivasis' by the state or private individuals.

7. Identify any two kinds of right to freedoms along with any two grounds of restrictions that take away these freedoms.

Ans. Two kinds of right to freedoms along with their grounds of restrictions are given below

Freedoms	Restrictions (grounds)
Freedom of speech and expression.	Sovereignty and integrity of India, or the security of the state, or friendly relations with foreign states, or public order, or decency or morality, or contempt of court, or defamation, or incitement to an offence.
Freedom to assemble peaceably and without arms.	Sovereignty and integrity of India, or public order.

8. Explain any one Fundamental Right of a person who is either accused or convicted of a crime.

Ans. Article 20 provides for safeguards to persons who are accused of having committed crimes. This article provides the human rights framework to the criminal justice system. The rights of persons accused of crimes.

One of the safeguards provided is that no person can be convicted for the commission or omission of an act that does not amount to an offence by any law in force at the time of such act.

9. Explain 'Right to life and personal liberty' as given in the Indian Constitution.

Ans. The meaning of right to life includes
(i) right to human dignity
(ii) right to basic requirements of life
(iii) right to participate in activities and expression
(iv) right to tradition, heritage and culture and so on.

Personal liberty means various rights that provide for personal liberty of a person i.e., everyone has the right to do his or her will freely. The meaning of 'Right to life and personal liberty' is broad and embraces many aspects including
(i) Human dignity
(ii) Basic necessities of life
(iii) Engaging in activities and expression
(iv) Tradition, heritage, and culture
(v) Privacy
(vi) Pollution free environment
(vii) Livelihood

10. Explain 'Right to education' provided in the Fundamental Rights chapter of the Constitution.

Ans. The right to education is explained in Article 21A. It states that 'The state shall provide free and compulsory education to all children of the age of six to fourteen years in such manner as the state may, by law, determine.' This article provides for right to education to all between the age of six and fourteen, and obligates state to implement this.

11. Identify any one safeguard provided to someone if she/he is arrested and detained.

Ans. One of the safeguards provided to someone who is arrested and detained under Article 22 is that no one can be detained in custody without providing grounds for arrest.

12. What is meant by human trafficking, that is prohibited by the Indian Constitution?

Ans. Human trafficking is the trade of humans for the purpose of forced labour, sexual slavery or commercial sexual exploitation for the trafficker or others. This may encompass providing a spouse in the context of forced marriage, or the extraction of organs, or tissues, including for surrogacy. Article 23 prohibits human trafficking, beggar and forced labour.

Human trafficking can occur within a country or trans-nationally. It is a crime against the person because of the violation of the victim's rights of movement through coercion and because of their commercial exploitation. Human trafficking is the trade in people, especially women and children and does not necessarily involve the movement of the person from one place to another.

13. Describe 'Right to freedom of religion' as provided in the Indian Constitution.

Ans. Under Article 25, all persons have the right to freedom of conscience and freedom to profess, practice and propagate religion as long as their acts do not threaten public order, morality and health.

14. Explain judicial remedies that are available for the enforcement of Fundamental Rights.

Ans. Article 32 of the Constitution provides for legal or judicial remedies for the protection of the rights against their violation by the state or other institutions/individuals. For the enforcement of any of the Fundamental Rights, the Supreme Court may issue instructions, orders or writs, including writs in the nature of habeas corpus, mandamus, prohibition, quo warranto and certiorari, as applicable. Similarly under Article 126 of the Contitution of India the High Courts also have power to issue writs.

15. What is meant by Public Interest Litigation (PIL)? Find out one PIL that was initiated on the basis of a letter written to the Supreme Court or on the basis of a newspaper report.

Ans. PIL refers to litigation undertaken to secure public interest and demonstrates the availability of justice to socially-disadvantaged parties and was introduced by Justice PN Bhagwati.

The first ever PIL is listed as Hussainara Khatoon Vs. State of Bihar and dates back to 1979. A public interest activist lawyer filed this case on behalf of thousands of prisoners of the Bihar jail against the inhuman conditions of the prison.

16. Describe any one salient feature of the Directive Principles of State Policy. Give one example of directive principle that has been elevated to Fundamental Rights.

Ans. One salient feature of the Directive Principle of State Policy is that the provisions of Directive Principles are not enforceable by any court of law, but they provide guidance in carrying out and drafting laws and policies regarding human and social development.

The Right to Education has been elevated to Fundamental Rights by the Supreme Court, which is an important example of directive principle that has been elevated to Fundamental Rights.

17. Give any one example of fundamental duties provided in the Constitution.

Ans. Respecting the Constitution and institutions, the National Flag and the National Anthem are the examples of fundamental duties.

Exam Pattern Questions

Objective Type Questions

Multiple Choice Questions (MCQs)

1. Sadanand is a florist who relies on local flowers for his livelihood. The district administration prohibits the plucking of wild flowers to conserve the local flora and fauna. Is Sadanand's Constitutional right infringed upon? **CBSE 2019**

(a) Yes, his sole means of earning a livelihood was affected.
(b) Yes, Article 21 gives the Fundamental Right to life.
(c) No, the government is powerful and can make any law.
(d) No, because the government is sovereign and enacts laws for the common good.

2. Which of the following provisions of the Indian Constitution is not based on 'equality principle'? **CBSE 2019**

(a) Abolition of untouchability.
(b) Equality of opportunity in matters of state or public employment.
(c) Prohibiting the state from discriminating against anyone based on grounds of religion, race, caste or place of birth.
(d) Prohibiting human trafficking, beggary and forced labour.

3. Jatin, a resident of Sompur was visiting the neighbouring city of Malikgarh, where he was prevented from entering a public park by the local authority as he did not belong to Malikgarh. Which Fundamental Right of Jatin has been violated? **CBSE SQP 2022**

(a) Article 14 (b) Article 15
(c) Article 17 (d) Article 32

4. Indian police have extensive powers for crime detection and investigation. But, such powers should not impinge upon the rights of the accused. This right has been guaranteed under **CBSE SQP 2021**

(a) Article 20(3) (b) Article 21
(c) Article 22 (d) Article 20(4)

5. Phulmaniya travels from Ranchi to Kolkata to work as domestic help. On landing in Kolkata, she was subjected to forced surrogacy. Which Fundamental Right of Phulmaniya was violated? **CBSE 2018**

(a) Right to equality
(b) Right against exploitation
(c) Right to life and personal liberty
(d) Right to freedom

6. Which of the following is not a part of Article 21? **CBSE SQP 2021**

(a) Right to Life
(b) Right to Food
(c) Right to Livelihood
(d) Right to Constitutional Remedies

7. The safeguard provided under Article 22 is not applicable to which among the following?

(a) Person from enemy country
(b) Citizens
(c) Person detained under preventive detention laws
(d) Both (a) and (c)

8. Which article prohibits human trafficking, beggar and forced labour?

(a) Article 22 (b) Article 23
(c) Article 24 (d) Article 25

9. Directive Principles of State Policy (DPSP) are provided under which Part and Article of the Indian Constitution? **CBSE 2017**

(a) Part IVA, Article 51A
(b) Part III, Article 51A
(c) Part IV, Articles 36-51
(d) Part III, Article 12-35

10. Equal pay for equal work for both men and women is a

(a) Fundamental Right (b) DPSP
(c) Fundamental Duty (d) None of these

11. A petition was filed in the High Court highlighting the plight of sewage cleaners working for the State Jal Board. It highlighted the problem of exposure to toxic fumes, suffocation and accidental death, while working. In this context, which of the following statements is applicable? **CBSE 2020**

(a) Fundamental Duty has been breached by the state.
(b) Fundamental Rights can not be enforced if the violation is not willful.
(c) Fundamental Rights can be enforced against the state through Public Interest Litigation.
(d) Directive Principles of State Policy are not enforceable judicially so no action.

12. In the city of Bheempur, all factories and mills were asked to submit the complete data about their employees (both wage earners and salaried). Tajeshwar Chemical Works submitted the following data

No. of People	Age Group	Gender	
		Male	Female
4	12 years to 14 years	3	1
6	15 years to 18 years	4	2
5	20 years to 30 years	3	2
5	31 years to 40 years	3	2

- Salaries were paid according to government provisions.
- The workers in the age group of 12 years to 14 years and 15 years to 18 years were compulsorily sent to a school run by Rajeshwar Chemical Works, after the working hours of the factory were over.

Rajeshwar Chemical Works was served a notice for the violation of Fundamental Rights.

Choose the correct option that describes the situation of Rajeshwar Chemical Works. **CBSE 2017**

(a) No right has been violated as Rajeshwar Chemical Works was paying proper wages/salary to all its workers.
(b) Fundamental Rights under Article 24 has been violated as children under the age of 14 years are working there.
(c) Fundamental Right under Article 14 has been violated as an equal number of males and females have not been employed.
(d) Fundamental Right under Article 19 has been violated as the workers in the age group of 12 years to 18 years were compulsorily sent to school every evening.

13. A large number of persons had been carrying on the business of dyeing and printing in the Rajkot area for the last 25 years providing employment to about 30,000 families.

From these business places untreated dirty water was being discharged on the roads thereby causing damage to the public health. A notice, therefore, was given to close this business till necessary measures to protect public health as provided under the environmental statutes were taken by those business men.

Choose the correct option that describes the above situation.

(a) Notice can not be justified as it will cause loss of employment to 30,000 families.
(b) Notice can not be justified as it amounts to violation of the Fundamental Right of the persons who have been carrying on the business for the last 25 years.
(c) The notice can not be justified on the ground of damage to public health as the persons in that area have been voluntarily residing for long and have become used to that environment.
(d) The notice can be justified as the right to business is not absolute and reasonable restriction can be imposed by law in the interest of the public.

14. Ubaid refuses to give a sample of his blood after he is stopped by the police for driving over the speed limit. The police suspect him to be driving under the influence of alcohol, which is prohibited under the law.

(a) Ubaid is protected by Article 20(3) in his refusal to give a blood sample.
(b) Ubaid is not protected by Article 20(3) as he was under the influence of alcohol.
(c) Ubaid is not protected by Article 20(3) in his refusal to give a blood sample since he is not accused of any offence yet.
(d) Refusal to give a blood sample is a crime and Ubaid must be punished for the same.

15. Article 19 also provides 'reasonable restrictions' on these freedoms, which means that these rights are conditional. Identify the right guaranteed under Article 19. **CBSE SQP 2020**

(a) Right to Freedom (b) Right to Life
(c) Right to Education (d) Right against Exploitation

16. The state wanted to prohibit Ajit from making a speech because Ajit wanted to mobilise people to commit riots.

(a) The state can prohibit someone from making inciting speeches that may provoke others to commit violence.
(b) The state can not restrict anyone from making speeches.
(c) The state is sovereign and thus can restrict anyone from making any speeches.
(d) The state can not restrict Ajit because he is an influential person.

17. Smita was an author who published a book on the independence struggle of our country. A few people were not happy with the content of the book and thus the state restricted the sale of this book.

(a) The state has absolute authority to restrict the sale of the book.
(b) The state can restrict the sale of the book on the ground of defamation.
(c) The state can not restrict the sale of the book because of a few unruly protestors.
(d) The state can not restrict the sale of a book because freedom of speech and expression is absolute.

18. 'This article is most fundamental, it is expensive and covers many other rights and is applicable to both the citizens as well as non-citizens'. A person can be deprived of his right to life and personal liberty.

(a) By the state in an absolute manner.
(b) By the courts without any reason.
(c) Only by procedure established by law.
(d) This right can not be taken away.

19. Rahul, a journalist, publishes an article criticising the government's handling of a sensitive national security issue. The government orders Rahul's arrest and seize of his publications, citing potential disruption of public order.

Under Article 19(1)(a) of the Indian Constitution, which guarantees freedom of speech and expression, can the government's action be justified as a reasonable restriction?

(a) Yes, as the restriction is necessary for maintaining public order.
(b) No, as the restriction violates Rahul's Fundamental Right to free speech.
(c) Yes, but only if the government provides Rahul with a fair trial.
(d) No, unless the government proves Rahul's article incited violence.

20. ...... provides for safeguards to persons who are accused of having committed crimes.

(a) Article 20 (b) Article 21
(c) Article 21A (d) Article 22

21. .... guarantees the aggrieved ones, whose Fundamental Rights have been violated or denied, to petition directly to the Supreme Court for the enforcement of Fundamental Rights.

(a) Article 226 (b) Article 32
(c) Article 26 (d) Article 30

22. The second part of Article 21 describes that one's right to life and personal liberty can be taken away only by CBSC 2023

(a) the Supreme Court of India.
(b) a procedure that is fair and reasonable.
(c) the state.
(d) law, when it violates any other Fundamental Right.

23. Meme, a suspected terrorist from an enemy country, is caught preparing an imminent attack in a high-profile area in the national capital. He was arrested by the local police. Which of the following will apply in this situations? CBSE 2023

(a) No one can be detained in custody without providing the grounds for arrest.
(b) Arrested person has a right to consult and be defended by a legal practitioner of choice.
(c) No person can be detained beyond 24 hours without the authority of Magistrate.
(d) No safeguards apply for meme.

24. Ravindra, a prisoner, is subjected to solitary confinement for 23 hours a day, without access to natural light, adequate ventilation or basic amenities. He challenges this treatment as a violation of his Fundamental Rights.

Under Article 21 of the Indian Constitution, which protects life and personal liberty, can Ravindra's right to humane treatment be enforced as a Fundamental Right?

(a) Yes, but only if Ravindra's treatment amounts to torture.
(b) No, as Article 21 only protects life and personal liberty, not prison conditions.
(c) Yes, as the right to dignity and humane treatment is implicit in Article 21.
(d) No, unless Ravindra's treatment violates an international human rights treaty.

25. Which among the following options is a special law for protection of minorities in India? CBSE 2024 C

(a) Article 21 of the Constitution of India
(b) Article 14 of the Constitution of India
(c) Protection of Civil Rights Act, 1955
(d) Universal Declaration of Human Rights

26. Match the following.

Column I	Column II
A. Freedom to Manage religious affairs	1. Article 14
B. Right to Equality	2. Article 21
C. Right to Education	3. Article 26
D. Right to Life	4. Article 21A

Codes

	A	B	C	D
(a)	3	1	4	2
(b)	3	2	1	4
(c)	2	1	4	3
(d)	3	1	2	4

27. Match the articles with the corresponding Fundamental Rights.

Column I	Column II
A. Articles 14-18	1. Right to Freedom
B. Articles 19-22	2. Cultural and Educational Rights
C. Articles 23-24	3. Right to Equality
D. Articles 25-28	4. Right against Exploitation
E. Articles 29-30	5. Right to Freedom of Religion

Codes

	A	B	C	D	E
(a)	1	2	3	4	5
(b)	4	1	2	5	3
(c)	3	1	4	5	2
(d)	2	3	5	1	4

28. **Match the following freedoms with appropriate restrictions.**

Column I (Freedoms)	**Column II** (Restrictions)
A. Freedom to practice any profession	1. Protection of interest of Scheduled Tribes
B. Freedom to move freely throughout the territory of India	2. State prescribed professional or technical qualification
C. Freedom to assemble peacefully and without arms	3. Public order
D. Freedom of speech and expression	4. Defamation

Codes

	A	B	C	D		A	B	C	D
(a)	2	1	3	4	(b)	1	2	3	4
(c)	4	3	2	1	(d)	4	2	1	3

29. **Statement I** Under Article 21 of the Constitution of India, the Right to Life includes the Right to Livelihood, and the state must ensure that no person is deprived of their means of living arbitrarily. **CBSE 2025**

Statement II In the case of Olga Tellis Vs. Bombay Municipal Corporation, the Supreme Court ruled that evicting slum dwellers without providing them alternative housing violates their Right to Livelihood under Article 21.

Choose the correct statement

(a) Both Statements are correct.
(b) Both Statements are incorrect.
(c) Statement I is correct, but Statement II is incorrect.
(d) Statement II is correct, but Statement I is incorrect.

30. **Statement I** Article 14 ensures that all individuals are treated equally under the law, but it allows for reasonable classification based on valid distinctions. **CBSE 2025**

Statement II The Prohibition of Child Marriage Act, 2006, setting different legal marriage ages for men and women, violates Article 14 as it treats individuals unequally.

Choose the correct statement

(a) Both Statements are correct.
(b) Both Statements are incorrect.
(c) Statement I is correct, but Statement II is incorrect.
(d) Statement II is correct, but Statement I is incorrect.

31. **Statement I** Under Article 25, freedom of religion is absolute and cannot be restricted by the state for any reason. **CBSE 2025**

Statement II The Supreme Court has ruled that the use of loudspeakers for religious prayers can be restricted under noise pollution regulations as it affects public order and health.

Choose the correct statement

(a) Both Statements are correct.
(b) Both Statements are incorrect.
(c) Statement I is correct, but Statement II is incorrect.
(d) Statement II is correct, but Statement I is incorrect.

Assertion-Reason Questions

Directions (Q.Nos. 32-41) In the questions given below, there are two statements. Read the statements and choose the correct option.

Codes

(a) Both A and R are true and R is the correct explanation of A.
(b) Both A and R are true, but R is not the correct explanation of A.
(c) A is true, but R is false.
(d) A is false, but R is true.

32. **Assertion** (A) Article 18 of Indian Constitution abolished all titles except for military and academic titles.

Reason (R) Titles violate the essence of Article 14 of the Indian Constitution. **CBSE 2024**

33. **Assertion** (A) Any public-spirited person can file petition or write letters to court on behalf of aggrieved person.

Reason (R) Courts have liberalised the doctrine of locus standi of the enforcement of Fundamental Rights through Public Interest Litigations (PILs). **CBSE 2025**

34. **Assertion** (A) India is a secular state.

Reason (R) Article 26 of the Constitution of India guarantees the freedom to mange religious affairs.

35. **Assertion** (A) In 1948, the United Nations General Assembly adopted the Universal Declaration of Human Rights (UDHR) as 'a common standard of achievement for all peoples and nations'.

Reason (R) The Universal Declaration of Human Rights provides and defines the various kinds of human rights that are applicable to all human beings.

36. **Assertion** (A) It is the duty of the state to apply the Directive Principles of State Policy in making laws and policies on social and human development.

Reason (R) DPSPs can be enforced in the court of law.

37. **Assertion** (A) Article 51A of the Indian Constitution prescribes fundamental duties of every citizen.

Reason (R) The courts might raise the status of these duties to that of Fundamental Rights in future

38. **Assertion** (A) Safeguarding public property and abjuring violence is a DPSP.

Reason (R) Valuing and preserving the rich heritage and culture is a fundamental duty.

39. Assertion (A) The freedoms under Article 19 of the Constitution of India are not absolute, but conditional.

Reason (R) The State can "authoritatively and reasonably" limit or take away the freedoms under Article 19. **CBSE 2024 C**

40. Assertion (A) Parents of children between the age of 6 to 14 years have a duty to provide opportunities for education to their children.

Reason (R) Article 21A provides Right to Education as a Fundamental Right. **CBSE 2024 C**

41. Assertion (A) The Sustainable Development Goals (SDGs) are inextricably linked to human rights, as achieving the SDGs requires the realisation of human rights.

Reason (R) The United Nations General Assembly's Transforming Our World: The 2030 Agenda for Sustainable Development explicitly recognises that the SDGs are grounded in the Universal Declaration of Human Rights and international human rights law.

Answers

1. (d) No, because the government is sovereign and enacts laws for the common good.
2. (d) Prohibiting human trafficking, beggary and forced labour.
3. (b) Article 15
4. (a) Article 20(3)
5. (c) Right to life and personal liberty
6. (d) Right to Constitutional Remedies
7. (d) Both (a) and (c)
8. (b) Article 23
9. (c) Part IV, Articles 36-51
10. (b) DPSP
11. (a) Fundamental duty has been breached by the state.
12. (c) Fundamental Right under Article 14 has been violated as an equal number of males and females have not been employed.
13. (d) The notice can be justified as the right to business is not absolute and reasonable restriction can be imposed by law in the interest of the public.
14. (c) Ubaid is not protected by Article 20(3) in his refusal to give a blood sample since he is not accused of any offence yet.
15. (a) Right to Freedom
16. (a) The state can prohibit someone from making inciting speeches that may provoke others to commit violence.
17. (c) The state can not restrict the sale of the book because of a few unruly protestors.
18. (c) Only by procedure established by law.
19. (a) Yes, as the restriction is necessary for maintaining public order.
20. (a) Article 20
21. (b) Article 32
22. (b) a procedure that is fair and reasonable.
23. (b) Arrested person has a right to consult and be defended by a legal practitioner of choice.
24. (c) Yes, as the right to dignity and humane treatment is implicit in Article 21.
25. (c) Protection of Civil Rights Act, 1955
26. (a) 3 1 4 2
27. (c) 3 1 4 5 2
28. (a) 2 1 3 4
29. (a) Both Statements are correct.
30. (c) Statement I is correct, but Statement II is incorrect.
31. (d) Statement II is correct, but Statement I is incorrect.
32. (a) Both A and R are true and R is the correct explanation of A.
33. (a) Both A and R are true and R is the correct explanation of A.
34. (b) Both A and R are true, but R is not the correct explanation of A.
35. (a) Both A and R are true and R is the correct explanation of A.
36. (c) A is true, but R is false.
37. (b) Both A and R are true, but R is not the correct explanation of A.
38. (d) A is false, but R is true.
39. (a) Both A and R are true and R is the correct explanation of A.
40. (a) Both A and R are true and R is the correct explanation of A.
41. (a) Both A and R are true and R is the correct explanation of A.

Subjective Questions

Very Short Answer Type Questions

1. Analyse the concept of Human Rights.

Ans. Human Rights are rights inherent to all human beings, regardless of race, sex, nationality, ethnicity, language, religion or any other status. Human rights include the right to life and liberty, freedom from slavery and torture, freedom of opinion and expression, the right to work and education and many more.

2. When was the Universal Declaration of Human Rights adopted? What are its objectives?

Ans. In 1948, the United Nations General Assembly adopted the Universal Declaration of Human Rights (UDHR) as 'A common standard of achievement for all peoples and nations'.

The Universal Declaration of Human Rights provides and defines the various kinds of human rights that are applicable to all human beings.

3. State four parts of the Indian Constitution which contains the human rights framework. **CBSE 2017**

Ans. The four parts of our Indian Constitution which contain the human rights framework are

(i) Preamble

(ii) Fundamental Rights

(iii) Directive Principles of State Policy

(iv) Fundamental Duties

4. A violent clash took place between the security forces of Azamgarh and Mirzapur over border dispute, which claimed lives of six Azamgarh police personnel and injured dozens of others. The government informed the Parliament that there were a total of seven inter-state border disputes at present in the country. **CBSE SQP 2022**

(i) Which institution is authorised to resolve such disputes?

(ii) Mention the Constitutional provision under which it can intervene.

Ans. (i) The President can constitute an inter-state council to resolve such disputes.

(ii) Article 263 of the Constitution gives powers to the President to set up an inter-state council for resolution of disputes between states.

5. When can the state reasonably take away the right to freedom of speech and expression?

Ans. The state can 'reasonably' limit or take away the right to 'freedom of speech and expression' when there is a threat to

(i) the sovereignty and integrity of India

(ii) the security of the state

(iii) friendly relations with foreign states

(iv) public order, or decency or morality

(v) in relation to contempt of court

(vi) or defamation

(vii) incitement (provocation to commit) to an offence.

6. Rachita is a student leader. She makes a hate speech targeting members of a certain community in the college premises. The college authorities stop her speech mid-way and Rachita accuses them of violating her Fundamental Rights. Identify which Fundamental Right applies in this situation. State whether the restriction is justified. **CBSE 2020**

Ans. As per the above statement, Rachita being stopped from her speech does not violate her Fundamental Right because her freedom of speech can be a threat to public order. Therefore, the restrictions are justified.

7. In a bustling city, a real estate developer acquires a vast tract of land that has been home to several low-income families for generations. The developer plans to build luxurious high-rise apartments and a shopping complex on this land, displacing the existing families without providing adequate compensation or resettlement options. The families, many of whom have been living there for decades, face eviction and loss of their livelihoods.

Identify the Fundamental Right in the Indian Constitution that is violated in this instance. What is the role of the state in the given situation? **CBSE 2024 C**

Ans. The Fundamental Rights violated in this instance is Article 21: Right to Life and Liberty, which includes the right to livelihood, shelter and protection from forced eviction. The state's role is to

- protect the rights of low-income families.
- ensure fair compensation and resettlement options.
- enforce laws and policies to prevent forced evictions.
- balance development with social justice and human.

8. Praveen was arrested on the suspicion of having murdered his friend. He was produced before the Magistrate within 24 hours of his arrest. No concrete evidence could be presented by the police against Praveen. After being brought back from the court he was taken to custody to make him confess his crime.

Is the police justified in its action? Which provision of Article 22 of the Constitution of India is being violated by the police? **CBSE 2018**

Ans. In the given situation, the police is not justified in its actions as it has violated Article 22(2) of the Constitution which provides that no person can be detained in custody beyond the period of 24 hours without the authority of the Magistrate.

9. State the provisions of preventive detention laws in India to which the safeguard of Article 22 does not apply. **CBSE 2020**

Ans. One of the preventive detention laws to which the safeguard of Article 22 does not apply is the Maintenance of Internal Security Act of 1971. It was enacted during the Indira Gandhi administration, popularly known as 'emergency' and many political opponents were detained without safeguards against arrest and detention and other human rights.

10. During a nationwide emergency, the government implements strict measures to maintain law and order, suspending certain Constitutional rights. As part of these measures, a particular group of individuals is detained by the authorities for questioning, due to suspected involvement in unlawful activities. The group refused to co-operate on the grounds that they were entitled to safeguards under Article 22 of the Constitution which the authorities denied.

In this context, explain why Article 22 safeguards may not apply. **CBSE 2019**

Ans. Article 22 safeguards may not apply as all the Fundamental Right except Article 20 and 21 are suspended during national emergency, and in the given situation as well the government has implemented strict measures to maintain law and order and has announced nationwide emergency.

11. Give any two differences between Fundamental Rights and Human Rights. **CBSE 2025**

Ans. Two differences between Fundamental Rights and Human Rights are

Fundamental Rights	Human Rights
Fundamental Rights are specific to a particular country and are enshrined in its Constitution.	Human Rights have universal acceptance and apply to all individuals regardless of nationality.
Fundamental Rights are enforceable by national courts.	Human Rights are generally recognised by international declarations like the UDHR and may not always be legally enforceable within a country.

12. Explain how does Article 27 protect the freedom of payment of taxes for the promotion of any religion?

Ans. Article 27 prohibits forcing anyone to pay any taxes on revenues that are used in payment of expenses for the promotion or maintenance of any religion or section. For example, donations in temples that are used for the upkeep of the temple cannot be taxed.

13. Tamil, Telugu, Gujarati Speaking people living in Delhi are among the many minority communities. What rights do they have with regard to their language and culture while living in Delhi? **CBSE SQP 2024**

Ans. Tamil, Telugu, Gujarati speaking people living in Delhi are linguistic and cultural minorities. They are afforded protection under Article 29 and 30 of the Indian Constitution.

(i) Any minority group having a distinct language, script or culture of its own shall have the right to conserve the same. No citizen shall be denied admission into any educational institution maintained by the state or receiving aid out of state funds on grounds only of religions, race, caste language or any of them.

(ii) All minorities, whether based on religion or language, have the right to establish and administer educational institutions of their choice. In making any law providing for the compulsory acquisition of any property of an educational institution established and administered by a minority.

14. 'The Right of Consititutional Remedies is the most important Fundamental Right'. Justify the given statement.

Ans. The Right to Constitutional Remedies is the most important Fundamental Rights because Fundamental Rights are justiciable rights. They are enforceable, as every individual has the right to seek help from courts if they are violated.

Encroachment or violation of Fundamental Right is our day-to-day life is a matter of great concern. This is why our Constitution does not permit the legislature and the executive to curb these rights. It provides legal remedies for the protection of our Fundamental Rights.

When any of our rights are violated, we can seek justice through courts. We can directly approach the Supreme Court that can issue directions, orders or writs for the enforcement of Fundamental Rights.

15. A minority education society owns a chain of schools. These schools are recognised by the state and wholly funded by it.

To promote the spirit of unity and oneness, all the students in these schools have to attend a special religious prayer every morning irrespective of their religious beliefs.

A group of students refused to participate in the prayer. The school authorities, after giving warning for being indisciplined, suspended the students for a week. Parents of these students alleged violation of Fundamental Right of their children.

Is the action of school authorities justified? Stating the relevant Constitutional provision, given reason for your answer. **CBSE 2024**

Ans. The action of school authorities of suspending students is unjustified because the school is wholly funded by the state and Article 28 of Indian Constitution states that, No religion instruction shall be provided in any educational institution wholly maintained out of state funds.

It also violates Article 25 of the Constitution which talks about freedom of religion.

16. Mention two salient features of Directive Principles of State Policy. **CBSE 2019**

Or **State any two key features of the Directive Principles of State Policy in the Indian Constitution.** **CBSE 2025**

Ans. Two salient features of the Directive Principles are

(i) It is the duty of the state to apply these principles in making laws and policies on social and human development.

(ii) These principles are largely of the nature of economic and social rights.

17. In a remote tribal region of India, there is a unique community that follows ancient customs and traditions, different from mainstream practices. The local government plans to implement developmental projects in the region to improve infrastructure and living conditions. However, some members of the tribal community express concerns about the potential impact of these projects on their distinct culture and way of life.

In this context, assess the significance of Part IV of the Indian Constitution in guiding the local government's actions. **CBSE 2024 C**

Ans. Part IV (Directive Principles of State Policy) of the Indian Constitution is significant in guiding the local government's actions. Specifically

- **Article 46** The state must protect the rights and interests of Scheduled Tribes, including their cultural heritage.
- **Article 39** The state must ensure that development projects do not harm the weaker sections of society, including tribal communities.

These provisions direct the local government to balance development with the protection of tribal culture and interests.

18. A group of citizens in a city regularly engages in public protests against government policies. During one protest, some individuals damage public property, disrupt traffic, and use offensive language. The protestors claim that they are exercising their right to freedom of speech and expression. Is the claim by the protestors justified? How do the fundamental duties under Article 51A of the Constitution of India apply in this situation? **CBSE 2025**

Ans. The protesters' claim is not fully justified, as the right to freedom of speech and expression under Article 19 is subject to reasonable restrictions, including public order and morality. Article 51A of the Constitution imposes fundamental duties, such as safeguarding public property and maintaining harmony, which the protesters violated by damaging property and disrupting traffic.

Short Answer Type Questions

1. What do you understand about International Human Rights? Explain.

Ans. In 1948, the United Nations General Assembly adopted the Universal Declaration of Human Rights (UDHR) as 'A common standard of achievement for all peoples and nations'. The Universal Declaration of Human Rights provides and defines the various kinds of human rights that are applicable to all human beings.

The Universal Declaration of Human Rights provides and defines the various kinds of human rights that are applicable to all human beings. They include the fundamental, civil, political, economic, social and cultural rights. For example, Freedom of speech, assembly, conscience and religion, Right to education, Right to livelihood and decent standard of living, Right to life, liberty and security of person, Right to equality, Freedom from all forms of discriminations including discrimination based on gender and race.

2. Write a short note on the right to equality. Also state how Article 15 also upholds the equality principle.

Ans. Article 14 provides to all the right to equality before law and equal protection of the law. It prohibits discrimination on grounds of religion, race, caste, sex or place of birth. It means that law treats everyone equally without consideration of their rank or status or other backgrounds. The principle of equality means that one uniform law cannot be applied to all equally as some may not be similarly placed as others. So 'equality' treats equals similarly and unequals differently.

Article 15 is based on the equality principle. It prohibits state from discriminating against anyone based on the grounds of religion, race, caste, sex or place of birth. Also, it prohibits anyone and the state from using these grounds to restrict (restrain) any citizen from entering shops, public restaurants, hotels and places of public entertainment, or the use of wells, tanks, bathing ghats, roads and places of public resort.

3. Explain the provisions of safeguards in the Indian Constitution, to persons accused of having committed crimes. CBSE 2020

Ans. For answer refer to text under the heading Right to Freedom (Article 20) on page no. 218 to 220.

4. Given below are two situations. Read them and answer the questions that follow. CBSE 2019

(i) Sunil was sentenced to death on charges of murder and robbery. He was held in solitary confinement by jail authorities since the date of his conviction by the session court. Appeal against the decision is pending in the High Court.

(ii) Kharak Singh, an accused in dacoity case was let off due to the lack of evidence by the court. Uttar Pradesh police regulations allowed domiciliary visits at night, secret picketing of Kharak Singh's house, tracking/verifying his movement and periodic inquiries by officers.

(a) Identify the Fundamental Rights violated in the above two situations.

(b) Explain the provisions of the article that are alleged to be violated.

(c) On what grounds can Sunil and Kharak Singh challenge the action of the authorities?

Ans. (a) Articles 20 and 21 are violated in the given situations.

(b) Article 20 provides for safeguards to persons who are accused of having committed crimes. This article provides the human rights framework to the criminal justice system. Article 21 states 'No person shall be deprived of his life or personal liberty except according to procedure established by law.'

(c) Sunil and Kharak Singh can challenge the action of the authorities on the ground that the due process of law has not been followed.

5. Article 21 of the Indian Constitution provides that a person can be deprived of his/her 'Right to life or personal liberty' only by procedure established by law. Elucidate the above statement with the help of an example. CBS ESQP 2022

Ans. Article 21 states that a person's right to life and personal liberty can only be taken away through a fair and legal procedure. This ensures protection from arbitrary actions by the government.

For example, if a person is sentenced to death penalty, it must follow a proper legal trial, ensuring a fair hearing and appeal process. In Maneka Gandhi Vs. Union of India (1978), the Supreme Court ruled that laws restricting personal liberty must be just, fair and reasonable.

6. What are Human Rights? Explain how Fundamental Rights and Human Rights are important to create a better environment for people and to help them preserve their dignity. CBSE SQP 2024

Ans. Human rights are basic rights that we have because we exist as human beings. These are not granted by any state. Human rights belong to all human beings irrespective of their nationality, race, caste, creed, gender, etc. All individuals enjoy the same human rights, without any discrimination. Human rights are safeguards that a human being seeks to live with dignity and equality. Therefore, human rights are universal and inalienable rights.

The principle of universality of human rights means that we are all equally entitled to our human rights. Human rights are inalienable; therefore, these should not be taken away, except in specific situations and according to due process.

For instance the right to liberty may be restricted if a person is found guilty of a crime by a court of law.

A few examples of human rights are those basic rights that ensure fairness, equality, freedom and respect to all people. These rights abolish various unjust practices like exploitation, discrimination and inequality. Human rights include most fundamental right like the right to life, rights to food, education, work, health, liberty, etc. Fundamental Rights are basic rights of the citizens of a country. Fundamental Right are enshrined in the Constitution and they are enforceable in the court of law. If there is any kind of violation of Fundamental Right, one can approach the court for the protection of such rights.

7. What are the key principles outlined in the Universal Declaration of Human Rights (UDHR) and how do they reflect the foundational values of human dignity, freedom and equality? CBSE 2025

Ans. The Universal Declaration of Human Rights (UDHR) outlines fundamental principles that uphold human dignity, freedom, and equality. The key principles include

- **Liberty of a person (Article 3)** Ensures the right to life, liberty and personal security.
- **Equality before the law (Article 7)** Guarantees equal protection without discrimination.
- **Prohibition on torture (Article 5)** Forbids torture and inhumane treatment.
- **Right to work and equal pay (Article 23)** Ensures fair wages and employment rights.
- **Right to social security (Article 25)** Protects access to social well-being and security.

These principles emphasise the universal, inalienable nature of human rights, forming the foundation of international human rights law?.

8. Garvit is arrested on the apprehension that he will indulge in acts of rioting, leading to public disorder near a community centre during the festival season. **CBSE 2022**

(i) Identify and explain the legal provision under which Garvit is arrested.

(ii) Are the safeguards provided under Article 22 of the Indian Constitution available to Garvit?

Ans. (i) Garvit can be arrested on the apprehension that he will indulge in acts of rioting because Preventive Detention Laws and Article 19 provides that the state can 'reasonably' limit or take away the right to 'freedom of speech and expression' when there is a threat to the sovereignty and integrity of India, or the security of the state, or friendly relations with foreign states, or public order, or decency or morality, or in relation to contempt of court, or defamation, or incitement to an offence.

(ii) The provisions regarding preventive detention in India are governed by Article 22. Persons who are detained or arrested are protected by this article. Therefore, Article 22 does not apply before the arrest or imprisonment of a person or group of people; it only does so later. Therefore, the safeguards provided under Article 22 of Indian Constitution is not available to Garvit while being detained.

9. Explain the provisions enshrined in the Constitution of India that make India a secular entity by giving its citizens freedom of conscience and religion. **CBSE 2019**

Ans. The Constitutional provisions that make India a secular entity by giving its citizens the freedom of conscience and religion have been enshrined under Article 25.

Under Article 25, all persons have the right to freedom of conscience and freedom to profess, practice and propagate religion as long as their acts do not threaten public order, morality and health.

Further, the citizens have also been granted the freedom to manage religious affairs under Article 26.

Article 26 provides the right to every religious denomination, including their sub-sections or sects, to

(i) establish and maintain institutions for religious and charitable purposes

(ii) manage their own matters of religious affairs

(iii) own and acquire movable (e.g., vehicles, furniture) and immovable (e.g., house, trees) property

(iv) administer such property in accordance with law.

10. What do you understand by freedom as to attendance at religious instruction or religious worship in certain educational institutions? Also state the exceptions, if any.

Ans. Article 28 prohibits religious instructions in educational institutions that are wholly maintained out of state funds.

For example, government run schools like Sainik Schools and Kendriya Vidyalaya Schools cannot impart religious instructions to students.

However, some educational institutions are exempted from this rule such as those which are administered by the state, but are established by endowments or trusts that require religious instruction in such educational institutions.

Furthermore, state recognised or state aided educational institutions cannot force any student to take part in any religious instruction or to attend any religious worship conducted in such institutions. These provisions along with others make India a secular (absence of any state religion) state.

11. Prem is a bonded labourer working for a construction baron. He is paying off a debt his father had incurred and had not been able to pay off-before his death. His two sons, Bhim (aged 10) and Arjun (aged 11) have to drop out of school and work in a glass factory to make their ends meet. A journalist highlights Prem's plight in a newspaper article as it was common for most of the families in village Bhandha from where he was reporting. He also wrote a letter to the Hon'ble Supreme Court requesting its intervention in the situation. **CBSE 2022**

(i) Identify and explain the Fundamental Rights of Prem and his sons, that have been violated.

(ii) How would the newspaper article and the letter written to the Supreme Count help the villagers?

Ans. (i) The Fundamental Rights of Prem and his sons that have been violated are Article 23 and 24 of Constitution of India. Article 23 prohibits human trafficking, beggar and forced labour. Article 24 prohibits employment of children below the age of 14 years in factories, mining and other hazardous employment.

(ii) The newspaper article and the letter written to the Supreme Court could help the villagers by creating awareness about the bondage labour and child labour to the masses. It also made Supreme Court aware about the violation of Fundamental Rights given by the Constitution of India, which makes the newspaper article and letter a meaningful means to get justice.

12. Identify and explain the constitutional provision that applies to each of the following cases

(i) A government school refuses to admit a student based on their religion, stating that it follows a particular religious ideology.

(ii) A religious group wants to construct a charitable hospital and run it under their management without government interference.

(iii) A citizen files a petition in the Supreme Court, claiming that the demolition of their home without alternative housing violates their Fundamental Rights.

Ans. (i) This case violates Article 29, which protects the rights of minorities to preserve their culture, language and education. It also violates Article 30, which ensures that no citizen can be denied admission to state-funded educational institutions based on religion.

(ii) This relates to Article 26, which grants religious groups the right to establish and manage religious and charitable institutions. However, their activities must follow the law and not harm public order or health.

(iii) This case falls under Article 21, which guarantees the right to life and livelihood. The Supreme Court has ruled that eviction without rehabilitation violates this right.

13. With regard to the provisions of 'Fundamental Rights' enshrined in Part III of the Indian Constitution, consider the following situations and answer the questions that follow. **CBSE 2016**

(i) State Government gave reservations to Scheduled Castes, Scheduled Tribes in public employment, who have not been adequately represented in the services under the state.

(ii) Dipender is a rickshaw puller and was not allowed to enter a public restaurant because he belonged to a backward class.

(iii) Marriage of Khushi, aged 18 years and Yash, aged 20 years was disallowed by the village panchayat.

Ans. (i) Article 16 provides for equality of opportunity in matters of public or state employment and bars any discrimination to any citizen on grounds of religion, race, caste, sex, descent, place of birth or residence. However, this article allows the state to provide reservation or affirmative (positive) action programs for government jobs to backward classes like Schedule Castes and Scheduled Tribes who because of historical and continued disadvantages based on caste status and otherwise have not been adequately represented in the services under the state.

(ii) The given situation is a violation of Article 15 of the Constitution. Article 15 is based on the equality principle. It prohibits state from discriminating against anyone based on grounds of religion, race, caste, sex or place of birth. Also, it prohibits anyone and the state from using these grounds to restrict (restrain) any citizen from entering shops, public restaurants, hotels and places of public entertainment or the use of wells, tanks, bathing ghats, roads and places of public resort.

(iii) This is not a violation of any Fundamental Right since the legal age for marriage is 18 years for women and 21 years for men.

Long Answer Type Questions

1. What features of Fundamental Rights give them a high pedestal in the Constitutional framework? **CBSE SQP 2020**

Ans. Articles 12-35 in Part III of the Constitution contain the provisions on Fundamental Rights. Some of the salient features of Fundamental Rights that give them a high pedestal in the Constitutional framework are

- They are enforceable by the Higher Courts in India which means that a person whose Fundamental Right has been violated can approach the Supreme Court or the High Court for its redressal.
- Article 32 provides the right to the aggrieved ones, whose Fundamental Rights have been violated or denied, to petition the Supreme Court for the enforcement of Fundamental Rights.
- Article 13 elevates the authority of Fundamental Rights. It ensures that the state or other competent authority does not make laws including ordinances, orders, bye laws, rules, regulations, notifications, customs or usages that contradicts or takes away or breaches the Fundamental Rights.
- Fundamental Rights are mostly enforceable against the state and in some cases against private persons. An example of the former is the right to freedom of speech and expression, for the latter is the prohibition of employment of children below the age of fourteen years in factories, mines, and in places of hazardous activities.

2. (i) State the freedoms which are available to the citizens of India under Article 19 of the Indian Constitution. **CBSE 2017**

(ii) Which of the following can be a reasonable restriction? Give reasons for your answer.

(a) Restrictions on the sale of a book because of protests by a group of people.

(b) Prohibition on making inciting speeches that may provoke others to commit violence.

Ans. (i) Article 19 prescribes and protects the following kinds of freedoms to all citizens
- Freedom of speech and expression.
- Freedom to assemble peaceably and without arms.
- Freedom to form associations or unions.
- Freedom to move freely throughout the territory of India.
- Freedom to reside and settle in any part of the territory of India.
- Freedom to practice any profession, or to carry on any occupation, trade or business.

(ii) (a) The state can 'reasonably' limit or take away the right to 'freedom of speech and expression' when there is a threat to
- the sovereignty and integrity of India
- the security of the state
- friendly relations with foreign states
- public order, or decency or morality
- in relation to contempt of court, or defamation
- incitement (provocation to commit) to an offence.

Since restrictions on the sale of a book due to protests by a group of people does not fall within the purview of any of the options given above, it will not classify as a reasonable restriction.

(b) According to Article 19 inciting speeches may provoke others to commit violence, classify as a reasonable restriction.

3. **(i) Explain the cultural and educational rights as granted by the Constitution of India.** **CBSE 2016**

(ii) Critically assess the situations given below in light of 'Cultural and Educational Rights'.

(a) A government aided school in Punjab denied admission to Rachit because his mother tongue was Bengali and he does not understand Punjabi (Gurumukhi).

(b) In the annual budget for education the state government allocated ₹ 36.5 crores for government and state funded schools and ₹ 16.5 crores for schools run by religious minorities.

Ans. (i) Articles 29 and 30 of the Indian Constitution provide cultural, linguistic and educational rights.

Article 29 of the Constitution of India protects the right of minorities to conserve their distinct language, script, or culture. It also prohibits educational institutions, maintained by the state or receiving aid out of state funds, from denying admissions to any citizen on grounds of religion, race, caste or language.

Article 30 provides all minorities, whether based on religion or language, the right to establish and administer educational institutions of their choice. It also prohibits state from discriminating educational institutions, while granting them aid, on grounds of religion or language.

(ii) For answer refer to text under the heading '

(a) Article 29 also prohibits educational institutions, maintained by the state or receiving aid out of state funds, from denying admissions to any citizen on grounds of religion, race, caste or language. Thus, this constitutes a violation.

(b) Article 30 provides all minorities, whether based on religion or language, the right to establish and administer educational institutions of their choice. It also prohibits state from discriminating educational institutions, while granting them aid, on grounds of religion or language.

4. **Describe the evolution of Right to Education from a policy goal to a Fundamental Right.** **CBSE SQP 2022**

Ans. The Evolution of Right to Education from a policy goal to a Fundamental Right are discussed below
- Article 21A provides for right to education to all between the age of six to fourteen and obligates state to implement this.
- Prior to 2002, the Indian Constitution considered elementary education for children between age six to fourteen as a policy goal provision in the Directive Principles of State Policy.
- Directive Principles of State Policy are not enforceable in a court of law as they are as aspirational goals to be achieved over a period of time.
- In 1992-93, however, the Supreme Court affirmed that depriving one from education amounts to depriving one's right to life. This meant that elementary education was raised to the status of Fundamental Right from that of a policy goal (directive principles) and hence it is enforceable.
- Accordingly, in 2002, Article 21A providing the right to elementary education was created as a Fundamental Right.

5. **Describe the scope of, right to equality in the Indian Constitution.**

Ans. The right to equality in the Indian Constitution is a Fundamental Right that guarantees all citizens equal treatment before the law and equal opportunities in certain matters.

The right to equality is covered under Article 14-18 of the Indian Constitution.
- **Article 14** This article is divided into two parts : equality before the law and equal protection of laws. Equality before the law means that everyone is treated equally in the eyes of the law, while equal protection of the law means that the same law applies to everyone

- **Article 15** This artical prohibits discrimination on the grounds of race caste, religion sex or place of birth. It also allows the state to make special provisions for women and childen.
- **Article 16(1)** This article covers equality of opportunity in matters of public employment.
- **Article 17** Talks about abolition of untouchability
- **Article 18** Talks about abolition of all titles except military and academic.

6. A group of workers in Rajasthan are evicted from their homes, which were built on government land, without prior notice or alternative arrangements. They claim that their right to livelihood and shelter, as recognised in the Olga Tellis case, has been violated. With no resources to hire a lawyer, they approach a non-profit organisation for help.

In light of the above scenario, answer the following questions

(i) **Which Article of the Constitution guarantees protection against the violation of Fundamental Rights?**

(ii) **What is Public Interest Litigation (PIL), and how can it help the evicted workers?**

(iii) **How did the Supreme Court interpret the Right to Livelihood in the Olga Tellis case?**

Ans. (i) Article 32 of the Indian Constitution guarantees protection against the violation of Fundamental Rights. It allows people to directly approach the Supreme Court if their rights are denied. Similarly, Article 226 allows people to approach the High Courts for the same.

(ii) Public Interest Litigation (PIL) is a way for individuals or organisations to file a case in court for the protection of public rights. Since the workers cannot afford a lawyer, a non-profit organisation can file a PIL on their behalf to seek justice. The court can then review whether their eviction was lawful and if they should be given alternative housing.

(iii) In the Olga Tellis case (1985), the Supreme Court ruled that the Right to Livelihood is part of the Right to Life (Article 21). The court stated that evicting people without providing them with alternative shelter violates their Fundamental Rights.

7. (i) **Differentiate between Fundamental Rights and Directive Principles of State Policy on any three grounds.** **CBSE SQP 2022**

(ii) **How can the status of Directive Principles of State Policy be changed? Explain with the help of an example.**

Ans. (i) The Difference between Fundamental Rights and Directive Principle of State Policy

Basis For Comparison	Fundamental Rights	Directive Principles
Meaning	Fundamental Rights are the essential rights of all the citizens of the country.	Directive Principle are the guidelines which are referred while formulating policies and laws of the country.
Defined in	Part III of the Constitution	Part IV of the Constitution
Nature	Negative	Positive

(ii) Articles 36-51 in Part IV of the Constitution lays down the guiding principles of governance for the State are called the 'Directive Principles of State Policy'. The provisions of directive principles are not enforceable by any court of law, but they provide guidance in carrying out and drafting laws and policies regarding human and social development. Supreme Court has raised the status of many provisions of directive principles to that of Fundamental Right by suggesting they violate one's right to life (Article 21). Thus, the status of Directive Principles of State Policy could be changed by Supreme Court or by the amendments in constitution. The best example of it is right to education.

8. **What are 'Fundamental Duties'? State their salient features. How are Fundamental Duties different from Fundamental Rights?** **CBSE 2018**

Ans. Article 51A of the Constitution prescribes fundamental duties of every citizen. In that, certain conduct and behaviour are expected of the citizens.

The salient features of fundamental duties are

(i) The fundamental duties cannot be enforced in a court of law for violation of the duties, and no one can be punished for the violation.

(ii) Fundamental duties contain standards to be followed by the citizens.

(iii) They remind citizens not to behave irresponsibily, but help to build a free, democratic and strong society.

Fundamental duties are different from Fundamental Rights in the following ways

(i) Fundamental Rights are enforceable while fundamental duties are non- justiciable.

(ii) Fundamental Rights are the rights which are compulsorily provided to the people whereas fundamental duties are those duties which citizens are expected to follow.

SELF ASSESSMENT TEST

Objective Type Questions

1. Which Clause of the Magna Carta prevented the English government from jailing or punishing an individual 'except by the lawful judgement of his peers and by the law of the land'?

(a) Clause 28 (b) Clause 29 (c) Clause 30 (d) Clause 31

2. **Statement I** Under Article 32, individuals can directly approach the Supreme Court for the enforcement of Fundamental Rights, making it a Fundamental Right itself.

Statement II Article 226 grants the High Courts wider jurisdiction than Article 32, as it allows them to issue writs for violations of both Fundamental Rights and legal rights.

Choose the correct statement

(a) Both Statements are correct. (b) Both Statements are incorrect.

(c) Statement I is correct, but Statement II is incorrect. (d) Statement II is correct, but Statement I is incorrect.

3. The Preamble guarantees which of the following kinds of justice?

(a) Social (b) Economic (c) Political (d) All of these

4. Which Article prohibits the employment of children in factories?

(a) Article 23 (b) Article 24 (c) Article 25 (d) Article 26

Very Short Answer Type Questions

5. What is the obligation of the States according to the International Human Rights Law?

6. How are the rights of persons accused of any crime protected under Article 20?

Short Answer Type Questions

7. Identify and explain the Constitutional provision that applies to each of the following cases

(i) A temple in a village denies entry to a certain section of society based on caste, stating it is an age-old tradition.

(ii) A private minority school refuses government aid, asserting its right to manage its institution without state interference.

(iii) A citizen challenges a law in the Supreme Court, claiming it restricts their right to freely practice and propagate their religion.

8. What is human trafficking? State some examples of human trafficking.

9. How does the Constitution protect the right to freedom of religion?

Long Answer Type Questions

10. Write a short note on the Preamble to the Constitution. What are the objectives that it seeks to achieve?

11. A minority community in Tamil Nadu decides to establish an educational institution to preserve and promote their language and culture. However, when they apply for government aid, they find that the authorities impose additional conditions that other institutions do not have to follow. The community members feel discriminated against and argue that their rights under Articles 29 and 30 are being violated.

In light of the above scenario, answer the following questions

(i) What rights do minorities have under Articles 29 and 30 regarding educational institutions?

(ii) Can the government impose conditions on minority-run institutions while granting aid? Explain with reasons.

(iii) How should the community approach the legal system to challenge this alleged discrimination?

14 CHAPTER

The quasi-judicial bodies are public administrative agencies under the realm of the executive branch and are largely vested with authority similar to courts.

Complaint Mechanisms of Quasi-Judicial Bodies

▼ **YOUR STUDY GOALS**

14.1 Quasi-Judicial Bodies
14.2 Various Human Rights Commission
14.3 National Commission for Minorities
14.4 National Commission for Women (NCW)
14.5 National Commission for Scheduled Castes and Scheduled Tribes
14.6 National Commission for Protection of Child Rights (NCPCR)

▼ **YOUR PRACTICE GOAL**

- Objective Type Questions (18 Qs ; MCQs, A-R, Statements, Matching)
- Subjective Questions (10 VSAs, 10 SAs, 5 LAs)

14.1 Quasi-Judicial Bodies

- Quasi-judicial bodies have the power to resolve disputes and also impose punishments. Examples of quasi-judicial institutions include
  - National and state human rights commissions
  - Central and state information commissions
  - Consumer redressal forums and commissions
  - Income tax tribunals and so on
- The most fundamental bodies specifically to human rights are the National Human Rights institutions that include
  - National Human Rights Commission (NHRC)
  - National Commission for Minorities
  - National Commission for Women (NCW)
  - National Commission for Scheduled Castes
  - National Commission for Scheduled Tribes
  - National Commission for Protection of Child Rights (NCPCR)
- These commissions are **independent or autonomous**[1] and **transparent bodies** that are created under specific legislations to promote and protect human rights. For example, the National and State Human Rights Commissions are governed by the Protection of Human Rights Act, 1993.

---

1 **Autonomous** It means having the freedom to govern itself or control its own affairs.

- National commissions have jurisdiction over the entire nation. The parallel state commissions take matters of human rights violations from the respective states.

14.2 Various Human Rights Commission

The various Human Rights Commissions are discussed below

National Human Rights Commission (NHRC)

- The National Human Rights Commission was established under a specific legislation called the **Protection of Human Rights Act** that was enacted by the Parliament in **1993**.
- It is an independent institution with powers and functions to promote and protect human rights.
- An act also provides for the Constitution of State Human Rights Commissions at state levels for access to complaint mechanisms at the state level.

Composition of NHRC

The National Commission is headed by the Chairperson who is a former Chief Justice of the Supreme Court. The other members of commission are

- One member who is a former judge of the Supreme Court.
- Another member who is present or former Chief Justice of a High Court.
- Two other members having a knowledge or experience in matters relating to human rights.
- Besides, there is a Secretary-General who is the Chief Executive Officer of the commission. He performs administrative duties of the commission.

Appointment of the Members of NHRC

- The Chairperson and the members are appointed by the President of India on recommendation of a committee which consists of the
  - Prime Minister,
  - The Speaker of the House of the People (Lok Sabha)
  - Minister of Home Affairs at the center
  - Leader of opposition in the Lok Sabha
  - Leader of opposition in the Council of States (Rajya Sabha)
  - Deputy Chairman of the Rajya Sabha.
- The committee is required to consult the Chief Justice of India whenever a sitting judge of the Supreme Court or sitting Chief Justice of a High Court is appointed to the commission.
- The government also appoints police officers and investigative staff and other administrative, technical and scientific personnel, for the efficient functioning of the commission.
- National Commission is based in New Delhi.

Functions of the Commission

- The commission is vested with the functions of **inquiry and investigation.**
- It conduct inquiry and investigation into the alleged (suspected) violation of human rights or abetment (aiding or supporting), or negligence in the prevention of such violation by a public servant.
- The complaint can be filed by the victim or his/her representative, or the court may direct the commission with a complaint, or the commission may initiate inquiry and investigation on its own **(suo motu)**[2]. For example, the commission may inquire **suo motu** based on some human rights violations by news or report published through the media.
- Suo motu inquiry is especially useful when the victims belong to weaker sections of the society and have limited access to justice delivery mechanisms.

2 **Suo motu** It means on its own motion' and relates to an action taken by court of its own accord without any request by the parties involved.

Powers of the Commission

The commission has the powers of a Civil Court.

- **While conducting an enquiry** or investigation, following powers can be utilised
  - Summon (call) and enforce the attendance of witnesses and examine them on oath.
  - Ask for presentation of any document before itself.
  - Receive evidence on affidavits.
  - Request public record from any court or office.
  - Examine witnesses or documents.
- **Procedure of NHRC after Completion of Inquiry** Once the inquiry is completed, the commission can make recommendations to governmental authority in cases where any public servant is the perpetrator of human rights violation.
  - The recommendation may include payment of compensation to the victims or suggest initiation of proceedings for prosecution of the public servant.
  - The commission can also approach the Supreme Court or the High Court for directions and orders.
  - The commission may also ask the state authority to provide immediate interim relief to the victim.
- **Intervening in Court Proceedings**

  For example, the commission can request the Supreme Court to transfer pending riot cases out of a state in which the riots had happened. It is to ensure that the witnesses are not threatened in any manner and that the evidence is not damaged.
- **Inspection of Jails or Other Government Institutions** The commission may visit any jail or other governmental institutions, where prisoners are lodged or detained, to study the living conditions of the inmates, and make recommendations to the government.
- **Awareness and Sensitisation** The powers of the commission related to awareness and sensitisation[3] are
  - The commission can review various human rights laws either in the Constitution or other statutes, and recommend measures to the government for their effective implementation.
  - The commission can also evaluate various factors, including acts of terrorism, which prevent the enjoyment of human rights, and recommend appropriate remedial measures to the government.
  - The commission's role includes studying various international human rights laws and making recommendations for their effective implementation at the domestic level (within the state).
  - The commission can undertake and promote research in the field of human rights as well as spread human rights literacy among various sections of society. It promote awareness of the safeguards available for the protection of these rights through publications, media, seminars and other available means.
  - The commission can encourage and support the efforts of non-governmental organisations and institutions involved with human rights work.

Complaint Mechanism of NHRC

The complaint mechanism procedure with the National Human Rights Commission is easy and straight forward as follows

- Any one aggrieved of human rights violation or their representatives can lodge a complaint with the commission in any language.
- The complaint can be filed online at www.nhrc.nic.in or by paper petition using the complaint format provided on the website.

3 **Sensitisation** It means the quality or condition of responding to certain stimuli in a sensitive manner.

- The complaint can be sent either by post or fax or through E-mail.
- There is no fee for filing a complaint.
- The complaint must be filed within a year of the occurrence of the human rights violation.
- Once the complaint is pending before the commission, one can check the status of the complaint online.

Following types of complaint(s) are not ordinarily entertainable

- The matter that is illegible (unreadable).
- The matter that is vague, anonymous or pseudonymous.
- The matter that is trivial or frivolous in nature
- The matters which are pending before a State Human Rights Commission or any other commission.
- Any matter after the expiry of one year from the date on which an act constituting violation of human rights is alleged to have been committed.
- Allegation is not against any public servant.
- The issue related to civil dispute, such property rights, contractual obligations, etc.
- The issue related to service matters.
- The issue related to labour/industrial disputes.
- Allegations that do not make out any specific violation of human rights.
- The matter that is sub-judice (already pending) before a court/tribunal.
- The matter that is covered by judicial verdict/decision of the commission.

Quick Test 1

1 Give one example of Quasi-Judicial Institutions.
2 In which year the Protection of Human Rights Act was enacted by the Parliament?
3 Who is the head of National commission?
4 The complaint can be filed online for human rights violation at which site?

14.3 National Commission for Minorities

- National Commission for Minorities Act, 1992 was enacted to safeguard the human rights of minorities, including protection against inequality and discrimination and also to create National Commission for Minorities.
- Minorities' human rights are enshrined in the Constitution as well as other laws enacted by Parliament and the State Legislatures.
- The minorities here are referred to as religious minorities of Muslims, Christians, Sikhs, Buddhists, Jains and Zoroastrians (Parsis).
- Many states also have instituted the State Minorities Commissions and are located in the respective state capitals.
- Persons who belong to the minority communities can approach the State as well as National Minorities Commission for remedying human rights violations.

Composition of the Commission

The National Minorities Commission consists of a Chairperson, a Vice-Chairperson and five other members who are nominated by the Central Government from amongst the minority communities and are persons of eminence (repute), ability and integrity.

Functions of the Commission

The functions of the commission include the following

- Evaluating the progress of the development of minorities.
- Monitoring the working of the safeguards provided in the Constitution and in other laws enacted by Parliament and the State Legislatures.
- Making recommendations for the effective implementation of safeguards for the protection of the interests of minorities by the Central Government or the State Governments.
- Looking into specific complaints regarding deprivation of rights and safeguards of the minorities, and taking up such matters with the appropriate authorities.
- Initiating studies on problems arising out of any discrimination against minorities and recommending measures for their removal.
- Conducting studies, research, and analysis on the issues relating to socio-economic and educational development of minorities.
- Suggesting appropriate measures in respect of any minority to be undertaken by the Central Government or the State Governments.
- Making periodical or special reports to the Central Government on any matter concerning minorities and in particular, the difficulties confronted by them.

Powers of the Commission

The National Commission for Minorities is vested with powers of a Civil Court like the National Human Rights Commission. When the commission tries any suit or hears a complaint, it has the powers to

- summon and enforce the attendance of any person and examine him/her on oath.
- require the discovery and production of any document.
- receive evidence of affidavits.
- request any public record or copy from any court or office.
- issue commissions for the examination of witnesses and documents.

Complaint Mechanism of the Commission

- There are many grounds on which the commission typically declines admitting the complaint. These are
  - The commission does not entertain or admit cases or complaints that do not relate to minority status or rights.
  - The complaint should not be pending before another court or commission, i.e., matters that are **sub judice**[4].
  - If the complainant has not availed of other ordinary judicial/quasi-judicial/ administrative institutions that are available for **redressal**[5], the commission does not admit such matters unless the complainant has reasonable justification.
  - The complaint should not relate to events that are more than one year old.
  - Complaints should not be vague, anonymous, **pseudonymous**[6] or frivolous.
  - The commission does not entertain complaints that are not directly addressed to it.
- The National Commission for Minorities, like the NHRC, can also take action suo motu based on newspaper reports or other findings.
- Applications of complaints are required to be sent to the commission and addressed directly to the Secretary, National Commission for Minorities, New Delhi.
- It does not charge any fee for lodging a complaint. The updated contact details are available on the commission's website at **www.nchm.nic.in.**

4 **Sub Judice** It means that a particular case or matter is under trial or being considered by a judge or court.

5 **Redressal** It means remedy or compensation for wrong or grievance.

6 **Pseudonymous** It means writing or written under a false name.

14.4 National Commission for Women (NCW)

The National Commission for Women was **established in 1992** under the National Commission for Women Act, 1990.

Composition of NCW

The Commission consists of

- A **Chairperson and five members** who are nominated by the Central Government from and amongst persons of ability, integrity, and standing. They should have experience in any one of the following areas,
  - law or legislation
  - trade unionism
  - management of an industry potential of women
  - women's voluntary organisations (including women activist)
  - administration
  - economic development
  - health, education or social welfare.
- Atleast one member each belongs to the Scheduled Castes and Scheduled Tribes communities.
- Member-secretary takes care of the administrative matters.

Functions of the Commission

The commission has the following functions

- To investigate and examine matters relating to the safeguards provided for women under the Constitution and other laws.
- To present annual and other reports to the Central Government about the working of the safeguards.
- To make recommendations to central and states for the effective implementation of safeguards for improving the conditions of women.
- To review provisions of the Constitution and other laws affecting women, and make recommendations about remedial legislative measures required to address inadequacies or shortcomings in the laws.
- To take up cases with the appropriate authorities about violation of women human rights as provided in the Constitution and other laws.
- To look into complaints and also take suo motu notice of matters on deprivation of women's rights, non-implementation of laws required to achieve equality, and development and non-compliance of policy decisions, guidelines or instructions pertaining to women welfare.
- To initiate special studies or investigations into specific problems or situations arising out of discrimination and atrocities against women, and to identify the constraints and recommend strategies.
- To undertake promotional and educational research, and to suggest ways for ensuring due representation of women in all spheres.
- To identify factors responsible for preventing women's advancement,
- To participate and advice on the planning process of socio-economic development of women.
- To evaluate the progress of the development of women under the union and any state.
- To inspect a jail, remand home, women's institution or other place of custody where women are kept as prisoners, and take up remedial action with the concerned authorities for if found necessary.
- To fund litigation involving issues affecting a large body of women.
- To make periodical reports to the government on any matter concerning to women and in particular various difficulties under which women toil.

Powers of the Commission

The commission has investigating powers similar to that of a Civil Court which are as follows

- Summon and enforce the attendance of any person and examining him/her on oath.
- Require the discovery and production of any document.
- Receive evidence on affidavits.
- Request any public record or copy from any court or office.
- Issue commissions for the examination of witnesses and documents.

Quick Test 2

1. In which year National Commission for Minorities Act was enacted by the Parliament?
2. which religious communities are listed as minorities in the Minorities Act?
3. In which year the National Commission for Women was established?
4. How many members are nominated by the Center for the National Commission for Women?

14.5 National Commission for Scheduled Castes and Scheduled Tribes

- Article 338 of the Constitution of India provides for establishing a special officer for the Scheduled Castes and Scheduled Tribes to investigate all matters relating to the safeguards provided for the Scheduled Castes and Scheduled Tribes in the Constitution and report to the President.
- National Commission for Scheduled Castes and National Commission for Scheduled Tribes were constituted under Article 338 of the Constitution.
- They aim to protect their human rights and prevent their exploitation, and to encourage and defend their social, educational, economic and cultural securities as provided in the Constitution and other legislations.

  For example, the state provides reservation or affirmative action programmes for government jobs to backward classes like Schedule Castes and Scheduled Tribes who have not been adequately represented in the services under the state because of historical and continued disadvantages based on caste status and otherwise.
- Examples of special laws for protection of minorities include
  (i) Protection of Civil Rights Act, 1955
  (ii) Scheduled Caste and Scheduled Tribe (Prevention of Atrocities) Act, 1989

Functions of the Commissions

Both commissions have similar functions under Article 338 to investigate and monitor all matters relating the safeguards provided for the Scheduled Castes and Scheduled Tribes in the Constitution and other laws. Other functions are

- To evaluate the working of the safeguards.
- To inquire into specific complaints with respect to the **deprivation**[7] of rights and safeguards of the Scheduled Castes and Scheduled Tribes.
- To participate and advise on the planning process of socio-economic development of the Scheduled Castes and Scheduled Tribes, and to evaluate the progress of their development under the union and any state.
- To present reports annually and periodically to the President on,
  - working of the safeguards and recommendations for the effective implementation of the safeguards and protection, as well as welfare.
  - socio-economic development of the Scheduled Castes and Scheduled Tribes.

7 **Deprivation** It means the lack of denial of something considered to be a necessity.

Powers of Communications

Both commissions have the powers of a Civil Court just like the other human rights commissions which are as follows

- Summon and enforcing the attendance of any person from any part of India and examining him/her on oath.
- Require the discovery and production of any document.
- Receive evidence on affidavits.
- Request any public record or copy from any court or office.
- Issue commissions for the examination of witnesses and documents.
- Article 338 requires the Union and State Governments to consult the commission on important policies affecting Scheduled Castes and Scheduled Tribes.

Complaint Mechanism of the Commissions

- The commissions receive complaints from an individual or group of persons alleging denial of the safeguards provided in the Constitution, by an authority or an organisation.
- The commissions follow up with the authorities and organisations against whom the complaint is lodged. The websites of the Commissions are **www.ncsc.nic.in** for the Scheduled Castes and **www.ncst.nic.in** for the Scheduled Tribes.

14.5 National Commission for Protection of Child Rights (NCPCR)

The National Commission for Protection of Child Rights is an Indian statutory body established by the Commission for Protection of **Child Rights Act, 2005**. The commission emphasises on the principle of **universality and inviolability** of child rights and recognises the tone of urgency in all the child related policies of the country. For the commission, protection of all children in upto to 18 years age group is of equal importance. Thus, policies define priority actions for the most vulnerable children, focusing on backward regions, specific communities, or children in difficult situations.

The NCPCR believes that focusing only on specific groups of children may exclude many other vulnerable children. This selective approach weakens efforts to protect child rights as a whole. To ensure all children benefit, there must be a broader environment supporting child rights.

- The commission sees all child rights as interconnected and equally important.
- A child's ability to enjoy rights at 18 depends on access to entitlements from birth.
- Therefore, policy interventions are crucial at every stage of childhood to ensure comprehensive protection.

Functions of NCPCR

The functions of the NCPCR under Commission for Protection of Child Rights (CPCR) Act, 2005 are

- Examine and review the safeguards provided by or under any law for the protection of child rights, and recommend measures for their effective implementation.
- Present reports to the Central Government about working of those safeguards.
- Inquire into violation of child rights and recommend initiation of proceedings in such cases.
- Examine all factors that inhibit the enjoyment of rights of children affected by terrorism, communal violence, riots, natural disaster, domestic violence, HIV/AIDS, trafficking, maltreatment, torture and exploitation, pornography and prostitution, and recommend appropriate remedial measures.
- Look into the matters relating to the children in need of special care and protection including
  - children in distress
  - children in conflict with law
  - children of prisoners
  - marginalised and disadvantaged children
  - juveniles and children without family

- Study treaties and other international instruments and undertake periodical review of existing policies, programmes and other activities on child rights, and make recommendations for their effective implementation in the best interest of children.
- Undertake and promote research in the field of child rights.
- Spread child rights literacy among various section of society and promote awareness of the safeguards available for protection of these rights, through publications, the media, seminar and other available means.
- Undertake formal investigation where concern has been expressed either by children themselves or by a concerned person on their behalf.
- Promote, respect and consideration of the views of children and all government departments and organisations dealing with child.
- Produce and disseminate information about child rights.
- Compile and analyse data on children.
- Promote the incorporation of child rights into the school curriculum, training of teachers or personnel dealing with children.

Powers of NCPCR

The powers of NCPCR are

- Inquire into complaints and take suo moto notice of matters related to
  - Deprivation and violation of child rights.
  - Non-implementation of laws providing for protection and development of children.
  - Non-compliance of policy decisions, guidelines or instructions which aimed at mitigating hardships and ensuring welfare of the children, and to provide relief to such children or take up the issues arising out of such matters with appropriate authorities.
- Performing other functions as it may consider necessary for the promotion of child rights.

Complaint Mechanism of NCPCR

Complaints may be made to the commission in any language listed in the 8th Schedule[8] of the Constitution.

(i) No fee shall be chargeable on such complaints.

(ii) The complaint shall disclose a complete picture of the matter leading to the complaint.

(iii) The commission may seek further information/affidavit as may be considered necessary.

While making a complaint, it is to be ensured that the complaint is

- clear and legible, not vague, anonymous or pseudonymous.
- genuine, not trivial or frivolous.
- not related to civil disputes such as property rights and contractual obligations.
- not related to service matters.
- not pending before any other commission duly constituted under the law or sub-judice before a court/tribunal.
- not already decided by the commission.
- not outside the purview of the commission on any other grounds.

Quick Test 3

1. Which article of the Constitution provides for establishing a special officer for the Scheduled Castes and Tribes?
2. In which year the Scheduled Caste and Scheduled Tribe (Prevention of Atrocities) Act was passed?
3. In which year the Commission for Protection of Child Rights Act was passed?
4. Which national commission emphases on the principle of universality and inviolability of child rights?

8 8th Schedule of the Indian Constitution provides with the list of official languages in India in its 8th schedule.

Mind Map

COMPLAINT MECHANISMS OF QUASI-JUDICIAL BODIES

1 Quasi-Judicial Bodies

Definition
- Public administrative agencies with authority similar to courts.

Key Features
- Resolve disputes and impose penalties.
- Operate under the executive branch.

For examples
- National and State Human Rights Commissions.
- Central and State Information Commissions.
- Consumer Redressal Forums.
- Income Tax Tribunals.

2 National Human Rights Commission (NHRC)

Established Protection of Human Rights Act, 1993.

Composition
- **Chairperson** Former Chief Justice of India.
- **Members** Former judges of the Supreme Court or High Courts, human rights experts.
- **Secretary-General** handles administrative duties.

Functions
- Investigate human rights violations (suo motu or through complaints).
- Recommend compensation or prosecution of violators.
- Visit prisons and government institutions for inspection.
- Create awareness and sensitise the public on human rights issues.

Powers
- Civil court powers for summoning, document requisition, and evidence examination.

3 National Commission for Minorities (NCM)

Established National Commission for Minorities Act, 1992.

Minority Groups
- Muslims, Christians, Sikhs, Buddhists, Jains and Zoroastrians (Parsis).

Functions
- Evaluate the development of minorities.
- Monitor constitutional and legal safeguards.
- Recommend measures for minority protection.
- Investigate complaints of rights deprivation.

Complaint Mechanism
- Cases unrelated to minority issues or pending elsewhere are not entertained.

4 National Commission for Women (NCW)

Established National Commission for Women Act, 1990.

Composition
- Chairperson and five members from various fields.

Functions
- Investigate safeguards for women.
- Recommend legislative changes for women's welfare.
- Take up cases of discrimination and violence.
- Promote research and awareness on women's rights.

Powers
- Civil court-like authority to summon witnesses and documents.

5 National Commission for Scheduled Castes (NCSC) and Scheduled Tribes (NCST)

Established Article 338 of the Constitution.

Objective
- Protect human rights of SCs and STs.
- Promote social, educational, and economic development.

Functions
- Investigate safeguards under the Constitution.
- Monitor reservation policies and welfare programs.
- Submit reports to the President on SC/ST conditions.

Powers
- Civil court-like powers for inquiries.

6 National Commission for Protection of Child Rights (NCPCR)

Established Commission for Protection of Child Rights Act, 2005.

Scope
- Focus on children up to 18 years old.

Functions
- Monitor implementation of child rights laws.
- Investigate violations related to trafficking, abuse, or exploitation.
- Promote child rights awareness and inclusion in education.

Complaint Mechanism
- Accepts complaints in any language, free of cost.
- Excludes frivolous or vague complaints.

7 Complaint Mechanisms

General Procedure
- Complaints must relate to the commission's jurisdiction.
- Cannot be sub-judice or vague.

Specific Guidelines
- **NHRC** Online and written complaints allowed; suo motu action possible.
- **NCM** Focus on minority rights and grievances.
- **NCW** Address gender discrimination and violence.
- **NCPCR** Protect children in conflict with law or at risk.

CBSE TEXTBOOK FOLDER

1. Explain any one power or function of the National Human Rights Commission.

Ans. The commission is vested with the functions of inquiry and investigation. It conduct inquiry and investigation into the alleged (suspected) violation of human rights or abetment (aiding or supporting) or negligence in the prevention of such violation by a public servant.

The complaint can be filed by the victim or his/her representative, or the court may direct the commission with a complaint, or the commission may initiate inquiry and investigation on its own (suo motu).

2. Who are minorities whose interests the National Commission for Minorities intends to protect?

Ans. A minority group, by its original definition, refers to a group of people whose practices, race, religion, ethnicity or other characteristics are fewer in numbers than the main groups of those classifications. However, in present day society, a minority group refers to a category of people who experience relative disadvantage as compared to members of a dominant social group.

3. Ms. Bagchee is a Jewish woman who has married outside her community, because of which she is disallowed to perform certain religious customs. What could be the grounds of disqualification of her complaint to the National Commission for Minorities?

Ans. The ground that disqualifies one's complaint from being admitted by the National Commission for Minorities is that it does not entertain or admit cases or complaints that do not relate to minority status or rights.

4. Ms. Nisha Joseph is a Christian and her services were terminated by a school managed by state run by non-governmental organisation without any substantial reasons. What is the remedy available to her for redressal of this issue?

Ans. Ms. Nisha Joseph belongs to the minority communities and therefore she can approach the state as well as National Minorities Commission for remedying human rights violations. National Commission for Minorities Act, 1992 safeguard the human rights of minorities including protection against inequality and discrimination.

5. Smt. Savitri is troubled by the exploitation that is being faced by her deaf and dumb daughter who has been abandoned by her husband and in laws, allegedly due to her disabilities. Which forum can she approach for redressal of issues being faced by her? State its powers and functions.

Ans. Smt. Savitri can approach National Commission for Women for redressal of issues faced by her daughter.

The function of National Commission for Women are as follows

- To review provisions of the Constitution and other laws affecting women and make recommendations about remedial legislative measures required to address inadequacies or shortcomings in the laws.
- To take up cases with the appropriate authorities about violation of women human rights as provided in the Constitution and other laws.
- To look into complaints and also take suo moto notice of matters on deprivation of women's rights, non-implementation of laws required to achieve equality and development, and non-compliance of policy decisions, guidelines or instructions pertaining to women welfare.
- To initiate special studies or investigations into specific problems or situations arising out of discrimination and atrocities against women, and to identify the constraints and to recommend strategies.
- To participate and advice on the planning process of socio-economic development of women.
- To evaluate the progress of the development of women under the union and any state.

6. Why were the National Commission for Scheduled Castes and the National Commission for Scheduled Tribes created?

Ans. Article 338 of the Constitution of India provides for establishing a special officer for the Scheduled Castes and Scheduled Tribes to investigate all matters relating to the safeguards provided for the Scheduled Castes and Scheduled Tribes in the Constitution and report to the President.

National Commission for Scheduled Castes and National Commission for Scheduled Tribes were constituted under Article 338 of the Constitution. They aim to protect their human rights and prevent their exploitation, and to encourage and defend their social, educational, economic and cultural securities as provided in the Constitution and other legislations.

Examples of special laws for protection of minorities include

- Protection of Civil Rights Act, 1955 and the
- Scheduled Caste and Scheduled Tribe (Prevention of Atrocities) Act, 1989

Functions of the Commissions

Both commissions have similar functions under Article 338 to investigate and monitor all matters relating the safeguards provided for the Scheduled Castes and Scheduled Tribes in the Constitution and other laws.

Other functions are

- To evaluate the working of the safeguards.
- To inquire into specific complaints with respect to the deprivation of rights and safeguards of the Scheduled Castes and Scheduled Tribes.

7. Ravi avails benefits of being a member of scheduled caste in his service under the Central Government. In a matter of promotion with his department he moved to the Central Administrative Tribunal. As the matter is pending for a long time, he decides to obtain a speedier redressal of his cause and moves to the National Commission for Scheduled Castes.

Decide if the matter will be entertained by the commission. Also set out the various grounds on which the commission can reject a complaint made to it.

Ans. The National Commission for Schedule Castes can reject the Ravi's complaint because the matter is pending in Central Administrative Tribunal.

The various grounds on which National Commission on Schedule Caste can reject the complaint are

- It does not entertain or admit cases or complaints that do not relate to Schedule Castes and their rights.
- Complaint should not be pending before another court or commission, i.e., matters that are sub-judice.
- If the complainant has not availed of other ordinary judicial/quasi-judicial/ administrative institutions that are available for redressal, the commission does not admit such matters unless the complainant has reasonable justification.
- The complaint should not relate to events that are more than one year old.
- Complaint should not be vague, anonymous, pseudonymous or frivolous.
- Commission does not entertain complaints that are not directly addressed to it.

Exam Pattern Questions

Objective Type Questions

Multiple Choice Questions (MCQs)

1. Quasi-judicial bodies are ....

(a) public administrative agencies
(b) private administrative agencies
(c) social administrative agencies
(d) None of the above

2. The National Human Rights Commission (NHRC) receives a media report about systematic human rights violations in a remote tribal village, involving negligence by the local public authorities. The victims, being part of a weaker section of society and lack access to legal mechanisms to file a complaint. How can the NHRC act in this situation give legal provisions?

(a) The NHRC cannot act unless the victims file an official complaint.
(b) The NHRC can initiate a suo motu inquiry to investigate the allegations.
(c) The NHRC can directly prosecute the public servants involved without further investigations.
(d) The NHRC can only recommend the local government to take action without any inquiry.

3. During a jail inspection, the NHRC finds that the living conditions of inmates violate basic human dignity and human rights. What measures can the NHRC take based on its powers under the law?

(a) File a direct case in the Supreme Court and demand prosecution of jail authorities.
(b) Recommend immediate remedial actions to the government, including compensation to inmates if applicable.
(c) Directly pass orders for improving jail conditions without consulting the government.
(d) Cancel the licenses of the jail staff involved in these violations.

4. Who is the Chairperson of the National Human Rights Commission?

(a) Former Chief Justice of the Supreme Court
(b) Former Chief Justice of any High Court
(c) Any High Court Judge
(d) Any Supreme Court Judge

5. Who may file a complaint before the National Commission of Human Rights?

(a) Victim (b) Relatives of the victim
(c) Court itself (d) None of these

6. 'A', is a Christian who wanted to report a violation done with him. Which of the following commissions can be approached by him?

(a) National Commission for Minorities
(b) National Commission for SCs and STs
(c) National Commission for Human Rights
(d) All of the above

7. Which Article of the Constitution of India provides for establishing a special officer for the Scheduled Castes and Scheduled Tribes to investigate all matters relating to the safeguards provided for the Scheduled Castes and Scheduled Tribes in the Constitution and report to the President?

(a) Article 367
(b) Article 368
(c) Article 337
(d) Article 338

8. Which among the given statements is TRUE for the National Commission for Scheduled Castes and Scheduled Tribes?

(a) The Commission has the powers of a Civil Court while investigating matters.
(b) The Commission can only present reports to the Prime Minister.
(c) The Commission does not deal with complaints regarding the deprivation of rights.
(d) The Commission cannot request public records from courts or offices.

9. A media report highlights poor living conditions in a detention center, prompting the NHRC to conduct a suo motu inspection. During the inspection, officials discover inhumane treatment of detainees, including the denial of basic medical care. What immediate action can the NHRC take based on its statutory powers?

(a) Direct the detention center to resolve the issue within 24 hours without consulting the government.
(b) Recommend immediate interim relief and compensation for detainees to the state authority.
(c) Penalise the officials involved in the violation without further inquiry.
(d) Conduct a public hearing to determine the next steps before taking any action.

10. Which of the following scenarios best demonstrates the role of the National Commission for Scheduled Castes and Scheduled Tribes in safeguarding the rights of marginalised communities?

(a) A private company refuses to hire an individual based on their personal preferences.
(b) A government agency denies a Scheduled Tribe community access to reserved educational scholarships.
(c) A local club restricts membership based on financial status.
(d) A celebrity voices support for social equality in an interview.

11. Sunita, a Dalit woman, alleges that she was brutally assaulted by police officers in custody. She approaches the National Human Rights Commission (NHRC) seeking justice, as her complaints to local authorities were ignored. What is the correct course of action for the NHRC in Sunita's case?

(a) NHRC can directly investigate and prosecute the police officers.
(b) NHRC can recommend compensation to Sunita, but cannot investigate.
(c) NHRC can investigate, but only after Sunita exhausts all judicial remedies.
(d) NHRC can intervene and recommend action to the State Government.

12. 12 years old girl, Jyoti, is forced to work as a domestic help in a household, earning minimal wages and facing physical abuse. A local NGO files a complaint with the National Commission for Protection of Child Rights (NCPCR). What can the NCPCR do in Jyoti's case?

(a) Directly rescue Jyoti and prosecute the employers.
(b) Recommend compensation to Jyoti, but cannot investigate.
(c) Investigate, conduct hearings and make recommendations to authorities.
(d) Only provide counseling to Jyoti.

13. In 1992, the National Commission for Women was established under the ....

(a) National Commission for Women Act, 1990
(b) National Commission for Women Act, 1993
(c) National Commission for Women Act, 1992
(d) National Commission for Women Act, 1989

14. Match the following.

Column I	Column II
A. National Commission for Women	1. 1993
B. National Human Rights Commission	2. 1992
C. Protection of Civil Rights Act	3. 1961
D. Dowry Prohibition Act	4. 1955

Codes

	A	B	C	D		A	B	C	D
(a)	2	1	4	3	(b)	1	2	3	4
(c)	3	2	1	4	(d)	3	4	1	2

15. Statement I The National Human Rights Commission (NHRC) has the power to conduct suo motu inquiries into human rights violations, even if no formal complaint has been filed.

Statement II The NHRC can directly prosecute public officials found guilty of human rights violations without referring the case to any other authority.

Choose the correct statement

(a) Both Statements are correct.
(b) Both Statements are incorrect.
(c) Statement I is correct, but Statement II is not correct.
(d) Statement II is correct, but Statement I is not correct.

16. **Statement I** The National Commission for Scheduled Castes and Scheduled Tribes can enforce its recommendations as legally binding decisions.

Statement II The Commission can inquire into complaints regarding the deprivation of rights and suggest remedial measures.

Choose the correct statement

(a) Both Statements are correct.
(b) Both Statements are incorrect.
(c) Statement I is correct, but Statement II is not correct.
(d) Statement II is correct, but Statement I is not correct.

Assertion-Reason Questions

Directions (Q. Nos. 17-18) In the questions given below, there are two statements. Read the statements and choose the correct option.

Codes

(a) Both A and R are true and R is the correct explanation of A.
(b) Both A and R are true, but R is not the correct explanation of A.
(c) A is true, but R is false.
(d) A is false, but R is true.

17. **Assertion** (A) The National Commission for Minorities was enacted in the year 1992.

Reason (R) The primary objective is to safeguard the human rights of minorities, including protection against inequality and discrimination.

18. **Assertion** (A) The National Commission for Minorities does not entertain or admit cases or complaints that do not relate to minority status or rights.

Reason (R) It is vested with powers of a Civil Court.

Answers

1. (a) public administrative agencies
2. (b) The NHRC can initiate a suo motu inquiry to investigate the allegations.
3. (b) Recommend immediate remedial actions to the government, including compensation to inmates if applicable.
4. (a) Former Chief Justice of the Supreme Court
5. (d) None of these
6. (a) National Commission for Minorities
7. (d) Article 338
8. (a) The Commission has the powers of a Civil Court while investigating matters.
9. (b) Recommend immediate interim relief and compensation for detainees to the state authority.
10. (b) A government agency denies a Scheduled Tribe community access to reserved educational scholarships.
11. (d) NHRC can intervene and recommend action to the State Government.
12. (c) Investigate, conduct hearings and make recommendations to authorities.
13. (a) National Commission for Women Act, 1990
14. (a) 2 1 4 3
15. (c) Statement I is correct, but Statement II is not correct.
16. (d) Statement II is correct, but Statement I is not correct.
17. (a) Both A and R are true and R is the correct explanation of A.
18. (b) Both A and R are true, but R is not the correct explanation of A.

Subjective Questions

Very Short Answer Type Questions

1. What do you understand about the term 'quasi-judicial' bodies?

Ans. The quasi-judicial bodies are public administrative agencies under the realm of the executive branch and are largely bestowed (vested) with authority similar to courts. These bodies have the power to resolve disputes and also impose punishments.

2. Give some examples of quasi-judicial bodies operating in the country.

Ans. Examples of quasi-judicial institutions are

(i) National and state human rights commissions
(ii) Central and state information commissions
(iii) Consumer redressal forums and commissions
(iv) Income tax tribunals.

3. "The National Human Rights Commission (NHRC) plays a crucial role in safeguarding human rights in India". Justify the given statement.

Ans. The NHRC protects human rights by investigating violations, conducting inquiries, and recommending actions against offenders. It can summon witnesses, inspect jails, and raise awareness. Though it cannot enforce decisions, its recommendations help ensure justice and protect people's Fundamental Rights.

4. A local journalist publishes a report about poor living conditions in a government-run juvenile home. The National Human Rights Commission (NHRC) takes suo motu action and initiates an inquiry into the matter. Identify the key functions of the NHRC demonstrated in the situation given above.

Ans. The key functions of the NHRC demonstrated in the situation given above are

- **Inquiry and Investigation** NHRC initiates suo motu inquiry into human rights violations.
- **Inspection** NHRC visits government institutions to assess living conditions.
- **Recommendations** NHRC suggests corrective measures to authorities.
- **Awareness** NHRC promotes human rights and accountability.

5. How are the members of the National Commission for Human Rights appointed?

Ans. The Chairperson and the members of the National Commission for Human Rights are appointed by the President of India on recommendation of a committee which consists of the Prime Minister, the Speaker of the House of the People (Lok Sabha), Minister of Home Affairs at the center, Leader of opposition in the Lok Sabha, Leader of opposition in the Council of States (Rajya Sabha) and Deputy Chairman of the Rajya Sabha.

6. Analyse the composition of the National Commission for Minorities.

Ans. The National Minorities Commission consists of a Chairperson, a Vice-Chairperson and five other members who are nominated by the Central Government from amongst the minority communities who are persons of eminence (repute), ability and integrity.

7. Give two grounds on which the National Commission for Minorities can decline a complaint.

Ans. There are many grounds on which the commission typically declines admitting the complaint such as

(i) It does not entertain or admit cases or complaints that do not relate to minority status or rights.

(ii) The complaint should not be pending before another court or commission, i.e. matters that are sub-judice.

8. Malika Arora was mercilessly beaten by her husband and in-laws for insufficient dowry. The police refused to file an FIR because her in-laws are very affluent merchants in the area. **CBSE 2019**

(i) Identify the body she can approach for relief.

(ii) State any two powers of this body similar to that of a Civil Court.

Ans. (i) National Commission for Women

(ii) The commission has investigating powers similar to that of a Civil Court which are as follows

- Summon and enforce the attendance of any person and examining him/her on oath,
- Require the discovery and production of any document.

9. What was the objective behind the Constitution of the National Commission for SCs and STs?

Ans. The National Commission for Scheduled Castes and for Scheduled Tribes were instituted under Article 338 of the Constitution to protect their human rights and prevent their exploitation and to encourage and defend their social, educational, economic and cultural securities as provided in the Constitution and other legislations.

10. Discuss the complaint mechanism of the National Commission for SCs and STs.

Ans. The National Commissions for SCs and STs receive complaints from an individual or group of persons alleging denial of the safeguards provided in the Constitution by an authority or an organisation. The commissions follow up with the authorities and organisations against whom the complaint is lodged.

Short Answer Type Questions

1. Give any four functions of the National Human Rights Commission. **CBSE 2020**

Ans. The functions of the National Human Rights Commission are

(i) **Inquiry and Investigation** One of the Commission's roles is to conduct inquiry and investigation into the alleged (suspected) violation of human rights or abetment (aiding or supporting) or negligence in the prevention of such violation by a public servant.

(ii) **Intervening in Court Proceedings** The commission may, with the permission of the court, intervene in court proceedings concerning human rights violations.

(iii) **Inspection of Jails or Other Governmental Institutions** The commission may visit any jail or other governmental institutions, where prisoners are lodged or detained, to study the living conditions of the inmates and make recommendations to the government.

(iv) **Awareness and Sensitisation** The commission can review various human rights laws either in the Constitution or other statutes and recommend measures to the government for their effective implementation.

2. State the recommendations that can be made by the National Human Rights Commission when public servant is identified as a perpetrator of human rights violation. **CBSE 2024**

Ans. The commission make recommendation to governmental authority in cases where any public servant is the perpetrator of human rights violation.

The recommendation may include payment of compensation to the victim or suggest initiation of proceeding for prosecution of the public servant.

3. Ms. Ananya, a social activist, filed a complaint with the National Human Rights Commission (NHRC) regarding the custodial torture of a young man from a Scheduled Tribe in her district. The victim's family was unaware of the complaint procedure and lacked the resources to take legal action. The NHRC took suo motu cognisance of the case after reading a newspaper report and initiated an inquiry.

(i) **Was the NHRC justified in taking suo motu action in this case? Explain with reason.**

(ii) **What powers does the NHRC have to conduct an inquiry in such a case?**

(iii) **What possible recommendations can the NHRC make after completing its inquiry?**

Ans. (i) Yes, the NHRC was justified in taking suo motu action because it has the authority to investigate human rights violations even if no formal complaint is filed. This is especially important for marginalised groups like Scheduled Tribes, who may not have access to justice.

(ii) To conduct an inquiry, the NHRC has powers like summoning witnesses, asking for documents, and inspecting records.

(iii) After the inquiry, the NHRC can recommend actions such as compensation for the victim, punishment for the guilty officers, legal reforms, or better safeguards to prevent future custodial torture. These steps help protect human rights and ensure justice.

4. A national daily had the following news article on the plight of children in rural areas of a district- "......A daily wage earner had a big family to support. To arrange for resources to marry his daughter he gave away his two sons, Golu and Mohan, to a bangle-making unit in Ghosabad district.

In another instance in the same district, there have been reports of trafficking of young girls between the ages of 5-10 years".

(i) **Identify the quasi-judicial body that has jurisdiction over such matters.** **CBSE SQP 2024**

(ii) **State any four functions of this organisation that aim to build an atmosphere in favour of protecting children's rights.**

Ans. (i) NCPCR (National Commission for Protection of Child Rights) has jurisdiction over such matters.

(ii) Functions of the quasi-judicial body are

(a) Examine and review the safeguards provided by or under any law for the time being in force for the protection of child rights and recommend measures for their effective implementation.

(b) Present to be central government, annually and at such other intervals, as the commission may deem fit, reports upon working of those safeguards.

(c) Inquire into violation of child rights and recommend initiation of proceedings in such cases.

(d) Examine all factors that inhibit the enjoyment of rights of children affected by terrorism, communal violence, riots, natural disaster, domestic violence HIV/AIDS, trafficking, maltreatment, torture, exploitation, pornography and prostitution and recommend appropriate remedial measures for their protection and well-being.

5. A newspaper publishes an article reporting the death of a 14 years old boy in an observation home. According to the report, the deceased was placed there following charges of theft and died by suicide. Twenty other boys lodged in the same facility were reported to be anxious and shocked. A social worker charged that the staff was unskilled and insensitive in handling juveniles. Identify the body that is vested to take suo-moto cognisance of the matter and initiate inquiry in India.

List its powers in conducting investigation into the matter.

Ans. National Commission for Protection of Child Rights (NCPCR) is the body that is vested to take suo moto cognizance of the matter and initiate inqury in India.

The powers of NCPCR is to inquire into complaints and take suo moto notice of matters related to

- Deprivation and violation of Child Rights.
- Non implementation of laws providing for protection and development of children.
- Non compliance of Policy decisions, guidelines or instructions aimed at mitigating hardships and ensuring welfare of the children and to provide relief to such children.

6. State any four functions of the National Commission for Women.

Ans. The National Commission for Women has been charged with the following functions

(i) To investigate and examine matters relating to the safeguards provided for women under the Constitution and other laws.

(ii) To present annual and other reports to the Central Government about the working of the safeguards.

(iii) To make recommendations to central and states for the effective implementation of safeguards for improving the conditions of women.

(iv) To review provisions of the Constitution and other laws affecting women and make recommendations about remedial legislative measures required to address inadequacies or shortcomings in the law.

7. A 12 years old child, Rohan' is working in a factory in Delhi. He is made to work for long hours and is paid very low wages. Rohan's parents are unaware of his working conditions. A local NGO files a complaint with the NCPCR. What can NCPCR do in this situation?

Ans. The NCPCR has the power to conduct inquiries, rescue children from the exploitative situations, and take legal actions against those who are responsible. In this case NCPCR can conduct inquiry, rescue Rohan and take legal action against the factory owner for violating child labour laws.

8. Assess the role and the mandate of the National Commission for Protection of Child Rights (NCPCR) and how it works to ensure the welfare and protection of children in India. CBSE 2024 C

Ans. The National Commission for Protection of Child Rights (NCPCR) is a statutory body established under the Commissions for Protection of Child Rights Act, 2005. Its mandate includes

- Monitoring and investigating child rights violations.
- Advising the government on child rights policies and laws.
- Inspecting and reviewing institutions and services for children.

The NCPCR works to ensure the welfare and protection of children in India by

- Receiving and addressing complaints related to child rights.
- Conducting research and studies on child rights issues.
- Collaborating with state commissions and other stakeholders to promote child rights .

9. Write any four powers of the National Commission for Women, which are similar to that of a Civil Court. CBSE 2017

Ans. The National Commission have investigating powers similar to that of a Civil Court as follows

(i) Summon and enforce the attendance of any person and examining him/her on oath.

(ii) Require the discovery and production of any document.

(iii) Receive evidence on affidavits.

(iv) Request any public record or copy from any court or office.

10. In a juveniles custodial home, several juveniles report being subject to harsh disciplinary measures, including excessive physical punishment and prolonged isolation. Some also mentioned that their complaints about inadequate food and unsanitary living conditions are being ignored by the school administration. Identify the national body which can be approached. How can this body address the violation of the rights of juveniles? CBSE 2025

Ans. The National Commission for Protection of Child Rights (NCPCR) is the national body that can be approached regarding the rights violations of juveniles in custodial homes. The Commission has the authority to

(i) **Inspect custodial homes** and other institutions meant for children to ensure they meet safety and welfare standards.

(ii) **Recommend remedial actions** for cases of maltreatment, torture, or inadequate living conditions, ensuring the enforcement of child protection laws.

Long Answer Type Questions

1. List any eight functions of the National Human Rights Commission. CBSE 2017

Ans. Eight functions of the National Human Rights Commission are

(i) The commission can make recommendations to governmental authority in cases where any public servant is the perpetrator of human rights violation. The recommendation may include payment of compensation to the victims or suggest initiation of proceedings for prosecution of the public servant.

(ii) The commission can approach the Supreme Court or the High Court for directions and orders.

(iii) The commission may ask the state authority to provide immediate interim relief to the victim.

(iv) The commission may, with the permission of the court, intervene in court proceedings concerning human rights violations.

(v) The commission may visit any jail or other governmental institutions, where prisoners are lodged or detained, to study the living conditions of the inmates and make recommendations to the government.

(vi) The commission can review various human rights laws either in the Constitution or other statutes and recommend measures to the government for their effective implementation.

(vii) The commission can evaluate various factors, including acts of terrorism, which prevent the enjoyment of human rights and recommend appropriate remedial measures to the government.

(viii) The commission's role includes studying various international human rights laws and making recommendations for their effective implementation at the domestic level (within the state).

2. Explain the types of complaints not entertainable by National Human Rights Commission.

Ans. For answer, refer to text under the heading 'National Human Rights Commission (NHRC)' on page no. 245.

3. Ashok files a complaint with the National Commission for Minorities (NCM) alleging discrimination against people speaking a certain language in the recruitment for State Government jobs. The NCM however declines his complaint. **CBSE 2022**

(i) State the ground/grounds on which the NCM may refuse to entertain Ashok's case.

(ii) Who are regarded as 'Minorities' for being safeguarded by National Commission for Minorities?

(iii) State any three functions performed by National Commission for Minorities.

Ans. (i) The grounds on which the NCM may refuse to entertain Ashok's case are

(a) If ordinary judicial/quasi-judicial/ administrative remedies are available elsewhere.

(b) If the case is not based on or relating to Minority status/rights/safeguards.

(c) If the case in point is vague, anonymous, pseudonymous or frivolous.

(ii) The minorities under National Commission for Minorities Act, 1992 are referred to religious minorities of Muslims, Christians, Sikhs, Buddhists, Jains and Zoroastrians (Parsis).

(iii) Three functions performed by NCM for minorities are

(a) Monitor the working of the safeguards provided in the Constitution and in laws enacted by Parliament and the State Legislatures.

(b) Make recommendations for the effective implementation of safeguards for the protection of the interests of minorities by the Central Government or the State Government.

(c) Look into specific complaints regarding deprivation of rights and safeguards of the minorities and take up such matters with the appropriate authorities.

4. Explain the Constitution and any eight functions of the National Commission for Women. **CBSE 2016**

Ans. In 1992, the National Commission for Women was established under the National Commission for Women Act, 1990. It consists of a chairperson and five members who are nominated by the Central Government from amongst persons of ability, integrity, and standing who have had experience in any one of the following areas

- law or legislation
- trade unionism
- management of an industry potential of women
- women's voluntary organisations (including women activist)
- administration
- economic development
- health, education, or social welfare

Atleast one member from amongst belongs to the Scheduled Castes and Scheduled Tribes communities. The member-secretary takes care of the administrative matters.

For answer refer to text under the heading 'National Commission for Women' on page no. 249.

5. Discuss the complaint mechanism of the National Commission for Minorities.

Ans. For answer, refer to text under the heading 'National Commission for Minorities' on page no. 247 and 248.

SELF ASSESSMENT TEST

Objective Type Questions

1. Which of the following actions best illustrates the enforcement powers of the National Commission for Scheduled Castes and Scheduled Tribes?
   (a) Summoning officials to provide evidence regarding discrimination against Scheduled Castes in government recruitment.
   (b) Conducting cultural awareness programs about tribal heritage.
   (c) Releasing a public statement encouraging equal rights for all communities.
   (d) Organising a festival to celebrate the traditions of Scheduled Tribes.

2. **Statement I** The National Commission for Protection of Child Rights (NCPCR) can take suo motu cognisance of cases involving child rights violations.

   Statement II The NCPCR is responsible for reviewing international treaties and recommending their implementation at the national level.

   Choose the correct statement
   (a) Both Statements are correct.
   (b) Both Statements are incorrect.
   (c) Statement I is correct, but Statement II is not correct.
   (d) Statement II is correct, but Statement I is not correct.

Very Short Answer Type Questions

3. "The National Commission for Women (NCW) is essential for protecting women's rights in India". Justify the given statement.
4. How many members are nominated for the National Commission for Women?
5. "Several employees belonging to the Scheduled Caste community at a manufacturing unit in Maharashtra have alleged that they were denied promotions and assigned menial tasks despite having the required qualifications. The workers filed complaints, but no action was taken by the management".
   (i) Identify the quasi-judicial body that has jurisdiction over such matters.
   (ii) State any four functions of this body that help in safeguarding the rights of Scheduled Castes.

Short Answer Type Questions

6. How can the NHRC create awareness and sensitise people?
7. Briefly discuss the objectives and functions of National Commission for Minorities.

Long Answer Type Question

8. Arjun and Sameera decide to establish a Non-Governmental Organisation (NGO) to support underprivileged children in rural areas. They start operations without officially registering the NGO, relying on public donations and voluntary contributions. Over time, they expand their activities, providing educational resources and health care assistance. However, disagreements arise over financial transparency and decision-making. Arjun insists on complete autonomy in fund allocation, while Sameera believes they should follow a structured governance model to ensure accountability.
   (i) Identify the type of legal entity that Arjun and Sameera should ideally register their NGO as, under Indian law.
   (ii) State the key features of this type of legal entity.
   (iii) Discuss the potential risks of operating an unregistered NGO and suggest measures they should take to formalise their operations and resolve theirs conflict.

15
CHAPTER

International Law and its Institutions

International law is a framework of rules and principles binding the relations between states and governing their conduct amongst themselves.

▼ YOUR STUDY GOALS

15.1 Meaning of International Law
15.2 Historical Evolution of International Law
15.3 Sources of International Law
15.4 International Human Rights
15.5 International Law and Municipal Law
15.6 International Law and India

▼ YOUR PRACTICE GOAL

– Objective Type Questions (21 Qs ; MCQs, A-R, Statements, Matching)
– Subjective Questions (16 VSAs, 13 SAs, 7 LAs)

Every state has its own respective laws (domestic laws) which regulate the conduct of its citizens. These laws regulate the private, social, commercial and other activities of the individuals. These internal laws (municipal laws) also help in regulating the conduct and affairs of the state machinery.

Internationl law becomes more and more important because it answers all the following questions

- What happens when there is a dispute between two or more states parties?
- Which body of law governs their conduct?
- Which jurisdiction is to be applied in case of disputes related to private parties across different jurisdictions?

15.1 Meaning of International Law

- Every country is referred to a 'State' in international law.
- According to **Bentham,** international law is a collection of rules governing relations between states. This original definition did not include two important elements of modern international law i.e. individuals and international organisations.
- It is a form of law which relies on consent based governance to a great extent, as states are not ordinarily obliged to abide by it, unless they expressly consent to a particular course of conduct.

- Certain aspects are exceptions to the consent requirement, such as principles of customary international law and authoritative norms or jus cogens.
- 'Jus cogens' is a latin phrase that means 'compelling law'. It designates norms from which no derogation is permitted by way of particular agreements.
- Jus cogens are norms of customary international law which are so important that they cannot be changed through treaties.

15.2 Historical Evolution of International Law

- The term 'International Law' was first coined by the English philosopher, **Jeremy Bentham** in 1780. The Dutch jurist **Hugo Grotius** (1583-1645) is considered to be the founding **Father of Modern International Law** and has greatly influenced the development of this field. Grotius emphasised the freedom of the high seas (1625; On the Law of War and Peace).
- The origin of international law is embedded in history. It can be traced to co-operative agreements between people in the ancient middle East but the essential structure of international law was mapped out during European Renaissance.

International law is categorised into two types

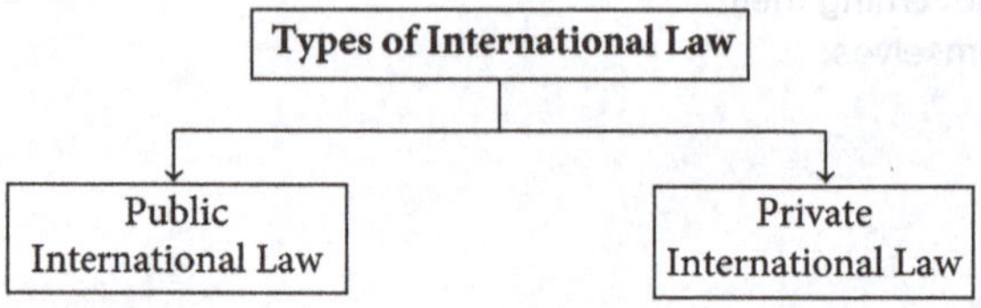

Public International Law

- Public International Law is the law that regulates relations between states.
- Public International Law is different from other types of laws because it is concerned with inter-state regulation.
- This means it deals with regulating the conduct of one state with another.
- It is not concerned with the relations between private entities (legal and natural persons) and even the domestic laws of any country.
- The **primary objective** of Public International Law is to provide for a framework of rules and regulations which help in fostering[1] stable and organised international relations.
- Some key areas where Public International Law is applicable are
  - Peace and security trade
  - Human rights intellectual property
  - Climate change
  - Science and security
  - Airspace
  - Fisheries
  - Weapons international crimes
  - Biodiversity
  - Finance development
  - Extradition
  - Sea
  - Natural resources

The World Trade Organisation (WTO)

- World Trade Organisation (WTO) is one of the global international organisation that deals with trade between nations.
- It was established in 1995 and is located in **Geneva, Switzerland.** WTO has **164 members** representing 98 per cent of the world trade.

1 Fostering It means encouraging the development of something desirable.

- WTO is the only global international organisation dealing with the rules of trade between nations.
- It is an inter-governmental organisation that regulates and facilitates international trade.
- The goal of WTO is to help producers of goods and services, and exporters and importers to conduct their business.
- There are a number of ways of looking at the World Trade Organisation as follows
    - It is an organisation for trade opening.
    - It is a forum for governments to negotiate trade agreements.
    - It is a place for them to settle trade disputes.
    - It operates a system of trade rules.

Private International Law

- Private international law, often referred to as **'conflict of laws'**, is a set of rules and principles that govern inter-state interactions and transactions of private parties.
- It is a body constituted of conventions, model laws, domestic laws of states and secondary legal sources. It commonly involves issues like
    - which jurisdiction should be permitted to hear the case.
    - which jurisdiction law should be applied to the issues in the case.
- For example, there is conflict of laws in marriage laws with respect to marriage related issues between couples belonging to different jurisdictions.

International Organisations under Private International Law

- There are certain international bodies which have been working towards harmonising private laws of different countries and bringing uniformity in their application. The bodies include organisations such as
    - The Hague Conference on Private International Law
    - The International Centre on the Settlement of Investment Disputes (ICSID)
    - The International Institute for Unification of Private Law (UNIDROIT)
    - The United Nations Commission for International Trade Law (UNCITRAL)
- The Hague Conference originated in 1893 and convened by the government of Netherlands. It focuses on developing conventions on a wide array of aspects of private law.
- The UNCITRAL works towards developing model laws and guides, related to international trade and commercial laws, including the UNCITRAL arbitration rules.
- Some of the international conventions/model laws in the sphere of Private International Law which have gained more resistance in recent times are
    - The United Nations Convention on Contracts for the Sale of International Goods **(CISG)**
    - The UNCITRAL Model Law on International Commercial Arbitration
    - The Geneva Convention on the execution of foreign arbitral awards
- The CISG is also referred to as the **Vienna Convention**, on sale of goods. It is a multilateral treaty which provides options for avoiding choice of law issues by providing a framework of accepted substantive rules with respect to contract disputes.
- The UNCITRAL Model Law has provided a framework for domestic laws on international arbitration. It is being adopted by an increasing number of countries, including India which joined it in 1996.

Difference between Public and Private International Law

Public International Law is a set of rules which governs the inter-course between nations through determining the rights and obligations of the governments of the nations. On the other hand, **Private International Law** comprises of certain rules and regulations which are established or agreed upon by private citizens from different nations who enter into transactions and that would govern them if a dispute were to arise.

International Law Vs. Domestic Law

International law is an independent system of law that exists outside the legal orders of particular states. International law differs from domestic (municipal) legal systems as follows

- United Nations (UN) General Assembly consists of representatives of around **190 countries.** It has no power to issue binding laws.
- The resolutions passed by UN General Assembly serve only as recommendations, except in certain cases such as to determine the UN budget, while admitting new members of the UN and electing new judges to the **International Court of Justice (ICJ)** along with the Security Council.
- The international court system does not have absolute jurisdiction in international law.
- Also, there is no international police force or system of law enforcement and there is no supreme executive authority.
- The UN Security Council may authorise the use of force in specific cases to compel states to comply with its decisions, only where there is a prior act or threat of aggression. Any such enforcement action can be vetoed by any of the Security Council's five permanent members (China, France, Russia, the United Kingdom and the United States).
- Thus, international law is a weak law as compared to municipal law. But unlike municipal law, international law functions in a decentralised manner.
- As per **Oppenheim's** view, International law is a true law. But according to **Austin's** view, international law is not a true law, as any rule which is not enacted by any superior or legislative authority, cannot be regarded as a law.

International Law and International Relations

- International law is a distinct part of international relations.
- States normally conform to relevant rules and principles of international laws while responding to any international situation, if and when it arises.
- The rules of international law are based on reciprocity[2] or self-interest.
- Breach in international rules by a state may result in loss of its credibility and that may affect it in future relations with other states.
- For example, if a state violates a treaty to its advantage, it may induce other states to breach other treaties. This may ultimately cause harm to the state that first violated the treaty.
- When international rules and principles are followed by states, it creates value of certainty, predictability and sense of common purpose in international affairs.
- International law is a complex system. It is founded upon the concept of equality of states, which is one of the basic principles of international law.
- However in reality, some states continue to be more important than others in creating and maintaining international law.

2 **Reciprocity** It means the practice of exchanging things with others for mutual benefit.

Role of Globalisation

Globalisation in the 1980's resulted in increase in international and regional organisations both in number and influence.

- This has resulted in expansion of international law to cover the rights and obligations of international organisations.
- New international law is now frequently created through processes that require near-universal consensus. For instance, in the area of environment, bilateral negotiations have been supplemented and at times been replaced by multilateral ones.
- They have transformed the process of individual state consent into community acceptance.
- This consensus building process has resulted in various environmental agreements and **Law of the Sea Treaty (1982).**
- The Kyoto Protocol was adopted in **Kyoto, Japan, in 1997** and took effect in **2005**.
- It is an international treaty aimed at combating global warming. It called for participating countries to reduce their emissions of greenhouse gases and carbon di-oxide emissions.

Quick Test 1

1. Who coined the term 'International Law' for the first time?
2. What are the two types of international law?
3. What is the full form of UNCITRAL?
4. Which international law regulates relation between states?
5. In which year Law of Sea Treaty was signed?

15.3 Sources of International Law

- The most authoritative source of international law is Article 38(1) of the Statute of the International Court of Justice.
- It provides that when a court deals with disputes relating to international law, it shall apply the following
  - International conventions, whether general or particular, establishing rules expressly recognised by the contesting states
  - International custom, as evidence of general practice accepted by law
  - The general principles of law recognised by civilised nations
- Article 38(1) of the ICJ divides the sources of international law, which the court will consider in its decisions, into sources of **primary** and **secondary nature.**
- The primary sources include conventions (or treaties), customary law, and general principles of law recognised by civilised nations as per Article 38 (1).
- Judicial decisions and the teachings of publicists are sometimes referred to as secondary sources or evidence of international law.

General Principles of Law Recognised by Civilised Nations

General principles are considered as the **third source** of internatinal law.

- They are used primarily to fill gaps when treaties or customary international law do not provide a rule of decision.
- They could be general principles of justice, natural law, analogies to private law, principles of comparative law or general conceptions of international law.
- The general principles of law are also found in textbooks, general surveys or manuals, treatises, encyclopedias.

- According to **Scholars**, when new treaties and customary law develop to address areas of international concern that are not previously covered, the significance of general principles will lose importance, as these gaps in international law are filled.
- **Article 38(1)** is technically limited in application to the International Court of Justice (ICJ), as the function of the court is to decide disputes submitted to it in accordance with international law and all members of the UN are IPSO Facto[3] members, it is widely accepted that this is considered as enumerating the general norm on sources of international law.
- **Hierarchy of Provisions under ICJ** The provisions of the statute of the ICJ do not suggest any hierarchy, however they are generally applied in the following order in case of disputes

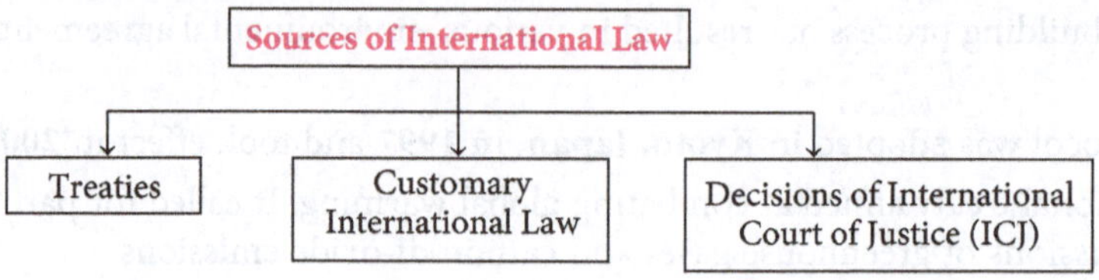

Treaties

- A treaty/international convention/charter refers to a legally binding, written, agreement in which states agree to act in a particular manner as specified in the agreement.
- Treaties are often complex documents, particularly with regards to those involving more than two parties as they are binding upon them and are to be entered into in good faith.
- Agreements between different nations without the intention of creating binding obligations are not considered treaties, however, they may have political effects.
- A treaty is not required one consolidated document but may consist of more than one related document.
- Treaties may be drafted between states by their leaders or government departments depending on the circumstances.
- However, there are a number of stages that are involved in order to convert a final draft into a binding treaty.
- The final text has to be 'adopted' in an international conference by way of two-third majority.

Methods to Express Consent to be Bound by a Treaty

A state may express its consent to be bound by a particular treaty in certain cases. The most common of these are

- **Consent by Signature** In certain cases, treaties may be given force by way of **signatures of representatives** who have been given the full powers, i.e. authorisation in writing from their state to be able to take decisions on its behalf.
- **Consent by Exchange of Instruments** In some cases, consent may be recorded by way of **exchanging certain instruments,** (documents which contain the terms agreed to by both sides) when these instruments provide that they will be in effect on such exchange.
- **Consent by Ratification** Ratification is simply understood to be the act by which a state **establishes its consent to be bound by a treaty** on the international plane. This was initiated as a measure to ensure that the **representative who signed a treaty had due authority,** by seeing whether the state agrees to 'ratify' the same.
- Ratification differs from country to country. It usually requires a sign that the state consents to follow the provisions of the treaty. It could be established through the assent by the President of the state or require a vote of a majority in the legislature.

3 IPSO facto It is a Latin phrase which means 'by the fact itself'. It means that a specific phenomenon is a direct consequences, a resultant effect of the action in question.

Customary International Law

- Customs are the **second source** of international law.
- Customary international law consists of rules that come from a general practice accepted as law and exists independent of treaty law.
- Customary international law refers to binding legal rules that have developed on global or regional levels through continued practice.
- It is important in current times when there is armed conflict, because it fills gap in treaty law and thus strengthens the protection offered to victims.
- An observed custom is extremely flexible and could be derived from the **law of nature** or **mutual consent of states**. Customary international law is comprised of two elements
  - (i) Consistent and General International Practice by States It is the widespread repetition of similar international acts over time by states (state practice).
  - (ii) Subjective Acceptance of the Practice as Law by the International Community It is the requirement that the acts must occur out of a sense of obligation **(opinion juris[4])**.
- International custom generally refers to a description of state practice. It develops from a general and consistent practice of states followed by them from a sense of legal obligation.
- Once a certain practice is understood to be customary law, states are obliged to act as the rule of customary international law prescribes.
- The **North Sea Continental Shelf cases** in **1969** (Germany Vs. Denmark and the Netherlands) confirmed that **both** state practice (the objective element) and opinio juris (the subjective element) **are essential pre-requisites** for the formation of a customary law rule. This is consistent with Article 38 (1) (b) of the Statute of the ICJ.
- Many other sources have been included to identify and cover more and more customs and practices in the international domain such as unsigned treaties and United Nations declarations.
- International customary law is probably the most disputed and discussed source of international law. For example, it is not clear when a particular state practice becomes a legally binding state practice. It is also unclear how one can identify a rule of international custom, or how one can prove its existence.

North Sea Continental Shelf Cases

- These were a series of disputes that came to International court of Justice in 1969. The case involved agreements among denmark, Germany and the Neatherlauds regarding the 'Delimitation' of areas, rich in oil and gas, of the continental shelf in the North sea.
- In these cases, the court explained the criteria necessary to establish state practice which is widespread and representative participation. It stated that uniform and consistent practice was necessary to demonstrate opinio juris. The North Sea Continental Shelf cases also eliminated the misbelief that duration of the practice (i.e. the number of years) was an essential factor in forming customary international law.

Decisions of International Court of Justice (ICJ)

- The court may have jurisdiction to decide cases in which the parties agree to appear before the court and agree to be bound by the decision of the ICJ.
- **Article 59** of the Statute of the ICJ states that decisions of the ICJ have no binding force except on the parties to the dispute, therefore, past decisions of the ICJ are not binding.
- However, ICJ does refer to its past opinions when deciding new cases.
- The court may also be a forum in a treaty between parties. In certain cases, it is compulsory to refer to the court with regards to certain disputes.

4 **Opinion Juris** It is a shortened form of Latin phrase 'opinio juris sive necessitatis', which means, 'an opinion of law or necessity'. It prevents generally unwanted general practice from becoming customary law.

- Under **Articles 65-68** of the Statute of the ICJ, the court may also give advisory opinions to countries.
- These are not binding but are only referrals to the ICJ, to understand the point of law on the matter.
- Article 38 of the Statute of the ICJ mentions judicial decisions as a subsidiary means for determining rules of law.

Quick Test 2

1. Which is the most authoritative source of International law, explain in brief?
2. What are the methods to express consent to be bound by treaty?
3. What are the North Sea Continental Shelf cases?

15.4 International Human Rights

- International human rights pose a variety of questions under the framework of international law.
- There are various problems related to enforcement and sanctions with regards to human rights.
- The Second World War had a great impact on the development of human rights law as there was a need for a system to give rise to protection of human rights. This led to a wide rise of activism and literature on the same. Some of the key conventions and treaties promoting and protecting human rights in the international sphere are

(i) Article 4 of the International Covenant on Civil and Political Rights (ICCPR)
- It states that there are certain rights such as the right to life, freedom of thought, prohibition of slavery, etc that are believed to be **non-derogable** (cannot be derogated or disrespected).
- They constitute a special place in the hierarchy of rights.
- There are also certain rights that have entered the framework of customary international law like the prohibition of torture, genocide and slavery and the principles of non-discrimination.
- These have become certain **inalienable rights** that do not require any specific treaty to be given effect to.

(ii) **Universal Declaration of Human Rights** It deals with various provisions, some of which are
- Liberty of a person **(Article 3)**
- Equality before law **(Article 7)**
- Prohibitions on torture **(Article 5)**
- Socio-economic rights such as right to work and equal pay **(Article 23)**
- Right to social security **(Article 25)**

This declaration is not a binding document. There have been many instances where it has been referred to, by cases of the International Court of Justice. It is an extremely important document for the purpose of international human rights.

(iii) **Vienna Declaration and Programme of Action (1993)** It emphasised that all human rights were universal, indivisible, interdependent and interrelated.
- This led to the creation of the post of the **UN High Commissioner for Human Rights** who would principally be responsible for UN human rights activities. The High Commissioner can make recommendations to other UN bodies and can also co-ordinate between them.
  Some important legislations and arrangements for protecting human rights are
  (a) Convention on the prevention and punishment of the crime of genocide.
  (b) The international convention on the elimination of all forms of racial discrimination.
- There are various bodies such as the commission on human rights, which has been known as the **Human Rights Council** since **2006**.
- It looks into matters of human rights issues. However, it has faced criticisms on its political selectivity and failure to objectively review the issues in certain countries.

Ergaomnes

- Generally human rights violations are dealt with by the state in which they occur. However, there are certain human rights, established under treaty that may constitute ergaomnes obligations for the state parties.
- This means that there are some violations that are so serious, that any state may take action against such crimes, regardless of whether they occurred in their jurisdiction or not.
- All states have a shared interest in elimination of such violations. This is one of the most empowering features of International Human Rights Law, where it allows the international community to also seek an active role to protect the rights of citizens of other countries.

Quick Test 3

1 Which provision of Universal Declaration of Human Rights talks about equality before law?
2 Which article of International Covenant on Civil and Political Rights talks about non-derogable rights?
3 In which year, the Vienna Declaration and Programme of Action was passed?

15.5 International Law and Municipal Law

- The interplay between municipal and international law is complex. Some authors believe that international law and the law of the domestic jurisdiction, (also referred to as the municipal law of the country) are completely different entities which cannot affect or overrule each other. However, it is not so in practice.
- Some principles with respect to difference between international law and municipal (domestic) law are
  - You can not use a domestic law to justify the breach of an international one.
  - No one can declare that their consent to a treaty has been invalidated by way of a change of its municipal law.
  - The lack of domestic legislation cannot be brought up as a defense, if there is an international obligation on the state to not to do a certain act.
  - There have been various cases on points that state that international law is prevalent over domestic law. However, it does not mean that domestic legislations carry no force.
  - Some international treaties require that countries adopt domestic legislation in accordance with the international obligations to which they have already agreed.

Application of International Law by Countries to its Jurisdiction

- Each country has its own method of dealing with the application of international law to its jurisdiction.
- The provisions of international law are often used to supplement various propositions of the domestic law when they are both concurrent with each other.
- However, whenever there is a dispute between international and domestic law, supremacy of either depends mainly on the forum where the case is being contested.
- International forums generally give preference to treaty law and other international sources whereas domestic forums give preference to statutes of the jurisdiction.

International Law in United Kingdom and United States of America

- In countries such as the United Kingdom, there is a **doctrine of transformation.**
- It states that any international agreement must be transformed into municipal law, before it can be domestically considered applicable.
- This means that the provisions of the treaty need to be transformed into local law by passing a domestic legislation with concurrent provisions of the international obligations.

- In the United States of America, **customary international law** is federal law and if the federal courts in the US determine it to be binding, then it is binding on the state courts as well.
- However, no act of legislature may be invalidated only on the basis of violation of customary international law.

15.6 International Law and India

- **Article 51** of the Indian Constitution specifically states that the state shall endeavor to 'foster respect for international law and treaty obligations in the dealings of organised peoples with one another'.
- Under **Article 253** of the Constitution of India, the Parliament and the Union of India have the power to implement treaties and can even interfere in the powers of the State Government in order to give power to provisions of an international treaty.

Application of International Law in India

- India generally follows the pattern of only affirming a treaty through ratifying it by the assent of the executive, unless the treaty requires ratification by way of an act of the legislature.
- In the landmark case of **Kesavananda Bharati Vs. State of Kerala,** it was observed that the Court must interpret the provisions of the Constitution in accordance with the Charter of the United Nations.

Role of International Treaties with Relation to the Indian Constitution

- There has been an evolution in the role of international treaties with relation to the Indian Constitution. For example, if India is a party to an international agreement to stop the killing of a species of turtle, it restricts the right to trade of certain fishermen by prohibiting killing of the turtle.
- If this treaty is to be enforced in India, the **Indian Parliament needs to pass a domestic legislation** regarding prohibition of the killing of such turtle species.
- International treaties cannot override domestic law on their own.
- Hence, these treaties will not have the same force in law if there is a contradictory law provided by the legislature.

Dispute Resolution

- In doestic cases, disputes may be resolved by way of application to court, mediation, conciliation or even arbitration.
- In international law, there may be disputes regarding a large number of issues relating to treaties or some basic covenants of international law.
- If such disputes arise between states or even between individuals and the state, there are certain institutions and mechanisms to resolve such disputes.
- There are two important international dispute resolution centres which are

International Court of Justice

- The International Court of Justice, also known as the **World Court**, is the **principal judicial organ of the United Nations**.
- It settles legal disputes submitted to it by states in accordance with international law and gives advisory opinions on international legal issues from UN bodies and agencies.
- In **1946,** the General Assembly of the United Nations, enacted the statute of the ICJ which gave rise to the institution of the International Court of Justice at the Hague, Netherlands.
- All members of the UN are party to this statute, by default under **Article 93** of the United Nations Charter, and non-members may also become parties under this article.

- The judgement by the ICJ is final. It is binding on the parties to a case and cannot be appealed.
- The ICJ has no enforcement powers, but if states don't act in accordance with the ICJ, then the Security Council (the organ of the UN) may take action, who is primarily responsible for maintaining peace and security.

Peace Palace Library

Peace Palace Library is located in the **Hague, Netherlands.** It is one of the oldest libraries dedicated to international law. It has collected international law publications **since 1913**. The main objective of Peace Palace Library is to assist the institutions residing in the Peace Palace, including the International Court of Justice, the Permanent Court of Arbitration, and the Hague Academy of International Law.

International Criminal Court

- The International Criminal Court (ICC) is a tribunal, set up through the Rome Statute in 2002. It was setup with the purpose of prosecuting criminals for **four major crimes** that are
  - Crimes against humanity
  - Genocide (deliberate killing of a large group of people, especially those belonging to a particular nation or ethnic group)
  - War crimes
  - Crime of aggression
- The ICC may prosecute criminals for crimes committed in a country which accepts the jurisdiction of the court.
- The cases may be referred by the country directly to the ICC or through the prosecutor of the ICC, who is the person appointed to try cases on behalf of the ICC.
- The ICC has limited jurisdiction over the ICJ with regards, to certain issues concerning to criminal matters listed under the Rome Statute.
- The difference in ICC and ICJ is similar to the difference between civil and criminal courts in the domestic context.
- However, the jurisdiction of the ICC is more restricted than that of ordinary criminal courts.

Other Dispute Resolution Mechanism

- Many times, the treaties signed by the states lays down the procedure to be followed in case of a dispute by themselves. For instance, the **General Agreement on Trade and Tariffs** (GATT) provides for a dispute resolution panel within its own provisions.
- Treaties often employ mediation, arbitration and other dispute resolution mechanisms to arrive at an agreeable decision. The United Nations has even created its own forum to deal with issues related to investment disputes, in association with the World Bank.
- These are some of the dispute resolution mechanisms available with regards to international disputes available to resolve disputes in international law.
  - There are many other forums that can be created which are dependent on agreements between parties and the provisions of the treaties.
  - The provisions of ICJ are also wide enough to deal with most disputes that may arise between member states.

Quick Test 4

1. Which article of Indian Constitution states about International relation and treaty obligations?
2. In which place the International Court of Justice is located?
3. In which year International Criminal Court was set up?
4. What is the full form of GATT?

Mind Map

INTERNATIONAL LAW AND ITS INSTITUTIONS

1 Meaning of International Law

Definition

- Framework of rules and principles governing relations among states and entities.
- Coined by Jeremy Bentham in 1780.

Key Elements

- Governed by consent among states.
- Includes customary international law and authoritative norms (jus cogens).
- **Jus Cogens** Compelling norms from which no derogation is allowed.

2 Historical Evolution

Origin

- Rooted in co-operative agreements from the ancient Middle East.
- Structured during the European Renaissance.

Pioneers

- Hugo Grotius, the founding father of modern international law.
- Advocated freedom of the high seas (1625).

3 Types of International Law

Public International Law

- Governs relations between states.

Applications

- Peace and security, human rights, environmental protection.
- Trade, intellectual property, extradition and natural resources.

Institutions

- United Nations, World Trade Organisation (WTO).

Private International Law

- Addresses legal disputes involving private parties across jurisdictions.

Key Issues

- Determination of jurisdiction.
- Applicable laws in cross-border cases.

Institutions

- Hague Conference, UNCITRAL and ICSID.

4 Sources of International Law

Article 38(1) of ICJ Statute

- Treaties and conventions.
- **Customary law** Derived from state practices (opinio juris).
- General principles recognised by civilised nations.
- Judicial decisions and scholarly writings (secondary sources).

5 International Organisations

United Nations

- Promotes peace, security and co-operation.

World Trade Organisation (WTO)

- Facilitates international trade and resolves disputes.

International Court of Justice (ICJ)

- Principal judicial organ of the UN for state disputes.

International Criminal Court (ICC)

- Prosecutes crimes like genocide, war crimes, and crimes against humanity.

6 International Law Vs. Municipal Law

Key Differences

- International law lacks centralised enforcement.
- Municipal laws are binding within state jurisdictions.

For examples

- UK adopts international laws through transformation.
- Indian Constitution (Article 51) respects international treaties.

7 Key Case Laws

North Sea Continental Shelf Cases

- Defined equitable principles for boundary disputes.

Vishaka Vs. State of Rajasthan

- Used international conventions to establish domestic obligations.

Sheela Barse Vs. Secretary, Children's Aid Society

- Implemented conventions on child protection.

8 Human Rights in International Law

Universal Declaration of Human Rights (UDHR)

- Non-binding but widely referenced.

ICCPR Article 4

- Non-derogable rights include freedom from torture, slavery and discrimination.

Ergaomnes Obligations

- Universal responsibility to act against grave violations.

9 Role of Globalisation

Impact

- Expansion of international and regional organisations.

For examples

- Kyoto Protocol on climate change.
- Law of the Sea Treaty (1982).

CBSE TEXTBOOK FOLDER

1. Distinguish between Public International Law and Private International Law.

Ans. Public international law (or the law of nations) is a body of customary or conventional rules which are considered as legal binding by civilised states in their intercourse with each other and is concerned solely with the rights and obligations of sovereign states. On the other hand, Private International Law (or the conflict of laws) may be defined as the rules voluntarily chosen by a given state for the decision of cases which have a 'foreign' element or complexion. The Public International Law is concerned solely with rules concerning the rights and obligation of the states (i.e. countries) interest whereas, speaking individuals and their dealings are the sole concerns of Private International law.

2. What happens in case of conflict between a treaty provision and a domestic law?

Ans. Whenever there is a conflict between international and domestic law, supremacy of either depends mainly on the forum, i.e. where the case is being contested. International forums generally give preference to treaty law and other international sources whereas domestic forums give preference to statutes of the jurisdiction.

3. Explain the existing dispute resolution mechanism in international law.

Ans. The dispute resolution mechanism in international law consist of two important international dispute resolution centres which are

(i) **International Court of Justice** The International Court of Justice, also known as the World Court, is the principal judicial organ of the United Nations. It settles legal disputes submitted to it by states in accordance with international law and gives advisory opinions on international legal issues from UN bodies and agencies. The judgment by the ICJ is final. It is binding on the parties to a case and cannot be appealed. The ICJ has no enforcement powers, but if states don't act in accordance with the ICJ, then the Security Council (the organ of the UN) may take action, who is primarily responsible for maintaining peace and security.

(ii) **International Criminal Court** The International Criminal Court (ICC) is a tribunal, set up through the Rome Statute in 2002. It was setup with the purpose of prosecuting criminals for four major crimes that are

(a) Crimes against humanity

(b) Genocide (deliberate killing of a large group of people, especially those belonging to a particular nation or ethnic group)

(c) War crimes

(d) Crime of aggression

The ICC may prosecute criminals for crimes committed in a country which accepts the jurisdiction of the court. The cases may be referred by the country directly to the ICC or through the prosecutor of the ICC, who is the person appointed to try cases on behalf of the ICC.

The ICC has limited jurisdiction over the ICJ with regards, to certain issues concerning to criminal matters listed under the Rome Statute. The difference in ICC and ICJ is similar to the difference between civil and criminal courts in the domestic context, however, the jurisdiction of the ICC is more restricted than that of ordinary criminal courts.

4. What is the role of the UN High Commissioner for Human Rights?

Ans. The office of the United Nations High Commissioner for Human Rights (commonly known as the Office of the High Commissioner for Human Rights (OHCHR)) is a United Nations agency that works to promote and protect the human rights that are guaranteed under international law and stipulated in the Universal Declaration of Human Rights of 1948.

5. Explain the various sources of International Law.

Ans. The various sources of international law are

- Article 38(1) of the Statute of the International Court of Justice
- Treaties
- Customs
- Decisions of ICJ

6. In an international conference, aimed at formulating a resolution on an environment issue between the member countries, Indian representative headed for a consent, subject to approval by Indian Parliament. The Parliament, on considering the matter, refused to give assent and thus the terms of resolution were not implemented in India.

(i) Identify the mode of entering into the treaty opted in the given condition.

(ii) Analyse the situation when it would be binding on the Indian representative to give assent to the resolution.

Ans. (i) The mode of ratification is used for entering into the treaty.

(ii) In certain cases, treaties may be given force by way of signatures of representatives who have been given the full powers, i.e. authorisation in writing from their state to be able to take decisions on its behalf.

Exam Pattern Questions

Objective Type Questions

Multiple Choice Questions (MCQs)

1. International law is based on consent-based governance as states are not obliged to abide by it, unless they expressly consent to a particular course of conduct. What is the exception to the above rule of consent requirement? **CBSE SQP 2022**

(a) Ergaomnes (b) Jus cogens
(c) Stare decisis (d) Treaties

2. A multinational corporation operates in a country where labour laws are lax, and it engages in exploitative practices against workers. The government of another country, which has strict labour laws, decides to file a complaint in the International Court of Justice (ICJ) against the corporation. Which of the following is the most likely outcome?

(a) The ICJ immediately issues binding sanctions against the corporation.
(b) The ICJ declares the corporation's practices illegal under international labour law and enforces its jurisdiction.
(c) The ICJ dismisses the complaint as it lacks jurisdiction over non-state actors like corporations.
(d) The ICJ requests member states to assemble a force to penalise the corporation.

3. In which of the following areas is the Public International Law applicable?

(a) Peace and security trade
(b) Weapons international crimes
(c) Human rights intellectual property
(d) All of the above

4. During an armed conflict, State 'A' uses weapons banned under a specific treaty to which it is not a party. State 'B', a party to the treaty, brings the case before the International Court of Justice (ICJ), citing that the use of such weapons violates customary international law. How should the ICJ assess the claim?

(a) The ICJ cannot consider the case because State A is not a party to the treaty.
(b) The ICJ will evaluate whether the treaty provision is widely accepted as customary international law.
(c) The ICJ will immediately hold State A responsible as the treaty terms apply universally.
(d) The ICJ will declare that customary international law does not apply in cases of armed conflict.

5. Four nations, India, USA, United Kingdom and France enter into an international trade treaty. The Indian delegation provisionally consented to the treaty as the final consent will follow once the Indian Parliament votes in favour of the said treaty. Which method of consent is being followed by the Indian delegation? **CBSE SQP 2022**

(a) Consent by signature
(b) Consent by exchange of instruments
(c) Consent by ratification
(d) No consent is required

6. In which of the following cases was it observed that the court must interpret the provisions of the constitution in light of the Charter of the United Nations?

(a) Kesavananda Bharati Vs. State of Kerala
(b) Maneka Gandhi Vs. Union of India
(c) Magan Bhai Patel Vs. Union of India
(d) Kharak Singh Vs. State of Punjab

7. Which statement best reflects the application of opinio juris in customary international law?

(a) Opinio juris refers to the repeated actions of states over time, regardless of whether they believe those actions are legally required.
(b) It ensures that only treaties, and not state practice, contribute to the formation of customary international law.
(c) It signifies that states follow a particular practice not just out of habit but because they believe it is a legal obligation.
(d) Opinio juris applies only when a state formally declares its legal obligation through a written agreement.

8. The Supreme Court held that India had ratified conventions regarding the protection of children and thus, placed an obligation on the State Government to implement these principles. In the given content, identify the case.

(a) Sheela Barse Vs. Secretary Children's Aid Society
(b) Magan Bhai Patel Vs. Union of India
(c) Kesavananda Bharati case
(d) Maneka Gandhi case

9. Which among the following is NOT an outcome of the North Sea Continental Shelf Cases?

(a) Recognition of state practice and opinio juris as essential for customary international law

(b) Establishment of the principle of equitable distribution in maritime delimitation
(c) Confirmation that the duration of state practice is a necessary condition for customary law formation
(d) Clarification that specially affected states play a significant role in developing customary international law

10. India signs the Paris Agreement on Climate Change, an international treaty aimed at mitigating global warming. However, India's domestic laws, specifically the Environment Protection Act, 1986, do not fully align with the treaty's provisions. What is the status of the Paris Agreement in India's legal system?

(a) The Paris Agreement automatically overrides India's domestic laws.
(b) India's domestic laws must be amended to align with the Paris Agreement.
(c) The Paris Agreement has no legal effect in India until incorporated into municipal law.
(d) India's international obligations under the Paris Agreement are separate from its domestic laws.

11. According to ………… of its Statute, the International Court of Justice whose function is to decide in accordance with international law such disputes as are submitted to it, has to apply, inter alia (among other things), 'International custom'.

(a) Article 38 (b) Article 39
(c) Article 41 (d) Article 42

12. Statement I Under Article 253 of the Constitution of India, the Parliament and the Union of India have the power to implement treaties and can even interfere in the powers of the State government to give power to provisions of an international treaty.

Statement II In the case of Magan Bhai Patel Vs. Union of India, the court held that India had ratified conventions regarding the protection of children and this placed an obligation on the State Government to implement these principles. **CBSE SQP 2024**

Choose the correct statement

(a) Both Statements are correct.
(b) Both Statements are incorrect.
(c) Statement I is correct, but Statement II is not correct.
(d) Statement II is correct, but Statement I is not correct.

13. Statement I Opinio juris prevents unwanted general practice from becoming customary law.

Statement II Opinio juris is the belief that an action was carried out as a legal obligation. **CBSE 2025**

Choose the correct statement

(a) Both Statements are correct.
(b) Both Statements are incorrect.
(c) Statement I is correct, but Statement II is not correct.
(d) Statement II is correct, but Statement I is not correct.

14. Statement I According to Article 38(1) of the Statute of the International Court of Justice, international custom is considered a primary source of international law and serves as evidence of a general practice accepted as law.

Statement II The North Sea Continental Shelf cases established that duration of state practice is an essential factor in forming customary international law.

Choose the correct statement

(a) Both Statements are correct.
(b) Both Statements are incorrect.
(c) Statement I is correct, but Statement II is not correct.
(d) Statement II is correct, but Statement I is not correct.

15. Match the following.

Column I	Column II
A. Hague Conference	1. Main judicial arm of the UN
B. International Court of Justice	2. Developing conventions on a wide array of aspects of private law
C. World Bank	3. Right to life, freedom of thought, prohibition of slavery
D. ICCPR	4. Aid the economies of various nations which had suffered immense losses subsequent to the Second World War

Codes

	A	B	C	D		A	B	C	D
(a)	2	1	4	3	(b)	1	2	3	4
(c)	3	2	4	1	(d)	2	4	1	3

16. Match the following

Column I	Column II
A. Article 3	1. Liberty of a person
B. Article 7	2. Equality before law
C. Article 5	3. Prohibitions on torture
D. Article 23	4. Socio-economic rights such as right to work and equal pay

Codes

	A	B	C	D		A	B	C	D
(a)	2	1	4	3	(b)	1	2	3	4
(c)	3	2	4	1	(d)	2	4	1	3

Assertion-Reason Questions

Directions (Q. Nos. 17-21) In the questions given below, there are two statements. Read the statements and choose the correct option.

Codes

(a) Both A and R are true and R is the correct explanation of A.
(b) Both A and R are true, but R is not the correct explanation of A.

(c) A is true, but R is false.
(d) A is false, but R is true.

17. **Assertion** (A) The ICC has limited jurisdiction over the ICJ with regards to certain issues pertaining to criminal matters listed under the Rome Statute.
Reason (R) The divide is similar to the divide of civil and criminal courts in the domestic context. However, the jurisdiction of the ICC is more restricted than that of ordinary criminal courts.

18. **Assertion** (A) The International Criminal Court (ICC) is a tribunal set up through the Rome Statute in 2002 with the purpose of prosecuting criminals for 4 major crimes.
Reason (R) ICC may also give advisory opinions under Articles 65-68 of the Statute of the ICJ to countries.

19. **Assertion** (A) Customary international law is considered a primary source of international law.
Reason (R) Customary international law is derived from the consistent and uniform practice of states, which is accepted as law.

20. **Assertion** (A) Treaties are the most important source of international law.
Reason (R) Treaties are binding agreements between states, creating specific obligations and rights.

21. **Assertion** (A) The Universal Declaration of Human Rights (UDHR) is a binding instrument.
Reason (R) The UDHR was adopted by the United Nations General Assembly as a non-binding resolution.

Answers

1. (b) Jus cogens
2. (c) The ICJ dismisses the complaint as it lacks jurisdiction over non-state actors like corporations.
3. (d) All of the above
4. (b) The ICJ will evaluate whether the treaty provision is widely accepted as customary international law.
5. (c) Consent by ratification
6. (a) Kesavananda Bharati Vs. State of Kerala
7. (c) It signifies that states follow a particular practice not just out of habit but because they believe it is a legal obligation.
8. (a) Sheela Barse Vs. Secretary Children's Aid Society
9. (c) Confirmation that the duration of state practice is a necessary condition for customary law formation
10. (d) India's international obligations under the Paris Agreement are separate from its domestic laws.
11. (a) Article 38
12. (c) Statement I is correct, but Statement II is not correct
13. (a) Both Statements are correct.
14. (c) Statement I is correct, but Statement II is not correct.
15. (a) 2 1 4 3
16. (b) 1 2 3 4
17. (a) Both A and R are true and R is the correct explanation of A.
18. (c) A is true, but R is false.
19. (a) Both A and R are true and R is the correct explanation of A.
20. (d) A is false, but R is true.
21. (c) A is true, but R is false.

Subjective Questions

Very Short Answer Type Questions

1. What do you understand about international law?

Ans. International law came to be known as a framework of rules and principles binding the relations between states and governing their conduct amongst themselves.

2. What are the two types of international law?

Ans. The two types of international law are
(i) Public International Law
(ii) Private International Law

3. Give some examples of some organisations working in the domain of private international law.

Ans. Some examples of international organisations that work in the domain of private international law are
- The Hague Conference on Private International Law
- The International Centre on the Settlement of Investment Disputes (ICSID)
- The International Institute for Unification of Private Law (UNIDROIT)
- The United Nations Commission for International Trade Law (UNCITRAL)

4. What is public international law?

Ans. Public international law is the law that regulates relations between states.

It is different from other types of laws because it is concerned with interstate regulation, i.e. it deals in regulating the conduct of one state with another and is not concerned with the relations between private entities (legal and natural persons) and even the domestic laws of any country.

5. What is the primary objective of public international law?

Ans. The primary objective of public international law is to provide for a framework of rules and regulations which help in fostering stable and organised international relations.

6. Kenwe Shurochi ex-President of Lukaya, is convicted of grave acts of brutality against his own citizens during a civil war. Identify the international institution that was set up to prosecute the accused in this instance. List the major crimes that come under its jurisdiction. **CBSE 2022**

Ans. The international institution is the International Criminal Court (ICC). It is tribunal set up through the Rome Statute in 2002 with the purpose of prosecuting criminals for four major crimes

- Crimes against Humanity
- Genocide
- War Crimes
- Crime of Aggression

7. In a regional summit in South Asia, there is widespread acceptance of the need to strengthen the bonds between nations by promoting cultural heritage and the equal dignity of all cultures. Identify the International Organisation that works towards this objective. Why was the need for creation of this organisation felt? **CBSE 2022**

Ans. The International Organisation that works towards strengthening bonds between nations by promoting cultural heritage and the equal dignity of all cultures is UNESCO. United Nations Educational, Scientific and Cultural Organisation was set up to promote co-ordination between members keeping in mind the fact mere economic and political arrangements are not enough to ensure growth and stability in member states.

8. Judicial precedent is an important source of law in domestic legislation but not in international law. The judicial precedent of ICJ is a secondary source of law. Comment. **CBSE SQP 2024**

Ans. Judicial decisions and the teachings of publicists are sometimes referred to as 'secondary sources' or evidence of international law.

The court may have jurisdiction to decide cases in which the parties agree to appear before the court, on their own behest, and agree to be bound by the decision of the ICJ.

Article 59 of the Statute of the ICJ states that decisions of the ICJ have no binding force except on the parties to the dispute, therefore, past decisions of the ICJ are not binding.

However, ICJ does refer to its past opinions when deciding new cases. The ICJ tends to examine its previous decisions, determine which cases should not be applied and rarely departs from the relevant case law.

Also, Article 38 of the Statute of the International Court of Justice (ICJ) mentions Judicial decisions as a 'subsidiary means for the determination of rules of law.'

9. 'International customary law is the most disputed and discussed source of international law'. Comment. **CBSE SQP 2024**

Ans. Customary international law is comprised of two elements

(i) consistent and general international practice by states -it is the widespread repetition of similar international acts over time by states (state practice) and

(ii) a subjective acceptance of the practice as law by the international community - the requirement that the acts must occur out of a sense of obligation (opinion juris).

International customary law is probably the most disputed source of international law. For example, it is not clear when a particular state practice becomes a legally binding state practice. It is also unclear how one can identify a rule of international custom, or how one can prove its existence.

10. What do you understand by a Treaty/International Convention?

Ans. A Treaty/International Convention/Charters refers to a legally binding written agreement in which states agree to an act in a particular manner as specified in the agreement.

11. Neha, an environmental activist, signs an international petition urging governments to ban single-use plastics. She later learns that India has signed an international treaty on plastic waste management but has not yet passed domestic legislation to enforce the ban.

Identify the four key principles that determine whether an international treaty can be enforced as law in India.

Ans. The four key principles that determine whether and international treaty can be enforced as law in India are

- **Legislative Approval** If a treaty affects citizens' rights, Parliament must pass a law to enforce it.
- **No Automatic Enforcement** Treaties do not automatically become Indian law.
- **No Override of Domestic Law** Treaties cannot contradict existing Indian laws.
- **Judicial Interpretation** Courts may refer to treaties if no conflicting law exists.

12. How are treaties ratified by 'consent by signature'?

Ans. In certain cases, treaties may be given force by way of signatures of representatives who have been given the full powers, i.e. authorisation in writing from their state to be able to take decisions on its behalf.

13. What does Article 4 of the International Covenant on Civil and Political Rights provide for?

Ans. Article 4 of the International Covenant on Civil and Political Rights (ICCPR) states that there are certain rights such as the right to life, freedom of thought, prohibition of slavery, etc that are believed to be non-derogable (can not be derogated or disrespected) and constitute a special place in the hierarchy of rights.

14. A nation engages in human rights violations within its own borders, including acts of genocide against a specific ethnic group. Under ergaomnes obligations, what are the legal responsibilities of the international community, even if there is no direct threat to neighbouring states? CBSE 2025

Ans. Under ergaomnes obligations, when a nation commits human rights violations, including genocide, the international community has a legal responsibility to act. Some violations are so grave that any state may take action against such crimes, regardless of jurisdiction. International human rights law empowers global intervention beyond domestic limitations

15. Aman, an international law student, was researching the role of the International Criminal Court (ICC) in prosecuting war crimes. He came across a case where a country's leader was accused of genocide but claimed that his nation had never accepted the jurisdiction of the ICC. Curious about how international courts handle such cases, Aman decided to study the Rome Statute and the differences between the ICC and the ICJ.

(i) **Why couldn't the International Criminal Court (ICC) prosecute the leader if his country had not accepted its jurisdiction?**

(ii) **How is the ICC different from the International Court of Justice (ICJ) in terms of its function?**

Ans. (i) The ICC cannot prosecute the leader if his country hasn't accepted its jurisdiction because the court only has authority over member states of the Rome Statute. However, the UN Security Council can refer cases, even if the country is not a member.

(ii) The ICC deals with criminal cases like genocide and war crimes, prosecuting individuals. The ICJ, on the other hand, settles disputes between countries and gives legal opinions. The ICJ's rulings are for states, while the ICC punishes criminals.

16. "International dispute resolution mechanisms prioritise negotiation and mediation before resorting to formal litigation". Analyse this statement in the context of the role of the International Court of Justice (ICJ) and other dispute resolution methods in international law.

Ans. International dispute resolution focuses on peaceful methods like negotiation and mediation before taking legal action. The ICJ settles disputes only when countries agree to its jurisdiction. Other methods, like arbitration and UN mediation, help resolve conflicts without formal litigation, promoting diplomacy and reducing tensions between nations.

Short Answer Type Questions

1 (i) **Why is private international law? How is it different from public international law?** CBSE 2020

(ii) **Why is private international law referred to as 'Conflict of Laws'?**

Ans. (i) Private international law is a set of rules and principles that govern interstate interactions and transactions of private parties.

On the other hand, public international law is the law that regulates relations between states.

(ii) Private international law is called the conflict of laws because the central concern is the determination of which nation's laws will govern a transnational matter.

2. What is meant by Ratification of Treaty? Why is it initiated? CBSE 2017

Ans. Ratification is simply understood to be an act by which a state establishes its consent to be bound by a treaty on the international plane.

Ratification was initiated as a measure to ensure that the representative who signed a treaty had due authority, by seeing whether the state agrees to 'ratify' the same. Ratification differs from country to country, but usually requires a sign that the state consents to follow the provisions of the treaty i.e. could be assent by the President of the state or require a vote of a majority in the legislature.

In multilateral treaties, involving a number of countries, ratification is usually the most preferred method of expressing assent where one party collects the ratification of the others.

3. In the given scenarios, how can international law be applied in domestic legislation in India? State the relevant case laws. CBSE SQP 2022

(i) **India is a party to an international agreement to stop taking out oil from particular species of trees**

to prevent forest fires. This restricts the right of trade of certain villagers.

(ii) India is a party to international convention relating to discrimination against women. Indian courts created legally binding obligations regarding sexual harassment.

(iii) In this case, the Supreme Court held that India had ratified conventions regarding the protection of children and this placed an obligation on the State Government to implement these principles.

Ans. (i) The given scenario is similar to case of Magan Bhai Patel Vs. Union of India, the court held that if a treaty or international agreement restricts the rights of the citizens or modifies the laws of the state, it would require to have a legislative measure.

(ii) The case of Vishaka Vs. State of Rajasthan, in which the Indian courts used the provisions of the Convention on Elimination of all forms of Discrimination against Women, (CEDAW), to create legally binding obligations regarding sexual harassment.

(iii) The given scenario is similar to the case of Sheela Barse Vs. Secretary Children's Aid Society, it was a case in which there were no contradictory laws and as they were supplementing the law already in force, the court held that the treaty could be applied directly to Indian law.

4. What do you understand about International Human Rights? Which is one of the most influential documents in this regard?

Ans. International Human Rights pose a variety of questions under the framework of international law. There are various problems related to enforcement and sanctions with regards to human rights. The Second World War had a profound impact on the development of human rights law as there was a need for a system to give rise to protection of human rights. This led to a wide rise of activism and literature on the same.

One of the most influential documents in this regard is the Universal Declaration of Human Rights which deals with various provisions, few of them are

- liberty of a person (Article 3)
- equality before law (Article 7)
- prohibitions on torture (Article 5)
- socio-economic rights such as right to work and equal pay (Article 23)
- right to social security (Article 25)

5. For adoption of International Treaties in domestic law, India and UK follow different practices in accordance with their legal provisions. **CBSE SQP 2020**

(i) State the practices followed in the UK and India.

(ii) With reference to Magan Bhai Patel Vs. Union of India, explain how the Supreme Court of India implemented this practice.

Ans. (i) In countries such as the United Kingdom, there is a doctrine of transformation which states that before any international agreement can be considered applicable domestically, it must be transformed into municipal law. This means that the provisions of the treaty need to be transformed into local law, passing a domestic legislation with concurrent provisions as the international obligations.

India generally follows the pattern of only affirming a treaty by way of ratifying it by the assent of the executive, unless the treaty requires ratification by way of an act of the legislature. In the landmark case of Kesavananda Bharati Vs. State of Kerala, it was observed that the Court must interpret the provisions of the Constitution in light of the Charter of the United Nations.

(ii) In the case of Magan Bhai Patel Vs. Union of India, the court decided that if a treaty or international agreement restricts the rights of the citizens or modifies the laws of the state, it would be required to have a legislative measure.

For example, if India is a party to an international agreement to stop the killing of a species of turtle, it restricts the right to trade of certain fishermen by prohibiting killing of the turtle. If this treaty is to be enforced in India, the Indian Parliament needs to pass a domestic legislation regarding prohibition of the killing of such turtle species.

6. What did the Supreme Court hold in the Sheela Barse case?

Ans. In the case of Sheela Barse Vs. Secretary Children's Aid Society, the Supreme Court decided that India had ratified conventions regarding the protection of children and this placed an obligation on the State Government to implement these principles. This was a case in which there were no contradictory laws and as they were supplementing the law already in force the court held that the treaty could be applied directly to Indian law.

7. The Federal Republic of Germany and Denmark are parties to a treaty that establishes the bounderies of their respective continental shelves in the North sea. The treaty provides that the boundaries are to be determined by the principle of equidistance, but also includes a provision that allows for deviations from this principle of necessary to ensure 'equi table' boundaries. A dispute arises between the parties regarding the interpretation and application of this provision.

Which key principle was established by the International Court of Justice in the North Sea Continental Shelf cases (1969)?

Ans. The ICJ held that the principle of equidistance is not the only relevant factor in determining continental shelf boundaries, but should be applied in conjunction with other relevant factors to achieve an 'equitable' boundary. The principle has since become a cornerstone of international law regarding continental shelf boundaries.

8. Identify and explain the type of dispute resolution method being used in each of the following cases

(i) Two neighbouring countries have a border dispute. They agree to sit together with a neutral third-party mediator who helps facilitate discussions, but the final decision remains in their hands.

(ii) A trade disagreement arises between two nations. They decide to submit their case to a panel of arbitrators, who review the facts and deliver a binding decision that both countries must follow.

(iii) A territorial conflict between two states is taken to the International Court of Justice (ICJ), where both parties present their arguments, and the court delivers a legally binding judgment.

Ans. (i) **Mediation** A neutral third party helps the countries discuss and resolve their dispute, but the final decision is made by the countries themselves. It is a peaceful method to avoid conflict.

(ii) **Arbitration** A panel of arbitrators listens to both sides and makes a binding decision. Both nations must follow the ruling, making it a formal dispute resolution method.

(iii) **Litigation (ICJ)** The International Court of Justice (ICJ) acts like a global court, where both states present their case, and the court's decision is legally binding on them.

9. (i) Why is Private International Law referred to as 'Conflict of Laws' ?

(ii) State any two model laws in the sphere of Private International Law that have been framed to harmonise private laws of different countries. **CBSE 2024 C**

Ans. (i) The term Conflict of Law (or private international law) refers to a set of procedural rules that determines which legal system and which jurisdiction applies to a given dispute.

(ii) Two model laws in the sphere of Private International Law are

(a) Hague Convention on the Law Applicable to Contracts for the International Sale of Goods (1986) Harmonises laws governing international sales contracts.

(b) UNCITRAL Model Law on International Commercial Arbitration (1985) Standardises arbitration procedures for international commercial disputes.

10. There was a treaty between two neighbouring countries namely Arunland and Poratia regarding sharing of special economic zones. A dispute arose between them regarding fulfillment of certain terms and conditions of this treaty obligation. Both the countries are not members of the United Nations. Arunland refused to fulfill its treaty obligations. Aggrieved by this, Portia approached the International Court of Justice (ICJ) for its advice. **CBSE 2016**

(i) Can the International Court of Justice (ICJ) give its advisory opinions to the country ? If yes, under which provision?

(ii) State the advisory jurisdiction of the International Court of Justice (ICJ).

(iii) State any two values communicated by the International Court of Justice.

Ans. (i) Yes, ICJ can give advisory opinions under Articles 65-68 of the Statute of the ICJ to countries. These are only binding, but are only referrals to the ICJ to understand the point of law on the matter.

(ii) Under Articles 65-68 of the ICJ, the court may give advisory opinions to countries. These are not binding but are only referrals to the ICJ, to understand the point of law on the matter.

(iii) Two values communicated by ICJ are

- It serves as the judicial arm of the UN.
- It facilitates the peaceful resolution of disputes between the member states.

11. The Republic of Costa Rica and Nicaragua are in dispute over a border river's navigation rights. Costa Rica claims Nicaragua's construction of a canal violates their 1858 treaty. Nicaragua refuses to negotiate, leading Costa Rica to file a complaint with the International Court of Justice (ICJ). What primary function of the ICJ? State its jurisdiction.

Ans. The International Court of Justice, also known as the World Court, is the principal judicial organ of the United Nations.

It settles legal disputes submitted to it by states in accordance with international law and gives advisory opinions on international legal issues from UN bodies and agencies.

The court may have jurisdiction to decide cases in which the parties agree to appear before the court and agree to be bound by the decision of the ICJ. Article 59 of the Statute of the ICJ states that decisions of the ICJ have no binding force except on the parties to the dispute, therefore, past decisions of the ICJ are not binding.

However, ICJ does refer to its past opinions when deciding new cases.

12. **How was the ICC set up? State the cases over which it can exercise its jurisdiction.**

Or **In the context of International Dispute Resolution Mechanism, answer the following questions** **CBSE 2018**

(i) **When and why was the ICC set up?**

(ii) **What is the jurisdiction of ICC?**

(iii) **When can ICC take up a case?**

Ans. (i) The International Criminal Court (ICC) is a tribunal set up through the Rome Statute in 2002 with the purpose of prosecuting criminals for four major crimes

(a) Crimes against Humanity

(b) Genocide

(c) War Crimes

(d) Crime of Aggression

(ii) The ICC may prosecute criminals for crimes committed in a country which accepts the jurisdiction of the court. The cases may be referred by the country directly to the ICC or through the prosecutor of the ICC, who is person appointed to try cases on behalf of the ICC.

(iii) ICC can take up cases only if countries agree to submit to the jurisdiction, in which the person who has committed the crime is a national of the country, or if it was committed in the territory of that country.

The cases may be referred by the country directly to the ICJ or through the prosecutor of the ICC, who is the person appointed to try cases on behalf of the ICC.

13. **Jerbo Mustafa was indicted on charges of committing 'crimes of aggression' in Aleppo. In this context,** **CBSE 2019**

(i) **Identify the international organisation that can initiate action against him and the statute that led to its creation.**

(ii) **State the categories of crimes that can be dealt with by this organisation.**

(iii) **Discuss the manner in which this organisation takes up cases.**

Ans. (i) International Criminal Court can initiate action against Jerbo Mustafa.

(ii) For answer refer to Q.No. 12 (i) of Short Answer Type Question.

(iii) For answer refer to Q.No. 12 (iii) of Short Answer Type Question.

Long Answer Type Questions

1. (i) **Why is Private International Law referred to as "Conflict of Laws"?**

(ii) **Explain the provisions of the following conventions that make them important in the sphere of Private International Law.**

(a) **Vienna Convention on Sale of Goods**

(b) **United Nations Commission for International Trade Law (UNCITRAL) Model Law.** **CBSE 2022**

Ans. (i) Private International Law, often referred to as "Conflict of Laws", is a set of rules and principles that govern interstate interactions and transactions of private parties. It is a body constituted of conventions, model laws, domestic laws of states and secondary legal sources. It commonly involves issues like which

- Jurisdiction should be permitted to hear the case, and
- Jurisdiction's law should be applied.

It is different from public international law, as the latter is a set of rules which governs the inter-course between nations through determining the rights and obligations of the governments of the nations, while the former comprises of certain rules and regulations which are established or agreed upon by private citizens from different nations who enter into transactions and that would govern them if a dispute were to arise.

(ii) (a) The CISG, also referred to as the Vienna convention on sale of goods, is a multilateral treaty which provides options for avoiding choice of law issues by providing a framework of accepted substantive rules with respect to contract disputes. It is considered one of the most influential documents in private international law, and nowadays is deemed to be incorporated into any otherwise applicable domestic laws, unless expressly excluded.

(b) The United Nations Commission for International Trade Law has provided a framework for domestic laws on international arbitration and is being adopted by an increasing number of countries, with India joining the list in 1996. The UNCITRAL works towards developing model laws and guides, related to international trade and commercial laws, including the UNCITRAL Arbitration Rules.

2. The term 'International law' has been defined in a variety of ways by different jurists. Discuss. **CBSE 2017**

Ans. International law has been defined in various ways by different jurists. Some of them are

- According to Oppenheim, Law of Nations or International Law is the name for the body of customary law and conventional rules which are considered binding by civilised states in their intercourse with each other.
- According to Alf Ross, International law is the body of legal rules binding upon states in their relations with one another.
- According to Lawrence, International law is the rules which determine the conduct of general body of a civilised state in their mutual dealings.
- According to modern definition of international law, it came to be known as a framework of rules and principles binding the relations between states and governing their conduct amongst themselves. It is a form of law which relies on consent-based governance to a great extent, as states are not ordinarily obliged to abide by it, unless they expressly consent to a particular course of conduct. However, certain aspects are exceptions to the consent requirement, such as principles of customary international law and peremptory norms or jus cogens.

3. The countries of Novara and Elderia are in a dispute over the construction of a dam on the river Nelara with Elderia bringing the case to the International Court of Justice (ICJ). Novara argues that past ICJ rulings in similar cases should guide the decision, while Elderia insists on a fresh interpretation of the law. Analyse how Articles 59, 38 and 38(1) of the Statute of ICJ would influence the court's decision-making in this case. **CBSE 2025**

Ans. Articles 59, 38, and 38(1) of the Statute of the ICJ play a crucial role in the dispute between Novara and Elderia over the construction of the Nelara dam.

- Article 59 states that ICJ decisions are binding only on the parties involved and in that specific case, meaning past rulings do not create binding precedents.
- Article 38 recognises judicial decisions as a subsidiary source of international law, allowing the ICJ to refer to past judgments while ensuring flexibility in interpretation.
- Article 38(1) outlines the primary sources of law the ICJ must apply, including international conventions, customary law, and general legal principles.

While Novara argues for reliance on past decisions, Elderia's demand for a fresh interpretation aligns with the ICJ's discretion to consider each case based on evolving legal principles and factual distinctions.

4. A matter relating to right to fisheries over high seas arose between two neighbouring countries of Travia and Gistonia. The matter is pending before the International Court of Justice (ICJ). **CBSE SQP 2022**

(i) State the most authoritative source of international law.

(ii) Explain the jurisdiction of ICJ.

(iii) Mention any other two dispute resolution mechanism available to Travia and Gistonia.

Ans. (i) For answer, refer to text under the heading 'Sources of International Law' on page no. 267.

(ii) For answer refer to Q.No. 3 (i) of CBSE Textbook Folder.

(iii) United Nations Convention or Contracts for the Sale of International Goods (CISG), and the UNCITRAL Model Law on International Commercial Arbitration, are other two dispute resolution mechanism available to Travia and Gistonia.

5. Trepal, a mountainous country, rich in medicinal herbs, has a flourishing domestic market of ayurvedic medicines. Gokushar Ltd. received a big order for its famous Guduchi Herbal Tea from its neighboring country, Drance. This was one of the biggest orders that the company ever received. But the very first lot was rejected by Drance as the Herbal Tea failed the 'stringent quality and generic medicine test'. Drance also canceled the remaining order. Gokushar Ltd. was very disappointed and approached the government agencies of his country for help.

(i) Which category of International law is involved in the problem stated above?

(ii) Which organisation will be instrumental in resolving the problem between the two countries? State the role of this organisation in the modern-day scenario. **CBSE 2024**

Ans. (i) The category of International Law involved in this problem is International Trade Law. It deals with rules and agreements that govern trade between countries, ensuring fair practices and resolving disputes.

(ii) The **World Trade Organization (WTO)** will be instrumental in resolving this issue. The WTO is responsible for regulating global trade and ensuring smooth trade relations between countries.

Role of WTO in the modern-day scenario

(a) **Trade Dispute Resolution** It helps settle disputes when countries have disagreements over trade policies, like in this case of rejected goods.

(b) **Setting Trade Rules** It creates fair trade rules that all member countries must follow.

(c) **Ensuring Fair Practices** It ensures that no country imposes unfair restrictions on imports and exports.

(d) **Promoting Global Trade** It encourages free trade by reducing unnecessary barriers and tariffs.

Gokushar Ltd. can seek help from the government to raise this issue under WTO trade dispute mechanisms.

6. In a global crisis, two neighbouring countries Alpha and Omega are engaged in a tense territorial dispute over a resource-rich region. Amid rising tensions and military buildups, the international community represented by the UN intervenes to mediate the conflict and prevent further escalation. All attempts to restore normalcy failed and Omega raided the disputed area to take control over it. Alpha, pleaded the violation of UN Declaration on Non-aggression among neighbouring countries.

Analyse the reasons for failure of international law to avert this attack on Alpha by Omega. **CBSE 2024 C**

Ans. The failure of international law to avert Omega's attack on Alpha can be attributed to several reasons

(i) **Lack of enforceability** International law relies on voluntary compliance, and the UN lacks a standing army to enforce its decisions.

(ii) **Veto Power** Permanent members of the UN Security Council, including Omega, can veto resolutions, rendering the UN ineffective.

(iii) **National Interests** Omega prioritised its national interests over international obligations, demonstrating the prevalence of state sovereignty over international law.

(iv) **Inadequate mediation** The UN's mediation efforts may have been insufficient or ineffective, failing to address the underlying issues driving the conflict.

(v) **Absence of clear boundaries** The disputed region's unclear boundaries and conflicting claims created an environment conducive to conflict.

These factors highlight the limitations and challenges of international law in preventing conflicts, particularly when national interests and sovereignty are at stake

7. Countries Betaland and Gammaland have a long standing practice of allowing fishing activities in a disputed maritime area. Examine how this practice may form a customary norm and its implication in resolving the dispute between the two countries. **CBSE 2024 C**

Ans. The long-standing practice of allowing fishing activities in the disputed maritime area between Betaland and Gammaland may form a customary norm in international law. Customary norms are established through consistent state practice and opinio juris (a belief that the practice is legally binding).

The implications of this customary norm in resolving the dispute are

- **Establishing a precedent** The consistent practice of allowing fishing activities creates a precedent for future disputes.
- **Defining territorial rights** The customary norm may influence the definition of territorial rights and maritime boundaries.
- **Informing negotiations** The established practice can serve as a basis for negotiations, facilitating a mutually acceptable solution.
- **Shaping international law** The customary norm may contribute to the development of international law, particularly in the areas of maritime law and territorial disputes.

By recognising and respecting this customary norm, Betaland and Gammaland can work towards a resolution that balances their interests and promotes co-operation.

SELF ASSESSMENT TEST

Objective Type Questions

1. Which of the following organisations can take up cases of genocide?
   (a) ICC (b) ICJ (c) WHO (d) UNESCO
2. Article 4 of the ……….. states that there are certain rights such as the right to life, freedom of thought, prohibition of slavery, etc. that are said to be non-derogable (can not be derogated or disrespected) and constitute a special place in the hierarchy of rights.
   (a) International Covenant on Civil and Political Rights (ICCPR)
   (b) Universal Declaration of Human Rights (UDHR)
   (c) GATT
   (d) WHO
3. Which of the following Articles of the Statute of the ICJ states that decisions of the ICJ have no binding force except on the parties to the dispute?
   (a) Article 59 (b) Article 60 (c) Article 58 (d) Article 62

Very Short Answer Type Questions

4. Can international law be directly applied in the domestic jurisdiction?
5. A recent news report highlighted a dispute between two neighboring countries over the construction of a hydroelectric dam on a shared river
   "Country 'A' has accused Country 'B' of violating international water-sharing agreements by constructing a dam that restricts water flow into its territory. Country 'B' claims the project is within its rights and beneficial for its development. Diplomatic negotiations have failed, and tensions are rising".
   (i) Identify the international judicial body that can adjudicate such disputes between states.
   (ii) Explain any four functions of this body in resolving international disputes.

Short Answer Type Questions

6. Discuss the concept of international law in the Indian context.
7. A state may express its consent to be bound by a particular treaty in certain cases. What are the various ways of giving consent?

Long Answer Type Question

8. Zenovia, a country known for its advanced technology industry, signed a trade agreement with Verland, allowing the free exchange of electronic goods. However, Verland recently imposed high import duties on Zenovian smart devices, claiming they pose a threat to its domestic manufacturers. Zenovia argues that this action violates the trade agreement and disrupts fair competition.
   (i) Which category of international law is applicable in this dispute?
   (ii) Identify the international organisation responsible for resolving such trade conflicts and explain its role in modern global trade.

16

CHAPTER

Legal Profession in India and Other Countries

The modern legal profession in India traces its origins to the colonial period, emerging with the establishment of Mayor's courts in Madras and Calcutta in 1726. After the passing of Legal Practitioner's Act, 1846, the legal profession became available to the duly qualified and certified practitioners with good character.

YOUR STUDY GOALS

16.1 Legal Profession
16.2 Lawyers and Professional Ethics
16.3 Legal Education
16.4 Opportunities for Law Graduates

YOUR PRACTICE GOAL

- Objective Type Questions (40 Qs ; MCQs, A-R, Statements, Matching)
- Subjective Questions (25 VSAs, 11 SAs, 9 LAs)

16.1 Legal Profession

- The practitioners could now practice irrespective of their nationality and religion.
- However, women were still excluded from the legal profession.
- It was through the Legal Practitioner's (Women) Act, XXIII of 1923 that they were allowed to practice in courts.

The Advocates Act, 1961

This act was passed in 1961 with an objective to amend and consolidate the law relating to legal practitioners and to provide for the Constitution of the Bar Councils and an All-India Bar. The main provisions of the act are

One Category of Practitioner's

- The old categories of practitioners (vakils, barristers, pleaders of several grades and mukhtars) were abolished and consolidated into a single category called **'advocates'** who enjoy the right to practice in courts throughout India.
- An advocate on the state rolls is entitled to practice before any tribunal, or authority of India, or any court including the Supreme Court.

- In order to be eligible for enrolment, an advocate must be
  - a citizen of India
  - atleast 21 years of age
  - must have an LLB degree from an Indian University.
- There is an additional requirement of an All India Bar Examination since **2010**, which is to be cleared by and advocate, in order to be able to start practice.
- A foreign national who is not a national of a specific country, may be enrolled on a reciprocal basis with the country of his citizenship and his foreign degree may be recognised by the council for the purpose.
- In the absence of such reciprocity, foreign nationals cannot practice law in India.
- The Bar Council has released a list of foreign degrees that it recognises.

Senior Advocate and Advocate on Record

There are two kinds of advocates according to the Advocates Act. They are senior advocates and advocates-on-record. They are discussed below

- **Senior Advocates** They are designated by the Supreme Court of India or by any High Court. The Court can designate any advocate, with his consent, as senior advocate, if in its opinion such advocate is deserving of such distinction **(Section 16, Advocates Act, 1961)**. A designated senior advocate wears a gown with a flap at the back.
- A senior advocate is not entitled to appear without an Advocate-on-record in the Supreme Court or without a junior in any other court or tribunal in India. He is not entitled to the following
  - File a vakalatnama in any court or tribunal
  - Accept instructions to draft pleading or affidavits
  - Advice on evidence or to do any drafting work of an analogous kind in any court or tribunal.
- **Advocates-On-Record** (AOR) They are entitled to file any matter or document before the Supreme Court. They can also file an appearance or act for a party in the Supreme Court. Only an AOR can file a vakalatnama in the Supreme Court on behalf of a client. Any correspondence by the Supreme Court is sent to the AOR.
- If one wants to practice as an Advocate-on-Record (AOR) in the Supreme Court, then he or she should follow the given process
  - He/She needs to practice for 4 years as an advocate.
  - Thereafter he/she must inform to the Supreme Court that he has started taking training with a senior advocate on record because he intends to become an advocate-on-record.
  - After completion of one year's training, he/she has to appear for an examination conducted by the Supreme Court itself.
  - After an advocate passes this examination, he/she must have a registered office within a radius of 10 miles from the Supreme Court building and a registered clerk.

The Bar Council of India

- The Bar Council of India was established by Parliament under the Advocates Act, 1961.
- The Advocates Act had established an All India Bar Council to regulate the Indian legal profession which includes both the **practice of law** and **legal education.**
- It constitutes the Attorney-General and Solicitor General of India as ex-officio members of the Bar Council.
- It also includes one member elected to it by each State Bar Council.
- Its Chairman and Vice-Chairman are elected by its own.
- The Bar Councils, with the consent of the High Court, make rules for
  - the rights and duties of advocates of High Court and professional conduct.
  - legal education and examinations.

History of Bar Council of India

In **1923**, the Government of India appointed the **Indian Bar Committee**, popularly known as the **Chamier Committee**, to address the existing disparities in the legal profession. Its Chairman was **Sir Edward Chamier,** a retired Chief Justice of the Patna High Court.

In its report the committee refused to organise the bar on an all-India basis. However, the committee suggested the establishment of Bar Council for each of the High Courts. The committee suggested that a Bar Council should have **power to make rules** in matters such as

- qualifications and admission of persons to be advocates of the concerned High Court.
- legal education.
- discipline and professional conduct of advocates.
- terms on which advocates of another High Court could appear occasionally in the concerned High Court or any other matter prescribed by the High Court.

According to the **Chamier Committee** recommendations, the central legislature enacted the Indian Bar Councils Act, 1926.

The act had the following provisions

- The Constitution and incorporation of Bar Councils.
- To confer powers and impose duties on the Bar Councils.
- To consolidate the regulations pertaining to the legal profession.

Functions of Bar Council of India

The Bar Council of India performs regulatary as well as representative functions.

Regulatory Functions

- To set standards for legal education and grants recognition to universities whose degree in law will serve as qualification for enrolment as an advocate.
- To regulate the content, syllabus, duration of the law degree, according to which every university can lay down its own provisions. The council has a Legal Education Committee for this purpose.
- To protect the rights, privileges and interests of advocates and through the creation of funds for providing financial assistance to organise welfare.

Representative Functions

- To lay down standards of professional conduct and **etiquette**[1]
- To lay down a procedure to be followed by its **disciplinary**[2]

- To promote and support law reform.
- To deal with and dispose of any matter which may be referred to it by a State Bar Council.
- To promote legal education and to lay down standards of legal education.
- To recognise universities whose degree in law shall be a qualification for enrollment as an advocate.
- To conduct seminars and talks on legal topics by eminent jurists and publish journals and papers of legal interest.
- To organise legal aid for the poor.
- To recognise the foreign qualifications in law obtained outside India, for the purpose of admission as an advocate in India.
- To manage and invest the funds of the Bar Council.
- To provide for the election of its members who shall run the Bar Councils.

---

1 **Etiquette** It means the customary code of polite behaviour in society or among members of a particular profession or group.

2 **Disciplinary** It means concerning or enforcing discipline.

State Bar Councils

- The Advocates Act, 1961 has created a State Bar Council in each state. It consists of
  - the Advocate General of the state as an ex-officio member.
  - **15-25 members** elected for a period of **five years.**
  - **two members** are to be nominated by the Bar Council of India from amongst advocates on the electoral roll of the State Bar Council, to discharge the functions of the State Bar Council.
- Application for enrollment is made to the State Bar Council.
- Every State Bar Council shall prepare and maintain a roll of advocates.
- In this roll, the names and addresses of all shall be entered who are admitted to be advocates on the roll of the State Bar Council.

Functions of State Bar Councils

The functions of a State Bar Council are

- To admit persons as advocates on its roll.
- To prepare and maintain such roll.
- To entertain and determine cases of misconduct against advocates on its roll.
- To safeguard the rights, privileges and interests of advocates on its roll.
- To promote the growth of bar associations for the purposes of effective implementation of the welfare schemes.
- To promote and support law reform.
- To conduct seminars and organise talks on legal topics by eminent jurists and publish journals and paper of legal interest.
- To organise legal aid to the poor in the prescribed manner.
- To manage and invest the funds of the Bar Council.
- To provide for the election of its members.
- To visit and inspect universities.
- To perform all other functions conferred on it by or under this act.
- To do all other things necessary for discharging the aforesaid functions.
- A State Bar Council may constitute one or more funds for the purpose of
  - giving financial assistance to organise welfare schemes for the indigent, disabled or other advocates
  - giving legal aid or advice in accordance with the rules made in this behalf
  - establishing law libraries.

Quick Test 1

1. Under which act were women allowed to practice law in India?
2. In order to be eligible for enrollment, advocate must be how many years old?
3. Who can file vakalathnama in Supreme Court?
4. Under which act Bar Council of India was established?

16.2 Lawyers and Professional Ethics

The Bar Council of India Rules include professional standards for lawyers. The key duties and responsibilities of an advocate are given below

Professional Duties of an Advocate

An Advocate's duties towards the court includes

- To act in a dignified manner.
- To respect the court.
- Not to communicate with a judge in private and impair impartiality.
- Not to act in an illegal manner towards the opposition.
- To refuse to represent clients who insist on adopting unfair means.
- To uphold and maintain the values of the profession.

Duties Towards Clients

An Advocate's duties towards the client include

- Being bound to accept briefs.
- Not to withdraw from service.
- Not to appear in matters where he/she is a witness.
- Not to suppress material or evidence.
- To maintain client confidentiality and not to instigate litigation or to charge contingency fee (fee depending on success or favourable result of matters).
- To ensure that his/her duties do not conflict with the client's interests.
- Not to negotiate directly with the opposing party, and to carry out legitimate promises.
- If these rules and standards of conduct are violated, then it lead to disciplinary action against advocates which may result in suspension or debarment.

Advertising by Lawyers in India

- In India, advertising by lawyers has been strictly restricted by the Bar Council of India.
- An advocate is prohibited from promoting himself through circulars, advertisements, touts, personal communications, interviews other than through personal relations, furnishing or inspiring newspaper comments or producing his photographs to be published in connection with cases in which he has been engaged or concerned.
- An amendment to this rule allows advocates to furnish certain information on their websites after intimating and taking approval from the Bar Council of India.
- However, only 5 pieces of information can be put up on the internet which are
  - (i) The name of the advocate or the firm
  - (ii) The contact details
  - (iii) Details of enrollment with the bar
  - (iv) His professional and academic qualification
  - (v) The areas of practice

Advertising by Lawyers in Other Countries

- Different countries across the world allow advertising by lawyers to varying degrees. The position in the USA is different from that in India, where lawyers have a right to advertise, but subject to reasonable restrictions.

- There are different rules of professional ethics for different states and there is also the **Model Rules of Professional Conduct** which serves as an indicative reference point. These include
  - **Rule 7.1** of the model rules prohibits false and misleading communication about services.
  - **Rule 7.2** addresses advertising and referrals.
  - **Rule 7.3** articulates no-solicitation periods (e.g. families and victims of mass disasters are off limits for 30-45 days).
- Lawyers in the US can provide information about class actions, can approach clients by handing out business cards and can advertise on internet forums.
- For class actions, appeal through referrals is permissible, newspaper and magazine ads and even mass e-mails are permitted as long as they are not misleading, and no financial incentive is promised.
- Personal injury ads are common in the USA. Often known as **ambulance chasers**, the personal injury lawyers are strong in their advertising on bill boards, newspapers, flyers and even distasteful ads on the television.
- However, ambulance chasing is not representative of professional practice in India.
- This is because these classes of lawyers solicit business by lurking around hospitals or by ads in newspapers and in Yellow Pages with toll free numbers and free consultations.
- The issue of allowing advertising and appeal by lawyers requires balancing the interest of the public which includes
  - getting information on legal rights and services through advertisements.
  - enhancement of access to justice and the legal profession.
  - the possible misuse of advertising techniques by lawyers which may lead to a loss of credibility of the profession as a whole.
- Countries like the USA, UK and France are more flexible with granting permission for legal ads whereas Hong Kong, Singapore and Malaysia are moving towards progressive relaxation. For example, in Malaysia, the Legal Profession (Publicity Rules), 2001 is a simple, comprehensive code that regulates ads in legal and non-legal directories, controls publication of journals, magazines, brochures and newsletters and interviews in the media, bars publicity through clients and even regulates greeting cards.
- In Hong Kong, lawyers are forbidden to advertise on television, radio and in the cinemas, but are permitted to advertise in print media.

Liberalisation of the Legal Profession

- In 1990's, RBI granted permission for the first time, to three law firms to establish their **liaison**[3] offices in India.
- Later, in 1995, the **General Agreement on Trade in Services** (GATS) under World Trade Organisation (WTO) came into force.
- Under GATS, a credible and reliable system for liberalising legal services was created that applies to liberalise legal profession and corporate legal services.
- Thus, legal advisory, legal documentation services, legal certification services, legal advisory and information services and other legal services were liberalised.
- The Bar Council of India has consistently passed several resolutions between 2002 and 2007 that oppose the opening up of the Indian legal profession to foreign lawyers or foreign law firms.
- In 2011, in a judgment delivered by the Bombay High Court on a Public Interest Litigation (PIL) filed by lawyer's collective, a non-profit organisation, the High Court decided that foreign law firms could not be permitted to set up liaison offices in India.

3 **Liaison** It means a communication for establishing and maintaining mutual understanding and co-operation.

- Contrary to this the Madras High Court, in response to a PIL filed by AK Balaji, permitted foreign lawyers to practice in India on a 'fly in and fly out' basis.

Women and the Legal Profession in India

- Indian women were granted the right to take up legal profession through Legal Practitioners (Women) Act after many struggles.
- In **1916,** the Calcutta High Court and in **1922,** the Patna High Court had decided that women were not entitled to be enrolled as vakil or pleader.
- In the Patna High Court case of Ms. Hazra, the court decided that the sections of the Legal Practitioner's Act referred to males and not females.
- Since **1793,** no woman had ever been admitted to the roll of pleaders.
- It was the Allahabad High Court who first enrolled **Ms. Cornelia Sorabji** as the **first Indian lady vakil of Allahabad High Court** on 24th August, 1921.
- Since then, the number of women entering into the profession has increased but gender bias is still present in the profession.
- However, recent studies have indicated that gender-based disadvantages are gradually being eliminated, especially in the corporate law sector.
- According to data tabled by law ministry in Parliament in 2022, only 15.3 per cent of lawyers in India are women.

Quick Test 2

1. Mention any one duty of advocate towards client.
2. When did General Agreement on Trade in Services (GATS) came into force?
3. Who are ambulance chasers?
4. Who was the first Indian vakil of Allahabad High Court?

16.3 Legal Education

India

- The Bar Council of India prescribes the minimum standards of imparting legal education in India.
- There are **two ways** to obtain a degree to practice law and enroll with the Bar Council. These are
  (i) A 3-year LLB programme which requires a prior undergraduate degree.
  (ii) A 5-year integrated BA, LLB/BBA, LLB/BSc, LLB programme which commences immediately after secondary school.
- The University Grants Commission (UGC), the Law Commission of India and various state governments led to the establishment of various national law schools in India in the last two decades.
- This movement was introduced by Professor **N.R. Madhava Menon.** He was involved in the setting up of the first National Law School in Bangalore in 1987 as National Law School of India University (NLSIU).
- There are now **24 National Law Schools in India.** 22 of these now have a common entrance test- CLAT (Common Law Admission Test).
- National Law School University, Delhi conducts a separate entrance test called the AILET- All India Law Entrance Test, while a number of others law schools in India have adopted the Law School Admission Test (LSAT). Some other institutions conduct their own separate entrance tests.

Globalisation and Legal Profession in Other Countries

- Globalisation literally refers to the integration of economy and legal structure of a nation with the world order.
- The term 'globalisation of law' refers to a utopian condition in which the whole world lives under a single set of legal rules.
- Such rules might be imposed by an international body, adopted by global consensus, or arrived at by parallel development in all parts of the globe.
- There is a need for transnational law in today's world of increasing international trade and inter-dependence. The increase in globalisation led to increase in the flow of people and information across borders and further increase in opportunities for trained lawyers.
- Generally, the opportunities are available in common law based jurisdictions such as the United States and the United Kingdom and Australia and Canada to an extent.
- However, unlike many other professions, lawyers trained and licensed in one jurisdiction may not be licensed to practice in other jurisdictions.
- Lawyers trained in other jurisdictions will have to requalify in order to practice in the foreign jurisdictions.
- This is because different countries have different legal systems and laws are framed according to the social, political and civil conditions of the country.

United States of America (USA)

- In the United States, after completing a four-year undergraduate degree in any discipline, students can apply for the Law School Admission Test (LSAT) exam.
- Thereafter, they can apply to a law school and enrol in a three- year JD (Juris Doctor) programme.
- The pedagogical method adopted in law schools involves the case study method as well as the Socratic Method.

Licensing Requirements

In the states of United States of America, following licensing requirement are needed for legal profession

- Each state in the United States separately administers a mandatory bar exam. Bar applicants must also satisfy the character and fitness requirements of the state.
- Most states also have mandatory or minimum Continuing Legal Education (CLE) requirements. CLE is professional education of lawyers that takes places after they are admitted to the bar. It requires minimum hourly commitments which lawyers must undertake in order to maintain their license.
- Nearly all states require candidates to pass the Multistate Bar Examination (MBE) and the Multistate Professional Responsibility Examination (MPRE).
- Some states also require the passing of the Multistate Essay Examination (MEE) and/or the Multistate Performance Test (MPT).

Foreign Lawyers Practicing in the US

- Foreign lawyers to practice legal profession in the US, may appear for bar examinations. However, laws from state to state vary in this matter.
- Students who have completed an LLM (Master of Laws) may qualify to sit, for the bar exam in California, New Hampshire, New York, Virginia, North Carolina.
- The criteria for eligibility to take the bar examination or to otherwise qualify for bar admission are set by each state's bar association.

- Some states may allow some foreign-educated lawyers to take the bar examination without earning their degree locally through the following process
  (i) Foreign-educated lawyers must get their law degree reviewed and analysed by the **American Bar Association** (ABA).
  (ii) Once reviewed, the application is either accepted or deferred. If accepted, foreign lawyers are allowed to sit for that state's bar exam.
- In New York, foreign lawyers are allowed to sit for the bar without completing any further law school study in the US.
- Even if the application is deferred, applicants may be asked to complete course work at an ABA-approved college before sitting for the bar exam.
- This course includes a one-year LLM programme at an ABA accredited school.

Foreign Legal Consultant (FLC)

Foreign lawyers may also take up work as a **Foreign Legal Consultant (FLC)**. As an FLC, it is possible to advise on home country law and international law, but not to appear in court.

FLCs are recognised in Alabama, Arizona, Connecticut, District of Columbia, Florida, Georgia, Hawaii, Illinois, Indiana, Michigan, Minnesota, Missouri, New Jersey, New York, Ohio, Oregon, Texas and Washington. California does not allow FLCs.

The American Bar Association (ABA)

- The American Bar Association acts as a voluntary professional body at the federal level for US lawyers. **ABA was founded in 1878.**
- It is the largest voluntary professional body in the world and has a significant international profile.
- Members of the legal profession in other countries can become international associates of the ABA.
- ABA supports the legal profession with practical resources for legal professionals while improving the administration of justice, accrediting law schools, establishing model ethical codes and more.
- Its goals include, serving the members, improving the profession, eliminating bias and enhancing diversity and advancing the rule of law.
- The ABA has been accrediting schools since **1923**. It also publishes the ABA journal.

Regulation of Legal Profession by State Bar Associations

- Bar associations in the US are divided into two categories which are unified and non-unified.
- In states with a unified bar, the State Bar Association have the responsibilities of regulating lawyers (admission, discipline and so on) with activities to support their members as a professional body.
- Membership is mandatory in order to practice in such states.
- There are **32 states** with **unified bars**, including California, Texas and Florida.
- In states with a non-unified bar, responsibility for admitting and regulating lawyers lies with the state, Supreme Court or board of bar examiners.

United Kingdom (UK)

- Legal education in the UK consists of a three-year LLB, directly after secondary school.
- Graduates from fields other than law and non-graduates can become solicitors, but LLB is the most straightforward path.
- Clinical education continues after the LLB through the **Legal Practice Course (LPC)** and training contracts.

- Graduates are required to complete the **Bar Vocational Course (BVC)** to become a barrister, instead of the LPC. Then, they have to seek a 'pupillage' instead of a training contract.
- There are a number of differences between barristers and solicitors, but the most significant among them is that barristers can appear in all courts while solicitors can only appear in higher courts, if they qualify to become solicitor advocates.
- To qualify as a barrister or solicitor students are required to obtain a qualifying law degree. For an LLB to meet the requirements of a qualifying law degree, the course must cover legal research skills and the seven foundation subjects as follows

  (i) Obligations I (Contract Law)
  (ii) Obligations II (Tort Law)
  (iii) Foundations of Criminal Law
  (iv) Foundations of Equity & the Law of Trusts
  (v) Foundations of the Law of the European Union
  (vi) Foundations of Property Law
  (vii) Foundations of Public Law

- The requirement for completion of the academic stage is a lower second class UK Honours degree. Students who have not taken an undergraduate degree in law can still become lawyers.
- For students with undergraduate degrees in subjects besides law, it is possible to enrol in the Graduate Diploma in Law Course (GDL), which is commonly known as **Common Professional Examination** (CPE) or a conversion course.
- This is a one year full-time or two years part-time course, which covers the seven foundation subjects.
- Legal education in Scotland is slightly different than the rest of the UK. The LLB degrees awarded in other parts of the UK are not recognised as part of the qualification process in Scotland (and vice-versa).

Foreign Lawyers and Practicing in the UK

- It is possible to practice law for qualified lawyers coming from outside England and Wales.
- The Solicitors Regulation Authority (SRA) does not impose any formal experience requirements, in order to re-qualify as solicitors in England and Wales.
- Some law firms may express their own requirements which can differ from the SRA guidelines.
- Candidates can take the qualified Lawyers Transfer Scheme in order to qualify under this jurisdiction.
- Lawyers coming from EU Member States can depend upon EU Directive 77/249 in this area.

16.4 Opportunities for Law Graduates

- Law is an exciting and challenging profession.
- Law graduates in India have various options and opportunities open to them after their graduation.
- Following are some of the opportunities available to graduates after they obtain their degrees in law
  - **Litigation** Graduates may practice as an advocate in a court of law. This can be achieved by working under experienced advocates, or being attached to litigation departments of law firms or companies in order to practice in the Courts of India.
  - **Law Firm Practice** Law firms vary in size and practice areas. They may range from boutique law firms specialising in specific areas of law (such as Intellectual Property Rights and Tax law), to mid-sized law firms as well as large law firms which are full service law firms with different practice groups such as

    – general corporate
    – mergers and acquisitions
    – employment law
    – taxation
    – international trade
    – insurance
    – intellectual property
    – project finance and infrastructure

- Transactional law at law firms typically involves practicing in commercial and economic laws and advising on issues concerning to a commercial transaction between two or more parties. This would usually include
  - advising on the laws applicable to the transaction.
  - drafting contracts and other documents.
  - helping clients with the commercial negotiations .
  - management and execution (i.e. successful completion) of the transaction.
  - Corporate lawyers would also advise on regulatory issues and legal compliance. Centres for Legal Process Outsourcing (LPOs) also have a lot of transactional work.
- **Corporate Sector** Large corporations often have an in-house legal practice. An in-house counsel will give legal advice to the company. They have expertise in the business of the company and are responsible for ensuring that the business of the company is being run in compliance with applicable laws and when required will bring in external lawyers.

  Several organisations such as commercial banks, multi-national companies, investment firms, insurance companies, e-commerce ventures, media houses are hiring law graduates for managing their legal departments.
- **Public Policy** Lawyers have an important role in formulating and advising on public policy. Several organisations employ law graduates for policy making and have institutionalised fellowships where law graduates can be Research Assistants.

  For example, a law graduate interested in public policy can apply to serve as a Legislative Assistant under the **Legislative Assistants to Members of Parliament (LAMP)** fellowship programme run by **PRS Legislative Research.**

  Institutions such as **Competition Commission of India** (CCI) and **Securities Exchange Board of India** (SEBI) also employ law graduates for policy making in the respective fields. Law firms have established Government Policy Departments where they employ for policy research.
- **Legal Research and Academia** Law graduates may take up teaching and research as a profession. At least a postgraduate degree in law or related disciplines is expected to build a career in academics.

  Universities employ postgraduates in law as lecturers/Assistant Professors at the beginning of their careers. Short-term positions and opportunities as Visiting Professors/Adjunct Professors are also available in academia.
- **Non-Governmental Organisations** Not-for-profit organisations, especially organisations with a social justice orientation have positions for law graduates. These range from small grass-root level organisations to large, well-funded organisations.

  They may be general in nature **providing free legal aid,** legal education and legal awareness to more specialist organisations involved in areas such as women and child rights, environmental law, employment laws, consumer rights and public health.
- **Government Institutions** Government departments, statutory authorities, public sector undertakings and regulatory bodies also provide interesting opportunities to lawyers.

  Graduates may opt for jobs in the government sector in institutions such as National Human Rights Commission, Law Commission of India and National Commission for Women, etc.
- **Further Study** Law is an interdisciplinary subject and graduates may opt for further studies in related disciplines such as business, economics, anthropology and sociology.

  Traditionally, law graduates pursue Master of Laws (LLM) degree followed by research degrees such as M Phil or PhD. A variety of opportunities are available in India and abroad for advanced studies in law.

- **Judicial Services/Clerkships** The court system provides several avenues to law graduates. The higher judiciary, that is, judges of the High Courts and Supreme Courts have law clerks cum research assistants who assist a judge in researching cases, maintaining paperwork, etc. Judicial clerks often sit in court hearings with the judges.

  Graduates may write the All India Judicial Services Examination to avail positions in the Indian Judiciary. Qualifying candidates began in sub-ordinate courts and may then progress to hold offices in the High Courts and even the Supreme Court of India.
- **Judge Advocate General (JAG) Officer** The Judge Advocate General's (JAG) Department is the legal branch of the Indian Army. It deals with military related disciplinary cases and litigation.

  It assists in providing legal assistance to the army in human rights matters and the rule of law among other things.

  The department consists of legally qualified army officers who are educated in military law and provide legal help to the military in all aspects.

  The JAG's Department is also responsible for emerging fields of military law such as those related to cyber laws, space laws, terrorism and human rights violations. The service rendered in the JAG's Department is considered to be judicial service as per the regulations for the Indian army.

Quick Test 3

1. What is globalisation?
2. When did American Bar Association founded?
3. What is the full form of LAMP?
4. Mention any one opportunity for law graduation.

Mind Map

LEGAL PROFESSION IN INDIA AND OTHER COUNTRIES

1 Introduction to Legal Profession

Historical Context

- Emerged during the colonial period with Mayor's Courts in 1726 (Madras, Calcutta).

Legal Practitioners Act, 1846

- Allowed qualified practitioners to practice irrespective of religion or nationality.

Key Milestone

- **Legal Practitioners (Women) Act, 1923** Allowed women into the profession.

2 The Advocates Act, 1961

Objective

- Consolidate law on legal practitioners.
- Establish Bar Councils and All India Bar.

Key Features

- Abolished old practitioner categories (vakils, barristers, pleaders).
- **Created a unified category** Advocates.
- Advocates can practice in any court in India.

Eligibility for Enrollment

- Indian citizenship.
- Minimum 21 years of age.
- LLB degree from a recognised university.
- Must pass the All India Bar Examination (since 2010).

3 Types of Advocates

Senior Advocate

- Designated by Supreme Court/High Court.
- **Restrictions** Cannot file vakalatnama, draft pleadings, or appear without a junior.

Advocate-on-Record (AOR)

- Authorised to file matters in the Supreme Court.
- Requires four years of practice, training under an AOR, and passing a Supreme Court exam.

4 Bar Councils

Bar Council of India (BCI)

- Established under the Advocates Act, 1961.

Functions

- Regulate professional conduct and legal education.
- Approve law degrees and maintain disciplinary jurisdiction.
- Organise legal aid and seminars.
- Recognise foreign law qualifications.

State Bar Councils

- Constituted in each state.

Functions

- Maintain advocate rolls.
- Handle misconduct cases.
- Provide welfare schemes and legal aid.

5 Professional Ethics for Lawyers

Duties Towards Court

- Act with dignity and respect.
- Avoid private communication with judges.

Duties Towards Clients

- Maintain confidentiality.
- Avoid conflicts of interest.
- Refuse unfair practices.

Advertising Restrictions

- Limited information allowed (e.g., name, contact, qualifications).
- Bar Council approval required for online listings.

6 Legal Education in India

Programmes

- 3-year LLB for graduates.
- 5-year integrated LLB (BA LLB, BBA LLB).

Institutions

- National Law Schools (e.g., NLSIU, established 1987).
- **Entrance Exams** CLAT, AILET, LSAT.

Regulated by

- Bar Council of India.

7 Globalisation and Legal Profession

Global Impact

- Liberalisation of legal services under WTO and GATS.

Challenges for Foreign Lawyers

- Re-qualification required in jurisdictions like the US and UK.

Key Frameworks

- American Bar Association (ABA).
- Solicitors Regulation Authority (SRA) in the UK.

8 Opportunities for Law Graduates

Litigation

- Practice in courts under experienced advocates.

Corporate Sector

- In-house legal counsel for companies.

Law Firms Practice

- Specialised areas (e.g., M&A, IP law, taxation).

Public Policy

- Roles in policy-making bodies like CCI, SEBI.

Academia and Research

- Teaching positions and fellowships.

NGOs

- Focused on legal aid and awareness.

Judiciary

- Judicial Services Examination for subordinate courts.

Military Law

- Judge Advocate General (JAG) roles.

CBSE TEXTBOOK FOLDER

1. Write short notes on the following

(i) **Women and the Legal Profession**

(ii) **Professional Ethics for lawyers**

(iii) **Eligibility and qualification to practice as an Advocate in India**

(iv) **Legal Education in India**

Ans. (i) Indian women were granted the right to take up legal profession through Legal Practitioners (Women) Act after many struggles. In 1916, the Calcutta High Court and in 1922, the Patna High Court had decided that women were not entitled to be enrolled as vakil or pleader.

In the Patna High Court case of Ms. Hazra, the court decided that the sections of the Legal Practitioner's Act referred to males and not females. Since 1793, no women had ever been admitted to the roll of pleaders. It was the Allahabad High Court who first enrolled Ms. Cornelia Sorabji as the first Indian lady vakil of Allahabad High Court on 24th August, 1921.

Since then, the number of women entering into the profession has increased but gender bias is still present in the profession. However, recent studies have indicated that gender-based disadvantages are gradually being eliminated, especially in the corporate law sector.

(ii) **Professional Ethics for Lawyers** An advocate has following duties

- To act in a dignified manner.
- To respect the court.
- Not to communicate with a judge in private and impair impartiality.
- Not to act in an illegal manner towards the opposition.
- To refuse to represent clients who insist on adopting unfair means.
- In addition, being an officer of the court, an advocate is expected to uphold and maintain the values of the profession.

(iii) **Eligibility and Qualification to Practice as an Advocate in India** In order to be eligible for enrollment, an advocate must be

- a citizen of India
- atleast 21 years of age
- must have an LLB degree from an Indian University

(iv) **Legal Education in India** Legal education in India is regulated by the Bar Council of India. There are two ways to obtain a degree to practice law and enroll with the Bar Council

(a) A 3-year LLB programme which requires a prior undergraduate degree

(b) A 5-year integrated BA, LLB/BBA., LLB/BSc, LLB program which commences immediately after secondary school.

Some universities offer both the five year and the three year degree programmes.

2. What changes did the Advocates' Act bring about in India?

Ans. After the enactment of the Advocates Act, 1961, all the old categories of practitioners (vakils, barristers, pleaders of several grades and mukhtars) were abolished and consolidated into a single category called advocates who enjoy the right to practice in courts throughout India.

The Advocates Act also established an All India Bar Council for the first time, with the Attorney-General and Solicitor General of India as ex-officio members of the Bar Council.

3. Discuss the main points of difference between Senior Advocate and Advocate-on-record.

Ans. The difference between senior advocate and advocate-on-record are as follows

(i) A senior advocate is an advocate who has been officially designated as such by either the Supreme Court or the High Court. An advocate-on-record (AOR) is an advocate who has passed a qualifying examination conducted by the Supreme Court.

(ii) A senior advocate argues cases in court upon instructions from another advocate. The AOR is hold accountable, by the Supreme Court, for the conduct of the case. Any notice and correspondence from the Supreme Court are sent to the AOR, and not to the party.

(iii) A senior advocate cannot file a vakalathnama. Only an AOR can file a vakalath, a petition, an affidavit or any other application on behalf of a party in the Supreme Court.

4. Compare the rules regarding advertising by als in India and other countries.

Ans. The right of advocates to advertise their services or solicit clients has been a controversial issue in the field of legal ethics and professionalism. In India, advertising by lawyers has been strictly restricted by the Bar Council of India.

An advocate is prohibited from promoting himself through circulars, advertisements, touts, personal communications, interviews other than through personal relations, furnishing or inspiring newspaper comments or producing his photographs to be published in connection with cases in which he has been engaged of concerned. An amendment to this rule allows advocates to furnish certain information on their websites after intimating and taking approval from the Bar Council of India.

However, different countries across the world allow advertising by lawyers to varying degrees. Lawyers in the US can provide information about class actions, can approach clients by handing out business cards and can advertise on internet forums. Countries like the USA, UK and France are more flexible with granting permission for legal ads whereas Hong Kong, Singapore and Malaysia are moving towards progressive relaxation. In Malaysia, for example, the Legal Profession (Publicity Rules), 2001, is a simple, comprehensive code that regulates ads in legal and non-legal directories, controls publication of journals, magazines, brochures and newsletters and interviews in the media, bars publicity through clients and even regulates greeting cards. In Hong Kong, lawyers are forbidden to advertise on television, radio and in the cinemas but are permitted to advertise in print media.

5. How is the Bar Council of India organised? What are its roles and functions? Trace the history of the Bar Council.

Ans. The Bar Council of India was established by Parliament under the Advocate Act, 1961. It performs the regulatory functions by prescribing standards of professional conduct and etiquette and by exercising disciplinary jurisdiction over the bar. It also sets standards for legal education and grants recognition to universities whose degree in law will serve as qualification for enrolment as an advocate.

BCI performs the following functions

(i) To lay down standards of professional conduct and etiquette for advocates.

(ii) To lay down a procedure to be followed by its disciplinary committee and the disciplinary committees of each State Bar Council.

(iii) To safeguard the rights, privileges and interests of advocates.

(iv) To promote and support law reform.

The history of the concept of Bar Councils dates back to the recommendations of the Chamier Committee and the Indian Bar Councils Act, 1926, through which Bar Councils were established for each of the High Courts with 15 members each. But these councils were merely advisory in nature. After the independence of the country in 1950, a resolution was passed by the Bar Council of Madras which advocated the need for establishment of an all India Bar Council and other similar reforms. Based on the recommendations of the All India Bar Committee, the government introduced a bill in the Parliament in 1961, which later resulted into the Advocates Act, 1961, under which the Bar Council of India and the respective State Bar Councils were established.

6. Compare the rules regarding entry of foreign lawyers in the United States and the UK.

Ans. **Foreign Lawyers in the USA**

Foreign lawyers to practice legal profession in the US, may appear for bar examinations. However, laws from state to state vary in this matter.

Students who have completed an LLM may qualify to sit the bar exam in California, New Hampshire, New York, Virginia, North Carolina.

The criteria for eligibility to take the bar examination or to otherwise qualify for bar admission are set by each state's bar association.

Some states may allow some foreign-educated lawyers to take the bar examination without earning their degree locally through the following process

- Foreign-educated lawyers must get their law degree reviewed and analysed by the American Bar Association (ABA).
- Once reviewed, the application is either accepted or deferred. If accepted, foreign lawyers are allowed to sit for that state's bar exam.

Foreign Lawyers in the UK

Legal education in the UK consists of a three-year LLB, directly after secondary school. Graduates from fields other than law and non-graduates can become solicitors, but LLB is the most straightforward path. Clinical education continues after the LLB through the Legal Practice Course (LPC) and training contracts.

Graduates are required to complete the Bar Vocational Course (BVC) to become a barrister, instead of the LPC. Then, they have to seek a 'pupillage' instead of a training contract. There are a number of differences between barristers and solicitors, but the most significant among them is that barristers can appear in all courts while solicitors can only appear in higher courts, if they qualify to become solicitor advocates. To qualify as a barrister or solicitor students are required to obtain a qualifying law degree.

Exam Pattern Questions

Objective Type Questions

Multiple Choice Questions (MCQs)

1. The modern legal profession in India has colonial roots emerging with the advent of Mayor's courts in which of the following places?

(a) Madras (b) Calcutta
(c) Both (a) and (b) (d) Bombay

2. Who were native practitioners qualified to appear and practise in the High Courts of pre-independence India?

(a) Barristers (b) Vakils
(c) Pleaders (d) None of these

3. Which of the following is not a development of the Advocates Act, 1961? CBSE SQP 2020

(a) All old categories of practitioners were abolished and consolidated into a single category called 'advocates'.
(b) Established Bar Council of India.
(c) Created State Bar Council in each State.
(d) Scraped off the provisions of Indian Bar Council Act of 1926.

4. Pratap is a legally qualified Indian Army recruit. He specialises in human rights matters. Which of the following is best suited for his services? CBSE 2024 C

(a) Competition Commission of India
(b) Centre for Legal Process Outsourcing
(c) Securities and Exchange Board of India
(d) Judge Advocate General's Department

5. In order to be eligible for enrollment, an advocate must be ....

(a) a citizen of India.
(b) atleast 21 years of age.
(c) must have an LLB degree from an Indian University.
(d) All of the above

6. Which court in India can designate an advocate as a senior advocate? CBSE 2022

(a) High Court only
(b) Supreme Court only
(c) Supreme Court or any of the High Courts
(d) District Court only

7. Whose services can be availed for by the Chairman of the legal services institution in cases of great public importance and where serious threats to life and liberty of the applicant exists? CBSE SQP 2022

(a) Advocate-on-Record (b) Solicitor General
(c) Senior Advocate (d) Retired Judge

8. The Advocates-on-record practice in .... CBSE SQP 2020

(a) High Court
(b) Supreme Court
(c) Both High Courts and Supreme Court
(d) Any Court in India

9. With regard to a senior advocate in India, pick the odd one out. CBSE 2019

(a) Argues cases in court upon instructions from another advocate.
(b) Officially designated as such by the Supreme Court or High Court.
(c) Wears gowns that have flaps on the shoulder.
(d) Can directly keep an engagement to appear in a case or draft pleadings.

10. Who regulates legal education in India? CBSE SQP 2020

(a) Legal Education Committee
(b) State Bar Council
(c) Bar Council of India
(d) Recognised Universities of India

11. Aman, a lawyer was suspended as he breached the rules laid down by the Bar Council of India. From the options given below, what misconduct may have led to his suspension? CBSE SQP 2022

(a) He charged contingency fee from his client in a land dispute.
(b) He negotiated with the opposite party through the opposing advocate.
(c) He refused to represent client who insisted on adopting unfair means.
(d) He refused to appear in a matter where he was the witness.

12. An advocate can seek permission for advertising from CBSE SQP 2020

(a) State Bar Council where he is registered
(b) Bar Council of India
(c) Bar Council of the court where he practices
(d) High Court of the state where he practices

13. Rahul cleared his five years integrated programme in B.A. LL.B five years ago. When can he start practicing as an advocate? CBSE SQP 2022

(a) Rahul can practice as an advocate as he has cleared B.A. LL.B exam.
(b) Rahul can practice as advocate if he clear All India Bar Examination.

(c) Rahul can practice law only after he does LL.M, as he cleared his LL.B five years ago.
(d) Rahul can practice law after training with a senior Advocate-on-record for one year.

14. Arjun Bedi, a practicing advocate, decided to expand his clientele by advertising his services. Through which of the following is promotion of his services permissible in India, in this context? **CBSE 2019**

(a) Interviews in the newspaper.
(b) Furnishing and inspiring newspaper comments.
(c) Circulars and advertisements.
(d) Website information regarding areas of practice.

15. Mei Ling is a practicing lawyer in Hong Kong. She is considering launching a marketing campaign to attract more clients. Which of the following is a feasible option for her? **CBSE 2025**

(a) Proceed with the campaign on all media, since lawyers are free to advertise without restrictions.
(b) Proceed with the campaign on print media.
(c) Launch the campaign but exclude testimonials, success rates and any comparative statements.
(d) Avoid all forms of advertising as it is entirely prohibited in Hong Kong.

16. How many members are nominated to the State Bar Council by the Bar Council of India? **CBSE 2024 C**

(a) 1 (b) 2 (c) 3 (d) 4

17. The first Indian lady vakil to be enrolled was **CBSE 2020**

(a) Ms. Hazra (b) Anna Chandy
(c) Ms. Cornelia Sorabji (d) Fathima Beevi

18. Prabhav graduated in a 5 year BA-LLB programme from NLU, Delhi. He applied for registration as an Advocate to the Bar Council of India, Delhi office. His application was not considered. What can be the probable reason for the same? **CBSE SQP 2020**

(a) 5 year law programme is not recognised in Delhi
(b) Application for enrollment is to be made to the State Bar Council.
(c) Both (a) and (b)
(d) None of the above

19. In the United States, students after completing a four-year undergraduate degree in any discipline, students take

(a) LSAT exam (b) CLAT exam
(c) AILET exam (d) JD exam

20. What is/are the pedagogical methods involved in US law schools?

(a) The Case Study method
(b) The Socratic method
(c) Interdisciplinary approach
(d) Both (a) and (b)

21. Mandatory or minimum continuing legal education is a requirement of ....

(a) UK (b) US states
(c) Australian states (d) None of these

22. Which of the following is a very popular US State for Bar Examinations?

(a) California (b) Texas (c) Michigan (d) Alaska

23. Legal qualifications of which of the following is different from the rest of the UK?

(a) Whales (b) Ireland (c) Scotland (d) London

24. Professional education of lawyers in the US after admission to bar is called .... **CBSE 2019**

(a) Continuing Legal Education
(b) Bar Vocational Course
(c) Graduate Diploma in Law Course
(d) Multistate Bar Examination

25. Michael Browne has an undergraduate degree in Anthropology and aspires to become a lawyer in the UK. Which of the following will enable her to do so? **CBSE 2020**

(a) Pupillage
(b) Common Professional Examination
(c) Bar Vocational Course
(d) Legal Practice Course

26. In the year 1940, Naveen passed a BA course from a recognised university. He wanted to become a 'Pleader' in India. He was required to pass the 'Pleadership Examination' which was held by the .... prior to the enactment of the Advocates Act, 1961. **CBSE 2016**

(a) Mayor's Court (b) High Court
(c) Supreme Court (d) Mofussil Court

27. Raveena is working with a reputed law firm. Her areas of specialisation typically involve practicing in commercial and economic laws and advising on issues pertaining to commercial transactions between two parties. She also advises on the laws applicable to the transactions, drafts contracts and other documents and helps clients with the commercial negotiations.

Raveena is specialised in .... **CBSE 2020**

(a) Corporate Law (b) Taxation Law
(c) Transactional Law (d) Legal Process Outsourcing

28. Rashi did her LLB from the University of London, UK after schooling in India. She applied for registration to the Delhi State Bar Council for enrollment as an Advocate. She is 20 years old with a Gold Medal in her LLB. Her application for registration was rejected.

What could be the probable reason for the same?

(a) Rashi did not clear the All India Bar Examination.
(b) Rashi does not possess an LLM degree
(c) Rashi has not done her LLB from India
(d) Rashi hasn't attained 21 years of age

29. Rohan, an Indian lawyer, wants to provide legal services in the UK. Prior to 2009, he was restricted from doing so due to regulatory barriers. However, with the liberalisation of legal services, the UK's Legal Services Act, 2007, and India's subsequent notifications, Rohan can now provide legal services in the UK, either individually or in partnership with UK law firms.

What development enabled Rohan to provide legal services in the UK?

(a) India's signing of the WTO's GATS agreement
(b) The UK's Legal Services Act, 2007
(c) Establishment of the Bar Council of India
(d) Amendment to the Indian Advocates Act, 1961

30. Advocates Act, 1961 recognises only one class of practitioners called ....

(a) Pleades (b) Joli uiors (c) Barristers (d) Advocates

31. Alex graduated with Science from the University of London. He developed an interest in law and wants to become a solicitor. Identify the requirement he needs to fulfill the same. **CBSE 2024 C**

I. Training Contracts **II. Pupillage**
III. Legal Practice Course Bar
IV. Vocational **V. Course**

Choose the correct option

(a) I and II (b) III and IV
(c) II and III (d) I and III

32. Match the following.

Column I	Column II
A. AILET	1. First NLU
B. NLSIU	2. Regulated by BCI
C. Legal Education in India	3. Established by Parliament under the Advocates Act, 1961
D. Bar Council of India	4. Entrance test by Delhi

Codes

	A	B	C	D		A	B	C	D
(a)	1	2	3	4	(b)	4	1	2	3
(c)	4	2	1	3	(d)	2	1	3	4

33. Statement I The Advocates Act, 1961, abolished all old categories of legal practitioners and established a single category called "Advocates".

Statement II Under the Advocates Act, 1961, only Senior Advocates can file a vakalatnama in any court or tribunal in India.

Choose the correct statement

(a) Both Statements are correct.
(b) Both Statements are incorrect.
(c) Statement I is correct, but Statement II is not correct.
(d) Statement II is correct, but Statement I is not correct.

34. Statement I The Legal Practitioners' (Women) Act, 1923, allowed women to practice law in India.

Statement II Cornelia Sorabji was the first Indian woman to be enrolled as a lawyer in the Supreme Court of India.

Choose the correct statement

(a) Both Statements are correct.
(b) Both Statements are incorrect.
(c) Statement I is correct, but Statement II is not correct.
(d) Statement II is correct, but Statement I is not correct.

35. Statement I Only senior advocate can file a vakalatnama in the Supreme Court of India.

Statement II Any advocate enrolled in a State Bar Council can directly file a case in the Supreme Court.

Choose the correct statement

(a) Both Statements are correct.
(b) Both Statements are incorrect.
(c) Statement I is correct, but Statement II is not correct.
(d) Statement II is correct, but Statement I is not correct.

Assertion-Reason Questions

Directions (Q. Nos. 36-40) In the questions given below, there are two statements. Read the statements and choose the correct option.

Codes

(a) Both A and R are true and R is the correct explanation of A.
(b) Both A and R are true, but R is not the correct explanation of A.
(c) A is true, but R is false.
(d) A is false, but R is true.

36. Assertion (A) The office of the Attorney General for the Union of India and the Advocate General for the concerned states are Constitutional offices.

Reason (R) The Constitution of India has also laid down the qualifications necessary for being considered for the position of the Attorney General and the Advocate General.

37. Assertion (A) The Solicitor Regulation Authority (SRA) does not impose any formal experience requirement for requalifying as solicitor in England and Wales.

Reason (R) It is not possible to be a barrister and solicitor. **CBSE 2025**

38. Assertion (A) Giving effect to the Chamier Committee recommendations, the Central Legislature enacted the Indian Bar Councils Act, 1926.

Reason (R) The Act was to provide for the Constitution and incorporation of Bar Councils, to confer powers and impose duties on the Bar Councils and to consolidate the regulations pertaining to the legal profession.

39. Assertion (A) A senior advocate is not entitled to appear in the Supreme Court without an Advocate-on-record.

Reason (R) Advocates-on-record are entitled to file an appearance or act for a party in the Supreme Court. **CBSE 2025**

40. Assertion (A) For qualified lawyers coming from outside England and Wales, it is still possible to practice.

Reason (R) The Solicitors Regulation Authority (SRA) does not impose any formal experience requirements in order to re-qualify as solicitors in England and Wales.

Answers

1. (c) Both (a) and (b)
2. (b) Vakils
3. (d) Scraped off the provisions of Indian Bar Council Act of 1926.
4. (d) Judge Advocate General's Department
5. (d) All of the above
6. (c) Supreme Court or any of the High Courts
7. (c) Senior Advocate
8. (b) Supreme Court
9. (d) Can directly keep an engagement to appear in a case or draft pleadings.
10. (c) Bar Council of India
11. (b) He negotiated with the opposite party through the opposing advocate.
12. (b) Bar Council of India
13. (b) Rahul can practice as advocate if he clear All India Bar Examination.
14. (d) Website information regarding areas of practice.
15. (c) Launch the campaign but exclude testimonials, success rates and any comparative statements.
16. (b) 2
17. (c) Ms. Cornelia Sorabji
18. (d) None of the above
19. (a) LSAT exam
20. (d) Both (a) and (b)
21. (b) US states
22. (a) California
23. (c) Scotland
24. (a) Continuing Legal Education
25. (d) Legal Practice Course
26. (b) High Court
27. (c) Transactional Law
28. (d) Rashi hasn't attained 21 years of age
29. (b) The UK's Legal Services Act, 2007
30. (d) Advocates
31. (d) I and III
32. (b) 4 1 2 3
33. (c) Statement I is correct, but Statement II is not correct.
34. (c) Statement I is correct, but Statement II is not correct.
35. (b) Both Statements are incorrect.
36. (a) Both A and R are true and R is the correct explanation of A.
37. (c) A is true, but R is false.
38. (a) Both A and R are true and R is the correct explanation of A.
39. (a) Both A and R are true and R is the correct explanation of A.
40. (a) Both A and R are true and R is the correct explanation of A.

Subjective Questions

Very Short Answer Type Questions

1. 'The modern legal profession has its roots in the colonial period'. Justify the given statement.

Ans. The modern legal profession in India began during the colonial period with the Mayor's Courts in Madras and Calcutta (1726).

It developed further with the Legal Practitioners Act (1846), allowing qualified individuals to practice law. The Advocates Act (1961) later unified the profession.

2. State any two outcomes of the enactment of Advocates Act, 1961. **CBSE SQP 2022**

Or **What happened to the old categories of legal practitioners after the enactment of the Advocates Act, 1961?**

Ans. The two outcomes of the enactment of Advocates Act, 1961 are as follows

(i) All the old categories of practitioners (vakils, barristers, pleaders of several grades and mukhtars) were abolished and consolidated into a single category called 'advocates'.

(ii) The Advocates Act also established an All India Bar Council for the first time, with the Attorney-General and Solicitor General of India as ex- officio members of the Bar Council.

3. In what circumstances do legal services institutions avail the services of senior advocates? **CBSE 2022**

Ans. The services of senior advocates may be availed if the Chairman of the legal services institution forms an opinion to that effect in cases of great public importance and where serious threats to life and liberty of the application exists.

4. Mr. Swami is a qualified Lawyer practising since 1990 in the High Court of Delhi and in the Supreme Court of India. He has special knowledge and expertise in the field of Civil and Criminal Laws. While appearing in a court room he usually dresses in black and white, wears a white band around his neck and a black gown having flaps on the shoulders. On 18th November, 2015, Mr. Mehta directly approached and appointed Mr. Swami as his advocate, to file an appeal in the Delhi High Court against the decision of the District Court. Mr. Swami accepted ₹ 1 lakh in cash as his consultation charges. On 19th November, 2015 i.e. on the very next day, without wasting any time Mr. Swami started drafting pleadings as 29th November, 2015 was the last day to file the appeal. **CBSE 2016**

(i) Mr Swami comes under which category of legal practitioner as recognised by the Advocates Act, 1961?

(ii) Giving reason, state whether the conduct of Mr. Swami is justified as per the provisions of the Advocates Act, 1961?

Ans. (i) Mr. Swami comes under the category of Senior Advocate.

(ii) The conduct of Mr. Swami is not justified as per the provisions of Advocates Act, 1961 because a senior advocate can not file a vakalatnama, appear in the court without another advocate or advocate-on-record, can not directly accept an engagement to appear in a case or draft pleadings.

5. Write down any two functions of the Bar Council of India.

Ans. Two functions of the BCI include

(i) To lay down standards of professional conduct and etiquette for advocates.

(ii) To lay down a procedure to be followed by its disciplinary committee and the disciplinary committees of each State Bar Council.

6. What are the prospects of a law graduate in formulation and advising on public policy? **CBSE 2024 C**

Ans. A law graduate has promising prospects in formulating and advising on public policy. They can work with government agencies, think tanks, NGOs, or private companies, utilising their legal expertise to analyse and develop policies. Career paths include Policy Analyst, Legislative Counsel, or Public Policy Advisor.

7. State the representative functions of the Bar Council of India. **CBSE 2024 C**

Ans. The Bar Council of India (BCI) has the following representative functions

- Represents the Indian bar in international conferences and forums.
- Maintains relations with foreign bar associations and councils.
- Sends representatives to the Parliament and state legislatures.
- Participates in the appointment of judges to the Supreme Court and High Courts.
- Represents the interests of the legal profession before the government and judiciary.

8. Rohan Abbas, an upcoming criminal lawyer, after taking approval from the Bar Council of India, prepared a five piece information that he can put on the internet to solicit clients. The information included his name, contact details, his professional and academic qualifications. Apart from these, mention the other two pieces of information that Rohan can give to advertise his services. **CBSE 2020**

Ans. The other two pieces of information that can be given are

(i) Details of his enrollment with the bar.

(ii) His areas of practice.

9. Name the body responsible for regulating the minimum legal standards to be maintained by institutions that impart legal education in India.

Ans. The Bar Council of India (BCI) is envisaged under the Advocates Act as a body for regulating the minimum standards to be maintained by institutions imparting legal education in India.

10. What are the primary functions of any State Bar Council?

Ans. The State Council's main functions include

- admitting law graduates on its roll
- determining cases of misconduct against advocates on the roll, and
- organising legal aid, among other functions.

11. State any two professional duties of an advocate.

Ans. Two professional duties of an advocate are **CBSE 2019**

(i) To act in a dignified manner

(ii) To respect the court

12. During a court proceeding, an advocate finds out that their client intends to provide false evidence. What should the advocate do in this situation to adhere to their professional duty toward the court and uphold ethical standards? CBSE 2025

Ans. An advocate must refuse to represent a client who insists on adopting unfair means, including providing false evidence. Advocates are required to uphold the dignity of the court and maintain professional ethics.

Suppressing material or misleading the court is against their duty and may lead to disciplinary action.

13. India is expected to liberalise the legal sector under the General Agreement on Trade and Services (GATS) and other free trade agreements. In light of this, evaluate the judgement of Bombay and Madras High Courts. CBSE SQP 2022

Ans. In 2011, in a judgment delivered by the Bombay High Court on a Public Interest Litigation (PIL) was filed by lawyer's collective, a non-profit organisation, the High Court held that foreign law firms could not be permitted to set up liaison offices in India. Contrary to this position, the Madras High Court, in response to a PIL filed by A.K. Balaji, permitted foreign lawyers to practice in India on a "fly in and fly out" basis.

14. What is the pedagogical method adopted in law schools in US?

Ans. The pedagogical (teaching) method adopted in law schools involves

(i) The Case Study method (ii) The Socratic method

15. Can foreign educated lawyers in the US take the bar exam without earning the degree locally?

Ans. Yes, some states of US may allow some foreign educated lawyers to take the bar examination without earning their degree locally. However in such a case, foreign educated lawyers must begin the process by getting their law degree reviewed and analysed by the American Bar Association (ABA).

16. What is the American Bar of Association?

Ans. The American Bar Association acts as a voluntary professional body at the federal level for US lawyers. ABA was founded in 1878. It is the largest voluntary professional body in the world and has a significant international profile. Members of the legal profession in other countries can become international associates of the ABA.

17. How can you become a solicitor in the UK?

Ans. In the UK, to become a solicitor, it is necessary to take the Legal Practice Course (LPC), which is a one year full-time or two years part-time course. In some cases, students may be fortunate enough to have a training contract offer from a law firm at this stage.

18. Describe, citing any two examples, how the rules of advertising by lawyers differs from country to country. CBSE 2025

Ans. The rules of advertising by lawyers vary across countries. In India, the Bar Council of India strictly restricts legal advertising, allowing only limited information on lawyers' websites with prior approval. In contrast, the USA permits lawyer advertisements with regulations prohibiting misleading claims and setting solicitation restrictions.

19. Neha and Rani are good friends and have also completed a degree in law. As fresh graduates, Neha is keen to contribute in policy making and Rani wants to specialise in commercial and economic laws. Mention the fields that they can specialise in. CBSE SQP 2022

Ans. Neha and Rani could choose public policy and corporate sector. Lawyers have an important role in formulating and advising on public policy. Several organisations employ law graduates for policy making and have institutionalised fellowships where law graduates can be Research Assistants.

An inhouse counsel will give legal advice to the company, have expertise in the business of the company and be responsible for ensuring that the business of the company is being run in compliance with applicable laws and when required will bring in external lawyers.

20. Aman is a law graduate who is keen on working for an organisation with a social justice orientation. Explain the option available to Aman as a law graduate in this context.

Ans. Aman as a law graduate, who is keen on working for an organisations with a social justice orientation can opt for not-for-profit organisations.

These range from small grass-root level organisations to large well-funded organisations. They may be general in nature providing free legal aid, legal education and legal awareness.

21. Which legislation is responsible for regulating the legal profession in India?

Ans. The legal profession in India, which includes both the practice of law as well as professional legal education, is regulated by the Advocates Act, 1961.

22. What is the primary work domain in a transactional law firm?

Ans. Transactional law at law firms typically involves practicing in commercial and economic laws and advising on issues pertaining to a commercial transaction between two or more parties. This would usually include advising on the laws applicable to the transaction, drafting contracts and other documents, and helping clients with the commercial negotiations and the management and execution (i.e. successful completion) of the transaction.

23. State any two categories of legal practitioners that existed under the British rule in India.

Ans. Two categories of legal practitioners that existed under British rule were

(i) **Attorneys** Attorneys previously only referred to British attorneys or solicitors, but now this definition is sometimes used to refer to advocates as well.

(ii) **Solicitors** Prior to the enactment of the Advocates Act, solicitors referred to British solicitors who were permitted to practise in the High Courts in pre-Independence India. Today, in the Bombay and Calcutta High Courts there is a separate class of legal practitioners, known as solicitors, who prepare the case, but do not argue in court.

24. Why does allowing advertising by lawyers require a balancing act?

Ans. The issue of allowing advertising and solicitation by lawyers requires balancing the interest of the public which includes getting information on legal rights and services through advertisements and enhancement of access to justice and the legal profession on one hand and the possible misuse of advertising techniques by lawyers which may lead to a loss of credibility of the profession as a whole

25. Who is a Judge Advocate General (JAG) Officer? State the role of the JAG's Department. (Any two)

Ans. Judge Advocate General is the legal and judicial chief of the army and advises the Chief of the Army Staff on legal matters.

(i) The JAG's Department is also responsible for emerging fields of military law such as those related to cyber laws, space laws, terrorism and human rights violations.

(ii) It deals with military related disciplinary cases and litigation and assists in providing legal assistance to the army in human rights matters and the rule of law among other things.

Short Answer Type Questions

1. Evaluate the changes effected by the Advocates Act, 1961 that revolutionised the legal profession and legal education in India. CBSE 2020

Ans. After the enactment of the Advocates Act, 1961, all the old categories of practitioners (vakils, barristers, pleaders of several grades and mukhtars) were abolished and consolidated into a single category called advocates who enjoy the right to practice in courts throughout India.

The Advocates Act also established an All India Bar Council for the first time, with the Attorney-General and Solicitor General of India as ex-officio members of the Bar Council. The All India Bar Council has one member elected to it by each State Bar Council and it elects its own Chairman and Vice-Chairman.

2. State the requirements to be fulfilled by law aspirants, both Indian and foreign national, to be able to start practice in India. CBSE 2019

Ans. In order to be eligible for enrolment, an advocate must be

- a citizen of India
- atleast 21 years of age
- must have an LLB degree from an Indian University.

Further, a foreign national may be enrolled on a reciprocal basis with the country of his citizenship and his foreign degree may be recognised by the council for the purpose.

In the absence of such reciprocity, foreign nationals cannot practice law in India.

Moreover, the council has released a list of foreign degrees that it recognises.

There is an additional requirement of an All India Bar Examination since 2010, which has to be cleared by Advocates in order to be able to start practice all over India.

3. Explain the categories of legal practitioners in India after the Advocates Act, 1961. CBSE 2019

Ans According to the Advocates Act, 1961 only one category of legal practitioners exist, i.e, advocates.

Advocates have been classified as senior advocates and other advocate-on-record. These are discussed below

- **Senior Advocates** They are designated by the Supreme Court of India or by any High Court. The court can designate any advocate, with his consent, as senior advocate, if in its opinion such advocate is deserving of such distinction (Section 16, Advocates Act, 1961). A designated senior advocate wears a gown with a flap at the back.

- **Advocates-On-Record** (AOR) They are entitled to file any matter or document before the Supreme Court. They can also file an appearance or act for a party in the Supreme Court. No other High Court in India has a similar provision. Only an AOR can file a vakalatnama in the Supreme Court on behalf of a client. Any correspondence by the Supreme Court is sent to the AOR.

4. Ms. Rina hired Advocate P. Sharma, enrolled with the Bar Council of Delhi, to represent her in a property dispute. She won the case, and the court awarded her ₹ 15,000 as compensation. However, Advocate P. Sharma withdrew the amount on her behalf but did not inform or return the money to her. When Ms. Rina confronted him, he claimed that the amount was adjusted against his legal fees, without prior agreement.

(i) **Was Advocate P. Sharma's conduct ethical? Justify your answer.**

(ii) **Which authority can take action against Advocate P. Sharma?**

(iii) **What possible consequences can Advocate P. Sharma face for this act?**

Ans. (i) Advocate P. Sharma's conduct was unethical because he withdrew Ms. Rina's compensation without informing her and used it without consent. Lawyers must act honestly and keep clients informed about their case and finances.

(ii) The State Bar Council of Delhi can take action against Advocate P. Sharma. If needed, the Bar Council of India can also review the matter.

(iii) Advocate P. Sharma may face disciplinary action, including warnings, suspension, or disbarment. He may also have to return the money and face legal consequences for professional misconduct. Lawyers must always act in the best interest of their clients.

5. What are the different categories of Bar Associations present in the US and how do they vary in terms of their scope, membership and specific areas of focus in supporting legal professionals ? **CBSE 2024 C**

Ans. In the US, there are several categories of Bar Associations, varying in scope, membership, and focus

- **National Bar Associations** American Bar Association (ABA) is the largest, focusing on national issues and advocacy.
- **State and Local Bar Associations** e.g., New York State Bar Association, Los Angeles County Bar Association, serving local legal communities.
- **Specialized Bar Associations** e.g., American Intellectual Property Law Association (AIPLA), National Bar Association (NBA) for African American lawyers, focusing on specific practice areas or demographics.
- **Minority Bar Associations** e.g., Hispanic National Bar Association (HNBA), Asian American Bar Association of New York (AABANY), supporting under-represented groups.

These associations provide various benefits, including CLE programs, networking opportunities, and advocacy for legal professionals.

6. 'Ambulance chasing' is common place in the USA, but it is not representative of professional practice in India. Justify the statement and explain the norms of advertising by advocates in India. **CBSE 2018**

Ans. Ambulance chasing is not representative of professional practice in India. This is because these classes of lawyers solicit business by lurking around hospitals or by ads in newspapers and in Yellow Pages with toll free numbers and free consultations.

The issue of allowing advertising and solicitation by lawyers requires balancing the interest of the public which includes

- getting information on legal rights and services through advertisements
- enhancement of access to justice and the legal profession
- the possible misuse of advertising techniques by lawyers which may lead to a loss of credibility of the profession as a whole.

7. Give a short note on the background of the American Bar Association.

Ans. In 1878, the ABA supports the legal profession with practical resources for legal professionals while improving the administration of justice, accrediting law schools, establishing model ethical codes and more. Membership is open to lawyers, law students and others interested in the law and the legal profession.

Its goals include

- serving the members
- improving the profession
- eliminating bias
- enhancing diversity and
- advancing the rule of law

One of its most important responsibilities is the creation and maintenance of a code of ethical standards for lawyers. The ABA has been accrediting schools since 1923 and it also publishes the ABA journal.

8. Riya, a law graduate in India, is exploring career options in law beyond courtroom practice. Explain any three such opportunities available to Riya. How can she apply her legal skills in these fields? **CBSE 2025**

Ans. Riya, as a law graduate, can explore various career options beyond courtroom practice

(i) **Corporate Sector** She can work as an in-house legal counsel for corporations, ensuring compliance with laws and advising on business transactions.

(ii) **Public Policy** She can contribute to policy-making by working with organisations like PRS Legislative Research or regulatory bodies like SEBI.

(iii) **Legal Research and Academia** She can pursue higher studies and work as a researcher or professor, contributing to legal education and policy research.

9. Teresa Williams is a lawyer based in Malaysia and she is keen on expanding her clientele in the country. Assess the regulations that will apply when she advertises her services. **CBSE 2022**

Ans. In India, advertising by lawyers has been strictly restricted by the Bar Council of India.The regulations that will apply when she advertises her services suggests only 5 pieces of information can be put up on the internet.

- The name of the advocate or the firm
- The contact details
- Details of enrolment with the Bar
- His professional and academic qualification
- The areas of practice.

10. Examine the scope for qualified lawyers from outside England and Wales to practice in the UK. **CBSE 2018**

Ans. It is possible to practice law for qualified lawyers coming from outside England and Wales.

The Solicitors Regulation Authority (SRA) does not impose any formal experience requirements in order to re-qualify as solicitors in England and Wales. Some law firms may express their own requirements which can differ from the SRA guidelines. Candidates can take the Qualified Lawyers Transfer scheme in order to qualify under this jurisdiction.

Lawyers coming from EU member states can depend upon EU Directive 77/249 in this area. European lawyers can practice to the same level as they could in their own country. However, it is not possible to be a barrister and solicitor simultaneously.

11. Rahul, a practicing lawyer in Delhi, has started a You Tube channel where he provides free legal advice and shares his experiences as a lawyer. He also promotes his law firm and offers consultation services to viewers. Rahul claims that his videos are educational and informative, but his competitors argue that he is indirectly advertising his services. Discuss the ethics of Rahul's actions in light of the Bar Council of India's rules on lawyer advertising.

Ans. Rahul's actions on YouTube raise ethical concerns regarding lawyer advertising in India. The Bar Council of India's Rules prohibit lawyers from soliciting or advertising their services. However, Rahul's educational content can be seen as informative rather than solicitous. The key issue is whether his promotional messages constitute indirect advertising.

The Bar Council of India Rules allow lawyers to provide information about their qualifications, experience and areas of practice. Rahul should ensure transparency by clearly separating educational content from promotional material. To comply with ethics, Rahul could provide disclaimers stating his videos are for informational purposes only and not intended as solicitations.

By walking this fine line, Rahul can maintain the educational value of his channel while adhering to professional ethics. Regular monitoring and adjustments will be necessary to avoid potential conflicts.

Long Answer Type Questions

1. (i) **State the eligibility criteria for being enrolled as an advocate in India.** **CBSE 2017**

(ii) **How can an advocate in India become an advocate-on-record?**

(iii) **How do lawyers in India play an important role in formulating and advising on public policy?**

Ans. (i) In order to be eligible for enrolment, an Advocate must be

- a citizen of India
- at least 21 years of age
- must have an LLB degree from an Indian University

(ii) An advocate can become an advocate-on record (AOR) by passing a qualifying examination conducted by the Supreme Court. The examination is taken by an advocate who has been enrolled with a Bar Council for at least five years and has completed one year training with an AOR of not less than five years standing.

(iii) Lawyers have an important role in formulating and advising on public policy. Several organisations employ law graduates for policy making and have institutionalised fellowships where law graduates can be Research Assistants. For example, a law graduate interested in public policy can apply to serve as a Legislative Assistant under the Legislative Assistants to Members of Parliament (LAMP) Fellowship programme run by PRS Legislative Research. Institutions such as Competition Commission of India (CCI) and Securities Exchange Board of India (SEBI) also employ law graduates for policy making in the respective fields.

Law firms have established Government Policy Departments where they employ law graduates for policy research.

2. Explain the main provisions of the Advocates Act, 1961 in reference to the following points **CBSE 2017**

(i) Composition of the All India Bar Council.
(ii) Any two functions of the BCI.
(iii) Composition of the State Bar Council.
(iv) Any two functions of the State Bar Council.

Ans. (i) The All India Bar Council has one member elected to it by each State Bar Council and it elects its own Chairman and Vice-Chairman.

(ii) Two functions of BCI are

(a) To lay down standards of professional conduct and etiquette for advocates.

(b) To lay down a procedure to be followed by its disciplinary committee and the disciplinary committees of each State Bar Council.

(iii) The State Bar Council in each state consists of the Advocate General of the state as an ex-officio member, and 15-25 advocates elected for a period of five years.

(iv) Two functions of the State Bar Council are

(a) To accept persons as advocates on its roll.

(b) To prepare and maintain such roll.

3. Describe the professional duties of an advocate in India. **CBSE 2018**

Ans. An advocate has following duties

- To act in a dignified manner.
- To respect the court.
- not to communicate with a judge in private and impair impartiality.
- Not to act in an illegal manner towards the opposition.
- To refuse to represent clients who insist on adopting unfair means.
- An Advocate is expected to uphold and maintain the values of the profession.

Furthermore, an Advocate's duty towards the client includes

- being bound to accept briefs
- not to withdraw from service
- not to appear in matters where he/she is a witness
- not to suppress material or evidence
- to maintain client confidentiality and not to instigate litigation or to charge contingency fee (fee depending on success or favourable result of matters),
- to ensure that his/her duties do not conflict with the client's interests.
- not to negotiate directly with the opposing party (only through the opposing advocate) and to carry out legitimate promises made.

4. Compare the rules regarding legal education in India and the USA. **CBSE 2016**

Ans. The Bar Council of India was established by Parliament under the Advocates Act, 1961.

The Advocates Act had established an All India Bar Council to regulate the Indian legal profession which includes both the practice of law and legal education. It constitutes the Attorney-General and Solicitor General of India as ex-officio members of the Bar Council. It also includes one member elected to it by each State Bar Council. Its Chairman and Vice-Chairman are elected by its own. The Bar Councils, with the consent of the High Court, make rules for

- the rights and duties of advocates of High Court and professional conduct.
- legal education and examinations.

In the United States, after completing a four-year undergraduate degree in any discipline, students can apply for the Law School Admission Test (LSAT) exam. Thereafter, they can apply to a law school and enrol in a three- year JD (Juris Doctor) programme. The pedagogical method adopted in law schools involves the Case Study method as well as the Socratic method.

In the states of United States of America, following licensing requirement are needed for legal profession

- Each state in the United States separately administers a mandatory bar exam. Bar applicants must also satisfy the character and fitness requirements of the state.
- Most states also have mandatory or minimum continuing legal education (CLE) requirements. CLE is professional education of lawyers that takes places after they are admitted to the bar. It requires minimum hourly commitments which lawyers must undertake in order to maintain their license.
- Nearly all states require candidates to pass the Multistate Bar Examination (MBE) and the Multistate Professional Responsibility Examination (MPRE).
- Some states also require the passing of the Multistate Essay Examination (MEE) and/or the Multistate Performance Test (MPT).

5. Susanna is UK based lawyer, who is considering law practice in India. Outline the eligibility for enrolment as an advocate in India and the rules that govern enrolment of foreign nationals. **CBSE 2022**

Ans. An advocate on the state rolls is entitled to practice before any tribunal, or authority of India, or any court including the Supreme Court.

In order to be eligible for enrolment, an advocate must be

- a citizen of India
- atleast 21 years of age
- must have an LLB degree from an Indian University.

There is an additional requirement of an All India Bar Examination since 2010, which is to be cleared by and advocate, in order to be able to start practice.

A foreign national who is not a national of a specific country, may be enrolled on a reciprocal basis with the country of his citizenship and his foreign degree may be recognised by the council for the purpose.

In the absence of such reciprocity, foreign nationals cannot practice law in India. The Bar Council has released a list of foreign degrees that it recognises.

6. Describe any six opportunities available to law graduates in India. **CBSE 2019**

Ans. For answer, refer to text under the heading 'Opportunities for Law Graduates' on page no. 296 and 297.

7. Write short notes on the following **CBSE 2016**

(i) Women and the Legal Profession.

(ii) Professional Ethics for Lawyers in India, as laid down by the BCI.

Ans. (i) For answers refer to Q. 1 (i) of CBSE Textbook folder.

(ii) For answers refer to Q. 1 (ii) of CBSE Textbook folder.

8. India has a well-established legal profession governed by the Advocates Act, 1961. A foreign lawyer, Mr. Edward, who holds a legal degree from a reputed university in his country, wishes to practice law in India. However, he is informed that his degree is not automatically recognised by the Bar Council of India.

(i) Which legal provision determines the eligibility of foreign lawyers to practice law in India?

(ii) What role does the Bar Council of India play in regulating foreign lawyers seeking to practice in India?

(iii) In the absence of reciprocity, what alternatives are available for foreign lawyers to offer legal services in India?

Ans. (i) The eligibility of foreign lawyers to practice law in India is determined by the Advocates Act, 1961. Under this act, only Indian citizens with an LLB degree from a recognised university and enrollment with a State Bar Council can practice law. However, foreign nationals may be permitted if their home country grants similar rights to Indian lawyers under a reciprocal arrangement recognised by the Bar Council of India.

(ii) The Bar Council of India (BCI) regulates foreign lawyers by setting standards for legal education, enrollment, and professional conduct. It has the authority to recognise foreign law degrees and establish rules regarding foreign legal practitioners. The BCI also maintains a list of recognised foreign law degrees. Without reciprocity, foreign nationals cannot enroll as advocates or practice law in Indian courts.

(iii) In the absence of reciprocity, foreign lawyers can offer legal services in alternative ways. They may work as legal consultants, advising clients on international law. They can also collaborate with Indian law firms or provide legal documentation and advisory services. The fly-in, fly-out (FIFO) model allows them to offer legal advice on a temporary basis.

9. Illustrate the journey of women in the legal profession in India, highlighting the challenges they faced, the milestones achieved and the current scenario. Consider the following points in your answer

(i) Early beginnings: When were women first allowed to practice law in India?

(ii) Breaking barriers: Who were the pioneering women lawyers and judges?

(iii) Current scenario: What is the representation of women in the legal profession today?

(iv) Challenges: What obstacles do women still face in the legal profession?

(v) Milestones: What significant achievements have women made in the legal field?

Ans. The journey of women in the legal profession in India has been a remarkable one. Women were first allowed to practice law in 1923, with Cornelia Sorabji being the first woman to enroll as an advocate.

Pioneering women like Anna Chandy and Leela Seth broke barriers, becoming the first woman judge and chief justice, respectively. Today, women constitute around 15% of the legal profession, with many holding prominent positions. However, challenges persist, including gender bias, stereotyping, and work-life balance issues. Despite this, women have made significant strides, with notable achievements like India's first woman Chief Justice, Leela Seth, and the current Attorney General, R. Venkataramani, being a woman. The journey is ongoing, with women continuing to shatter glass ceilings and pave the way for future generations.

SELF ASSESSMENT TEST

Objective Type Questions

1. It was the first pan-India (all India) law concerning the regulation of the Indian legal profession. A religious test for enrolment as a pleader was abolished, and persons of any nationality and religion could be enrolled as a pleader.
   (a) The Legal Practitioners Act of 1846
   (b) The Legal Practitioners Act of 1923
   (c) The Legal Practitioners Act of 1840
   (d) None of these
2. Who among the following legal officers can act as advisors to the Central Government?
   (a) The Attorney General of India,
   (b) The Solicitor General of India, and
   (c) The Additional Solicitor General of India.
   (d) All of these
3. **Assertion (A)** The State Bar Councils are responsible for admitting advocates to their rolls and safeguarding their rights, privileges and interests.

   Reason (R) The Bar Council of India directly enrolls advocates and manages all State Bar Councils without any involvement from the respective State Bar Councils.

   Codes
   (a) Both A and R are true and R is the correct explanation of A.
   (b) Both A and R are true, but R is not the correct explanation of A.
   (c) A is true, but R is false.
   (d) A is false, but R is true.

Very Short Answer Type Questions

4. 'Senior Advocates are designated as such by the Supreme Court of India or by any High Court'. Justify the given statement.
5. What do you understand about the concept of ambulance chasing? Is it applicable in the Indian context?

Short Answer Type Questions

6. Briefly state the history of the legal profession in India.
7. Mr. Rajiv engaged Advocate K. Mehta, registered with the Bar Council of Maharashtra, to handle his tenant eviction case. After winning the case, the court ordered the tenant to pay ₹ 20,000 to Mr. Rajiv. Advocate K. Mehta collected the amount but did not inform Mr. Rajiv or hand over the money. When questioned, he stated that it was adjusted as his legal fees without prior discussion.
   (i) Was Advocate K. Mehta's action legally and ethically acceptable? Explain.
   (ii) Which authority can take action against Advocate K. Mehta?

Long Answer Type Questions

8. Briefly discuss the legal education system prevalent in the UK.
9. The legal profession in India is regulated under the Advocates Act, 1961, which categorizes practitioners into 'Advocates' and 'Senior Advocates'. Meera, a highly experienced lawyer with extensive knowledge in Constitutional law, wishes to be designated as a Senior Advocate. However, she learns that there are specific criteria and restrictions associated with this designation.
   (i) Which legal provision governs the designation of Senior Advocates in India?
   (ii) What are the key differences between a Senior Advocate and an Advocate-on-Record in the Supreme Court?

17 CHAPTER

Legal Services

Legal services refer to the advice and assistance provided by a lawyer or attorney who practices law-related services.

YOUR STUDY GOALS

YOUR PRACTICE GOAL

- Objective Type Questions (22 Qs ; MCQs, A-R, Statements, Matching)
- Subjective Questions (10 VSAs, 9 SAs, 8 LAs)

17.1 Meaning of Legal Services

- Legal services include legal aid which means giving the persons limited means, grants, advice or counsel to represent them in court for civil and criminal matters.
- It aims to create a bridge between the poor and rich in the society in order to provide equality to seek justice in the court of law.
- Legal aid ensures that no one is prohibited from legal advice and help because of lack of funds.
- Thus, the provision of legal aid to the poor is based on humanitarian considerations and the main aim of these provisions is to help those who are socially and economically backward.
- The free legal services include
  - Payment of court fee, process fees and all other charges payable or incurred in connection with any legal proceedings.
  - Providing service of lawyers in legal proceedings.
  - Obtaining and supply of certified copies of orders and other documents in legal proceedings.
  - Preparation of appeal, paper book including printing and translation of documents in legal proceedings.
- Litigation is not a luxury but it should be used as a last resort.
- Free legal services also include provision of aid and advice to the beneficiaries to access the benefits under the welfare statutes and schemes framed by the Central Government or the State Government and to ensure access to justice in any other manner.

Types of Legal Services

Legal services are of two types

(i) Pre-litigation legal services (ii) Post-litigation legal services

The pre-litigation legal services include

- Legal education
- Legal advice
- Legal awareness
- Pre-litigation settlement

Post litigation services include all those services that are required to be rendered by an advocate to his client.

Legal Background

- In a participatory democracy, it is essential that citizens have faith in their judicial institution.
- A judiciary that is fair and independent is an important component in sustaining their trust and confidence. An impartial independent judiciary is the guardian of individual rights in a democratic society. For citizens to have faith in their court system, all people must have access to the courts when necessary.
- Thus, access to approach to the courts whenever required constitutes an important element of people's faith in the judiciary.
- It is also the responsibility of the state to ensure that fair and impartial justice is made available at the door-steps of the poor and economically weaker sections, irrespective of their caste, creed, religion, geographical position, free of cost.
- It is because the court system is the mechanism recognised and accepted by all to peacefully resolve disputes. Denying access to the courts forces dispute resolution into other arenas and results in vigilantism and violence.
- Human rights and human dignity form the premises for socio-legal foundations of free legal aid. As part of human rights, it is necessary to recognise the principle of equality and ensure access to justice.
- These foundations reflect the incorporation of legal obligation in the international treaties, regional treaties, the working of monitoring bodies under these treaties or in the national legal systems.

17.2 The Legal Services Authority Act, 1987

- In the year 1987, the Legal Services Authorities Act was enacted by the Parliament which came into force on 9th November, 1995.
- The Legal Services Authorities Act of 1987 provides free legal aid to certain categories of citizens. The act states to constitute legal services authorities to provide free and competent legal services to the weaker sections of the society for ensuring that opportunities for securing justice are not denied to any citizen by reason of economic or other disabilities.
- Article 39A of the Constitution of India provides free legal aid to the poor and weaker sections of society and ensures justice for all.
- Articles 14 and 22 (1) of the Constitution also make it obligatory for the state to ensure equality before the law and a legal system that promotes justice on the basis of equal opportunity for all.
- The 14th Report of the Law Commission of India on Reform of Judicial Administration, 1958 mentioned the idea of providing free legal aid to the poor by the state.
- The report highlighted the responsibility of the legal community to administer legal aid schemes and the state to fund legal representation to the accused in criminal proceedings, appeals and jails.
- In 1960, the Union Government initiated the national legal aid scheme which faced financial shortages and ended. In 1973, in the second phase, the Union Government constituted a committee under the chairmanship of Justice Krishna Iyer to develop a legal aid scheme for states.
- The committee devised a strategy in a decentralised mode with legal aid committees in every district, state and the centre.

- A committee on judicature was set up under the chairmanship of **Justice P.N. Bhagwati** to implement the legal aid scheme. This committee suggested legal aid camps and nyayalayas in rural areas and recommended the inclusion of free legal aid provision in the Constitution.

Entitlement to Legal Services

- **Sections 12 and 13 of the Legal Services Authority Act** deals with the criteria of eligibility to the legal services and its procedures. Every person, who has to file or defend a case, shall be entitled to legal services under this act, if that person is
  - a member of a Scheduled Caste or Scheduled Tribe.
  - a victim of trafficking in human beings or beggar, as referred in **Article 23** of the Constitution.
  - a woman or a child.
  - a person with disability as defined in clause (i) of Section 2 of the Persons with Disabilities (Equal Opportunities, Protection of Rights and Full Participation) Act, 1995.
  - a person under circumstances of unjustified want such as being a victim of a mass disaster, ethnic violence, caste atrocity, flood drought, earthquake or industrial disaster.
  - an industrial workman.
  - a person in custody, according to clause (g) of Section 2 of the Immoral Traffic (Prevention) Act, 1956 (104 of 1946).
  - a person in a juvenile home according to clause (j) of Section 2 of the Juvenile Justice Act, 1986 (53 of 1986).
  - a person in a psychiatric hospital or psychiatric nursing home according to clause (g) of Section 2 of the Mental Health Act, 1987 (14 of 1987).
  - a person who has receipt of annual income of
    - less than ₹ 9,000 or such other higher amount as may be prescribed by the State Government, if the case is before the court than the Supreme Court.
    - less than ₹ 12,000 or such other higher amount as may be prescribed by the Central Government, if the case is before the Supreme Court.

17.3 The Legal Services Authorities (Amendment) Act, 2002

The Parliament has made certain amendments in the Legal Services Authorities Act by passing an act known as the Legal Services Authorities (Amendments) Act, 2002, for encouraging pre-litigation legal services, specially in public utility service. The purpose of this amendment is to bring out certain changes in the Legal Services Act, 1987, especially

- the establishment of permanent Lok Adalats to settle disputes concerning public utility services at pre-litigation state.
- pre-litigation conciliation and settlement concerning public utility services.

Public Utility Service

Public utility service means any

- transport service for the carriage of passengers of goods by air, road or water
- postal, telegraph or telephone service
- supply of power, light or water to the public by any establishment
- system of public conservancy or sanitations
- service in hospital or dispensary
- insurance service

Public utility service also includes any service which the Central Government or the State Government, in the public interest, declare to be a public utility service by notifications.

Provisions of Permanent Lok Adalat

Some important provisions of permanent Lok Adalat are

- The permanent Lok Adalat shall, during conduct of conciliation proceedings, assist the parties in their attempt to reach an amicable settlement of the dispute in an independent and impartial manner.
- It shall be the duty of every party to the application to co-operate in good faith with the permanent Lok Adalat and to comply with the direction of the permanent Lok Adalat, to produce evidence and other related documents before it.
- In case the parties reach at an agreement on the settlement of the dispute, they shall sign the settlement agreement and the permanent **Lok Adalat shall pass an award in terms** thereof.
- Where the parties fail to reach at an agreement, the permanent Lok Adalat shall decide the dispute.
- The permanent Lok Adalat while conducting conciliation proceedings or deciding a dispute shall be guided by the principles of natural justice, objectivity, fair play, equity and other principles of justice.
- It shall not be bound by the Code of Civil Procedure, 1908 (5 of 1908) and the Indian Evidence Act, 1872 (1 of 1872).
- The award of permanent Lok Adalat shall be final and deemed to be a decree of a Civil Court.

17.4 National Legal Services Authority (NALSA)

- The National Legal Services Authority (NALSA) has been constituted under the **Legal Services Authorities Act, 1987** while exercising the power of 5.29 to monitor and evaluate the implementation of legal aid programmes and to lay down policies and principles for making legal services available under the act. In every state, a State Legal Services Authority and in every High Court, a High Court Legal Services Committee have been constituted.
- District Legal Services Authorities and Taluk Legal Services Committees have been constituted in the districts. Most of the Taluks have to give effect to the policies and directions of the NALSA, and provide free legal services to the people and conduct Lok Adalats in the state.
- Supreme Court Legal Services Committee has been constituted to administer and implement the legal services programmes, as it relates to the Supreme Court of India. NALSA lays down policies, principles, and guidelines and frames effective and economical schemes for the State Legal Services Authorities, to implement the Legal Services Programmes throughout the country. The State Legal Services Authorities, District Legal Services Authorities, Taluk Legal Services Committees, etc have to discharge the following main functions.
    - provide Free and Competent Legal Services to the eligible persons
    - organise Lok Adalats for easy settlement of disputes
    - organise legal awareness camps in rural areas

NALSA Regulations, 2010

- In 2010, the National Legal Services Authority (NALSA) of India adopted the National Legal Services Authority (Free and Competent Legal Services) Regulations in exercise of its power under **Section 29** of the Legal Services Authorities Act, 1987.
- The NALSA regulations are applicable to the Legal Service Committees of the Supreme Court, High Courts, the States, Districts and Taluks.

Some broad features of the relevant regulation are as follows

Selection of Panel Lawyers

- The legal services institution is vested with the authority to invite applications from legal practitioners with requisite professional experience to indicate the types of cases as they may be entrusted with.
- The panel shall be prepared by the Executive Chairman of the legal service institution in consultation with the Attorney-General (for Supreme Court), Advocate-General (for High Courts), Government pleader (for Districts/Taluks) and the Bar Association President.
- The legal practitioner shall have three years or more of experience at the bar for being considered for empanelment.
- Personal traits like competence, integrity, suitability and experience shall be considered.
- Separate panels shall be maintained for different types of cases.
- The Panel has to be reconstituted every three years without disturbing the work of panel lawyers already representing ongoing cases.
- Some of the conditions for panel lawyers are as follows
  - If the panel lawyer wishes to withdraw from a case entrusted to him, then he shall communicate this to the member secretary and the latter may permit him to do so.
  - The panel lawyer is barred from taking any fee, remuneration or other valuable consideration from any person for whom legal services are rendered under the Regulation or Act.
  - The panel lawyer may be withdrawn from a case or his name shall be removed from the panel on account of non-performance of duties satisfactorily, or for actions against the object and purpose of the Act or Regulations.

Payment of Fee

The NALSA Regulations specify the rules regarding the payment of fees for panel lawyers which shall be in accordance with the State regulations, without any delay on receipt of completion of proceedings for them.

Service of Senior Advocates

The services of senior advocates may be availed in the following cases

- If the Chairman of the legal services institution forms an opinion to that effect in cases of great public importance.
- Where serious threats to life and liberty of the applicant exists.

Initiatives of NALSA

Legal Service Mobile App To enable equitable access to justice, NALSA has launched Legal Services Mobile App on Android and IOS versions to enable easy access to legal aid to common citizens.

DISHA Scheme The **Department of Justice** (DoJ) has launched a comprehensive, holistic, integrated and systemic solution on access to justice at pan India level through a scheme titled Designing Innovative Solutions for Holistic Access to Justice (DISHA). **It is being implemented from 2021-26.** All Access to justice programmes have been merged under the DISHA scheme and upscaled to all India levels.

Quick Test 1

1. What is the importance of legal aid?
2. When did Legal Services Authority Act, 1987 came into force?
3. Mention any one provision of permanent Lok Adalat.
4. Which committee has been constituted to administer and implement the legal services programmes?

17.5 The Indian Legal System

- The adversarial system that was brought by the colonial era made the access to justice difficult because it ended the era of informal dispute settlement prevalent in Indian society. The pre-British system was accessible as it was not technical or formal and was conducted in a language known to parties.
- The formal nature of proceedings in an adversarial system which requires pleadings and court fees, make access to justice difficult, for poor masses in India.
- In **M.H. Hoskot Vs. state of Maharashtra ([1978] 35CC 544)** the SC observed that our judicature bases itself on the Anglo-American model of dispensing justice. The system compels to collaborate lawyer-power thereby steering the wheels of equal justice under the law by providing free legal aid to certain categories of persons. Thus, in an adversarial system, the poor are represented by the advocates appointed by the government to ensure equal representation in the court of law, which forms one of the most important aspects of a true democracy.

Legal Aid under the Indian Constitution

- In 1976, **42nd Amendment** of the Indian Constitution inserted the **Article 39-A** in the Directive Principles of State Policy as 'Equal Justice and Free Legal Aid'.
- According to this article, the state shall secure that the operation of the legal system promotes justice, on the basis of equal opportunity, and shall provide free legal aid, by suitable legislation or schemes or in any way, to ensure that opportunities for securing justice are not denied to any citizen by reason of economic or other disabilities.
- However, this Constitutional guarantee was violated more often because a technical application of statutory law or Constitutional obligation is inadequate. Only a fair procedure can ensure the concept of equality and access to justice. Under **Article 15** of the Constitution of India, the state shall not discriminate against any citizen on grounds of religion, race, caste, sex, place of birth or any of them. On the basis of this principle, no citizen shall be subject to any disability on the grounds only of religion, race, caste, sex, place of birth or any of them. **Article 14** of the Constitution of India provides that the state shall not deny to any person equality before the law or the equal protection of the laws within the territory of India.

Free Legal Aid under Criminal Law

- **Section 340(1)** of the Code of Criminal Procedure, **1898,** provided that if a man was charged with an offence punishable with death, the court could provide him with counsel upon his request.
- However, in the Code of Criminal Procedure, **1973,** India facilitated statutory implementation of free legal aid subsequently.
- **Section 304(1)** also provides that in a trial before the sessions judge, if the accused has not sufficient means to engage a pleader, the court should assign a pleader for his defence at the expense of the state.
- In criminal cases, prosecution is initiated by the state, and when legal aid is provided to the accused, the expenditure of both the parties is managed by the state.

Legal Aid in Context of Social Justice and Human Rights

- Many people are denied human rights only because they **cannot afford the cost** required for the enforcement of their rights. In order to do social justice to them and to make human rights meaningful, legal aid becomes essential.
- A right to access to justice is **sine-qua-non**[1] for social justice. The access to justice itself is one of the most basic human rights, and without it, the realisation of many other human rights may become difficult.
- Infact, the right to access justice or legal aid is evolved by judicial creativity for the benefit of poor persons. It is neither possible nor proper to separate the right to legal aid from the range of human rights.
- Human rights are only declarations without legal aid.

1 **sine-quo- non** It refers to an essential condition, component, or requirement that is indispensable.

- Legal aid is only a way for providing social justice to all.
- Legal aid is an integral part of human rights and it requires urgent considerations.
- In present legal system of most countries, justice is not given but sold.

Legal Aid under International Law

- International law addresses the provision for free legal service from the perspective of human rights. A direct provision for legal services is incorporated in the **International Covenant on Civil and Political Rights** (ICCPR).
- India has ratified the International Covenant on Civil and Political Rights which came into force in **1976.** It is bound by the international obligation to provide free legal assistance as per the requirements of the covenant. The Supreme Court of India has adopted the method of giving effect to international legal obligations when these obligations exist in the Indian legal system expressly.
- The court also recognised international legal obligations as part of the law of the land when Indian law can be interpreted in accordance with international law.
- A number of international treaties may be interpreted referring to the need for free legal services while aiming at effective legal remedy and access to justice, such as
  - International Covenant on Economic, Social and Cultural Rights (ICESCR)
  - Convention on Elimination of Discrimination Against Women (CEDAW)
  - International Convention on Elimination of All Forms of Racial Discrimination.
- There are a number of declarations and principles adopted by the UN which refer to effective legal remedy, of which free legal services (in genuine cases) form an essential component.
- **Article 8** of the Universal Declaration on Human Rights (UDHR) provides that everyone has the right to an effective remedy by the competent national tribunals, for acts violating the Fundamental Rights granted by the Constitution or by the law.

Denial or Withdrawal of Legal Aid

- Legal aid can be denied at the initial stage before the application for legal aid is accepted. It can also be withdrawn at the later stage after the application has been accepted. Legal aid can be denied or withdrawn in the following circumstances
  - If a person is found **ineligible** under **Section 12** of the Legal Services Authorities Act, 1987.
  - If the aided person who applied under the income category is found to possess sufficient means.
  - It the aided person obtained legal services by mis-representation or fraud.
  - If the aided person **does not cooperate** with the Legal Services Authority/Committee or with the legal services advocate.
  - If the person engages a legal practitioner other than the one assigned by the Legal Services Authority/Committee.
  - In the event of death of the aided person, except in the case of civil proceedings where the right or liability survives.
- It the application for legal service or the matter in question is found to be an abuse of the process of law or of legal services.

Quick Test 2

1. What is the provision of Article 39-A of the Indian Constitution?
2. When did International Covenant on Civil and Political Rights came into force?
3. What is the provision under Article 8 of UDHDR?
4. Mention any one circumstance under which legal aid can be denied.

Mind Map

LEGAL SERVICES

1 Meaning of Legal Services

Definition
- Includes legal aid through advice, grants, or counsel for representation in civil and criminal matters.
- Aims to bridge social and economic disparities by ensuring equal access to justice.

Scope
- Payment of court fees, legal representation, document preparation and welfare access.

Types
- **Pre-litigation Services** Legal education, advice, awareness and settlements.
- **Post-litigation Services** Representation in court, appeals and enforcement of decrees.

2 Legal Services Authority Act, 1987

Objective
- Ensure access to justice for economically weaker and socially backward sections.

Constitutional Basis
- **Article 39A** Free legal aid and equal justice.
- **Articles 14 & 22(1)** Equality before the law and legal representation.

Eligibility
- Scheduled Castes, Scheduled Tribes, women, children, persons with disabilities, victims of disasters or violence, and individuals below prescribed income levels.

3 Amendments to the Act

Legal Services Authorities (Amendment) Act, 2002
- Introduced Permanent Lok Adalats for pre-litigation disputes.
- Focused on public utility services like transport, insurance and electricity.

Key Features of Lok Adalats
- Guided by natural justice principles.
- Awards are final and deemed as civil court decrees.

4 Role of National Legal Services Authority

Establishment
- Constituted under the Legal Services Authority Act, 1987.

Functions
- Lay down policies and principles for legal services.
- Monitor implementation of legal aid programmes.
- Organise Lok Adalats and legal awareness campaigns.

Regulations 2010
- Panel lawyer selection.
- Guidelines for fee payment and use of senior advocates.

Initiatives
- **DISHA Scheme** Holistic access to justice.
- Legal Services Mobile App.

5 Legal Aid under the Constitution

- **Article 39A** Equal justice and free legal aid.
- **Article 15** Prohibits discrimination based on religion, race, caste, sex, or birthplace.
- **Article 14** Equality before the law and equal protection under the law.

Criminal Law
- **Section 304(1) CrPC** Free legal aid for defendants in sessions court trials.

6 Legal Aid under International Law

ICCPR (International Covenant on Civil and Political Rights)
- Recognises legal aid as a human right.

Universal Declaration of Human Rights (UDHR)
- **Article 8** Right to an effective remedy by competent tribunals.

Other Treaties
- CEDAW (Convention on Elimination of Discrimination Against Women).
- ICESCR (International Covenant on Economic, Social and Cultural Rights).

7 Denial or Withdrawal of Legal Aid

Grounds
- Ineligibility under Section 12 of the Act.
- Sufficient financial means of the applicant.
- Misrepresentation or fraud.
- Lack of co-operation or engagement of another legal practitioner.

8 Social Justice and Human Rights

Impact
- Ensures access to justice for marginalised groups.
- Promotes equality and reduces systemic disparities.

Challenges
- Over-reliance on formal legal systems.
- Need for effective implementation and widespread awareness.

9 Key Case Laws

M.H. Hoskot Vs. State of Maharashtra (1978)
- Mandated free legal aid for the poor.

10 Conclusion

- Legal aid bridges gaps in access to justice and promotes social and economic equity.
- Requires continuous monitoring, awareness programmes, and integration with international obligations for meaningful implementation.

CBSE TEXTBOOK FOLDER

1. Mention any four categories of persons entitled to free legal aid under Legal Services Authority Act by Central Authority.

Ans. Persons entitled to free legal aid under Legal Services Authority Act by Central Authority are

- A person with disability as defined in Clause (i) of Section 2 of the Persons with Disabilities (Equal Opportunities, Protection of Rights and Full Participation) Act, 1995
- A person under circumstances of unjustified want such as being a victim of a mass disaster, ethnic violence, caste atrocity, flood drought, earthquake or industrial disaster
- A person in custody, according to Clause (g) of Section 2 of the Immoral Traffic (Prevention) Act, 1956
- A person in a juvenile home according to Clause (j) of Section 2 of the Juvenile Justice Act, 1986

2. How has the amendment of the Legal Services Authorities Act in 2002 widened its scope by establishing permanent Lok Adalats?

Or **Why was the Legal Services Authorities Act of 1987 amended in year 2022? Describe the changes that were introduced in the Principal Act.** **CBSE 2022**

Ans. The Parliament of India realised that litigation-oriented legal services cannot bring out desired results, therefore, for encouraging pre-litigation legal services especially in public utility service, the Parliament has made certain amendments in the Legal Services Authorities Act by passing an act known as the Legal Services Authorities (Amendment) Act, 2002.

The purpose of this amendment is to bring out certain changes in the Legal Services Act, 1987 (hereinafter referred to as the Principal Act) especially for the establishment of permanent Lok Adalats to settle disputes concerning public utility services at pre-litigation state.

3. Discuss the main provisions for legal aid under the Indian Constitution.

Or **Explain the provisions of the Indian Constitution that deals with the concept of legal aid.** **CBSE 2022**

Ans. The main provisions for legal aid under the Indian Consitution are

- In 1976, 42nd Amendment of the Indian Constitution inserted the Article 39-A in the Directive Principles of State Policy as 'Equal Justice and Free Legal Aid'. According to this article, the state shall secure that the operation of the legal system promotes justice, on the basis of equal opportunity, and shall provide free legal aid, by suitable legislation or schemes or in any way, to ensure that opportunities for securing justice are not denied to any citizen by reason of economic or other disabilities.
- Under Article 15 of the Constitution of India, the state shall not discriminate against any citizen on grounds of religion, race, caste, sex, place of birth or any of them. On the basis of this principle, no citizen shall be subject to any disability on the grounds only of religion, race, caste, sex, place of birth or any of them.

4. Discuss three main provisions of National Legal Services Authorities Regulations 2010.

Or **Describe the broad features of NALSA Regulations 2010.** **CBSE 2020**

Ans. The provisions of National Legal Services Authorities Regulations 2010 are

(i) **Selection of Panel Lawyers** The legal services institution is vested with the authority to invite applications from legal practitioners with requisite professional experience to indicate the types of cases as they may be entrusted with.

The panel shall be prepared by the Executive Chairman of the legal service institution in consultation with the Attorney-General (for Supreme Court), Advocate-General (for High Courts), Government pleader (for Districts/Taluks) and the Bar Association President.

The legal practitioner shall have three years or more of experience at the bar for being considered for empanelment. Personal traits like competence, integrity, suitability, and experience shall be considered.

(ii) **Payment of Fee** The NALSA Regulations specify the rules regarding the payment of fees for panel lawyers which shall be in accordance with the state regulations, without any delay on receipt of completion of proceedings for them.

(iii) **Service of Senior Advocates** The services of senior advocates may be availed in the following cases

- If the Chairman of the legal services institution forms an opinion to that effect in cases of great public importance.
- Where serious threats to life and liberty of the applicant exists.

Exam Pattern Questions

Objective Type Questions

Multiple Choice Questions (MCQs)

1. In a rural district of India, a legal aid clinic is established to assist impoverished individuals in navigating the court system. A farmer, unable to pay court fees, approaches the clinic with a land dispute case. Despite legal aid representation, the opposing party delays the case through repeated adjournments, leading to the farmer's financial and emotional distress.

Which systemic flaw in the adversarial system does this scenario highlight?

(a) The inherent bias against unrepresented litigants in the adversarial system.
(b) The overreliance on government-appointed advocates for the poor.
(c) The misuse of procedural mechanisms to delay justice, disadvantage weaker parties.
(d) The inability of the adversarial system to address language barriers and cultural differences.

2. The Chairman of the Supreme Court Legal Services Committee (SCLSC) is .... **CBSE 2017**

(a) a judge of the Supreme Court.
(b) the Governor of the concerned state.
(c) the Attorney General.
(d) the Chief Justice of the High Court of the concerned State.

3. Bipin approached permanent Lok Adalat for resolution of his dispute with Electricity Board on the issue of inflated electricity bill. Permanent Lok Adalat are set up under **CBSE SQP 2020**

(a) Legal Services Authorities (Amendment) Act, 2002
(b) Legal Services Authorities Act, 1987
(c) Article 39A of Constitution of India
(d) Article 14 of Constitution of India

4. In a criminal trial, a defendant from an economically disadvantaged background is represented by a government-appointed lawyer. The prosecutor, representing the state, presents complex evidence that requires extensive cross-examination. The defense lawyer, lacking resources and expertise, fails to challenge the evidence effectively, leading to the defendant's conviction.

What democratic principle is compromised in this scenario?

(a) The principle of judicial independence.
(b) The principle of equality before the law.
(c) The principle of proportionality in sentencing.
(d) The principle of public access to legal proceedings.

5. Which among the following is NOT a function of the National Legal Services Authority (NALSA)?

(a) Organising Lok Adalat for amicable settlement of disputes.
(b) Providing free and competent legal services to eligible persons.
(c) Enacting new laws for legal aid and dispute resolution.
(d) Organising legal awareness camps in rural areas.

6. Supreme Court Legal Services Committee is created by

(a) Supreme Court (b) Central Government
(c) State Government (d) High Court

7. The panel lawyer selected under NALSA Regulations is .... **CBSE 2018**

(a) allowed to charge fees from client.
(b) not allowed any remuneration.
(c) given remuneration from the Consolidated Fund of India.
(d) barred from taking any fees from the client.

8. Raghav was empaneled in the year 2020 under the Delhi Legal Services Authorities Act as an expert for matrimonial cases. In which year will he have to reapply for being a panelist in the reconstituted panel? **CBSE SQP 2020**

(a) 2021 (b) 2023 (c) 2025 (d) 2026

9. Equal justice and free legal aid has been incorporated in which Article of the Constitution?

(a) Article 38
(b) Article 39
(c) Article 39A
(d) Article 40

10. In light od the principles enshrined in Article 39A, which of the following circumstances contradicts its core objective of equal justice and free legal aid? **CBSE 2025**

(a) The state provides legal aid to economically disadvantages citizens facing criminal prosecution.
(b) A wealthy individual is given legal aid despite having adequate resources to access private legal counsel.
(c) A marginalised person is granted legal representation in a civil matter by the state.
(d) The state facilities access to justice for those affected by socio-economic disabilities.

11. **Read the given situations and decide which of the following is eligible to receive free legal aid?** **CBSE SQP 2020**

(a) Raghu in a property dispute with his brother.
(b) Pankaj working as an accounts officer in government sector undertaking services related issues.
(c) Mr. Seth, a senior citizen, fighting for his pension.
(d) Mrs. Verma, branch manager of a bank accused of money laundering.

12. **The Constitution of India provides that the state shall not deny to any person equality before the law or the equal protection of the laws within the territory of India. Identify the article.**

(a) Article 14 (b) Article 15 (c) Article 16 (d) Article 17

13. **Given below are the different stages in the development of the legal aid movement in India. Arrange them chronologically.**

I. Article 39A was inserted by the 42nd Amendment Act of the Indian Constitution.
II. The Committee on National Implementation of Legal Aid was constituted with Justice Bhagwati as its head.
III. The Union Government initiated the national legal aid scheme which faced financial shortages and died a natural death.
IV. The Union Government constituted a committee under the Chairmanship of Justice Krishna Iyer to develop a legal aid scheme for states. **CBSE SQP 2022**

Choose the correct option.

(a) I, II, III, IV (b) I, III, II, IV
(c) III, IV, I, II (d) IV, III, II, I

14. After winning a case, Mr. Kumar needs to ensure that the court's decision is enforced. His lawyer, Ms. Singh, assists him in executing the court decree. She helps him recover the awarded amount by garnishing the opponent's bank account and auctioning his property. Ms. Singh also ensures that the court-ordered injunction is implemented, restraining the opponent from further illegal activities.

What post-litigation service is Ms. Singh providing to Mr. Kumar?

(a) Filing an appeal (b) Executing the court decree
(c) Drafting a legal notice (d) Mediating a settlement

15. **In 1980, the Committee on National Implementation of Legal Aid was constituted with .... as its head.**

(a) Justice Iyer (b) Justice Bhagwati
(c) Justice Swaminatham (d) None of these

16. **........... of the Universal Declaration on Human Rights (UDHR) provides that everyone has the right to an effective remedy by the competent national tribunals for acts violating the Fundamental Rights granted by the Constitution or by the law.**

(a) Article 7 (b) Article 8 (c) Article 9 (d) Article 6

17. **Match the following.**

Column I		Column II
A. Article 39-A	1.	Pre-litigation legal service
B. 14th Law Commission Report	2.	Inserted by 42nd Constitution Amendment Act
C. Legal education	3.	2010
D. National Legal Services Authority (Free and Competent Legal Services) Regulations	4.	Idea of providing free legal aid to the poor by the state.

Codes

	A	B	C	D		A	B	C	D
(a)	1	2	3	4	(b)	2	4	1	3
(c)	1	3	2	4	(d)	4	1	3	2

18. **Statement I** Article 39-A of the Indian Constitution mandates the state to provide free legal aid to ensure access to justice for all citizens, particularly the weaker sections of society.

Statement II The Legal Services Authorities Act, 1987, was enacted to give statutory backing to the provisions of Article 39 A.

Choose the correct statement

(a) Both Statements are correct.
(b) Both Statements are incorrect.
(c) Statement I is correct, but Statement II is not correct.
(d) Statement II is correct, but Statement I is not correct.

19. **Statement I** According to Section 304(1) of the Code of Criminal Procedure, if an accused does not have sufficient means to engage a lawyer, the court must assign a pleader at the state's expense.

Statement II The provision for free legal aid under criminal law was first introduced in the Code of Criminal Procedure, 1973.

Choose the correct statement

(a) Both Statements are correct.
(b) Both Statements are incorrect.
(c) Statement I is correct, but Statement II is not correct.
(d) Statement II is correct, but Statement I is not correct.

Assertion-Reason Questions

Directions (Q. Nos. 20-22) In the questions given below, there are two statements. Read the statements and choose the correct option.

Codes

(a) Both A and R are true and R is the correct explanation of A.
(b) Both A and R are true, but R is not the correct explanation of A.
(c) A is true, but R is false.
(d) A is false, but R is true.

20. **Assertion** (A) The Preamble of the Legal Services Act sets forth the need to address the grievances of weaker sections of the society

Reason (R) The society is rapidly progressing and the reflections of the same can be found on all fronts.

21. **Assertion** (A) Mere declaration and passing of resolutions about human rights are not enough.

Reason (R) The guarantee for the enforcement of these rights is equally essential.

22. **Assertion** (A) The Parliament has made certain amendments in the Legal Services Authorities Act by passing an act known as the Legal Services Authorities (Amendments) Act, 2002.

Reason (R) The purpose of this amendment is to bring out certain changes in the Legal Services Act, 1987 especially for the establishment of permanent Lok Adalats to settle disputes concerning public utility services at pre-litigation state.

Answers

1. (c) The misuse of procedural mechanisms to delay justice, disadvantage weaker parties.
2. (a) a judge of the Supreme Court.
3. (a) Legal Services Authorities (Amendment) Act, 2002
4. (b) The principle of equality before the law.
5. (c) Enacting new laws for legal aid and dispute resolution.
6. (b) Central Government
7. (d) barred from taking any fees from the client.
8. (b) 2023
9. (c) Article 39A
10. (b) A wealthy individual is given legal aid despite having adequate resources to access private legal counsel.
11. (c) Mr. Seth, a senior citizen, fighting for his pension.
12. (a) Article 14
13. (b) I, III, II, IV
14. (b) Executing the court decree
15. (b) Justice Bhagwati
16. (b) Article 8
17. (b) 2 4 1 3
18. (a) Both Statements are correct.
19. (c) Statement I is correct, but Statement II is not correct.
20. (a) Both A and R are true and R is the correct explanation of A.
21. (a) Both A and R are true and R is the correct explanation of A.
22. (a) Both A and R are true and R is the correct explanation of A.

Subjective Questions

Very Short Answer Type Questions

1. Enumerate the components of pre-litigation legal service. **CBSE 2018**

Ans. The pre-litigation legal services include

- Legal education
- Legal advice
- Legal awareness
- Pre-litigation settlement, etc.

2. 'Litigation is not a luxury but it should be used as a last resort'. Analyse the statement with respect to pre litigation services.

Ans. These days, the number of litigations is increasing day by day, which is against the smooth administration of justice. So far, emphasis was given only on post-litigation assistance or help. Now, it is being realised that pre-litigation legal services are more useful than post-litigation legal services. The pre-litigation legal services include; Legal education, legal advice awareness and pre-litigation settlement.

Post-litigation services include all those services that are required to be rendered by an advocate to his client. These services should be resorted only when pre-litigation services fail to give any result.

3. In 1987, the Legal Services Authorities Act was enacted to provide free legal aid to marginalised sections of society. The act established the National Legal Services Authority (NALSA) and State Legal Services Authorities (SLSAs) to implement legal aid programmes. The act aimed to ensure that legal services were accessible to all, regardless of economic or social status.

What was the primary objective of the Legal Services Authorities Act, 1987?

Ans. The primary objective of the Legal Services Authorities Act, 1987 is to provide free legal aid to marginalised sections of society, ensuring access to justice for all

4. Enlist any four legal services given to any beneficiary under the provision of free legal aid. **CBSE 2025**

Ans. The four legal services provided under free legal aid include

(i) Payment of court fees, process fees, and other charges related to legal proceedings.

(ii) Providing the services of lawyers in legal proceedings.

(iii) Obtaining and supplying certified copies of orders and other documents.

(iv) Preparation of appeal, paper books, including printing and translation of documents.

5. In 1960, the legal aid scheme died a natural death due to paucity of funds. In 1973, the movement was revived by the Union Government with formation of a committee to develop legal aid scheme for states.

(i) Who was the Chairman of this committee?

(ii) How did this committee develop a strong foundation for initiating legal aid scheme in India? **CBSE 2022**

Ans. (i) Justice Krishna Iyer was appointed as the Chairman of committee for legal aid.

(ii) The committee dealt with the nexus between law and poverty, and spoke of PIL. It emphasised the need for active and widespread legal aid system that enabled law to reach the people, rather than requiring people to reach the law.

6. Where are the NALSA Regulations applicable?

Ans. The NALSA Regulations are applicable to the Legal Service Committees of the Supreme Court, High Courts, the states, districts and taluks.

7. What is the composition of NLSA?

Ans. The NLSA consists of

- the Chief Justice of India as Patron-in-Chief,
- a judge of the Supreme Court nominated by the President as as Executive Chairman, and
- other members nominated by the government in consultation with the CJI.

8. What is the primary purpose of the Legal Services Authorities (Amendment) Act, 2002?

***Or* State the purpose of the Legal Services Authorities (Amendment) Act, 2002.** **CBSE 2025**

Ans. The purpose of Legal Services Authorities (Amendment) Act, 2002 is to bring out certain changes in the Legal Services Act, 1987, especially for the establishment of permanent Lok Adalats to settle disputes concerning public utility services at pre-litigation state.

9. Arvind is being tried for misappropriation of office funds in trial before the sessions judge. He does not have sufficient means to engage a pleader. What remedy is available to Arvind? **CBSE 2020**

Ans. If Arvind is unable to engage a pleader, the court is required to assign a pleader for his defence at the expense of the state.

10. Many people cannot afford the cost of enforcing their human rights. How does legal aid help in ensuring social justice and making human rights meaningful for the poor?

Ans. Legal aid helps the poor by providing free legal support, ensuring access to justice, and making human rights enforceable. It removes financial barriers, prevents social injustice, and guarantees fair treatment, making human rights meaningful and accessible to everyone, regardless of wealth.

Short Answer Type Questions

1. (i) Mr. Mahavir is physically and mentally harassed by his son and daughter-in-law and wishes to file a case against them under the Indian Penal Code. He is a senior citizen and runs a small tea stall for his survival. He approaches Delhi District Legal Services Authority for help.

(ii) What kind of help can be provided by the Delhi District Legal Services Authority?

(iii) Will Delhi District Legal Services Authority be able to help Mr. Mahavir? Give reason for your answer. **CBSE SQP 2022**

Ans. (i) The Delhi District Legal Services Authority may provide legal services to the eligible persons, to conduct Lok adalats for cases pending before Hon'ble High Court and to encourage the settlement of disputes by way of negotiation, arbitration and conciliation.

(ii) The Legal Services Authorities Act of 1987 provides free legal aid to certain categories of citizens

(a) A member of a Scheduled Caste or Scheduled Tribe;

(b) A victim of trafficking in human beings or beggar as referred in Article 23 of the Constitution

(iii) A woman or a child those who have the financial means, who can afford to have a lawyer, should desist from taking the help of legal aid institutions. Thus, Mr. Mahavir needs to come into the given criteria for the legal aid services.

2. State the composition of the Central Authority constituted under Legal Services Authorities Act.

Ans. The Central Government constitutes the National Legal Services Authority (NLSA) and the Supreme Court Legal Services Committee (SCLSC) for exercising powers and functions as determined by the Central Authority.

The NLSA consists of

- the Chief Justice of India as patron-in-chief,
- a judge of the Supreme Court nominated by the President as Executive Chairman, and

- other members nominated by the Government in consultation with the CJI.

The SCLC consists of

- judge of the Supreme Court as the Chairman, and Other members prescribed by the Government and nominated by the CJI.

3. Neither is it possible nor is it proper to isolate the right to legal aid from the range of human rights. Comment.

Ans. It is neither possible nor proper to separate the right to legal aid from the range of human rights. Human rights are only declarations without legal aid. They become lucrative only when they are enforced. The right to legal aid enables accomplishment of these human rights and makes them worthwhile for the poor masses in the world. Many people are denied human rights only because they cannot afford the cost required for the enforcement of their rights. In order to do social justice to them and to make human rights meaningful, legal aid becomes essential. Legal aid is only a way for providing social justice to all. Legal aid is an integral part of human rights and it requires urgent considerations.

4. Mr. Arjun, a daily wage labourer, was accused of theft and could not afford a lawyer for his defense. The court appointed a legal aid lawyer to represent him.

(i) Under which law was Mr. Arjun entitled to free legal aid?

(ii) What are the rights of an accused person in such cases?

(iii) Can legal aid be withdrawn in any situation? If yes, under what circumstances?

Ans. (i) Mr. Arjun was entitled to free legal aid under Article 39-A of the Indian Constitution and Section 304(1) of the Code of Criminal Procedure (CrPC), 1973, which ensures legal representation for accused persons who cannot afford a lawyer. The Legal Services Authorities Act, 1987, further strengthens this right.

(ii) An accused person has the right to a fair trial, legal representation, protection against self-incrimination, and the presumption of innocence until proven guilty. Free legal aid ensures they receive a proper defense.

(iii) Legal aid can be withdrawn if the person is found ineligible, misrepresents facts, refuses cooperation, hires another lawyer, or abuses the process.

5. With regard to the responsibility of the Central Government to provide legal aid service **CBSE 2016**

(i) What is the composition of the Central Authority?

(ii) State any four functions of the Central Authority.

Ans. (i) For answer, refer to Q.No. 2 of Short Answer Type Questions.

(ii) Four functions performed by the Central Authority are

(a) Lay down policies and principles for making legal services available under the provisions of this act.

(b) Frame the most effective and economical schemes for the purpose of making legal services available under the provisions of this Act.

(c) Utilise the funds at its disposal and make appropriate allocation of funds to the State Authorities and District Authorities.

(d) Take necessary steps by way of social justice litigation with regard to consumer protection, environment protection or any other matter of special concern to the weaker sections of the society.

6. Explain legal aid in context of social justice and human rights in India. **CBSE SQP 2022**

Ans. The growth of legal aid movement is seen as one of the late conscious attempts in social adjustment that followed the slow and often unconscious process of social engineering. Social engineering may be defined as the science and art of making appropriate adjustments to human relationships as well as to promote the welfare of the community as a whole. The basic philosophy of legal aid is to ensure equal justice to all, especially to the poor, so that no one is deprived of equal rights in the eyes of the law or denied access to the court only because of poverty, illiteracy or other incapacities.

As part of the human rights, it is necessary to recognise the principle of equality and ensure access to justice. These foundations reflect the incorporation of legal obligation in the international treaties, regional treaties, the working of monitoring bodies under these treaties or in the national legal systems.

7. Identify the provision for legal aid under the Indian Constitution. What does the judgement of M.H. Hoskot Vs. State of Maharashtra state about the legal aid services in India? **CBSE SQP 2022**

Ans. In 1960, some guidelines were drawn by the Government for legal aid schemes. Article 39A of the Constitution - inserted by the 42nd Amendment Act in 1976 - offered a remedy to this problem by directing the state to provide free legal aid by suitable legislation or schemes or in any other way, to ensure that opportunities to secure justice are not denied to any citizen by reason of economic or other disabilities.

The judgement of M.H. Hoskot Vs. State of Maharashtra state about the legal aid services in India that "The state had the consitutional mandate to provide free legal aid to an accused who cannot afford legal services due to poor economic conditions also ensuring the free and fair trial".

8. Ramesh, a daily wage labourer, was falsely accused of theft and imprisoned. His family, living below the poverty line, couldn't afford legal representation. The court referred the case to the Legal Services Authority, which provided Ramesh with a lawyer. The lawyer argued the case, and Ramesh was acquitted. The Legal Services Authority also provided Ramesh with compensation for wrongful imprisonment.

Who are entitled to legal services in India, as per the Legal Services Authorities Act, 1987?

Ans. For answer refer to text under the heading 'The Legal Services Authority Act, 1987' on page no. 315.

9. Riya, a low-income individual is facing a legal battle and applies for legal aid. After providing all necessary documents and proof of her financial status Riya's application for legal aid is denied. In this context, state why legal aid may be denied or withdrawn. **CBSE 2024 C**

Ans. Legal aid may be denied or withdrawn in the following situations

- **Misrepresentation or Fraud** If Riya provides false information or conceals facts about her financial status or case.
- **Lack of Merit in the Case** If the legal aid authority determines that Riya's case lacks legal merit or is frivolous.
- **Non-Co-operation** If Riya fails to co-operate with the legal aid authority or her assigned lawyer.
- **Change in Financial Circumstances** If Riya's financial situation improves, making her ineligible for legal aid.

The legal aid authority may reassess Riya's application if she provides additional information or appeals the decision.

Long Answer Type Questions

1. Discuss the main provisions for Free Legal Aid under the Indian Constitution.

Ans. For answer, refer to text under the heading Legal Aid under the Indian Constitution on page no. 319

2. Explain the importance of the following provisions to create equal opportunity and ensure access to justice for all. **CBSE 2018**

(i) Article 39-A of the Constitution
(ii) Section 304(1) of CrPC
(iii) NALSA Regulations, 2010

Ans. (i) For answer, refer to text under the heading Legal Aid under the Indian Constitution on page no. 319.

(ii) For answer, refer to text under the heading 'Free Legal Aid under the Criminal Law, on page no. 319.

(iii) For answer, refer to text under the heading 'NALSA Regulations, 2010' on page no. 317.

3. Explain the term 'legal aid'. Why is it important for every legal system to provide for legal aid? Discuss the provisions in the Indian Constitution that have paved way for the various provisions of legal aid in India. **CBSE 2025**

Ans. Legal aid refers to the provision of free legal assistance to individuals who cannot afford legal representation or access to justice due to financial constraints. It ensures that justice is not denied to anyone based on economic limitations.

Legal aid is important in a legal system as it upholds the principle of equality before the law, allowing marginalised sections of society to exercise their rights effectively.

The Indian Constitution lays the foundation for legal aid under Article 39A, introduced by the 42nd Amendment, mandating the state to provide free legal assistance to economically weaker sections. Additionally, Articles 14 and 22(1) reinforce the right to legal representation, ensuring fair treatment under the law. The Legal Services Authorities Act, 1987, further institutionalised legal aid through bodies like the National Legal Services Authority (NALSA), which implements legal aid schemes and organises Lok Adalat for dispute resolution.

4. A poor and illiterate woman Sarita, is a victim of domestic violence. Her husband has thrown her out their matrimonial home, and she has no access to her children. Sarita approaches a legal aid clinic, where she meets a lawyer who provides her with free legal assistance. The lawyer helps Sarita to file a case against her husband seeking maintenance, custody of her children and protection from domestic violence.

How does the provision of legal aid to Sarita advance social justice and human rights?

Ans. It advances both social justice and human rights by providing access to justice, promoting gender equality and protecting Sarita's rights as a woman. The provision of legal aid to Sarita advances social justice by providing access to justice for a poor and marginalised person. It also advances human rights by promoting gender equality and protecting Sarita's right as a woman, including her right to be free from domestic violence and to have access to her children. Legal aid helps reduce poverty by enabling Sarita to access resources and services she otherwise couldn't afford. It advances women's rights by providing Sarita with legal assistance to challenge patriarchal norms and seek justice for domestic violence.

5. Explain the process of Constitution of the panel for providing free legal aid under the NALSA Regulations 2010. **CBSE SQP 2024**

Ans. Under the NALSA (National Legal Services Authority) Regulations 2010, the process for constituting a panel for providing free legal aid is as follows

- The District Legal Services Authority (DLSA) identifies and selects advocates with a minimum 3 years of experience. The selected advocates are then recommended to the Secretary, DLSA.
- The Secretary, DLSA, constitutes a panel of advocates, ensuring representation from various fields of law.
- The panel is valid for a specified period, typically 2-3 years. During this period, panel members provide free legal aid to eligible clients, including legal advice, drafting and representation in court.
- The DLSA monitors and reviews the performance of panel members, and may remove or replace them as needed.
- This process enables the provision of quality legal aid to marginalised and underprivileged sections of society, promoting access to justice and legal empowerment.

6. With regards to the selection of panel lawyers under the NALSA Regulations, 2010, answer the questions given below.

(i) Mention the basic requirement an advocate must fulfill to be considered for empanelment.

(ii) State the composition of the selection board for empanelling advocates for High Court Legal Services Committee.

(iii) Under what circumstances can a panel lawyer be removed from any case?

(iv) When can the services of a senior advocate be availed by the legal services authorities?

Ans. (i) An advocate must have a minimum of three years of experience at the bar to be considered for empanelment. Additionally, competence, integrity, suitability, and experience in handling different types of cases are key criteria for selection.

(ii) The selection board for empanelment of advocates in the High Court Legal Services Committee consists of the Executive Chairman of the legal services institution in consultation with the Advocate-General, Government Pleader and the Bar Association President.

(iii) A panel lawyer can be removed from any case if their performance is unsatisfactory or if their actions go against the objectives of the Legal Services Authorities Act or NALSA Regulations.

(iv) The services of a senior advocate may be availed in cases of great public importance or where there is a serious threat to the life and liberty of the applicant, as determined by the Chairman of the legal services institution?.

7. Explain sequentially the enactment of The legal Services Authorities Act, 1987. **CBSE SQP 2024**

Ans. The enactment of The Legal services Authorities Act, 1987, occurrerd sequentially as follows.

- **Introduction** The act was introduced in the Parliament of India to constitute legal services authorities for providing free legal aid to weaker sections of society.
- **Passage** The act was passed by both Houses of Parliament, namely, the Lok Sabha and the Rajya Sabha.
- **Assent** The president of India gave assent to the act on 11th December, 1987.
- **Notification** The act was notified in the official Gazette of India on 11th December, 1987.
- **Commencement** The act came into force on 9th November, 1995, with the establishment of the National Legal Services Authority (NALSA).
- **Amendments** The act has undergone several amendments including in 1994, 2002 and 2017, to expand its scope and strengthen legal services authorities.

8. The 14th Law Commission of India mooted the idea of providing legal aid to the poor by the State and paved the way for a legislation to this regard in 1987. Sequentially explain the developments that led to the environment of Legal Services Authority Act, 1987. What changes were introduced in the Act of 1987 by its amendment in 2002? **CBSE 2024 C**

Ans. The developments leading to the Legal Services Authority Act, 1987, were

- **14th Law Commission Report (1958)** Recommended state-funded legal aid for the poor.
- **Committee on Legal Aid (1973)** Established to explore legal aid mechanisms.
- **Legal Aid Scheme (1980)** Launched by the Government of India to provide legal aid.
- **Legal Services Authorities Act, 1987** Enacted to establish a nationwide network of legal services authorities.

The 2002 amendment introduced significant changes

- **Expansion of beneficiaries** Included marginalised groups, such as women, children, and persons with disabilities.
- **Establishment of Lok Adalats** Permanently established Lok Adalats for speedy and cost-effective dispute resolution.
- **Increased funding** Provided for enhanced funding for legal services authorities.
- **Strengthened institutional framework** Fortified the institutional framework for providing legal aid and services.

SELF ASSESSMENT TEST

Objective Type Questions

1. "In the state of nature, indeed, all men are born equal, but they cannot continue in this equality, society makes them lose it, and they recover it only by the protection of the laws" was said by
   (a) Montesquieu (b) Smith (c) Rawls (d) P.N. Bhagwati
2. The services of senior advocates may be availed if
   (a) the Chairman of the legal services institution forms an opinion to that effect in cases of great public importance.
   (b) serious threats to life and liberty of the applicant exist.
   (c) Both (a) and (b)
   (d) None of the above
3. The panel lawyer may be withdrawn from a case or his name removed from the panel on account of
   (a) non-performance of duties satisfactorily (b) for actions against the object and purpose of the act
   (c) for actions against the object of the Regulations. (d) All of these
4. 'Insurance service' comes under the ambit of
   (a) Public utility service (b) Private utility service (c) State utility service (d) Central utility service

Very Short Answer Type Questions

5. 'An impartial and independent judiciary is the guardian of individual rights in a democratic society'. Justify the given statement.
6. Rahul, who belongs to a Scheduled Caste and earns below the prescribed income limit, is accused of a crime. He applies for free legal aid, and a lawyer is assigned to him by the Legal Services Authority. Later, it is found that Rahul misrepresented his financial status.
   Identify the conditions under which legal aid can be denied or withdrawn in this situation.
7. Which section of the Legal Services Authority Act deal with the criteria of eligibility to the legal services?

Short Answer Type Questions

8. Identify and explain the type of legal aid eligibility or denial in each of the following cases
   (i) Ramesh, a factory worker, is accused of a crime but cannot afford a lawyer. He applies for free legal aid under the Legal Services Authorities Act, 1987.
   (ii) Sita, a woman from a Scheduled Tribe, seeks free legal aid for a land dispute case but is found to have sufficient financial resources.
   (iii) Akash, an undertrial prisoner, requests free legal aid but refuses to co-operate with the assigned legal services advocate.
9. How has the concept of free legal aid been incorporated under International Law?
10. What is the criteria for providing free legal services in India?

Long Answer Type Question

11. India has ratified the International Covenant on Civil and Political Rights (ICCPR), which mandates free legal assistance for those in need. However, many underprivileged individuals still struggle to access justice due to systemic barriers.
    (i) Which category of International Law is relevant to the issue of free legal aid?
    (ii) How does the Indian legal system incorporate international obligations regarding free legal aid?
    (iii) What role do international treaties play in ensuring access to justice for marginalised communities?

PROJECT WORK

Understanding Case Laws

Declaration

I hereby declare that this document, titled "Understanding Case Laws", is an original work completed by me. The information presented has been gathered from various sources, including textbooks, online research, and official reports, to provide an insightful understanding cases.

I affirm that this work has not been copied from any existing material, and all sources of information have been duly acknowledged.

Signature: ____________________

Name: ____________________

Date: ____________________

Acknowledgement

I want to sincerely thank to Mr./Mrs. .... , my Legal Studies instructor, for her direction and assistance with my paper. I was able to better organise and explain my ideas as a result of her insightful criticism and recommendations. Their ongoing encouragement has always encouraged me to aim high and follow my passions.

I also want to express my gratitude to the library personnel for giving me access to a variety of books on legal studies and tools. This project would not have been possible without their help.

Finally, I want to highlight the importance of court cases in our society and how they influence the development of our legal system. The goal of this project is to shed light on some of the most significant court issues and their ramifications for society.

Date............

....
Name of Student

Certificate

This is to Certify that the project work

.... is the bonafide

work of .... (Name of the student) who

carried out the work under my supervision

....

Name and Signature of
Teacher/Supervisor

Contents

Understanding Case Laws

Introduction

The legal system of India is intricate and multidimensional, which has developed over time as a result of the efforts of legislators, judges and attorneys. Based on a blend of common law, statutory law, and civil law, the Indian legal system is always changing to meet the changing requirements and values of society. The system is based on three types of laws

- **Common Law** This is law that comes from judges' decisions in previous cases. It's like a rulebook that judges follow based on what has happened in the past.
- **Statutory Law** These are laws made by the government and Parliament. They are written down and passed in official documents.
- **Civil Law** This deals with resolving disputes between individuals or organisations such as property disputes, family matters and business issues.

The legal system in India keeps changing to make sure it stays relevant and fair for society. One important part of this system is **landmark cases**. These are cases that have made big changes or set important examples for how laws should be interpreted. When judges decide these cases, they create rules and guidelines that help future judges to make decisions in similar cases. These landmark decisions help in shaping the way about how the law works and guide the decisions that come afterward.

Importance of Understanding Case Laws

Understanding the case laws is a significant aspect of studying law. The importance of understanding case laws are as follow

- **Shows How Laws are Applied in Real Life** Laws on paper are just rules, but case laws show how these rules work in real situations. By studying them, we learn how courts apply laws to actual disputes and cases. For example, understanding a case about a contract dispute helps us to see how a court interprets contract law when two parties are in conflict.

- **Helps in Understanding Legal Principles** Case laws clarify complex legal principles by showing how they are used in practice. For instance, in family law, a case law about child custody will help you understand how courts apply the principles of best interest for the child.
- **Establishes Precedents for Future Cases** Courts follow previous decisions in similar cases, which are called precedents. Understanding case laws help to see how past judgements influence future decisions. This is important for consistency in the legal system, as similar cases should lead to similar results, ensuring fairness.
- **Guides Legal Decision-making** Case laws guide lawyers, judges and lawmakers in future decisions. They help in interpreting laws and understanding how similar cases have been handled before.
- **Explains Rights and Remedies** Case laws help in understanding how individuals can seek justice when their rights are violated. For instance, consumer protection cases show how consumers can seek compensation for defective products.
- **Clarifies Legal Justice and Fairness** Case laws help to see how courts balance justice. For example, understanding Constitutional cases about individual rights or public interest helps to see how courts protect personal freedoms while maintaining public order. This helps in better understanding the core values of the legal system, such as fairness and equality before the law.
- **Demonstrates How Laws Reflect Social Changes** Case laws show how the legal system adapts to societal changes. For example, cases involving women's rights or environmental protection demonstrate how the law evolves in response to new social concerns.
- **Helps Understand Legal Remedies and Punishments** In criminal cases, case laws help to understand the punishments and legal remedies for crimes. For example, in cases of theft or murder, case laws show how the law determines the appropriate punishment.

Types of Cases

In India, cases are divided into different types based on the nature of the issue. The different types of cases are as follow

- **Civil Cases** Civil cases deal with disputes between individuals, organisations, or the government over legal rights and duties. These cases usually involve issues like property, contracts, family matters and money.
- **Criminal Cases** Criminal cases deal with actions that are harmful to society and the state. These are cases where a person is accused of committing a crime, like theft, assault, or murder.
- **Constitutional Cases** Constitutional cases involve the interpretation of the Indian Constitution. These cases deal with Fundamental Rights, the powers of the government and other Constitutional matters.
- **Family Cases** Family cases deal with issues related to family relationships such as marriage, divorce, child custody, inheritance and maintenance.

- **Labour and Employment Cases** Labour and employment cases focus on the rights of workers and employers. These cases deal with disputes related to wages, working conditions, workplace safety and termination.
- **Consumer Cases** Consumer cases deal with disputes between consumers and sellers, service providers or businesses. The focus is on protecting consumers from unfair trade practices, defective products or poor services.
- **Environmental Cases** Environmental cases focus on protecting the environment, natural resources and wildlife. These cases deal with pollution, deforestation or any action that harms the environment.
- **Public Interest Cases** Public interest cases focus on issues that affect the general public or large sections of society. These cases are filed to address matters of public concern or social justice, which are often brought by individuals or groups for the welfare of society.

Difference Between Civil, Criminal and Constitutional Case

The difference between Civil, Criminal and Constitutional Cases are as follows

Criteria	Civil Case	Criminal Case	Constitutional Case
Nature of Dispute	Private disputes between individuals or organisations.	Public issues where society or state is harmed.	Issues related to the interpretation of the Constitution.
Parties Involved	Plaintiff (person who files the case) Vs. Defendant (person being sued).	Prosecution (government) Vs. Defendant (accused).	Individuals or organisations Vs. Government or the state (may involve rights violations or power disputes).
Purpose	To compensate the victim or resolve private disputes.	To punish the accused and maintain public order.	To protect Constitutional rights and ensure laws follow the Constitution.
Examples	Divorce, property disputes, breach of contract.	Murder, theft, assault.	Violation of Fundamental Rights, powers of the government, law challenges.
Outcome	Compensation, orders to do or not do something.	Punishment (jail, fines, etc.).	Strike down unconstitutional laws, enforce Fundamental Rights, judicial review.

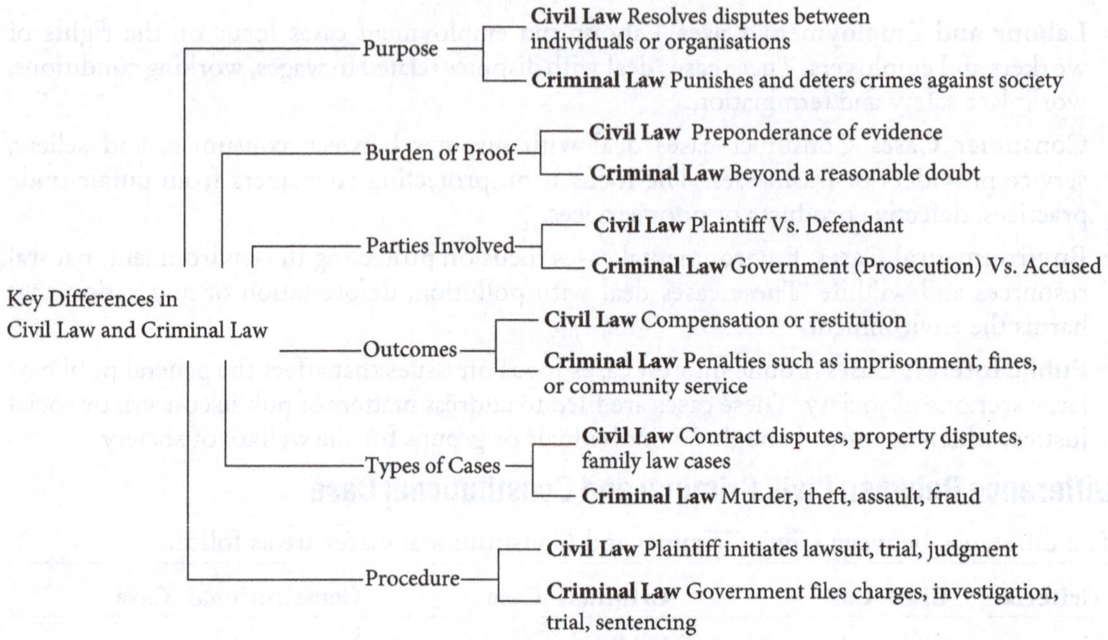

Key differences in Civil Law and Criminal Law

The Cases

The three decided cases based on Civil, Criminal and Constitutional in nature are as follows

1. M.C. Mehta Vs. Shri Ram Foods and Fertiliser Industries (1987)

Name of the Case M.C. Mehta Vs. Shri Ram Foods and Fertiliser Industries

Parties to the Case

- **Petitioner** M.C. Mehta (Environmental Activist)
- **Respondent** Shri Ram Foods and Fertiliser Industries (Industrial Corporation)

Citation to the Case

Citation- [1987] 2 SCC 411

Bench

The case was decided by the Supreme Court of India.

- Honourable Chief Justice- R.S. Pathak
- Honourable Justices- P.N. Bhagwati, O. Chinnappa Reddy, S.M. Fazal Ali and E.S. Venkataramiah.

Nature of the Case

The case is a Public Interest Litigation (PIL), which falls under **Civil Law** and involves Environmental Law.

Facts of the Case and Issues Involved

Facts

- In the 1980s, M.C. Mehta, an environmentalist filed a PIL in the Supreme Court regarding the severe pollution being caused by Shri Ram Foods and Fertiliser Industries in the area of Delhi.
- The factory was releasing harmful pollutants such as harmful chemicals and gases into the atmosphere and surrounding environment.
- The pollution was having serious detrimental effects on public health, including respiratory problems, contamination of water bodies and damage to agricultural lands in the vicinity.
- The petitioner argued that the factory was violating public health, environmental and Constitutional rights by its actions.

Issues Involved

- Whether Shri Ram Foods and Fertiliser Industries were causing environmental harm by discharging toxic pollutants into the atmosphere.
- Whether the industry was violating the right to life and environmental protection under Article 21 of the Constitution of India.
- Whether the factory should be shut down or if measures should be taken to prevent further environmental damage.
- The extent of responsibility of industries in controlling environmental pollution and its impact on public health.

Decision of the Case, including Ratio Decidendi and Obiter Dicta

- The Supreme Court in this case ruled in favor of the petitioner. The court observed that the factory was indeed causing significant harm to the environment and violating public rights under the Constitution.
- The court directed that the factory take immediate steps to reduce pollution levels and implement safer, cleaner production which processes to avoid any further damage to the environment.
- The court emphasised that industries must prioritise environmental protection as part of their operations, and pollution control mechanisms should be in place.

Ratio Decidendi

- **Environmental Responsibility** The court reaffirmed the principle that industries have a Constitutional duty to prevent environmental pollution. The right to a clean and healthy environment is implied under **Article 21** of the Constitution, which guarantees the right to life. The discharge of toxic substances into the environment without proper control or treatment was a violation of the public's right to health and the environment.
- **Precautionary Principle** The court applied the precautionary principle, which suggests that if there is a threat of serious damage to the environment, measures should be taken even if

scientific evidence is not fully conclusive. The court held that the burden of proof lies with the industry to show that their actions will not cause harm to the environment.

- **Polluter Pays Principle** The court introduced the **'Polluter Pays Principle'**, which asserts that the polluting party must bear the costs of the damage caused by its actions. Shri Ram Foods and Fertiliser Industries were ordered to compensate for the environmental harm caused.

Obiter Dicta

- The court observed that industrial development should not come at the cost of public health or the environment. It emphasised that industries must adhere to environmental protection norms and avoid harming public resources.
- The court also noted that the environment should be treated as a public good, and any actions threatening it could lead to severe repercussions.

Analysis

The judgement in M.C. Mehta Vs. Shri Ram Foods and Fertiliser Industries marked a pivotal moment in the development of environmental law in India, setting the foundation for stronger regulations around industrial pollution.

While the ruling has numerous benefits, including reinforcing the Constitutional right to a clean environment and holding industries accountable through the **Polluter Pays Principle**, it also presents challenges in terms of implementation and economic impact.

Alternatives like incentivising cleaner technologies, fostering public-private partnerships, and implementing phased regulations could provide more balanced solutions that encourage environmental responsibility while supporting industrial growth.

2. State of Maharashtra Vs. Mayer Hans George (1965)

Name of the Case State of Maharashtra Vs. Mayer Hans George

Parties to the Case

- **Appellant (State)** State of Maharashtra
- **Respondent** Mayer Hans George (A German national and businessman)

Citation to the Case

Citation- AIR 1965 SC 722

Bench

- The case was decided by the Supreme Court of India.
- Honourable Chief Justice–K. Subba Rao
- Honourable Justices–J. C. Shah, S. K. Das and V. Ramaswami

Nature of the Case

This case is a **Criminal Law** case.

Facts of the Case and Issues Involved

Facts

- Mayer Hans George, a German national, had been living in India for several years and was involved in running a business in Mumbai.
- He had been working in India under an employment contract and was in possession of certain foreign exchange.
- The case arose after Mayer Hans George was accused of violating the Foreign Exchange Regulation Act, 1947 (FERA), which regulated the flow of foreign exchange in India.
- He was charged with unlawfully retaining foreign exchange and transferring funds without the approval of the Reserve Bank of India.
- Mayer Hans George had engaged in some transactions that violated the provisions of the law regarding the possession and use of foreign currency without the proper permissions.

Issues Involved

- Whether Mayer Hans George's actions in transferring foreign exchange without proper authorisation were in violation of the Foreign Exchange Regulation Act, 1947.
- Whether the charges against him under FERA were justified, considering his defense regarding his intentions and knowledge of the law.
- Whether the conviction imposed by the lower court was proper in light of the facts and the law under which he was charged.

Decision of the Case, including Ratio Decidendi and Obiter Dicta

- The Supreme Court of India upheld the conviction of Mayer Hans George, finding that his actions were indeed in violation of the Foreign Exchange Regulation Act, 1947.
- The court ruled that the unauthorised transfer of foreign exchange violated the regulatory provisions of the act, regardless of his personal knowledge or intent.
- The court emphasised that the law was designed to prevent unauthorised dealings with foreign currency and to regulate the economy in a manner that protected national interests.
- Therefore, the conviction was upheld, and Mayer Hans George was held guilty of violating the provisions of the Foreign Exchange Regulation Act.

Ratio Decidendi

- **Strict Liability Under FERA** The court clarified that the Foreign Exchange Regulation Act imposed strict liability, meaning the person could be convicted for an offense under the act without needing to prove intent or knowledge. Even if the accused had no intention to violate the law, the mere act of violating the provisions was sufficient to constitute an offence.
- **Public Policy Consideration** The court emphasised the importance of regulating foreign exchange as a matter of national interest. The act was designed to control the inflow and outflow of foreign currency and any violation could have adverse effects on the economy. Hence, the law applied strictly to all individuals, regardless of nationality or knowledge.

Obiter Dicta

- The court mentioned in passing that the government had the right to impose restrictions on the possession, use and transfer of foreign exchange in the interest of the nation's economic stability. This was part of the larger policy framework to prevent capital flight and ensure that foreign exchange was used for the benefit of the country's economy.
- The court also observed that foreign nationals living or doing business in India must comply with Indian laws, including those governing foreign exchange, even if they were unaware of the specific provisions. Ignorance of the law could not be a valid defense in such cases.

Analysis

The decision in State of Maharashtra Vs. Mayer Hans George was an important ruling for the enforcement of India's **Foreign Exchange Regulation Act** (FERA) and set a precedent for how violations related to foreign exchange are treated under Indian law.

While the judgement strengthened the rule of law and emphasised the need for strict regulation of foreign exchange, alternative solutions such as incorporating knowledge requirements, raising awareness among foreign nationals and introducing more lenient approaches for first-time offenders could provide a better balance between ensuring legal compliance and fairness in dealing with unintentional violations.

3. Kesavananda Bharati Vs. State of Kerala (1973)

Name of the Case Kesavananda Bharati Vs. State of Kerala

Parties to the Case

- **Petitioner** Kesavananda Bharati (a religious leader and petitioner in this case)
- **Respondent** State of Kerala (Represented by the government)

Citation to the Case

Citation- AIR 1973 SC 1461

Bench

The case was decided by the Supreme Court of India.

- Honourable Chief Justice– S. M. Sikri
- Honourable Justices– A.N. Grover, A.N. Ray, D.G. Palekar, H.R. Khanna, J.M. Shelat, K.K. Mathew, K.S. Hegde, M.H. Beg, P. Jaganmohan Reddy, S.N. Dwivedi and Y.V.Chandrachud.

Nature of the Case

The case is a **Constitutional Law** case. It primarily revolves around the interpretation of the Basic Structure Doctrine of the Indian Constitution.

Facts of the Case and Issues Involved

Facts

- Kesavananda Bharati, the petitioner, was a religious leader and the head of a religious institution in Kerala. His institution owned large land holdings and was affected by the Kerala Land Reforms Act, 1963, which sought to impose restrictions on land holdings and redistribute excess land to landless people.
- Bharati challenged the Constitutional validity of certain provisions of the Kerala Land Reforms Act, claiming they violated his Fundamental Rights under Article 19 (right to freedom of speech and protection of property) and Article 31 (right to property) of the Indian Constitution.
- His petition also raised the broader issue of whether Parliament had the authority to amend the Constitution, specifically whether the Constitutional amendment (such as those modifying the Fundamental Rights) could alter the basic structure of the Constitution.

Issues Involved

- Whether the Kerala Land Reforms Act infringed upon the Fundamental Rights of Kesavananda Bharati and his institution.
- Whether Parliament had the power to amend the Constitution, including its Fundamental Rights, or whether such amendments could affect the basic structure of the Constitution.
- Whether the Basic Structure Doctrine (i.e., the idea that certain fundamental features of the Constitution cannot be altered by amendments) could be adopted by the Supreme Court.

Decision of the Case, including Ratio Decidendi and Obiter Dicta

- The Supreme Court, by a majority of 7-6, held that Parliament cannot alter or destroy the basic structure of the Constitution through amendments.
- The court ruled that the basic structure doctrine was a part of the Constitution, and no amendment by Parliament could change or amend the basic structure of the Constitution, including Fundamental Rights.
- In this case, the court upheld the Kerala Land Reforms Act but emphasised that any future amendments to the Constitution that may affect its basic structure will be subject to judicial review.
- The court did not provide a definitive list of what constitutes the "basic structure" of the Constitution, leaving it to be determined case by case, but certain features like democracy, secularism, republican form of government, separation of powers, and Fundamental Rights were considered part of the basic structure.

Ratio Decidendi

- **Basic Structure Doctrine** The most significant outcome of this case was the establishment of the basic structure doctrine. The court held that although Parliament has the power to amend the Constitution, it cannot alter or destroy its basic structure. This means that fundamental principles of the Constitution, including democracy, rule of law, and separation of powers, cannot be changed by Constitutional amendments.

- **Judicial Review of Constitutional Amendments** The court also made it clear that amendments made by Parliament are subject to judicial review, especially when they affect the fundamental features of the Constitution. This was a landmark decision as it introduced the concept of judicial checks on Parliament's power to amend the Constitution.
- **Parliament's Power to Amend** The court recognised that Parliament does have the power to amend the Constitution under Article 368, but this power is not absolute. It cannot be used to alter the essential elements or structure of the Constitution.

Obiter Dicta

- The court emphasised that the basic structure doctrine was a safeguard against arbitrary use of power by the legislature and was necessary to preserve the democratic framework established by the Constitution.
- It also noted that any changes to the Constitution should be consistent with its core principles, which are intended to protect the rights and freedoms of the people, as well as the democratic form of government.
- The court suggested that while the scope of "basic structure" may evolve over time, it should always preserve the fundamental democratic principles inherent in the Constitution.

Analysis

The Kesavananda Bharati Vs. State of Kerala decision is a landmark ruling that played a pivotal role in safeguarding India's Constitutional integrity. The establishment of the basic structure doctrine ensured that the fundamental principles of the Constitution could not be altered arbitrarily, preserving democratic values and the rule of law. However, the ruling has also drawn criticism for its lack of clarity and its potential for judicial overreach. While the decision strengthened judicial oversight and balanced the powers of the legislature and judiciary but alternative solutions such as clearer definitions of basic structure, a more flexible approach to amendments and greater dialogue between the branches of government could have better addressed the evolving needs of India's democratic system.

Conclusion

Understanding case laws is vital in grasping how the Indian legal system works and evolves over time. Landmark cases like M.C. Mehta Vs. Shri Ram Foods, State of Maharashtra Vs. Mayer Hans George and Kesavananda Bharati Vs. State of Kerala has significantly shaped various areas of law including environmental, criminal and Constitutional law.

These cases highlight the dynamic nature of law, showing how it adapts to societal changes and legal challenges. By studying these cases, we gain insight into how the law protects rights, enforces responsibilities and ensures justice. Landmark decisions not only influence legal practices but also help in maintaining fairness, public order,and the protection of Fundamental Rights, ensuring a balanced and evolving legal system in India.

Sources

- CBSE Textbook, Legal Studies, Class 12th.
- Case Law References: M.C. Mehta Vs. Shri Ram Foods and Fertiliser Industries, [1987] 2 SCC 411, State of Maharashtra Vs. Mayer Hans George, AIR 1965 SC 722 and Kesavananda Bharati Vs. State of Kerala, AIR 1973 SC 1461.
- Foreign Exchange Regulation Act (FERA), 1947.
- Constitution of India, various articles such as Articles 21, 13, and the Basic Structure Doctrine.

Viva Voce Questions

1. ***What is the Indian legal system based on?***

Ans. The Indian legal system is based on three types of laws

- **Common Law** Laws developed from judges' decisions in past cases.
- **Statutory Law** Laws made by the government or Parliament.
- **Civil Law** Deals with disputes between individuals or organisations.

2. ***What are landmark cases?***

Ans. Landmark cases are important cases that create major changes or set important examples for how laws should be interpreted. These cases help shape future legal decisions and guide judges in similar cases.

3. ***Why is it important to understand case laws?***

Ans. Understanding case laws is important because they show how laws are applied in real life, help understand legal principles, establish precedents for future cases and guide legal decision-making. They also clarify how justice and fairness are maintained.

4. ***What is the difference between Civil, Criminal and Constitutional cases?***

Ans. The difference between Civil, Criminal and Constitutional cases are

- **Civil Cases** Deal with private disputes between individuals or organisations (For example, property disputes).
- **Criminal Cases** Involve crimes against society or the state (For example, theft or murder).
- **Constitutional Cases** Deal with the interpretation of the Constitution, including Fundamental Rights (For example, right to freedom).

5. ***What does 'precedent' mean in the legal system?***

Ans. A precedent is a previous legal decision that serves as a guide for judges to decide future cases. It ensures consistency and fairness in the legal system.

6. ***What is the purpose of case laws?***

Ans. The purpose of case laws is to explain how legal principles are applied in real situations, guide future decisions, protect rights, and ensure fairness in society.

7. ***Give an example of a Civil Case.***

Ans. An example of a civil case is a property dispute between two individuals or a contract breach between two businesses.

8. ***Give an example of a Criminal Case.***

Ans. An example of a criminal case is a person being charged with theft or murder.

9. ***What are Family Cases about?***

Ans. Family cases deal with issues like marriage, divorce, child custody, inheritance, and maintenance within a family.

10. ***What is a Public Interest Case?***

Ans. A public interest case is filed to address issues that affect society or large groups of people. These cases are usually for social justice or welfare.

11. ***What are some of the issues dealt with in Environmental Cases?***

Ans. Environmental cases address issues like pollution, deforestation, wildlife protection and preserving natural resources.

12. ***What does the 'Polluter Pays Principle' mean?***

Ans. The 'Polluter Pays Principle' means that the person or organisation causing pollution must bear the costs of cleaning up and fixing the environmental damage they caused.

13. ***In the case of M.C. Mehta Vs. Shri Ram Foods, what was the key issue?***

Ans. The key issue in the case was whether the factory was causing environmental harm by releasing harmful pollutants into the environment, violating public health rights under Article 21 of the Constitution.

14. ***What is the 'Precautionary Principle' in environmental law?***

Ans. The 'Precautionary Principle' states that if there is a risk of serious environmental harm, measures should be taken even if full scientific evidence is not available. The burden of proof lies with the polluter.

15. ***In the case of State of Maharashtra Vs. Mayer Hans George, what law was violated?***

Ans. Mayer Hans George violated the Foreign Exchange Regulation Act (FERA), 1947, by transferring foreign exchange without proper authorisation.

16. ***What is the Basic Structure Doctrine?***

Ans. The basic structure doctrine, established in the Kesavananda Bharati case, says that certain fundamental features of the Indian Constitution cannot be altered by amendments, such as democracy, secularism, and the separation of powers.

17. ***Why did Kesavananda Bharati challenge the Kerala Land Reforms Act?***

Ans. Kesavananda Bharati challenged the Kerala Land Reforms Act because he believed it violated his Fundamental Rights, especially the right to property under Article 31 of the Indian Constitution.

18. ***What was the outcome of the Kesavananda Bharati case?***

Ans. The Supreme Court ruled that Parliament cannot alter the basic structure of the Constitution through amendments. It also upheld the Kerala Land Reforms Act but emphasised that any future amendments that affect the basic structure would be subject to judicial review.

19. ***What does 'judicial review' mean in the context of constitutional amendments?***

Ans. Judicial review means that the judiciary can examine the amendments made by Parliament and check whether they violate the basic structure of the Constitution. If they do, the judiciary can strike them down.

SAMPLE QUESTION PAPER 1

A Highly Simulated Sample Question Paper for CBSE Class XII

LEGAL STUDIES

General Instructions

1. The question paper contains 4 sections – A, B, C and D.
   - Section A contains 20 Multiple Choice Questions for 20 marks.
   - Section B contains 8 Short Answer Type Questions for 2 marks each.
   - Section C contains 8 questions for 3 marks each.
   - Section D contains 4 Long Answer Type Questions for 5 marks each.
2. Internal Choice is given in the paper. There is no overall choice.

Time : 3 hours **Max. Marks : 80**

FULLY SOLVED

SECTION A

1 A juvenile detained in a reformatory home seeks legal aid to challenge the conditions of the home, claiming they violate basic human rights. The legal aid authority refuses to provide assistance, arguing that the annual income of the juvenile's family exceeds ₹ 12,000. How does this decision align with the Legal Services Authority Act, 1987? (1)

(a) The juvenile is not entitled for legal aid as he was in custody and he violets the law.

(b) The juvenile is entitled to legal aid as being in custody qualifies them for assistance, regardless of family income.

(c) Legal aid can only be provided if the family income falls below ₹12,000, even for those in custody.

(d) The juvenile must prove their detention which directly impacts their financial independence to avail legal aid.

2 A tenant files a case in a Junior Civil Judge Court, claiming compensation for property damage caused by the landlord's negligence. After a few hearings, the court determines that the compensation claim exceeds its pecuniary jurisdiction. What is the appropriate course of action in this scenario? (1)

(a) The Junior Civil Judge Court transfers the case to a higher court with appropriate pecuniary jurisdiction.

(b) The Junior Civil Judge Court must dismiss the case as it cannot exceed its pecuniary limits.

(c) The tenant must file a fresh case in the District Court and restart the proceedings.

(d) The tenant must seek approval from the State Government to allow the case to proceed in the same court.

3 **Assertion** (A) Dr. B.R. Ambedkar, the Chairman of the Drafting Committee of the Constituent Assembly, has termed Article 13 as the 'Heart of the Constitution'.

Reason (R) This Article provides explicitly the powers of judicial review to the courts in the matters of Fundamental Rights. (1)

Codes

(a) Both A and R are true and R is the correct explanation of A.

(b) Both A and R are true, but R is not the correct explanation of A.

(c) A is true, but R is false.

(d) A is false, but R is true.

4 **Assertion** (A) Arbitration proceedings are confidential and not open to public scrutiny.

Reason (R) The Arbitration and Conciliation Act, 1996, emphasises party autonomy and privacy, allowing parties to opt for confidential proceedings. (1)

Codes

(a) Both A and R are true and R is the correct explanation of A.
(b) Both A and R are true, but R is not the correct explanation of A.
(c) A is true, but R is false.
(d) A is false, but R is true.

5 You are working as a data scientist at a large e-commerce company, and your team has been tasked with predicting customer churn. You have collected a dataset that includes customer information, purchase history, and user engagement data. However, after training your model on the dataset, the model is overfitting to the training data, achieving very high accuracy but poor performance on the validation set. What should be your next course of action to improve the model's generalisation ability? (1)

(a) Increase the complexity of the model by adding more features to the dataset.
(b) Perform cross-validation and increase the dataset size.
(c) Decrease the model complexity by reducing the number of layers or parameters.
(d) Apply data augmentation techniques to generate synthetic data.

6 **Assertion** (A) All contracts are agreements but all agreements, are not contracts.
Reason (R) An agreement must be enforceable by law in order to be a contract. (1)

Codes

(a) Both A and R are true and R is the correct explanation of A.
(b) Both A and R are true, but R is not the correct explanation of A.
(c) A is true, but R is false.
(d) A is false, but R is true.

7 Which statement best reflects the distinction between tort and breach of contract? (1)

(a) In tort, the primary remedy is performance of the contract, whereas in breach of contract, the remedy is always in the form of damages.
(b) In tort, damages are always liquidated, while in breach of contract, damages are unliquidated.
(c) In tort, the duty is bound towards specific persons, while in breach of contract, the duty is generally towards the public.
(d) In tort, damages may be compensatory or exemplary, whereas in breach of contract, damages are generally compensatory.

8 Which among the given statements is TRUE regarding the Transfer of Property Act, 1882? (1)

(a) The Transfer of Property Act, 1882 provides the basic principles for transfer of both movable and immovable properties.
(b) Transfer of immovable property requires mere delivery to be valid.
(c) The Transfer of Property Act, 1882 applies to transfers by will or succession.
(d) The Transfer of Property Act, 1882 does not require registration for the transfer of immovable property valued above ₹ 100.

9 Which of the following is NOT a right of the owner of a copyright? (1)

(a) Right to Reproduce Work
(b) Right of Adaptation
(c) Right of Paternity
(d) Right of Maternity

10 A chemical plant in City 'X', located near densely populated residential areas, releases toxic gases due to an accident which causes widespread health issues. The affected residents sue the company for damages. The company argues that the accident was caused by a rare mechanical failure despite regular maintenance. Based on the principle of absolute liability, what should the court decide? (1)

(a) The company is not liable since the accident was unintentional and caused by a rare mechanical failure.
(b) The company is partially liable and should share the damages with the residents.
(c) The company is fully liable for the harm caused, irrespective of the preventive measures taken.
(d) The company can avoid liability by proving that the residents were aware of the risks of living near the plant.

11 A company in India is involved in a commercial dispute with a foreign partner based in the UK. The arbitration clause in the contract specifies that disputes should be resolved under the English Arbitration Law, and the venue for arbitration is London. However, one of the parties seeks interim relief under Section 9 of the Indian Arbitration and Conciliation Act, claiming urgent action is needed to prevent harm. The Indian court is now deciding whether it has jurisdiction to grant this relief. What should the Indian court decide regarding the application for interim relief? (1)

(a) The Indian court has jurisdiction to grant interim relief because the case is filed in India.
(b) The Indian court cannot grant interim relief because the arbitration proceedings are governed by English law, and relief should be sought in England.

FULLY SOLVED

(c) The Indian court has jurisdiction to grant interim relief as the substantive law governing the contract is Indian law.

(d) The Indian court must dismiss the application due to the arbitration clause specifying English jurisdiction.

12 An employee at a factory is working near a machine that operates without any proper safeguards. The employee's clothing gets caught in the machine, and they are seriously injured. The company had knowledge of this hazard but never took action to rectify the issue. The employee sues the company for negligence. Which of the following elements is most critical for the employee to prove in their negligence lawsuit? (1)

(a) The company's breach of statutory duty

(b) The employee's contributory negligence

(c) The company's intentional act to harm the employee

(d) The company's failure to provide a safe working environment

13 A man steals food from a store, claiming he did so to feed his starving children. He argues that his motive was not criminal but based on necessity. However, he knowingly took the property without consent. How does the law view his act? (1)

(a) His act is criminal, but his motive will reduce the severity of the punishment.

(b) The act is not criminal because the motive justifies it.

(c) His act is criminal, and the motive does not affect the criminality of the act.

(d) The man will not be charged because his motive was altruistic.

14 **Assertion** (A) The National Commission for Minorities was enacted in the year 1992.

Reason (R) The primary objective is to safeguard the human rights of minorities, including protection against inequality and discrimination. (1)

Codes

(a) Both A and R are true and R is the correct explanation of A.

(b) Both A and R are true, but R is not the correct explanation of A.

(c) A is true, but R is false.

(d) A is false, but R is true.

15 A high-ranking government official accepts an honorary title from a foreign state, without obtaining consent from the President of India. Identify the Article of the Indian Constitution which is violated by this act? (1)

(a) Article 12 – Definition of 'State'

(b) Article 18 – Abolition of titles

(c) Article 15 – Prohibition of discrimination

(d) Article 32 – Right to Constitutional Remedies

16 **Assertion** (A) The office of the Attorney General for the Union of India and the Advocate General for the concerned States are Constitutional offices.

Reason (R) The Constitution of India has also laid down the qualifications necessary for being considered for the position of the Attorney General and the Advocate General. (1)

Codes

(a) Both A and R are true and R is the correct explanation of A.

(b) Both A and R are true, but R is not the correct explanation of A.

(c) A is true, but R is false.

(d) A is false, but R is true.

17 **Statement I** Public International Law applies to states, international organisations and individuals.

Statement II Public International Law only regulates relations between states and does not bind individuals or non-state actors. (1)

Choose the correct statement.

(a) Both Statements are correct.

(b) Both Statements are incorrect.

(c) Statement I is correct, but Statement II is not correct.

(d) Statement II is correct, but Statement I is not correct.

18 **Statement I** Institutional arbitration is administered by organisations like the International Court of Arbitration (ICA) and the London Court of International Arbitration (LCIA).

Statement II Institutional arbitration requires parties to follow rigid rules and procedures, limiting party autonomy. (1)

Choose the correct statement.

(a) Both Statements are correct.

(b) Both Statements are incorrect.

(c) Statement I is correct, but Statement II is not correct.

(d) Statement II is correct, but Statement I is not correct.

19 Rahul, a car dealer, offered to sell a vehicle to Rohan for ₹ 5 lakhs. Rohan accepted the offer and paid ₹ 50,000 as earnest money. The agreement stated that the balance would be paid within 30 days. However, Rahul sold the car to another buyer before the deadline. Rohan sued Rahul for breach of contract. Rahul claimed that the agreement was not

FULLY SOLVED

valid since it was not in writing and registered, as required under the Indian Contract Act. What is the most likely outcome of Rohan's lawsuit? (1)

(a) Rahul wins, as the agreement was not in writing and registered.
(b) Rohan wins, as the payment of earnest money indicates a valid contract.
(c) The case will be dismissed due to lack of jurisdiction.
(d) Rahul's sale to another buyer is valid, superseding Rohan's claim.

20 A high-profile criminal case in India has reached its trial stage, where the defense team is actively cross-examining witnesses. The judge is closely observing the testimony and objections raised by both parties, but does not intervene or investigate the facts further, focusing only on the evidence presented by the parties. Which of the following legal systems best describes this trial process? (1)

(a) Inquisitorial System
(b) Adversarial System
(c) Hybrid System
(d) Investigative Model

SECTION B

21 The Supreme Court appointed a retired judge along with three members to recommend measures for controlling vehicular pollution in India. Following this, lead-free petrol was introduced, and CNG became the primary fuel for public transport in Delhi.
Identify four significant outcomes of this judicial intervention in controlling vehicular pollution. (2)

22 "The Lokpal and Lokayukta Act, 2013 is a significant step towards combating corruption in India, yet challenges remain in its implementation". Comment.

Or Explain the composition of the Lokpal as per the Lokpal and Lokayuktas Act, 2013. How is the chairperson of the Lokpal selected? (2)

23 Priya was shopping at a supermarket when she slipped on a wet floor and injured herself. There was no warning sign indicating that the floor was wet. She decides to file a case against the supermarket for her injuries.

(i) Identify the type of tort involved in this situation.
(ii) Explain any two essential elements required to establish liability in such cases. (2)

24 Discuss different types of intellectual property rights in India and specify their names. (2)

25 What is the composition of the National Human Rights Commission? (2)

26 "International law is also called law of nations." Justify the given statement. (2)

Or "International law is an independent system of law that exists outside the legal orders of particular states, yet its enforcement remains a challenge." Analyse this statement with respect to the differences between international law and domestic law.

27 Neha and Rani are good friends and have also completed a degree in law. As fresh graduates, Neha is keen to contribute in policy making and Rani wants to specialise in commercial and economic laws. Mention the fields that they can specialise in. (2)

28 How has the Supreme Court diluted the provision of 'locus standi'? (2)

Or Differentiate between Article 32 and Article 226 in one point only.

SECTION C

29 Rohit has a Saving Bank Account with Zono Bank. Being an employee of TTS Co. Ltd, his salary and other allowances were being directly credited to his account with the bank. He alleged that the bank had issued a cheque book without his knowledge to someone else and had passed cheques which were not drawn by him. The total amount so fraudulently withdrawn from his account amounted to ₹ 100,000. (3)

(i) Identify the agency he can approach for the redressal of his grievance.
(ii) State its functions.

30 How has the series of three judicial decisions, popularly known as the Three Judges Case, helped in the development of the modern collegium system? (3)

Or Name the statutory body established under the Lokpal and Lokayuktas Act, 2013, which is responsible for investigating corruption cases against public servants. List its composition and powers in tackling corruption.

31 Identify and explain the type of tribunal involved in each of the following cases

(i) Ramesh, a central government employee, has a dispute regarding his promotion and wants to challenge the decision of his department.
(ii) A telecom company disagrees with a fine imposed by the Telecom Regulatory Authority of India (TRAI) and seeks resolution.

FULLY SOLVED

(iii) An environmental activist files a case against a factory for polluting a nearby river, demanding strict action and compensation. (3)

32 In a Continental European Country, only the legislature has the power to create laws and rules. Here the judge is allowed to decide the presentation of specific form of evidence and the role of judge is an active one in a way that he is even allowed to take active part in investigation. (3)

(i) To which system of adjudication does the judge belong to?

(ii) State the type of jurisdiction followed in the country.

(iii) State any one advantage and any one disadvantage of the system of adjudication identified above.

33 When can a case be refered to Lok Adalat? State the powers of Lok Adalats while trying a suit. (3)

Or How does the concept of Lok Adalat came into being?

34 Susheela is a minor who looks older than her age. Subroto is a major who enters into a contract with Susheela thinking that she is a major too. Later, Subroto found that Susheela is a minor. (3)

(i) Is the contract valid? Give reasons.

(ii) State the exception to the rule regarding capacity to contract by a minor as stated in the Indian Contract Act, 1872.

35 What constitutes tort of negligence? (3)

36 Briefly discuss the two cases on movable and immovable property. (3)

Or Write a short note on the doctrine of lis pendens.

SECTION D

37 A legal dispute arose between two companies over the payment for goods supplied. One company claimed the other had not honored the contract terms, while the other argued defects in the goods. Both companies agreed to resolve the issue outside the court.

(i) Identify the ADR method used in this case.

(ii) List any four benefits of using this method for commercial disputes. (5)

38 Discuss the Indian principal of absolute liability. (5)

Or Discuss how tort law protects us against the different kinds of harms.

39 Amit and Neha enter into an agreement to resolve a business dispute through arbitration instead of going to court. They appoint an arbitrator, but midway through the proceedings, Neha challenges the arbitrator's decision, claiming it is biased and seeks to set aside the arbitral award in court. (5)

In light of the above scenario, answer the following questions:

(i) Identify the type of dispute resolution method used by Amit and Neha.

(ii) Explain the key features of this dispute resolution method.

(iii) Discuss under what grounds an arbitral award can be set aside as per the Arbitration and Conciliation Act, 1996, and how Amit and Neha should proceed to resolve the issue.

Or Deep Mohanty and Raghav Nair are neighbours in an apartment complex. Large flowering pots kept on the balcony of Deep's flat have caused seepage and weakened the ceiling above Raghav's balcony. The latter demands that Deep remove the plants and a dispute ensues.

Identify and explain the alternative dispute resolution mechanism that is best suited in the given situation. Also explain its process.

40 Describe the historical background and development of intellectual property rights. (5)

Or What is a trademark and how is it different from a tradename?

FULLY SOLVED

Answers

1. (b)	**2.** (a)	**3.** (a)	**4.** (a)	**5.** (b)	**6.** (a)	**7.** (d)
8. (a)	**9.** (d)	**10.** (c)	**11.** (b)	**12.** (d)	**13.** (c)	**14.** (a)
15. (b)	**16.** (a)	**17.** (d)	**18.** (d)	**19.** (a)	**20.** (b)	

21. Four significant outcomes of this judicial intervention in controlling vehicular pollution are

(i) **Lead-Free Petrol** Lead-free petrol was introduced in major cities to reduce harmful emissions.

(ii) **CNG Adoption** Delhi became the first city to have public transport running entirely on CNG.

(iii) **Cleaner Air** Pollution levels decreased, improving public health.

(iv) **Policy Changes** Stricter fuel and emission norms were implemented nationwide.

22. The Lokpal and Lokayukta Act, 2013 helps fight corruption by investigating complaints against public officials.

However, challenges like delays in appointing members, lack of independence, and political interference affect its effectiveness. Proper implementation, transparency, and public awareness are needed to make it a strong tool against corruption in India.

Or The Lokpal consists of a chairperson and up to 8 members, with 50 per cent being judicial members. The chairperson must be a former Chief Justice of India, a Supreme Court judge, or an eminent expert in anti-corruption matters. The President appoints the chairperson based on recommendations from a selection committee.

23. (i) The type of tort involved is negligence because the supermarket failed to take proper care to prevent harm.

(ii) Two essential elements to establish liability are

(a) **Duty of Care** The supermarket had a duty to keep the premises safe.

(b) **Breach of Duty** Not placing a warning sign led to an unsafe condition.

24. There are seven different kinds of IP rights recognised in India. They are copyright, trademarks, patents, geographical indications, plant varieties, industrial designs, and designs for semi-conductor integrated circuits.

25. The National Human Rights Commission is headed by the Chairperson who is a former Chief Justice of the Supreme Court.

The other members of commission are

- One member who is a former judge of the Supreme Court,
- Another member who is present or former Chief Justice of a High Court, and
- Two other members with knowledge or experience in matters relating to human rights.

Besides, there is a Secretary General who is the Chief Executive Officer of the Commission who largely discharges administrative duties of the commission.

26. International law is also called the law of nations because it governs relations between countries, ensuring peace, trade and co-operation. It sets rules for diplomacy, human rights and global security. By regulating interactions between states and international bodies, it promotes order and justice in global affairs, making it truly a law of nations.

Or International law governs relations between states but lacks a central authority for enforcement, unlike domestic law, which is backed by a sovereign government. While treaties and customs guide international law, compliance depends on state consent. Without a global enforcement body, adherence relies on diplomacy, mutual interests, and international organisations.

27. Neha and Rani could choose public policy and corporate sector. Lawyers have an important role in formulating and advising on public policy. Several organisations employ law graduates for policy making and have institutionalised fellowships where law graduates can be Research Assistants. An inhouse counsel will give legal advice to the company, have expertise in the business of the company and be responsible for ensuring that the business of the company is being run in compliance with applicable laws and when required will bring in external lawyers.

28. The Supreme Courts has diluted the doctrine of locus standi (right to appear before or petition the court) through its judicial review practice, for the enforcement of Fundamental Rights of those who lack access to Courts due to poverty or social and economic disabilities.

Or Article 32 provides a person to initiate writs (Habeas corpus, Mandamus, Prohibition, Quo-warranto and Certiorari) in the Supreme Court for the enforcement of Fundamental Rights.

On the other hand, Article 226 provides a person to initiate similar writs in the High Courts for the enforcement of Fundamental Rights.

29. (i) The Agency Rohit can approach for the redressal of his grievance is Banking Ombudsman, who is a senior official appointed by the Reserve Bank of India to redress customer complaints against deficiency in certain banking services.

(ii) The Function of Banking Ombudsman are as follows

- A Banking Ombudsman is responsible for matters relating to non-payment or delay in collection of cheques, bills, drafts, etc.
- Failure to issue or delay in issues of banker's cheques, failing to honour guarantee or letter of credit commitments all fall under the ambit of the responsibilities of a Banking Ombudsman.
- A Banking Ombudsman receives complaints regarding non-adherence to any of the banking guidelines laid down by the RBI.

30. A series of three judicial decisions popularly known as the Three Judges Cases helped in the development of the modern collegium system in the following ways

- The first Judges case (1981) gave primacy to the Executive and stated that the CJI's recommendation to the President can be refused for cogent reasons. It gave vast powers to the Executive for the next 12 years, in making judicial appointments.
- In the second Judges case (1993), the decision in the first case was modified. It decided that the Chief Justice of India has primacy in the matter of appointments to the Supreme Court and the High Courts.
- In 1998, the Supreme Court in a Presidential reference (1998 advisory decision) emphasised upon the role of 'consultation' and held that the process of appointment of Judges to the Supreme Court and the High Courts is an integrated participatory consultative process.

Or The Lokpal is the statutory body established under the Lokpal and Lokayuktas Act, 2013, to investigate corruption cases against public servants. It consists of a chairperson and up to 8 members (50% judicial). It has powers similar to the police and CVC, including inquiry, investigation and recommending prosecution.

FULLY SOLVED

31. (i) **Central Administrative Tribunal (CAT)** Ramesh's case relates to a government service dispute. CAT handles such issues for central government employees, providing a quicker resolution than regular courts.

(ii) **Telecom Disputes Settlement and Appellate Tribunal (TDSAT)** The telecom company's dispute with TRAI falls under TDSAT, which resolves conflicts related to telecom, broadcasting and internet services.

(iii) **National Green Tribunal (NGT)** The environmental activist's case concerns pollution, which is handled by NGT. It ensures environmental protection and can impose fines or order corrective actions against polluting industries.

32. (i) The judge belongs to the adversarial system of adjudication.

(ii) The country follows a civil law system of jurisdiction.

(iii) An advantage of adversarial system is that in this system the use of cross-examination can be an effective way to test the credibility (genuineness) of witnesses presented, A disadvantage of adversarial system is that in this system, the cost of the justice system falls upon the parties.

33. Lok Adalat takes up cases which are civil in nature (including marriage, and family disputes) and compoundable criminal cases. It accepts cases pending in regular court under their jurisdiction.

The Lok Adalat shall have the same powers as are vested in a Civil Court under the Code of Civil Procedure (1908). Further, a Lok Adalat shall have the requisite powers to specify its own procedure for the determination of any dispute coming before it.

Or In ancient times, the disputes were referred to 'panchayats' which were established at village level. Panchayats used to resolve the dispute through arbitration. It has proved to be a very effective alternative to litigation.

This concept of settlement of dispute through mediation, negotiation or through the arbitral process known as decision of 'Nyaya Panchayat', is conceptualised and institutionalised in the philosophy of Lok Adalat. It involves people who are directly or indirectly affected by dispute resolution. The evolution of the movement called Lok Adalat was a part of the strategy to relieve heavy burden on the Courts with pending cases and to give relief to the litigants who were in a queue to get justice.

34. (i) As per the Indian Contract Act, 1872, a contract entered into with a minor is void. In the given situation, the contract is void as Susheela is a minor. The fact that she looked older cannot validate the contract.

(ii) As per the Indian Contract Act, 1872, a contract entered into with a minor is void in all cases except where the contract has been entered into for the benefit of the minor. For example, a contract to provide essential supplies to the minor till he attains the age of 18.

35. Negligence is defined as the breach (violation) of the duty to take care, which results in damages.

In other words, it means the wrong-doer or the defendant has been careless in a way that harms the interest of the victim or the claimant.

For example, when the defendant carries out an act of constructing something on her premises, she owes a duty of care towards the claimant (and anyone in proximity).

The standard of duty of care depends on whether the claimant was on the site or in the neighbourhood, as well as whether the claimant was a lawful visitor or a trespasser.

36. A movable property is a property that can be moved from one place to another. It is governed by the Sale of Goods Act. Immovable Property refers to a property that cannot be moved from one place to another. It is governed by the Transfer of Property Act.

Two cases on movable and immovable property are

- In Shanta Bai Vs. State of Bombay (1958), the distinction between movable and immovable property was observed. If the intention is to reap fruits from the trees, it will be regarded as an immovable property. But if the intention is to cut down the tree and use it as timber, it would be regarded as movable property.
- In Marshall Vs. Green, there was sale of trees wherein the trees were cut and taken away. The Court held that the sale was not that of immovable property.

Or The doctrine of lis pendens emerged from the Latin maxim 'ut lite pendent nihil innoveteur' which means that 'nothing new should be introduced in a pending litigation'. When a suit or litigation is pending on an immovable property, that immovable property cannot be transferred.

The main objectives of doctrine of lis pendens are

- To avoid endless litigation.
- To protect one of the parties to the
- litigation against the order of the Court.
- To avoid the abuse of any legal process.

Further, to constitute lis pendens, the following conditions should be satisfied

- There must be a suit or proceeding involving the immovable property.
- Such a suit or proceeding must be pending before the Court that is competent to try it.
- The right to the immovable property must be in question in the suit or proceeding.
- The property in litigation should be transferred.
- The transferred property should affect the rights of the other person to the transfer.

37. (i) The ADR (Alternative Dispute Resolution) method used in this case is Arbitration. Arbitration is a process where disputing parties refer their case to a neutral third-party arbitrator or panel, who makes a legally binding decision.

FULLY SOLVED

This method is widely used in commercial disputes as it offers a private and efficient alternative to litigation.

(ii) Four benefits of Arbitration for commercial disputes are

(a) **Speedy Resolution** Arbitration is faster than traditional court proceedings, reducing the time spent in legal battles. This helps businesses resolve disputes quickly and continue their operations.

(b) **Cost-Effective** Court cases can be expensive due to prolonged hearings, lawyer fees and court costs. Arbitration minimises these expenses, making it a more affordable option.

(c) **Confidentiality** Unlike court cases, which are public, arbitration proceedings are private, ensuring business-sensitive information remains protected.

(d) **Expert Decision-Making** In arbitration, parties can select an arbitrator with expertise in their industry, ensuring a well-informed decision. This is particularly beneficial for technical commercial disputes.

38. In India, principle of absolute liability was introduced by the Supreme Court in the aftermath of the two instances of gas leaks from factories injuring many.

The first case was about the infamous Bhopal gas leak disaster of 1984 where a factory of the Union Carbide Corporation located in Bhopal had a major leakage of the gas methyl isocyanate that killed, and injured many people.

In the second incident of 1985 in Delhi, a factory of the Shri Ram Foods and Fertiliser Industries leaked oleum (acid) gas that killed one person that had few others hospitalised and created huge panic among the residents.

In the second case, the court decided that if an industry/enterprise is engaged in some inherently dangerous activity for commercial gain and that activity is capable of causing unfortunate damage, then the industry officials are absolutely liable to pay compensation to the aggrieved parties.

The industry cannot plead that all safety measures were taken care of by them and that there was no negligence on their part. They will not be allowed any exceptions neither can they take up any defence like that of 'Act of God' or 'Act of Stranger'.

Or Tort law protect us against the different kinds of harms in the following ways

- **Property Interests in Land** The law of tort protects the claimant's interests in her landed property by preventing intentional intrusions or trespass of the property by the defendant or the wrong-doer.
- **Other Types of Property** Law of tort prohibits taking away of tangible property deliberately, which amounts to the tort of 'conversion'.
- **Bodily Injury** Law of tort protects the claimant against any harm to his/her interests of bodily integrity. Tort of battery and assault applies to any intentional harm caused to the body.
- **Economic Interests** Injury caused by both intentional act as well as negligence can cause economic harm to the claimant. The economic interests are also protected by the law of tort to a lesser extent.

39. (i) Amit and Neha have chosen Arbitration, a type of Alternative Dispute Resolution (ADR). In this method, disputes are settled by an independent third party (arbitrator) instead of going to court.

(ii) Key features of arbitration are

(a) **Binding Decision** The arbitrator's decision (arbitral award) is final and enforceable like a court judgment.

(b) **Private Process** Arbitration is conducted in a confidential setting, unlike court trials.

(c) **Flexibility** The parties can choose their arbitrator and set their own rules for proceedings.

(d) **Less Formal & Faster** Arbitration avoids lengthy legal procedures, making it quicker than court litigation.

(iii) Under the Arbitration and Conciliation Act, 1996, an arbitral award can be set aside by the court if

(a) The arbitrator was biased or lacked impartiality.

(b) The arbitration agreement was not valid.

(c) The party was not given a proper opportunity to present their case.

(d) The award was against public policy or beyond the arbitrator's authority.

Amit and Neha should approach the court to review the arbitrator's bias claim or mutually agree to appoint a new arbitrator.

40. The importance and role of intellectual property protection emerged with the establishment of the World Trade Organisation (WTO) in the Trade-Related Intellectual Property Systems (TRIPS) Agreement. It was negotiated at the end of the Uruguay Round of the General Agreement on Tariffs and Trade (GATT) treaty in 1994.

The TRIPS Agreement came into effect on 1st January, 1995 and is the most comprehensive multilateral agreement on intellectual property. It encompasses all forms of intellectual property and aims at harmonising and strengthening standards of protection, and providing effective enforcement of intellectual property rights at both national and international levels. India being signatory to the TRIPS Agreement has passed several legislations for the protection of intellectual property rights to meet the international obligations.

Some of these legislations are listed below

- Trade Mark Act, 1999
- Designs Act, 2000
- Copyright Act, 1957 (as amended)
- Patents Act, 1970 (as amended)
- Geographical Indications of Goods (Registration and Protection) Act, 1999
- Protection of Plant Varieties and Farmers' Rights Act, 2001

Or For answer refer to Q. No. 3 Long Answer Type Question on page no. 159-160.

FULLY SOLVED

SAMPLE QUESTION PAPER 2

A Highly Simulated Sample Question Paper for CBSE Class XII

LEGAL STUDIES

UNSOLVED

General Instructions

1. The question paper contains 4 sections – A, B, C and D.
- Section A contains 20 Multiple Choice Questions for 20 marks.
- Section B contains 8 Short Answer Type Questions for 2 marks each.
- Section C contains 8 questions for 3 marks each.
- Section D contains 4 Long Answer Type Questions for 5 marks each.

2. Internal Choice is given in the paper. There is no overall choice.

Time : 3 hours **Max. Marks : 80**

SECTION A

1 The dispute regarding the sharing of water resources between the State of Tamil Nadu and Kerala with respect to Mullaperiyar dam can be brought before the Supreme Court under the exercise of which jurisdiction? (1)

(a) Advisory jurisdiction (b) Original jurisdiction
(c) Appellate jurisdiction (d) Judicial review

2 In a pollution-related disaster, a factory owner argues that they cannot compensate the victims due to financial constraints. However, the victims demand adequate compensation, citing the Deep Pocket Principle. How is the court most likely to rule in this situation?

(a) The court exempts the factory owner from compensation due to financial limitations.
(b) The court orders limited compensation, considering the financial condition of the factory owner.
(c) The court mandates full compensation, prioritising the victims' rights over the owner's financial constraints.
(d) The court transfers liability to the government, as the factory owner is unable to pay.

3 A criminal case involving a serious offence is heard by a Chief Judicial Magistrate Court. During the trial, the accused's lawyer argues that the case should be tried in a Sessions Court due to the severity of the charges. What action is the Chief Judicial Magistrate Court most likely to take in this scenario?

(a) The Chief Judicial Magistrate Court retains the case and concludes the trial as per its authority.
(b) The Chief Judicial Magistrate Court dismisses the lawyer's argument and continues the trial.
(c) The Chief Judicial Magistrate Court commits (transfers) the case to the Sessions Court for trial.
(d) The Chief Judicial Magistrate Court forwards the case to the High Court for jurisdictional clarification.

4 A Public Interest Litigation (PIL) is filed in India challenging the government's environmental policies. The court, recognising the complexity of the issue and the potential for a settlement, refers the case to mediation. The mediator is an environmental law expert, chosen by both parties, who will facilitate discussions and seek a resolution that aligns with the public interest. Identify which form of Alternative Dispute Resolution is being used in this scenario?

(a) Arbitration (b) Conciliation
(c) Mediation (d) Judicial Settlement

5 The Lokpal and Lokayukta Act, 2013 aims to combat acts of bribery and corruption of public servants- a term that has been given a fairly wide interpretation in the act. As per the legislation, an enquiry of corruption can be initiated against which of the following persons? (1)

(a) Against the ex-Prime Minister of India accused of corruption in matters pertaining to international relations.

(b) Against the ex-Prime Minister of India accused of corruption in matters relating to internal security.

(c) Against any person who has been a member of either House of the Parliament.

(d) Against any member of the Parliament against whom allegation of corruption is raised for anything said or a vote given by him in the Parliament.

6 Which among the given statements is TRUE for a valid contract under the Indian Contract Act, 1872? (1)

(a) A valid contract must have lawful consideration and a lawful object.

(b) An agreement becomes a contract only when registered under the Indian Registration Act.

(c) A minor can enter into a valid contract if they provide written consent.

(d) A contract without consideration is always void, with no exceptions.

7 Which statement best reflects the principle of duty of care in the law of negligence? (1)

(a) A person is only responsible for harm caused if they intended to cause injury to another person.

(b) A duty of care exists only in contractual relationships and does not apply in other situations.

(c) A person owes a duty of care to those who could be reasonably foreseen as being affected by their actions.

(d) The duty of care applies only to professionals such as doctors and lawyers, not to ordinary individuals in daily life.

8 **Assertion** (A) Madam Pillai Vs. Badar Kali was a case law that determined the validity of oral transfer.

Reason (R) The court held that the plaintiff acquired a title by way of oral transfer and she is entitled to the property though the instrument of sale was not registered. (1)

Codes

(a) Both A and R are true and R is the correct explanation of A.

(b) Both A and R are true, but R is not the correct explanation of A.

(c) A is true, but R is false.

(d) A is false, but R is true.

9 Ravi, a famous painter, creates an original artwork and shares it on social media. Without his permission, a printing company copies his artwork onto posters and sells them for profit. (1)

In the above scenario, which intellectual property right has been violated?

(a) Trademark Infringement

(b) Patent Violation

(c) Copyright Infringement

(d) Trade Secret Misappropriation

10 A State Government in India is creating a policy to address urban air pollution, aligning with the sustainable development principles in Agenda 21. This policy focuses on promoting the use of Electric Vehicles (EVs) and adopting cleaner technologies. This approach emphasises sustainable transportation and reducing environmental impact while balancing economic growth. Which of the following policies is most aligned with the principles laid out in Agenda 21?

(a) Creating a national EV incentive programme and restricting the sale of non-electric vehicles.

(b) Encouraging the widespread planting of trees in urban areas without a focus on vehicle emissions.

(c) Prohibiting the use of all vehicles in urban areas.

(d) Limiting the use of public transportation to reduce air pollution.

11. **Assertion** (A) limited liability partnership is different from a normal partnership.

Reason (R) It is a type of legal entity that combines the limited liability and flexibility of a partnership. (1)

Codes

(a) Both A and R are true and R is the correct explanation of A.

(b) Both A and R are true, but R is not the correct explanation of A.

(c) A is true, but R is false.

(d) A is false, but R is true.

12 An individual unknowingly violates a newly enacted law about the use of social media, where sharing certain types of content is prohibited. The individual claims ignorance of the law. Is the individual exempt from criminal liability?

(a) Ignorance of the law is an acceptable excuse under Indian law.

(b) Ignorance of the law is no excuse, and the individual can still be held liable.

(c) If the law was not properly communicated to the public.

(d) The individual may receive a reduced sentence due to ignorance.

13 Rajesh, a 12-year-old boy, works in a hazardous chemical factory to support his family. The factory owner claims that since Rajesh volunteered for the job, there is no legal violation. Based on the provisions of the Indian Constitution, which Article is violated in this situation, and why?

(a) Article 23- Prohibits forced labour and human trafficking, and Rajesh is being coerced.

(b) Article 24- Prohibits employment of children under 14 in hazardous environments.

(c) Article 26- Ensures equal access to religious institutions.

(d) Article 25- Protects freedom of conscience and religious practices.

14 You are a project manager working on a software development project for a client. The team is behind schedule, and the client insists on an earlier delivery date. In a meeting, you suggest working overtime, but the development team expresses concern about burnout and quality issues. The client pressures you to find a solution to meet the deadline. What is the best course of action in this situation? (1)

(a) Push the team to work overtime to meet the deadline and deliver the product as requested.

(b) Present the risks of burnout and quality issues to the client and propose a realistic extension for the deadline.

(c) Tell the client that the team is not available for overtime, regardless of the deadline.

(d) Agree to work overtime but do not inform the team about the potential risks involved.

15 **Assertion** (A) The International Criminal Court (ICC) is a tribunal set up through the Rome Statute in 2002 with the purpose of prosecuting criminals for 4 major crimes.

Reason (R) ICC may also give advisory opinions under Articles 65-68 of the Statute of the ICJ to countries. (1)

Codes

(a) Both A and R are true and R is the correct explanation of A.

(b) Both A and R are true, but R is not the correct explanation of A.

(c) A is true, but R is false.

(d) A is false, but R is true.

16 **Statement I** A transfer of property must be effected by a registered deed, as per the Registration Act, 1908.

Statement II All transfers of property, regardless of value, require payment of stamp duty under the Indian Stamp Act, 1899. (1)

Choose the correct statement

(a) Both Statements are correct.

(b) Both Statements are incorrect.

(c) Statement I is correct, but Statement II is not correct.

(d) Statement II is correct, but Statement I is not correct.

17 Parliament passes a constitutional amendment removing judicial review from the Constitution, arguing that it is necessary to expedite governance. A public interest litigation challenges this amendment in the Supreme Court, citing that it violates the basic structure of the Constitution. What is the most likely outcome based on the principles established in the Kesavananda Bharati case?

(a) The amendment is upheld, as Parliament has the absolute power to amend the Constitution under Article 368.

(b) The amendment is upheld, as judicial review is not explicitly listed in the Constitution as a fundamental right.

(c) The amendment is struck down, as judicial review is an essential feature of the basic structure of the Constitution.

(d) The court refers the matter to Parliament, as it lacks the authority to review constitutional amendments.

18 **Assertion** (A) The National Commission for Minorities was enacted in the year 1992.

Reason (R) The primary objective is to safeguard the human rights of minorities, including protection against inequality and discrimination. (1)

Codes

(a) Both A and R are true and R is the correct explanation of A.

(b) Both A and R are true, but R is not the correct explanation of A.

(c) A is true, but R is false.

(d) A is false, but R is true.

19 **Statement I** The Supreme Court Legal Services Committee provides free legal aid to eligible persons, including women, children and marginalised communities.

Statement II The Supreme Court Legal Services Committee is headed by the Chief Justice of India and functions under the Legal Services Authorities Act, 1987. (1)

Choose the correct statement

(a) Both Statements are correct.

(b) Both Statements are incorrect.

(c) Statement I is correct, but Statement II is not correct.

(d) Statement II is correct, but Statement I is not correct.

20. A high-ranking Group 'A' officer in the Ministry of Finance is accused of using their position to misappropriate public funds. The case is brought before the Lokpal for investigation. The officer's lawyer argues that the Lokpal cannot proceed as there is no special court to adjudicate the case. How should the Lokpal address this claim? (1)

(a) The Lokpal postpones the investigation until a special court is constituted.

(b) The Lokpal proceeds with the investigation and prosecutes the officer through an existing court.

(c) The Lokpal dismisses the case, as the absence of a special court invalidates the process.

(d) The Lokpal directs the Central Government to establish a special court before proceeding.

SECTION B

21 "The courts that function below the High Courts are popularly known as subordinate judiciary." Comment.

Or "The Constitution of India lays out the framework of the Indian judicial system". Comment (2)

22 Why is mediation a better method of resolution of disputes arising from strained resolutions? (2)

23 State the meaning of acceptance under the Indian Contract Act. (2)

24 Rahul and Priya enter into an agreement where Rahul agrees to sell his house to Priya for ₹ 50 lakh. They finalise the deal orally and Priya pays an advance amount. However, Rahul later refuses to transfer ownership, claiming that no written contract was signed. Priya insists that the agreement is valid and seeks legal recourse. (2)

(i) Identify any two legal issues arising in this case.

(ii) Explain whether an oral agreement for the sale of immovable property is legally valid under the Transfer of Property Act, 1882.

25 Rahul agrees to rent his apartment to Sita for ₹ 15,000 per month. Sita accepts the offer and agrees to pay the rent on the first day of each month. They draft and sign a rental agreement specifying the terms and conditions. (2)

Identify the four essentials of a valid contract in the situation given above.

26 Explain the key differences between a sole proprietorship and a partnership in terms of ownership liability and decision-making. (2)

Or Discuss the advantages and disadvantages of a Limited Liability Partnership (LLP) compared to a traditional partnership.

27 State four parts of the Indian Constitution which contains the human rights framework. (2)

28 Give some examples of some organisations working in the domain of private international law. (2)

Or In a regional summit in South Asia, there is widespread acceptance of the need to strengthen the bonds between nations by promoting cultural heritage and the equal dignity of all cultures. Identify the international organisation that works towards this objective. Why was the need for creation of this organisation felt?

SECTION C

29 "A factory in a small town was found to be dumping hazardous chemical waste into a nearby river, severely affecting the health of the local residents. Several complaints were lodged, but the pollution continued, causing irreversible damage to the environment and aquatic life".

(i) Identify the statutory body responsible for addressing such environmental concerns.

(ii) State any four functions of this organisation that help in preventing and controlling environmental pollution. (3)

30 State the requirements to be fulfilled by law aspirants, both Indian and foreign national, to be able to start practice in India. (3)

31 During an international trade dispute, Country 'X' imposes additional tariffs on imports from Country 'Y', citing national security concerns. Country 'Y' claims this violates the World Trade Organisation (WTO) agreements and files a complaint with the WTO dispute settlement body.

(i) Is the action taken by Country 'X' justified under international trade law? Provide reasons.

(ii) Which authority has the jurisdiction to resolve the dispute between Country 'X' and Country 'Y'?

(iii) What possible consequences might Country 'X' face if found in violation of WTO rules? (3)

32 Identify the statutory body established under the Protection of Human Rights Act, 1993, to promote and protect human rights in India. Mention its composition and powers. (3)

Or Name the statutory body created under the National Commission for Women Act, 1990, to safeguard women's rights in India. List its functions and explain how it addresses issues related to women's welfare and protection.

33 What do you understand by freedom as to attendance at religious instruction or religious worship in certain educational institutions? Also state the exceptions, if any. (3)

Or What do you understand about International Human Rights? Explain.

UNSOLVED

34 State any four functions of the National Commission for Women. (3)

35 Identify and explain the type of business entity in each of the following cases

(i) Ramesh starts a small grocery store in his neighbourhood, managing everything on his own. He makes all business decisions and keeps all the profits, but he is also personally responsible for any losses.

(ii) Meera and Ankit decide to start a clothing brand together. They agree to share profits and losses equally, and they jointly manage the business.

(iii) A group of architects forms a business where they work together but enjoy limited liability protection, ensuring that each partner is only responsible for their own mistakes. (3)

36 What are the roles of fundamental duties in protecting and promoting environmental protection in India? (3)

Or What are the significances of the united nations conference on Environment and Development?

SECTION D

37 Ravi and Ankit, two neighboring shop owners, had a long-standing dispute over the placement of a signboard that partially blocked the entrance of Ankit's shop. After multiple arguments, they decided to take the matter to court. However, a well-wisher advised them to approach an alternative dispute resolution forum where their issue could be settled quickly and amicably without a lengthy legal battle. (5)

(i) Which alternative dispute resolution method would be most suitable for resolving Ravi and Ankit's dispute?

(ii) Explain the benefits of this dispute resolution method in comparison to a formal court proceeding.

38. Arjun and Meera, concerned about increasing pollution levels in their city, decide to start an eco-friendly packaging business. They set up a small manufacturing unit that produces biodegradable packaging materials. However, before commencing operations, they are informed that they must obtain necessary environmental clearances and approvals from the authorities. Additionally, they learn that their business must comply with pollution control regulations to prevent harm to the environment. (5)

In light of the above scenario, answer the following questions

(i) Identify the statutory body responsible for granting environmental clearances and regulating pollution control in India.

(ii) Explain the key objectives and functions of this body in ensuring environmental sustainability.

(iii) Discuss the significance of such regulations for businesses and how Arjun and Meera can ensure compliance with environmental laws.

39 Give a short note on the background of the American Bar Association. (5)

Or

Explain the categories of legal practitioners in India after the Advocates Act, 1961.

40 Give any four functions of the National Human Rights Commission. (5)

Or

Write a note on the National Commission for SCs and STs. What are their objectives?

UNSOLVED

Answers

1. (b)	**2.** (c)	**3.** (c)	**4.** (c)	**5.** (c)	**6.** (a)	**7.** (c)
8. (a)	**9.** (c)	**10.** (a)	**11.** (a)	**12.** (b)	**13.** (b)	**14.** (b)
15. (c)	**16.** (c)	**17.** (c)	**18.** (c)	**19.** (c)	**20.** (b)	

SAMPLE QUESTION PAPER 3

A Highly Simulated Sample Question Paper for CBSE Class XII

LEGAL STUDIES

General Instructions

1. The question paper contains 4 sections – A, B, C and D.
- Section A contains 20 Multiple Choice Questions for 20 marks.
- Section B contains 8 Short Answer Type Questions for 2 marks each.
- Section C contains 8 questions for 3 marks each.
- Section D contains 4 Long Answer Type Questions for 5 marks each.
2. Internal Choice is given in the paper. There is no overall choice.

Time : 3 hours ***Max. Marks : 80***

UNSOLVED

SECTION A

1 You are the CEO of a mid-sized tech startup, and you're considering raising capital to scale operations. You receive an offer from a venture capital firm that is interested in investing but requires you to give up 40 per cent equity in exchange for the investment. You currently hold 100 per cent of the company's equity. What is the most important factor you should consider before accepting the offer? (1)

(a) The valuation of your company post-investment.

(b) The amount of capital being offered.

(c) The operational expertise and network the venture capital firm can provide.

(d) The potential for a future acquisition of the company.

2 Rahul, an accused, is convicted of murder by the Trial Court and sentenced to imprisonment. He appeals to the High Court, which dismisses his appeal. Rahul then files an appeal to the Supreme Court under Article 136 of the Constitution. Which of the following is true regarding this appeal? (1)

(a) The Supreme Court has to necessarily hear the appeal and decide the matter on merit.

(b) The Supreme Court may grant special leave to appeal if it is satisfied that the appeal raises a substantial question of law or justice.

(c) The Supreme Court has no power to entertain the appeal as the High Court has already dismissed it.

(d) The Supreme Court will only hear the appeal if the President of India grants permission.

3 A driver runs a red light and collides with another vehicle, causing the driver of the other car to sustain severe injuries. The injured driver decides to file a tort claim against the reckless driver for negligence. The defendant argues that the collision was due to mechanical failure, which was not their fault. Which of the following defenses is most likely to be successful in this case?

(a) Contributory negligence

(b) Comparative negligence

(c) Force majeure

(d) No-fault liability

4 Mohan purchases a mixer-grinder from M/s Makil and Bros. The grinder malfunctions within the warranty period. Both the manufacturer and the seller fail to rectify the problem and a dispute ensues. The dispute may best be resolved through (1)

(a) mediation (b) conciliation

(c) arbitration (d) negotiation

5 **Statement I** The Lokpal and Lokayuktas Act, 2013, establishes the institution of ombudsman at the central level to investigate complaints against public servants. (1)

Statement II The Ombudsman in India has the power to impose penalties and punishments on public servants found guilty of corruption and misconduct.

Choose the correct statement

(a) Both Statements are correct.
(b) Both Statements are incorrect.
(c) Statement I is correct, but Statement II is not correct.
(d) Statement II is correct, but Statement I is not correct.

6 Ashwin agreed to supply 20 litres of oil to Bholu on 1st June, 2014. On 1st June, 2014, Ashwin did not supply the oil. Which of the following is correct? (1)

(a) Bholu cannot recover compensation from Ashwin.
(b) Bholu can recover compensation from Ashwin for 10 litres of oil.
(c) Bholu cannot recover compensation as the suit is barred by limitation.
(d) Bholu is entitled to receive compensation as there is a breach of contract.

7 **Assertion** (A) A contract lawyer would look up the Contract Act to look for rules to be applicable in a given fact situation. A tort lawyer would look for rules as developed by Courts in similar cases.

Reason (R) Torts are mostly a common law subject. (1)

Codes

(a) Both A and R are true and R is the correct explanation of A.
(b) Both A and R are true, but R is not the correct explanation of A.
(c) A is true, but R is false.
(d) A is false, but R is true.

8 A group of local farmers has been practicing crop rotation on their lands to improve soil fertility and reduce the need for chemical fertilisers. The local government is planning a large industrial project nearby that could lead to soil degradation and water contamination. Identify which provision of the Indian Constitution can the farmers use to advocate for the protection of their agricultural practices? (1)

(a) Article 38 (b) Article 51A(g)
(c) Article 48A (d) Article 21

9 Which among the given statements is TRUE for a Trademark? (1)

(a) A trademark only includes wordmarks and logos, excluding packaging and colours.
(b) A trademark provides protection for a brand name and helps distinguish products and services.
(c) Trademark rights in India are protected under the Copyright Act, 1957.
(d) A trade name and a trademark provide the same level of brand protection.

10 **Assertion** (A) Sustainable development is important for the well-being of human society.

Reason (R) Sustainable development is a kind of development that meets the needs of the present without compromising the ability of future generations to meet their own needs. (1)

Codes

(a) Both A and R are true and R is the correct explanation of A.
(b) Both A and R are true, but R is not the correct explanation of A.
(c) A is true, but R is false.
(d) A is false, but R is true.

11 After winning a case, Mr. Kumar needs to ensure that the court's decision is enforced. His lawyer, Ms. Singh assists him in executing the court decree. She helps him recover the awarded amount by garnishing the opponent's bank account and auctioning their property. Ms. Singh also ensures that the court-ordered injunction is implemented, restraining the opponent from further illegal activities. What post-litigation service is Ms. Singh providing to Mr. Kumar? (1)

(a) Filing an appeal
(b) Executing the court decree
(c) Drafting a legal notice
(d) Mediating a settlement

12 **Statement I** The initial stage of crime, where an individual forms an intention to commit an offense, is known as the 'Intention' stage.

Statement II The stage of crime where an individual takes concrete steps to prepare for the commission of the offense, but has not yet committed it, is known as the 'Preparation' stage. (1)

Choose the correct statement

(a) Both Statements are correct.
(b) Both Statements are incorrect.
(c) Statement I is correct, but Statement II is not correct.
(d) Statement II is correct, but Statement I is not correct.

13 **Assertion** (A) Article 51A of the Constitution prescribes fundamental duties of every citizen.

Reason (R) Human Rights include most Fundamental Rights like right to like, like to food, eduction, work, health and liberty etc. (1)

Codes

(a) Both A and R are true and R is the correct explanation of A.
(b) Both A and R are true, but R is not the correct explanation of A.
(c) A is true, but R is false.
(d) A is false, but R is true.

UNSOLVED

14 12-year-old girl, Jyoti, is forced to work as a domestic help in a household, earning minimal wages and facing physical abuse. A local NGO files a complaint with the National Commission for Protection of Child Rights (NCPCR). What can the NCPCR do in Jyoti's case? (1)

(a) Directly rescue Jyoti and prosecute the employers.

(b) Recommend compensation to Jyoti, but cannot investigate.

(c) Investigate, conduct hearings, and make recommendations to authorities.

(d) Only provide counseling to Jyoti.

15 The court held that if a treaty or international agreement restricts the rights of the citizens or modifies the laws of the state it would be required to have a legislative measure. Identify the case. (1)

(a) Magan Bhai Patel Vs. Union of India
(b) Maneka Gandhi Vs. Union of India
(c) Sheela Barse Vs. Union of India
(d) None of these

16 A foreigner enters India with a large quantity of narcotic substances, unaware of a new law regulating the importation of narcotics. The individual claims ignorance of the law and denies criminal intent. Under Indian law, how should their liability be determined?

(a) The person cannot claim ignorance of the law as a defense, as ignorance does not exempt liability in such cases.

(b) Liability arises because laws concerning narcotics fall under strict liability where intent is not mandatory for prosecution.

(c) The individual's liability depends on their ability to demonstrate that their action lacked any connection to intentional wrongdoing.

(d) The foreigner's liability is dismissed, as being unaware of the law negates criminal responsibility under this context.

17 **Assertion** (A) The ICC has limited jurisdiction over the ICJ with regards to certain issues pertaining to criminal matters listed under the Rome Statue.

Reason (R) The divide is similar to the divide of civil and criminal courts in the domestic contexts. However, the jurisdiction of the ICC is more restricted than that of ordinary criminal courts. (1)

Codes

(a) Both A and R are true and R is the correct explanation of A.

(b) Both A and R are true, but R is not the correct explanation of A.

(c) A is true, but R is false.

(d) A is false, but R is true.

18 The Government of India appointed Justice Rajendra Singh as a High Court Judge. However, shortly after his appointment, Justice Singh made several judgments against the government in high-profile cases. The government, displeased with his decisions, attempted to transfer Justice Singh to a smaller court in a remote location. Justice Singh challenged the transfer order, arguing it was an attempt to undermine his independence. What principle is Justice Singh invoking to challenge the transfer order? (1)

(a) Separation of Powers
(b) Judicial Review
(c) Independence of Judiciary
(d) Parliamentary Supremacy

19 Which statement best reflects the significance of Article 32 in the Indian Constitution?

(a) Article 32 allows the Parliament to modify Fundamental Rights through ordinary legislation.

(b) Article 32 provides the right to approach the Supreme Court for the enforcement of Fundamental Rights if they are violated.

(c) Article 32 restricts the power of the Supreme Court to hear matters related to Fundamental Rights.

(d) Article 32 allows only the President to seek judicial review of laws affecting fundamental rights.

20. Article 368 of the Constitution confers power to the Parliament to amend the Constitution. Article 13 (2) states that the state shall not make any law which takes away the Fundamental Rights. To overcome this restriction, the Parliament adopted the 24th Amendment to the Constitution which altered Articles 13 and 368 in such a way that allowed itself with unlimited powers of amendment, including the authority to amend Fundamental Rights. Identify the case which restricted this power in 1973 by establishing the doctrine of basic structure. (1)

(a) Maneka Gandhi Vs. Union of India
(b) Nathuni Yadav and Ors Vs. State of Bihar
(c) Hussainara Khatoon Vs. State of Bihar
(d) Kesavananda Bharati Vs. State of Kerala

SECTION B

21 Give two grounds on which the National Commission for Minorities can decline a complaint. (2)

22 Mr. P.L. wants to start a business to export bananas in the cities. But, he is confused about the registration process and he doesn't know about the laws as well. How will he start his business? In this situation, some question is raised in his hand. If you are his lawyer how will you help him? (2)

(i) What kind of property is used in this business?

(ii) Which act is used in this situation?

Or How can an immovable property of a value more than ₹ 100 be transferred?

23 The Supreme Court of India has often interpreted Directive Principles of State Policy (DPSPs) in a way that elevates them to the status of Fundamental Rights. Analyse this statement with suitable case laws. (2)

Or Fundamental duties, though not enforceable in a court of law, play a significant role in shaping responsible citizenship. Justify the given statement.

24 The Central Pollution Control Board issues a notice to a manufacturing company for violating air and water pollution standards. The company, in response, claims that it was unaware of the specific environmental regulations it breached. (2)

Identify the key legal provisions that regulate air and water pollution in India and explain their significance in ensuring environmental protection.

25 A chemical manufacturing company releases untreated industrial waste into a nearby river, causing severe pollution and affecting the health of residents in the surrounding areas. The affected community decides to take legal action against the company for its negligence. What legal remedies are available under the law of torts for the affected residents, and how can the company be held accountable for its actions? (2)

26 What is the jurisdiction of the disputes brought before Lok Adalat? (2)

27 How can a judge from the lower Judiciary be removed from his office? (2)

28 "The High Courts function as organs of judicial administration at the state-level." Comment. (2)

SECTION C

29 Briefly discuss the method of appointing a Supreme Court Judge. (3)

Or How has the serious of three judicial decisions, popularly known as the Three Judges Case, helped in the development of the modern collegium system.

30 How can you say that the Central Government has sanctioned the working of several ombudsmen in the country? Give some examples. (3)

31 Identify and explain the type of liability that is being imposed in each of the following cases (3)

(i) A chemical factory negligently disposes of hazardous waste into a nearby river, leading to severe pollution and health hazards for the local community. The affected residents sue the factory for compensation.

(ii) A zoo keeps a wild tiger in an enclosure, but due to unforeseen circumstances, the tiger escapes and injures a visitor. The zoo had taken all necessary precautions to secure the enclosure, yet the visitor files a lawsuit.

(iii) A gas leak from an industrial plant causes a major explosion, affecting thousands of people in the nearby town. The plant management claims they followed all safety measures, but the government holds them accountable for the disaster.

32 Explain the provisions enshrined in the Constitution of India that make India a secular entity by giving its citizens freedom of conscience and religion. (3)

Or

Name the international declaration adopted by the United Nations General Assembly in 1948 as a common standard for all nations to uphold human rights. List the key categories of rights defined under this declaration and explain its significance in promoting global human rights.

33 There was a treaty between two neighbouring countries namely Arunland and Poratia regarding sharing of special economic zones. A dispute arose between them regarding fulfilment of certain terms and conditions of this treaty obligation. Both the countries are not members of the United Nations. Arunland refused to fulfil its treaty obligations. Aggrieved by this, Portia approached the International Court of Justice (ICJ) for its advice. (3)

(i) Can the International Court of Justice (ICJ) give its advisory opinions to the country? If yes, under which provision?

(ii) State the advisory jurisdiction of the International Court of Justice (ICJ).

(iii) State any two values communicated by the International Court of Justice.

34 Mr France wants to start his business and in-home space. But he is confused about the legal entity. What type of legal entity gives good profit to him?

In this above situation, which legal entity is good for him, and write advantages of that entity also? (3)

35 In a Continental European Country, only the legislature has the power to create laws and rules. Here the judge is allowed to decide the presentation of specific form of evidence and the role of judge is an active one in a way that he is even allowed to take active part in investigation. (3)

(i) To which system of adjudication does the judge belong to?

(ii) State the type of jurisdiction followed in the country.

36 Why trademark should be necessary to be registered in this 21st century? (3)

Or What is required to qualify as a patentable matter? Discuss.

SECTION D

37 Rohan and Meera are government employees facing workplace discrimination issues. They decide to seek legal recourse but want a faster and less expensive resolution instead of approaching traditional courts. They learn about a special body that handles service-related disputes for government employees. (5)

In light of the above scenario, answer the following questions

(i) Identify the type of tribunal Rohan and Meera should approach for resolving their dispute.

(ii) Explain the key features and functions of this tribunal.

(iii) Discuss how tribunals help in reducing the burden on traditional courts and provide speedy justice. What advantages do tribunals offer compared to regular court proceedings?

38 Briefly discuss the difference between sale and lease in points. (5)

Or How can property be transferred under the Transfer of Property Act?

39 Shabana became a Family Court lawyer in Lokhandwala area of Mumbai. While dealing in her first case, her client Mamta was accused by her husband of being infidel and both don't want to live together anymore. (5)

(i) Describe in detail the role played by lawyers and counselors in family courts.

(ii) What is the criticism of the existing status of lawyers pertaining to family courts ?

Or What are the different statutes which come within the purview of the Family Courts Act? Describe.

40 (i) State the provisions of the most authoritative sources of International Law. (5)

(ii) Explain the provisions of the following conventions that make them important in the sphere of Private International Law.

(a) Vienna Convention on Sale of Goods

(b) United Nations Commission for International Trade Law (UNCITRAL) Model Law.

Answers

1. (a)	2. (b)	3. (c)	4. (a)	5. (d)	6. (d)	7. (a)
8. (c)	9. (b)	10. (a)	11. (b)	12. (b)	13. (b)	14. (c)
15. (a)	16. (b)	17. (a)	18. (c)	19. (b)	20. (d)	

UNSOLVED

CBSE
Examination Paper 2025

LEGAL STUDIES

Time : 3 Hours **Max. Marks : 80**

General Instructions

Read the following instructions very carefully and strictly follow them :

(i) The Question Paper contains 4 sections A, B, C and D.

Section-A contains 20 Multiple Choice Questions for 20 marks.

Section-B contains 8 Short Answer Type Questions for 2 marks each.

Section-C contains 8 questions for 3 marks each.

Section-D contains 4 Long Answer Type Questions for 5 marks each.

(ii) Internal choice is given in the paper. There is no overall choice.

Section-A

1. In a landmark case, the Supreme Court was handling a highly technical environmental dispute involving multiple stakeholders and scientific complexities. Given the intricate details of environmental policies and scientific evidence, the court appointed an amicus curiae, an expert in environmental law and science, to assist by providing impartial information and insights on the matter. The amicus curiae made recommendations based on international standards, which helped the court in reaching its final decision.

Based on the concept of amicus curiae, which of the following statements is correct? **(1)**

(a) The amicus curiae advocates for the interests of the public and acts as a representative for the government.

(b) The amicus curiae serves as the legal advisor to the party that requests their assistance in the case.

(c) The amicus curiae assists the court by providing impartial expertise on complex issues, without representing any party in the case.

(d) The amicus curiae is only allowed to assist in cases related to constitutional matters.

2. A High Court in India issues a verdict in a complex property dispute, which left one party dissatisfied with the decision. The aggrieved party now seeks to approach the Supreme Court for special leave to appeal under Article 136, the Supreme Court can grant special leave to appeal against any judgement, decree or order in any matter passed by **(1)**

(a) any court or tribunal in India

(b) only High Court

(c) only subordinate court

(d) only tribunals

3. Assertion (A) Any public-spirited person can file petition or write letters to court on behalf of aggrieved persons. **(1)**

Reasoning (R) Courts have liberalised the doctrine of locus standi of the enforcement of Fundamental Rights through Public Interest Litigations (PILs).

(a) Both A and R are true and R is the correct explanation of A.

(b) Both A and R are true, but R is not the correct explanation of A.

(c) A is true, but R is false.

(d) A is false, but R is true.

4. Arjun, at the request of the local community leader, builds a playground for the children in his neighborhood, spending a considerable amount of his own money. Later, Ravi, a local snack vendor, sets up a stall near the playground to sell snacks to children and promises to give Arjun 10% of his profits from all sales as a token of appreciation for building the playground. However, Ravi fails to pay Arjun the promised percentage, and Arjun decides to take legal action to recover it. Based on contract law principles, which of the following is correct? **(1)**

(a) Arjun is entitled to the percentage of profits as Ravi benefited from his efforts in building the playground.
(b) Arjun cannot claim the percentage of profits, as the playground was built at the request of the community leader and not Ravi.
(c) Ravi must pay Arjun the promised percentage since he made a verbal commitment to do so.
(d) Ravi has to pay Arjun only if Arjun can prove the playground was built specifically for his benefit.

5. Ravi, at a local market, was involved in an argument with Mohan over a disputed transaction. In the heat of the argument, Ravi suddenly pushed Mohan forcefully, causing Mohan to stumble backward and fall. Mohan suffered a minor injury to his back as a result of the fall. Mohan believes that Ravi's action was an intentional physical contact that resulted in harm, and he is considering suing Ravi for the tort of battery.

Which of the following statements is correct regarding the tort of battery in this case? **(1)**

(a) Ravi's action of pushing Mohan constitutes battery, as it was an intentional and direct application of physical force.
(b) Ravi is not liable for battery because the physical contact was not severe enough to cause significant injury.
(c) The tort of battery requires that the defendant's action must cause permanent injury, which is not the case here.
(d) Ravi is not liable for battery because his action was a part of self-defense act, even if there was no immediate threat to his safety.

6. Raj signs a contract to perform at a music festival. A few days before the festival, Raj develops a severe illness and doctors advise him complete rest. He misses the performance. Organisers of the event had to cut a sorry figure as Raj's performance was the highlight of the music festival.

Which of the given statements best describes Raj's inability to perform at the festival? **(1)**

(a) It is breach of contract as Raj failed to fulfill his obligation.
(b) It is discharge due to impossibility of performance because the illness makes performance impossible.
(c) It is discharge by performance as Raj was willing to perform if he hadn't been ill.
(d) It is breach of contract as a health issue does not discharge a contract.

7. Neha, a photographer, takes a beautiful photograph of a sunset and posts it on her personal blog. A local travel magazine uses the image without Neha's permission. The publishers credit Neha as the photographer but do not pay her or seek her consent. Neha considers taking legal action against the magazine. In this context which of the following options is correct? **(1)**

(a) Neha cannot take legal action because the magazine credited her as the photographer.
(b) Neha can take legal action because her photograph is protected by copyright and the magazine used it without permission.
(c) Neha cannot take legal action because the photograph was available for the general public on her blog.
(d) Neha can only take legal action if she had registered the photograph with a copyright office.

8. A company, XYZ Corp. operates a large dam to generate electricity. Due to an unforeseen design flaw the dam suddenly bursts, causing massive flooding in a nearby town. The company had taken all standard safety measures and had no knowledge of the design flaw. The affected residents sue the company for damages, Which of the following is applicable in this instance? **(1)**

(a) The company is not liable because the flaw was unforeseen.
(b) The company is absolutely liable because the operation of the dam is inherently dangerous and the damages occurred regardless of the fault.
(c) The company is liable only if it is proven that they ignored warning signs of the flaw.
(d) The company is not liable because it followed all safety protocols.

9. Mohan lends his rare antique vase to his friend Sumit for a week. Instead of returning it, Sumit accidentally drops and shatters the vase while showing it to another friend. When Mohan asks for his vase to be returned, Sumit apologises but says there is nothing he can do now that the vase is destroyed. Mohan decides to take legal action. Identify the legal claim he should pursue? **(1)**

(a) He should file a claim for trespass to chattels because Sumit damaged the vase while it was in his possession.
(b) He should file a claim for trespass to chattels because Sumit used the vase without permission.

(c) He should file a claim for conversion because Sumit destroyed the vase, depriving him of its use permanently.
(d) He should file a claim for conversion because Sumit delayed returning the vase.

10. From the options given below, which statement accurately describes the process of property registration in India? **(1)**
(a) The buyer and seller exchange property documents without involving any government authority.
(b) The property is officially transferred from the seller to the buyer through a government-authorised deed, affixed by a seal of the Registrar's office.
(c) The buyer must pay property taxes before the sale is completed without the need for any legal documentation.
(d) The property ownership is verified by a local official but no formal record is kept.

11. In a criminal trial in a country in continental Europe, the judge, Judge Helena plays an active role in investigating the case. She questions the witnesses, evaluates the evidences presented by the parties and orders additional forensic test. The defense lawyer, Mr. Jameson, expresses concern that the judge's active involvement in the investigation may undermine the fairness of the trial. In the given content, identify the probable disadvantage of the justice dispensation system that is concerning for the defense lawyer. **(1)**
(a) The active role of judge would prevent delays and prolonged trials.
(b) Stronger party in the case, with more resources and expert lawyers may not be able to influence the judges.
(c) The judge can no longer remain neutral to evaluate the case with an open mind.
(d) Less reliance is placed on cross examination and other techniques used by lawyers.

12. An advantage of .... is that there is no strict application of the procedural laws and the disputing parties can directly interact with the judges. **(1)**
(a) Mediation (b) Lok Adalat
(c) Conciliation (d) Tribunal

13. Omega Builders and Delta Constructions have a dispute over project delays. The court suggest mediation, but Omega Builders is unsure if their case qualifies. According to the Afcons Infrastructure Ltd. Vs. Cherian Varley Construction Co. ruling, which disputes are generally excluded from mediation? **(1)**
(a) Commercial contracts
(b) Matrimonial and Custody issues
(c) Criminal offenses
(d) Consumer disputes

14. **Statement I** Opinion juris prevents unwanted general practice from becoming customary law.
Statement II Opinion juris is the belief that an action was carried out as a legal obligation. **(1)**
Choose the correct option
(a) Both Statements are correct.
(b) Both Statements are incorrect.
(c) Statement I is correct but Statement II is not correct.
(d) Statement II is correct but Statement I is not correct.

15. **Assertion (A)** The Solicitor Regulation Authority (SRA) does not impose any formal experience requirement for requalifying as solicitor in England and Wales. **(1)**
Reasoning (R) It is not possible to be a barrister and solicitor.
(a) Both A and R are true and R is the correct explanation of A.
(b) Both A and R are true but R is not the correct explanation of A.
(c) A is true, R in false.
(d) A is false R is true.

16. Mei Ling is a practicing lawyer in Hong Kong. She is considering launching a marketing campaign to attract more clients. Which of the following is a feasible option for her? **(1)**
(a) Proceed with the campaign on all media, since lawyers are free to advertise without restrictions.
(b) Proceed with the campaign on print media.
(c) Launch the campaign but exclude testimonials, success rates and any comparative statements.
(d) Avoid all forms of advertising as it is entirely prohibited in Hong Kong.

17. **Assertion (A)** A Senior Advocate is not entitled to appear in the Supreme Court without an Advocate-on-record. **(1)**
Reasoning (R) Advocates-on-record are entitled to file an appearance or act for a party in the Supreme Court.
(a) Both A and R are true and R is the correct explanation of A.
(b) Both A and R are true, but R is not the correct explanation of A.
(c) A is true, R is false.
(d) A is false, R is true

18. In light of the principles enshrined in Article 39A, which of the following circumstances contradicts its core objective of equal justice and free legal aid? **(1)**
(a) The state provides legal aid to economically disadvantages facing criminal prosecution.
(b) A wealthy individual is given legal aid despite having adequate resources to access private legal Counsel.

(c) A marginalised person is granted legal representation in a civil matter by the state.
(d) The state facilities access to justice for those affected by socio-economic disabilities.

19. "Most accused persons do not lead defence evidence in India". Identify the reason for this from the options given below. **(1)**
(a) The burden to prove the offence beyond reasonable doubt is on the prosecution.
(b) The judge decides the case on its merit according to the evidences presented by the defence.
(c) The assertion that the accused has committed offence is sufficient to prove the guilt by prosecution.
(d) The accused is presumed guilty at the first instance when the trial begins.

20. **Statement I** The Evidence Law helps the judges to separate the 'Wheat from the Chaff'. **(1)**

Statement II The function of the law of evidence is to provide a mechanism for the investigation and trial of offenders.

Choose the correct option
(a) Both Statements are correct.
(b) Both Statements are incorrect.
(c) Statement I is correct, but Statement II is not correct.
(d) Statement II is correct, but Statement I is not correct.

SECTION-B

21. Explain the principle of judicial review. **(2)**

22. Sunil and Asha are co-founders of a tech-startup. Recently they had a contractual disagreement with their software vendor regarding the delivery timeline of a critical project. Sunil insisted on filing a lawsuit whereas Asha suggested resolution by appointing a neutral third party who could facilitate the parties in achieving an acceptable, voluntary agreement. Sunil agreed and their matter was resolved within two weeks **(2)**
(i) Identify the method of dispute resolution adopted by Sunil and Asha.
(ii) Give any two advantages of adopting alternate disputes resolution mechanism by the parties.

23. A nation engages in human rights violations within its own borders, including act of genocide against specific ethnic group. Under erga omnes obligations, what are the legal responsibilities of the international community, even if there is no direct threat to neighbouring states? **(2)**

24. (a) Describe, citing any two examples, how the rules of advertising by lawyers differs from country to country. **(2)**

Or (b) During a court proceeding, an advocate finds out that their client intends to provide false evidence. What should the advocate do in this situation to adhere to their professional duty toward the court and uphold ethical standards?

25. (a) State the purpose of the Legal Services Authorities (Amendment) Act 2002. **(2)**

Or (b) Enlist any four legal services given to any beneficiary under the provision of free legal aid.

26. Jai, a business owner, enters into an agreement with Sana, a government official. Jai promises to pay Sana 10 lakhs in exchange for her influence in securing a lucrative government contract for his company. Both parties sign the agreement and begin to execute it. Identify the nature of this agreement and discuss the legal consequences for both parties involved. **(2)**

27. A group of citizens in a city regularly engages in public protests against government policies. During one protest, some individuals damage public property, disrupt traffic, and use offensive language. The protestors claim that they are exercising their right to freedom of speech and expression. Is the claim by the protestors justified? How do the Fundamental Duties under Article 51A of the Constitution of India apply in this situation? **(2)**

28. (a) State any two key features of the Directive Principles of State Policy in the Indian Constitution.

Or (b) Give any two differences between Fundamental Fights and Human Rights.

SECTION-C

29. (a) "Independence of judiciary is vital for the respect of due process of law". Elaborate. **(3)**

Or (b) "Article 50 of the Constitution of India directs the State to take steps to separate the judiciary from the executive". In light of Article 50, discuss the importance of the separation of powers between the judiciary and the executive. State any two provisions enumerated in Article 50 that contribute to the independence of the judiciary in India.

30. (a) How is an arbitral award both similar and different from a court pronounced judgement or order? **(3)**

Or (b) State the features of ad-hoc arbitration.

31. Riya, a law graduate in India, is exploring career options in Law beyond court room practice. Explain any three such opportunities available to Riya. How can she apply her legal skills in these fields? **(3)**

32. Mrs. Kapoor, an elderly landowner, verbally expressed her wish to transfer her agricultural land worth ₹ 20 Lakhs to her son Raj without any legal documentation. **(3)**

Her other son Aman, who has been managing the land wants it to be transferred in his name as had been incharge of the land. Additionally, a neighbour, Mr. Sharma, offers Aman money to buy the land directly.

In the given situations, who has the right to transfer the property under the provisions of Transfer of Property Act (TPA) 1882? State any two essentials for a valid transfer based on the scenario given above.

33. (a) Name the statutory body that was constituted under the Water (Prevention and Control of Pollution) Act, 1974. State the two principal functions to be performed by this body. **(3)**

Or (b) State the significance of the Stockholm Declaration, 1972. Establish the relationship between Stockholm Declaration, 1972 and Earth Summit, 1992.

34. What are the key principles outlined in the Universal Declaration of Human Rights(UDHR) and how do they reflect the foundational values of human dignity, freedom and equality? **(3)**

35. In a Juveniles custodial home, several juveniles report being subject to harsh disciplinary measures, including excessive physical punishment and prolonged isolation. Some also mentioned that their complaints about inadequate food and unsanitary living conditions are being school administration. Identify the national body which can be approached. How can this body address the violation of the rights of juveniles? **(3)**

36. Sneha started a beauty care brand called "Glow Essence", offering organic skin care products. Within a year her brand gained popularity for its quality and natural ingredients. However, Sneha discovered that another company was selling low quality skin care products under the similar name leading to confusion among customers. This damaged her brand's reputation. On consulting a legal expert Sneha learned that "Glow Essence" is a trade name and not a trade mark. She initiated the registration process. **(3)**

(i) Differentiate between a trade name and a trade mark .

(ii) Explain, how registration of "Glow Essence" benefit Sneha.

SECTION-D

37. (a) Explain the concept of 'trade secrets' in intellectual property law. Discuss the legal protection provided to trade secrets under Indian law. How do these protections differ from patents and copyrights in terms of duration and scope? **(5)**

Or (b) All agreements per se are not contracts. They must meet certain criteria to qualify as such. Elaborate.

38. (a) With regards to the selection of panel lawyers under the NALSA Regulations, 2010, answer the questions given below **(5)**

(i) Mention the basic requirement an advocate must fulfil to be considered for empanelment.

(ii) State the composition of the selection board for empanelling advocates for High Court Legal Services Committee.

(iii) Under what circumstances can a panel lawyer be removed from any case?

(iv) When can the services of a Senior Advocate be availed by the legal services authorities?

Or (b) Explain the term 'legal aid'. Why is it important for every legal system to provide for legal aid? Discuss the provisions in the Indian Constitution that have paved way for the various provisions of legal aid in India.

39. The countries of Novara and Elderia are in a dispute over the construction of a dam on the river Nelara with Elderia bringing the case to the International Court of Justice (ICJ). Novara argues that past ICJ rulings in similar cases should guide the decision, while Elderia insists on a fresh interpretation of the law. Analyse how Articles 59, 38 and 38(1) of the Statute of ICJ would influence the court's decision-making in this case. **(5)**

40. Vikram, a skilled graphic designer, has been running his design studio as a sole proprietorship. Over time, his business has grown, and he started handling larger projects with higher risks. While he enjoys the simplicity of managing his sole proprietorship, he is worried about his personal liability if something goes wrong. On the advice of his friend, Vikram is considering converting his business into a One Person Company (OPC) to limit his liability and improve his business's credibility. Based on the above case, compare Sole proprietorship and One Person Company (OPC), Which form of business entity would be better for Vikram and why? **(5)**

Answers

1. (c)	2. (a)	3. (a)	4. (b)	5. (a)
6. (b)	7. (b)	8. (b)	9. (c)	10. (b)
11. (c)	12. (b)	13. (c)	14. (a)	15. (c)
16. (c)	17. (a)	18. (a)	19. (a)	20. (c)

21. The principle of judicial review means that courts can check if a law or government action follows the Constitution. If a law goes against the Constitution, courts can cancel it. This helps protect people's rights and ensures fairness in government decisions.

22. (i) The method of dispute resolution adopted by Sunil and Asha is mediation. In this process, a neutral third party helps both sides communicate and reach a mutually acceptable solution without going to court.

(ii) Two advantages of Alternate Dispute Resolution (ADR) are

(a) **Saves Time** It is less time consuming as people resolve their disputes expeditiously in a short period as compared to courts.

(b) **Cost-Effective** It is less costly than litigation.

23. Under erga omnes obligations, when a nation commits human rights violations, including genocide, the international community has a legal responsibility to act. Some violations are so grave that any state may take action against such crimes, regardless of jurisdiction. International human rights law empowers global intervention beyond domestic limitations

24. (a) The rules of advertising by lawyers vary across countries. In India, the Bar Council of India strictly restricts legal advertising, allowing only limited information on lawyers' websites with prior approval. In contrast, the USA permits lawyer advertisements with regulations prohibiting misleading claims and setting solicitation restrictions.

Or (b) An advocate must refuse to represent a client who insists on adopting unfair means, including providing false evidence. Advocates are required to uphold the dignity of the court and maintain professional ethics. Suppressing material or misleading the court is against their duty and may lead to disciplinary action.

25. (a) The Legal Services Authorities (Amendment) Act, 2002, was enacted to promote pre-litigation legal services, particularly for public utility services. It introduced permanent Lok Adalats to resolve disputes at the pre-litigation stage and emphasised conciliation and settlement to reduce litigation and improve access to justice.

Or (b) The four legal services provided under free legal aid include

(i) Payment of court fees, process fees, and other charges related to legal proceedings.

(ii) Providing the services of lawyers in legal proceedings.

(iii) Obtaining and supplying certified copies of orders and other documents.

(iv) Preparation of appeal, paper books, including printing and translation of documents?.

26. The agreement between Jai and Sana is illegal and void under the Indian Contract Act, as it involves unlawful consideration and object, i.e., bribery. Such agreements cannot be enforced by law. Both parties may face legal consequences under the Prevention of Corruption Act, 1988, which penalises bribery and corruption involving public servants.

27. The protesters' claim is not fully justified, as the right to freedom of speech and expression under Article 19 is subject to reasonable restrictions, including public order and morality. Article 51A of the Constitution imposes fundamental duties, such as safeguarding public property and maintaining harmony, which the protesters violated by damaging property and disrupting traffic.

28. (a) Two key features of the Directive Principles of State Policy (DPSP) are

(i) The state has a duty to apply these principles in making laws and policies on social and human development.

(ii) The provisions of directive principles are not enforceable by any court of law, but they provide guidance for drafting laws and policies?.

Or (b) Two differences between Fundamental Rights and Human Rights are

Fundamental Rights	Human Rights
Fundamental Rights are specific to a particular country and are enshrined in its Constitution.	Fundamental Rights are enforceable by national courts.
Human Rights have universal acceptance and apply to all individuals regardless of nationality.	Human Rights are generally recognised by international declarations like the UDHR and may not always be legally enforceable within a country.

29. (a) The independence of the judiciary is essential for upholding the due process of law, ensuring that the state respects legal rights, fairness, liberty and Fundamental Rights. Only an independent judiciary can operationalise this concept. In criminal law, it guarantees a fair trial, even for foreign nationals and individuals accused of crimes against the state, such as terrorists. Thus, judicial independence remains a vital principle in modern democracy?.

Or (b) Article 50 of the Indian Constitution mandates the separation of the judiciary from the executive to ensure an independent judicial system. This separation helps maintain the rule of law, prevents misuse of power and upholds citizens' rights. Two key provisions contributing to judicial independence include

(i) Judges are provided with security of tenure, ensuring they remain free from external influence.

(ii) Judges cannot be easily removed except for proven misbehaviour or incapacity, safeguarding their impartiality.

30. (a) An arbitral award is similar to a court judgment as it is binding on the parties and can be enforced like a court order. Arbitrators also have the authority to grant interim relief, similar to judges. However, an arbitral award lacks precedential value, meaning future arbitrations are not bound by previous awards, unlike judicial rulings that follow the doctrine of stare decisis.

Or (b) Ad-hoc arbitration is governed by the parties themselves without involving a formal arbitral institution. It can be domestic or international. The parties are not bound by institutional rules and have the freedom to set their own arbitration procedures. This type of arbitration is cost-effective and provides flexibility in choosing arbitrators, timelines and procedures. However, it may face delays due to the absence of a structured framework and administrative support.

31. Riya, as a law graduate, can explore various career options beyond courtroom practice

(i) **Corporate Sector** She can work as an in-house legal counsel for corporations, ensuring compliance with laws and advising on business transactions.

(ii) **Public Policy** She can contribute to policy-making by working with organisations like PRS Legislative Research or regulatory bodies like SEBI.

(iii) **Legal Research and Academia** She can pursue higher studies and work as a researcher or professor, contributing to legal education and policy research?.

32. (a) Under the Transfer of Property Act, 1882, only a competent owner or an authorised individual can transfer property. Mrs. Kapoor's verbal expression lacks legal validity as a transfer must be formalised through proper documentation. Aman cannot claim ownership merely by managing the land. A sale to Mr. Sharma would require valid ownership proof and a registered deed.

Two essentials of a valid transfer include

(i) The transfer must be between two or more living persons.

(ii) It must comply with necessary formalities like registration.

33. (a) The statutory body constituted under the Water (Prevention and Control of Pollution) Act, 1974, is the Central Pollution Control Board (CPCB). It functions under the Ministry of Environment and Forest Protection. Two of its principal functions include

(i) Advising the Central Government on matters related to the prevention and control of water and air pollution, along with improving air quality.

(ii) Planning and executing nationwide programmes for the prevention, control, or abatement of water and air pollution.

Or (b) The Stockholm Declaration of 1972 was the first international agreement addressing global environmental issues. It emphasised the responsibility of humans to protect the environment and acknowledged the link between development and environmental conservation.

The Earth Summit of 1992 in Rio de Janeiro built upon this by formulating a global action plan, Agenda 21, to promote sustainable development. The Earth Summit marked the 20th anniversary of the Stockholm Declaration and reinforced its principles by incorporating economic, social, and environmental concerns into sustainable development goals.

34. The Universal Declaration of Human Rights (UDHR) outlines fundamental principles that uphold human dignity, freedom and equality. The key principles include

- **Liberty of a Person (Article 3)** Ensures the right to life, liberty and personal security.
- **Equality Before the Law (Article 7)** Guarantees equal protection without discrimination.
- **Prohibition on Torture (Article 5)** Forbids torture and inhumane treatment.
- **Right to Work and Equal Pay (Article 23)** Ensures fair wages and employment rights.
- **Right to Social Security (Article 25)** Protects access to social well-being and security.

These principles emphasise the universal, inalienable nature of human rights, forming the foundation of international human rights law?.

35. The National Commission for Protection of Child Rights (NCPCR) is the national body that can be approached regarding the rights violations of juveniles in custodial homes. The commission has the authority to

(i) Inspect custodial homes and other institutions meant for children to ensure they meet safety and welfare standards.

(ii) Recommend remedial actions for cases of maltreatment, torture, or inadequate living conditions, ensuring the enforcement of child protection laws?.

36. (i) A trade name is the official name under which a company operates, while a trademark is a distinctive mark, logo, symbol, or phrase that differentiates a company's goods or services from others. A trade name does not provide brand protection, whereas a trademark ensures legal security for brand identity.

(ii) Registering "Glow Essence" as a trademark will prevent unauthorised use by others, helping Sneha secure her brand identity and reputation. It grants her exclusive rights, allowing legal action against infringers and protecting customers from confusion.

37. (a) Trade secrets in intellectual property law refer to confidential business information that provides a competitive edge. This includes formulas, processes, client lists and business strategies. In India, there is no specific legislation for trade secrets, but they are protected under contract law, equity principles and common law remedies. Section 272 of the Indian Contract Act, 1872, offers legal recourse for breach of confidentiality. Unlike patents and copyrights, trade secrets do not have a fixed duration and remain protected as long as they remain undisclosed. Patents require public disclosure and last 20 years, while copyrights protect creative works for the author's lifetime plus 60 years.

Or (b) According to the Indian Contract Act, 1872, an agreement becomes a contract only when it meets certain legal criteria. An agreement is formed when one party makes an offer and another accepts it. However, for an agreement to be legally enforceable as a contract, it must fulfill the following essential conditions

(i) **Competent Parties** Both parties must be legally capable of entering into a contract.

(ii) **Lawful Consideration and Object** The agreement must involve a valid exchange that is not illegal.

(iii) **Free consent** Both parties must agree without coercion, fraud, or misrepresentation.

(iv) **Not Expressly Declared Void** Certain agreements, like those against public policy, are unenforceable.

38. (a) (i) An advocate must have a minimum of three years of experience at the bar to be considered for empanelment. Additionally, competence, integrity, suitability, and experience in handling different types of cases are key criteria for selection.

(ii) The selection board for empanelment of advocates in the High Court Legal Services Committee consists of the Executive Chairman of the legal services institution in consultation with the Advocate-General, Government Pleader and the Bar Association President.

(iii) A panel lawyer can be removed from any case if their performance is unsatisfactory or if their actions go against the objectives of the Legal Services Authorities Act or NALSA Regulations.

(iv) The services of a Senior Advocate may be availed in cases of great public importance or where there is a serious threat to the life and liberty of the applicant, as determined by the Chairman of the legal services institution.

Or (b) Legal aid refers to the provision of free legal assistance to individuals who cannot afford legal representation or access to justice due to financial constraints. It ensures that justice is not denied to anyone based on economic limitations. Legal aid is important in a legal system as it upholds the principle of equality before the law, allowing marginalised sections of society to exercise their rights effectively.

The Indian Constitution lays the foundation for legal aid under Article 39A, introduced by the 42nd Amendment, mandating the state to provide free legal assistance to economically weaker sections. Additionally, Articles 14 and 22(1) reinforce the right to legal representation, ensuring fair treatment under the law. The Legal Services Authorities Act, 1987, further institutionalised legal aid through bodies like the National Legal Services Authority (NALSA), which implements legal aid schemes and organises Lok Adalats for dispute resolution.

39. Articles 59, 38, and 38(1) of the statute of the ICJ play a crucial role in the dispute between Novara and Elderia over the construction of the Nelara dam.

- Article 59 states that ICJ decisions are binding only on the parties involved and in that specific case, meaning past rulings do not create binding precedents.
- Article 38 recognises judicial decisions as a subsidiary source of international law, allowing the ICJ to refer to past judgments while ensuring flexibility in interpretation.
- Article 38(1) outlines the primary sources of law the ICJ must apply, including international conventions, customary law and general legal principles.

While Novara argues for reliance on past decisions, Elderia's demand for a fresh interpretation aligns with the ICJ's discretion to consider each case based on evolving legal principles and factual distinctions.

40. A sole proprietorship is a business owned and managed by a single individual. It has minimal legal formalities, no separate legal identity, and the owner has unlimited liability, meaning personal assets can be used to cover business debts. Decision-making is quick, and profits go directly to the owner. However, it has limited financial resources and lacks continuity.

A **One Person Company (OPC)**, as per the Companies Act, 2013, is a private company with a single member. It has a separate legal entity, limited liability, and better access to funding. Unlike a sole proprietorship, an OPC provides perpetual succession, as a nominee takes over in case of the owner's demise.

For Vikram, shifting to an OPC would be beneficial as it limits his personal liability, enhances credibility, and allows easier fundraising. Since his business is growing and involves higher risks, an OPC offers legal protection while maintaining single ownership.